Austr

a Lonely Planet travel survival kit

Mark Honan

Austria

1st edition

Published by
    Lonely Planet Publications
    Head Office: PO Box 617, Hawthorn, Vic 3122, Australia
    Branches: 155 Filbert St, Suite 251, Oakland, CA 94607, USA
                    10 Barley Mow Passage, Chiswick, London W4 4PH, UK
                    71 bis rue du Cardinal Lemoine, 75005 Paris, France

Printed by
    Colorcraft Ltd, Hong Kong

Photographs by
    Mark Honan
    Richard Nebeský
    Geert Cole
    Simon Bracken
    Austrian National Tourist Office (Sydney)

    Front cover: The ceiling of Salzburg's cathedral (Mark Honan)

Published
    March 1996

National Library of Australia Cataloguing in Publication Data

Honan, Mark
    Austria

    Includes index.
    ISBN 0 86442 328 4 (pbk).

    1. Austria – Guidebooks. I. Title. (Series: Lonely Planet travel guidebook).

914.360453

text & maps © Lonely Planet 1996
photos © photographers as indicated 1996
climate charts compiled from information supplied by Patrick J Tyson, © Patrick J Tyson, 1996

Mark Honan

After a university degree in philosophy opened up a glittering career as an office clerk, Mark decided 'the meaning of life' lay elsewhere and set off on a two-year trip around the world. As a freelance travel writer, he then went camper vanning around Europe to write a series of articles for a London magazine. When the magazine went bust Mark joined a travel agency, from where he was rescued by Lonely Planet. Mark wrote the *Vienna city guide*, the Austria, Liechtenstein and Switzerland chapters for Lonely Planet's *Western* and *Central Europe* shoestring books, and coordinated, and wrote part of, *Central America on a shoestring*. He also wrote the *Switzerland* guide, which he is currently updating.

From the Author

Thanks to the following for providing support, advice and/or insider tips: Tanja Widmann, Ewa Ferens, Reinhard Wind, Imregard Lauria, Janin Kus, Franz Schubert and Werner Heriszt. The Austrian National Tourist Office (particularly Marion Telsnig) and local tourist offices were invaluable in their assistance. Ed Baxter wrote the draft for the piece on Viennese actionism. Ed and the Kat gave useful information on ski resorts.

From the Publisher

This book was edited and proofed by Anne Mulvaney and Kim Johns. Kay Dancey designed the maps, title page and illustrations. Andrew Smith, Ann Jeffree, Jacqui Saunders, Chris Klep, Matt King, Jane Hart and Marcel Gaston assisted with maps. Lou Callan assisted with the German language section. Thanks to Mary Neighbour, Jane Hart and Rob van Driesum for their help, and thanks to the Austrian National Tourist Office (Sydney) for assistance with illustrations.

Warning & Request

Things change – prices go up, schedules change, good places go bad and bad places go bankrupt – nothing stays the same. So if you find things better or worse, recently opened or long since closed, please write and tell us and help make the next edition better.

Your letters will be used to help update future editions and, where possible, important changes will also be included in a Stop Press section in reprints.

We greatly appreciate all information that is sent to us by travellers. Back at Lonely Planet we employ a hard-working readers' letters team to sort through the many letters we receive. The best ones will be rewarded with a free copy of the next edition or another Lonely Planet guide if you prefer. We give away lots of books, but, unfortunately, not every letter/postcard receives one.

Contents

Map Legend

BOUNDARIES

International Boundary

Regional Boundary

ROUTES

Freeway

Highway

Major Road

Unsealed Road or Track

City Road

City Street

Railway

Underground Railway

Tram

Walking Track

Walking Tour

Ferry Route

Cable Car or Chairlift

AREA FEATURES

Parks

Built-Up Area

Pedestrian Mall

Market

Cemetery

Forest

Beach or Desert

Rocks

HYDROGRAPHIC FEATURES

Coastline

River, Creek

Intermittent River or Creek

Rapids, Waterfalls

Lake, Intermittent Lake

Canal

Swamp

SYMBOLS

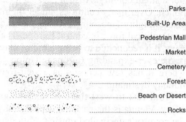

✪ CAPITAL		National Capital
◉ Capital		Regional Capital
● CITY		Major City
● City		City
● Town		Town
● Village		Village

Place to Stay, Place to Eat

Cafe, Pub or Bar

Post Office, Telephone

Tourist Information, Bank

Transport, Parking

Museum, Youth Hostel

Caravan Park, Camping Ground

Church, Cathedral

Mosque, Synagogue

Buddhist Temple, Hindu Temple

Hospital, Police Station

Embassy, Petrol Station

Airport, Airfield

Swimming Pool, Gardens

Shopping Centre, Golf Course

Winery or Vineyard, Zoo

One Way Street, Route Number

Stately Home, Monument

Castle, Tomb

Cave, Hut or Chalet

Mountain or Hill, Lookout

Lighthouse, Shipwreck

Pass, Spring

Beach, Surf Beach

Archaeological Site or Ruins

Ancient or City Wall

Cliff or Escarpment, Tunnel

Railway Station

Note: not all symbols displayed above appear in this book

Introduction

For a small country, Austria packs a terrific punch. Over many centuries, under the rule of the mighty Habsburgs, it was the dominant political force in central Europe. These days, it is reconciled to being a minor player in the ever-expanding European Union, but where it has few peers is as a year-round holiday destination.

From east to west there is something to enjoy. Vienna is the national capital, hub of the country's unrivalled music tradition and home to some of the most impressive architecture in Europe. Cruises on the Danube River provide an escape to a landscape of castles and vine-terraced hills. Salzburg is a city where the Baroque reached great heights in music, art and architecture. Innsbruck is a stunningly-situated city, with snow-capped peaks a backdrop to its historic buildings.

You will know images of Austria before you even get there. Much of the country is dominated by the powerful and beautiful Alps. The provinces of Vorarlberg and Tirol in particular are resplendent with defining images of the magic of the mountains – relaxed chalet villages, top-notch winter sport resorts, isolated hiking trails, traditional Alpine festivals and much more. Austria has no coastline but has hundreds of lakes, ideal for sport or relaxation. Several cities have world-class museums and art collections. An efficient tourist industry, good transport, charming hotels and atmospheric restaurants make it easy and pleasurable simply to be there.

This book contains a chapter on each of Austria's nine provinces, with the provincial capital starting off each chapter. As well, there are chapters for the Salzkammergut lake region and the Hohe Tauern National Park region. Starting with Vienna, the chapters loosely follow a clockwise tour of the country, though the delights of Austria may be experienced in any order. In half a day you could pass directly from the flat plains of Lake Neusiedl to the soaring magnificence of the Alps.

Austria undeniably has something for

everybody. Expensive? Perhaps, but it costs nothing to walk amid the stupendous Alpine scenery, to cycle along the castle-strewn Wachau stretch of the Danube, or to admire the exuberant décor of the many Baroque churches. It costs nothing to wander around imperial Vienna and enjoy the offerings of legions of street artists, or gape in awe at the lavish façades of the grandiose public buildings. And it costs nothing to gaze in wonder at the superb symmetry of Salzburg's many church spires. Sure, it costs something to get there and stay there but you'll find it's a cost well worth paying.

Facts about the Country

HISTORY

The Danube Valley was populated during the Palaeolithic Age, evidenced by a 25,000-year-old statuette, the *Venus of Willendorf*, which was found in the area. In 1991 the body of a late Stone Age man was discovered in a glacier in the Ötztal Alps. When the Romans arrived on the scene in the 1st century BC there were already Celtic settlements in the Danube Valley, the result of migrations east from Gaul some 500 years earlier. Celts had also long been mining salt in Hallstatt and trading along the north-south Alpine trading routes. The Romans established settlements from Brigantium (Bregenz) to Carnuntum (Petronell), 40 km east of a military camp known as Vindobona (Vienna). The Danube River, known to the Romans as Danuvius, marked the northern border of the empire and served to discourage advances by Germanic tribes from the north.

By the 5th century, the Roman Empire had collapsed and the Romans were beaten south by invading tribes. The importance of the Danube Valley as an east-west crossing meant successive waves of tribes and armies tried to wrest control of the region. Before and after the Romans withdrew came the Teutons, Slavs, Huns, Goths, Franks, Bavarians, Avars and Magyars. In the 7th century the Bavarians controlled territory between the Eastern Alps and the Wienerwald (Vienna Woods), with the Slavs encroaching on the region from the south-east.

Charlemagne

Charlemagne, the king of the Franks and eventually Holy Roman Emperor, brushed aside all those in his path and established a territory in the Danube Valley known as the Ostmark (Eastern March) in 803. This was west of Vienna and bordered by the rivers Enns, Raab and Drau. Upon his death in 814 the Carolingian Empire was divided into three parts, and determined invasions by the Magyars meant the Ostmark was overrun.

Otto I, the Great, controller of the eastern portion of Charlemagne's old empire, defeated the Hungarians at Augsburg and re-established the Ostmark in 955. Seven years later Pope John XII crowned Otto the Holy Roman Emperor of the German princes. In 996 the Ostmark was first referred to as Ostarrichi, a clear forerunner of the modern German Österreich (Austria), meaning eastern empire. Various celebrations are planned for 1996 to mark Austria's 1000th anniversary. (Commemorating a name rather than an event seems a little contrived, but it's certainly sufficient excuse for a party.)

The Babenbergs

Leopold von Babenberg, a descendant of a noble Bavarian family, became the margrave, or count, of the Ostmark in 976. The Babenbergs gradually extended their sphere of influence: during the 11th century, Vienna and most of modern-day Lower Austria fell into their hands; in 1192, Styria and much of Upper Austria were also safely garnered. This was a period of trade and prosperity for the region. In 1156 the Holy Roman Emperor, Friedrich Barbarossa, elevated the territory to that of a duchy. The same year, the Babenbergs, under Duke Heinrich II, established their permanent residence in Vienna.

In 1246 Duke Friedrich II died in a battle with the Hungarians over the Austro-Hungarian border. He left no heirs, which allowed the Bohemian king, Ottokar II, to move in and take control. Ottokar held sway over a huge area (all the way from the Sudeten, on the northern border of the present-day Czech Republic, to the Adriatic Sea) and refused to swear allegiance to the new Holy Roman Emperor, Rudolf of Habsburg. His pride was costly: Ottokar died in a battle against his powerful adversary at

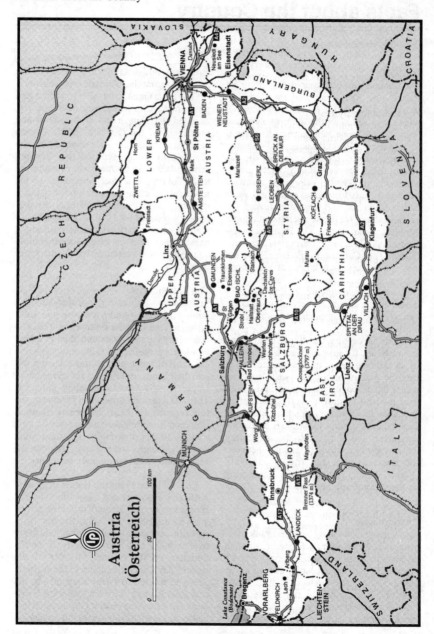

Austria (Österreich)

Marchfeld in 1278. Rudolf granted his two sons the fiefdoms of Austria and Styria in 1282. Thus began the rule of one of the most powerful dynasties in European history. The Habsburgs were to retain the reins of power right up to the 20th century.

The Habsburg Dynasty

The Habsburgs initially suffered a few reversals (including some humiliating defeats against the Swiss) but managed to consolidate their position: Carinthia and Carniola were annexed in 1335, followed by Tirol in 1363. Rudolf IV (ruled 1358-65) went as far as to forge some documents (the *Privilegium maius*) to elevate his status to that of an archduke. He also laid the foundation stone of Vienna's St Stephen's Cathedral and founded Vienna University. These acts helped to placate the wealthy Viennese families, whose privileges had been reduced in the previous century.

In 1453 Friedrich III managed to genuinely acquire the status that was faked by Rudolf IV and was elected Holy Roman Emperor. Furthermore, he persuaded Pope Paul II to raise Vienna to a bishopric in 1469. Friedrich's ambition knew few bounds. His motto was A E I O U, usually interpreted to mean *Austria Est Imperator Orbi Universo*, though some scholars stake a claim for *Alles Erdreich Ist Österreich Untertan*, or even *Austria Erit In Orbe Ultima*. If the exact wording is under dispute, the meaning isn't, for either way it expressed the view that the whole world was Austria's empire. To try to prove this, Friedrich waged war against King Matthias Corvinus of Hungary, who occupied Vienna (1485-90). He also made no friend of the Archbishop of Salzburg, who sided with his opponents. Salzburg was a powerful ecclesiastical principality until the 19th century.

Friedrich instigated the famous and extremely successful Habsburg policy of acquiring new territories through politically motivated marriages. The intermarriage policy had a genetic side-effect, albeit discreetly played down in official portraits: a distended lower jaw became a family trait.

In 1477 Friedrich's son, Maximilian, gained control of Burgundy and the Netherlands by marriage to Maria of Burgundy. Maximilian's eldest son, Philip, was married to the infanta of Spain in 1496. The person to eventually gain the most was Philip's son, Charles. He became Charles I of Spain in 1516 (which included control of vast overseas territories) and also Charles V of the Holy Roman Empire in 1519.

Charles' acquisitions were too diverse for one person to rule effectively. He handed over the Austrian territories to his younger brother Ferdinand in 1521, who also inherited Hungary and Bohemia through his marriage to Anna Jagiello after her brother, King Lewis II, died in battle in 1526.

The Turkish Threat

Ferdinand became preoccupied with protecting his territories from the incursions of the Turks, who were rampant under the leadership of Suleiman the Magnificent, sultan of the Ottoman Empire. Styria was particularly vulnerable. The Turks overran the Balkans and it was they who had killed Lewis II in their conquest of Hungary. In 1529 the Turks reached Vienna, but their 18-day siege of the city foundered with the onset of an early winter. They withdrew but remained a powerful force, and it was this ongoing threat that prompted Ferdinand I to move his court to Vienna in 1533, the first Habsburg to permanently reside in the city. This move increased the city's prestige.

In 1556 Charles abdicated as emperor and Ferdinand was crowned in his place. Charles' remaining territory was inherited by his own son, Philip II, thereby finalising the split in the Habsburg line. In 1571 Maximilian II granted religious freedom to his subjects, upon which the vast majority of Austrians turned to Protestantism. But in 1576, Maximilian's grandson, Rudolf II, became emperor and embraced the Counter-Reformation and much of the country reverted to Catholicism – not without coercion. The problem of religious intolerance was the cause of the Thirty Years' War which started in 1618 and had a devastating effect

The Turks & Vienna

Rulers of the Ottoman Empire viewed Vienna as 'the city of the golden apple', and it wasn't the Apfelstrudel they were after in their two great sieges of the city. The first, in 1529, was undertaken by Suleiman the Magnificent, but the 18-day endeavour was unable to break the Austrians' resolve. The Turkish sultan subsequently died at the siege of Szigetvár, yet his death was kept secret for several days in an attempt to preserve the morale of the army. The subterfuge worked for a while. Messengers were led into the presence of the embalmed body, which had been placed in a seated position on the throne, and relayed their news to the corpse. The lack of the slightest acknowledgment by the sultan towards his minions was interpreted as regal impassivity.

At the head of the Turkish siege of 1683 was General Kara Mustapha. Amid the 25,000 tents of the Ottoman army that surrounded Vienna he installed his 1500 concubines. These were guarded by 700 black eunuchs. Their luxurious quarters contained gushing fountains and regal baths, established in haste but with great opulence.

Again, the Turks' efforts were to no avail – perhaps the concubines proved too much of a distraction. Mustapha failed to put garrisons on the Kahlenberg, and was surprised by a quick attack from Charles of Lorraine heading a German army which was supported by a Polish army. Mustapha was pursued from the battlefield and defeated at Gran. At Belgrade he was met by an emissary of the sultan. The price of failure was death, and Mustapha meekly accepted his fate. When the Austrian imperial army conquered Belgrade in 1718, the grand vizier's head was dug up and carried to Vienna in triumph, where it is preserved in the Historical Museum of the City of Vienna (but is no longer exhibited). ∎

on the whole of central Europe. In 1645 a Protestant Swedish army marched within sight of Vienna but did not attack. Peace was finally achieved in 1648, and through the Treaty of Westphalia Austria lost territory to France.

For much of the rest of the century, Austria was preoccupied with halting the advance of the Turks into Europe. Vienna, already depleted by a severe epidemic of the bubonic plague, found itself in 1683 again under Turkish siege. The Viennese were close to capitulation when they were rescued by a Christian force of German and Polish soldiers. Combined forces subsequently swept the Turks to the south-eastern edge of Europe. The removal of the Turkish threat saw a frenzy of Baroque building in many cities. Under the musical emperor, Leopold I, Vienna became a magnet for musicians and composers.

The Years of Reform

The death of Charles II, the last of the Spanish line of the Habsburgs, saw Austria become involved in the War of the Spanish Succession (1701-14). At its conclusion Charles VI, the Austrian emperor, was left with only subsidiary Spanish possessions (such as the some of the Low Countries and parts of Italy). Charles then turned to the problem of ensuring his daughter, Maria Theresa, would succeed him as he had no male heirs. To this end he drew up the Pragmatic Sanction, co-signed by the main European powers, and Maria Theresa duly ascended the Habsburg throne in 1740. However, to ensure she stayed there it was first necessary to win the War of the Austrian Succession (1740-48).

Maria Theresa, aided by Britain and the Netherlands, had to fight off three rivals to the throne, including the elector of Bavaria. Prussia took advantage of the Europe-wide conflict to wrest control of Silesia from Austria, which it retained in the ensuing peace. In the Seven Years' War (1756-63) the European powers changed alliances. Austria, now opposed by Britain, sought without success to regain Silesia from Prussia.

Maria Theresa's rule lasted 40 years, and is generally acknowledged as a golden era in which Austria developed as a modern state. Centralised control was established, along with a civil service. The army and economy were reformed and a public education system introduced. Vienna's reputation as a centre for music grew apace.

Maria Theresa's son, Joseph II, who ruled from 1780 to 1790 (he was also jointly in charge from 1765), was an even more zealous reformer. He issued an edict of tolerance for all faiths, secularised religious properties and abolished serfdom. Yet Joseph moved too fast for the general population and was ultimately forced to rescind some of his measures.

Empress Maria Theresa (1717-80) ruled Austria for 40 prosperous years

The Crumbling Empire

The rise of Napoleon proved to be a major threat to the Habsburg empire. He inflicted major defeats on Austria in 1805 and 1809. Franz II, the grandson of Maria Theresa, had taken up the Austrian crown in 1804 and was forced by Napoleon in 1806 to relinquish the German crown and the title of Holy Roman Emperor. The cost of the war caused state bankruptcy and a currency collapse in 1811.

European conflict dragged on until the Congress of Vienna in 1814-15, in which Austria and its capital regained some measure of pride. The proceedings were dominated by the Austrian foreign minister,

Klemens von Metternich. Austria was left with control of the German Confederation until forced to relinquish it in the Austro-Prussian War in 1866. Thereafter Austria had no place in the new German empire unified by Bismarck.

On the home front, all was not well in post-Congress Vienna. The arts and culture as pursued by the middle class flourished (the so-called Biedermeier period), but the general populace had a harder time. Metternich had established a police state and removed civil rights. Coupled with poor wages and housing, this led to revolution in Vienna in March 1848. The war minister was hanged from a lamppost, Metternich was ousted and Emperor Ferdinand I abdicated. The subsequent liberal interlude was brief, and the army helped reimpose an absolute monarchy. The new emperor, Franz Joseph I (1830-1916), a nephew of Ferdinand, was just 18 years old.

Technical innovations led to an improvement in Austria's economic situation. Franz Joseph became head of the dual Austro-Hungarian monarchy, created in 1867 by the *Ausgleich* (Compromise), which was Austria's response to defeat by Prussia the previous year. Common defence, foreign and economic policies ensued but unity was not complete, as two parliaments remained. Another period of prosperity began, which particularly benefited Vienna. Universal suffrage was introduced in Austro-Hungarian lands in 1906.

Peace in Europe had been maintained by a complex series of alliances (Austria-Hungary was linked through the secret Triple Alliance to the German empire and Italy). The situation changed in 1914 when Franz Joseph's nephew, and heir to the Austrian throne, Franz Ferdinand, was assassinated in Sarajevo on 28 June. A month later Austria-Hungary declared war on Serbia and WW I began.

The Republic

In 1916 Franz Joseph died and his successor, Charles I, abdicated at the conclusion of the war in 1918. The Republic of Austria was

The Emperor & the Minister

France declared war on Austria in 1792 and enjoyed significant victories in northern Italy, but it was Napoleon, who became the French emperor in 1804, who inflicted the heaviest defeats on Franz II and his subjects. In 1805 Austria joined a coalition with Britain and Russia to try to restore the French monarchy. Within a year Austria was defeated at Ulm, Vienna was taken and Austro-Russian forces were defeated at Austerlitz. Under the treaty at Pressburg in December 1805, Austria lost territory to both France and Bavaria.

Napoleon was at the peak of his power in 1809 when Austria joined another coalition with Britain. An Austrian defeat at Wagram the same year led to the Treaty of Vienna, by which Austria lost more land. Also in 1809, Klemens von Metternich (1773-1859) was appointed Austria's foreign minister. A hereditary prince, Metternich was something of a reactionary who supported the monarchy and the status quo and sought to suppress liberal and egalitarian forces. He was instrumental in arranging the marriage of Franz II's daughter, Marie Louise, to Napoleon in 1810. The marriage was meant to buy peace with France, yet it wasn't long before Metternich helped create the decisive coalition which engineered Napoleon's downfall at Waterloo in 1815. ■

created on 12 November 1918, marking the end of the centuries-old Habsburg dynasty and the right of the monarchy to participate in government. Under the peace treaty signed by the Allied powers on 10 September 1919, the Republic's planned union with Germany was prohibited, and it was forced to recognise the independent states of Czechoslovakia, Poland, Hungary and Yugoslavia. Previously, these countries, along with Romania and Bulgaria, had been largely under the control of the Habsburgs. The loss of so much land caused severe economic difficulties in Austria – the new states declined to supply vital raw materials to their old ruler and many urban families were soon on the verge of famine. But by the mid-1920s the federal government had stabilised the currency and established new trading relations.

The Rise of Fascism

After WW I, Vienna's socialist city government embarked on a programme of enlightened social policies. The rest of the country, however, was firmly under the sway of the conservative federal government, causing great tensions between the capital and the state. These tensions were heightened when, in July 1927, right-wing extremists were acquitted of an assassination charge (a dubious decision which was seen as politically motivated) and the Palace of Justice in Vienna was torched by demonstrators. Police fired on the crowd and 86 people were killed.

Political and social tensions, such as the polarisation of political factions and rising unemployment, coupled with a worldwide economic crisis, gave the federal chancellor, Engelbert Dolfuss, an opportunity in 1933 to establish an authoritarian regime. In February 1934 civil war between the left and right erupted, with hundreds of people killed over four days. The right wing proved victorious. In July the outlawed National Socialists (Nazis) assassinated Dolfuss. His successor, Kurt von Schuschnigg, was unable to stand up to increased threats from Germany. In 1938 he capitulated and included National Socialists in his government.

On 11 March 1938 German troops marched into Austria and encountered little resistance. Adolf Hitler, a native of Austria who had departed Vienna decades before as a failed and disgruntled artist, returned to the city in triumph, and held a huge rally at Heldenplatz. Austria was incorporated into the German Reich under the *Anschluss* on 13 March. A national referendum in April supported this union.

The arrival of the Nazis had a devastating

effect on Austrian Jews, though many liberals and intellectuals also fled the Nazi regime. Representing 10% of Vienna's population, the Jews had enjoyed normal civil rights. After May 1938, Germany's Nuremberg Racial Laws were applicable in Austria and Jews were stripped of many of their civil rights; they were excluded from some professions and universities; and they were forced to wear the yellow Star of David. Vienna's Jewish community was rocked by racial violence on the night of 9 November 1938, when their shops were looted and all but one of their temples burnt down. Many Jews fled the country, but about 60,000 Jews were sent to the concentration camps, where all but 2000 perished.

Austria was part of Germany's war machine during WW II from 1939 to 1945. The government was a puppet of the German Nazis, and Austrians were conscripted to the German army, although there were undercurrents of resistance to Germany: 100,000 Austrians were imprisoned for political reasons and 2700 resistance fighters executed. Allied bombing was particularly heavy in Vienna in the last two years of the war and most major public buildings were damaged or destroyed, plus about 86,000 homes. As the war neared its end, Allied troops overran Austria from east and west. The Soviets reached Vienna first, entering the city on 11 April.

Post-WW II

Austria was declared independent again on 27 April 1945 and a provisional federal government established under Karl Renner. The country was restored to its 1937 frontiers and occupied by the victorious Allies – the USA, the Soviet Union, UK and France. The country was thus divided into four zones, one for each occupying power. Vienna, within the Soviet zone, was itself divided into four zones, with control of the city centre alternating between the four powers on a monthly basis. Austria's and Vienna's situation was very similar to that of Germany and Berlin; the Soviet zones in the latter were eventually sealed off, but Austria remained united as its postwar communists (unlike those in Germany's Soviet sector) failed to gain electoral support.

Delays caused by frosting relations between the superpowers ensured that the Allied occupation dragged on for 10 years. It was a tough time for the people – the rebuilding of national monuments was slow and expensive and the black market dominated the flow of goods. On 15 May 1955 the Austrian State Treaty was ratified, with Austria proclaiming its permanent neutrality. The Allied forces withdrew, and in December 1955 Austria joined the United Nations. As the capital of a neutral country on the edge of the Warsaw Pact, Vienna attracted spies and diplomats in the Cold War years. Kennedy and Khrushchev met there in 1961, and Carter and Brezhnev in 1979.

Austria's international image suffered when former secretary-general of the United Nations, Kurt Waldheim, was elected as president in 1986, and it was revealed he had served in a German Wehrmacht unit implicated in WW II war crimes. There was no specific evidence against Waldheim, but his rank as a lieutenant made it hard to accept his denials that he was personally involved. Waldheim made virtually no mention of his three years military service in the Balkans in his biography, *In the Eye of the Storm*, published in 1985. He was barred from making state visits by several countries.

In 1992, Waldheim was succeeded by Thomas Klestil; like Waldheim, he was a candidate of the right-wing Austrian People's Party (ÖVP). In the federal government, the Social Democrats have enjoyed sole or coalition power (with the ÖVP) since the 1970s.

In the postwar years Austria has worked hard to overcome economic difficulties. It established a free trade treaty with the European Union (EU, then known as the EEC) in 1972, and full membership was applied for in July 1989. Terms were agreed early in 1994 and the Austrian people endorsed their country's entry into the EU in the referendum on 12 June 1994; a resounding 66.4%

were in favour. Austria formally joined the EU on 1 January 1995.

GEOGRAPHY

Austria occupies an area of 83,855 sq km, extending for 560 km from west to east, and 280 km from north to south. The Alps are a dominating feature of the country. Two-thirds of Austria is mountainous, with three chains running west to east and forcing most east-west travel into clearly defined channels.

The Northern Limestone Alps, on the border with Germany, reach nearly 3000 metres and extend eastwards almost as far as the Wienerwald. They are separated from the High or Central Alps, which form the highest peaks in Austria, by the valley of the Inn River. Many of the ridges in the Central Alps are topped by glaciers and most of the peaks are above 3000 metres. North-south travel across this natural barrier is limited to a

handful of high passes and road tunnels. The Grossglockner is the highest peak at 3797 metres. The Southern Limestone Alps, which include the Karawanken range, form a natural barrier along the border with Italy and Slovenia.

Away from the mountains, the mighty Danube (Donau) River is the country's most famous natural feature. The Salzach River joins the Inn River near Braunau, which in turn joins the Danube at Passau, on the German border. The main rivers in the south-east are the Mur and the Drau. Lakes are numerous, but particularly in the Salzkammergut region and Carinthia. Lake Neusiedl, in the east, is central Europe's largest steppe lake. In the west, Austria has a small share (along with Germany and Switzerland) of Lake Constance (Bodensee), through which the Rhine River flows.

The most fertile land is in the Danube Valley; cultivation is intensive and 90% of

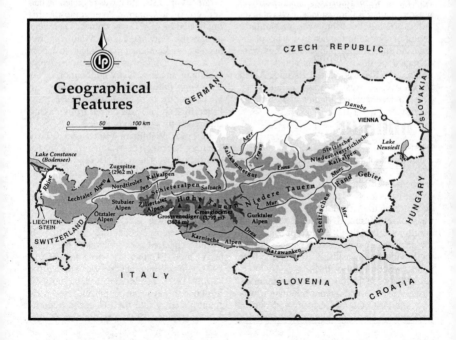

Austria's food is home-grown. North of the Danube the land is mostly flattish and forested. Burgenland is also relatively flat, as is the area south-east of Graz. Lower Austria, Burgenland and Styria are the most important wine-growing regions.

CLIMATE

Austria comes within the central European climatic zone, though the eastern part of the country has what is called a Continental Pannonian climate, characterised by a mean temperature in July above 19°C and annual rainfall usually under 80 cm. Austria's average rainfall is 71 cm per year, with the west of the country receiving significantly higher figures. Mountains tend to draw the clouds, though the Alpine valleys often escape much of the downfall.

Visitors need to be prepared for a range of temperatures depending on altitude – the higher, the colder. But the sun is also very intense at high elevations, which receive more sunshine in autumn and winter than the Alpine valleys. Some people find the *Föhn*, a hot, dry wind which sweeps down from the mountains mainly in early spring and autumn, rather uncomfortable.

Average maximum temperatures in Vienna are: January 1°C, April 15°C, July 25°C and October 14°C. Average minimum temperatures are lower by about 10°C (summer) to 4°C (winter). Temperatures in Salzburg and Innsbruck are similar to those in Vienna, except that winter is a few degrees cooler.

FLORA & FAUNA

Nearly half of Austria (46%) is forested. At low altitudes oak and beech are common. At higher elevations conifers predominate, such as pine, spruce and larch. At around 2200 metres trees yield to Alpine meadows. Beyond 3000 metres, only mosses and lichens cling to the stark crags.

Alpine flowers add a palette of colour to the high pastures from about June to September. Alpine flowers have adapted to cope

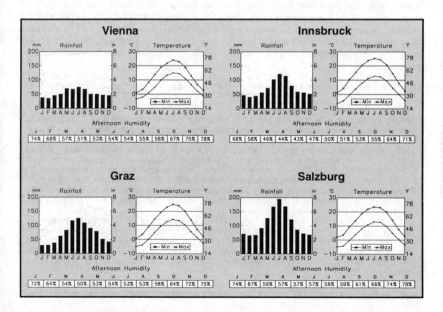

with harsh conditions: long roots counter harsh winds, bright colours (a consequence of strong ultra-violet light) attract the few insects, and hairs and special leaf shapes protect against frost and dehydration. Orchids, edelweiss, dandelions and poppies all survive at higher altitudes. Mountains have a fragile ecosystem and environmental measures have been in place in Austria for many years to protect these areas. Most Alpine flowers are protected and should not be picked.

Fauna in the lowlands is typical for central Europe, though Lake Neusiedl is a unique sanctuary for numerous species of bird. In Alpine regions, the ibex (a mountain goat with huge curved horns) was under threat but is now breeding again. The ibex can master the art of leaping around mountains from the day it is born. In July it may migrate to an elevation of 3000 metres or more. The chamois (a small antelope) doesn't go quite so high, but it's equally at home scampering around on mountainsides. It can leap four metres vertically and its hooves have rubbery soles and rigid outer rims – ideal for maintaining a good grip on loose rocks. The chamois is more often seen than the ibex. They have similar habits and tend to rest in the noon heat. Marmots, chunky rodents

related to the squirrel, are also indigenous to the Alps. Butterflies are numerous in the Alpine meadows.

GOVERNMENT

The head of state is the president, who is chosen by the electorate for a six-year term. The chancellor, appointed by the president, is the head of the federal government and the most influential political figure. Franz Vranitzky has been chancellor since 1986.

The country is divided into nine federal provinces *(Bundesländer)*, each of which has its own head of government *(Landeshauptmann)* and provincial assembly *(Landtag)*. As well as being Austria's capital, Vienna has been a federal province in its own right since 1922. The term of office for each Landtag is four or five years, depending upon the province. Each has a degree of autonomy over local issues and elects representatives to the Federal Council *(Bundesrat)*, the upper house of the national legislative body. The lower house, the National Council *(Nationalrat)*, is elected every four years by voters over the age of 18.

In national politics, the 1970s saw the dominance of the Socialist Party, now called the Social Democrats (SPÖ). In the 1990 election, the SPÖ formed a ruling coalition

---

Austria's Mountain Creatures

Marmots are a type of rodent seen in the mountains, particularly in the Tirol Alps. They generally live in colonies comprising about two dozen animals. Members mark out the group's territory using pungent secretions from their cheeks. They all take part in lookout duty, watching not only for predators but also for alien marmots, which they will attack. Sentries raise themselves on their hind legs to better scan the surrounding area. The warning cry they give upon spotting a predator (such as a fox or golden eagle) is recognised by the chamois, which shares the same enemies.

For living quarters, the marmot builds a complex network of burrows which may have up to 100 exits. Marmots have powerful claws to aid digging and, although they can use their four limbs together, it usually takes several generations to finish a burrow. They sleep on beds of dried grass, which they regularly clean out and replace.

Their long hibernation (concluding in April) leaves only five months to complete the breeding cycle and replenish energy for the next hibernation. These monogamous creatures therefore start mating soon after emerging in spring. The young are born blind and stay underground for the first four weeks of life. Once on the surface, they must quickly acquire the family smell (to be recognised as part of the group) and learn the warning cries. Marmots commonly feed on grass and plants. ∎

Keeping Austria Beautiful

Austria is one of the most environmentally-conscious countries in Europe. Trams, which do not add to air pollution, are used in most cities. Bicycles are another popular way to get around.

Recycling is well established. Austrians diligently separate tin cans, paper and plastic from their refuse, for recycling. This isn't dictated by conscience: they are compelled to do so by law. In addition, 'hazardous' materials such as aerosol cans must be put aside and are collected twice-yearly by municipal authorities. Recycling bins are a common sight in city streets.

Glass containers (especially beer bottles) often have a return value, and some supermarkets have an automatic bottle-returning area (*Flaschen Rücknahme*). It's all very efficient. You put your bottle into the recess and the machine works out what type it is and the appropriate return value. After depositing the bottles, you press a button and the machine gives you a credit note against the rest of your shopping.

In the Tirol, look for hotels bearing a sign reading 'Umweltsiegel Tirol – Wirtshaften mit Natur'. This means the place has met various environmental standards, eg not providing a breakfast consisting of wasteful, individually-packaged ingredients. ■

with the Austrian People's Party (ÖVP). This coalition retained power in the October 1994 general election, though both parties won fewer seats than in 1990.

Despite this leftist coalition, Austria has been perceived from abroad to retain a sneaking affection for fascism. Such a view gained ground with the casual acceptance by Austrians of former president Waldheim and his murky past. The political party that made the strongest gains in the 1994 national election was the far-right Freedom Party (FPÖ) which soared to a 22.8% share of the vote. The party is led by the personable but ruthless populist, Jörg Haider, who stands on an anti-immigration, anti-foreigner platform. Some political pundits are predicting that the FPÖ will overhaul the ÖVP as Austria's second-largest party in the 1998 election. The FPÖ's support is strongest in the south – it won 33% of the vote in Carinthia's provincial election in 1994. Three years earlier Haider had been forced to resign as Carinthia's governor after he praised the employment policy of Hitler's Nazis.

ECONOMY

Industries controlled by government or the big banks have been a feature of life in postwar Austria. In common with much of Europe, the federal government recently embarked on a programme of privatisation. But the nationalised sector remains significant, and privatisation hasn't gained any momentum in Vienna where the local (provincial) assembly still has fingers in many economic pies. The national economy is bolstered by a large contingent of foreign labour, particularly from Eastern Europe. Guest workers, mostly poorly paid, account for about 8.5% of the workforce.

Austria is relatively poor in natural resources – production in labour-intensive manufacturing industries was developed after WW II and now accounts for 75% of Austria's exports. Machinery, metallurgical products and textiles are particularly important. Linz is one of Austria's main iron and steel centres, feeding from iron ore mined at Eisenerz. Deposits of oil and natural gas are supplemented by hydroelectric power and imported coal (Austrians have voted against developing a nuclear power industry). Forestry employs about 25% of the population and agriculture 10%. The country's cosseted farmers lost some of their protection with Austria's entry into the EU, and face the challenge of improving their productivity in the open market.

Austria generally has a trade deficit in visible earnings, which is offset by income from tourism. This industry is hugely important for the whole country, but particularly for Tirol, where annually there are 75 overnight tourist stays per local inhabitant. One-third of Tirol's private farms list providing tourist accommodation as their primary or secondary source of income. Austria is increasingly gearing itself towards big-spending tourists, with a rise in the number of four and five-star hotels and a fall in those with one or two stars. The majority of visitors are Germans (Germany is also Austria's largest trading partner).

Austrian citizens enjoy wide-ranging welfare services including free education and health care, and a benign pensions and housing policy. The country came through the 1990s recession virtually unscathed: in 1994 unemployment was under 5% and inflation under 3%.

POPULATION & PEOPLE

Austria has a population of 7.9 million; Vienna accounts for 1.54 million, followed by Graz (243,000), Linz (203,000), Salzburg (144,000) and Innsbruck (118,000). On average, there are 94 inhabitants per sq km. Native Austrians are mostly of Germanic origin. Vienna and the south-east have the most ethnic diversity: industrial expansion in the late 19th century brought an influx of European migrants, particularly from the Czech-speaking parts of the former Habsburg Empire.

In May 1993 around 600,000 foreigners were living legally in the country; roughly 65,000 of these were war refugees from the former Yugoslavia. Other foreigners hailed mainly from Turkey, Poland, Germany, the Czech Republic and Slovakia. Between 1990 and 1992 Vienna alone experienced an increase of immigration over emigration of 91,043. In September 1992 a survey established that the public perception of what posed the greatest current threat to the country was being 'overrun by waves of refugees' (voiced by an incredible 38% of respondents). Given such sentiments, it's not surprising that the federal government has tightened immigration controls considerably

– only 25,000 residency permits were allocated in 1994.

National service is compulsory for Austrian males (six months plus two months at a later time), though they may opt out of the military in favour of civil service duties. Women are not conscripted and cannot even volunteer to join the armed services.

EDUCATION

Austria's schooling system is uniform throughout the country. Children have nine years of compulsory education, from age six to 15. At age 10 children embark on either a basic secondary education (at a *Hauptschule*) or an extended secondary education (at a *Gymnasium*). The former lasts four years, and leads to a one-year technical course or extended vocational training. Gymnasium pupils may also opt for vocational training after four years, or they can graduate at age 18 and try for university.

Austria has 12 universities and six fine arts colleges, offering places for over 200,000 students. A university education, like schooling, is free for Austrians. Over 10% of all students are foreigners, though they are usually charged tuition fees.

ARTS
Music

Above all other artistic pursuits, Austria is known for music. Composers throughout Europe were drawn to Austria and especially Vienna in the 18th and 19th centuries by the willingness of the Habsburgs to patronise this medium. In fact many of the royal family were themselves gifted musicians – Leopold I was a composer, and Charles VI (violin), Maria Theresa (double bass) and Joseph II (harpsichord and cello) were all players. The various forms of classical music – symphony, concerto, sonata, opera and operetta – were explored and developed by the most eminent exponents of the day.

As early as the 12th century Vienna was known for its troubadours (*Minnesänger)* and strolling musicians. In 1498 Maximilian I relocated the court orchestra from Innsbruck to Vienna. Opera originated in Italy

Part of a Haydn musical score for a keyboard sonata

around 1600 yet it was in Vienna that it attained its apotheosis. The genre was reformed by Christoph Willibald von Gluck (1714-87) who married the music to a more dramatic format (as in *Orpheus & Eurydice* and *Alceste).*

Classicism Opera was taken to further heights by Wolfgang Amadeus Mozart (1756-91), who succeeded Gluck as court composer (albeit at less than half of the former's salary!) in 1787. Mozart achieved a fusion of Germanic and Italianate styles (his librettos were first in Italian and later – an innovation – in German). Pundits consider Mozart's greatest Italian operas to be *The Marriage of Figaro* (1786), *Don Giovanni* (1787) and *Così fan Tutte* (1790); the librettist in each case was Italian writer Lorenzo da Ponte. Mozart's *The Magic Flute* (1791) was a direct precursor of the German opera of the 19th century.

Mozart's mentor was Josef Haydn (1732-1809), the dominant musical figure of the 18th century. Haydn has been credited with ushering in the classicist era in Viennese music. He spent 38 years as musical director for the Esterházy family in nearby Eisenstadt. In the course of his life he wrote two great oratorios, *The Creation* (1798) and *The Seasons* (1801), as well as concertos, symphonies, operas, Masses and sonatas.

Ludwig van Beethoven (1770-1827) hailed from Bonn and came to Vienna at the age of 21 to study under Haydn, although he was already a virtuoso pianist. He stayed in the city up to the time of his death, living at as many as 80 addresses. He was greatly

inspired by the Viennese countryside (eg in the *Pastoral Symphony* of 1808). Among his piano sonatas, overtures and concertos are the opera *Fidelio* and the *Ninth Symphony* (concluding with the majestic *Ode to Joy).* Beethoven began to lose his hearing at age 30, understandably a cause of deep depression to him, and was profoundly deaf while composing some of his major works.

Franz Schubert (1797-1828), a native Viennese, was responsible for giving the ancient German lieder tradition a new lease of life, creating a craze of what became known as 'Schubertiade' musical evenings.

The Waltz The waltz originated in Vienna at the beginning of the 19th century and went down a storm at the Congress of Vienna. The early masters of this genre were Johann Strauss the Elder (1804-49), who was also the composer of the *Radetzky March*, and Josef Lanner (1801-43).

But the man who really made this metier his own was Johann Strauss the Younger (1825-99), composer of 400 waltzes. Young Strauss became a musician against the wishes of Strauss senior (who had experienced years of struggle), and set up a rival orchestra to his father's. He composed Austria's unofficial anthem, the *Blue Danube* (1867), and *Tales from the Vienna Woods.*

This joyful if lightweight style became so popular that more 'serious' composers began to feel somewhat disenfranchised. The operetta form became equally fashionable. The younger Strauss proved also to be a master of this style, especially with his eternally popular *Die Fledermaus* (1874) and *The Gipsy Baron* (1885). Franz Lehár (1870-1948) was another notable operetta composer.

Other 19th-Century Composers Anton Bruckner (1824-96) was raised in Upper Austria and was long associated with the abbey in St Florian. He became settled in Vienna with his appointment as organist to the court in 1868. Bruckner is known for dramatically intense symphonies and church music. Hugo Wolf (1860-1903) rivalled Schubert in lieder composition, though he later went insane.

In the late 19th century Austria was still attracting musicians and composers from elsewhere in Europe. Johannes Brahms (1833-97) and Gustav Mahler (1860-1911) were both German. Brahms enjoyed Vienna's village atmosphere and said it had a positive effect on his work, which was of the classical-romantic tradition. Mahler is known mainly for his nine symphonies, and was director of the Vienna Court Opera from 1897 to 1907. Richard Strauss (1864-1949) was also German, and was drawn more to Salzburg than Vienna.

The New School Vienna's musical eminence continued in the 20th century with the innovative work of Arnold Schönberg (1874-1951), who founded what has been dubbed the 'New School' of Vienna. Schönberg developed theories on 12-tone composition, yet some of his earlier work (eg *Pieces for the Piano op. 11* composed in 1909) went completely beyond the bounds of tonality. The most influential of his pupils were Alban Berg (1885-1935) and Anton von Webern (1883-1945), who both explored the 12-tone technique. Schönberg was also a competent artist.

Music Today The wine taverns (*Heurigen*) in Vienna have a musical tradition all their own, with the songs often expressing very maudlin themes. It's known as *Schrammelmusik*, and is usually played by musicians wielding a combination of violin, accordion, guitar and clarinet. In the field of rock and pop Austria has made little impact (unless you count the briefly emergent Falco), though both Vienna and Graz have a thriving jazz scene, and Vienna was home to Joe Zawinul of Weather Report.

Today, Austrian orchestras, such as the Vienna Philharmonic, have a worldwide reputation, and institutions like the Vienna Boys' Choir, the Staatsoper (State Opera), the Musikverein and the Konzerthaus are unrivalled. Salzburg and Graz are also major music centres and all three cities host important annual music festivals. Linz has the International Bruckner Festival, Feldkirch its Schubertiade festival, and Innsbruck its Early Music concerts. The Bregenz festival is famous for its stage on Lake Constance. A visit to some sort of musical event is an essential part of any trip to Austria.

Architecture
Significant Roman ruins can still be seen in Austria, such as at Petronell and Magdalensberg. Romanesque buildings generally have been extended and modified using later architectural styles (eg St Stephen's Cathedral in Vienna). One of the purest examples of the Romanesque style is the Gurk cathedral in Carinthia. It has not only retained its Romanesque shape, but also has Romanesque sculptures and frescoes. Porcia Palace in Spittal an der Drau is also Romanesque.

The Gothic style didn't really take hold in Austria until the accession of the Habsburgs. The most impressive Gothic structure in Austria is St Stephen's Cathedral. It displays a typical characteristic of the Gothic style in Austria with its three naves of equal height. Secular Gothic buildings include the Golden Roof in Innsbruck, the Kornmesserhaus in Bruck an der Mur and the Bummerlhaus in Steyr.

Baroque While Renaissance architecture had little penetration in Austria (except in Salzburg), Baroque proved to be a high point in terms of both architecture and painting. Building fervour was fuelled by the removal of the Turkish threat in 1683. Learning from the Italian model, Graz-born Johann Bernhard Fischer von Erlach (1656-1723) developed a national style called Austrian Baroque. This mirrored the exuberant ornamentation of Italian Baroque but gave it a specifically Austrian treatment through dynamic combinations of colour coupled with irregular or undulating outlines. Examples of Fischer von Erlach's work in Vienna include the National Library and St Charles' Church. His son, Josef Emmanuel (1693-1742), carried on where he left off. Other prominent Baroque architects were Johann Lukas von Hildebrandt (1668-1745),

responsible for the Belvedere Palace in Vienna and Mirabell Palace in Salzburg, and Jakob Prandtauer (1660-1726), known for the abbeys at Melk and St Florian.

Rococo, the extreme version of Baroque, was a great favourite with Empress Maria Theresa. She chose this fussy style for most of the rooms of Schönbrunn Palace when she commissioned Nicolas Pacassi to renovate it in 1744. Austrian rococo is sometimes referred to as late-Baroque Theresian style.

19th & 20th Century The rococo style was succeeded by neoclassicism. This was a less showy style of which Vienna's Technical

Architectural Styles

Romanesque This style dates from the 10th to 13th centuries. Romanesque churches are characterised by thick walls, closely spaced columns and heavy, rounded arches.

Gothic This style was popular from the 13th to 16th centuries. It was made possible by engineering advances that permitted thinner walls and (in churches) taller, more delicate columns and great expanses of stained glass. Distinctive features include pointed arches and ribbed ceiling vaults, external flying buttresses to support the walls, and elaborately-carved doorway columns.

Renaissance The 16th century saw a new enthusiasm for classical forms and an obsession with grace and symmetry. Italian architects were imported to Austria to create Renaissance buildings, and they usually incorporated both Italian and local features.

Baroque This resplendent, triumphal style is closely associated with the rebuilding (and the re-imposition of Catholicism) in Austria after the Thirty Years' War. Marble columns, emotive sculpture and painting, and rich, gilded ornamentation contributed to extravagant and awe-inspiring interiors.

Rococo This is essentially late, over-the-top Baroque. Florid in the extreme, elaborate and 'light-weight', it was popular with architects in the late 18th century.

Historicism The revival of old architectural styles became popular after the 1848 revolutions. Neoclassical, neo-Gothic and neo-Renaissance styles came to the fore. Neoclassicism favoured grand colonnades and pediments, and often huge and simple symmetrical buildings.

Modern The sensuous and decorative style popular at the turn of the century was Art Nouveau (Jugendstil). Its main practitioners in Austria were Vienna's Secession movement architects. The more sinuous and decorative features of this style soon became subservient to functional considerations both in design and building materials. ■

University is an example. The period between the Congress of Vienna (1814-25) and the revolutions of 1848 was called the Vormärz (pre-March), or Biedermeier when applied to art.

In the second half of the 19th century, historicism took hold; this is seen principally in Vienna's Ringstrasse developments instigated by Franz Joseph I. A great diversity of retrograde styles can be seen here, such as French Gothic (Votive Church), Flemish Gothic (Rathaus), Grecian (Parlament building), French Renaissance (Staatsoper) and Florentine Renaissance (Museum of Applied Arts).

The backlash came at the end of the 19th century with the emergence of Art Nouveau (Jugendstil), an art and architecture style that spread through much of Europe. In Vienna the movement flowered with the founding of the Secession movement in 1897. Otto Wagner (1841-1918), designer of the Postsparkasse (Post Office Savings Bank) and the Church am Steinhof, was one of the leading architects in the field. Wagner led the movement towards a more functional style in the early 20th century. Adolf Loos (1870-1933) was even more important in moving towards a new functionalism. He was a bitter critic of the Ringstrasse buildings, yet also became quickly disillusioned with the ornamentation in Secessionist buildings.

The dominance of the Social Democrats in the Vienna city government of the Republic (1918) gave rise to a number of municipal building projects, not least the massive Karl-Marx-Hof apartment complex. Postwar architecture was mostly utilitarian. More recently some strange multicoloured, haphazard-looking structures have been erected in Vienna, the work of the maverick artist and architect, Friedensreich Hundertwasser. Austria's premier postmodern architect is Hans Hollein, whose work includes the Haas Haus in Vienna.

Painting

Examples of Gothic church art in Austria are best seen in the Middle Ages collection in the Orangery in Vienna's Lower Belvedere.

Early Renaissance art is represented in Austria by the Danube school, which combined landscapes and religious motifs; exponents included Rueland Frueauf the Younger, Wolf Huber, Max Reichlich and Lukas Cranach.

Baroque artists responsible for many church frescoes were Johann Michael Rottmayr and Daniel Gran. An important canvas painter was Franz Anton Maulbertsch, who combined mastery of colour and light with intensity of expression.

The leading Biedermeier painters were Georg Ferdinand Waldmüller and Friedrich Gauermann, who captured the age in portraits, landscapes and period scenes. Some of Waldmüller's evocative if idealised peasant scenes can be seen in the Historical Museum of the City of Vienna. Rudolf von Alt was an exponent of watercolour. Another Biedermeier artist was Moritz Michael Daffinger, who appears on the AS20 note.

Prominent painters of the historicism period were Hans Makart (1840-84) and August von Pettenkofen. Anton Romako (1832-89) anticipated the age of expressionism.

The pre-eminent Art-Nouveau painter, and a founder of the Viennese Secession movement, was Gustav Klimt (1862-1918). Trained in the traditional mould, he soon developed a colourful and distinctive style, full of sensuous female figures, flowing patterns and symbolism.

Egon Schiele (1890-1918) and Oskar Kokoschka (1886-1980) were important exponents of Viennese expressionism. The work of these Austrian painters is best viewed in the Austrian Gallery in the Belvedere Palace. See also the Egon Schiele museum in Tulln.

Sculpture & Design

Sculpture mirrored the changes in architecture over the years. The *Verdun Altar* in Klosterneuburg abbey dates from the Romanesque period. Austria has some beautiful Gothic altars carved using limewood: the best known can be seen in St Wolfgang, and was the work of Michael Pacher (1440-98).

Innsbruck's Hofkirche has the best Renaissance sculpture in the tomb of Maximilian. The same church has impressive statues in bronze, including several by that master of all trades, Albrecht Dürer.

Fine examples of Baroque sculpture are the *Donner Fountain* by George Raphael Donner in Vienna's Neuer Markt, and Balthasar Permoser's statue of Prince Eugene in the Lower Belvedere. Baroque even extended to funeral caskets, as created by Balthasar Moll for Maria Theresa and Francis I. All these are in Vienna, but the Baroque style is evident throughout the country.

Neoclassical sculpture is typified in the equestrian statue of Emperor Joseph II in Josefsplatz in Vienna's Hofburg. Salzburg has several distinctive equine fountains in its old town centre.

The Biedermeier period was strongly represented in furniture, examples of which can be seen in Vienna's Museum of Applied Arts. After Biedermeier, the technique of bending wood in furniture became popular, particularly in the backs of chairs. The bentwood chair became known as the Viennese chair.

In 1903 the Wiener Werkstätte (Vienna Workshops) were founded. They created a

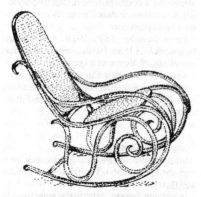

The bentwood chair, also known as the Viennese chair, was developed in the 19th-century Biedermeier period

range of quality, if expensive, household products, as well as garments and jewellery. Aesthetic considerations were given priority over practicality, resulting in some highly distinctive styles, such as Josef Hoffmann's silver tea service (displayed in the Museum of Applied Arts). Another key figure involved in the Wiener Werkstätte was Kolo Moser (1868-1918).

Literature

The outstanding Austrian work of the Middle Ages was the *Nibelungenlied* (The Song of the Nibelungs), written around 1200 by an unknown hand. This epic poem told a tale of passion, faithfulness and revenge in the Burgundian court at Worms. Its themes were adapted by Richard Wagner in his *The Ring of the Nibelungen* operatic series.

The first great figure in the modern era was the playwright Franz Grillparzer (1791-1872), who anticipated Freudian themes in his plays, which are still performed at the Burgtheater in Vienna. Other influential playwrights who still regularly get an airing are Johann Nestroy (1801-62), known for his satirical farces, and Ferdinand Raimaund, the 19th-century author of *The Misanthrope*. Adalbert Stifter (1805-68) is credited as being the seminal influence in the development of an Austrian prose style.

Austria's literary tradition really took off around the turn of the century, when the Vienna Secessionists and Sigmund Freud were also creating waves. Influential writers who emerged at this time included Arthur Schnitzler, Hugo von Hofmannsthal, Karl Kraus and the poet Georg Trakl. Kraus' apocalyptic drama *Die letzten Tage der Menschheit* (The Last Days of Mankind) employed a combination of reports, interviews and press extracts to tell its tale – a very innovative style for its time. Kraus (1874-1936) had previously founded *Die Fackel* (The Torch), a critical literary periodical. Peter Altenberg was a poet who depicted the bohemian lifestyle of Vienna.

Robert Musil was a major 20th-century writer, but only achieved international recognition after his death. He was born in

Klagenfurt in 1880 and died in poverty in Geneva in 1942, with his major literary achievement, *Der Mann ohne Eigenschaften* (The Man Without Qualities) still unfinished. Fortunately, enough of this work was completed for it to fill three volumes and reveal a fascinating portrait of the collapsing Austro-Hungarian monarchy.

Another major figure in the 20th century was Heimito von Doderer (1896-1966). He grew up in Vienna and first achieved recognition with his novel *The Strudlhof Staircase*. His magnum opus was *Die Dämonen* (The Demons), an epic fictional depiction of the end of the monarchy and the first years of the Austrian Republic.

The Vienna Group (Wiener Gruppe) was formed in the 1950s by H C Artmann. Its members incorporated surrealism and dadaism in their sound compositions, textual montages and actionist happenings. Public outrage and police intervention were a regular accompaniment to their meetings. The group's activities came to an end in 1964 when Konrad Bayer, its most influential member, committed suicide.

Thomas Bernhard (1931-89) was born in Holland but grew up and lived in Austria. He was obsessed with negative themes such as disintegration and death but in later works, like *Cutting Timber*, he turned to polemic attacks against social conventions and institutions. He also wrote plays and short stories. Bernhard was influenced by Ludwig Wittgenstein's writings, and even wrote an autobiographical novel about his friendship with the philosopher's nephew.

The best known living writer is Peter Handke (born 1942). His output encompasses innovative and introspective prose works (*The Left-Handed Woman*) and stylistic plays (*The Hour When We Knew Nothing of Each Other*).

Contemporary female writers include the provocative novelist Elfriede Jelinek (*Oh Wilderness, Oh Protection From It* and *Lust*), and Friederike Mayröcker, the author of *Phantom Fan* and *Farewells,* who was once described by a critic as 'the avant-garde's bird of paradise'.

Theatre & Film

Austria's tradition in the theatre was bolstered by the quality of operas and operettas produced in the golden age of music. In addition, Greek dramas, avant-garde, mime, comedy, farce and other genres are regularly performed. Vienna is home to the four federal theatres and opera houses – the Staatsoper, Volksoper, Akademietheater and Burgtheater. The Burgtheater is a premier venue in the German-speaking world. Vienna also has a number of municipal theatres and there are major theatres in all the provincial capital cities.

Austrian endeavours in the film industry go mostly unnoticed outside the German-speaking world. There are a few exceptions. The film director Fritz Lang (1890-1976) was responsible for the innovative science fiction silent film *Metropolis* (1926), and *M* (1931) starring Peter Lorre. Well-known actors are Klaus Maria Brandauer who starred in *Mephisto* (1980) and other films; and of course there's ex-Mr Universe Arnold Schwarzenegger, whose bulk fills the screen in such action epics as *The Terminator* (1985) and *Total Recall* (1990).

PHILOSOPHY & SCIENCE

The Vienna Circle was a group of philosophers centred on Vienna University in the 1920s and 1930s. The term logical positivism was created to describe their views. They owed an initial debt to the work of the Austrian philosopher and scientist Ernst Mach (whose name lives on as a measure of the speed of a body in relation to the speed of sound). The Vienna Circle formulated the verifiability principle, which sought to find meaning in phenomena by the method of its verification. Many members emigrated when the Nazis arrived in 1938. The movement remained influential, though it lost some of its appeal when philosophers couldn't agree whether the verifiability principle itself should be subject to empirical verification.

Sir Karl Popper (1902-94) was loosely connected with the Vienna Circle, but mainly in a critical capacity. He was born in Vienna and lived and worked there until he also emigrated rather than face the Nazis. He had an impact on the way the nature of scientific enquiry was understood, with his views that the hallmark of science is falsifiability rather than verifiability. He pointed out that general scientific laws could never be logically proved to always apply, they could only be disproved if and when contrary data became manifest. Scientific laws are therefore accepted until they are seen to require revision, thus leading to the advancement of scientific endeavour. Popper was also known for his work in the field of social and political philosophy.

Ludwig Wittgenstein (1889-1951) made a significant impact with his philosophical writings, not least on the Vienna Circle. He was born in Vienna and died in Cambridge, England, where he spent the latter part of his career as a research fellow at the university. Much of his output was concerned with the scope and limitations of language. His *Tractatus* was an adamant treatise ordered as a series of logical statements. By analysing language using language he ended up in the paradoxical situation of having to say what he admitted could only be shown. Nevertheless, Wittgenstein was so convinced that this work had achieved all that it was possible for such a text to do, that it effectively heralded an end to philosophical enquiry. He retreated to the obscurity of a teaching post in western Austria but later came out of retirement and proceeded to all but contradict his earlier work. His new theories were less rigid and attempted to illuminate the inventiveness of language. Wittgenstein has been hailed as one of the most influential 20th-century philosophers, yet in his personal life he cut a rather lonely figure. One of his great fears was that his writings would be destroyed by fire (only the *Tractatus* was published in his lifetime), and he obsessively stored these in a fireproof safe.

Sigmund Freud (1856-1939), the founder of psychoanalysis, had a love-hate relationship with Vienna, the city where he lived and worked for most of his life. He too fled the Nazis in 1938. Freud believed the repression

The cover of 'Studies in Hysteria', published in 1895 by Sigmund Freud & Josef Breuer

of infantile sexuality was the cause of neurosis in adult life. Central to his treatments was getting the patient to recognise unconscious conflicts. Early on he employed hypnosis to uncover these conflicts, but later abandoned hypnosis in favour of free association and the study of symbolism in dreams. *The Interpretation of Dreams* (1900) was his first major work.

His final psychoanalytical work was *The Ego and the Id* (1923), a new theory in which the tensions between the id (basic urges), the ego (the conscious personality) and the superego (idealised ingrained precepts) were explored. Although Freud's views have always been attacked, his legacy to the 20th century remains enormous. A mental landscape of Oedipus complexes, phallic objects and Freudian slips are only a few of the manifestations. Generations of patients supine on couches are another.

CULTURE
Traditional Lifestyle
The people in Alpine areas often live up to the Austrian stereotype. Women can still be seen in the *Dirndl*, a full, pleated skirt with tight bodice, worn with traditional apron,

bonnet and blouse with short, puffed sleeves. The men, meanwhile, are anything but self-conscious in collarless loden jackets, green hats, wide braces and shorts or knee breeches. Although such costumes are worn on a day-to-day basis in out-of-the-way places, as a tourist you're more likely to see them during celebrations and processions.

In early summer, hardy herders climb to Alpine pastures with their cattle and live in summer huts while tending their herds. They gradually descend to village level as the grassland is grazed. Both the departure and the return is a cause for celebration and processions. The cattle wear heavy bells and decorated headdresses.

Rural ritual retains a foothold in the consciousness of Alpine village folk, and finds exuberant expression in the many festivals scattered through the year. These often act out ancient traditions, such as welcoming the spring with painted masks and the ringing of bells. Yodelling and playing the alphorn are also part of the tradition. Alpine wrestling, where the object is to pin both your opponent's shoulders to the ground at the same time, is another event featured in festivals.

Society & Conduct

It is customary to greet people you come across with the salute *Grüss Gott* and to say *Auf Wiedersehen* when departing. This applies to shop assistants, café servers and the like. When being introduced to someone it is usual to shake hands, likewise when you take your leave. This applies even in younger, informal company.

Some older Viennese still cling to the language and etiquette of the empire, known as *Kaiserdeutsch* or *Schönbrunndeutsch*. This can be seen as pompous or charming depending upon your point of view; it may manifest itself at introductions, with men addressing women as *Gnädige Frau* (gracious lady) and formally adding *Küss die Hand* (I kiss your hand), perhaps backing this up by actually performing the act or clicking the heels. Formal titles should also be used *(Herr* for men and *Frau* for women).

Men would be advised to wear a jacket and tie when dining in some of the top restaurants mentioned in this book. Austrians tend to dress up when going to the opera or theatre, so the wearing of jeans and running shoes (trainers) by foreigners at such events is tolerated but rather frowned upon. You will find conservative behaviour exhibited in various other ways too, such as in the rigid respect for the 'don't walk' red figure on traffic lights; even if there's no traffic anywhere in sight, people will obediently wait for the lights to change.

On the beach, nude bathing is usually limited to restricted areas (look for a sign saying FKK), but topless bathing is common in many parts. Women should be wary of taking their tops off as a matter of course. The rule is, if nobody else seems to be doing it, don't. It is no problem for men to wear shorts away from the beach.

RELIGION

Religion plays an important part in the lives of many Austrians. In the countryside you'll often see small roadside shrines decorated with fresh flowers. Freedom of religion is guaranteed under the constitution. Even the religious rights of children are protected: up to age 10 their religious affiliation is in the hands of parents, yet from age 10 to 12 the child must be consulted about their preferred religion, and from age 12 to 14 a change of religion cannot be imposed upon any child. Upon reaching 14, children have full independence to choose their own faith.

The national census of 1991 revealed that 78% of the population is Roman Catholic, 5% Protestant and 9% non-denominational. Nearly 5% of Austrians belong to other religious groups and the rest of the population declined to reveal their affiliation. Most Protestants are concentrated in Burgenland and Carinthia.

LANGUAGE

The national language is German, though for a small country, there is a surprising diversity in regional accents and dialects. This is due in part to the isolating influence of high mountain ranges, causing language to evolve differently in different communities. Austrians will tell you that they have difficulty understanding the accents of compatriots from other regions; indeed, the Vorarlberg dialect is much closer to Schwyzerdütsch (Swiss-German, a language all but incomprehensible to most non-Swiss people) than it is to standard High German.

Fortunately for visitors, Austrians can switch to High German when necessary, and can often speak some English, too. Young people are usually quite fluent in English. As might be expected, understanding of English is more widespread in cities and tourist areas than in out-of-the-way rural districts. Tourist office and train information staff almost invariably speak English; hotel receptionists and restaurant servers usually do as well, especially in higher class places. Nevertheless, knowledge of some German phrases would be an asset and would help endear you to the locals. One characteristic of German is that all nouns are written with a capital letter.

In some areas of the country, a significant minority may have a different first language to German. In Burgenland about 25,000 people speak Croatian, and in Carinthia about 20,000 people speak Slovene.

Lonely Planet's *Western Europe phrasebook* includes German.

Pronunciation

Unlike English or French, German has no real silent letters: you pronounce the **k** at the start of the word *Knie* (knee), the **p** at the start of *Psychologie* (psychology), and the **e** at the end of *ich habe* (I have).

Vowels As in English, vowels can be pronounced long, like the 'o' in 'pope', or short, like the 'o' in 'pop'. As a rule, German vowels are long before one consonant and short before two consonants: the **o** is long in the word *Dom* (cathedral), but short in the word *doch* (after all).

a	short as in
au	as in 'vow'
ä	short as in 'act',
äu	as in 'boy'
e	short as in 'bet', or long
ei	as in 'aisle'
eu	as in 'boy'
i	short as in 'inn', or long as in 'see'
ie	as in 'see'
o	short as in 'pot', or long as in 'note'
ö	like the 'er' in 'fern' (sometimes written as **oe**)
u	as in 'pull'
ü	similar to the 'u' in 'pull' but with lips stretched back (sometimes written as **ue**)

Consonants Most German consonants sound similar to their English counterparts. One important difference is that **b**, **d** and **g** sound like 'p', 't' and 'k', respectively, when they appear at the end of a word.

b	as in the English 'b', but as 'p' when at the end of a word
ch	like the 'ch' in Scottish 'loch'
d	as in the English 'd', but as 't' when at the end of a word
g	as the hard 'g' in English, but as 'k' when at the end of a word; or like the 'ch' in the Scottish 'loch' when at the end of a word following 'i'
j	like the 'y' in 'yet'
qu	'k' plus 'v'
r	can be trilled like the Italian 'r' or guttural like the French 'r', depending on the region
s	as in 'sun', but like the 'z' in 'zoo' when followed by a vowel
sch	as in 'ship'
sp, st	the **s** sounds like the 'sh' in 'ship' when at the start of a word
tion	the **t** sounds like the 'ts' in 'hits'
ß	as in 'sun' (written as 'ss' here)
v	as the 'f' in 'fan'
w	as the 'v' in 'van'
z	as the 'ts' in 'hits'

as in 'day'
or long as in 'hair'
or long as in 'father'
'cut', or long as in
...ative

...en.

Plea...
Thank you.
That's fine/You're   *Bitte se...*
  welcome.
Sorry/Excuse me.   *Entschuldigung.*

Some Useful Phrases
Do you speak English?
  Sprechen Sie Englisch?
Does anyone here speak English?
  Spricht hier jemand Englisch?
I (don't) understand.
  Ich verstehe (nicht).
Just a minute.
  Einen Moment.
Could you please write that down?
  Können Sie es bitte aufschreiben?
How much is it?
  Wieviel kostet es?

Getting Around
What time does ... leave?
  Wann fährt ... ab?
What time does ... arrive?
  Wann kommt ... an?
What time is the next boat?
  Wann fährt das nächste Boot?

next	*nächste*
first	*erste*
last	*letzte*

the boat	*das Boot*
the bus (city)	*der Bus*
the bus (intercity)	*der (Überland) Bus*
the tram	*die Strassenbahn*
the train	*der Zug*

Useful Signs

CAMPING GROUND	CAMPINGPLATZ
ENTRANCE	EINGANG
EXIT	AUSGANG
FULL	VOLL
NO VACANCIES	BESETZT
GUESTHOUSE	PENSION/
	GÄSTEHAUS
HOTEL	HOTEL
INFORMATION	AUSKUNFT
OPEN	OFFEN
	(or GEÖFFNET)
CLOSED	GESCHLOSSEN
POLICE	POLIZEI
POLICE STATION	POLIZEIWACHE
TRAIN STATION	BAHNHOF (Bf)
MAIN TRAIN STATION	HAUPTBAHNHOF
ROOMS AVAILABLE	ZIMMER FREI
TOILETS	TOILETTEN (WC)
YOUTH HOSTEL	JUGENDHERBERGE

I would like ...	*Ich möchte ...*
a one-way ticket	*eine Einzelkarte*
a return ticket	*eine Rückfahrkarte*
1st class	*erste Klasse*
2nd class	*zweite Klasse*

Where is the bus stop?
  Wo ist die Bushaltestelle?
Where is the tram stop?
  Wo ist die Strassenbahnhaltestelle?
Can you show me (on the map)?
  Können Sie mir (auf der Karte) zeigen?
I'm looking for ...
  Ich suche ...

far/near
  weit/nahe
Go straight ahead.
  Gehen Sie geradeaus.
Turn left.
  Biegen Sie links ab.
Turn right.
  Biegen Sie rechts ab.

MARK HONAN

MARK HONAN

MARK HONAN

MARK HONAN

MARK HONAN

MARK HONAN

A	B
C	D
E	F

A: Cogwheel railway driver, Schafberg, the Salzkammergut
B: Flea market, Naschmarkt, Vienna
C: Newsstand, Praterstern, Vienna

D: Relaxing at an Easter Sunday concert, Millstatt, Carinthia
E: Poster board, Vienna
F: Café life, Stephansplatz, Vienna

MARK HONAN

MARK HONAN

MARK HONAN

The colours and landscapes of Austria: snow covered mountains in
Hohe Tauern National Park, shimmering Traunsee in the Salzkammergut
and fields of vivid yellow surrounding St Florian Abbey, Upper Austria.

Around Town

I'm looking for ...	*Ich suche ...*
a bank	*eine Bank*
the city centre	*die Innenstadt*
the ... embassy	*die ... Botschaft*
my hotel	*mein Hotel*
the market	*den Markt*
the police	*die Polizei*
the post office	*das Postamt*
a public toilet	*eine Öffentliche Toilette*
the telephone centre	*die Telefonzentrale*
the tourist office	*das Verkehrsamt*

beach	*Strand*
bridge	*Brücke*
castle	*Schloss/Burg*
cathedral	*Dom*
church	*Kirche*
hospital	*Krankenhaus*
island	*Insel*
lake	*See*
main square	*Hauptplatz*
market	*Markt*
monastery/convent	*Kloster*
mosque	*Moschee*
mountain	*Berg*
old city	*Altstadt*
palace	*Palast*
ruins	*Ruinen*
sea	*Meer*
square	*Platz*
tower	*Turm*

Accommodation

Where is a cheap hotel?
Wo ist ein billiges Hotel?
What is the address?
Was ist die Adresse?
Could you write the address, please?
Könnten Sie bitte die Adresse aufschreiben?
Do you have any rooms available?
Haben Sie noch freie Zimmer?

I would like ...	*Ich möchte ...*
a single room	*ein Einzelzimmer*
a double room	*ein Doppelzimmer*
a room with a bath	*ein Zimmer mit Bad*

to share a dorm	*einen Schlafsaal teilen*
a bed	*ein Bett*

How much is it per night/per person?
Wieviel kostet es pro Nacht/pro Person?
Can I see it?
Kann ich es sehen?
Where is the bath/shower?
Wo ist das Bad/die Dusche?

Food

bakery	*Bäckerei*
grocery	*Lebensmittelgeschäft*
delicatessen	*Delikatessengeschäft*
restaurant	*Restaurant/ Gaststätte*
breakfast	*Frühstück*
lunch	*Mittagessen*
dinner	*Abendessen*

I would like the set lunch, please.
Ich hätte gern das Tagesmenü, bitte.
Is service included in the bill?
Ist die Bedienung inbegriffen?
I am a vegetarian.
Ich bin Vegetarierin (f)/Vegetarier (m).

Time & Dates

today	*heute*
tomorrow	*morgen*
in the morning	*morgens*
in the afternoon	*nachmittags*
in the evening	*abends*

Monday	*Montag*
Tuesday	*Dienstag*
Wednesday	*Mittwoch*
Thursday	*Donnerstag*
Friday	*Freitag*
Saturday	*Samstag/Sonnabend*
Sunday	*Sonntag*

January	*Januar*
February	*Februar*
March	*März*
April	*April*
May	*Mai*
June	*Juni*
July	*Juli*

August	*August*
September	*September*
October	*Oktober*
November	*November*
December	*Dezember*

Numbers

0	null
1	eins
2	zwei *(zwo* on phones and in public announcements)
3	drei
4	vier
5	fünf
6	sechs
7	sieben
8	acht
9	neun
10	zehn
11	elf
12	zwölf
13	dreizehn
14	vierzehn
15	fünfzehn
16	sechzehn
17	siebzehn
18	achtzehn
19	neunzehn
20	zwanzig
21	einundzwanzig
22	zweiundzwanzig
30	dreissig
40	vierzig
50	fünfzig
60	sechzig
70	siebzig
80	achtzig
90	neunzig
100	hundert
1000	tausend
one million	eine Million

Health

I'm ...	*Ich bin ...*
diabetic	*Diabetikerin* (f)
	Diabetiker (m)
epileptic	*Epileptikerin* (f)
	Epileptiker (m)
asthmatic	*Asthmatikerin*(f)
	Asthmatiker(m)

I'm allergic to antibiotics/penicillin.
Ich bin gegen Antibiotika/Penizillin allergisch.

antiseptic	*Antiseptikum*
aspirin	*Aspirin*
condoms	*Kondome*
constipation	*Verstopfung*
contraceptive	*Verhütungsmittel*
diarrhoea	*Durchfall*
medicine	*Medizin*
nausea	*Übelkeit*
sunblock cream	*Sunblockcreme*
tampons	*Tampons*

Emergencies

Help!	*Hilfe!*
Go away!	*Gehen Sie weg!*
Call a doctor!	*Holen Sie einen Arzt!*
Call the police!	*Rufen Sie die Polizei!*

Austrian Words

Though the grammar is the same as standard German, there are also many words and expressions that are used only by Austrians. Some words will be used throughout the country, others are only in use regionally, though they will probably be generally understood. Most would not automatically be understood by non-Austrian German speakers. On the other hand, the 'normal' German equivalent would be understood by Austrians.

Servus is an informal greeting, and can also be used when taking your leave. The word has been adopted as a motto by the Austrian national tourist office. *Grüss dich* or *Griassdi* (literally 'greet you') is also a familiar, informal greeting. It's especially used by people who don't want to bring God into the conversation (as in *Grüss Gott* – 'Greet God'). For 'goodbye', *Auf Wiederschauen* is the standard phrase; *Pfialdi* or *Ciao* is less formal.

It's quite possible you may want to tell people that you've been drinking. If you're tipsy you can say *Ich bin beschwipst* or *Ich habe einen Schwips*. If you're definitely worse for wear, the Viennese dialect is *I'hab en dulliö*. If you're very drunk, you could say *Ich bin zu*, though everyone will probably already know by then.

Some useful Austrian words are: *Blunzen* (black pudding); *Gerstl* (money); *Maut* (tip); *Obers* (cream); *Paradeiser* (tomatoes); *Scherzl* (crust of bread); *Stamperl* (glass of Schnapps); *Müch* (milk); and *Maroni* (roasted chestnut). See the Food section in the Facts for the Visitor chapter for more useful food-related words.

Words that are more specifically Viennese include:

Beisl
   small tavern for food and drink
Bim
   tram
Haberer
   friend
Stiftl
   glass (for wine)
Verdrahn
   to sell

Facts for the Visitor

VISAS & EMBASSIES

Visas are not required for EU, US, Canadian, Australian or New Zealand citizens. Visitors may stay a maximum of three months (six months for Japanese) although passports rarely receive an entry stamp. If you need to stay longer you could simply leave the country and re-enter. British, other EU nationals and Swiss nationals may theoretically stay as long as they like, though if they are taking up residency they should register with the local police at the beginning of their stay. Any other nationals seeking residency should apply in advance in their home country.

South African and some Arab and Third World nationals (eg Kenyans, Nigerians, Egyptians, Saudi Arabians) require a visa. The visa will be valid for up to three months; the procedure varies depending upon the nationality – some nationals may be required to show a return ticket. Visa extensions are not possible: you will need to leave the country and reapply.

Under the Schengen Accord, passports are not required for travel between EU countries and internal border controls have disappeared (except to/from Britain, Ireland and Denmark, which have opposed this treaty). Austria signed the accord in 1995, but owing to its extensive borders with non-EU countries, it will take two years to comply with the terms.

Visa and passport requirements are subject to change, so always double-check before travelling.

Austrian Embassies Abroad

Austrian embassies abroad include:

Australia
 12 Talbot St, Forrest, Canberra, ACT 2603 (☎ 06-295 1376)
Canada
 445 Wilbrod St, Ottawa, Ont KIN 6M7 (☎ 613-789 1444)
Ireland
 15 Ailesbury Court Apartments, 93 Ailesbury Rd, Dublin 4 (☎ 01-269 4577)
New Zealand
 Austrian Consulate, 22-4 Garrett St, Wellington (☎ 04-801 9709) – does not issue visas or passports; contact the Australian office for these services
South Africa
 1109 Duncan St, Momentum Office Part, 0011 Brooklyn, Pretoria (☎ 012-462 483)
UK
 18 Belgrave Mews West, London SW1 8HU (☎ 0171-235 3731)
USA
 3524 International Court NW, Washington, DC 20008 (☎ 202-895 6700)

Foreign Embassies in Austria

These are all in Vienna. For a complete listing, look in the Vienna telephone book under *Botschaften* (embassies) or *Konsulate* (consulates). Of the embassies mentioned below, consulate details in Vienna are the same unless indicated. For other Austrian cities, the main consulates are listed in the appropriate city sections. Double-check visa requirements if you plan to make excursions to neighbouring Hungary, the Czech Republic or Slovakia.

Australia
 4 Mattiellistrasse 2-4 (☎ 512 85 80)
Belgium
 4 Wohllebeng 6 (☎ 502 070)
Canada
 1 Laurenzerberg 2 (☎ 533 36 92)
Croatia
 17 Heuberggasse 10 (☎ 450 20 830)
Czech Republic
 14 Penzingerstrasse 11-13 (☎ 894 37 41)
 Visas cost AS246 for Australians and New Zealanders and AS512 for Canadians (not required for UK and US citizens); apply for visas weekdays from 8 to 11 am and collect the same day between 2 and 3 pm
Denmark
 Embassy – 1 Führichgasse 6 (☎ 512 79 040)
 Consulate – 9 Ferstelgasse 3 (☎ 402 22 970)

Finland
   1 Gonzagagasse 16 (☎ 531 590)
France
   Embassy – 4 Technikerstrasse 2 (☎ 505 47 470)
   Consulate – 1 Wipplinger Strasse 24-26 (☎ 535 62 09)
Germany
   3 Metternichgasse 3 (☎ 711 540)
Hungary
   1 Bankgasse 4-6 (☎ 533 26 31)
   Visas cost AS270 for Australian and New Zealand citizens (Britons, Canadians and Americans don't need a visa) and are issued within one hour. Apply on weekdays between 8.30 am and 12.30 pm.
Ireland
   3 Landstrasser Hauptstrasse 2, Hilton Center (☎ 715 42 460)
Italy
   Embassy – 3 Rennweg 3 (☎ 712 51 210)
   Consulate – 3 Ungarngasse 43 (☎ 713 56 71)
Japan
   Büro (Embassy/Consulate), 4 Argentinierstrasse 21 (☎ 501 710)
Netherlands
   2 Untere Donaustrasse 13-15 (☎ 24 85 870)
New Zealand
   Consulate – 19 Springsiedelgasse 28 (☎ 318 85 05)
   The New Zealand Embassy (☎ 0228-22 80 70) in Bonn, Germany, has responsibility for Austria.
Norway
   3 Bayerngasse 3 (☎ 715 66 920)
Poland
   13 Hietzinger Hauptstrasse 42C (☎ 877 74 440)
Romania
   4 Prinz Eugen Strasse 60 (☎ 505 32 27)
Slovakia
   19 Armbrustergasse 24 (☎ 37 13 09)
   Visas cost AS250 for Australians and New Zealanders and AS515 for Canadians (not required for UK and US citizens); apply for visas weekdays from 8 to 11 am and collect the same day between 2 and 3 pm.
Slovenia
   1 Nibelungengasse 13 (☎ 586 13 040)
South Africa
   19 Sandgasse 33 (☎ 32 64 930)
Sweden
   2 Obere Donaustrasse 49-51 (☎ 214 77 010)
Switzerland
   3 Prinz Eugen Strasse 7 (☎ 795 050)
UK
   Embassy – 3 Jaurèsgasse 12 (☎ 713 15 75)
   Consulate – 3 Jaurèsgasse 10 (☎ 714 61 17)
USA
   Embassy – 9 Boltzmanngasse 16 (☎ 313 39)
   Consulate – 1 Gartenbaupromenade 2 (☎ 313 39)

DOCUMENTS

As a precaution against loss or theft, keep a separate record of document numbers, or a photocopy of key pages. Ensure your passport is valid until well after you plan to end your trip; if it's not, renew it before you depart. Once you start travelling, carry your passport at all times and guard it carefully. Austrians are required to carry personal identification, so you also will need to be able to identify yourself.

Student & Youth Cards

An International Student Identity Card (ISIC) can get the holder all sorts of discounts on admission prices, air and international train tickets, even some ski passes. In Austria, student discounts sometimes only apply to those under 27 years of age. If you're under 26 but not a student, you can apply for a Federation of International Youth Travel Organisations (FIYTO) card; this is not so useful, but may work for reductions in lieu of an ISIC. Both cards should be issued by both student unions and by youth-oriented travel agents in your home country.

CUSTOMS

If arriving from a European country, you may bring in 200 cigarettes or 50 cigars or 250 grams of tobacco. From outside Europe, limits are double these amounts. The allowance for the importation of alcohol is always the same: 2.25 litres of wine and one litre of spirits. Tobacco and alcohol may only be brought in by those aged 17 or over. No duty is payable on items brought in for personal or professional use, nor on gifts or souvenirs up to a value of AS2500 (AS1000 if arriving via the Czech Republic, Hungary, Slovakia or Slovenia). It is planned that duty-free shops will be abolished by 1999 for people travelling within the EU, but there is considerable opposition from business interests.

Within the EU, the purchase of duty-paid goods (ie goods bought in 'normal' shops) is all but unrestricted, provided the goods are for personal use only (ie not for re-sale at a profit). Customs officials give generous leeway to profligate hedonists, but they are unlikely to believe that quantities above the following guideline limits are for personal use only: 90 litres of wine, 110 litres of beer, 10 litres of spirits, 800 cigarettes and 200 cigars. Other goods have no guideline limits.

MONEY

The Austrian schilling (AS, or ÖS in German) is a fully convertible, stable currency, and changing into or out of foreign currencies is not a problem. It's also easy to acquire cash in US dollars or Deutschmarks, which may be useful if you're travelling on to Eastern Europe.

Austrian banks are open Monday to Friday from 8 am to 3 pm, with late opening on Thursday until 5.30 pm; smaller branches close between 12.30 and 1.30 pm.

Train stations have extended hours for exchange at ticket counters or exchange offices.

Branch post offices can exchange money up to 5 pm on weekdays and on Saturday morning. Some main post offices in cities have longer hours for exchange.

Currency

The schilling is divided into 100 groschen. Banknotes come in denominations of AS20, AS50, AS100, AS500, AS1000 and AS5000. There are coins to the value of 500, 100, 50, 25, 10, five and one schillings, and for 50, 10, five and two groschen. There is no limit on the value of currency that can be brought into the country, but you can export no more than AS100,000 without special permission.

Exchange Rates

Australia	A$1	=	AS7.56
Canada	C$1	=	AS7.48
Czech Republic	Kcs 1	=	AS3.78
Germany	DM1	=	AS6.99
Hungary	Ft 100	=	AS7.61
Italy	ItL 1000	=	AS6.19
New Zealand	NZ$1	=	AS6.90
Switzerland	Sfr1	=	AS8.69
UK	UK£1	=	AS15.75
USA	US$1	=	AS9.95

Where to Exchange Money

Exchange rates can vary a little between banks. It pays to shop around, not only for exchange rates but also for commission

---

Who's on the Money

The people honoured on banknotes can reveal a lot about a society. Yet this is something so familiar it is barely looked at; many Austrians couldn't tell you which personalities appear on their currency.

Occupying a modest place on the AS20 note is Moritz M Daffinger (1790-1849), an artist and designer in applied arts; his image is backed with the Albertina graphic arts collection which includes some of his work. Sigmund Freud (1856-1939), psychoanalyst supreme, stares pensively from the AS50 note; on the reverse side is the Josephinium (the Museum of Medical History). The AS100 note is the domain of statesman and academic Eugen Böhm-Bawerk (1851-1914), who was president (1911-14) of the Academy of Sciences, which appears on the back.

Otto Wagner (1841-1918) is found on the AS500 note; the Art-Nouveau architect is coupled with the Post Office Savings Bank, one of his more famous creations. The AS1000 note belongs to Erwin Schrödinger (1887-1961), the physicist who won a Nobel Prize in 1933 for research into atomic theory. Finally, occupying pride of place on the AS5000 note (rather ironically, for a man who died a pauper), is Wolfgang Amadeus Mozart (1756-91); on the reverse side is Vienna's Staatsoper.

Austria has recognised artists, psychologists, politicians, architects, scientists and musicians. A fair spread, you might think. Except for one thing – none are women. Some years ago Angelika Kauffmann (18th-century portrait painter) and Berta von Suttner (1905 Nobel Peace Prize winner) occupied a place in the nation's pockets, and feminists were enraged when the banknotes were redesigned to produce today's all-male crop. ■

charges. Changing cash attracts a negligible commission but the exchange rate is usually between 1% and 4% lower than for cheques. American Express is the best place to change, especially if you have its cheques. See the Money entries for Vienna, Salzburg, Graz, Innsbruck, Klagenfurt and Linz for branch details. Otherwise, post offices charge the lowest commission rate: AS60 (up to the value of AS16,260), with no commission for cash. Unfortunately, the exchange rate given by the post office is not always the best.

Train stations charge AS64 minimum for cheques, and about AS20 for cash. Banks charge a minimum of AS45 to AS90. Avoid changing a lot of low-value cheques as commission costs will be higher – the exact figure is calculated by adding a basic charge plus a fee per cheque (though for some reason banks usually charge you for a minimum of three to five cheques even if you're only cashing one).

Big hotels also change money, but rates are invariably poor.

Cash

Avoid carrying large amounts of cash, but taking some will allow more flexibility of changing currencies upon arrival and departure. Towards the end of your trip, try not to change more than you think you'll need, as you will lose out if you have to reconvert the excess. Banks rarely accept coins in currencies other than their own, so spend your last coins on a cup of coffee or fuel if travelling by car.

Travellers' Cheques

All major travellers' cheques are equally acceptable, though you may want to use American Express, Visa or Thomas Cook because of their 'instant replacement' policies.

A record of the cheque numbers and the initial purchase details is vital when it comes to replacing lost cheques. Without this, you may well find that 'instant' is a very long time indeed. You should also keep a record of which cheques you have cashed. Keep these details separate from the cheques. Buy cheques in your home currency (as long as it's freely convertible and stable), because if you buy too many in schillings you'll lose on the 'spread' of the exchange rate when cashing in the excess back home.

International Transfers

International transfer of funds is rarely as straightforward as it should be – if you have a credit card, get a cash advance instead (see the following section on Credit Cards). Things will go more smoothly if you nominate a large bank in a major city to receive the funds, instead of some out-of-the-way branch. There are always charges made by the sending bank – a telegraphic transfer (expect to pay a charge of around US$30) is usually more expensive than an International Money Order (IMO). You sometimes need to allow up to two weeks for transfers. Although the 'Swift' system (electronic transfer of funds) within Europe can take just a few hours, from the UK you should allow two to three days.

You can also transfer money through American Express or Thomas Cook. There's no charge at the Austrian end to receive an American Express Moneygram. US nationals can also use Western Union but there may not be a convenient collecting office.

Credit Cards & ATMs

Using a credit card can limit or even remove the need to carry travellers' cheques. Not only can you pay for many goods and services by card, but you can also use them to get cash advances at most banks. Automated teller machines (ATMs) are extremely common and are accessible 24 hours a day.

ATMs are linked up internationally and have English instructions. You'll need to know your personal identification number (PIN) to get instant cash advances. Fees may work out lower than using travellers' cheques. There's no charge at the ATM end, but your credit card company will usually charge a 1% or 2% fee on the total withdrawn. You can avoid the monthly interest charged on your credit card account (due from the day of withdrawal) by leaving your account in credit at the start of your holiday. You may even earn interest on this credit balance.

In Austria, ATMs are known as Bankomats, and I've found them the most efficient way to manage money. These machines are numerous in cities and towns. Even villages should have at least one machine: look for the sign showing blue and green horizontal stripes. You can usually take up to AS2500 at each transaction, with Visa or MasterCard, or AS5000 for EuroCard.

Visa, EuroCard and MasterCard (known as Access in the UK) are equally acceptable, although a surprising number of shops and restaurants refuse to accept any credit cards at all. The same applies to American Express and Diners Club charge cards. Plush shops and restaurants will accept credit cards, though, and the same applies for hotels. Train tickets can be bought by credit card in main stations.

Guaranteed Cheques

Eurocheques are the most popular form of guaranteed personal cheque. They're a convenient way to organise your money if you're a European or have time to set up a European bank account (at least two weeks to apply for the cheques). Getting Eurocheques from a UK bank costs around £6 joining fee plus a yearly charge of around £6. Many hotels, restaurants and shops accept these. Each cheque is guaranteed up to a set sum; you may need to write more than one to cover larger purchases.

Another possible way to organise your money in Europe is to use the post office giro system, which operates through post office accounts. Contact your post office for details.

Costs

Vienna is the most expensive city in Austria, yet other cities and tourist resorts still tend to have higher prices than less-visited towns or rural places. The schilling has edged higher against most other major currencies in the last couple of years, making things costlier for visitors. A survey by the Union Bank of Switzerland in 1994 placed Vienna as the 15th most expensive city in the world (New York was 10th, London was 21st, and Sydney was 32nd).

In tourist areas, budget travellers can get by on about AS300 per day if they camp or stay in hostels, hitchhike (or have previously bought a rail pass), stick to student cafés, cheap lunch specials or self-catering, and only have the occasional drink. Staying in a cheap pension and dispensing with self-catering will require about AS600 a day – add AS120 for a room with private shower/WC. To stay in a mid-range hotel, have a cheap lunch, a decent dinner, some money to spend on evening entertainment and not be too concerned about how expensive a cup of coffee is, a daily allowance of at least AS1000 would be needed. These costs don't include extras like souvenirs, postage, tours or admission fees. Churches have free entry; museums occasionally do, but AS15 to AS45 is more usual. Other admission fees may be up to AS100. Transport must be allowed for, too (eg taking cable cars in the mountains can add significantly to costs). Off the beaten track, the main saving will be from lower accommodation prices.

Note that children pay lower prices; students and senior citizens often do, too.

Tipping

Hotel and restaurant bills include a service charge, but hotel porters and cleaning staff usually expect something for their services. It is also customary to tip in restaurants and cafés. Round up small bills and add an extra 5 to 10% to larger ones: simply say the total amount you want them to take when you hand over the money (it's not usual to leave the tip on the table). Taxi fares do not include an element for tips and the driver will expect around 10% extra. Tour guides, cloakroom attendants and hairdressers are also usually tipped.

Bargaining

Bargain hard in flea markets. Otherwise, prices are fixed, but it can't hurt to ask for 'a discount for cash' if you're making several purchases. In theory, hotel prices are not negotiable; in practice, you can normally haggle for a better rate in the low season or if you're staying more than a few days.

Consumer Taxes

Ice cream and hot and cold drinks are subject to a refreshment tax on top of the inevitable value-added tax (*Mehrwertsteuer; MWST*), which makes them expensive. Prices are always displayed inclusive of all taxes, even (usually) service charges in hotels and restaurants.

All non-EU tourists are entitled to a refund of the VAT (MWST) on purchases over AS1000. To claim the tax, a U34 form or tax-free cheque and envelope must be completed by the shop at the time of purchase, and then stamped by border officials when you leave the country. Vienna, Salzburg, Innsbruck, Linz and Graz airports have a counter for payment of instant refunds. There are also counters at Vienna's Westbahnhof and Südbahnhof train stations, and at major border crossings. The refund is best claimed upon departing Austria; otherwise you will have to track down an international refund office or claim by post.

Before making a purchase, ensure the shop has the required paperwork; some places display a 'Tax Free for Tourists' sticker. Also confirm the value of the refund; it's usually advertised as 13%, though it may vary for certain categories of goods.

WHEN TO GO

Summer sightseeing and winter sports make Austria a year-round destination. When to go depends on what you want to do or see. Look at Cultural Events later in this chapter for seasonal events, and study the climate charts in Facts about the Country.

The summer high season is in July and August, when crowds will be bigger and prices higher. But in Austria this isn't necessarily the best time to visit – it can be uncomfortably hot in the cities and many famous institutions close down (eg the opera season, Spanish Riding School and Vienna Boys' Choir). Consequently, June and September are also busy months for tourism. During winter you'll find things less crowded in the cities and the hotel prices lower (except over Christmas and Easter), but it can get very cold. Consider visiting in spring or autumn as a good compromise.

Winter sports are in full swing from mid-December to late March, with the high season over Christmas, New Year and in February. The length of the skiing season depends on the altitude of the resort – virtual year-round skiing is possible on glaciers. Alpine resorts are very quiet from late April to late May, and in November; at these times some bars, restaurants and hotels close down. Spring in the Alps is in June, when the Alpine flowers start coating the mountains with colour.

WHAT TO BRING

Pack as light as you can. Anything you forget to bring you can easily buy in Austria. Allow for colder weather in winter and at high altitudes (several layers of thin clothing are better than one thick one). Even if they prefer to dress informally, men will need proper shoes (not trainers or running shoes), smart trousers (not jeans) and a tie to get into casinos and some nightclubs; this is also the accepted attire for top restaurants and trips to the opera. Being able to present a smart appearance helps when dealing with officialdom (like at border controls).

Whether to take suitcases or a backpack is a matter of personal choice. If you're travelling by car it doesn't really matter what you take, but a backpack is better if you plan to do much walking. Unfortunately, it doesn't offer too much protection for your valuables; the straps tend to get caught on things and some airlines may refuse to be responsible if the pack is damaged or broken into. Travelpacks are a nifty combination of backpack and shoulder bag, where the backpack straps zip away inside the pack. During city sightseeing, a small daypack is better than a shoulder bag for deterring bag snatchers.

A padlock (and chain) is useful to lock your bag to a train or bus luggage rack, and may also be needed to secure a youth hostel locker. Swiss Army knives are the most versatile pocket knives available; get one with at least a bottle opener and corkscrew.

Other items that might be useful include a compass, a flashlight (torch), an alarm clock (or watch alarm), an adapter plug for electrical appliances, a universal bath/sink plug (a film canister sometimes works, too), sunglasses, clothes pegs and string (impromptu clothesline). Some hostels charge extra for sheets so you may save money if you have your own. If you take a water bottle you won't have to keep buying expensive drinks when sightseeing. Consider also acquiring a cup water heater to make your own hot beverages. A supply of passport photos is useful for visas for onward travel, rail/bus passes etc. Tampons and condoms are widely available in Austria.

Compile a packing list before you leave home, and don't forget wet-weather gear. Pack a few plastic carry bags: they can help keep your clothes separate, clean and dry. Tag your luggage both inside and out with your name and address.

TOURIST OFFICES

Local tourist offices are efficient and helpful. They may be called a number of different things in German, depending on the place (*Fremdenverkehrsverband*, *Verkehrsamt*, *Kurverein*, *Kurort*, *Tourismusbüro* or *Kurverwaltung*), but they can always be identified by a white 'i' on a green background and all provide basically the same information. In addition, each province has its own tourist board, though some of these are geared more to handling written or telephone enquiries than dealing with personal callers.

In this book their addresses are included at the beginning of each chapter. Between provincial offices and the local offices are sometimes regional offices which promote a designated area (eg the Salzkammergut tourist board in Bad Ischl).

A centrally situated local tourist office can be found in any town or village that tourists are likely to visit, and at least one of the staff will speak English. Most offices have a room-finding service, often without commission. Maps are always available and usually free. Staff can answer a range of enquiries, ranging from where and when to attend religious services for different denominations, to where to find vegetarian food.

Some local offices hold brochures on other localities, so you can sometimes stock up information in advance. If you're empty-handed and arrive somewhere too late in the day to get to the tourist office, try asking in the railway ticket office, as staff often hold a supply of hotel lists or city maps. Top hotels also usually have a supply of useful brochures in the foyer.

Tourist Offices Abroad
The Austrian National Tourist Office (ANTO) has branches in many countries; sometimes its functions are taken care of by the Austrian Trade Commission. Make contact by telephone or letter in the first instance – most offices prefer to send information rather than accept personal callers. ANTO offices abroad include:

Australia
    1st floor, 36 Carrington St, Sydney, NSW 2000 (☎ 02-9299 3621; fax 9299 3808)
Canada
    2 Bloor St East, Suite 3330, Toronto, Ont M4W 1A8 (☎ 416-967 3381; fax 967 4101); also in Vancouver and Montreal
Czech Republic
    Österreich Werbung, Krakovská 7, CR-12543 Prague 1 (☎ 2-26 85 18; fax 26 67 16)
Germany
    Österreich Information, Postfach 1231, D 82019, Taufkirchen, Munich (☎ 089-666 70 100; fax 666 70 200)
Hungary
    Osztrák Nezeti Idegenforgalmi Képviselet, Rippl Rónai utca 4, H 1068, Budapest (☎ 1-268 01 04; fax 268 01 08)

Facts for the Visitor – Useful Organisations 43

Ireland
    Eire Merrion Hall, Strand Rd, Sandymount, PO Box 2506, Dublin 4 (☎ 01-283 0488; fax 283 0531)
Italy
    Ente Nazionale Austriaco per il Turismo, Via Larga 23, I 20122, Milan (☎ 02-583 072 20; fax 02-583 073 78); also in Rome
South Africa
    Cradock Heights, 2nd floor, 21 Cradock Ave, Rosebank, 2196 Johannesburg (☎ 11-442 7235; fax 442 8304)
Switzerland
    Österreich Werbung, Zweierstrasse 146, Wiedikerhof, CH 8036, Zürich (☎ 01-451 15 51; fax 451 11 80)
UK
    30 St George St, London W1R OAL (☎ 0171-629 0461; fax 499 6038)
USA
    500 Fifth Ave, Suite 2009-2022, PO Box 1142, New York, NY 10108-1142 (☎ 212-944 6880; fax 730 4568); also PO Box 491938, Los Angeles, CA 90049 (☎ 310-477 3332; fax 477 5141)

There are also tourist offices in Amsterdam, Brussels, Paris, Madrid, Copenhagen, Stockholm and Tokyo. New Zealanders can get information from the Austrian consulate in Wellington (see the Austrian Embassies Abroad section earlier in this chapter).

USEFUL ORGANISATIONS

The Österreichisches Komitee für Internationalen Studentenaustausch (ÖKISTA) is a travel agency specialising in student and budget fares. International Student Identity Cards (ISIC) are issued for a AS60 fee, if you can prove your status. ÖKISTA has branches in Vienna, Graz, Linz, Innsbruck and Salzburg – see the relevant city section for details.

Within the UK, the Anglo-Austrian Society (☎ 0171-222 0366), 46 Queen Anne's Gate, Westminster, London SW1H 9AU, organises lectures and musical events relating to Austria, and arranges German-language tuition. Membership costs UK£8 a year, and allows reductions on some flights through its travel arm, Austria Travel (see the Getting There & Away chapter). The society

has a Vienna office (☎ 0222-512 98 03) at 1 Stubenring 24.

Other organisations appear under their appropriate headings within this chapter (eg 'Hostels' gives details of the youth hostel associations and 'Activities' includes information on the Austrian Alpine Club). See the Getting Around chapter for information on motoring organisations.

BUSINESS HOURS & HOLIDAYS

Shops are generally open Monday to Friday from 8 am to 6.30 pm and Saturdays to 1 pm. Some may open later one night of the week or up to 5 pm on the first Saturday of the month, *Langersamstag* ('long' Saturday) or sometimes *Einkaufsamstag* (shopping Saturday). Shops generally close for up to two hours at noon (except in big cities), and sometimes on Wednesday afternoon too. Public holidays are:

1 January
    New Year's Day
6 January
    Epiphany
Easter Monday (Ostermontag)
1 May
    Labour Day
Ascension Day (Christihimmelfahrt)
Whit Monday (Pfingstmontag)
Corpus Christi (Fronleichnam)
15 August
    Assumption
26 October
    National Day
1 November
    All Saints' Day
8 December
    Immaculate Conception
25 December
    Christmas Day (Weihnachten)
26 December
    St Stephen's Day.

Some people also take a holiday on Good Friday.

FESTIVALS & CULTURAL EVENTS

Most events are small-scale local affairs, so it's worth checking with local tourist offices. ANTO annually compiles a list of annual and one-off events taking place in Austria. The cycle of music festivals throughout the country is almost unceasing. Religious holidays provide an opportunity to stage colourful processions. Corpus Christi (which is the second Thursday after Whitsun) brings carnivals, with some held on lakes in the Salzkammergut. National Day on 26 October involves various events, including much patriotic flag-waving.

Austria celebrates the 1000th anniversary of its name in 1996 so you can expect a number of special events to be staged throughout the year.

More details of specific events are given in the text, but some of the annual highlights are:

January
    New Year concerts
    Lavish balls in Vienna (continues into February)
February
    Fasching (Shrovetide Carnival) week in early February
March or April
    Easter Festival in Salzburg
May
    Maypole dances on 1 May
    Gauderfest in Zell am Ziller
    Spring Festival in the Prater in Vienna
    Vienna International Festival of arts and music (continues into June)
June
    Midsummer night's celebrations on 21 June
    Donauinselfest in Vienna (last weekend in June)
    Schubertiade (Schubert Festival) in Feldkirch
July & August
    Summer of Music Festival in Vienna
    Salzburg Festival

The Danube Valley is famous for its wines, celebrated in harvest festivals around October

September
    Trade Fairs, especially in Vienna, Graz and Innsbruck
    Bruckner Festival in Linz
October
    Viennale Film Festival in Vienna
    Autumn Festival in Styria
    Cattle Roundup in Alpine areas
    Wine Harvest celebrations in Burgenland and Lower Austria
November
    Modern Vienna Festival
    St Martin's Day on 11 November (goose eating)
December
    St Nicholas Day parades on 5 and 6 December
    Christmas markets in Vienna, Salzburg, Innsbruck and elsewhere

POST & TELECOMMUNICATIONS
Post

Post office hours vary: typical hours are Monday to Friday from 8 am to noon and 2 to 6 pm (money exchange only till 5 pm) and Saturday from 8 to 11 am; main post offices may stay open until anywhere between 7 and 9 pm. A few main post offices in big cities are open 24 hours. Some post offices have photocopiers, though those in copy shops or universities are cheaper.

Sending Mail Postcards and letters within Austria cost AS5.50 and AS6 respectively. To Europe they cost AS6 and AS7 (up to 20 grams) and go by air; elsewhere the cost is AS7 and AS10. Sending by air mail (*Flugpost*) outside Europe incurs a surcharge of AS1.50 per five grams to the USA and Canada, and AS4 per five grams to Australia and New Zealand. Stamps are available in tobacconists (*Tabak*) as well as post offices. The weight limit for letter post (*Briefsendung*) is two kg, costing AS260 either to Europe (by air) or elsewhere (surface mail). Air mail takes about four days to the UK, seven days to the USA and about 10 days to Australasia.

Parcels To send packages, you can buy convenient cardboard containers at the post office. Postage rates can be high. The cheapest way is to use the *Petit Paquet* post instead of the *Pakete* post. To use this, you must leave one side open (you can fasten it with a clip or string but not tape), and fill out a customs declaration. It's for sending objects and must not contain a letter. The upper weight limit is two kg and the cost is AS80 (Europe by air; elsewhere by surface). Outside Europe there's again a surcharge for air mail (eg a two-kg Petit Paquet to Australia costs AS580). Packages containing books up to five kg can go at a cheaper rate.

If you want to send anything heavier (up to 20 kg), you have to use the normal Pakete post: to Europe it costs AS115 (one kg), AS155 (three kg), AS185 (five kg) and AS255 (10 kg); to the USA and Canada it costs AS135, AS175, AS215 and AS300; and to Australia and New Zealand it's AS140, AS180, AS230 and AS325. These rates are for surface mail (except for Europe); air mail rates are much higher, particularly for heavier packages.

Receiving Mail Poste restante is *Postlagernde Briefe* in German, though you can use either term when addressing letters. Mail can be sent care of any post office and is held for a month; a passport must be shown to collect. Ask people who are sending you letters to write your surname in capitals and underline it. *Postamt* means post office: this, together with the post code, street name and town, will be sufficient to ensure mail ends up at the correct post office.

American Express (see Money in this chapter) will also hold mail for 30 days for customers who have its card or cheques. Get in the habit of crossing sevens in the continental style when addressing mail (and get others to do likewise), as it reduces the possibility of mail being misdirected and eventually returned to sender or despatched to the recycling bin.

Telephone

The Austrian telephone system is being upgraded throughout the country, a process not expected to be completed till about 1997. An unfortunate consequence of this is that telephone numbers are changing. Most areas had completed the changeover to the digital system by the time this book went to press, but you'll still come across numbers that have been changed since publication.

Telephone calls within Austria are 33% cheaper on weekends and between 6 pm and 8 am on weekdays – phones are still expensive though, despite only costing AS1 for connection. On local calls (below 25 km), a one-hour call costs AS40. On long-distance calls, inserting at least AS9 is recommended; on normal rates, each schilling lasts 15 seconds between 25 and 100 km distance, and only 10 seconds each above 100 km. You may still come across the odd old-style telephone where you need to press the red button when the dialled party answers (though you still have to feed the money in first). When phoning within the pre-digital network, schillings tick away at the local rate while you're waiting for the dialled party to pick up the receiver.

Post offices invariably have telephones. Be wary of using telephones in hotels, as they are more expensive (at least twice the price of the normal AS1 per unit, and AS3.50 per unit in top hotels). You can save money and avoid messing around with change by buying a phonecard *(Telefon-Wertkarte)*. For AS48 you get AS50 worth of calls and for AS95 and AS190 you get AS100 and AS200 worth of calls respectively. Phonecard phones generally don't have queues.

Note that telephone numbers for the same town may not always have the same number of digits: the reason for this is that some telephone numbers have an individual line, others a party line, and sometimes numbers are listed with an extension which you can dial direct. This is relevant for reading phone numbers listed in the telephone book: if, for example, you see the number '123 45 67...-0', the '0' signifies the number has extensions. Whether you dial the '0' at the end or not, you'll get through to that subscriber's main telephone reception. If you know a specific extension of somebody you want to speak to, dial that instead of the '0' and you'll get straight through to that person.

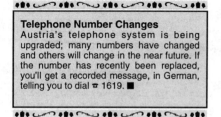

If you get the rising three-bleep anthem it means you've dialled an invalid number. Check the phone book or call ☎ 1611 for directory assistance. Patience is called for as it's nearly always engaged. Getting the fast beeps means it's engaged and you'll have to try again later. If you get the recorded message, hang on as you're now in the queue and will speak to a human being eventually. If the frustration of constant failure gives you sleepless nights, try calling in the early hours when you'll have more success.

International Calls For the directory of international telephone numbers, dial ☎ 1612 for Germany, ☎ 1613 for the rest of Europe, and ☎ 1614 for outside Europe. To direct-dial abroad, first telephone the overseas access code (00), then the appropriate country code, then the relevant city code (minus the initial '0' if there is one), and finally the subscriber number. If direct-dialling is not possible, call ☎ 09 for the international operator; as with the information lines, you may have to wait a while to be connected.

To reverse the charge (ie call collect), you also need to dial ☎ 09. You can reverse the charge to most countries on other continents (eg to Australia, New Zealand, the USA, Canada and South Africa) but *not* to most other countries in Europe (eg to the UK and Ireland).

A three-minute telephone call to the UK costs AS40 at the standard rate or AS26 at the cheap rate. International calls outside Europe are charged only at the standard rate; a three-minute call would cost AS54 to the USA, and AS84 to Australia or New Zealand.

Fax, Telex & Telegram
Luxury hotels offer these services but it might be cheaper to go to the post office. The exception is for receiving faxes: the post office will charge AS30 for the first page and AS10 for every other page; your hotel *may* not charge you anything. To send a fax from the post office costs AS10 for 10 pages plus the cost of the telephone time.

Telegrams can also be sent from the main post offices but they're very expensive, eg AS7.30 per word to the UK, and even each word of the address is charged! Sending a telex is much cheaper but places where you can send them from are very limited. In Vienna the only post office you can send telexes from is the Telegraphenzentralstation at 1 Börseplatz, open 24 hours. The cost per five lines varies, eg AS8 to the UK, AS25 to the USA and AS49 to Australia or New Zealand. In other cities, enquire at the main post office.

TIME
Austrians use the 24-hour clock for anything written down, instead of dividing the day up into am and pm. Austrian time is GMT/UTC plus one hour. If it's noon in Vienna it is 7 am in New York and Toronto, 4 am in San Francisco, 10 pm in Sydney and midnight in Auckland. Clocks go forward one hour on the last Saturday night in March and back again on the last Saturday night in September.

ELECTRICITY
The current used is 220 V, 50Hz AC. Sockets are the round two-pin type which are standard throughout most of Continental Europe. US and Canadian appliances will need a transformer if they don't have built-in voltage adjustment.

LAUNDRY
Look for *Wäscherei* for self-service (*Selbstbedienung*) or service washes (which are only slightly more expensive). The

minimum charge is around AS100 to wash and dry a five-kg load. Many youth hostels have cheaper laundry facilities, and most good hotels have an expensive laundry service, based on a price per item.

TOILETS
Toilet cubicles in some places, including many train stations, are attended or coin-operated; either way, expect to pay around AS5 (you can avoid the station charge by using the train toilets instead). There are many public toilets to be found: *Damen* is for women and *Herren* is for men.

WEIGHTS & MEASURES
The metric system is used. Like other Continental Europeans, Austrians indicate decimals with commas and thousands with points. You will sometimes see meat and cheese priced per *dag*, which is an abbreviation referring to 10 grams (to ask for this quantity say 'deca').

BOOKS
A great deal has been written about Austria and especially Vienna. Some bookshops in Austrian cities stock English-language titles, though they will cost more in schillings than a direct currency conversion of the cover price would indicate. Most books are published in different editions by different publishers in different countries. As a result, a book might be a hardcover rarity in one country while it's readily available in paperback in another. Fortunately, bookshops and libraries search by title or author, so your local bookshop or library should be best placed to advise you on the availability of the following titles.

Non-Fiction
Steven Beller's *Vienna and the Jews* is concerned specifically with the years 1867 to 1938. You could also try *Austria, Empire and Republic* by Barbara Jelavich. *A History of the Habsburg Empire 1526-1918* is a large tome by Robert A Kann. Two books available in Austria are *A Brief Survey of Austrian*

History and *Music and Musicians in Vienna*, both by Richard Rickett.

A number of other books deal with Austria from the slant of its musical heritage. *Mozart and the Enlightenment* by Nicholas Till is a scholarly work placing Mozart in historical context, with detailed analysis of his operatic works. *Mozart and Vienna* by H C Robbins Landon focuses on the Vienna years, and successfully evokes the city of the time by quoting extensively from a contemporary work, *Sketch of Vienna* by Johann Pezzl. *Mozart – his Character, his Work* by Alfred Einstein is self-explanatory from the title, as is *Gustav Mahler – Memories and Letters* by Alma Mahler. *Freud's Women* by Lisa Appignanesi & John Forrester, is a large volume which offers an insight into the psychoanalyst. There's also *The Life and Work of Sigmund Freud* by Ernest Jones.

Fiction
The Third Man is Graham Greene's famous Viennese spy story. John Irving's *Setting Free the Bears* is a fine tale about a plan to release the animals from Vienna's zoo. The zoo plot takes place in 1967, yet the book is also very evocative of life in Austria before, during and after WW II. Irving's *The Hotel New Hampshire* is also partially set in Vienna, and throws up an interesting perspective of the city. *Invisible Architecture* is a collection of three stories by Steven Kelly. The architecture in question is more to do with the make-up of the Viennese soul than the buildings in the city.

Mozart & the Wolf Gang by Anthony Burgess is a learned but still enjoyable celestial fantasy in which the great composers discourse on music and Mozart. *The Strange Case of Mademoiselle P* by Brian O'Doherty is a story about an attempted medical cure in Maria Theresa's Vienna. It's based on a real incident and is an insight into the petty power struggles in the imperial court, though it does rather peter out at the end.

The Salzburg Tales by Christina Stead is a Canterbury Tales-esque novel in which gatherers at the Salzburg Festival in the 1930s tell each other stories. It has some good character sketches of the audience, but apart from its setting sheds little light on Austria.

The works of various Austrian authors are available in English translations. Robert Musil's *The Man Without Qualities* is lengthy enough to be published in three volumes, despite the fact that the author died before he could complete the work. It's a vivid portrayal of Austria in the early years of the 20th century, as the Habsburgs' power waned and WW I loomed. An equally detailed work (some 1400 pages in three paperback volumes) is Heimito von Doderer's *The Demons*. It's more specifically Viennese, looking at all strata of society, starting in the 1920s.

Thomas Bernhard has several short works available. His text is seamless (no chapters or paragraphs, few full stops) and seemingly repetitive, but is surprisingly readable once you get into it. Try *Cutting Timber* for its incisive and rather dismissive view of Austrian society.

Guidebooks

A useful volume for hikers is *Mountain Walking in Austria* by Cecil Davies (paperback). It's not very up-to-date, but at least the information has a long shelf life. *Off the Beaten Track 'Austria'* (various authors, Moorland Publishing) concentrates on less well-known regions – Vienna and Salzburg aren't covered at all. The sights are arranged according to motoring tours.

Many guides deal specifically with Vienna, not least Lonely Planet's *Vienna City Guide*. *Thomas Cook Travellers Vienna* by Louis James is good for walking tours; Berlitz has a *Vienna* and a *Tyrol* pocket guide. Insight publishes one guide to *Vienna* and another to *Austria*, which have good background information and excellent pictures but are weak on the practical details.

Once in Vienna, *Falter's Best of Vienna* (AS45) is worth looking at. This seasonal magazine gives recommendations on the best places to eat, drink, shop, play and be entertained, as well as including some rather strange categories (eg best wall to lean against, best worker's Beisl with a parrot).

The same publisher releases an annual guide solely dedicated to eating, *Wien, wie es isst* (AS165, 408 pages). Both are in German only, which is a pity, as Falter is known for its witty wordplay.

For an enthusiastic assessment of a variety of restaurants, turn to *Eating Out in Austria* by Gretel Beer (Robert Hale Ltd). The detailed glossary of culinary terms is especially useful.

MAPS

Freytag & Berndt, at Schottenfeldgasse 62, A-1071 Vienna, has the most comprehensive coverage of the country. It publishes good town maps (1:10,000 to 1:25,000 scale) and has a *Wanderkarte* series for hikers, mostly on a 1:50,000 scale. Motorists should consider buying its *Strassen & Städte* road atlas (AS249). This covers Europe on a scale 1:350,000 and Austria on a scale 1:250,000, and includes many extensive town plans. Extremely detailed hiking maps are produced by the Austrian Alpine Club, on a scale 1:25,000. Michelin maps are also of a high standard.

To get around cities, maps provided by tourist offices are sufficient for most purposes. These are usually free, but where there's a charge (eg in Salzburg), you can probably make do with the hotel map instead.

MEDIA
Newspapers & Magazines

English-language newspapers are widely available in Austrian cities, usually on the same day on which they are published. Prices are between AS20 and AS35. The first to hit the stands each day are the *Financial Times* and the *International Herald Tribune* (AS26). *USA Today*, *Time*, *Newsweek* and most British newspapers are easy to find. The *Guardian Weekly* is a tabloid-size analysis of the week's news (AS30). There's a Buch und Presse shop in several of the larger train stations: they stock many newspapers and magazines from around the world.

Of the several German-language daily newspapers available, the magazine-size

Neue Kronen Zeitung (AS8) has the largest circulation; the tabloid-size *Die Presse* adopts a more serious approach. Austrian newspapers are often dispensed from bags attached to pavement posts, and rely on the honesty of readers to pay for the copies they take. Foreign titles are only available from newsstands or pavement sellers.

Radio & TV

Austria is fairly unusual in that it has a public sector monopoly on TV, and commercial radio licences were granted for the first time in 1995.

Blue Danube Radio is a news and music station, mostly in English but with some French programmes. News is broadcast at 30 minutes past the hour in German and English (sometimes also in French). At 1 pm it has a 'What's on in Vienna' segment. In some parts of the country you pick the station up on a different frequency, but usually somewhere between 100 and 104 FM. In Vienna it's on 103.8 FM.

National radio channels are Ö1 (87.8 and 92 FM), giving a cultural diet of music, literature and science; Ö2 (89.9 and 95.3 FM), broadcasting local and regional news and programmes; and Ö3 (99.9 FM), offering progressive entertainment and topical information. Radio City (96.06 FM) is a Bratislava station broadcasting German pop. The above frequencies are all for Vienna: they'll be different in other parts of the country.

There are just two national TV channels, ÖRF1 and ÖRF2. Many homes (and hotels) have cable and can pick up a whole host of channels from Germany and elsewhere, plus MTV, Eurosport, CNN (the 24-hour news network) and Superchannel (a US general entertainment channel). Local newspapers and events magazines give a full listing of programmes.

Note that videos in Austria use the PAL image registration system, as do the UK and Australia. This is not compatible with the NTSC system used in the USA, Canada and Japan.

FILM & PHOTOGRAPHY

There are no special restrictions on what you can or cannot photograph, though as in many other countries, some art galleries and museums insist you leave your camera in the cloakroom. Don't use a camera flash at the opera, theatre or similar events; it's very distracting for the performers, whether they be humans or Lipizzaner stallions.

Photography in snow can be tricky. The whiteness of snow can dominate a picture and cause the subject to be under-exposed (dark and dull on the photograph). Some cameras will allow you to compensate for this.

Film is widely available and reasonably priced, though you'll find prices a little higher than in Germany and Switzerland. Note that slide film *(Diafilm)* often excludes mounting *(Rahmung)* and sometimes processing *(Entwicklung)* too. Alternatively, there may be a coupon valid for processing only in Austria (check before buying).

The Niedermeyer chain store is one of the cheapest places to buy film: a 36-exposure roll costs AS69 for Kodak Gold 100 and AS129 for Kodachrome 64 (including processing but not mounting). Niedermeyer also has its own make of film which is much cheaper. Its main rival in price and range is the Foto Nettig chain; compare prices between these two stores. Foto Nettig is definitely the cheapest when it comes to developing: the price is AS35 per film plus AS1.90 per 9x13 cm print or AS2.90 per 10x15 cm print. Processing takes about three days. Both chains have a good range of cameras and lenses, for which prices are comparable to elsewhere in Europe.

HEALTH

No immunisations are required for entry to Austria, unless you're coming from an infected area (in which case you'll need to show an International Health Certificate). However, get a tetanus jab before you travel. Austria is a healthy place and if you're healthy when you arrive, there's no reason why you should experience any particular health problems. Even street snack stands have adequate sanitary standards. Be careful with food that has been cooked and left to go cold, which might happen in some self-service places.

Tap water is perfectly drinkable (except in the rare instance when you'll come across a sign announcing 'Kein Trinkwasser'). Beware of natural water, even crystal-clear Alpine streams. Take a water bottle on long walking trips. If you need to resort to natural water, it should be boiled for 10 minutes; and remember that at high altitude water boils at a lower temperature, so germs are less likely to be killed. Iodine is very effective in purifying water and is available in tablet form (such as Potable Aqua), but follow the directions carefully and remember that too much iodine can be harmful.

Medical Services

There is a charge for hospital treatment and doctor consultations, so some form of medical insurance is advised (cover provided by normal travel insurance would be sufficient). EU nationals can get free emergency medical treatment, though payment must still be made for the actual medication used, and also for most non-urgent treatment. Enquire before leaving home about the documentation required. British people normally need to show an E111 form (available from the DSS) to take advantage of reciprocal health agreements in Europe, so it's worth getting one if you're travelling through the Continent. However, in Austria you only need to show a British passport. The regional health insurance office *(Gebietskrankenkasse)* will know which other countries have reciprocal agreements with Austria (the USA, Canada, Australia and New Zealand don't), but it's wise to establish this from your own health department before you leave home. These regional offices also provide a health insurance scheme voucher for obtaining medical or dental treatment under reciprocal arrangements (in an emergency situation go straight to the hospital). If you go to a private hospital and the treatment is more expensive than it

would be in a public hospital, you'll have to pay the difference (even if you're covered under a reciprocal arrangement). In the following major cities, a Gebietskrankenkasse is located at:

Vienna
    10 Wienerbergstrasse 15-19 (☎ 601 220)
Graz
    Josef Pongratz Platz 1 (☎ 0860-80 10)
Salzburg
    Faberstrasse 19-23 (☎ 0662-88 89 0)
Innsbruck
    Klara Pölt Weg 2 (☎ 0512-59 15 0)

Chemist shops *(Apotheken)* are open normal shop hours, though in some places they operate an out-of-hours service in rotation.

Pre-Departure Preparations

Health Insurance Good travel insurance is essential, and you should enquire about the claims procedure in the event that medical treatment is required. A few insurers require notification *before* treatment is sought in order to meet the claim – tricky in an emergency situation. Other things to look for are whether the policy covers 'dangerous' sports (such as skiing and mountaineering) and if ambulances, helicopter rescue or emergency repatriation are included. Whatever your insurance, you will probably have to pay initial costs yourself (which you can claim back later) and the insurers will issue guarantees for subsequent charges.

Medical Kit A small, straightforward medical kit is a wise thing to carry. A possible kit list includes:

- Aspirin or Paracetamol (Acetamimophen in USA) – for pain or fever
- Antihistamine (such as Benadryl) – useful as a decongestant for colds, allergies, to ease the itch from insect bites or stings or to help prevent motion sickness
- Imodium or Lomotil – simply a change in your usual diet may be enough to cause stomach upsets
- Antiseptic, Mercurochrome and antibiotic powder or similar 'dry' spray – for cuts and grazes

- Calamine lotion – to ease irritation from bites or stings
- Bandages and Band-aids – for minor injuries
- Scissors, tweezers and a thermometer (note that mercury thermometers are prohibited by airlines)
- Insect repellent, sunscreen, suntan lotion and chapstick

You can buy all these items in Austria. A local product I've found excellent for clearing up blisters is *Hirschtalg* (Stag Fat). If you wear glasses, take a spare pair and your prescription. If you're taking medication, bring prescriptions with the generic rather than the brand name, and take a letter from your doctor to show you legally use the medication. Keep the medication in its original container. If you're carrying a syringe for some reason, have a note from your doctor to explain why you're doing so.

A Medic Alert tag is a good idea if your medical condition is not always easily recognisable (heart trouble, diabetes, asthma, allergic reactions to antibiotics etc).

Potential Problems

Sunburn On water, ice, snow or sand, and at higher altitudes, you can get sunburnt surprisingly quickly, even through cloud. Use a sunscreen and take extra care to cover areas that don't normally see sun – eg your feet. A hat provides added protection, and it may be a good idea to use zinc cream or some other barrier cream for your nose and lips. Calamine lotion is good to ease mild sunburn.

Sunglasses eliminate potential damage from reflected glare from water, ice or snow, but make sure they're treated to absorb ultra-violet radiation – if not, they'll actually do more harm than good.

Hypothermia If you are trekking at high altitudes or in a cool, wet environment, be prepared. Hypothermia occurs when the body loses heat faster than it can produce it and the core temperature of the body falls. It is surprisingly easy to progress from very cold to dangerously cold due to a combination of wind, wet clothing, fatigue and hunger, even if the air temperature is above freezing point. It is best to dress in layers, and wear a hat (a lot of heat is lost through the head). A strong, waterproof outer layer is essential, as keeping dry is vital. Carry basic supplies, including food that contains simple sugars to generate heat quickly, and lots of fluid to drink.

Symptoms of hypothermia are exhaustion, numb skin (particularly toes and fingers), shivering, slurred speech, irrational or violent behaviour, lethargy, stumbling, dizzy spells, muscle cramps and violent bursts of energy. Irrationality may take the form of sufferers claiming they are warm and trying to take off their clothes.

To treat hypothermia (in the absence of professional medical help), first get the patient out of the wind and/or rain, remove their clothing if it's wet and replace it with dry, warm clothing. Give them hot liquids – not alcohol – and some high-kilojoule, easily digestible food. This should be enough for the early stages of hypothermia, but if it has gone further, it may be necessary to place victims in warm sleeping bags and get in with them. Do not rub victims or remove their wet clothes in the wind. If possible, place the sufferer in a warm (but not hot) bath.

Altitude Sickness The higher you go, the thinner the air and the easier you need to take things (and the quicker you get drunk!). Acute Mountain Sickness or AMS occurs at high altitude and can be fatal. There is no hard and fast rule as to how high is too high; AMS can strike at altitudes of 3000 metres, although 3500 to 4500 metres is the usual range.

Headaches, nausea, dizziness, a dry cough, insomnia, breathlessness and loss of appetite are all signs to heed. Mild altitude problems will generally abate after a day or so, but if the symptoms persist or become worse the only treatment is to descend – even 500 metres can help.

Motion Sickness Eating lightly before and during a trip will reduce the chances of motion sickness. If you are prone to motion sickness, try to find a place that minimises disturbance – near the wing on aircraft, close to midships on boats, and near the centre on buses. Fresh air and a steady reference point like the horizon usually help, whereas reading or cigarette smoke don't. Commercial antimotion-sickness preparations, which can cause drowsiness, have to be taken before the trip commences – when you're feeling sick, it's too late. Ginger is a natural preventative and is available in capsule form.

Diarrhoea This can be caused by nothing more serious than a change of diet or climate. Dehydration is the main danger, particularly for children, so fluid replacement is essential. Weak black tea with a little sugar, or soda water/soft drinks allowed to go flat and diluted 50% with water are all good for this. With a severe case of diarrhoea (ie caused by contaminated food or water), seek medical help without delay.

Viral Gastroenteritis This is caused not by bacteria but, as the name suggests, by a virus. It is characterised by stomach cramps, diarrhoea, and sometimes by vomiting and/or a slight fever. All you can do is rest and drink lots of fluids.

Sexually Transmitted Diseases (STDs) While abstinence is the only 100% preventative, using condoms is also effective. Gonorrhoea and syphilis are the most common of these diseases: sores, blisters or rashes around the genitals, discharges, or pain when urinating are common symptoms. Symptoms may be less marked or not observed at all in women. Syphilis symptoms eventually disappear completely but the disease continues and can cause severe problems in later years. The treatment of gonorrhoea and syphilis is by antibiotics.

The most dangerous STD is of course HIV (Human Immunodeficiency Virus), which may develop into AIDS (Acquired Immune Deficiency Syndrome). It can also be spread by dirty needles, acupuncture, tattooing and ear or nose piercing.

Ticks Ticks might be a problem in forested areas and occasionally even in urban situations. If you see one that has buried itself into your skin, *don't* pull it off, but coax it out by covering it in petroleum jelly or oil. Salt or a lighted cigarette end may also be effective. A red blotch may appear, but long-term ill effects are rare. However, a very small proportion carry encephalitis (a cerebral inflammation that can cause death). In this case the blotch could be several cm across, perhaps pale in the centre; there may be flu-like symptoms or even no symptoms at all. Victims may feel extremely tired and weak. If you plan to spend a lot of time in forested areas, get an encephalitis immunisation before you leave. You'll see warnings about this hazard in many train stations.

Animal & Snake Bites Rabies is now rare in Europe, but you should still be wary of making contact with stray dogs or other mammals. Austria is home to several types of snakes, a couple of which can deliver a nasty although not fatal bite. They are more prevalent in the mountains. Wear boots when walking through undergrowth, don't put your hands into holes and crevices, and be careful when collecting firewood.

WOMEN TRAVELLERS

Women should experience no special problems. Fortunately, physical attacks and verbal harassment are less common than in many other countries. However, normal caution should be exercised when alone or in unfamiliar situations (which obviously occur quite often when travelling).

Austrian women do not enjoy equal social status to men in conservative parts of Austria, but this should not affect travellers. Vienna is more liberal about such matters, and a solo woman visiting a traditional male-oriented coffee house would not attract much notice.

TRAVELLING WITH CHILDREN

Successful travel with young children can require some special effort. Don't try to overdo things; even for adults, packing too much into the time available can cause problems. And make sure the activities include the kids as well, eg in Klagenfurt balance a tour of the museums with a trip to the Minimundus miniature park. Include children in the trip planning: if they have helped to work out where you will be going, they will be much more interested when they get there. See Lonely Planet's *Travel with Children* by Maureen Wheeler for more information.

DISABLED TRAVELLERS

If you have a physical disability, get in touch with your national support organisation at home (preferably the travel officer if there is one). They often have complete libraries devoted to travel, and can put you in touch with travel agents who specialise in tours for the disabled, or provide useful advice on independent travel.

The British-based Royal Association for Disability and Rehabilitation (RADAR) publishes a useful guide titled *Holidays and Travel Abroad: A Guide for Disabled People*, which gives a good overview of facilities available to disabled travellers in Europe. Contact RADAR (☎ 0171-250 3222) at 12 City Forum, 250 City Road, London EC1V 8 AF.

The Österreichischer Zivilinvalidenverband (☎ 0662-51 0 44), in Salzburg at Haunspergstrasse 39, looks after the needs of Austrian disabled people. Visitors will probably do better contacting instead the local tourist office for information on disabled access, parking (free in blue zones with the international disabled sticker), toilets, specialised shops and other matters. The Vienna office has the very detailed *Wien für Gäste mit Handicaps*. The Salzburg office also has good information.

Within Austria, hotels with three stars and above invariably have a lift (elevator) as well as stairs. More basic places often don't have a lift.

GAY & LESBIAN TRAVELLERS

Gays and lesbians should get in touch with their national organisation at home. This book lists some contact addresses and gay and lesbian venues (eg in Vienna), but your organisation should be able to give you much more comprehensive information. The *Spartacus International Gay Guide*, published by Bruno Gmünder (Berlin), is a good international directory of gay entertainment venues worldwide (mainly for men). Lesbians can turn to *Places of Interest for Women* (Ferrari Publications).

With the possible exception of Vienna, Austria is less liberal towards homosexuality than many European nations. Gay organisations are actually outlawed and it's against the law to promote homosexuality, though neither of these laws is usually enforced. The age of consent for gay and heterosexual sex is the same – 16. Strangely, there is no set age for lesbian sex, as the legislators apparently thought it would be impossible to distinguish between full sex and the intimate mutual washing of bodily parts. While lesbians welcome the lack of legislation, they see this as a typical (male) denial of female sexuality.

SENIOR TRAVELLERS

Senior citizens are entitled to many discounts in Austria on things like public transport, museum admission fees etc, provided they show proof of age. The minimum qualifying age for Austrians is 65 for men, and 60 for women. If the requisite age is lower in your own country, you *may* be able to persuade the Austrian official to give you a discount at that lower age.

In your home country, you may be entitled to all sorts of interesting travel packages and discounts (on car hire, for instance) through organisations and travel agents that cater for senior travellers. Start hunting at your local senior citizens' advice bureau.

SPECIAL DIETS

If you have dietary restrictions, tourist offices should be able to help with lists of suitable restaurants. Information on vegetarian places is given in this book for all major towns. See also the Food section in this chapter. The *Jewish Travel Guide* published by Jewish Chronicle Publications is a world-wide listing of kosher restaurants, synagogues and relevant institutions.

EMERGENCY

On the emergency (Euro-Notruf) telephone number you can request any emergency service: ☎ 112. Specific numbers are:

Ambulance: ☎ 144
Doctor (out of hours): ☎ 141
Police: ☎ 133
Fire: ☎ 122

The German for 'police' is *Polizei*, but in some parts of Austria they are called *Gendarmerie* instead.

DANGERS & ANNOYANCES
Theft

Crime rates in Austria are low by international standards but you should still always be security-conscious – you're never more vulnerable to theft than when travelling. Be wary of leaving valuables in hotel rooms. Staff will look after expensive items if you ask them, even in hostels. Don't even leave valuables in cars – especially not overnight. Beware of pickpockets (who thrive in crowds) and snatch-thieves (a daypack is more secure than a shoulder bag). Carry your own padlock for hostel lockers. Use a moneybelt and keep some emergency money hidden away from your main stash.

Generally, keep your wits about you, and be suspicious of anything out of the ordinary, even unlikely offers of help. Sadly, other travellers are sometimes the people you most have to guard against.

In the event of theft or loss, get a police report – this will be necessary for you to claim on travel insurance. Your consulate should be able to help if you're left in a desperate situation.

Drugs

Always treat drugs with a great deal of caution. Don't ever think about trying to carry drugs across the border. Dope (cannabis) is illegal but still available if you look hard enough. The police are reticent about revealing standard procedures for dealing with offenders. A small amount of dope for personal use would probably not be viewed seriously; possession of large amounts (above 300 grams) and dealing (especially to children) could result in a five-year prison term.

Other Concerns

Austrian train stations are a habitual haunt of drunks and vagrants who can be annoying and occasionally intimidating. Think twice

---

Avalanche Warning

Modern safety precautions mean the days of entire villages being buried by snow have passed, but the dangers of avalanches should not be underestimated. Each year, up to 200 people are killed by avalanches in the Alps.

Problems usually originate on slopes high above the prepared ski runs. Accordingly, mountain resorts now have a series of crisscross metal barriers built high on peaks to prevent snow slips. In addition, helicopters routinely drop explosive devices in the mountains to cause controlled slides and prevent the dangerous build-up of snow. Resorts also have a system involving flags or flashing lights to warn skiers of the likelihood of avalanches, and up-to-date reports on weather conditions are always available.

Despite these measures, skiers cannot afford to be complacent. Avalanche warnings should be heeded, and local advice sought before detouring from prepared runs. If skiers are buried in an avalanche snowfall, chances of rescue are improved if they carry an avalanche transceiver, a radio that transmits and receives a 457kHz signal. These cost around UK£160. A more expensive precaution (but of unproven value) is an ABS air balloon rucksack. ■

before sleeping overnight in a train station waiting room.

There has been something of a racist resurgence in southern Austria, with the anti-immigration, right-wing Freedom Party gaining ground. The Freedom Party is also making advances in traditionally socialist Vienna, despite (or because of) its wider ethnic mix.

Take care in the mountains: helicopter rescue is expensive unless you are covered by insurance (that's assuming they find you in the first place).

WORK

Since January 1993 EU nationals have been able to obtain work in Austria without needing a work permit, though after three months they should register with the Aufenthaltsbehörde (Residence Authority) office if there is one, or the Gemeindeamt (Council office) in smaller places. Contact your Austrian embassy at home for more information, or the Bundesministerium für Arbeit und Soziales (☎ 711 00), 1 Stubenring 1, Vienna. Nationals from outside the EU need to obtain both a work permit and a residency permit in advance from the Austrian embassy in their home country; for these to be granted you'll probably need a job offer, sufficient funds and confirmed accommodation in Austria.

Language skills are particularly crucial for any type of work in service industries. Your best chance of finding work is to start writing or asking around early – summer for winter work and winter for summer work. Try to get it all organised before places close for the off season. Some people do get lucky by arriving right at the beginning of the season and asking around.

In ski resorts, where there are often vacancies for jobs with unsociable hours, employers may be prepared to bend the rules on work permits, though regulations are now enforced more strictly than they were a few years ago. Although it is beyond their brief, tourist offices may be able to help you find work. Otherwise, you may be able to find casual work in return for free board and lodging and pocket money. Likely opportunities are in snow clearing, chalet cleaning, restaurants and ski equipment shops. If you manage to get a job just by asking around in ski resorts, the employer might be prepared to apply for the work permit on your behalf. A Volunteer Work Permit may be fairly easy to get; the drawback is that with this sort of permit you're not supposed to actually earn anything.

In October, grape-pickers are usually required in the wine-growing regions. Busking (street theatre) is not uncommon in Austria and may make you a few schillings if you have the required skills. Buskers are occasionally moved on by the police – ask about local regulations before you start up. Also ask about relevant permits before selling goods at flea markets.

One publication worth looking at is the fortnightly *Rolling Pin International* (AS25). It describes itself as 'the international newspaper of the hotel and tourism industries' and has articles in German and English. It carries job advertisements from around the world but by far the biggest section (about 10 pages) is for jobs in Austria; they're mostly in hotels. It should be available in most countries, but if you have difficulty finding a copy, contact the head office in Graz (☎ 0316-811 277), PO Box 44, A-8016. The principle of equal opportunity doesn't seem to apply: many jobs specify females only.

Useful books are *Working in Ski Resorts – Europe* by Victoria Pybus & Charles James, *Work Your Way Around the World* by Susan Griffith and *The Au Pair and Nanny's Guide to Working Abroad* by Susan Griffith & Sharon Legg; all are published in paperback by Vacation Work.

ACTIVITIES

Alpine mountains and lakes provide a superb setting for outdoor sports. In addition to the sports mentioned below, golf, tennis and horse riding are widely pursued. Cycling is also extremely popular: see the Getting Around chapter.

Skiing

All Austrians seem able to ski effortlessly. One reason for this is that schools organise skiing excursions for older pupils.

Skiing for tourists is reasonable value, and generally cheaper than in neighbouring Switzerland. Ski passes, which cover the costs of mountain transport, for little-known places may be almost half the price of the jet-set resorts like Kitzbühel. Vorarlberg and especially Tirol are the most popular areas, but there is also skiing in Salzburg province, Upper Austria and Carinthia. Ski passes are available from ski lifts, and usually from buses to the lifts, and also occasionally from tourist offices. Equipment can always be hired at resorts. You may initially get some strange looks if you ask to buy ex-rental stock, but great bargains can be picked up this way. Also keep your eyes open for discarded equipment that may still be perfectly usable.

Ski coupons for ski lifts can sometimes be bought, but usually there are general passes available for complete or partial days. Count on around AS240 to AS400 for a one-day ski pass, with substantial reductions for longer-term passes. The skiing season starts in December and lasts well into April in higher resorts. At the beginning and end of the season, and sometimes in January, ski passes may be available at a reduced rate as these times are low-season. Mid-April to May and November to mid-December falls between the summer and winter seasons in mountain resorts. Some cable cars will be closed for maintenance and many hotels and restaurants will be shut, but at least you'll avoid the crowds and find prices at their lowest. Year-round skiing is possible at several glaciers, such as the Stubai Glacier near Innsbruck.

This book is not a skiing guide. It does contain plenty of skiing information, but Austria has hundreds of top-notch ski resorts and no attempt has been made to cover them exhaustively. Don't assume the skiing is not good in a resort if it is not mentioned here. Rather, ski resorts have been selected if good skiing is allied to fame, scenery, and general attractions. For a detailed assessment of resorts based primarily on skiing criteria, turn to a specialist book or magazine, such as *The Good Ski Guide* published in the UK by Good Ski Guide Ltd.

The recent craze in ski resorts is snowboarding, the Alpine equivalent of surfing, dismissed by some as a phenomenon of 'young punks on planks' ('punks' is the more polite version of the phrase). This is as popular in Austria as it is elsewhere, and boards can be hired from ski shops. Cross-country skiing (*Langlauf*) is also extremely popular, and is the cheapest form of skiing because it's not necessary to buy lift passes in order to reach the trails and the slender cross-country skis are generally cheaper to hire than the sturdier downhill version. Rental prices for one day are around AS180 for downhill and AS90 for cross-country; ski shoes for downhill skiing are about AS80. Prices reduce over longer periods. Rental shops are often open daily.

There are numerous schools where you can learn to ski – Tirol province alone has

---

Clay-Court Master

Austria's top tennis player is clay-court specialist, Thomas Muster. In 1995, he became the first Austrian to win a Grand Slam tournament when he captured the French Open title. Muster, dubbed the 'Iron Man' by commentators, has shown great resilience in recovering from a major car accident, which occurred in 1989 in the USA. The resulting damage to ligaments in his left leg made it doubtful he would play tennis again. Muster won the French Open with his 35th successive victory on clay, an unbeaten run lasting eight months and catapulting him to No 3 in the world rankings. ■

1600 registered ski instructors. All the ski resorts listed in this book have at least one ski school and you can join a group class or pay for individual tuition on a per-lesson basis. It shouldn't be necessary to arrange these in advance. The ski school in Obertraun, a fairly low-profile resort, costs AS1100 for 20 hours tuition (AS400 per hour for individual tuition). In contrast, the ski school in flashy Lech charges AS1440 for 20 hours.

Hiking & Mountaineering

Hiking is popular with Austrians and visitors alike. Thousands of kms of trails explore the Alps. En route there are regular direction signs, and paths may also be indicated by red-white-red stripes on a convenient tree trunk. The practice of marking mountain trails according to their difficulty has started in Tirol and is becoming more widespread. Paths are colour-coded according to the skiing system: blue for easy, red for moderate (fairly narrow and steep), and black for difficult (only for the physically fit, some climbing may be required).

Most tourist offices have free or cheap maps of hiking routes. The best trails are away from the towns and in the hills. If you can afford it, take a cable car to get you started.

Mountaineering is a potentially dangerous activity, and you should never climb on your own or without proper equipment. Tirol has the most opportunities for mountain climbing. Be sure to consult local information phone numbers about weather conditions and avalanche warnings. The Kaisergebirge mountains in northern Tirol are a favourite with mountaineers, though there are other areas (eg the Ziller Valley).

The glossy *Mountains* booklet, available from ANTO or the Tirol regional office, contains contact addresses for mountain guides and mountaineering schools in the province, as well as details of Alpine huts and walking trails.

The Austrian Alpine Club (Österreichischer Alpenverein, ÖAV) caters for both hikers and mountaineers. Adult membership costs an initial AS70 plus AS460 per year, with substantial discounts for students and those aged under 25 or those over 60. ÖAV members pay half-price at Alpine huts and get other benefits, including insurance. The ÖAV head office (☎ 0512-58 78 28; fax 58 88 42) is at Wilhelm Greil Strasse 15, A-6010 Innsbruck. At the same address is its mountaineering school, the Bergsteigerschule (☎ 0512-59 5 47 34; fax 57 55 28). This

Austria offers numerous hiking opportunities on thousands of trails through the Alps

offers various mountain touring programmes for members, mostly in the summer.

Aerial Sports

Mountains are made for paragliding and hang-gliding. They are both popular, especially paragliding, and the equipment is more portable. Many resorts have places where you can hire the gear, get tuition, or simply go as a passenger on a flight. Ballooning is also taking off, despite the high costs.

Water Sports

The lakes are equally as developed for sports as the mountains. Water-skiing, sailing and windsurfing are common on most lakes; courses are usually available. The Austrian Sailing Federation (☎ 587 86 88) is at Grosse Neugasse 8, A-1040, Vienna. Carinthia and Salzkammergut are good regions for water sports. Although you can swim for free in some places, many lakeside beaches require an entrance fee (around AS20 to AS50 per day). Anglers should contact the local tourist office for a fishing permit valid for lakes and rivers. Rafting is another option on rivers. Paddleboats (*Pedalos*) are usually waiting for hire in lakeside resorts, as are rowing boats and motorboats.

Spa Resorts

There are spa resorts throughout the country. They are usually identifiable by the prefix *Bad* (Bath), eg Bad Ischl, Badgastein and Baden. Leisurely long walks and much wallowing in hot springs are typical ingredients of these salubrious locations.

Courses

In addition to the activity-based holidays and the schools for specific sports, there's a chance to learn new practical skills or academic disciplines. A variety of institutions offer a host of courses in the cities, either on an intensive full-time or evening-only basis. The most relevant for visitors is likely to be German-language classes. Language schools are included in the sections on Vienna, Salzburg and Innsbruck.

HIGHLIGHTS

Vienna and Salzburg are the most rewarding cities, followed by Innsbruck and Graz. Be sure to spend time at a traditional coffee house and a wine tavern (*Heuriger* or *Buschenschank*). Don't miss a visit to the opera or some other musical event. Take in the chaos and clutter of Vienna's flea market at the Naschmarkt. Spend some time in the Alps; perhaps take a Danube River cruise. Visit the ice caves at Wergen or Dachstein. For skiing and glitz, head for Kitzbühel or Lech; or for a less elitist skiing ambience, try St Anton. The following should help you prioritise your time.

Churches & Abbeys

St Stephen's Cathedral, in Vienna, is *the* Gothic church in Austria. The abbeys at Melk and St Florian illustrate Baroque to perfection. St Barbara Church in Bärnbach is unique. See the St Wolfgang altar in St Wolfgang's pilgrimage church, and the statues and mausoleum in Innsbruck's Hofkirche.

Museums & Galleries

The Kunsthistorisches Museum in Vienna is best for art; the Naturhaus, Salzburg, is best for natural history. For something a little more bizarre, try the Josephinium, the medical museum in Vienna. For ancient armaments, go to the armoury in Graz. Appreciate Austrian art in the Belvedere Palace, Vienna.

Palaces

In Vienna, enjoy Schönbrunn Palace for its grounds and Baroque rooms, and the Hofburg for its grand scale and many museum collections. In Salzburg, see Mirabell Palace for its gardens and Hellbrunn Palace for its water fountains. Also visit Schloss Eggenberg in Graz and Schloss Ambras in Innsbruck.

Picturesque Views

Take in the Nordkette peaks from Innsbruck's Maria Theresien Strasse, Friesach's castles from near the town moat,

Steyr at the confluence of its two rivers, Ehrenhausen's Hauptstrasse, and Hochosterwitz Castle with its spiralling defences. Don't miss Salzburg's domes from the Salzach, and the panorama from the Hohensalzburg fortress. Also view Graz from its Schlossberg, and the Schlossberg and Landhaus from the Graz armoury.

Scenic train rides include Innsbruck to Seefeld, Innsbruck to St Anton, Zell am See to Spittal and der Drau, and Semmering to Wiener Neustadt. The lake and mountain landscape from the Schafberg, Salzkammergut, is superb. Marvel at the unfolding magnificence of the Grossglockner Road. Linger over the view back to Krimml from the top of Krimml Falls. Expansive mountain vistas are part of the package at all ski resorts.

ACCOMMODATION

Accommodation is efficiently classified and graded according to the type of establishment and level of comfort. Tourist offices invariably have extensive information on everything available, including prices and facilities on-site. Often the office will find and book rooms for little or no commission. They tend not to locate the really budget places, but this service could save you a lot of time and effort, especially in somewhere like Vienna where finding a place to stay can be a problem.

In Austria there has been a general move towards providing higher quality accommodation at higher prices (eg rooms where guests use hall showers are gradually being upgraded and fitted with private showers). This makes life more difficult for budget travellers, who increasingly will have to rely on hostels.

It's wise to book ahead at all times, but reservations are definitely recommended in July and August and at Christmas and Easter. If a flexible itinerary precludes you making reservations a long way in advance, a telephone call the day before is better than nothing. However, some places will not accept telephone reservations. Confirmed reservations in writing are binding on either side and compensation may be claimed if you do not take a reserved room or if a reserved room is unavailable. Instant hotel reservations can be made from Britain via Austria On-line (☎ 0171-434 7390).

Breakfast is included in hostel, pension and hotel prices listed in this book, unless stated otherwise. Prices quoted here are high-season prices, which can be significantly higher than low-season prices in mid-range and top-end hotels. In hostels and budget pensions and hotels there is little, if any, variation in prices throughout the year.

Camping

There are over 400 camping grounds, which offer a range of facilities such as washing machines, electricity hook-up, cooking facilities (rarely) and on-site shop. Camping Gaz canisters are widely available. Camp sites are often scenically situated in an out-of-the-way place by a river or lake – fine if you're exploring the countryside but a bit of a pain if you want to sightsee in a town. For this reason, and because of the extra gear required, camping is more viable if you have your own transport. Sites charge between AS30 to AS60 per person, plus the same again for a tent and for a car, though some have a system of charging an all-inclusive rate for a site. For budget solo travellers, hostelling doesn't work out much more expensive.

Some sites are open all year but the majority close in the winter. If demand is low in spring and autumn, some camp sites will shut even if their literature says they should be open; telephone ahead at such times. In peak season, camp sites may be full unless you reserve, even though higher prices may apply.

The Austrian Camping Club (☎ 02243-85 877) is at An der Au, A-3400 Klosterneuburg.

Free camping is OK, except in urban areas, protected rural areas and on private land. Collect all your rubbish and dispose of it responsibly. On private land, check with the owner – they may allow you to camp, either for free or for a small charge.

Edelweiss is among Austria's many
Alpine flowers

Alpine Huts

There are 500 of these in the Eastern Alps,
and most are maintained by the Austrian
Alpine Club (ÖAV – see the Hiking & Mountaineering section in this chapter). Huts are
situated between about 900 and 2700 metres
and may be used by the general public. Meals
or cooking facilities are often available. Bed
prices for nonmembers are typically AS240
in a double or AS180 in a dormitory.
Members of the ÖAV or an affiliated club
pay half-price and have priority.

Hostels

Hostels are no longer specifically aimed at
youths, though most people who stay in them
are young, and noisy school groups can
sometimes disrupt the peace of such places.
Facilities in hostels are improving: four to
six-bed dorms with private shower/WC are
common, and some places even have double
rooms or family rooms. Having to do chores
is a thing of the past, but the annoying habit
of locking the doors during the day (usually
from 9 am to 5 pm) and at night (any time
between 10 pm and midnight) still persists in
many places. Only rarely can you check in
before 5 pm.

Austria has over 100 hostels affiliated to

Hostelling International (HI), plus a smattering of privately-owned hostels. Membership
cards are always required except in a few
private hostels. It'll be cheaper to become a
member in your home country than to wait
till you get to Austria. Nonmembers pay a
surcharge of AS40 per night for a guest card
(*Gästekarte*); after six nights the guest card
counts as a full membership card. Most
hostels accept reservations by telephone.
Some hostels have a fax reservation service:
you pay AS10 for the fax and a AS105
deposit which you get back when you claim
your bed at the hostel. Dormitory prices are
from AS110 to AS140 per night.

Youth hostel in German is *Jugendherberge*, though *Jugendgästehaus* or other
titles may be used instead.

Austria has two hostel organisations.
Hostels which are affiliated to the worldwide
HI network are linked to one or the other; this
is something of a historical legacy and makes
no difference to how the hostels are run.
Either head office in Vienna can give information on all HI hostels. The
Österreichischer Jugendherbergsverband
(☎ 0222-533 53 53) is on the corner of 1
Gonzagagasse 22 and 1 Schottenring 28;
either address is OK for mail. The
Österreichischer Jugendherbergswerk
(☎ 533 18 33) is at 1 Helfersdorferstrasse 4.
The latter has a travel arm called Supertramp
(☎ 0222-533 51) and a hiking shop on the
same premises.

Cheap dormitory-style accommodation is
sometimes available in ski resorts even if
there is no hostel. Look for *Touristenlager* or
Massenlager; unfortunately, such accommodation might only be offered to pre-booked
groups.

Hotels & Pensions

Hotels and pensions are rated from one to
five stars depending on the facilities they
offer, though as respective criteria vary you
can't assume a three-star pension is equivalent to a three-star hotel. Pensions tend to be
smaller than hotels, and usually provide a
more personal service and less standardised
fixtures and fittings. Pensions generally offer

a better size and quality of room for the price than hotels. Where they usually can't compete is in back-up services (eg room service, laundry service) and on-site facilities (eg private car parking, bar and/or restaurant). If none of that matters to you, stick with the pensions.

With very few exceptions, rooms in hotels and pensions are clean and adequately appointed. In tourist areas, expect to pay a minimum of around AS280/500 for a single/double with hall shower or AS330/600 with private shower. In less-visited places you may be able to save around AS50 per person. Prices quoted here are for the main high season, which means summer prices except in ski resorts. In the low season, prices should be noticeably lower, though in cities the difference will be less marked.

However, whether in city or country, if business is slow, mid-range and top-end hotels (and to a lesser extent pensions) are willing to negotiate on prices. It's always worth asking for a special deal as prices can come down quite substantially. Some places will also offer special weekend rates, or two nights for the price of one. Even in budget places, ask for a special price if you're planning to stay for more than a few days. Credit cards are rarely accepted by cheaper places.

In low-budget accommodation, a room with a private shower may mean a room with a shower cubicle rather than a proper en suite bathroom. Where there is a telephone in the room it's usually direct-dial, but this will still be more expensive than using a public telephone box. TVs are increasingly hooked up to satellite or cable (especially in places with three stars and above), which is a definite plus over TVs that only get the two national channels. Rooms which have a TV generally also have a mini-bar; prices will be comparable to ordinary bar prices in mid-range accommodation, but quite expensive in plush places.

Many hotels and pensions have rooms with three or more beds, or can place a fold-up bed in the room for a child; ask at the establishment. Smaller places with two stars or less tend not to have a lift (elevator); most

other places do. Some old Viennese apartment blocks have a lift that needs to be operated by a key, which the pension will give you.

All meals are often available, either for guests only, or more usually in a public on-site restaurant. A pension that has only breakfast available is a *Frühstückspension*; the hotel equivalent is *Hotel-Garni*. Other hotels and pensions will offer the option of paying for half or even full board. In budget places, breakfast is basic, maybe only a beverage, bread rolls, butter, cheese spread and jam. As you pay more, breakfast gets better; usually it's 'extended' *(Erweitert)* in two-star places, and could be a help-yourself buffet in places with three stars or more. A typical buffet will include the standard breakfast, plus cereals, juices and a selection of cold meats and cheeses. In five-star and some four-star places, you can expect hot food too (egg, sausage, bacon etc).

Other Accommodation

Self-catering holiday apartments *(Ferienwohnungen)* abound in mountain resorts, though it is sometimes necessary to book these well in advance. Hotels sometimes have self-contained apartment rooms.

A cheap and widely available option, particularly in more rural areas, is to take a room in a private house (AS120 to AS250 per person) or a farmhouse *(Bauernhof)*. In either case, look for signs saying *Zimmer frei* or *Privat Zimmer*.

A *Gasthaus* or *Gasthof* is a small-scale country inn. In these sorts of places you may not be able to check in on a day that the restaurant is closed for its rest day *(Ruhetag)* – phone ahead in this instance (somebody is normally there in the morning to organise the guests' breakfast).

Tourist offices can supply listings of accommodation, and often make reservations for little or no commission. The first night's stay can sometimes cost more.

In many resorts (not so often in cities) a guest card is issued to people who stay overnight, though entitlement may depend on a minimum length of stay. The card may offer discounts on useful things such as cable cars and admission prices. Check with the tourist office if you're not offered one at your resort accommodation – even camp sites and youth hostels should be included in these schemes. The guest card system is often financed by a resort tax, which may be anything from AS6 to AS25 per night, depending upon the place and type of accommodation. Prices quoted in accommodation lists are usually inclusive of such taxes.

FOOD

The main meal is taken at noon, whether in a restaurant, café or tavern. Many places have a set meal or menu of the day (Tagesteller or Tagesmenu) which gives the best value for money: a lunch menu with soup can sometimes cost as little as AS55 or AS60. A Mittagsmenu (midday menu) is similar to the Tagesmenu, although sometimes available in the evening also. Chinese restaurants are particularly good value in this respect, and the food is generally reliable. There are around 700 Chinese restaurants in Austria, and around 1000 pizzerias. Wine taverns (Heurigen or Buschenschenken) are fairly inexpensive places to eat, and are an Austrian institution, particularly in the suburbs of Vienna.

The cheapest deal around for sit-down food is in university restaurants (Mensas). Those mentioned in this book are open to everyone, though they usually only serve weekday lunches and may be closed during university holidays. Expect to find two or three different daily specials, including a vegetarian choice. Students may be able to get a discount of AS4 or so if they show an ISIC card. Mensas are good places to meet students (who usually speak English well) and find out about the 'in' places round town.

The main train stations all have several options for a cheap meal. Branches of Wienerwald offer unremarkable but reasonably priced chicken dishes, either on an eat-in or takeaway basis. Nordsee is its fishy equivalent. Self-service places are usually the cheapest and are often indicated by SB (Selbstbedienung).

For expensive dining, five-star hotels invariably have a gourmet restaurant. The more expensive restaurants usually add a cover charge (Gedeck), typically around AS25 at lunch and AS45 in the evening. In restaurants without a cover charge, the bread that appears on the table usually costs extra – if in doubt, ask.

If you plan on self-catering, Hofer is the cheapest of the several national supermarket chains, while Julius Meinl is the most expensive. If you just want to fill up with fast food, there's usually somewhere you can do this. A McDonald's awaits in every town, but sausage stands (Würstel Stand) selling various sausages with bread are more authentically Austrian. Deli shops sometimes offer hot food, such as spit-roasted

A Culinary Institution

The Würstel (sausage) stand is a familiar Austrian institution and may sell up to a dozen types of sausage. Each comes with a chunk of bread and a big dollop of mustard (Senf) – which can be sweet (Süss or Kremser Senf) or hot (Scharf). Tomato ketchup and mayonnaise are often provided. The thinner sausages are served two at a time, except in the less expensive 'hot dog' version, when the sausage is placed in a bread stick.

Types of sausage include: the Frankfurter, a standard thin, boiled sausage; the Bratwurst, a fat, fried sausage; and Burenwurst, the boiled equivalent of Bratwurst. Debreziner is a thin, spicy sausage from Hungary. Currywurst is Burenwurst with a curry flavour, and Käsekrainer is a sausage infused with cheese. Tiroler Wurst is a smoked sausage. If you want to surprise and perhaps impress the server, use the following Viennese slang to ask for a Burenwurst with sweet mustard and a crust of bread: 'A Hasse mit an Síassn und an Scherzl, bitte'. ∎

chicken (an Austrian favourite). Occasionally they have tables so you can eat on the premises.

Be wary of public holidays: restaurants that have a rest day *(Ruhetag)* often also close on these days. Although inns and restaurants often stay open till 11 pm or midnight, the kitchen is rarely open beyond 9 or 9.30 pm (except in pizzerias and Chinese restaurants).

Austrian Cuisine

Traditional Austrian food is generally quite heavy and hearty with meat strongly emphasised. In some parts of Austria vegetarians will have a fairly tough time finding varied meals. Even so, many places now offer at least one vegetarian dish, and there has been a noticeable move towards providing light, healthy meals (eg a *Fitnessteller*), especially in summer.

Jause is a light meal, served between normal eating times. You may come across regional variations in the German spellings used below.

Soup is the standard starter to a meal, particularly with a menu of the day. *Markknödelsuppe* is a clear bone marrow soup with dumplings. *Frittatensuppe* is a clear soup with shreds of pancake.

Dumplings *(Knödel)* are an element of many meals, and can appear in soups and desserts as well as main courses. They may be made of a variety of ingredients, eg liver *(Leberknödel)* or bread *(Semmelknödel)*.

Nockerln (sometimes called *Spätzle*, especially in the west) is small home-made pasta with a similar taste to Knödel. *Nudeln* is normally flat pasta (like tagliatelle), except when it's tiny noodles in a soup. In Carinthia, pasta is made into balls and combined with cheese *(Kasnudeln)*. *Kasnocken*, *Kässpätzle* and *Kasnödel* are variations on a similar theme.

Potato will usually appear as French fries *(Pommes Frites)*, boiled *(Kartoffel)*, roasted *(Bratkartoffel)* or as *Geröstete*, sliced small and sauteed. *Erdäpfel* is another word for potato.

Meat & Fish *Wiener Schnitzel* is Vienna's best known culinary concoction, and is consumed everywhere, not just in Vienna. It's a cutlet covered in a coating of egg and breadcrumbs and fried. The cutlet is either veal *(Kalb)* or, less expensively, pork *(Schwein)*; occasionally there are variations, such as turkey *(Puten)*.

Goulash *(Gulasch)* is also very popular. It's a stew with a rich sauce flavoured with paprika. Paprika pops up in various other dishes too, though note that *Gefüllte Paprika* will be a bell pepper (capsicum) stuffed with rice and meat.

Chicken may be called variously *Geflügel* (poultry), *Huhn* (hen) or *Hähnchen* (small cock) and is usually fried *(Backhuhn)* or roasted *(Brathuhn)*. A great variety of sausage *(Wurst)* is available, and not only at the takeaway stands. Beef *(Rindfleisch)*, lamb *(Lamm)* and liver *(Leber)* are mainstays of many menus. *Kümmelfleisch* is pork stew, flavoured with cumin. *Krenfleisch* is pork with horseradish. *Tafelspitz* is boiled beef, often served with *Apfelkren* (apple and horseradish sauce).

Austrians are fond of eating bits of beasts that some other nations ignore. *Beuschel* may be translated on menus as 'calf's lights'. It's thin slices of calf's lungs and heart in a thick sauce, usually served with a bread dumpling. It's quite tasty. Really. *Tiroler Bauernschmaus* is a selection of meats served with sauerkraut, potatoes and dumplings.

Common fish are trout *(Forelle)*, pike *(Hecht)*, pike-perch *(Fogosch)* and carp *(Karpfen)*. *Saibling* is a local freshwater fish, similar to trout.

Desserts & Cakes The most famous Austrian dessert is the *Strudel*, baked dough filled with a variety of fruits – usually apple *(Apfel)* with a few raisins and cinnamon. The Salzburg speciality, *Salzburger Nockerl*, is fluffy baked pudding made from eggs, flour and sugar. Pancakes are another popular dessert eg *Moosbeernocken* (blueberry pancakes). *Germknödel* are sour dough dumplings and *Buchteln* is noodles with vanilla cream. *Mohr im Hemd* is chocolate pudding with chocolate sauce. *Pofesen* is stuffed fritters.

Austria, and especially Vienna, is renowned for excellent pastries and cakes, which are very effective at transferring bulk from your money belt to your waistline. *Guglhupf* is a cake shaped like a volcano.

DRINKS
Nonalcoholic Drinks
Coffee is the preferred hot beverage rather than tea, though both are expensive in cafés and restaurants. Coffee houses *(Kaffeehaus* or *Café Konditorei)* are an established part of Austrian life, particularly in Vienna. Strong Turkish coffee is popular. Linger over a cup (from AS20) and read the free newspapers. Mineral or soda water is widely available, though tap water is fine to drink. Apple juice *(Apfelsaft)* is also popular. *Almdudler* is a soft drink found all over Austria; it's a sort of cross between ginger ale and lemonade.

Alcohol
Austrian wine comes in various categories that designate quality and legal requirements in the production, starting with the humble *Tafelwein*, through to *Landwein, Qualitäts-wein* and *Prädikatswein*; the latter two have subgroups. In restaurants, wine bought by the carafe or glass will be the cheapest choice. In autumn the whole country goes mad for *Sturm*, Heurigen wine in its semi-fermented state.

Austria is also known for its beer; some well-known makes include Gösser, Schwechater, Stiegl and Zipfer. It is usually a light, golden colour *(hell)*, though you can sometimes get a dark *(dunkel)* version too. In places where both types are on draught you can ask for a *Mischbiere*, a palatable mix of the two. *Weizenbier* or *Weissbier* (wheat beer) has a distinctive taste. It can be light or dark, clear or cloudy, and is usually served

---

The EU Effect
On 1 January 1995 Austria became a member of the EU, a move which has already greatly affected both Austrians and tourists. Some changes will be beneficial, but others not. Austria's cosseted farmers felt the impact immediately, though the EU agricultural policy still provides a high level of protection. Wholesale milk prices quickly dropped and may eventually be halved. General food shopping bills are expected to be reduced by between 5% and 10%, with reductions in staples such as bread, cheese, meat, fruit and vegetables. Austrian wine (another staple!) should become cheaper as supermarkets are flooded with Spanish and Portuguese imports. Clothes are expected to be 10% to 15% cheaper. However by mid-1995, price changes had only been noted in some of these goods, and even where wholesale prices had dropped, only about half of the reductions had been passed on to consumers (no legislation is planned to force retailers to reduce prices).

Other changes have less general relevance. EU residents living in Austria, for example, can now vote in Austrian local elections or even stand as a councillor, but prospective mayors should note they must have been born in Austria to take up that exalted office. (Pregnant visitors may want to bear that in mind!).

The notorious EU propensity to bureaucracy may yet be felt in Austria, such as in the stringent (or petty) regulations regarding the labelling and description of foodstuffs. Britain has had its own legislative battle as to what can be called a sausage. Austrians, meanwhile, are relieved that their cauliflower can still be called *Karfiol* instead of *Blumenkohl*, and mince meat is still known as *Faschiertes*, even if Germany considers it to be *Hackfleisch.* There has already been one example of the EU dictating on these matters, but pro-EU lobbyists are unlikely to be left with jam on their faces: the public should not be outraged by the modest insistence that exported Austrian jam be labelled *Konfitüre* instead of *Marmelade.* ■

MARK HONAN

MARK HONAN

MARK HONAN

MARK HONAN

MARK HONAN

MARK HONAN

A	B
C	D
E	F

A: Castle doorway, Linz, Upper Austria
B: Altes Landhaus façade, Innsbruck, Tirol
C: Arcaded corridor, Rathaus, Vienna
D: Doorway relief on fortified church, Eisenerz, Styria
E: Sculptures, St Florian Abbey, Upper Austria
F: Post office façade, Fleischmarkt, Vienna

Top: Souvenirs, Mariazell, Styria
Bottom: Ornament shop, Vienna

with a slice of lemon straddling the glass rim. Draught beer *(vom Fass)* comes in a 0.5-litre or 0.3-litre glass. In Vienna and some other parts of eastern Austria these are called respectively a *Krügerl* (sometimes spelled *Krügel*) and a *Seidel*. Elsewhere these will simply be *Grosse* (big) or *Kleine* (small). A small beer may also be called a *Glas* (glass). A *Pfiff* is ⅛ of a litre. *Radler* is a mix of beer and lemonade.

Austria produces several types of rum. Obstler is a spirit created from a mixture of fruits. Schnapps is also a popular spirit.

ENTERTAINMENT

Late opening is common in the cities, and in Vienna you can party all night long. It isn't hard to find bars or taverns featuring traditional or rock music.

Some cinemas show films in their original language. When this is the case, it should be stated on advertising posters: look for *OF (Original Fassung)* or *OV (Original Version)*. OmU *(Original mit Untertiteln)* means the film is in the original language with subtitles.

The main season for opera, theatre and concerts is September to June. Cheap, standing-room tickets are often available shortly before performances begin and they represent excellent value. Once inside, those standing tie a scarf to the rails or balcony to reserve their place when they go to the bar. If you're really on a budget, bear in mind you can often get into these places free after the first interval.

Gamblers can indulge at a dozen casinos around the country, including ones in Vienna, Graz, Linz, Innsbruck and Salzburg. Stakes for blackjack, roulette and other games are from AS50 (AS100 after 9 pm) up to much more than you can probably afford. There's no entry fee and you need to show identification to get in. To get you started on the gambling road, you only need to pay AS260 for your first AS300-worth of chips (these are a different colour, so you can't just cash them in and walk out!). Smart dress is required for the gaming tables (ie no trainers or jeans): a collared shirt, a tie (in winter) and jacket (a jacket and tie can sometimes be hired for a refundable deposit). Usual opening hours are 3 pm to 3 am.

THINGS TO BUY

Local crafts such as textiles, pottery, painted glassware, woodcarving and wrought-iron work make popular souvenirs. Unfortunately, Austria is no bargain when it comes to prices. The official outlet for goods that adhere to certain standards is the *Heimatwerk*. One of these exists in each major city (see city sections).

Top Viennese hotels dispense a free *Shopping in Vienna* booklet detailing all sorts of shopping outlets. Graz produces its own version.

Getting There & Away

Air travel is the quickest, easiest and sometimes cheapest means of transcontinental travel. If you're visiting Austria from outside Europe, it may be cheaper to fly to a European 'gateway' city and travel on from there. Munich, for example, is only two hours by train from Salzburg. There are some great fares available on certain routes thanks to severe competition between the airlines. Students, people aged under 26 and senior citizens often qualify for excellent deals.

Don't forget to arrange travel insurance. Paying for your ticket with a credit card often in itself provides limited travel accident insurance. For additional protection, limit your business dealings to travel agents who are bonded in some way (eg to ABTA in the UK), so you'll get reimbursed in the event of bankruptcy.

AIR

The main air transport hub is Vienna's airport (Flughafen Wien Schwechat), which handles nearly eight million passengers a year (10% of these travel to or from London). It has all the facilities expected of a major airport, such as tourist information, money-exchange counters (high commission rates) and car rental. See the Getting Around section in the Vienna chapter for information on transport from the airport to the city. Other Austrian airports which receive international flights are those at Linz, Graz, Salzburg, Innsbruck and Klagenfurt. These have scheduled or charter flights to a few European destinations and have transfer flights to/from Vienna for intercontinental passengers.

Austrian Airlines is the national carrier and has the most extensive services to Vienna. Lauda Air is another home-grown airline; ☎ 0660-66 55 is its toll-free number within Austria for reservations and information. Remember always to reconfirm your onward or return bookings by the specified time – usually 72 hours before departure on international flights.

There is no departure tax to pay at the airport when flying out of Austria; taxes do apply but they must be included in the airline ticket price. What may not be automatically included is the 'passenger service charge' of around US$15 that was introduced in 1995.

Buying a Plane Ticket

A plane ticket is a major expense, and it pays to spend some time researching the current state of the market. Start early: some of the cheapest tickets have to be bought months in advance (such as Apex tickets), and some popular flights sell out early. Alternatively, if your plans are flexible enough, you might risk waiting for last-minute bargains. Look for special offers that crop up from time to time.

Airlines release discounted tickets through selected travel agents, and they are often the cheapest deals going. Airlines don't sell these direct, but it's worth contacting them for information on routes and time-tables. Their low-season, student, youth and senior citizens fares can be very competitive. Return tickets usually work out much cheaper than two one-way tickets. Open Jaw returns allow you to fly into one city and out of another.

Round-the-World (RTW) tickets are another possibility, and are comparable in price to an ordinary return ticket. RTWs start at about UK£850, A$1800 or US$1300 depending on the season, and may be valid for up to a year. Special conditions might be attached to such tickets (eg you can't backtrack on a route). Also beware of cancellation penalties for these and other tickets.

Courier fares, where you get cheap passage in return for accompanying an urgent package through customs, offer incredibly low prices but there are usually special restrictions attached, and demand for couriers is decreasing in this electronic age.

If you are travelling from the USA, UK or South-East Asia, you will probably find that the cheapest flights are being advertised by obscure agencies. Most such firms are honest and solvent, but there are some rogue fly-by-night outfits around. If you feel suspicious about a firm, it's best to steer clear, or only pay a deposit before you get your ticket, then ring the airline to confirm that you are actually booked onto the flight before you pay the balance.

Established outfits, such as those mentioned in this book, offer more safety and are almost as competitive as you can get. The cheapest deals are only available at certain times of the year, or on weekdays, and fares are particularly subject to change. Always ask about the route: the cheapest tickets may involve an inconvenient stopover. Don't take schedules for granted, either: airlines usually change their schedules twice a year, on 26 March and 31 October.

Airlines can often make special arrangements for travellers with special needs if they're warned early enough. Children aged under two travel for 10% of the standard fare (or free on some airlines) as long as they don't occupy a seat. They don't get a baggage allowance. 'Skycots', baby food and diapers should be provided by the airline if requested in advance. Children aged between two and 12 can usually occupy a seat for half to two-thirds of the full fare, and do get a baggage allowance.

To/From Europe

Vienna has several daily nonstop flights to all major European transport hubs such as Amsterdam, Berlin, Frankfurt, Paris, Zürich and London. Austrian Airlines services all these places and many others. Lauda Air has daily flights to Vienna from Manchester and Munich; its twice-weekly flight from London Gatwick is usually the cheapest available through budget agencies (UK£149 for a one-month return). Lauda also flies daily from London Gatwick to Salzburg. See city sections for more on routes to provincial airports.

For shorter stays in Austria, a charter flight may be the most economical option. Usually there are restrictive conditions attached, such as your stay must include a Saturday night but may not exceed 12 days.

London is one of the world's major centres for buying discounted air tickets, and it'll cost less to fly than go by train. Cheap fares appear in *Time Out*, the *Evening Standard* and *TNT* (a free magazine dispensed at tube stations). The Sunday national papers are also a good source of ads for cheap fares. Mondial Travel (☎ 0181-314 1181), 154A Rushey Green, SE6, is a specialist for flights to Austria and can arrange fly/drive deals. Austria Travel (☎ 0171-222 2430), 46 Queen Anne's Gate, London SW1H 9AU, also has competitive fares, and sells city breaks and special interest tours (based round cycling, wine-tasting etc).

Trailfinders (☎ 0171-938 3232), 194 Kensington High St, London W8, has decent fares, plus a travel library, bookshop, visa service and immunisation centre. Its Manchester branch (☎ 0161-839 6969), is at 58 Deansgate; other branches are in Bristol and Glasgow. Campus Travel (☎ 0171-938 2188) 174 Kensington High St, London W8 has many interesting deals and very cheap travel insurance. Council Travel (0171-437 7767), 28A Poland St, London W1, is the USA's largest student and budget travel agency. Austrian Airlines (☎ 0171-434 7300) and Lauda Air (☎ 0171-630 5549) each has a London office.

STA Travel (☎ 0171-937 9921) is a worldwide agency for budget and student tickets, and has offices in London (117 Euston Rd, NW1, and 86 Old Brompton Rd, SW7) and other British cities, such as Manchester (☎ 0161-834 0668). Across Europe many travel agents have ties with STA Travel, where cheap tickets can be purchased and STA-issued tickets can usually be altered free of charge, including at ÖKISTA branches in Austria. Outlets in major transport hubs include: CTS Voyages (☎ 1-43 25 00 76), 20 Rue des Carmes, Paris; SRID Reisen (☎ 069-43 01 91), Berger Strasse 118, Frankfurt; ISYTS (☎ 01-322 1267 or

323 3767), 2nd floor, 11 Nikis St, Syntagma Square, Athens.

In Continental Europe, Athens is a recognised centre for cheap flights: check the many travel agents in the backstreets between Syntagma and Omonia squares. In Athens, as well as ISYTS above, try USIT (01-324 1884), Filellinon 3, or Pioneer Tours (☎ 322 4321), also at 11 Nikis St.

Amsterdam also has a good reputation for cheap fares: try Budget Air (☎ 020-627 12 51), Rokin 34; ICL Reizen (☎ 020-620 51 21), NZ Voorburgwal 256; Malibu Travel (☎ 020-623 68 14), Damrak 30; or the student agency, NBBS (☎ 020-624 09 89), Rokin 38.

Vienna has excellent connections to/from Eastern Europe, including Moscow, St Petersburg, Vilnius, Warsaw, Kiev and Bucharest. Austrian Airlines has extensive direct services to these and other places.

To/From the USA

The North Atlantic is the world's busiest long-haul air corridor: the *New York Times*, the *LA Times*, the *Chicago Tribune*, the *San*

Air Travel Glossary

Apex Apex, or 'advance purchase excursion', is a discounted ticket which must be paid for in advance. There are penalties if you wish to change it.

Baggage Allowance This will be written on your ticket: usually one 20 kg item to go in the hold, plus one item of hand luggage.

Bucket Shop An unbonded travel agency specialising in discounted airline tickets.

Bumped Just because you have a confirmed seat doesn't mean you're going to get on the plane (see Overbooking).

Cancellation Penalties If you have to cancel or change an Apex ticket there are often heavy penalties involved. Insurance can sometimes be taken out against these penalties. Some airlines impose penalties on regular tickets as well, particularly against 'no show' passengers.

Check In Airlines ask you to check in a certain time ahead of the flight departure (usually 1½ hours on international flights). If you fail to check in on time and the flight is overbooked the airline can cancel your booking and give your seat to somebody else.

Confirmation Having a ticket written out with the flight and date you want doesn't mean you have a seat until the agent has checked with the airline that your status is 'OK' or confirmed. Meanwhile you could just be 'on request'.

Discounted Tickets There are two types of discounted fares - officially discounted (see Promotional Fares) and unofficially discounted. The lowest prices often impose drawbacks like flying with unpopular airlines, inconvenient schedules, or unpleasant routes and connections. A discounted ticket can save you other things than money - you may be able to pay Apex prices without the associated Apex advance booking and other requirements. Discounted tickets only exist where there is fierce competition.

Full Fares Airlines traditionally offer first class (coded F), business class (coded J) and economy class (coded Y) tickets. These days there are so many promotional and discounted fares available from the regular economy class that few passengers pay full economy fare.

Lost Tickets If you lose your airline ticket an airline will usually treat it like a travellers' cheque and, after enquiries, issue you with another one. Legally, however, an airline is entitled to treat it like cash and if you lose it then it's gone forever. Take good care of your tickets.

No Shows No shows are passengers who fail to show up for their flight, sometimes due to unexpected delays or disasters, sometimes due to simply forgetting, sometimes because they made more than one booking and didn't bother to cancel the one they didn't want. Full fare passengers who fail to turn up are sometimes entitled to travel on a later flight. The rest are penalised (see Cancellation Penalties).

On Request An unconfirmed booking for a flight (see Confirmation).

Open Jaws A return ticket where you fly out to one place but return from another. If available this can save you backtracking to your arrival point.

Francisco Chronicle and the *San Francisco Examiner* all produce weekly travel sections in which you'll find numerous travel agents' ads.

Using the budget agencies, you should be able to fly New York to a European gateway city and return for US$350 to US$450 in the low season, or US$550 to US$650 in the high season. An APEX return on a daily Austrian Airlines flight from New York to Vienna costs around US$600. Austrian Airlines also flies daily from Chicago. From Los Angeles, Delta flies daily and Lauda Air flies three times a week (both via Munich). As well, Lauda Air has four flights a week from Miami (listed return fare US$980), also via Munich.

Council Travel (☎ 1-800-223 7402 toll free) and STA Travel (☎ 1-800-777 0112 toll free) sell discounted tickets from numerous outlets across the USA. One-way fares can be very cheap on a stand-by basis. Airhitch (☎ 212-864 2000) specialises in this sort of thing, and can get you from the USA to Europe one-way for US$160/269/229. Another interesting option is with Icelandair

---

Overbooking Airlines hate to fly empty seats and since every flight has some passengers who fail to show up (see No Shows) airlines often book more passengers than they have seats. Usually the excess passengers balance those who fail to show up but occasionally somebody gets bumped. This is most likely to be the passengers who check in late.

Promotional Fares Officially discounted fares like Apex fares which are available from travel agents or direct from the airline.

Reconfirmation At least 72 hours prior to departure time of an onward or return flight you must contact the airline and 'reconfirm' that you intend to be on the flight. If you don't do this the airline can delete your name from the passenger list and you could lose your seat. You don't have to reconfirm the first flight on your itinerary or if your stopover is less than 72 hours. It doesn't hurt to reconfirm more than once.

Restrictions Discounted tickets often have various restrictions on them - advance purchase is the most usual one (see Apex). Others are restrictions on the minimum and maximum period you must be away, such as a minimum of 14 days or a maximum of one year (see Cancellation Penalties).

Standby A discounted ticket where you only fly if there is a seat free at the last moment. Standby fares are usually only available on domestic routes.

Tickets Out An entry requirement for many countries is that you have an onward or return ticket, in other words, a ticket out of the country. If you're not sure what you intend to do next, the easiest solution is to buy the cheapest onward ticket to a neighbouring country or a ticket from a reliable airline which can later be refunded if you do not use it.

Transferred Tickets Airline tickets cannot be transferred from one person to another. Travellers sometimes try to sell the return half of their ticket, but officials can ask you to prove that you are the person named on the ticket. This is unlikely to happen on domestic flights, but on an international flight tickets may be compared with passports.

Travel Agencies Travel agencies vary widely and you should ensure you use one that suits your needs. Some simply handle tours while full-service agencies handle everything from tours and tickets to car rental and hotel bookings. A good one will do all these things and can save you a lot of money, but if all you want is a ticket at the lowest possible price then you really need an agency specialising in discounted tickets. A discounted ticket agency, however, may not be useful for other things, like hotel bookings.

Travel Periods Some officially discounted fares, Apex fares in particular, vary with the time of year. There is often a low (off-peak) season and a high (peak) season. Sometimes there's an intermediate or shoulder season as well. At peak times, when everyone wants to fly, not only will the officially discounted fares be higher but so will unofficially discounted fares, or there may simply be no discounted tickets available. Usually the fare depends on your outward flight - if you depart in the high season and return in the low season, you pay the high-season fare. ■

(☎ 800-223 5500), flying from New York to Luxembourg, via Reykjavík. This may be one of the cheapest deals. For courier flights, contact Discount Travel International (☎ 212-362 36 36) in New York or Way to Go (☎ 213-466 11 26) in Los Angeles.

The *Travel Unlimited* newsletter, PO Box 1058, Allston, MA 02134, publishes details of the cheapest air fares and courier possibilities for destinations all over the world from the USA and other countries, including the UK. It's a treasure trove of information. A single monthly issue of *Travel Unlimited* costs US$5, and a year's subscription US$25 (US$35 abroad).

To/From Canada

Check ads in the *Toronto Globe & Mail*, the *Toronto Star* and the *Vancouver Province*. Look for the budget agency, Travel Cuts. Its head office (☎ 416-979 2406) is at 187 College St, Toronto M5T 1P7, but it has offices in all major cities. From Toronto, Air Canada flies direct to Vienna on Monday and Wednesday; Swissair flies five times a week to Zürich, with onward connections to Vienna (C$750 return). Courier fares to London or Paris are much lower: contact FB On Board Courier Services on ☎ 514-633 0740 in Montreal or ☎ 604-338 1366 in Vancouver.

To/From Australasia

STA Travel and Flight Centres International are major dealers in cheap airfares. Check the travel agents' ads in the Telecom Yellow Pages, and the Saturday travel sections of Sydney's *Sydney Morning Herald* and Melbourne's *Age* newspapers. STA has offices at 224 Faraday St, Carlton, Vic 3053 (☎ 03-347 6911); 732 Harris St, Ultimo, NSW 2007 (☎ 02-281 9866); and 10 High St, PO Box 4156, Auckland (☎ 09-309 9995).

Flight Centres International has offices at 19 Bourke St, Melbourne 3000 (☎ 03-650 2899) and 82 Elizabeth St, Sydney 2000 (☎ 02-235 3522). From Australia to Vienna, Lauda Air flights are the most convenient. On Thursday, Lauda flies from Melbourne/Sydney, with a stopover in Bangkok; its Melbourne/Sydney flight on Saturday goes via Singapore. The listed low-season return fare is A$2250. Agencies may discount this fare by about 20%.

From New Zealand, there are no direct flights to Austria, and the cheapest flights will usually be via the USA. An RTW ticket may be the best deal.

To/From Africa

Nairobi is probably the best place in Africa to buy tickets to Europe, thanks to the many

---

Flying High

Austria's Niki Lauda, three-times Formula 1 racing champion, founded Lauda Air in 1979. It initially operated as a charter airline, with Lauda, a trained pilot, often taking the controls. In 1985, a partnership with the ITAS travel agency signalled a move to scheduled flights. The airline applied to the federal Ministry of Transportation in 1986 for the necessary concession and made its first scheduled flight in May the following year.

While all this was happening, the state-owned airline, Austrian Airlines, showed itself none too happy at facing domestic competition. It tried various measures to scuttle Lauda's endeavours: halving prices on certain routes, bad-mouthing the fledgling airline in the press and being uncooperative in air-traffic negotiations. But Lauda Air eventually prevailed. After three years of intensive political and public pressure (greatly aided by Lauda's status as a national hero), the airline received a worldwide concession in 1990 to operate scheduled flights.

Lauda Air flies to Europe, the USA, Asia and Australia, using a fleet of Boeing 767s, 737s and CRJ 100ERs. Lauda's personal tastes are reflected in the names given to the aircraft: Johann Strauss, Enzo Ferrari, James Dean and Bob Marley are among those honoured. ■

bucket shops and the strong competition between them. A typical one-way/return fare to London would be about US$550/800. Another option is to fly from Africa to Zürich and transfer from there: Swissair has direct flights to/from a number of places, including Nairobi and Johannesburg. Austrian Airlines flies direct to Vienna, usually twice a week from Cairo and Johannesburg.

Several West African countries such as Burkina Faso and the Gambia offer cheap charter flights to France, and charter fares from Morocco can be incredibly cheap if you're lucky enough to find a seat. If you intend departing from Cairo, it's often cheaper to fly to Athens and to proceed with a budget bus or train from there.

To/From Asia

Hong Kong is the discount airfare capital of Asia, and its bucket shops are at least as unreliable as those of other cities. Ask the advice of other travellers before buying a ticket. Many of the cheapest fares from South-East Asia to Europe are offered by Eastern European carriers. STA has branches in Hong Kong, Tokyo, Singapore, Bangkok and Kuala Lumpur.

To/from India, the cheapest flights tend to be with Eastern European carriers like LOT, or with Middle Eastern airlines such as Syrian Arab Airlines and Iran Air. Bombay is the air transport hub of Asia, with many transit options to/from South-East Asia, but tickets are slightly cheaper in Delhi. Try Delhi Student Travel Services in the Imperial Hotel, Janpath.

To Vienna, there are flights from Hong Kong and Singapore (both via Paris) and Beijing and Tokyo. Swissair flies to Zürich from Karachi, Bombay, Delhi, Bangkok, Singapore, Hong Kong, Beijing, Seoul, Tokyo and Manila.

BUS

Buses are generally slower, cheaper and less comfortable than trains. Eurolines (☎ 0171-730 0202), 52 Grosvenor Gardens, Victoria, London SW1, is the main European carrier. Other addresses for Eurolines include:

Budget Bus (☎ 020-627 51 51), Rokin 10, Amsterdam; Eurolines (☎ 1-43 54 11 99), 55 Rue Saint Jacques, 75005 Paris; Deutsche Touring (☎ 089-59 18 24), Arnulfstrasse 3, Munich; Lazzi Express (☎ 06-88 40 840), Via Tagliamento 27R, Rome; and Magic Bus (☎ 01-323 7474), Filellinon 20, Athens. These offices may be able to advise on other bus companies and deals.

On ordinary return trips, youth (under 26 years) fares are around 10% less than the adult full fare. At 8.30 am on both Friday and Saturday a bus departs from London's Victoria Station and arrives in Vienna at 11.30 am the next morning (UK£99 return). Eurolines also has Euro Explorer tickets: a return trip including London, Frankfurt, Budapest, Vienna, Brussels and back to London costs UK£140.

Eurobus, a new operation in 1995, has well-equipped buses which complete a figure of eight loop of Europe, taking in Amsterdam, Brussels, Paris, Zürich, Prague, Budapest and major cities in Germany and Italy. In Austria, the buses call at Vienna, Salzburg and Innsbruck (though Innsbruck's on a different part of the loop). Unlimited travel fares are: under 26 years, UK£169 for two months and UK£219 for three months; and 26 and over, UK£219 for two months, UK£270 for three months. Tickets are available in many countries worldwide, though you need to make your own way to a city on the loop to start off. Sales agents are STA in the UK and Supertramp in Austria.

Vienna's international bus station is at Wien Mitte, by the train station of the same name. Blaguss Reisen (☎ 501 80) in the bus station runs buses to Budapest daily at 7 am (3½ hours), departing from Wien Mitte. The fare is AS290 one-way or AS420 return. These tickets are available for the same price from the normal bus ticket counters. Wien Mitte also has several buses a day to/from Bratislava, via the Vienna airport and Hainburg. The fare is AS92 one-way or AS184 return. If you buy the return leg in Bratislava it'll only cost 92 Slovak crowns (about AS44 at the time of writing). Bus timetable information is available on ☎ 711 01 from 6 am to 9 pm. The Bundesbus counters in Wien Mitte are open daily from 6 am to 5.30 pm, and sell Eurolines tickets.

Austrobus (☎ 534 110; fax 534 11 200), 1 Dr Karl Lueger Ring 8, Vienna, has buses to Prague leaving from 1 Rathausplatz 5. Departures are at 7 am daily except Sunday, and 3 pm daily except Saturday (AS315; five hours).

TRAIN

Trains are a popular, convenient and pollution-free way to travel. They are also good meeting places, comfortable and reasonably frequent.

Stories about train passengers being gassed or drugged and then robbed occasionally surface, though bag-snatching is more of a worry. Sensible security measures include not letting your bags out of your sight (or at least chaining them to the luggage rack) and locking compartment doors overnight.

To/From Europe

European rail passes make train travel affordable, but unless you want to explore other countries in Europe as well, it may work out cheaper to pay the normal fare to Austria then use a national rail pass to explore the country (see the Getting Around chapter). Reservation costs (and most supplements) are not covered by rail passes, and pass holders must always carry their passport on the train for identification.

The *Thomas Cook European Timetable* is the trainophile's bible, giving a complete listing of train schedules, supplements and reservations information. It is updated monthly and is available from Thomas Cook outlets worldwide.

Austria benefits from its central location within Europe by having excellent rail connections to all important destinations. Vienna is one of the main rail hubs in central Europe; see its Getting There & Away section for details of the main train stations and the routes they serve.

Paris, Amsterdam, Munich and Milan are important cities for rail connections. Elsewhere in Austria, Salzburg has at least hourly

trains to/from Munich (AS272) with onward connections north. Express services to Italy go via Innsbruck or Villach. Villach also directs trains south-east. Trains to Slovenia go through Graz.

Travellers aged under 26 can pick up Billet International de Jeunesse (BIJ) tickets which cut fares by up to 50%. Various agents issue BIJ tickets in Europe, eg Campus Travel (☎ 0171-730 3402), 52 Grosvenor Gardens, London SW1, which sells Eurotrain tickets. British Rail International (☎ 0171-834 2345) at Victoria Station, and Wasteels (☎ 0171-834 7066) also sell BIJ tickets. From London, the fare to Vienna is UK£172 single or UK£291 return (UK£120 or UK£233 if under 26). This is via Ostend; an indirect routing would be slightly cheaper. If you want to take Eurostar through the Channel Tunnel, a London-Brussels return costs UK£155 – £79 if bought two weeks ahead – then Brussels-Vienna return is UK£170.

Express trains can be identified by the symbols EC (EuroCity, serving international routes) or IC (InterCity, serving national routes). The French TGV and the German ICE trains are even faster. Supplements can apply on fast trains, and it is a good idea (sometimes obligatory) to make seat reservations at peak times and on certain lines. Overnight trips usually offer a choice of couchette (around US$18) or a more expensive sleeper. Long-distance trains have a dining car or snacks available. Supplements sometimes apply on international trains. Reserving IC or EC train seats in 2nd class within Austria costs AS30; in 1st class, IC costs AS30 and EC AS50. In Austria you can sometimes pick up cheap fares on international return tickets valid less than four days.

The Orient Express is an old-style private train that serves European routes. It passes through Austria: enquire at travel agents.

European Rail Passes These may not work out much more expensive than a straightforward return ticket, and are worth considering if you want to explore several destinations. Treat rail passes as if they were cash, as replacement can be difficult or expensive, and always study the terms and conditions. Senior citizens can buy a Rail Europe Senior Card, entitling the holder to a 30% reduction on train fares in 20 European countries.

Eurail Pass This pass can only be bought by residents of non-European countries, and ideally should be purchased before arriving in Europe. Eurail passes are valid for unlimited travel on national railways and some private lines in Austria, Belgium, Denmark, Finland, France (including Monaco), Germany, Greece, Hungary, Italy, Luxembourg, the Netherlands, Norway, Portugal, Ireland, Spain, Sweden and Switzerland (including Liechtenstein). Britain is not covered. The pass is valid for some international ferries and reductions are given on steamer services in various countries (including Danube steamers).

A standard Youthpass for travellers under 26 is valid for unlimited 2nd-class travel for 15 days (US$398), one month (US$578) or two months (US$768). The Youth Flexipass, also for 2nd-class travel, is valid for freely chosen days within a two-month period: five days for US$255, 10 days for US$398 or 15 days for US$540.

The corresponding passes for those aged over 26 are available in 1st class only. The standard Eurail pass has five versions, costing from US$498 for 15 days unlimited travel, up to US$1398 for three months. The Flexipass costs US$348, US$560 or US$740 for five, 10 or 15 freely chosen days in two months.

Two or more people travelling together (minimum three people between 1 April and 30 September) can get good discounts on a Saverpass, which works like the standard Eurail pass. Eurail passes for children are also available.

A cheaper, restricted version, called the Europass, gives between five and 15 freely chosen days unlimited travel within a two-month period. You can travel in three to five of the following countries: France, Germany, Italy, Spain and Switzerland. Fares are US$355 to US$835, or US$250 to US$610

for those under 26. Austria can be added for a surcharge of US$45 (US$32 for those under 26). Chosen countries must be adjacent.

There is a Eurail and Europass Aid Office (☎ 83 95 74) in Vienna's Westbahnhof, open Monday to Friday from 9 am to 5 pm. Both the Eurail and the Europass give a 50% reduction on Erste Donau Dampfschiffahrts-Gesellschaft (DDSG) boats from Vienna to Budapest (see under Boat later in this chapter).

Inter-Rail Pass Inter-Rail passes are available in Europe to people who have been resident there for at least six months. Terms and conditions vary slightly between countries but in all cases there's only a discount of around 50% on normal fares in the country of origin.

Travellers over 26 can get the Inter-Rail 26+, valid for unlimited rail travel in Austria, Bulgaria, Croatia, the Czech Republic, Denmark, Finland, Germany, Greece, Hungary, Luxembourg, Netherlands, Norway, Poland, Romania, Ireland, Slovakia, Slovenia, Sweden and Turkey. The pass also gives free travel on shipping routes from Brindisi (Italy) to Patras (Greece), as well as 30 to 50% discounts on various other ferry routes (many more than covered by Eurail) and certain river and lake services (eg 50% off DDSG services from Passau to Vienna and Vienna to Budapest). A 15-day pass costs UK£209 and one month costs UK£269.

The Inter-Rail pass for those under 26 has been split into zones. Zone A is Ireland (and Great Britain if the pass is bought outside Great Britain); B is Sweden, Norway and Finland; C is Denmark, Germany, Switzerland and Austria; D is the Czech Republic, Slovakia, Poland, Hungary, Bulgaria and Romania; E is France, Belgium, Netherlands and Luxembourg; F is Spain, Portugal and Morocco; and G is Italy, Greece, Turkey and Slovenia. The price for any one zone is UK£179 for 15 days. Multi-zone passes are better value and are valid for one month: a two-zone pass is UK£209, a three-zone pass UK£229, and an all-zone pass UK£249.

An Inter-Rail pass can be purchased in Austria by people under 26 who are resident in Austria. It costs AS3000 for one zone, AS3600 for two, AS4000 for three and AS4500 for all zones.

Euro-Domino Pass There is a Euro-Domino pass (called a Freedom pass in Britain) for each of the countries covered in the zonal Inter-Rail pass, plus Croatia and the rest of the former Yugoslavia, except Slovenia. Adults (travelling 1st or 2nd class) and youths (under 26) can choose from three, five, or 10 days validity. It can be purchased by non-Europeans; passes are not valid for a European's own country of residence, though there is a 25% reduction in fares for the European country of departure and on transit routes to the countries paid for. If bought in Britain, the price of the pass for Austria is £83, £95 or £165; for those under 26 it's £62, £69 or £129.

European East Pass This is sold in the USA, Canada and Australia, and is valid for train travel in Austria, the Czech Republic, Slovakia, Poland and Hungary. The cost is US$200 for five days travel in 15 days, or US$325 for 10 days travel in one month.

Circular Tickets If these match your itinerary, they could be a cheaper alternative to a rail pass. Eurotrain has the Eastern Explorer ticket, including London, Amsterdam, Hanover, Berlin, Prague, Vienna, Salzburg, Zürich, Basel, Strasbourg, Luxembourg, Brussels, Bruges, then back to London. The ticket, available only to those aged under 26, is valid for two months and costs UK£240. British Rail International sells an Imperial Tour two-month ticket starting and ending in London with stopovers in Amsterdam, Berlin, Prague, Budapest, Vienna, Zürich and Brussels (UK£333, or UK£255 if under 26).

To/From Asia

It takes 47 hours on the direct train from Vienna to Moscow (via Kiev) and costs AS1308, plus AS410 for a compulsory sleeper. From there you can take four different trains for onwards eastern travel. Three of them (the trans-Siberian, trans-Mongolian and trans-Manchurian) follow the same route to/from Moscow across Siberia but have different eastern railheads. The fourth, the trans-Kazakhstan, runs between Moscow and Ürümqi (north-western China) across central Asia. Prices can vary enormously, depending on where you buy the ticket and

---

Crossing the Channel

Many ferry companies cover the English Channel crossing. The shortest routes (Dover to Calais, or Folkestone to Boulogne) are also the busiest. Ticket prices depend upon the length of the vehicle, the time of day or year and the type of ticket. Look for special deals on advance-purchase tickets.

The Channel Tunnel link between England and France opened in 1994. At 50 km, it's the longest undersea tunnel in the world and a remarkable engineering feat. The train service through the tunnel, Eurostar, runs from London's Waterloo to the Gare de Nord in Paris or the Midi/Zuid in Brussels. Either trip takes about three hours.

Le Shuttle is a vehicle-carrying service running between Folkestone and Calais. The crossing takes 35 minutes and there are between one and four departures daily every hour. Bicycles, motorcycles, cars, camper vans, caravans or trailers can be carried. Charges are similar to ferry prices: transporting a car and occupants varies from UK£136, in November and December, to UK£308, in the July and August peak times (for a return ticket). These Le Shuttle prices are valid for as many passengers as can be legally fitted into the vehicle (hitchers take note!). Ferry prices also usually cover all vehicle passengers. ■

what is included, but you won't save money compared to flying. If you have time (between six and nine days minimum) train travel is an interesting option, but only really worthwhile if you want to stop off and explore China and Russia on the way through. Possibilities for overland travel to/from Asia, whether by train, bus or private vehicle, should become more widespread as tourism expands in the region.

CAR & MOTORBIKE

Getting to Austria by road is simple, as there are fast, well-maintained *Autobahnen* (motorways) through all surrounding countries. German autobahns have no tolls or speed limits, whereas those in France (Autoroute) and Italy (Autostrada) have both. Switzerland has a one-off charge of Sfr30 (about US$21) for using its motorways. Swiss officials may insist you pay this even if you declare you're going to keep off the motorway system.

By road into Austria there are numerous entry points from Germany, the Czech Republic, Slovakia, Hungary, Slovenia, Italy and Switzerland. The only other country that borders Austria, Liechtenstein, is so small that it has just one entry point, near Feldkirch. The presence of the Alps limits options for approaching Tirol from the south (Switzerland and Italy). All main border crossing points are open 24 hours a day. Those served by minor roads are open between 6 to 8 am and 8 to 10 pm. The *Facts and Sights* map, available at tourist offices, indicates which are major and which are minor crossings.

To avoid a long drive to Austria, consider putting your car on a motorail service, which is run by the national railways: many head south from Calais and Paris. German Rail has services to Austria, eg Brussels to Salzburg costs UK£344/566 for single/return in the low season for a car and two adults, including a couchette.

Paperwork & Preparations

Proof of ownership of a private vehicle should always be carried (Vehicle Registra-

tion Document for British-registered cars) when touring Europe. A British or other European driving licence is acceptable for driving throughout Europe. If you have any other type of licence you should obtain an International Driving Permit (IDP) from an automobile association. If you're a member of one of these associations, ask for a Card of Introduction, which will make it easier to enjoy reciprocal benefits offered by affiliated organisations in Europe.

Third-party motor insurance is a minimum requirement in Europe: get proof of this in the form of a Green Card, issued by your insurers. Also ask for a 'European Accident Statement' form. Taking out a European breakdown assistance policy, such as the AA Five Star Service or the RAC Eurocover Motoring Assistance, is a good investment.

Every vehicle travelling across an international border should display a nationality plate of its country of registration. A warning triangle, to be used in the event of breakdown, is compulsory almost everywhere (including Austria). Recommended accessories are a first-aid kit (compulsory in Austria, Slovenia, Croatia, Yugoslavia and Greece), a spare bulb kit, and a fire extinguisher. In the UK, contact the RAC (☎ 0181-686 0088) or the AA (☎ 0256-20123) for more information.

Driving is on the right throughout Continental Europe, and priority is usually given to traffic approaching from the right. The RAC annually brings out its *European Motoring Guide*, which gives an excellent summary of regulations in each country, including parking rules. Motoring organisations in other countries have similar publications. Road signs are generally standard throughout Europe.

One thing to be aware of when driving through the continent is that Europeans are particularly strict on drink-driving laws. The blood-alcohol concentration (BAC) limit when driving is between 0.05% and 0.08%, but in some areas (Gibraltar, Eastern Europe, Scandinavia) it can be zero per cent.

For more on motoring regulations within Austria, see the Getting Around chapter.

Camper Van

Travelling in a camper van can be a surprisingly economical option for budget travellers, as it can take care of eating, sleeping and travelling in one convenient package. London is a good place to buy: look in *TNT* magazine, *Loot* newspaper and go to the Van Market in Market Rd, London N7. Expect to spend at least £1000 to £1500 (US$1600 to US$2400). The most common camper van is the VW based on the 1600 cc or 2000 cc Transporter, and spare parts are widely available in Europe. Discrete free camping, such as in autobahn rest areas, is rarely a problem, and is actually permitted in most places in Austria, Germany and Switzerland.

A drawback with camper vans is that they're expensive to buy in spring and hard to sell in autumn. A car and tent might do just as well instead.

Motorcycle Touring

Europe and Austria are ideal for motorcycle touring, with winding roads of good quality, stunning scenery to stimulate the senses, and an active motorcycling scene. The wearing of crash helmets for motorcyclists and passengers is compulsory everywhere in Europe. Austria, Belgium, France, Germany, Luxembourg, Portugal, Spain, Scandinavia, Croatia, Yugoslavia and most countries in Eastern Europe require that motorcyclists use headlights during the day; in other countries it is recommended.

Fuel

Leaded petrol is no longer available in Austria, but Super Plus has a special additive which allows it to be used for engines taking leaded petrol. Prices per litre are about AS10.50 for Super Plus, marginally more than for unleaded petrol, and AS7.70 for diesel. Plan to arrive in the country with a full or empty tank depending on where you're coming from: petrol is cheaper in Austria than in Germany or Italy and more expensive than in other neighbouring countries.

BICYCLE

This is one of the best ways to travel in terms of your bank balance, your health, and the environment. But it does require a high level of commitment to see it through.

Starting from Britain, consider joining the Cyclists' Touring Club (☎ 01483-417 217), Cotterell House, 69 Meadow, Godalming, Surrey GU7 3HS. It can supply information to members on cycling conditions in Europe as well as detailed routes, itineraries and cheap insurance. Membership costs £25 a year, or £12.50 for people aged under 18.

If coming from farther afield, bikes can be carried by aeroplane, but check with the carrier in advance, preferably before buying your ticket. To take it as a normal piece of luggage, you may need to remove the pedals or turn the handlebars sideways, but beware of possible excess baggage costs.

A primary consideration on long cycling trips is to travel light, but you should take a few tools and spare parts including a puncture repair kit and a spare inner tube. Panniers are essential to balance your possessions on either side of the bike frame. A bike helmet is also a very good idea, as is a good bike lock. Seasoned cyclists can average 80 km a day but there's no point overdoing it. The slower you travel, the more locals you're likely to meet.

Bicycles are not allowed on European motorways – not that you would want to use those tedious bits of concrete anyway. Stick to small roads or dedicated bike tracks where possible. If you get weary of pedalling or simply want to skip a boring section, you can put your feet up on the train. On slower trains, bikes can usually be taken on board as luggage, subject to a small supplementary fee. Fast trains (IC, EC etc) can rarely accommodate bikes: they need to be sent as registered luggage and may end up on a different train from the one you take. British Rail is not part of the European luggage registration scheme, so you would have to get to the Continent before you can send your bike in this way. In Austria, it costs AS120 to send a bike as international luggage.

Europe by Bike by Karen & Terry Whitehall outlines some worthwhile European bike tours.

HITCHING

Hitching is never entirely safe in any country in the world, and we don't recommend it. Travellers who decide to hitch should understand they are taking a small but potentially serious risk. People who do choose to hitch will be safer if they travel in pairs and let someone know where they are planning to go.

Throughout Europe, hitching is illegal on motorways – stand on the slip roads, or approach drivers at petrol stations, border posts and truck stops. In Austria, *Autohof* indicates a parking spot able to accommodate trucks. You can increase your chances of getting a lift by looking presentable and cheerful and making a cardboard sign indicating your intended destination in the local language. Showing a flag or some other indication of your country of origin can also help. Never hitch where drivers can't stop in good time or without causing an obstruction. Once you find a good spot, stay put and hope for the best. When it starts getting dark – forget it! Ferry tickets for vehicles sometimes include a full load of passengers, so hitchers may be able to secure a free passage by hitching before cars board the boat.

A safer way to hitch is to arrange a lift through an organisation, such as Allostop-Provoya in France and Mitfahrzentrale in Germany. You could also scan university notice boards. In Austria, Mitfahrzentrale is in Vienna and Bregenz.

BOAT

Getting to Europe by boat is not the option it used to be. Nowadays you can all but forget about trying to work your passage. Travel agents can tell you about luxury cruise ships across the Atlantic, or consult the *ABC Cruise & Ferry Guide* published by Reed Travel Group (☎ 01582-60 01 11), Church St, St Dunstable, Bedfordshire, England, LU5 4 HB. This volume is also useful if you want to take the more adventurous option of travelling as a paying passenger on a freighter. From Africa, the most important ferry routes are Morocco-Spain, Algeria/Tunisia/Morocco-France, and Tunisia-Italy.

Once in Europe, you can use the river network to get about; it's slower, more expensive, but probably more enjoyable than getting about by land. The Danube is now connected to the Rhine by a canal in Germany's Black Forest. In theory, it is possible to go all the way from the North Sea to Vienna by boat, but no major operator has started up straight-through services yet. Köln-Düsseldorfer (KD) Line (☎ 0221-2 08 80) based in Cologne has passenger services along the Rhine.

DDSG operates boats along the Danube. Its Vienna office (☎ 727 500) is at Handelskai 265, by the Reichsbrücke bridge. Fast hydrofoils travel eastwards to Bratislava and Budapest. The trip to Bratislava costs AS210 one-way and AS330 return; the journey takes one hour with two departures a day from mid-April to mid-October. Budapest costs AS750 one-way, AS1100 return and takes four hours 40 minutes with one departure daily from 1 April to 31 October (two daily from May to early September). If you can afford this mode of travel, it makes a pleasant change from going by bus or train.

Steamers ply the Danube from Vienna to Passau, a German border town, every day from May to late September. At least two a day sail in either direction along most of the route. In April and October steamers only sail between Vienna and Linz. The DDSG office in Linz (☎ 77 10 90) is at Untere Donaulände 1, and in Passau (☎ 0851-330 35) it's at Im Ort 14A, Dreiflusseck. In Bratislava, Slovakia, you can contact Blue Danube Travel (☎ 07 36 22 58), Fajnorovo nábre ie 2.

TOURS

For tailor-made tours, see your travel agent or look under Special Interests in the small ads in newspaper travel pages. Various packages are available with a musical theme. In the UK, Austrian Holidays (☎ 0171-434 7399), 10 Wardour St, London W1V 4 BQ, has holidays based around tourist sights, winter sights or the opera. See also Austria Travel under Air: To/From Europe earlier in this chapter. Similarly structured tours are available from other countries.

There are also bus tours based on hotel or camping accommodation. Operators in London include Contiki (☎ 0181-290 6422), Tracks (☎ 0171-937 3028) and Top Deck (☎ 0171-370 6487). They all have itineraries including Vienna and elsewhere in Austria.

For people aged over 60, Saga Holidays (Freephone ☎ 0800-300 500), Saga Building, Middelburg Square, Folkstone, Kent CT20 1AZ, England, offers an 11-night coach tour of Austria for UK£639 and a nine-night tour of the cities of the Habsburgs for UK£589. Both trips include return flights from London's Heathrow airport. Saga also operates in the USA as Saga International Holidays (☎ 0800-343 0272), 120 Boylston St, Boston, MA 02116.

WARNING

The information in this chapter is particularly vulnerable to change: prices for international travel are volatile, routes are introduced and cancelled, schedules change, special deals come and go, and rules and visa requirements are amended. Airlines and governments seem to take a perverse pleasure in making price structures and regulations as complicated as possible. You should check directly with the airline or a travel agent to make sure you understand how a fare (and any ticket you buy) works. In addition, the travel industry is highly competitive and there are many lurks and perks.

The upshot of this is that you should get opinions, quotes and advice from as many airlines and travel agents as possible before you part with your hard-earned cash. The details given in this chapter should be regarded as pointers and are not a substitute for your own careful, up-to-date research.

Getting Around

Transport systems in Austria are highly developed and generally very efficient, and reliable information is usually available in English. For detailed planning, consider buying an annual timetable (*Fahrplan*). The rail timetable costs AS100 and includes details of the more important ferry and cable car services. The bus timetable is produced in two volumes. However, information staff in train stations will look up specific information from these guides for you, or there may be a copy for you to peruse.

AIR

Domestic flights are operated by Tyrolean Airways, of which Austrian Airlines owns 42.8%. Vienna has several flights a day to Graz, Klagenfurt and Innsbruck and at least two a day to Salzburg and Linz. Austrian Airlines is a sales agent for Tyrolean Airlines. Rheintalflug (☎ 0222-711 10 69 15), flies from Vienna to Altenrhein, Switzerland, with free bus transfers to/from Bregenz in Vorarlberg. There are three flights a day (two on weekends) and fares are from AS3110 return. Check schedules as they vary according to the season.

Expense means that getting around by air is not a viable option for most people. The airfare between Vienna and Klagenfurt, for example, is AS1700 each way, or AS2130 return if travelling on a weekend (with reductions for partners and children in both cases). A family ticket for three people is AS3200. The air time is 55 minutes, plus check-in time and the hassle of getting to and from each airport. In comparison, the train takes 4½ hours and costs AS416 for a single ticket.

BUS

The Bundesbus (federal bus) network is primarily a back-up to the rail service, more to get to out-of-the-way places and local destinations than for long-distance travel. Some rail routes are duplicated by bus, but buses only really come into their own in the more inaccessible mountainous regions, eg some ski resorts in Tirol and Vorarlberg can only be reached by Bundesbus or private transport.

Bundesbuses are yellow or orange, and are run by either the post office or the rail network. As far as the traveller is concerned, there's no real difference between the two types: in this book buses are simply called Bundesbus throughout. They are clean and punctual and usually depart from outside train stations.

Bus fares work out at around AS130 per 100 km, though the longer the journey, the cheaper the per-km fare. However, unlike with the train, you can't buy a longer ticket and make stop-offs en route. Advance reservations are possible on some routes, but sometimes you can only buy tickets from the drivers. Neither European nor Austrian rail passes are valid for use on Bundesbuses. *Fahrpläne BundesBus* booklets are often available free of charge from bus station offices, major post offices and sometimes local or regional tourist offices. They're updated each year in late May and cover specific regions, eg one covers the Salzkammergut, another Pingau and the Hohe Tauern National Park, and so on. Bus information numbers are ☎ 0660-51 88 and ☎ 0660-80 20; calls are charged at the local rate.

Austrian citizens can get some excellent deals on buses, with reduced prices for senior citizens and families.

TRAIN

Austrian trains are comfortable, clean and reasonably frequent. The country is well covered by the state network, with only a few private lines. Eurail and Inter-Rail passes are valid on the former; enquire before embarking on the latter. The state network is at least as efficient as most other European national rail systems, especially considering such

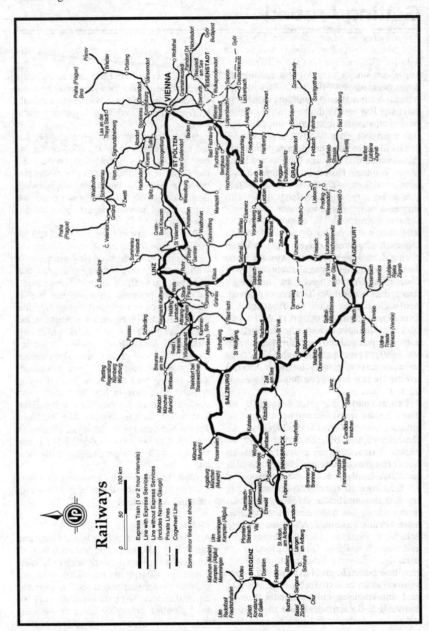

obstacles as the Alps. However, the ÖBB (Österreichischen Bundesbahnen; Austrian Federal Railways) does suffer in comparison with its Swiss neighbour, the SBB, which encounters similar terrain yet manages to run trains as if they were quartz watches on wheels. Austrian trains are often on time, but delays of five to 15 minutes are not uncommon. Think twice before you schedule very tight transport connections.

The German for train station is *Bahnhof* (abbreviated *Bf*); the main train station is the *Hauptbahnhof* (abbreviated *Hbf*). Some small rural stations are unstaffed, and at these you either buy the ticket from a platform dispenser or more usually on the train. Such stations are marked 'Hu' on timetables after the station name. All but the smallest stations will exchange foreign currency or travellers' cheques. Stations almost always have some facility for luggage storage, either at a staffed counter (AS20 per piece), or in 24-hour luggage lockers for AS20 (large enough for one backpack) or AS30 (two backpacks). Digital lockers may cost up to AS40, and some stations have lockers for skis. Luggage can be despatched between Austrian stations for AS80 per piece (up to 50 kg). This service covers transporting bicycles – see the following Bicycle section for more details.

Types of Train

The type and speed of a train can be identified by its prefix. EC (EuroCity), IC (InterCity) and SC (SuperCity) are all express trains, stopping only at major stations. They usually have a dining car where food and drink prices are quite reasonable. EN is an international night train, with sleeping cars and couchettes. E *(Eilzug:* literally, 'hurry train') is a fast train, but stopping at some smaller stations. D trains are medium fast. Slow, local trains have no letter prefix and stop everywhere. On small local trains servicing relatively deserted routes, there may be a button to press to request the train to stop (as on buses). Trains have smoking and non-smoking compartments, though Vienna's S-Bahn trains are non-smoking only.

The station platform *(Bahnsteig)* is divided into zones A, B and sometimes C: take care as a small rural train may be already waiting at one end while you're vainly waiting at the other for it to arrive. Usually you only realise when the train's pulling off (it's happened to me more than once). Even if you board the correct train, make sure you sit in the correct carriage, as trains occasionally split en route. Diagram boards show the carriage order (1st or 2nd class, dining car etc) of IC and EC trains. Long-distance trains always provide the choice of travelling 1st or 2nd class, though some local services are only 2nd class. Second class is comfortable enough; 1st class is roomier and less crowded.

Tickets & Information

Many stations have information centres where the staff speak English. Pick up the free booklet *Servus in Austria with Railways* at train station information offices, which tells you everything about travelling by rail, including special tickets, reservations and contact numbers. *Die Bahn im Griff* is a more detailed version in German.

Tickets can be purchased on the train but they cost around AS30 extra (unless you boarded at an unstaffed station or the ticket machine was out of order). In this book, fares are always quoted for 2nd class. Credit cards are accepted at over 200 stations, but only if the fare exceeds AS200. Eurocheque cards and cheques are accepted at all stations. Separate yellow posters in stations list arrivals *(Ankunft)* and departures *(Abfahrt)*.

Austrian train fares are expensive (eg AS156 for 100 km, AS276 for 200 km) but the cost can be reduced by national rail passes (see the following section on National Rail Passes). There's also a variety of discount tickets available, especially for youth groups. Streckenkarten are passes valid for hefty discounts on repeat fares for a specific trip, mostly of interest to commuters. Fares for children aged six to 15 are half-price; younger kids travel free if they don't take up a seat. Small pets (in suitable containers) travel free; larger pets are charged at half-price.

Ordinary return tickets (71 km or more each way) are valid for two months and you can break your journey as many times as you like, but you should tell the conductor so your ticket can be suitably endorsed. This is worth doing, as longer trips cost less per km. Single journeys of 71 km or more can also be broken up: these are valid for four days; singles for 70 km or under are valid only for one day. A return fare is usually the equivalent price of two singles. However, there is a 'Spar' ticket that covers unlimited trips on the same day on a particular route (of 50 km or less). This will enable you to get there and back for less than the price of two singles. Other exceptions are in Vorarlberg and Tirol: both provinces are divided into regional zones, and a zonal day pass is often less than the price of two singles. Sometimes, reduced rail fares on both national and international routes are available for those aged under 26: wave your passport and ask. In the larger towns, train information can be obtained on ☎ 1717.

Reserving train seats in 2nd class within Austria (on IC, SC or EC trains) costs AS30; in 1st class, IC reservations cost AS30, and SC and EC reservations cost AS50. To travel 1st class on SC and EC there's a AS50 surcharge anyway, so you may as well make a reservation for no extra charge. The exception is with some rail passes (Eurail, Bundes-Netzkarte and Puzzle), where SC and EC surcharges are included, but reservation charges aren't. Before you sit, check whether your intended seat has been reserved by someone else down the line.

National Rail Passes

The following passes can be purchased from travel agents or rail network offices, either inside or outside Austria.

The Bundes-Netzkarte is the national rail pass, valid on all state railways, including rack (cogwheel) railways and Wolfgangsee ferries (see the Salzkammergut chapter for details). It is valid for one month and costs AS5400 in 1st class and AS3600 in 2nd class.

It's the best deal if you're travelling extensively and intensively.

The Österreich Puzzle is not particularly puzzling – it's a kind of more flexible, regional Netzkarte which divides the country into four zones – north, south, east and west. You can buy a pass for each zone for AS990 (AS600 if under 26) giving you four days unlimited travel in 10 days. Zone areas overlap so you can cover the whole country without actually needing to buy the east zone. West covers Vorarlberg, Tirol, East Tirol and Salzburg province. South covers Salzburg province, East Tirol, Carinthia and Styria. East covers Styria, Burgenland, Vienna and Lower Austria. North covers Upper and Lower Austria, Vienna and Burgenland. First class costs 50% more.

The Kilometerbank allows up to six people to travel on journeys over 51 km. You can use the pass for shorter trips, but you'll still be debited the 51 km per person. The maximum trip per person is 700 km. Each km in 1st class debits 1.5 km. The cost is AS2100 for 2000 km, AS3150 for 3000 km, and AS5250 for 5000 km. These prices represent a discount of about 10% on normal fares. Kilometerbank may be the best deal if you want to take your time exploring the country, as it's valid for a year.

The Umweltticket (Environmental Ticket) is valid for half-price travel, and costs AS1080 for one year or AS1990 for two years. Senior citizens (women aged 60 and over, men 65 and over) and disabled people pay AS260 for one year. Austrian students pay AS140 and Austrian families pay AS170. The Grüne Bank (Green Bank) is like a debit card for the rail system and merely allows you to board the train without queuing for a ticket. It costs AS2000 and can be used to pay for Umweltticket or normal-price trips of over 51 km.

Private train companies in Austria accept Austrian rail passes (though the Achensee-bahn accepts only the Bundes-Netzkarte and the Austrian Puzzle pass).

CAR & MOTORBIKE

Rural driving is an enjoyable experience in

Austria. Roads are well maintained, well signposted and generally not too congested. Compared to train and bus, private transport gives more flexibility (eg the opportunity to stop when you want to admire that Alpine view), but it does tend to isolate you to some extent from local people and other travellers. The use of cars is often discouraged in city centres; consider ditching your trusty chariot and relying on public transport.

The fastest roads round the country are autobahns, identified on maps by national 'A' numbers or pan-European 'E' numbers (both are usually given in this book). These are generally not toll roads, though there are exceptions (eg the A13/E533 Brenner Pass autobahn). Their course is often shadowed by alternative fast routes (*Schnellstrassen* or *Bundesstrassen*). These principal routes are as direct as the terrain will allow, sometimes using tunnels to maintain their straight lines. In the mountains, you can opt instead for smaller, slower roads that wind over mountain passes. These can add many minutes and kms to your journey but are much more scenic. Take care on those bends, and stay in low gear on steep stretches. Some minor passes are blocked by snow from November to May. Carrying snow chains in winter is highly recommended and may be compulsory in some areas.

Toll roads are mostly in the mountainous regions. Toll roads and Alpine passes are mentioned in this book when relevant, but not all are covered. The useful *Facts and Sights*, a free brochure from ANTO, has a serviceable country map and lists all toll roads and prices, and all Alpine passes and their altitudes. For more detailed information, consult a motoring organisation.

Cars can be transported by motorail trains (*Autoreisezüge*). Vienna is linked by a daily motorail service to Feldkirch, Innsbruck, Salzburg and Villach. A daily motorail also goes from Graz and Villach to Feldkirch. Around 160 Austrian train stations offer park and ride facilities (free parking). In rural places, you may find petrol stations closed on Sunday. See the Getting There & Away chapter for more on fuel.

Road Rules & Signs

The minimum driving age is 18, both for Austrians and foreigners. Like the rest of Continental Europe, Austrians drive on the right side of the road. Speed limits are 50 km/h in towns, 130 km/h on autobahns and 100 km/h on other roads. Cars towing a caravan or trailer are limited to 100 km/h on autobahns. Seatbelts must be used, if fitted in the car, and children under 12 should have a special seat or restraint.

Motorcyclists and their passengers must wear a helmet, and dipped lights must be used in daytime. Motorcyclists should also carry a first-aid kit, though an Austrian biker assured me the police do not bother to enforce this regulation. Car drivers must carry a first-aid kit and a warning triangle.

Austrian police have the authority to impose fines of up to AS500 for various traffic offences. This can be paid on the spot (ask for a receipt) or within two weeks. The penalty for drink-driving (over 0.08% BAC) is a hefty on-the-spot fine and confiscation of your driving licence.

Give priority to vehicles coming from the right. On mountain roads, buses have priority; otherwise, priority lies with the vehicle which would find it most difficult to stop (generally the one facing downhill). Drive in low gear on steep downhill stretches – as a rule of thumb, use the same gear downhill as you did uphill.

Road signs generally conform to international standards. Triangular signs with a red border warn of dangers, and circular signs with a red border illustrate prohibitions. A crisscrossed white tyre on a blue circular background means snow chains are compulsory. *Umleitung* in German means 'diversion', though in Austria you may see *Ausweiche* instead. On maps or signs, look for the Austrian word *Maut*, indicating a toll booth.

Trams are a common feature in Austrian cities; take care if you've never driven amongst them before. Trams always have priority and no matter how much you might swear, they're never going to deviate from their tracks just to suit you. Vehicles should wait behind while trams are slowing down for passenger stops.

Urban Parking

Most town centres have a designated short-parking zone *(Kurzparkzone)*, meaning that on-street parking is limited to a maximum 1½ or three hours (depending upon the place) between specified times. These are known as blue zones from their blue markings; a parking voucher *(Parkschein)* should be purchased from a Tabak shop or pavement dispenser and displayed on the windscreen. Sometimes blue-zone parking is free, but you should get a clock face indicator from a Tabak shop or a police station, on which you can show the time you first parked. Outside the specified hours there are no parking restrictions in blue zones. On some streets stopping may be prohibited altogether (blue sign circled in red with a red cross) or only permitted for 10 minutes (blue sign circled in red with a single diagonal line – a *Halten* area). Plaques under the sign will state any exceptions or specific conditions (eg the 'Halten' sign may also be marked as a Kurzparkzone, allowing 1½ or three hours parking).

Parking tickets incur a fine of AS300 if you pay within two weeks. Don't assume you can get away with it if you're due to leave the country, as Austria has reciprocal agreements with some countries for the collection of such debts. Don't risk getting towed, as you'll find it expensive (at least AS1000) and inconvenient to retrieve your car.

Motoring Organisations

The main national motoring organisation is the Österreichischer Automobil-, Motorrad- und Touring Club, or ÖAMTC (☎ 0222-71 19 90), Schubertring 1-3, A-1010 Vienna. For 24-hour emergency assistance within Austria, dial ☎ 120. The ÖAMTC has many affiliations with motoring clubs worldwide and members of these clubs do not have to pay for assistance if they have the appropriate Letter of Introduction or ETI booklet (enquire with your club before leaving

home). If you are not a member of an affiliated motoring club, call-out charges are AS975 in the day and AS1325 at night. ÖAMTC also offers travel agency services.

The other national motoring club, the Auto-, Motor- und Radfahrerbund Österreichs (ARBÖ) (☎ 891 210), 15 Mariahilfer Strasse 180, is not a member of the AIT and has only a few international affiliations within Europe. It offers 24-hour emergency assistance on ☎ 123: nonmembers pay AS990 in the day or AS1090 at night.

Both organisations have branches throughout Austria.

Rental

For the lowest rates, organise car rental before departure. Holiday Autos (☎ 0171-491 1111) in London charges UK£179 for its lowest category car for one week, including an airport surcharge, unlimited mileage and collision-damage waiver (CDW), and has a lowest price guarantee. Its US office is in California (☎ 909-947 1737).

Within Austria, shop around to get the best deal; even the same company may have two or more different rates – *Lokal Tarif*, *City Tarif*, *Hotel Tarif* etc, plus you can pay by the km or go for unlimited rates. The following prices include 20% VAT (MWST). Hertz has the best unlimited-km rates: from AS732 from one to three days, AS648 per day for four to six days, and AS576 per day for seven days or more. The rate for a weekend (noon Friday to 9 am Monday) is AS1188 and includes 1000 km mileage.

Europcar prices are higher, but only marginally so for its weekend rates (AS1248). Eurodollar is known in Austria as ARAC Autovermietung. Rates are a little higher again. Main train stations in the larger cities offer car rental in conjunction with Eurodollar.

Avis is yet more expensive on its daily unlimited-km rate; its weekend rate is also slightly higher (AS1398) though the rental period is from 11 am Friday to 11 am Monday, which is three hours longer than its rivals. Budget is ill-named in Austria, and charges the highest rates of the multinational companies.

Autoverleih Buchbinder has 100 outlets in Austria but its prices are high. The weekend rate may look more competitive but the rental period is only from 4 pm Friday to 8 am Monday.

All these companies have branches in main cities, and may also have an airport office (though prices are 7% higher than in city offices). Local rental agencies often have cheaper rates than the multinationals; the local tourist office will have details.

The minimum age for renting small cars is 19 and for prestige models it is 25, and driving licences must have been held for a year or sometimes more. All companies offer a collision-damage waiver (CDW) for an additional charge (Europcar is the cheapest, starting at AS215 per day). Personal accident insurance is an optional extra and may not be necessary if you or your passengers hold travel insurance. Be sure to enquire about all terms and conditions before commencing a rental: Hertz, for example, has a surcharge of AS60 per day for drivers under 25. Pay attention to the make of cars on offer, too: most companies place an Opel Corsa within the cheapest category, but with Hertz it comes in the next group up.

Note also that some rental companies will not allow you to drive the car outside Austria; you may find this inconvenient going to/from Tirol as some routes pass into Germany or Italy.

If you're planning a long trip, investigate leasing a car instead of renting, as this might work out cheaper.

Purchase

Car prices are slightly higher than in Germany and Italy. All Austrian-registered cars must undergo an annual technical inspection. Car registration plates are issued to the owner, so whether you buy new or second-hand, the vehicle will come without plates. Likewise, if you sell a vehicle, you remove the plates and return them to the motor registration office (or transfer them to your new car).

Importing a vehicle into Austria is a tedious bureaucratic process, and all newly registered cars must be fitted with a catalytic converter.

BICYCLE

Cycling is a popular activity in Austria, and most regional tourist boards have brochures on cycling facilities and routes within their region. Separate bike tracks are common (in cities, make sure you're walking on the footpath, not the bike path). The Danube cycling trail is something of a Holy Grail for cyclists, though there are many other excellent bike tours in the country. Most are close to bodies of water, where there are fewer hills to contend with.

Bicycles can be hired from over 160 train stations and returned to any other station with a rental office (there's a AS40 charge if you don't return it to the same one). You'll need to show a passport or other photo ID to rent a bike. The rate is AS90 per day, or AS50 if you can show a train ticket valid for that day (or for arrival at that station after 3 pm the previous day). Mountain bikes where

Cycling is both a convenient mode of travel and a popular recreational activity

available cost AS150/200 per day with/without a ticket. Rental over five days costs AS200/360 (AS600/800 for mountain bikes). Rental periods operate per calendar day, even at rental counters that are open 24 hours.

Within Austria, you can take your bike with you on slower trains, on special 'Rad Tramper' trains along the Danube and on the Fahrradbus round Lake Neusiedl. A bicycle ticket (transferable) valid on trains costs AS30 per day, AS60 per week and AS210 per month. There is a fixed fare of AS80 for transporting a bike as luggage on a train. This may be the only option on fast trains, though a few also now allow you to accompany your machine (reservation for AS60 required, plus the bike ticket).

HITCHING

Hitching is never entirely safe in any country in the world, and we don't recommend it. Travellers who decide to hitch should understand that they are taking a small but potentially serious risk. However, many people do choose to hitch, and the advice that follows should help to make their journeys as fast and safe as possible.

Hitching in Austria is patchy, but not too bad overall (though the route west from Salzburg to Munich was identified in a hitching guide as one of the most difficult spots in Europe to get a lift). It is illegal for minors under 16 years to hitch in Burgenland, Upper Austria, Styria and Vorarlberg. Don't try to hitch from city centres: take public transport to suburban exit routes and hitch from there. See the Getting There & Away chapter for more on hitching.

WALKING

Many city centres are compact enough to enable major tourist sights to be seen on a walking tour, but walking really comes into its own in rural areas. Hikes are an excellent way to leave behind the wail of car horns and the opaque logic of train schedules.

There are 10 long-distance, national hiking routes, and three European routes pass through Austria. Options include the northern Alpine route from Lake Constance to Vienna, via Dachstein, or the central route from Feldkirch to Hainburger Pforte, via Hohe Tauern National Park. The Austrian Alpine Club has information (see Activities in the Facts for the Visitor chapter), and many bookshops sell detailed hiking maps.

BOAT

Services along the Danube are slow and expensive scenic excursions rather than functional transport. Nevertheless, a boat ride is definitely worth it if you like lounging on deck and having the scenery come to you rather than the other way round. See the Getting There & Away chapter for more on Danube services. There are boat services on the larger lakes throughout the country. On some (eg Lake Constance, Lake Wörth) special day passes are a good deal.

MOUNTAIN TRANSPORT

Austria now has 3500 transport facilities in steep Alpine regions, compared to just 26 in 1945. These fall into five main categories. A funicular (Standseilbahn) is a pair of counter-balancing cars drawn by cables along an inclined track. A cable car (Luftseilbahn) is a cabin dramatically suspended from a cable high over a valley, also with a twin that goes down when it goes up. A gondola (Gondelbahn) is a smaller version of a cable car except that it is hitched onto a continuously running cable once the passengers are inside. Nowadays the terms gondola and cable car are interchangeable and no distinction is made in this book. A cable chair (Sesselbahn) is likewise hitched onto a cable but is unenclosed. A ski lift (Schlepplift) is a T-bar hanging from a cable, which the skiers hold or sit on while their ski-clad feet slide along the snow. T-bars aren't as safe as modern cable cars (as they are vulnerable to careless skiers letting go) and are being gradually phased out.

LOCAL TRANSPORT

Buses efficiently and comprehensively cover urban areas, and in many larger cities they are supplemented by environmentally-friendly trams. Vienna also has an underground metro system which is great for getting round the city quickly, but you don't get to sightsee as you go. Most towns have an integrated transport system (meaning you can switch between bus and tram routes on the same ticket) and offer excellent value one-day or 24-hour tickets (AS20 to AS50). Weekly or three-day passes may be available too, as well as multi-trip tickets which work out cheaper than buying individual tickets. Tickets are usually transferable, so you can sell (or give!) unused portions to other travellers.

All these tickets are available in advance from Tabak shops, pavement dispensers, or occasionally tourist offices. In some towns you *must* buy these in advance – drivers will sell single tickets but not the better-value passes. Sometimes you even need to buy single tickets before boarding (as in Linz). Single tickets may be valid for one hour, 30 minutes, or a single journey, depending on the place. If you're a senior citizen, at school in Austria, or travelling as a family, you may be eligible for reduced-price tickets in some towns.

Keep alert when you're about to disembark a bus: if you haven't pressed the request button and nobody's waiting at the bus stop, the driver won't stop.

On-the-spot fines (AS400 to AS500) apply to people caught travelling without tickets. Depending on the inspector, you could have real problems if you haven't the cash to pay on demand. Some Austrians (mostly youngsters) risk riding 'black' *(schwarzfahren)*, even though it undermines the whole transport system.

Public transport runs from about 5 or 6 am to midnight, though in smaller towns evening services may be patchy or finish for the night rather earlier.

Taxi

Taxis are metered and fares comprise a flat fee plus a charge per km. Owing to the good public transport, you're unlikely to need a taxi unless returning to your hotel late at night. They tend to wait outside train stations and large hotels. There's usually a surcharge of around AS10 for calling a radio taxi.

TOURS

These vary from two-hour walks in a city centre to all-inclusive packages to regional attractions. Arrangements can usually be made through tourist offices or local travel agents. Sometimes you can pick up good deals on excursions via train and boat or bus. Look for brochures at train stations or enquire in train station travel offices. A brochure called *Erlebnis Bahn & Schiff* details all sorts of trips by ferry and/or steam train.

Vienna

Vienna conjures up countless images: elaborate imperial palaces; coffee houses crammed with rich cakes and Baroque mirrors; choirboys with angelic voices; Art-Nouveau masterpieces; and white stallions strutting in measured sequence in the Spanish Riding School. Then there's its all-pervasive music tradition – the mighty Danube (Donau) River may slice through 2840 km of Europe, from the Black Forest to the Black Sea, but it owes its fame largely to Vienna; thanks to the Strauss waltz, it will be forever pictured 'blue' in countless minds.

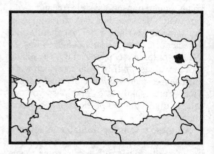

Vienna has gradually cast off its image as a haunt for genteel old ladies (dismissed as 'war widows' by young Austrians). The somewhat staid delights of its historical heritage remain, yet it is also a city where you can party all night, if that's what you want. Mix together the music, the nightlife, the stunning architecture and some of the best museums in Europe, and you get a city fully deserving of a leisurely exploration.

HISTORY

Vindobona, the military camp established by the Romans around 100 AD, was in the heart of Vienna's current Innere Stadt (first district). A civil town sprang up outside the camp and flourished in the 3rd and 4th centuries. At this time a visiting Roman emperor, Probus, introduced vineyards to the hills of the Wienerwald (Vienna Woods).

After the departure of the Romans, 'Wenia' is mentioned in the annals of the archbishopric of Salzburg in 881, and it became an important staging point for armies to and from the Crusades. The city continued to flourish as the seat of the Babenbergs, who granted Vienna a city charter in 1221.

Vienna developed apace under the Austro-Hungarian dual monarchy, and it hosted the World Fair in 1873. In 1919, voting rights were extended to all Viennese adults. The Social Democrats gained an absolute majority and embarked on an impressive series of social policies, particularly covering communal housing and health. The Karl-Marx-Hof is the best example of the municipal buildings created in this so-called 'Red Vienna' period. It originally contained 1325 apartments and stretches for one km along Heiligenstädter Strasse. In 1934, after the socialists were defeated in the civil war, Vienna's city council was dissolved and all progressive policies instantly stopped. Democracy was re-established in the city after WW II.

At the last election in Vienna (November 1991) the Social Democrats (SPÖ) achieved a narrow majority with 52 seats out of 100. The right-wing FPÖ made large gains with its anti-immigration, virtually racist campaign built around the slogan 'Vienna for the Viennese'. The assembly serves for a five-year term.

Vienna's provincial assembly also functions as the city council (Gemeinderat). Likewise, the offices of provincial governor and mayor are united in the same person. The Rathaus (City Hall) is the seat of these offices.

ORIENTATION

Vienna is at an elevation of 156 metres and occupies more than 400 sq km in the Danube Valley, with the hills of the Wienerwald

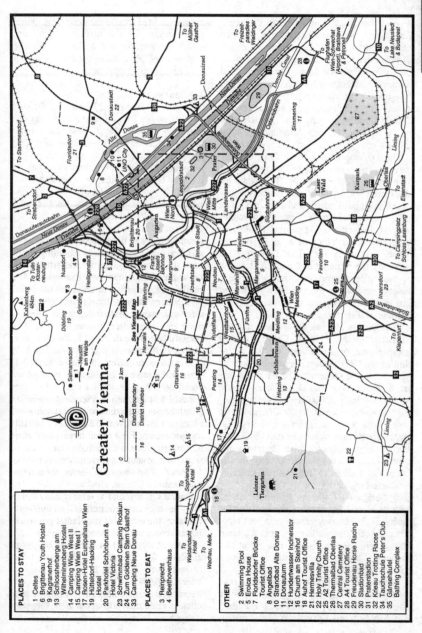

Greater Vienna

0   1.5   3 km

--- District Boundary
16   District Number

PLACES TO STAY

1   Celtes
6   Brigittenau Youth Hostel
9   Kagranerhof
13 Schlossherberge am Wilhelminenberg Hostel
14 Camping Wien West II
15 Camping Wien West I
19 Rosen-Hotel Europahaus Wien
20 Hütteldorf-Hacking Hostel
20 Parkhotel Schönbrunn & Hotel Victoria
23 Schwimmbad Camping Rodaun
24 Zum Goldenen Stern Gasthof
33 Camping Neue Donau

PLACES TO EAT

3   Reinprecht
4   Beethovenhaus

OTHER

2   Swimming Pool
5   Eroica House
7   Floridsdorfer Brücke Tourist Office
8   Angelibad
10 Strandbad Alte Donau
11 Donauturm
12 Hundertwasser Incinerator
16 Church am Steinhof
18 Auhof Tourist Office
21 Hermesvilla
22 Holy Trinity Church
25 A2 Tourist Office
26 Thermalbad Oberlaa
27 Central Cemetery
28 A4 Tourist Office
29 Freudenau Horse Racing
30 Stadionbad
31 Praterstadion
32 Krieau Trotting Races
34 Tauchschule Peter's Club
35 Gänsehäufel Bathing Complex

beyond the suburbs in the north and west. The Danube River divides the city into two unequal parts. The old city centre and nearly all the tourist sights are south of the river, mostly in the Innere Stadt. This is encircled by the Ringstrasse, or Ring, a series of broad roads sporting sturdy public buildings. Beyond the Ring is a larger traffic artery, the Gürtel (literally meaning 'belt'), which is fed by the flow of vehicles from outlying autobahns.

The Danube runs down a long, straight channel, built from 1870-75 to solve the problem of regular flooding. This was supplemented 100 years later by the building of the Neue Donau (New Danube) channel. The long, thin strip of land between the two channels is Donauinsel (Danube Island), a recreation area. A loop of water beyond the Neue Donau is the Alte Donau (Old Danube), the remnant of the original course of the river. It encloses the Donaupark, beaches and water-sport centres. North and east of the Alte Donau are relatively poor, residential districts.

The Donaupark has the Vienna International Center (UNO City), where international organisations are based, including the UN (its most important base after New York and Geneva). The park also has the Austria Center Vienna, Austria's largest convention hall. UNO City has extraterritorial status – it is leased to the UN for AS1 a year. Take your passport when visiting. Smaller trade fairs may be held in UNO City, though the main centre for trade fairs is the exhibition centre (*Messezentrum*) in the Prater. Guided tours of the Austria Center are conducted regularly.

St Stephen's Cathedral (Stephansdom), with its slender spire, is in the heart of the Innere Stadt and is Vienna's principal landmark. Leading south from here is Kärntner Strasse, an important pedestrian street that terminates at Karlsplatz, a major transport hub for the centre.

The majority of hotels and pensions are to the west of the city centre, roughly within a triangle bounded by Franz Josefs Bahnhof, Westbahnhof and Karlsplatz. Many restaurants are dotted around the same area, though the vicinity of the university, around Universitätsstrasse and Währinger Strasse, just north of Dr Karl Lueger Ring, is a good area for cheaper restaurants.

Addresses

Vienna is divided into 23 districts *(Bezirke)*, fanning out in approximate numerical order from the Innere Stadt. Take care when reading addresses. The number of a building within a street *follows* the street name. Any number *before* the street name denotes the district. This system has been used throughout this chapter. The middle two digits of postcodes correspond to the district, eg a postcode of 1010 means the place is in district one, and 1230 refers to district 23. Another thing to note is that the same street number may cover several adjoining buildings, so if you find that what is supposed to be a pizza restaurant at Wienstrasse 4 is really a rubber fetish shop, check the buildings either side before you resign yourself to a radical change of diet.

INFORMATION
Tourist Offices

The main tourist office (☎ 513 88 92, 513 40 15) is at 1 Kärntner Strasse 38. It is small and hectic but there is extensive free literature on hand. The city map is excellent, as is the *Youth Scene* magazine, which contains lots of useful information despite the chummy style. *Vienna Scene* aims at a more mature audience. The office has free lists of museums, events, hotels and restaurants. *Vienna From A to Z* (AS50) covers information on 300 sights, and includes walking tour itineraries of the centre. The office is open daily from 9 am to 7 pm, and has a room-finding service (AS40 commission per reservation).

Staff sell the Vienna Card (AS180), also available from hotels and transport ticket offices. New in 1995, this excellent card provides a 72-hour travel pass (see Getting Around in this chapter) plus numerous benefits, particularly admission and shopping discounts.

Advance requests for brochures, or things out of the ordinary, are dealt with at the head office of the Vienna Tourist Board (☎ 211 140; fax 216 84 92) at Obere Augartenstrasse 40, A-1025 Wien. They don't normally expect personal callers. Opening hours are Monday to Friday from 8 am to 4 pm.

The Lower Austria Information Centre (☎ 533 31 14), 1 Heidenschuss 2, is open Monday to Friday from 8.30 am to 5.30 pm. It's part of a private travel agency which also sells events tickets (commission charged).

The Austrian Information Office (☎ 587 20 00; fax 588 66 20), 4 Margaretenstrasse 1, is open Monday to Friday from 10 am to 5 pm (to 6 pm Thursday). Its web site can be found at http://austria-info.at/amusa/index.html, and tickets for arts events can be booked via e-mail on ticket@austria-info.at.

The city information office in the Rathaus is open Monday to Friday from 8 am to 6 pm. Somebody will also answer phone enquiries (☎ 403 89 89) on Saturday and Sunday from 8 am to 4 pm, as well as during office hours. It provides information on social, cultural and practical matters, geared as much to residents as tourists. Information and room reservations (commission charged) are also available in offices at entry points to the city:

Airport
    Arrivals hall, open daily from 8.30 am to 11 pm, except between October and May when it closes at 10 pm
Train stations
    Westbahnhof (open daily from 6.15 am to 11 pm) and Südbahnhof (open daily from 6.30 am to 10 pm)
Danube River
    DDSG landing stage near the Reichsbrücke, open April to mid-October from 9 am to 6 pm (8 pm May to September)
From the west by road
    A1 exit Wien-Auhof, open daily from 8 am to 10 pm (Easter to October), from 9 am to 7 pm (November) and from 10 am to 6 pm (December to pre-Easter)
From the south by road
    A2 exit Zentrum, Triesterstrasse, open daily from 9 am to 7 pm (Easter to June, and October) and 8 am to 10 pm (July to September)
From the east by road
    A4 exit Simmeringer Haide, Landwehrstrasse 6, open from 9 am to 7 pm (Easter to September)

From the north by road
    At the Floridsdorfer Brücke on Donauinsel, open from 9 am to 7 pm (Easter to September)

Information for cyclists is available at the bicycle office (☎ 505 84 35), 4 Frankenberggasse 11. It's open for personal callers Monday to Friday from 2 to 6 pm.

Another useful information source is the Youth Information Centre (☎ 526 46 37), 1 Dr Karl Renner Ring, in the below-ground Bellaria Passage, which can organise tickets for a variety of events at reduced rates for those aged between 14 and 26. There's plenty of information on rock concerts and other events. It's open from Monday to Friday from noon to 7 pm, and Saturday and school holidays from 10 am to 7 pm.

Money

There are banks and currency exchange offices all over the city, but compare commission rates before changing money. Exchange offices are open daily from 7 am to 10 pm in Westbahnhof, and from 6.30 am to 10 pm (9 pm November to March) in Südbahnhof. Bankomats are at all main train stations, the airport and at 200 branches of Bank Austria. Moneychangers at the airport charge at least AS90 commission, though the exchange rates are standard.

The American Express office (☎ 515 40), 1 Kärntner Strasse 21-23, is open Monday to Friday from 9 am to 5.30 pm, and Saturday from 9.30 am to noon. It has a travel section and financial services. There is no commission for travellers' cheques (Amex or otherwise). Cash exchanges attract a small commission on a sliding scale.

Post & Telecommunications

The main post office (Hauptpost 1011) is at 1 Fleischmarkt 19. It's open 24 hours a day for collecting and sending mail, changing money and using the telephone. Only a few services (like paying bills) are not round the clock. There are also 24-hour post offices at Südbahnhof, Westbahnhof and Franz Josefs Bahnhof.

Branch post offices are open Monday to

VIENNA

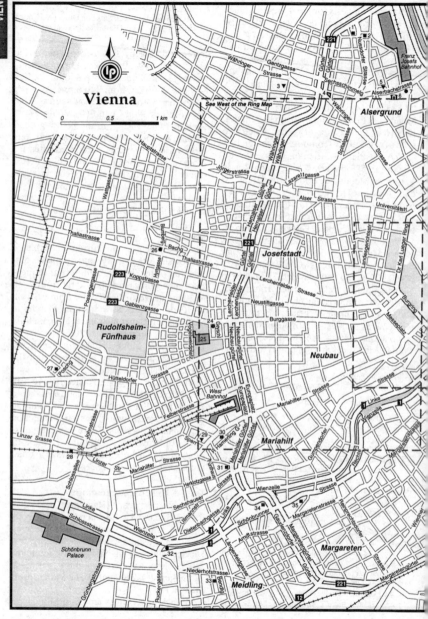

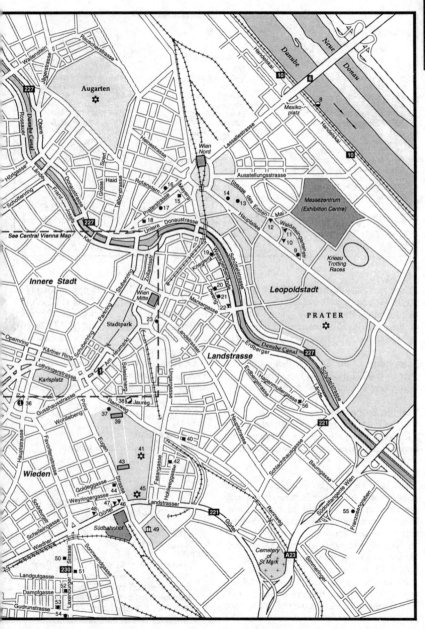

PLACES TO STAY		PLACES TO EAT			
1	Auge Gottes	3	Chez Robert	16	2 Rad-Börse
2	Hotel Arkadenhof	5	Feuervogel	17	Johann Strauss
15	Praterstern	10	Sta Cruz		Residence
18	Aphrodite	11	Café-Restaurant	19	KunstHausWien
27	Matauschek		Luftberg	20	Kalke Village
28	Rustler	12	Schweizerhaus	21	Hundertwasserhaus
30	Hostel Ruthensteiner	22	Steirereck	23	Mitfahrzentrale Wien
31	Altwienerhof	29	Madal Bal	24	Lugner City
33	Kolpingsfamilie	46	Kristall	25	Stadthalle
	Meidling	47	China Restaurant	26	BACH
34	Hotel Cryston	48	Wienerwald	32	U4 Nightclub
35	Goldenes Einhorn			36	Austrian Information
40	Artis	**OTHER**			Office
42	Pension Bosch			37	Orangery
44	Monopol	4	Volksoper	38	UK Embassy
50	Trend Hotel Favorita	6	Liechtenstein Palace	39	Lower Belvedere
51	Hotel Kolbeck Zur Linde	7	Foto Nettig	41	Botanical Gardens
52	Cyrus	8	DDSG Office	43	Upper Belvedere
53	Caroline	9	Bowling Alley	45	Alpine Garden
56	Turmherberge Don	13	Ferris Wheel	49	Museum of the 20th
	Bosco	14	Planetarium		Century
				54	Billa Supermarket
				55	Arena Music Venue

Friday from 8 am to noon and 2 to 6 pm, and Saturday from 8 to 11 am (closing noon for district head offices). They generally have a counter for changing money, but this closes at 5 pm on weekdays and 10 am on Saturday.

Telephone Code The telephone code for Vienna is 0222 if dialling from elsewhere in Austria, or 1 if calling from abroad.

Foreign Embassies

See the Facts for the Visitor chapter for the addresses, phone numbers and services of all major embassies and consulates in Vienna.

Cultural Centres

There is a huge range of English-language publications, for either leisure or research purposes, at the National Library (National-bibliothek) in the Neue Hofburg. It has huge reference and lending sections (free of charge), plus papyrus and music-score collections. Foreigners are permitted to borrow books. Upstairs is a room with newspapers such as the *Times* and the *International Herald Tribune*, and magazines and periodicals (many in English) covering all sorts of academic and recreational subjects. The main part of the library is open Monday to Friday from 9 am to 7.45 pm (to 3.45 pm from mid-June to 31 August) and Saturday to 5 pm. The British Council (☎ 533 26 16), 1 Schenkenstrasse 4, also has a library, with newspapers and magazines in English.

Go along to the Vedischen Kulturzentrum, 17 Rosenackerstrasse 26, at 5 pm on Sunday: there's yoga, Indian music and vegetarian food – it's all free!

Travel Agencies

Travel agencies in Vienna include:

Cedok
> 1 Parkring 10 (entry from Liebenberggasse) – specialist agency to the Czech Republic (☎ 512 43 72 85; fax 513 40 90)

Ibusz
> 1 Kärntner Strasse 26 – specialist agency to Hungary (☎ 512 78 79)

ÖKISTA
> Head office: 9 Garnisongasse 7 (☎ 401 480; fax 401 48 290). Opening hours are Monday to Friday from 9.30 am to 5.30 pm. Branches at: 9 Türkenstrasse 4-6 (☎ 401 48) and 4 Karlsgasse 3 (☎ 505 01 28). ÖS Reisen (☎ 402 15 61), 1 Reichsratstrasse 13, is a linked agency.

Österreichisches Verkehrsbüro
  1 Friedrichstrasse 7 – major national agency
  (☎ 588 000; fax 586 85 33)
Thomas Cook
  6 Mariahilfer Strasse 20 (☎ 526 58 02)

Bookshops

Wollzeile near St Stephen's is a street with many bookshops; Morawa at No 11 is the biggest. The British Bookshop (☎ 512 19 45), 1 Weihburggasse 24-6, has the largest selection of English-language books. Shakespeare & Co Booksellers (☎ 535 50 53), 1 Sterngasse 2, is a smaller place and has some second-hand books. Freytag & Berndt (☎ 533 20 94), 1 Kohlmarkt 9, stocks a vast selection of maps, and has travel guides in English. Reiseladen (☎ 513 75 77), 1 Dominikanerbastei 4, is a travel agency and travel bookshop with Lonely Planet guides.

Medical & Emergency Services

Medical treatment is available at the general hospital, the Allgemeines Krankenhaus (☎ 404 00) at 9 Währinger Gürtel 18-20. Other hospitals with emergency departments are Lorenz Böhler Unfallkrankenhaus (☎ 331 100), 20 Donaueschingenstrasse 13; Hanusch-Krankenhaus (☎ 94 21 510), 14 Heinrich Collin Strasse 30; and Krankenhaus Lainz (☎ 801 100), 13 Wolkerbergenstrasse 1.

The University Dental Hospital (Universitäts-Zahnklinik; ☎ 405 46 36) is at 9 Währinger Strasse 25A. For out-of-hours treatment, call ☎ 512 20 78.

Chemist shops are open normal shop hours, though they operate an out-of-hours service in rotation. Dial ☎ 1550 for recorded information in German on which chemist shops are open.

There are many police stations. The head office for the Innere Stadt (☎ 313 470) is at 1 Deutschmeisterplatz 3, and the police are also in the Stephansplatz and Karlsplatz U-Bahn stations.

Gay & Lesbian

Probably the best organisation to contact is Rosa Lila Villa (☎ 586 81 50), 6 Linke Wienzeile 102. There's telephone counselling, literature and advice on what's on offer in the city. Opening hours are Monday to Friday from 5 to 8 pm. On the premises is Café Willendorf, open daily from 7 pm to 2 am. The Homosexualle Initiative Wien (HOSI), 2 Novaragasse 40, also has telephone counselling (☎ 26 66 04) on Tuesday and Friday from 6 to 8 pm and Wednesday from 7 to 9 pm, and dancing for women only from 7 pm on Friday. It's open on Tuesday from 8 pm.

Laundry

Miele Selbstbedienung (☎ 405 02 55), 8 Josefstädter Strasse 59, is open Monday to Friday from 7 am to 8 pm and Saturday from 7 am to noon. To wash a six-kg load costs AS70 plus AS25 for soap powder and AS20 to dry. Dry cleaning is AS155 for four kg.

Münzwäscherei (☎ 587 04 73), 4 Margaretenstrasse 52, costs AS85 to wash (soap powder included) and AS25 to dry. It's open Monday to Friday from 7 am to 6 pm and Saturday from 8 to 11 am (closed for four weeks from mid-July).

CENTRAL VIENNA WALKING TOUR

This walk covers about 2.5 km. Major sights are considered in greater detail later in the chapter.

Kärntner Strasse

From the main tourist office, walk north up the pedestrian-only Kärntner Strasse, a walkway of plush shops, trees, café tables and street entertainers. Detour left down the short Donnergasse to look at the **Donner Fountain**, created in 1739, in Neuer Markt. The four naked figures (which were too revealing for Maria Theresa's taste) represent the four main tributaries to the Danube: the Enns, March, Traun and Ybbs. Across the square is the **Church of the Capuchin Friars** and the **Imperial Burial Vault**. Back on Kärntner Strasse, detour again down the second street on the left, Kärntnerdurchgang. Here you'll find the **American Bar** designed in 1908 by Adolf Loos, who was one of the prime exponents of a functional Art-Nouveau style, though the façade here is somewhat garish. Next door is a strip club, Chez Nous. This was formerly the base for the art club of the Vienna Group; ironically, many of the group's performance art events also involved naked postures.

Stephansplatz to Michaelerplatz

From Kärntner Strasse, the street opens out into Stock im Eisen Platz. Adjacent to the south-west corner is a nail-studded stump. It is said this tree trunk acquired its crude metal jacket in the 16th century from blacksmiths banging in a nail for luck when they left the city. Across the square is Stephansplatz and Vienna's prime landmark, **St Stephen's Cathedral** (Stephansdom). Facing it is the unashamedly modern **Haas Haus**, built by Hans Hollein and opened in 1990. Many Viennese were rather unhappy about this curving silver structure crowding their beloved cathedral, but tourists seem happy enough to snap the spindly reflections of St Stephen's spire in its rectangular windows.

Leading north-west from Stock im Eisen Platz is the broad pedestrian thoroughfare of **Graben**, another plush shopping street. Like Kärntner Strasse and Stephansplatz, it's a fine place to linger, soak up the atmosphere, absorb the hubbub of voices and appreciate the musicianship of street artists. Graben is dominated by the knobbly outline of the **Plague Column**, completed in 1693 to commemorate the 75,000 victims of the Black Death who perished in Vienna some 20 years earlier. Adolf Loos was busy in Graben, creating the Schneidersalon Knize at No 10 and, rather appropriately given his surname, the toilets nearby.

Turn left into Kohlmarkt, so named because charcoal was once sold here. At No 14 is one of the most famous of the Konditorei-style cafés in Vienna, **Demel**. Just beyond is Michaelerplatz, with the dome of St Michael's gateway to the **Hofburg** towering above.

The so-called **Loos Haus** (1910) on Michaelerplatz (the Goldman & Salatsch building) is a typical example of the clean lines of Loos' work. Yet Franz Joseph hated it, and described the windows, which lack lintels, as 'windows without eyebrows'. The excavations in the middle of the square are of Roman origin. **St Michael's Church** (Michaelerkirche) on the square betrays five centuries of architectural styles: 1327 (Romanesque chancel) to 1792 (Baroque doorway angels).

Ringstrasse

Pass through St Michael's Gate and the

Art Through Action

Viennese actionism, one of the most extreme modern art movements, spanned the years 1957 to 1968. It was linked to the Vienna Group and had its roots in abstract expressionism. Actionism sought access to the unconscious through the frenzy of an extreme and very direct art: the actionists started by pouring paint over the canvas and slashing it with knives, but soon moved to using bodies (live people and dead animals) as 'brushes', and blood, excrement, eggs, mud and whatever else came to hand as 'paint'. Finally they dispensed with the traditional canvas altogether; the artist's body became the canvas, and the site of art became a deliberated event (a scripted action staged privately or publicly).

It was a short step from self-painting to inflicting wounds upon the body and engaging in physical and psychological endurance tests. For 10 years the actionists scandalised the press and public, inciting violence and panic, and receiving plenty of publicity. Often poetic, humorous and aggressive, they became increasingly politicised, addressing the sexual and social repression they saw as pervading the Austrian state. *Art in Revolution* (1968), the last action in Vienna, resulted in six months hard labour all round. ∎

RICHARD NEBESKY

MARK HONAN

MARK HONAN

MARK HONAN

MARK HONAN

MARK HONAN

Top:	St Stephen's Cathedral, Vienna; tiled roof detail
Middle:	Museum of Fine Arts, Vienna; stone carvings detail
Bottom:	Secession building, Vienna; entrance detail

MARK HONAN

MARK HONAN

AUSTRIAN NATIONAL TOURIST OFFICE

Top: Brunnenhaus, Vienna
Left: Arnold Schwarzenegger poster advertising Viennale Film Festival
Right: Hundertwasserhaus, Vienna

courtyard to find yourself in Heldenplatz, with the vast curve of the **Neue Hofburg**, built between 1881 and 1908, on your left. Hitler addressed a rally from here during his triumphant return to Vienna in 1938. Walk past the line of fiacres, noting the Gothic spire of the **Rathaus** (1873-83) rising above the trees to the right. Ahead, on the far side of the Ring, stand the rival identical twins, the **Museum of Natural History** (1872-81) and the **Museum of Fine Arts** (1872-91). They were the work of Gottfried Semper, who did the exteriors, and Karl von Hasenauer, who did the interiors. Between the museums is a large statue of Maria Theresa, surrounded by key figures of her reign. She sits regally, holding her right hand out, palm upwards, as if in an early version of the 'gimme five' greeting.

The monumental architecture round the **Ringstrasse** is largely due to Emperor Franz Joseph. In 1857 he decided to tear down the redundant military fortifications and exercise grounds and replace them with grandiose public buildings in a variety of historical styles. Work began the following year and reached a peak in the 1870s. Ironically, the empire the buildings were supposed to glorify was lost after WW I. Plans for a grand walkway connecting the Hofburg and the museums, and for a companion wing to the Neue Hofburg, were shelved. A full tour of the Ring is recommended, or at least the section between the university and the Staatsoper (under two km). Break up your walk by relaxing en route in the Volksgarten with its many roses, or Rathauspark featuring statues and fountains. The **Burggarten**, formerly reserved for the pleasure of the imperial family and high-ranking officials, has statues of Mozart (erected 1896) and Franz Joseph.

From the Hofburg, walk anticlockwise round the Ring, passing a vast statue of a seated Goethe, until you reach the **Staatsoper** (State Opera), built from 1861 to 1869. This may appear the equal of any other Ringstrasse edifice, but initial public reaction was so poor that one of the designers, Eduard van der Nüll, committed suicide.

The building was all but destroyed in WW II and reopened only in 1955. The opulent interior is best explored during the interval of a performance, though you can also take a guided tour for AS50 (students AS30); schedules vary – see the timetable at the window on the Kärntner Strasse side of the building.

At the north-west corner of the Staatsoper is **Albertinaplatz**. The south-eastern extremity of the Hofburg is on your left, containing the famous Albertina collection of graphic arts. This is mostly closed for long-term renovations, though some facsimiles can be viewed Monday to Thursday from 10 am to 4 pm and Friday from 10 am to 1 pm (AS10). On the square is a troubling work by sculptor and graphic artist Alfred Hrdlicka (born 1928), created in 1988. This series of pale block-like sculptures commemorates Jews and other victims of war and fascism. Some of the stone originally came from the Mauthausen concentration camp.

Turn right into Philharmonikerstrasse, passing between the Staatsoper and the **Hotel Sacher**, purveyor of a famous cake, the Sachertorte. Sacher and Demel had a long-running dispute over who was the true creator of the authentic chocolate torte: the former was Metternich's cook, the latter was pastry cook to the Habsburgs.

Another few steps will bring you back to Kärntner Strasse, with the tourist office on your left.

INNERE STADT
St Stephen's Cathedral
The latticework spire of this Gothic masterpiece rises high above the city and is a focal point for visitors.

The cathedral was built on the site of a 12th-century church, of which the Giant's Gate (Riesentor, the main entrance) and the Towers of the Heathens (Heidentürme) are incorporated into the present building. Both are Romanesque in style; the church was recreated in Gothic style after 1359.

The dominating feature is the skeletal south tower, or **Südturm**, nick-named

'Steffl'. It stands 136.7 metres high and was completed in 1433 after 75 years of building work. Negotiating 343 steps will bring you to the viewing platform for an impressive panorama (open from 9 am to 5.30 pm, entry AS20). It was to be matched by a companion tower on the north side, but the imperial purse withered and the Gothic style went out of fashion, so the incomplete tower was topped off with a Renaissance cupola in 1579. Austria's largest bell, the **Pummerin** (boomer bell), was installed here in 1952; it weighs 21 tonnes. Entry to the north tower, accessible by a lift, costs AS40. It's open daily from 8 am to 5 pm; 9 am to 6 pm in July and August.

Interior walls and pillars are decorated with fine statues and side altars. A magnificent Gothic piece is the **stone pulpit**, fashioned in 1515 by Anton Pilgram. The expressive faces of the four fathers of the church (saints Augustine, Ambrose, Gregory and Jerome) are at the centre of the design, yet Pilgram himself can be seen peering out from a window below. The Baroque **high altar** in the main chancel shows the stoning of St Stephen. The left chancel has a winged altarpiece moved here from Wiener Neustadt and dating from 1447; the right chancel has the red marble tomb of Friedrich III, Renaissance in style. Under his guidance the city became a bishopric (and the church a cathedral) in 1469.

Don't ignore the decorations and statues on the outside of the cathedral: at the rear the agony of the Crucifixion is well captured, although some irreverent souls attribute Christ's pained expression to toothache. A striking feature of the exterior is the glorious **tiled roof**, showing dazzling chevrons on one end and the Austrian eagle on the other; a good perspective is gained from Schulerstrasse.

The **catacombs** in the cathedral are open daily, with tours approximately hourly between 10 am and 4.30 pm (AS35; in English if there's sufficient demand). The tour includes viewing a mass grave of plague victims, a bone house, and rows of urns containing the internal organs of the

Habsburgs. One privilege of being a Habsburg was to be dismembered and dispersed after death: their hearts are in the Augustinian Church in the Hofburg (viewed by prior appointment only; ☎ 533 70 except on Sunday) and the rest of their bits are in the Imperial Burial Vault (see the entry later in this chapter).

Hofburg

The huge Hofburg (Imperial Palace) is an impressive repository of culture and heritage. The Habsburgs were based here for over six centuries, from the first emperor (Rudolf I in 1279) to the last (Charles I in 1918). In that time new sections were periodically added. Sections include the early Baroque Leopold Wing, the 18th-century Imperial Chancery Wing, the 16th-century Amalia Wing and the Royal Chapel, which was commissioned by Friedrich III and refitted as Baroque by Empress Maria Theresa. This is where the Vienna Boys Choir sings Sunday Mass. The palace now houses the offices of the Austrian president.

The oldest part is the **Swiss Courtyard** (Schweizerhof), named after the Swiss guards who used to protect its precincts. It dates from the 13th century and now looks rather shabby. The Renaissance Swiss gate dates from 1553. The courtyard adjoins a much larger courtyard, **In der Burg,** with a monument to Emperor Franz II at its centre. The buildings around it are from differing eras.

Imperial Apartments The Kaiserappartements are as opulent as you might expect, with fine furniture, hanging tapestries and bulbous crystal chandeliers. Rooms in this part of the palace were occupied by Franz Joseph I and Empress Elisabeth. Entry costs AS70 (AS35 for students aged under 27) or AS85 (AS40) with the guided tour. It's open daily from 9 am to 5 pm. A combined ticket with the adjoining Silver Treasury (Silberkammer) of porcelain and tableware costs AS90 (AS105 with a tour).

Imperial Treasury This treasury (Schatzkammer) contains secular and ecclesiastical treasures of great value and splendour. The sheer wealth exhibited is staggering: Room 7 has a 2860-carat Colombian emerald, a 416-carat balas ruby and a 492-carat aquamarine. The imperial crown (Room 11) dates from the 10th century. The private crown of Rudolf II (1602) is a more delicate piece. Room 6 contains mementos of Marie Louise, daughter of Franz II and wife of Napoleon. Room 8 has two unusual objects formerly owned by Ferdinand I: a 75-cm-wide bowl carved from a single piece of agate, and a narwhal tusk, 243 cm long and once claimed to have been a unicorn horn.

The religious relics include fragments of the True Cross, one of the nails from the Crucifixion, and one of the thorns from Christ's crown. Ecclesiastical vestments display delicate and skilled work.

Written and audio guides are available on site. Allow anything from 30 minutes to two hours to get around; entry costs AS60 (students and senior citizens AS30) and it's open daily (closed Tuesday) from 10 am to 6 pm (to 9 pm on Thursday).

Prunksaal This archetypal Baroque structure was created by the Fischer von Erlachs from 1723 to 1726. It was commissioned by Charles VI; his statue stands under the central church-like dome, which itself has a fresco by Daniel Gran depicting the emperor's apotheosis. Leather-bound, scholarly tomes line the walls, and rare 15th-century volumes are stored in glass cabinets, with pages opened to beautifully-drawn sections of text. The hall is open Monday to Saturday from 10 am to 4 pm, and Sunday and holidays to 1 pm. Entry is AS50, or AS30 for students and senior citizens. The entrance is on Josefsplatz.

Collection of Old Musical Instruments This collection, the Sammlung Alter

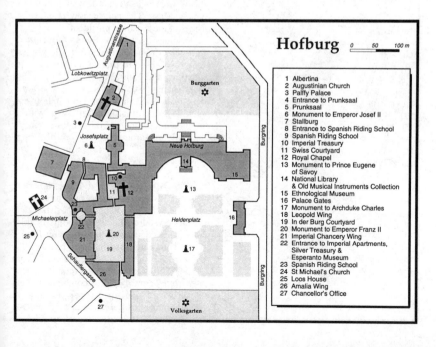

Hofburg

0   50   100 m

1 Albertina
2 Augustinian Church
3 Palffy Palace
4 Entrance to Prunksaal
5 Prunksaal
6 Monument to Emperor Josef II
7 Stallburg
8 Entrance to Spanish Riding School
9 Spanish Riding School
10 Imperial Treasury
11 Swiss Courtyard
12 Royal Chapel
13 Monument to Prince Eugene of Savoy
14 National Library & Old Musical Instruments Collection
15 Ethnological Museum
16 Palace Gates
17 Monument to Archduke Charles
18 Leopold Wing
19 In der Burg Courtyard
20 Monument to Emperor Franz II
21 Imperial Chancery Wing
22 Entrance to Imperial Apartments, Silver Treasury & Esperanto Museum
23 Spanish Riding School
24 St Michael's Church
25 Loos House
26 Amalia Wing
27 Chancellor's Office

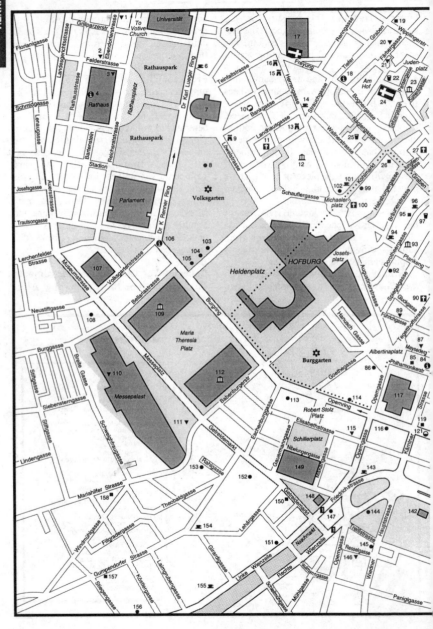

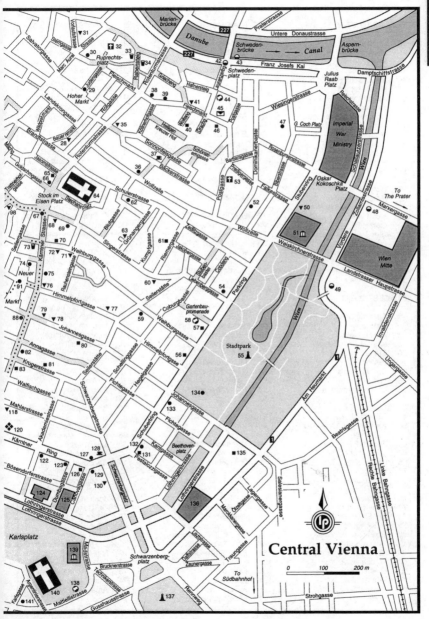

Central Vienna

0   100   200 m

PLACES TO STAY

19	Hotel Orient
26	Pension Nossek
40	Hotel Austria
46	Hotel Post
56	SAS Palais Hotel
57	Hotel Marriott
61	Appartement Pension Riemergasse
65	Hotel am Stephansplatz
70	Hotel Kaiserin Elisabeth
80	Music Academy Hotel
81	Hotel zur Wiener Staatsoper
83	Pension Am Operneck
85	Hotel Sacher & Café
95	Pension Aclon
119	Hotel Bristol
126	Hotel Imperial
131	Hotel am Schubertring
135	Hotel Inter-Continental & Vier Jahreszeiten Restaurant
150	Hotel-Pension Schneider
157	Kolping-Gästehaus
158	Quisisana

PLACES TO EAT

1	Catholic University Mensa
2	Naschmarkt
3	Wiener Rathauskeller
20	China Restaurant Peking
21	Brezel Gwölb
28	Wrenkh
31	China Restaurant Turandot
35	Pizza Bizi
41	Griechenbeisl
50	Academy of Applied Art Cafeteria
60	Zu den 3 Hacken
63	La Creperie
68	McDonald's
71	Weisser Rauchfangkehrer
72	Drei Husaren
76	Nordsee
77	Zum Kuckuck
78	Zur Fischerin Capua
79	McDonald's
87	Rosenberger Markt Restaurant
89	Kikkoman Hoshigaoka
98	Trzesniewski
110	Glacisbeisl
111	Würstel Stands
115	Restaurant Smutny
118	Korso
130	Naschmarkt Restaurant
146	Technical University Mensa

COFFEE HOUSES

6	Café Restaurant Landtmann
14	Café Central
37	Alt Wien
94	Café Bräunerhof
96	Café Hawelka
101	Demel
128	Café Schwarzenberg
143	Café Museum
154	Café Sperl
155	Café Drechsler

ENTERTAINMENT

7	Burgtheater
22	St Urbani-Keller
25	Esterházykeller
33	Roter Engel
34	Krah Krah
82	Casino
86	Bundestheaterkassen
97	Porgy & Bess
103	Volksgarten Pavillon Café
104	Volksgarten Waltzer Dancing
105	Volksgarten Nightclub
108	Volkstheater
113	Burg Kino
117	Staatsoper
125	Musikverein
136	Konzerthaus
151	Theater an der Wien
152	HTU Cinestudio
153	Top Kino

TRAVEL INFORMATION & TRANSPORT

4	City Information Office
18	Lower Austria Information Centre
42	Night Bus Departures
43	DDSG Canal Tour Landing Stage
48	Central Bus Station
49	City Air Terminal
52	Reiseladen (Travel Agency)
54	Cedok (Travel Agency)
84	Main Tourist Office
88	Ibusz (Travel Agency)
106	Youth Information Centre
114	Lauda Air
116	Avis
121	Lokalbahn to Baden

122	British Airways
123	Europcar
127	Hertz
129	Austrian Airlines & Swissair
132	Eurodollar
133	ÖAMTC
141	ÖKISTA Branch Office
147	Österreichisches Verkehrsbüro

CHURCHES & CATHEDRALS

11	Minorite Church
17	Church & Court of the Scots
24	Church am Hof
27	St Peter's Church
32	St Rupert's Church
53	Dominican Church
64	St Stephen's Cathedral
90	Church of the Capuchin Friars & Imperial Burial Vault
100	St Michael's Church
140	St Charles' Church

OTHER

5	Pasqualati House
8	Temple of Theseus
9	Liechtenstein Palace
10	Hungarian Embassy
12	State Museum of Lower Austria
13	Palace of the Lower Austrian Diet
15	Porcia Palace
16	Kinsky Palace
23	Clock Museum
29	Anker Clock
30	Shakespeare & Co Booksellers
36	Morawa (Bookshop)
38	Konsum Supermarket
39	Julius Meinl Supermarket
44	Canadian Embassy
45	Main Post Office
47	Postsparkasse
51	Museum of Applied Arts
55	Johann Strauss Statue
58	US Consulate
59	British Bookshop
62	Figaro House
66	Haas Haus & DO & CO Restaurant
67	Nail-Studded Stump
69	Billa Supermarket
73	Loos' American Bar
74	Inlingua Spracheschule
75	American Express
91	Donner Fountain

Musikinstrumente, is contained in the National Library and is the best part of the three-museums-in-one in the Neue Hofburg. Headphones (free) are activated by infrared as you walk round, giving a relaxing and evocative musical accompaniment to the instruments on display. Instruments of all shapes and sizes are to be found, including horns shaped like serpents, a mini keyboard disguised as a book, and violins with carved faces. Different rooms are dedicated to different composers (eg Haydn, Mozart and Beethoven) and contain instruments played by those notables.

It is open daily, except Tuesday, from 10 am to 4 pm and admission costs AS30 (children and senior citizens AS15). This includes entry to two adjoining collections. The **Ephesus Museum** has relief statues and a scale model of the famous archaeological site in Turkey. The **Collection of Arms & Armour** (Waffen und Rüstungen) dates mostly from the 15th and 16th centuries and has some fine examples of ancient armour; note the bizarre pumpkin-shaped helmet from the 15th century.

Imperial Burial Vault

The Kaisergruft is beneath the Church of the Capuchin Friars on Neuer Markt. It was instigated by Empress Anna (1557-1619), and her body and that of her husband, Emperor Matthias (1557-1619), were the first to be placed here. Since then, all but three of the Habsburg dynasty found their way here, the last being Empress Zita in 1989. The only non-Habsburg is the Countess Fuchs.

Fashion extends even to tombs: those in the vault range from the unadorned to the ostentatious. By far the most elaborate caskets are those portraying 18th-century Baroque pomp, such as the huge double sarcophagus containing Maria Theresa and Francis I. The tomb of Charles VI has been expertly restored. Both were the work of Balthasar Moll. The vault is open daily from 9.30 am to 4 pm and entry costs AS30 (students and senior citizens AS20).

Parlament

The Parlament building (1873-83) was designed by Theophil Hansen. It displays a Greek revival style, with huge pillars and figures lining the roof. The beautiful **Athena Fountain** in the front was sculptured by Karl Kundmann. Choosing a Grecian style of architecture was not a mere whim. Greece was the home of democracy and Athena was the Greek goddess of wisdom. It was hoped both qualities would be a permanent feature of Austrian politics.

The Parlament is the seat of the two federal assemblies. Guided tours (except during sessions) are conducted Monday to Friday at 11 am and 3 pm (also at 9 am, 10 am, 1 and 2 pm from mid-July to the end of August).

Am Hof

The Babenberg rulers of Vienna once had a fortress on Am Hof square before moving to the Hofburg, and there are also Roman ruins here. The **Church Am Hof**, on the south side, is a Baroque adaptation of its fire-damaged Gothic predecessor. On the north side, at No 10, is the former civic armoury (16th century). The Mariensäule column in the centre of the square is dedicated to the Virgin Mary and was erected in 1667.

Anker Clock

This picturesque Art-Nouveau clock (Ankeruhr) at 1 Hoher Markt 10-11 was created by Franz von Matsch in 1911. Over a 12-hour period, figures such as Josef Haydn and Maria Theresa slowly pass across the clock face – details of who's who are outlined on a plaque on the wall below. It draws crowds of tourists at noon when the figures trundle past, and organ music from the appropriate period is piped out. Walk north under the clock to visit St Rupert's Church (Ruprechtskirche), which was built in the 11th century and is the oldest church in Vienna.

Postsparkasse

This celebrated building, the Post Office Savings Bank, was the work of Otto Wagner. The design and choice of materials were both innovative: inside, note the sci-fi aluminium heating ducts and the naked stanchions – pared-down functionality *par excellence*. The main savings hall can be viewed Monday to Friday from 8 am to 3 pm, and Thursday to 5.30 pm. It's on the eastern side of the Innere Stadt, on Biberstrasse. Compare the modern appearance of the Postsparkasse with the classical-looking **Imperial War Ministry** on the Ring opposite, which was built around the same time (1909).

Museum of Fine Arts

The Kunsthistorisches Museum, on the south side of Maria Theresia Platz, is one of the finest museums in Europe and should not be missed. The Habsburgs were great collectors, and the huge extent of lands under their control led to many important art works being funnelled back to Vienna.

Rubens was appointed to the service of a Habsburg governor in Brussels, so it is not surprising that the museum has one of the best collections of his works. The collection of paintings by Pieter Brueghel the Elder is also unrivalled. The building itself has some

delightful features. The murals between the arches above the stairs were done by three artists, including a young Klimt (north wall), painted before he broke with classical tradition.

It's impossible to see the whole museum in one visit, so concentrate on specific areas. The sculpture and coin collections are closed for renovation for most of 1996, but the really important pieces (like Cellini's salt cellar) will have been moved to accessible rooms. Temporary exhibitions sometimes mean reorganisation, too. Guided tours in English depart at 3 pm (AS30) and provide an interesting analysis of a handful of main works. Written guides are also available on site. The museum is open Tuesday to Sunday from 10 am to 6 pm. On Thursday, late opening (to 9 pm) alternates between the picture gallery and the sculpture collection. Entry to the museum is AS45, or AS30 for students and senior citizens. Special exhibitions cost extra.

Ground Floor In the west wing is the Egyptian collection, including the burial chamber of Prince Kaninisut and the mummified remains of various animals. The Greek and Roman collection has the Gemma Augustea cameo (Saal XV), made from onyx in 10 AD.

The east wing contains sculpture and decorative arts, covering a range of styles. There's some exquisite 17th-century glassware and ornaments, and unbelievably lavish clocks from the 16th and 17th centuries (Saals XXXV and XXXVII). But the prime item here (Saal XXVII) is the salt cellar by Benvenuto Cellini, made in gold for Francis I of France in 1543. It depicts two naked deities, the goddess of the earth and the god of the sea, and has tiny wheels within so it can be pushed easily around the table.

First Floor The picture gallery on this floor is the most important part of the museum. Some rooms have information cards in English giving a critique of particular works. On this floor, smaller rooms lead off from a series of interconnected halls (saals).

East Wing This is devoted to German, Dutch and Flemish paintings. Saal X contains the Brueghel collection, amassed by Rudolf II. A familiar theme in Brueghel the Elder's work is nature, eg *The Hunters in the Snow* (1565). Brueghel's peasant scenes are also excellent, such as *The Battle Between Carnival & Lent* (1590).

The next gallery (Saal XI), shows the warm, larger-than-life scenes of Flemish Baroque, in vogue some 80 years after Brueghel. The motto in *The Feast of the Bean King* by Jacob Jordaens, to which the revellers are raising their glasses, translates as 'None resembles a fool more than the drunkard'.

Dürer (1471-1528) is represented in Room 14. His brilliant use of colour is shown in *The Holy Trinity Surrounded by All Saints*, originally an altarpiece. The *Martyrdom of 10,000 Christians* is another fine work.

The paintings by the mannerist Giuseppe Archimboldo in Room 19 use a device well explored by Salvador Dali – familiar objects arranged to appear as something else. The difference being that Archimboldo did it nearly 400 years earlier!

Rubens (1577-1640) synthesised northern European and Italian traditions. His dramatic Baroque scenes are in Saals XII and XIV and in Room 20. Note the open brushwork and diaphanous quality of the fur in the *Indefonso Altar*.

There are several Rembrandt self-portraits in Room 23. Vermeer's *The Allegory of Painting* (1665-66) is in Room 24. It's a strangely static scene of an artist in his studio, but one that transcends the mundane by its composition and use of light.

West Wing Saal I has Raphael's harmonious and idealised *Madonna in the Meadow* (1505). The triangular composition and the complementary colours are typical features of the Florentine high Renaissance. Compare this to Caravaggio's *Madonna of the Rosary* (1606) in Saal V, with the supplicants' dirty feet an example of the new realism in early Baroque. Caravaggio

emphasises movement in this picture by a subtle deployment of light and shadow.

Saal II has some evocative works by Titian, of the Venetian school. Next door in Room 2 is *The Three Philosophers* (1508), one of the few properly authenticated works by Giorgione. *Susanna at her Bath* (1555) by Tintoretto can be found in Saal IV. It recreates the Old Testament tale and successfully portrays both serenity and implicit menace. Tintoretto employs mannerist devices (contrasting light, extremes of facial features) to achieve his effect.

Saal VII has paintings by Bernardo Bellotto (1721-80), Canaletto's nephew. He was commissioned by Maria Theresa to paint scenes of Vienna. Several are shown here, though some landscapes are not faithful reproductions but have been creatively recomposed (eg the view from the Belvedere).

Room 10 has portraits of the Habsburgs. Juan Carreño's portrait of Charles II of Spain shows the characteristic Habsburg jaw. Most of the young women in Diego Velázquez' royal portraits are wearing dresses broad enough to fit round a horse, but the artist still manages to make the subjects come to life.

Museum of Natural History

The Naturhistorisches Museum, at the northern end of Maria Theresia Platz, is the scientific counterpart of the Museum of Fine Arts. The building is as grand but the exhibits aren't quite in the same league. It has minerals, meteorites and assorted animal remains in jars. Zoology and anthropology are covered in detail and there's a children's corner. The 25,000-year-old statuette, the *Venus of Willendorf*, is on display – the oldest museum piece in Vienna – and there are some good dinosaur exhibits. The museum also puts on special exhibitions. It's open daily, except Tuesday, from 9 am to 6 pm. In winter it's open only to 3 pm and the geological and palaeontological collections are closed. Admission costs AS30 (students AS15).

Museum of Applied Arts

The Museum für Angewandte Kunst

(MAK), 1 Stubenring 5, was built in high Renaissance style in 1871. The **exhibition rooms** highlight different styles, eg Renaissance, Baroque, Orient and Wiener Werkstätte. The layout of each room was the responsibility of a specific artist, and their reason for displaying the exhibits in a particular manner is explained. In one room Art-Nouveau chairs are back-lit and presented behind translucent white screens. There's a Klimt frieze upstairs, and some interesting pieces in the 20th-century Design & Architecture room (like Frank Gehry's cardboard chair).

In the basement is the **Study Collection**, which groups exhibits according to the type of materials used. There are some particularly good porcelain and glassware pieces, with casts showing how they're made. MAK is open daily except Monday from 10 am to 6 pm (to 9 pm Thursday). Admission costs AS90 (AS30 if no special exhibitions) for adults, AS45 (AS15) for students and senior citizens, or AS150 (AS50) for a family ticket.

Jewish Museum

This museum at 1 Dorotheergasse 11 documents the history of the Jews in Vienna, from the first settlements at Judenplatz in the 13th century to the present. Relations between the Jews and Viennese have not always been tranquil: Jews were expelled in 1420 (the 300 who remained were burned to death in 1421) and again in 1670. The darkest chapter came with the arrival of the Nazis in 1938 and the consequent curtailment of Jewish civil rights. Violence exploded on the night of 9 November 1938, known as the *Reichskristallnacht*. All the synagogues except the Stadttempel (1 Seitenstettengasse 4) were destroyed, and 6000 Jews were sent to concentration camps. Jews in Vienna now number 12,000, compared to 185,000 before 1938. The museum is open daily except Saturday from 10 am to 6 pm (9 pm Thursday) and admission is AS50 (students AS25).

Stadtpark

The city park lies just outside the Ring on the eastern side (Parkring), below the Museum of Applied Arts. It has a pond, winding walkways and several statues. The **Kursalon** at the south-west corner hosts waltz concerts in the afternoon and evening daily from April to 1 November; nearby in the park is a golden statue of Johann Strauss under a white arch; this is the image that often appears in tourist brochures.

SOUTH OF THE RING
Academy of Fine Arts

The Akademie der Bildenden Künste at 1 Schillerplatz 3 has a picture gallery, open Tuesday, Thursday and Friday from 10 am to 2 pm, Wednesday from 10 am to 1 pm and 3 to 6 pm, and weekends from 9 am to 1 pm. Hieronymus Bosch's *The Last Judgement* altarpiece is the most impressive exhibit, though Flemish painters are well represented. Admission costs AS30 (students AS15). The building itself has an attractive façade (1872-76) and was designed by Theophil Hansen. It was this academy that turned down would-be artist Adolf Hitler, forcing him to find a new career. Out the front there's a statue of Schiller.

Secession Building

In 1897 the Vienna Secession movement was formed by 19 progressive artists breaking from the conservative artistic establishment which met in the Künstlerhaus. Their aim was to present current trends in contemporary art and leave behind the historicism then in vogue. Among their number were Gustav Klimt, Josef Hoffman, Kolo Moser and Josef M Olbrich, a former student of Otto Wagner.

In 1898, Olbrich designed the movement's exhibition centre, which lies west of Karlsplatz on Friedrichstrasse. Its most striking feature is the enormous golden sphere (a 'golden cabbage head', according to some Viennese) rising from a turret on the roof. Above the door, the mask-like faces with dangling serpents instead of earlobes are also highly distinctive. The motto above the entrance asserts: 'Der Zeit ihre Kunst, der Kunst ihre Freiheit' ('To each time its art, to art its freedom'). The unspoken implication: to historicism its dustbin?

The 14th exhibition held in the building, in 1902, featured the famous *Beethoven Frieze* by Klimt. This 34-metre-long work was only supposed to be a temporary display, but has been painstakingly restored and is on view in the basement. The frieze, combining both dense and sparse images, shows willowy women with bounteous hair who jostle for attention with a large gorilla, while slender figures float and a choir sings. Beethoven would no doubt be surprised to learn that it is based on his Ninth Symphony.

The rest of this so-called 'temple of art' holds true to the original ideal of presenting contemporary art, though it may leave you wondering exactly where the altar is. 'Sometimes people just walk past the art, they think they're in empty rooms,' the lady at the desk told me. You have been warned! It's open Tuesday to Friday from 10 am to 6 pm, and weekends to 4 pm; entry costs AS60, students AS30. The Secession building also has an outside café.

Linke Wienzeile

This road runs south-west of the Secession building. Passing the Theater an der Wien, you soon reach two Art-Nouveau buildings created by Otto Wagner. No 38 features a façade of golden medallions by Kolo Moser, railings created from metal leaves and a brace of jesters on the roof who look like they could be shouting abuse at the traditional buildings nearby. No 40 is known as the **Majolica House** (1899) because Wagner used majolica tiles to create the flowing floral motifs on the façade.

Karlsplatz

Karlsplatz lies on the south side of Lothringerstrasse. Walking north-east across Ressel Park, you come to Wagner's **Stadt Pavillons**, the station buildings for Vienna's first public transport system, built from 1893 to 1902. Wagner was in charge of design for the metro lines, bridges and buildings. He incorporated floral designs and gold trim on a steel and marble structure. Wagner's Stadt Pavillon at Hietzing, near Schönbrunn on the outskirts of Vienna, is also worth a look.

North of the park, and west of Akademiestrasse, you can see two traditional Viennese buildings, the white **Künstlerhaus** and the rust-and-white **Musikverein** (1867-69).

St Charles' Church

This imposing church (Karlskirche), southeast of Ressel Park, was built from 1716 to 1739 in fulfilment of a vow made by Charles VI at the end of the 1713 plague. It was designed and commenced by Johann Bernhard Fischer von Erlach and completed by his son, Josef. Although predominantly Baroque, it combines several architectural styles. The twin columns are modelled on Trajan's Column in Rome, and show scenes from the life of St Charles Borromeo (who succoured plague victims in Italy), to whom

The Austrian Wagner

With Adolf Loos, Otto Wagner (1841-1918) was one of the most influential *fin de siècle* Viennese architects. He was trained in the classical tradition, and became a professor at the Academy of Fine Arts. His early work was in keeping with his education, and he was responsible for some neo-Renaissance buildings on the Ringstrasse.

As the 20th century approached, Wagner developed an Art-Nouveau style with flowing lines and decorative motifs. He joined the Secession movement in 1899 and attracted public criticism – this was one reason why his creative designs for Vienna's Historical Museum were never adopted. In 1905, Wagner, Klimt and others split from the Secession. Wagner began to strip away the more decorative aspects of his designs and concentrated instead on presenting the functional features of buildings in a creative way. ∎

the church is dedicated. The huge oval dome is 72 metres high; its interior features cloud-bound celestial beings painted by Johann Michael Rottmayr.

About 100 metres east of the church is Schwarzenbergplatz. Here is the **Russian Monument**, a reminder that the Russians liberated the city at the end of WW II. In front is a fountain, known as *Hochstrahlbrunnen*, and behind stands the Schwarzenberg Palace, co-created by Johann Bernhard Fischer von Erlach and Johann Lukas von Hildebrandt.

SCHÖNBRUNN PALACE

This sumptuous Baroque palace is one of Vienna's most popular attractions, receiving 25,000 visitors a week. It's in Schönbrunn Park, to the south-west of the Innere Stadt, and can be reached by U-Bahn No 4.

Leopold I commissioned Johann Bern-hard Fischer von Erlach to build a luxurious summer palace where a 'beautiful fountain' (*schöner Brunnen*) had previously stood. The building was completed in 1700, albeit much less grand than originally envisaged. Maria Theresa chose Nikolaus Pacassi to renovate and extend the palace (1744-49). The interior was fitted out in rococo style and had 2000 rooms, a chapel and a theatre. Like all imperial buildings associated with Maria Theresa, the exterior was painted a rich yellow, her favourite colour.

Napoleon lived in the palace in 1805 and 1809. In 1918 the last Habsburg emperor, Charles I, abdicated in the Blue Chinese Salon, after which the palace became the property of the new republic. In 1992 the palace administration was transferred to private hands; admission prices jumped, ren-ovations commenced and new tours were (and are being) created.

The Palace

The interior is suitably majestic with frescoed ceilings, tapestries, crystal chande-liers and gilded ornaments. However, the endless stucco and gold twirls can seem overdone. Franz Joseph evidently thought so too, for he had the rococo excesses stripped from his personal bedchamber in 1854.

The pinnacle of finery is reached in the **Great Gallery**. Gilded scrolls, ceiling fres-coes, chandeliers and huge crystal mirrors create the effect. Numerous lavish balls were held here, including one for the delegates at the Congress of Vienna (1814-15).

The **Mirror Room** is where Mozart played his first concert (1762) aged six in the pres-ence of Maria Theresa and the royal family. Afterwards young Wolfgang leapt onto the lap of the empress and kissed her. The **Round Chinese Room** had a table that could be drawn up and down through the floor for serving food, so that servants need not enter during secret consultations. The **Million Gulden Room** has Persian minia-tures set on rosewood panels and framed with rocaille frames.

The interior can be visited daily. Opening times are 8.30 am to 5 pm (1 April to 30 October) and 8.30 am to 4.30 pm (31 October to 30 March). Entry to see 22 of the rooms without a guide is AS80 (children AS30). Most people opt for the 40-minute guided tour that takes in 40 rooms and costs AS95 (children AS40). There are up to eight a day in English, but you may have to wait up to two hours in the height of summer (so book the tour and then explore the gardens). Separate guided tours of the **Bergl Rooms** are possible.

Wagenburg

The Imperial Coach Collection on the west side of the palace has both tiny children's wagons and great vehicles of state. The most ornate is the imperial coach of the court, built for Maria Theresa around 1765. It is extreme Baroque on wheels, with fussy gold orna-mentation and painted cherubs.

Allow 30 minutes to look around; the collection is open for viewing November to March from 10 am to 4 pm, May to Septem-ber from 9 am to 6 pm, and April and October from 9 am to 5 pm (AS30, students and senior citizens AS15).

Gardens

The beautifully tended formal gardens, arranged in the French style, are a symphony of colour in the summer. The extensive grounds have Roman ruins (now the site of summer concerts), the *Neptune Fountain* (a riotous ensemble from Greek mythology), and the crowning glory on the hill, the **Gloriette Monument**. The view towards the palace and Vienna is excellent, virtually as good as from its roof (entry AS20, May to October only). The palace grounds are open from 6 am until sunset.

On the west side of the grounds are the **Palm House** (Palmenhaus) and the **Butterfly House** (Schmetterlinghaus). Entry for each costs AS40 (AS25 for students to age 27) or AS65 (AS35) for a combined ticket. In the latter, butterflies are enticed onto fake flowers sprayed with honey.

The attractively laid-out **zoo** *(Tiergarten)* is the oldest zoo in the world (established 1752). Conditions for animals have been criticised as being cramped, but some have been recently improved. Admission costs AS80, or AS35 for students up to age 27. Opening times are 9 am to 4.30 pm (November to January), to 5 pm (February and October), 5.30 pm (March), 6 pm (April) and 6.30 pm (May to September). Feeding times vary for the different animals; sea lions dine sometime between 10.30 am and 3.30 pm, but 'land' lions have to wait until nearly closing time.

BELVEDERE PALACE

This splendid Baroque palace was built for Prince Eugene of Savoy from 1714 to 1723, and was the work of Johann Lukas von Hildebrandt. The Lower (Unteres) Belvedere was his summer residence while the Upper (Oberes) Belvedere was for banquets and other festivities. Between the two is a long garden laid out in French style, lined with statues of sphinxes and other mythical beasts. Running north from here is the much larger Botanical Gardens belonging to the university (free entry). The Habsburgs were rather irked that Prince Eugene should have a residence to match their own Hofburg, and the palace was eventually purchased by Maria Theresa.

The Belvedere is now home to the **Austrian Gallery**; the Baroque section is in the Lower Belvedere (entrance Rennweg 6A; take tram No 71) and 19th and 20th-century art is in the Upper Belvedere (entrance Prinz Eugen Strasse 27; take tram D). Opening hours are Tuesday to Sunday from 10 am to 5 pm; entry for both is AS60, or AS30 for students and senior citizens.

Upper Belvedere

This has the most important collection. Grand Baroque fixtures include Herculean figures and a fresco depicting the apotheosis of Prince Eugene. The 19th-century section has paintings from the Biedermeier period, including work by Georg Waldmüller, and

---

Great Military Exploits

One of Austria's greatest military heroes wasn't even Austrian. Prince Eugene of Savoy (1663-1736) was born in Paris. Told that he was too short to be accepted into the French army, he left France in 1683 to join the Habsburg forces and was just in time to help beat off the Turks besieging Vienna. He was given a regiment and within 10 years was promoted to field marshal.

Eugene's skills as a military strategist were evident in his victories against the Turks at Zenta in 1697, and during the campaign in the Balkans from 1714 to 1718 that finally drove the Turks out of all but a small corner of Europe. His capture of the fortress at Belgrade in 1718 helped end that war. Prince Eugene's skills as a statesman were also employed in the War of the Spanish Succession, where he negotiated for the Habsburgs with his former homeland. ■

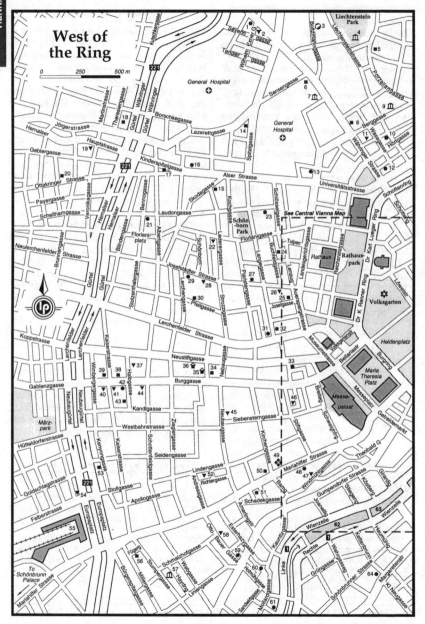

West of the Ring

0   250   500 m

General Hospital

General Hospital

Liechtenstein Park

See Central Vienna Map

Rathaus

Rathaus-park

Volksgarten

Heldenplatz

Maria Theresia Platz

Messe-palast

Schön-born Park

März-park

To Schönbrunn Palace

work by Hans Makart and Anton Romako which influenced the Viennese Art-Nouveau artists.

The 20th-century section of the gallery has the best exhibits. Klimt was a founder of the Secessionist Art-Nouveau school. His later pictures (such as the two portraits of Adele Bloch-Bauer) employ a harmonious but ostentatious (much metallic gold and silver) use of background colour to evoke or symbolise the emotions of the main figures. One of his best known but also most intriguing works here is *The Kiss* (1908). Pundits disagree as to whether the kiss in question is proffered willingly or under coercion. Some of Klimt's impressionistic landscapes are also on display.

Egon Schiele produced intense, melancholic work. See the hypnotic and bulging eyes on the portrait of his friend, *Eduard Kosmack* (1910). Schiele's dark, brooding colours and unforgiving outlines are a contrast to Klimt's golden tapestries and idealised forms. He lived with one of Klimt's models for awhile – Schiele's portraits of her

were much more explicit, bordering on the pornographic. *The Family* is Schiele's last work. He died of Egyptian flu shortly after, in 1918.

Other Austrian artists represented include Herbert Boeckl, Anton Hanak, Arnulf Rainer and Fritz Wotruba. There are several examples of the influential expressionist, Oskar Kokoschka. The gallery also has some exhibits from non-Austrian artists such as Munch, Monet, Van Gogh, Renoir and Cézanne.

Lower Belvedere

The Baroque section offers some good statuary, such as the originals from Donner's Neuer Markt fountain, and especially the apotheosis of Prince Eugene (again! This time in marble by the Baroque sculptor Balthasar Permoser). Eugene was presumably suffering delusions of grandeur by this time, for he commissioned the latter work himself; the artist, not to be outdone, depicted himself at the prince's feet. Paintings include portraits of Maria Theresa and

Francis I. A room is devoted to the vibrant paintings of Franz Anton Maulbertsch (1724-96).

The **Orangery** has a collection of Austrian medieval art, comprising religious scenes, altarpieces and statues. There are several impressive works by Michael Pacher, who was influenced by both early Low-Countries art and the early Renaissance of northern Italy.

OTHER SIGHTS
Votive Church
In 1853, Franz Joseph survived an assassination attempt when a knife-wielding Hungarian failed to find the Emperor's neck through his collar – reports suggested that a metal button deflected the blade. This church, at 9 Rooseveltplatz (north-west of the Ring), was commissioned in thanks at his lucky escape. Heinrich von Ferstel designed this twin-towered Gothic construction, completed in 1879.

Sigmund Freud Museum
This museum is housed at 9 Berggasse 19 (north-west of the Ring), in the apartments where Freud lived and worked from 1891 to 1938 (when he fled the Nazis). It contains his furniture, possessions, letters, documents and photographs; very detailed notes in English illuminate the offerings. Students and Freud freaks could spend awhile here; most casual observers would just skim through the three main rooms and wonder what on earth Freud wanted with that terracotta votive offering of male genitals (exhibit 24). There's also a fairly dull home movie of Freud, narrated by his daughter, Anna. The museum is open daily from 9 am to 4 pm (to 6 pm from July to September) and costs AS60 (AS40 for students and senior citizens).

Museum of Modern Art
The Museum Moderner Kunst is north-west of the Ring at 9 Fürstengasse 1, in the Baroque setting of the Liechtenstein Palace. The classical frescoes and stucco embellishments contrast well with the modern

Sigmund Freud (1856-1939), the founder of psychoanalysis, had a love-hate relationship with Vienna

exhibits. Rooms are devoted to various movements in 20th-century art: expressionism, cubism, futurism, constructivism, surrealism, pop art, photorealism, and Viennese actionism. Well-known artists represented include Picasso, Klee, Warhol, Magritte, Ernst and the sculptor, Giacometti. It's open daily except Monday from 10 am to 6 pm. Admission costs AS45, or AS25 for students and senior citizens.

A complementary collection is in the **Museum of the 20th Century** (open the same hours) at 3 Schweizer Garten, near Südbahnhof. Concept art, minimal art and land art from 1960 to the present are on display, and it also has temporary exhibitions and a sculpture garden. A combined ticket for both museums costs AS60 (AS30).

Josephinium
This is also known as the Museum of Medical History, and it's at 9 Währinger Strasse 25 (north-west of the Ring). Go to the 1st floor in the right-hand wing. It's a small museum but still fascinating, and a little bizarre. The prime exhibits are the ceroplastic and wax specimen models of the human

frame, created more than 200 years ago by Felice Fontana and Paolo Mascagni. They were used in the Academy of Medico-Surgery, instigated by Joseph II in 1785 to improve the skills of army surgeons who lacked medical qualifications. These models, showing the make-up of the body under the skin, were intended to give the students a three-dimensional understanding of the organs, bones, veins and muscles. Three rooms of this gory lot will make you feel like you've wandered onto the set of a tacky horror movie. One strange touch is the necklace on the female model lying down in the first room. Why this ornamentation? She's hardly dressed for a sophisticated night out, seeing that half her torso is missing.

The rest of the museum contains cases of arcane medical instruments, photos of past practitioners, accounts of unpleasant-looking operations, and some texts (one book is thoughtfully left open on a page dealing with the dissection of eyeballs). Opening hours are Monday to Friday (not public holidays) from 9 am to 3 pm and admission is AS10 (free for students).

Church am Steinhof
This distinctive Art-Nouveau creation was the work of Otto Wagner from 1904 to 1907. Kolo Moser chipped in with the mosaic windows. The design illustrates the victory of function over ornamentation prevalent in much of Wagner's work, even down to the sloping floor to drain cleaning water. It's about three km west of the Innere Stadt, at 14 Baumgartner Höhe 1, near the end of bus No 48A. The church is on the grounds of the Psychiatric Hospital of the City of Vienna. The interior can only be seen on Saturday at 3 pm (AS30), though other days are possible via tour companies (see the Tours entry later in this chapter).

Continue west along Linzer Strasse and turn right into Hüttelbergstrasse. Here you will find two **villas** designed by Wagner, at Nos 26 and 28. The most unusual (No 26) was built in 1888 and is now the Ernst Fuchs private museum. In the gardens (visible from the road) are some interesting statues, ceram-

ics and the ornate Brunnenhaus created by Fuchs.

Danube Tower
The Donauturm is the tallest structure in Vienna. Two revolving restaurants (at 170 and 160 metres high) allow you to enjoy a fine panorama. Go up to watch the sun set behind the Wienerwald. Meals in the restaurants cost AS75 to AS298. Admission costs AS60 (AS40 for children). The tower stands in the Donaupark on Donauinsel.

KunstHausWien
This art gallery, about 500 metres north-east of Wien Mitte train station at 3 Untere Weissgerberstrasse 13, looks like something out of a toyshop. It was designed by Friedensreich Hundertwasser; his innovative buildings feature coloured ceramics, uneven floors, patchwork paintwork, irregular corners and grass and trees on the roof.

The contents of the KunstHausWien are something of a paean in honour of Hundertwasser himself, presenting his paintings, graphics, tapestry, philosophy, ecology and architecture. Hundertwasser's quotes are everywhere, ranging from the profound to the cringe-worthy ('each raindrop is a kiss from heaven'). The gallery also puts on quality temporary exhibitions featuring other artists. Opening hours are daily from 10 am to 7 pm and entry costs AS70 (AS40 for students and seniors). Special exhibitions cost extra, and there's a café around the back.

While you are in the area, walk down the road to see the **Hundertwasserhaus**, a block of residential flats designed by Hundertwasser on the corner of Löwengasse and Kegelgasse. It is now one of Vienna's most prestigious addresses, albeit council-owned rented accommodation. Opposite is the **Kalke Village**, also Hundertwasser's handiwork, created from an old Michelin factory. It contains a café, souvenir shops and art shops.

Wurstelprater
East of the Innere Stadt, this large amusement park, usually referred to simply as the

Prater, is dominated by the giant **Ferris wheel** (*Riesenrad*) built in 1897. This achieved celluloid fame in *The Third Man* in the scene where Holly Martins confronts Harry Lime. The wheel is almost 65 metres high and weighs 430 tonnes. It rotates very slowly, allowing plenty of time to enjoy the view from the top (AS40). It operates as late as 11 pm in summer.

The amusement park has all sorts of funfair rides (AS10 to AS40), but it's a great place simply to wander around and soak up the atmosphere. As you walk, you're liable to bump into one of the colourful metal sculptures depicting humans caught up in strange hallucinogenic happenings. Some of these are rather witty, if seemingly inspired by the Beatles' animated film *Yellow Submarine*. Look for them on Rondeau and Calafatti Platz.

Cemeteries

Numerous famous composers have memorial tombs in the **Central Cemetery** (Zentralfriedho), 11 Simmeringer Hauptstrasse 232-244 (in the south-east of the city), including Gluck, Beethoven, Schubert, Brahms and Schönberg. Mozart also has a monument here, but he was actually buried in an unmarked grave in the **Cemetery of St Mark** (St Marxer Friedhof), 3 Leberstrasse 6-8. Many years after the true location had been forgotten grave-diggers cobbled together a poignant memorial from a broken pillar and a discarded stone angel. For St Mark, take tram No 71 to Landstrasser Hauptstrasse and follow the signs for a 10-minute walk.

From St Mark, take either tram No 71 or 72 to the central cemetery's Gate 2 for the graves of the composers and postwar Austrian presidents. Behind the memorial church are simple plaques devoted to those who fell in the world wars. These are in contrast to the ostentatious displays of wealth exhibited in the mausoleums of the rich, who couldn't take it with them but certainly tried. Most graves are neat and well

---

A Passionate Man

Friedensreich Hundertwasser was born as Friedrich Stowasser on 15 December 1928. In 1943, 69 of his Jewish relatives on his mother's side were deported to Eastern Europe and killed. In 1948, he spent three months at the Academy of Fine Arts in Vienna. Environmental themes were present even in his early work, eg *People (Complement to Trees)* from 1950, now on show in the KunstHausWien.

Hundertwasser's paintings employ vivid colours, metallic silver and spirals (reminiscent of Klimt's ornamental backgrounds); to Hundertwasser 'the straight line is Godless'. He faithfully adheres to this principle in his building projects, proclaiming that the uneven floors 'become a symphony, a melody for the feet and bring back natural vibrations to man'. He believes cities should be more harmonious with nature: buildings should be semisubmerged in undulating meadows, and homes should have 'tree tenants' that pay rent in environmental currency.

Hundertwasser has always been something of an oddity to the Viennese establishment. He complains that they won't allow him to carry out his more radical building projects. Nevertheless, he was commissioned to recreate the façade of the Spittelau (or Hundertwasser) incinerator. This was opened in 1992; it's the most unindustrial-looking heating plant you'll ever see (it's just north of Franz Josefs Bahnhof: take tram D to the Liechtenwerder Platz stop). Hundertwasser has stated that man is shielded from nature by three levels: cities, houses and clothes. He has tried to limit the insulating effect of the first two with his building projects. His solution to the third is to go naked, a concept he selectively carries out.

Hundertwasser remains one of Vienna's most idiosyncratic inhabitants. Whether he's organising a campaign to retain Vienna's traditional car number plates, designing postage stamps, redesigning national flags or simply painting pictures, he's always passionate, sometimes irritating and inevitably challenging. ■

Corpse Disposal – Viennese Style

It is said that nobody has such an attachment to their dead as do the Viennese. The one ambition many Viennese have in life is to afford a lavish funeral at death, which is why Joseph II caused such outrage in the 1780s with his scheme to introduce false-bottomed, reusable coffins.

In 1784, Vienna's huge central cemetery was opened, as there was simply no more space in the city cemeteries. To convince the populace that their future dearly-departed would rest better in this new location, the authorities shipped out the coffins of famous composers, where they now rest in group 32A. An unusual method was contemplated for transporting bodies to the suburban site: engineers drew up plans for a tube, many km long, down which coffins would be fired using compressed air. However, the high cost of the scheme (one million florins) led to its abandonment.

Each day at dawn, before the public is admitted to the central cemetery, hunters shoot male pheasants, hares and wild rabbits, as these inconsiderate creatures tend to disturb, or even eat, the flowers arranged carefully around the graves. Meanwhile, you won't find any cemeteries for pets in Vienna. It is expressly forbidden to bury animals in the soil, as the high water table might be contaminated by the seepage of chemicals used in inoculations and putting the animals down. Pet cremations are big business, although strictly controlled. ■

tended and garlanded with fresh flowers, though the old Jewish section is a tangle of broken and lopsided headstones and unfettered undergrowth.

MUNICIPAL MUSEUMS

There are 20 municipal museums run by the City of Vienna; entry costs AS30 (students AS10) or AS15 (students AS5). A book of 10 entry tickets costs AS80. Municipal museums are free for visits before noon on Friday (except holidays).

The **Historical Museum of the City of Vienna** is the best of them. It gives a detailed rundown on the development of Vienna from prehistory to the present day, and does a good job of putting the city and its personalities in context. Exhibits occupy three floors and include maps and plans, artefacts, many paintings (eg by Klimt, Schiele and the Biedermeier painters) and reconstructed rooms from the homes of Adolf Loos and Franz Grillparzer. Models show the impact of Ringstrasse developments, and there are some good period photographs. The museum is at 4 Karlsplatz 5, by St Charles' Church, and it's open daily except Monday from 9 am to 4.30 pm (AS30; AS45 for a family ticket).

The **Clock Museum**, 1 Schulhof 2, displays 1200 clocks and watches, ranging from the 15th century to a 1992 computer clock. Entry is AS30. The **Hermesvilla** is in the Lainzer Tiergarten (see Hiking under Activities later in this chapter); this former hunting lodge features the private apartments of Franz Joseph and Empress Elisabeth (AS30).

Several municipal museums are based in the former residences of the great composers, and generally contain assorted memorabilia and furniture of their exalted former inhabitants. Most are open daily except Monday from 9 am to 12.15 pm and 1 to 4.30 pm. A visit may take up to 30 minutes. Entry costs AS15 each for the following:

Eroica House
19 Döblinger Hauptstrasse 92. This house was named after Beethoven's Symphony No 3, which he wrote here.
Haydn Museum
6 Haydngasse 19. Haydn lived here for 12 years and composed most of the oratorios *The Creation* and *The Seasons*. He died here in 1809. The museum also has rooms devoted to Brahms.
Johann Strauss Residence
2 Praterstrasse 54. Strauss composed the *Blue Danube Waltz* here.

Wolfgang Amadeus Mozart (1756-91) composed *The Marriage of Figaro* in Vienna

Mozart's Apartment (Figaro House)
    1 Domgasse 5. Mozart spent 2½ productive years here and his work included *The Marriage of Figaro*.
Pasqualati House
    Mölkerbastei 8. Beethoven lived on the 4th floor of this house from 1804 to 1814.
Schubert Commemorative Rooms
    4 Kettenbrückengasse 6. Schubert lived here briefly before his death in 1828.

LANGUAGE COURSES

The tourist office's *Youth Scene* lists many places offering German language courses. ÖKISTA (☎ 401 480 241), 9 Garnisongasse 7, has a 10-week evening course for AS2200, starting in January, April and October (up to 15 students per class). Day classes start more frequently, with up to six students per class: they cost AS2800 (twice a week over four weeks) and AS5000 (every weekday over two weeks).

Other language schools generally stick with the six students per class limit. Centrum Deutsch (☎ 532 83 01), 1 Judenplatz 10, has four-week courses: AS2400 (two evenings weekly) or AS8900 (every weekday). Inlingua Sprachschule (☎ 512 22 25) 1 Neuer Markt 1, has similar prices, and also offers intensive courses or individual tuition. For information on organised tours of

Vienna see the Getting Around section at the end of this chapter.

GUIDED WALKING TOURS

Tourist guides conduct around 50 different walking tours, covering a range of themes (only some are in English). A leaflet from the tourist office details all of these and gives the various departure points. Tours last about 1½ hours and cost AS110 (AS60 if aged under 18).

An interesting tour is the Third Man Tour, conducted in English by Dr Brigitte Timmermann (☎ 220 66 20). It departs at 4 pm, usually on a Friday (not July or August); the meeting place is the U4 Friedensbrücke exit, and ideally you should bring a torch and a tram ticket. The tour takes in all the main locations used in the film, which include the underground sewers, home to 2½ million rats, and Harry Lime's apartment at Josefsplatz.

OUTDOOR ACTIVITIES

The best source of information is the city information desk in the Rathaus, rather than the tourist office. Staff can supply a detailed map of swimming and boating areas on Donauinsel.

The Prater is an important location for sports. It has tennis courts, a bowling alley (☎ 218 07 09; 2 Hauptallee 124), horse riding, sports stadia and swimming pools. A more compact sports complex is the Stadthalle (☎ 98 100), 15 Vogelweidplatz 15, which has a swimming pool, ice rink and bowling alley.

Hiking

To the west of the city, the rolling hills and marked trails of the Wienerwald are perfect for walkers. The Prater also has a wood with walking trails. Pick up the *Wandern in der Stadt* brochure from the Rathaus. A good trail is the one starting in Nussdorf (take tram D from the Ring) and reaching **Kahlenberg** (484 metres) for a fine view over the city from the north. On your return to Nussdorf you can undo all that exercise by imbibing a few drinks at a Heuriger. The round trip is an

The Story Behind the Story of *The Third Man*

'I had paid my last farewell to Harry a week ago, when his coffin was lowered into the frozen February ground, so that it was with incredulity that I saw him pass by, without a sign of recognition, among the host of strangers in the Strand.' Graham Greene wrote these words on the back of an envelope. There they remained for many years, as an idea without a context, until Sir Alexander Korda asked Greene to write a film about the Allies' occupation of postwar Vienna. The film was to be directed by Carol Reed, who had worked with Greene on *The Fallen Idol*.

Greene had an opening scene and a framework, but he still needed a plot. He flew to Vienna in 1948 and roamed the bomb-damaged streets, searching with increasing desperation for inspiration. Nothing came to mind until, with his departure imminent, Greene lunched with a British intelligence officer. The conversation proved more nourishing than the meal. The officer told him about the underground police who patrolled the huge network of sewers beneath the city. He also held forth on the subject of the black-market trade in penicillin, which the racketeers exploited with no regard for the consequences. Greene put these ideas together and created his story.

Another chance encounter completed the picture. Following filming one night, Carol Reed went drinking in the Heurigen area of Sievering. There he discovered Anton Karas playing a zither, and was mesmerised by the hypnotic rhythms the instrument produced. Although Karas could neither read nor write music, Reed flew him to London where he recorded the soundtrack. The bouncing, staggering refrain that was Harry Lime's theme dominated the film, became a chart hit and earned Karas a fortune.

In a final twist of serendipity, the most memorable lines of dialogue in the film came not from the measured pen of Greene, but from the improvising mouth of Orson Welles, who played Harry Lime. They were delivered in the Prater, under the towering stanchions of the Ferris wheel: 'In Italy for 30 years under the Borgias they had warfare, terror, murder, bloodshed – they produced Michelangelo, Leonardo da Vinci and the Renaissance. In Switzerland they had brotherly love, 500 years of democracy and peace, and what did that produce? The cuckoo clock. So long Holly'.

And in Vienna they had the ideal setting for a classic film. ■

11-km hike, or you can save your legs by taking the Nussdorf-Kahlenberg 38A bus in one or both directions.

Another place to roam around is the **Lainzer Tiergarten** animal preserve, open from late March to 1 November between 8 am and dusk. Get there by Tram No 62 to Hermesstrasse and then bus No 60B to the end station.

Swimming Pools

Most pools are open daily in the summer. Entry costs about AS45 with reduced admission prices after midday and possibly also 4 pm. Many places are open-air, and open from May to mid-September, such as the Stadionbad (☎ 749 81 94), a large complex of pools in the Prater. Bus Nos 83A and 80B run there from the U3 stop, Schlachthausgasse. Some places also have sauna facilities, such as Thermalbad Oberlaa (☎ 68 16 11 249), 10 Kurbadstrasse 14, open all year.

Beaches

There are swimming spots (easy access to the water, no charges) on both banks of the Neue Donau; some of these are for nude bathing and are marked FKK (*Freikörperkultur*) on maps and signs. There are several such spots near the Weidinger ferry at the southern end of Donauinsel, and on the northern tip of the island.

Private bathing complexes line the Alte Donau. They cost about AS50 or AS60 (including a locker) and are open May to September. Strandbad Alte Donau gives access to the Alte Donau (where the water has been known to be murky) and has separate outdoor swimming pools. Gänsehäufel is the biggest bathing complex, and has a nude section.

Water Sports

On the east bank of the Neue Donau by the Reichsbrücke bridge (U3 to Donauinsel) there's sailing, rowing and sailboard hire. About two km south on the same bank is Tauchschule Peter's Club (☎ 23 06 09), a diving centre. Continuing south, near the Weidinger ferry is Freizeitparadies Weidinger (☎ 220 50 65), where you can hire surfboards and pedal boats.

The Alte Donau is the favoured area for sailing. Hofbauer (☎ 219 34 30), 22 Obere Alte Donau, rents sailing boats and also has a branch on the Neue Donau at the Reichsbrücke bridge.

FESTIVALS

No matter what time of year you visit Vienna, there will be something special happening.

On New Year's Eve various celebrations are arranged in the Innere Stadt, and one of the evening's musical events is relayed onto a giant screen at Stephansplatz. The Opera Ball at the Staatsoper is one of the most lavish of 300 or so balls in January and February.

The Vienna International Festival (from mid-May to mid-June) has a wide-ranging programme of the arts and is considered the highlight of the year. Contact Wiener Festwochen (☎ 586 16 76), Lehárgasse 11, A 1060 Wien, for details as early as January. At the end of June, look for three days of free rock, jazz and folk concerts, plus general outdoor fun in the Donauinselfest. In the first two weeks of July there's the Jazz Festival at the Staatsoper and the Volkstheater. For information contact Jazz-Fest Wien (☎ 712 42 24), 3 Esteplatz 3/13.

Vienna's Summer of Music (from mid-July to mid-August) fills an otherwise flat spot in the music calendar. Contact Klangboden (☎ 4000 8400), Laudongasse 29, A 1080 Wien, to reserve tickets in writing before 15 April. Tickets are available from 1 June at the box office, 1 Friedrich Schmidt Platz 1, open daily from 10 am to 7 pm. Reduced student tickets go on sale 10 minutes before the performance.

In November and December there's the Modern Vienna Festival, featuring modern-classical and avant-garde music. It's based in the Musikverein and the Konzerthaus; ☎ 712 46 86 for information and tickets. Vienna's traditional Christmas market takes place in front of the Rathaus from mid-November to 24 December. Trees are decorated in Rathauspark, and inside the Rathaus there are free concerts of seasonal music.

PLACES TO STAY

Vienna can be a nightmare for low-budget travellers. Even those who can afford a range of options may find their accommodation choice full, especially in the summer. Reserve ahead or at least enquire by telephone before you trek all over town. Advance reservations are especially recommended at Christmas and Easter and between June and October.

From July to September student residences are converted to seasonal hotels, giving a much-needed boost to beds at the lower end of the market. A few rooms in private homes are on offer, mostly in the suburbs, but economic affluence over recent years has reduced the supply; expect a three-day minimum stay.

Accommodation Agencies

Several agencies can help with accommodation. Tourist offices (see the Facts for the Visitor chapter) charge a commission of AS30 to AS40 per reservation, irrespective of the number of rooms being booked. They can help find private rooms but don't have lists to give out. They can give you the useful *Jugendherbergen* pamphlet detailing youth hostels and camping grounds, and a booklet of hotels and pensions, revised summer and winter.

ÖKISTA (☎ 401 48), 9 Türkenstrasse 8, charges AS50 to find rooms for a minimum three nights. For longer stays, it charges a AS500 fee to find a room in a family house (from AS170 per night). The Mitwohnzentrale (☎ 402 60 61), 8 Laudongasse 7, can find private rooms from AS160 and apartments from AS400; a minimum stay is three days. The office is open Monday to Friday from 10 am to 2 pm and 3 to 6 pm and commission is 24% of the rent. If you're looking for long-term accommodation, try these agencies.

Another approach for longer term accommodation is to check university notice boards, or scan the ads in the magazines *Bazar*, *Findegrube* and *Falter*, available at newsstands. Kolping-Gästehaus (see the following entry on Budget Hotels & Pensions) has cheap monthly rates for stays of (preferably) at least three months.

Choosing a Location

Staying within the Innere Stadt is convenient for the sights, though inevitably you have to pay more. Most hotels and pensions are between the Ring and the Gürtel; these are better value and still within easy striking distance of the centre. Places in the suburbs have the lowest prices but are less accessible; these are a more viable option if you're not too interested in late-night attractions in the city.

If you have a car, parking costs can be expensive in the city centre. A better option might be to find somewhere farther out where you can safely leave your car, and then rely on public transport. Even if you want a late night and have to take a taxi home, the taxi fare will still be less than a day's garage fees. Hotels outside the Ring with private garages charge around AS70 to AS200 for 24 hours (about half the price of places within the Ring); the farther from the centre the cheaper it gets. Street parking is no problem away from the centre.

Camping

Wien West II (☎ 914 23 14), 14 Hüttelbergstrasse 80, is open all year except February. Down the road at No 40 is *Wien West I* (☎ 914 14 49), open in July and August. Both cost AS60 per adult and AS56 per tent or caravan (add AS5 per category in July or August). To get there, take U4 or S45 to Hütteldorf, then bus No 152. *Camping Neue Donau* (☎ 220 93 10), 22 Am Kleehäufel, is the same price and is open from mid-May to mid-September. It's the closest site to the city

centre (and consequently less scenic) and the only one east of the Danube. Take U3 to Schlachthausgasse, then bus No 83A.

Take bus No 62A from the U4 Philadelphiabrücke stop to *Schwimmbad Camping Rodaun* (☎ 88 41 54), 23 An der Au 2, which is open from late March to mid-November. Prices are AS60 per adult and AS47 to AS60 for a tent. Beyond the city to the south is the largest site, *Campingplatz Schloss Laxenburg* (☎ 02236-713 33), on Münchendorfer Strasse. It has swimming pools and boat rental and costs AS58 for an adult and AS56 for a tent or car (open 1 April to 31 October).

Hostels

Near the Centre No hostels invade the imperial elegance of the Ring. The nearest are two linked HI *hostels*, at 7 Myrthengasse 7 (☎ 523 63 16) and, around the corner, at 7 Neustiftgasse 85 (☎ 523 74 62). Both are well run and have knowledgeable staff. Enjoy the good showers, lockers and personal bedside light (sheer luxury!). Beds are AS140, lunch or dinner AS60 and laundry AS50 per load. Curfew is at 1 am. You can check in any time during the day at Myrthengasse, including for Neustiftgasse when that closes from 11.15 am (10.15 am Sunday) to 3.45 pm. Telephone reservations are accepted and strongly advised.

Believe it or Not (☎ 526 46 58), Apartment 14, 7 Myrthengasse 10, is a small private hostel. There's no clue on the main door that it's anything other than a private house. It has a friendly atmosphere, but one room has triple-level bunks and can get hot in summer. There's no breakfast; use the kitchen facilities instead. Beds are AS160 in summer or AS110 from November to Easter, except Christmas, and you get your own key for late entry.

Hostel Zöhrer (☎ 43 07 30), 8 Skodagasse 26, is a private hostel close to the Ring, and is reasonable value. Four to six-bed dorms are AS170 and doubles (bunk beds) are AS460, all with private shower. There's a kitchen, courtyard and own-key entry; reception is open from 8 am to 10 pm but there's no curfew and the doors aren't shut during the day.

Turmherberge Don Bosco (☎ 713 14 94), 3 Lechnerstrasse 12, south-east of the Ring in a church tower, has the cheapest beds in town; AS70 plus AS25 for sheets if required. However, the place hasn't been modernised in the last 35 years – some rooms are cramped and have few lockers (no locks). Breakfast is not included though there are basic kitchen facilities. It has 50 beds and is closed from December to February. Curfew is 11.25 pm and you can check in before noon or after 5 pm (telephone reservations accepted).

Near Westbahnhof, *Hostel Ruthensteiner* (☎ 893 42 02), 15 Robert Hamerling Gasse 24, is open 24 hours. Dorms are AS129 plus AS20 for sheets if required. Basic singles/doubles are AS209 a person. Breakfast costs AS25 and there's a kitchen and shady rear courtyard. Non-HI members must pay AS40 extra.

The modern *Kolpingsfamilie Meidling* (☎ 813 54 87), 12 Bendlgasse 10-12, is near the U6 stop 'Niederhofstrasse', south of Westbahnhof. Beds cost from AS100 (eight to 10-bed dorms) to AS145 (four-bed dorms). All dorms have a private shower, and some have a WC; the four-bed dorms have a balcony. There are lockers but no keys, and a patio round the back. Non-HI members pay AS20 extra, which is a bit of a cheek as they don't provide the guest-card stamp. Breakfast costs AS42 and sheets if required are AS65. Curfew is at 1 am, though reception is open 24 hours.

Brigittenau (☎ 332 82 940), 20 Friedrich Engels Platz 24, is a HI hostel with 334 beds, just a couple of minutes walk from the Danube (take tram N to its terminus). Dorms cost AS140, dinners AS60, and there's a large garden. It has a 1 am curfew, though reception is open 24 hours; doors are locked from 9 am to 3 pm.

Lauria (see Budget Hotels & Pensions) also has dormitory accommodation.

In the Suburbs HI *Hütteldorf-Hacking*, (☎ 877 02 63), 13 Schlossberggasse 8, has varying-sized dorms for AS139, a total of 277 beds. There's a lounge with various games available, and doors are locked from 9 am to 4 pm. Don't expect to enjoy much nightlife: there's an 11.45 pm curfew and it takes well over half an hour to return from the city centre, either by U4, or U3 to Westbahnhof and then S3, S45 or S50 (all alighting at Hütteldorf).

HI *Schlossherberge am Wilhelminenberg* (☎ 45 85 03 700) is at 16 Savoyenstrasse 2. Four-bed dorms with a shower/WC are AS214 and double occupancy of a dorm costs AS780. It's shut from 9.30 am to 2 pm and curfew is at 11.45 pm. It's a nice location but a long way from the centre: from the city, take tram J and then bus No 46B, or tram 44 and then bus No 146B.

Student Rooms

These rooms *(Studentenheime)* are available to tourists from 1 July to 30 September while students are on holiday. In their student incarnation they usually have a kitchen and dining room on each floor, but when they reinvent themselves as seasonal hotels these useful facilities generally remain locked. Rooms are perfectly OK but nothing fancy; some have a private shower/WC. Expect single beds (though beds may be placed together in double rooms), a work desk and a wardrobe. Most are outside the Innere Stadt.

Auge Gottes (☎ 34 25 85) at 9 Nussdorfer Strasse 75 has newly decorated singles/doubles for AS296/496; doubles with private shower are AS596 and triples/quads AS690/920 with own shower. *Auersperg* (☎ 512 74 93), 8 Auersperg-strasse 9, is near the Ring and has 24-hour reception. Singles/doubles are from AS355/580, or AS500/820 with private shower/WC.

At *Haus Döbling* (☎ 34 76 31), 19 Gymnasiumstrasse 85, singles/doubles all have private shower and hall WC. 'Hostel service' costs AS270/340; 'hotel service' (bathroom towels, beds made up etc) costs AS300/400; there are more than 300 beds.

At *Haus Pfeilgasse* (☎ 408 34 45), 8

Pfeilgasse 4-6, singles/doubles are AS250/420 and triples AS540. The shower and WC are in the corridor. It has the same reception (open 24 hours) as Hotel Avis. *Josefstadt* (☎ 406 52 11) is close to the Ring at 8 Buchfeldgasse 16. Its singles/doubles with shower are AS405/640 and triples with shower are AS930. *Katholisches Studentenhaus* (☎ 34 92 64), 19 Peter Jordan Strasse 29 has singles/doubles with hall shower/toilet for AS200/332 (no breakfast). Reception is on the 1st floor.

Music Academy (☎ 514 84 48), 1 Johannesgasse 8, has singles/doubles for AS380/600, or AS450/900 with private bath/WC; triples/quads are AS720/880, some with private shower/WC. It's a central location, with 24-hour reception. At *Porzellaneum* (☎ 317 72 82), 9 Porzellangasse, singles or doubles are AS160 per person without breakfast; reception is open 24 hours. *Rosen-Hotel Europahaus Wien* (☎ 97 25 38), west of the Gürtel at 14 Linzer Strasse 429, has rooms without own shower for AS280/460. Tram No 49 goes there from the city centre.

Budget Hotels & Pensions

Near the Centre *Lauria* (☎ 52 22 555), Kaiserstrasse 77, has minimal outside advertising and own-key entry. Hostel beds cost AS160 and there are good kitchen facilities but the price does not include breakfast. Rooms are clean and well decorated, some with large pictorial scenes; all have a TV. Staff are on duty from 8 am to 1 pm though you can phone ahead to arrange check-in for later. There's a choice of doubles (AS530), triples (AS700), quads (AS850) and fully equipped apartments (ranging from AS1400 for four people to AS2200 for eight). A two-day minimum stay usually applies for advance bookings, and credit cards are accepted.

Hospiz Hotel (☎ 523 13 04), 7 Kenyongasse 15, is run by the YMCA (known as CVJM in Austria) though anyone can stay. Simple singles/doubles are AS360/640, or AS380/680 with private shower, and there are triples/quads. Prices are around AS30 per

person lower in winter and reception is open from 7.30 am to 10 pm. In the summer, if you can't find anywhere else, you can sleep on a mat in the gym for AS140, but you must pack your gear out of the way for the day and evening. An extra mattress in a room is AS140. There's no lift and many stairs.

Kolping-Gästehaus (☎ 587 56 31), 6 Gumpendorfer Strasse 39, has singles without shower for just AS250 and triples (bunk beds) with shower for AS870. Doubles with shower are AS800, or AS900 also with WC. Rooms are fine, though it's a newish building with an institutionalised aura (long-term students stay here).

Auer (☎ 43 21 21), 9 Lazarettgasse 3, is small and pleasant with a Viennese feel. Singles/doubles start from AS320/490; doubles with private shower are AS550.

Pension Wild (☎ 406 51 74), 8 Langegasse 10, is quieter than the name suggests and very close to the Ring. Singles/doubles start from AS450/560 and there are some triples/quads from AS810/1000. Make use of the hall shower or indulge in a sauna and steam bath downstairs for AS30. It's run by an elderly Frau who speaks a quirky combination of English and German. Reception is open 24 hours and the kitchen facilities are a bonus.

Hotel Westend (☎ 597 67 29), 6 Fügergasse 3, is close to Westbahnhof and has reasonable singles/doubles for AS330/590 in a building with a circling stairway. Reception is open 24 hours.

Pension Kraml (☎ 587 85 88) is nearby at 6 Brauergasse 5. Small and friendly, it has rooms for AS280/590 and large doubles with private shower from AS750. Triples with a sink are AS780 and there's also a family apartment from AS950.

Pension Falstaff (☎ 317 91 27), 9 Müllnergasse 5, has singles/doubles for AS345/570 (negotiate to not pay the AS30 fee to use the hall shower) or AS465/790 with private shower. The rooms are long but some lack width; fittings are ageing but adequate. It's convenient for tram D to the Ring and Nussdorf.

Praterstern (☎ 214 01 23), 2 Mayergasse

6, east of the Ring, has rooms for AS280/530, but you may be charged up to AS50 to use the hall shower. Rooms with private shower/WC are AS415/675, and there's a pleasant rear garden. Cheaper rates are possible without breakfast.

Close to Südbahnhof, *Monopol* (☎ 505 85 26), 4 Prinz Eugen Strasse 68, has rooms from AS300/700, though there may be a charge to use the hall shower. Rooms with private bath/WC are AS700/1020.

Close to the centre is *Quisisana* (☎ 587 33 41), 6 Windmühlgasse 6. It charges AS350/560, or AS380/680 for rooms with private shower. Rooms vary in size and quality but are generally good value.

Ten minutes walk south from Südbahnhof is *Hotel Kolbeck Zur Linde* (☎ 604 17 73), 10 Laxenburger Strasse 19. Rooms are AS380/660; those with private shower/WC and cable TV are AS580/980. The patterned floor tiles in the corridor are typically Viennese. Reception is open 24 hours.

Down the road at No 14 is *Cyrus* (☎ 604 42 88), with rooms for AS380/600 (with shower and sometimes WC), and triples for AS750. The singles for AS250 (with hall shower) are usually full. Nearby is *Caroline* (☎ 604 80 70), 10 Gudrunstrasse 138, a pension on a shopping street with singles/doubles from AS430/750 including shower/WC and cable TV.

Pension Ani (☎ 408 10 60), 9 Kinderspitalgasse 1, costs from AS390/580 for rooms with shower, or you can pay more for bigger rooms with a private WC. The owner said he would give a discount to students and young people.

Pension Esterházy (☎ 587 51 59), 4 Nelkengasse 3, just off Mariahilfer Strasse, has decent-sized rooms for AS300/490 without breakfast; another hall shower and toilet are being built which should solve that particular shortage. Reception hours are limited so phone the day before (between 4 and 9 pm preferred).

Pension Bosch (☎ 798 61 79), 3 Keilgasse 13, is in a traditional building in a residential street. Rooms (from AS480/670 with shower, AS570/820 with shower/WC) have

good, old-fashioned furnishings with personal touches. Double rooms have twin beds.

Goldenes Einhorn (☎ 544 47 55), 5 Am Hundsturm, is a small, simple place opposite a post office and small market. Singles/doubles (no breakfast) cost from AS270/440; doubles with private shower are AS520.

East of the Danube, *Kagranerhof* (☎ 203 11 87), 22 Wagramer Strasse 141, offers rooms for AS290/490 with hall shower. To get there, take the U1 to Kagran.

In the Suburbs *Zum Goldenen Stern Gasthof* (☎ 804 13 82), at 12 Breitenfurter Strasse 94, south of Schönbrunn Park, has singles/doubles with hall shower for only AS220/400. However, it's very basic, too basic even to make the tourist office lists. To get there, take the train or S-Bahn 1 or 2 to Hetzendorf. Breitenfurter Strasse is two minutes walk to the south.

Matauschek (☎ 982 35 32), at 14 Breitenseer Strasse 14, is less than 10 minutes walk west of the Johnstrasse U3 stop. Singles/doubles cost AS300/520, or AS450/700 with private shower.

Rustler (☎ 982 01 62), 14 Linzer Strasse 43, is an efficiently run place close to Schönbrunn (or take tram No 52 from Westbahnhof). It has a pretty garden (complete with garden gnomes), double glazing and a small bar/breakfast room. Singles/doubles are AS330/550 and triples AS750; add about AS150 per room for private shower and the same again for private WC.

Waldandacht (☎ 97 16 50), 14 Wurzbachtalgasse 23, is as far as you can get into the Wienerwald without crossing into Lower Austria, and has 10 doubles with hall shower for AS500. Take the S50 to Weidlingau-Wurzbachtal.

Hotels – mid-range
Inside the Ring *Pension Nossek* (☎ 533 70 41), 1 Graben 17, is good value considering its ideal location. Clean, comfortable singles (AS480 to AS770) and doubles (AS950 to AS1500) are individually priced depending

on the size, view and private facilities. Around the corner, *Pension Aclon* (☎ 512 79 400) at 1 Dorotheergasse 6-8 has rooms starting at AS480/700.

Schweizer Pension Solderer (☎ 533 81 56), 1 Heinrichsgasse 2, has singles/doubles from AS400/660 with hall shower. Rooms with private shower/WC are AS700/920, or AS600/800 with shower only. Reception is open from 7 am to 10 pm.

Pension Am Operneck (☎ 512 93 10), 1 Kärntner Strasse 47, opposite the tourist office, has rooms for AS590/860 with private shower and WC.

Hotel Orient (☎ 533 73 07), 1 Tiefer Graben 30, has a *fin-de-siècle* hallway, and rooms decked out in a variety of interesting styles. Scenes for *The Third Man* were shot here. Singles/doubles with private shower start at AS700/850, while singles with hall shower (AS20 charge) are AS450. Some rooms are rented in the day for discrete liaisons, but it's by no means a seedy place.

Hotel Post (☎ 515 83), 1 Fleischmarkt 24, has pricey rooms with shower/WC for AS880/1120; rooms without shower are a better deal from AS480/760.

Near the Centre *Alla Lenz* (☎ 523 69 89), 7 Halbgasse 3-5, is an excellent top-of-the-range pension with a rooftop swimming pool (free to guests), a café, and a garage next door (AS150 per day). All rooms were renovated in 1994: singles/doubles start at AS700/980 (lower in winter) and have air-con, private shower and WC, telephone and cable TV.

Nearby, *Pension Atrium* (☎ 523 31 14), 7 Burggasse 118, has clean, renovated rooms from AS550/840 with shower/WC and TV, plus one apartment.

Altwienerhof (☎ 892 60 00), 15 Herklotzgasse 6, is a small, family-run hotel offering good-value, decent-sized rooms. Singles/doubles from AS480/980 have a shower/WC and there are a few cheaper rooms without showers.

Pension Continental (☎ 93 24 18), at 7 Kirchengasse 1, has good, big rooms from AS800/1000 with bath or shower, WC and

cable TV. It enjoys a good location overlooking Mariahilfer Strasse and has private parking.

Hotel Cryston (☎ 813 56 82), 12 Gaudenzdorfer Gürtel 63, has good singles/doubles from AS650/980 with shower/WC, and double glazing to eliminate traffic noise. There's also free private parking and a breakfast buffet. Those who take the cheaper rooms (AS420/640 for singles/doubles without showers) pay AS10 to use a hall shower, and get the buffet breakfast and use of parking spaces.

Hotel Am Schottenpoint (☎ 310 87 87) is at 9 Währinger Strasse 22. The entrance is through a small gallery with frescoes and a stucco ceiling, but the rest hasn't got quite the same style. Singles/doubles are AS960/1360, or AS890/1120 in winter.

In the Suburbs *Hotel Victoria* (☎ 877 55 36) is next to the plush Parkhotel Schönbrunn (see Hotels – top end) and has its reception there. It's an excellent deal as guests can use all the facilities at the Schönbrunn. Singles/doubles start at AS775/1100 and have shower, WC, TV and telephone; a few small singles without shower start at AS455.

West of the city in Wienerwald is *Sophienalpe* (☎ 46 24 32), 14 Sophienalpe 13, with an indoor swimming pool and a restaurant. There's no adequate public transport so you really need a car to stay here. Singles/doubles with private shower/WC cost from AS450/700.

Schloss Wilhelminenberg (☎ 45 85 03), 16 Savoyenstrasse 2, is also on the edge of the woods and has a big garden and stately appearance. Prices start at AS825/1100 and rooms have cable TV, shower and WC. There's also a youth hostel on the grounds (see Hostels). To get there take tram J or 46 and then bus No 46B, or tram 44 and bus No 146B.

Müllner Gasthof (☎ 22 35 99), 22 Esslinger Hauptstrasse 82, is a small place and good value, though it's closed in July and August. Singles/doubles with shower/WC and cable TV are AS480/900, and there's

VIENNA

free parking. It's one of the few places east of the Danube: if you don't have a car, you need to take the U1 to Kagran and then a long trip on bus No 26A.

Hotels – top end

All rooms in this category should have, as a minimum, a private shower or bath and WC, cable TV, direct-dial telephone, mini-bar and radio. These hotels will have all the facilities business visitors might require.

Inside the Ring *Appartement Pension Riemergasse* (☎ 512 72 200), 1 Riemergasse 8, is in a private block and can arrange parking for AS150 a day. All apartments have kitchenette, cable TV and bath/WC. Prices range from AS920 for a single to AS1960 for four in the smaller apartments. Breakfast costs AS66; credit cards are not accepted.

Hotel zur Wiener Staatsoper (☎ 513 12 74), 1 Krugerstrasse 11, has an attractive stuccoed façade. Rooms (AS950/1300) are compact, quiet and have white fittings. Garage parking is discounted to AS160 per day.

The plain frontage of *Hotel Kaiserin Elisabeth* (☎ 515 26), 1 Weihburggasse 3, belies its pleasant interior and long history (Mozart stayed here). Nicely decorated rooms are AS950/1900 with shower/WC and cable TV, and AS1450/2300 with bath also.

Hotel Austria (☎ 515 23), 1 Am Fleischmarkt 20, is down a quiet cul-de-sac, and has pleasantly furnished rooms for AS730/1064, or AS1105/1614 with private shower/WC.

Hotel am Stephansplatz (☎ 53 405), 1 Stephansplatz 9, is the closest you can sleep to St Stephen's without building a nest in the belfry. Comfortable, sizeable rooms cost from AS1190/1630.

Near the Centre *Hotel Maté* (☎ 404 55), 17 Ottakringer Strasse 34-36, has standard four-star rooms but the hotel has five-star facilities, including a swimming pool, solarium, sauna and fitness room (all free for

guests). Prices start at AS1050/1720, with reductions in winter.

Thüringerhof (☎ 43 95 81 83), 18 Jörgerstrasse 4-8, has rooms from AS850/1100, some very spacious. There's parking for AS50 and a rooftop terrace.

Hotel Arkadenhof (☎ 310 08 37), 9 Viriotgasse 5, is a comfortable, stylish, small-scale hotel. Rooms have all facilities (including air-con) and cost AS1380/1880 (AS200 less per person in winter). A comparable if larger place is the *Theater-Hotel* (☎ 405 36 48), Josefstädter Strasse 22, with an Art-Nouveau aura. Rooms cost AS1410/2200, 25% less in winter.

The unimaginatively named *Hotel am Schubertring* (☎ 717 02), 1 Schubertring 11, is conveniently central. Maze-like corridors lead to well-equipped singles/doubles costing from AS1350/1650, less in winter. They have either Biedermeier or Art-Nouveau furniture.

In a typically grand Viennese building, the *Hotel Atlanta* (☎ 405 12 30), 9 Währinger Strasse 33, is a good four-star hotel. Rooms are reasonably spacious and well furnished with elegant touches. Singles/doubles are AS980/1450 and triples AS1550. From November to March prices are reduced by about AS250 per person.

Close to the Theater an der Wien, the theatrical connection of *Hotel-Pension Schneider* (☎ 58 83 80), Getreidemarkt 5, is obvious when you enter the lobby and see the signed photos of the actors and opera stars who have stayed here. Singles are AS960 to AS1320, doubles AS1600, and there are excellent self-contained two-person apartments for AS2050. Prices are lower in the winter.

Aphrodite (☎ 211 48), 2 Praterstrasse 28, is a four-star hotel with a unique extra: it offers beauty treatments for both men and women (eg a two-day programme costs AS3300). The rooms bedazzle with many mirrors so that you can admire your progress, and there's a rooftop terrace, swimming pool, sauna and fitness room, which are all free for guests. Rooms are AS1200 per person and all have private bath/WC. There are a few singles with shower/WC for AS1000.

Trend Hotel Favorita (☎ 601 46), 10 Laxenburger Strasse 8-10, has singles/doubles from AS1290/1580 and good facilities for businesspeople. The sauna/steam bath is free for guests.

In the Suburbs *Celtes* (☎ 44 41 51), 19 Celtesgasse 1, is in the Neustift Heurigen area (take bus No 35 from the city centre). It's good value at AS850/1200 for singles/doubles with private shower/WC and satellite TV. The doubles for AS1400 are larger and have a bath.

Parkhotel Schönbrunn (☎ 878 04; fax 878 04 3220), 13 Hietzinger Hauptstrasse 10-20, is easily accessible from the centre by U4 (get off at the Hietzing stop). It was built partially with money from Emperor Franz Joseph who considered it his guesthouse. The lobby and grand ballroom all have the majesty of a five-star place, and the rooms surround a large garden with sun lounges, trees and grass. There's also a 12-metre-long swimming pool and a fitness room (both free for guests) as well as a solarium and sauna. The best rooms are in the older part but they're more expensive. Singles/doubles with bath/WC start at AS1385/1900, and there are some cheaper rooms with shower/WC.

Hotels – over the top

Nearly all Vienna's five-star hotels are within the Innere Stadt. Standard or 'economy' (something of a misnomer in this category) rooms are comfortable and with all the expected fittings and facilities, but they're not necessarily much better than those in a good four-star place; really you're paying the premium for the ambience, reputation, better service and the grandeur of the reception and lobby areas. All offer 'superior' rooms and suites.

At *Hotel Bristol* (☎ 51 516; fax 51 516 550), 1 Kärntner Ring 1, opulence and character go hand-in-hand; singles/doubles are from AS3000/3800. *Hotel Sacher* (☎ 51 456; fax 51 457 810), 1 Philharmoniker-strasse 4, has elegance and tradition with rooms starting at AS1900/3700. *Hotel Imperial* (☎ 501 100; fax 501 10 440), 1 Kärntner Ring 16, is a truly palatial, expensive (rooms from AS4100/5100) period hotel; the lobby was rebuilt in 1994.

The *Inter-Continental* (☎ 711 22; fax 713 44 89), 3 Johannesgasse 28 has a huge stylish lobby; rooms are from AS2350/2730 with traditional furnishings; the solarium, sauna and fitness room are free for guests.

At the *Marriott* (☎ 515 18; fax 515 18 6722), 1 Parkring 12A, a harmonious, galleried lobby shelters shops, cafés and fake pink flamingos; rooms are standard five-star quality (from AS2400 for a single) with surprisingly ancient TVs. The excellent facilities (fitness room, sauna and 13-metre-long swimming pool) are free for guests.

The *SAS Palais Hotel* (☎ 515 17; fax 512 22 16) is at 1 Parkring 16. It has a traditional Viennese aura, with good-quality singles/doubles from AS2300/3800; the solarium, fitness room and breakfast are only free at the higher 'Royal Club' price.

PLACES TO EAT

There are thousands of restaurants covering all budgets and all styles of cuisine. Coffee houses and Heurigen are almost a defining characteristic of Vienna, and these are places where you can also eat well. Beisl is a common Viennese name for a small tavern or restaurant. If you haven't the time or money for a sit-down meal, there are many takeaway places, including the Würstel stands, another institution of Vienna; they provide a quick snack of sausage and bread for about AS20 to AS35.

There are dozens of Chinese restaurants that are generally reliable and may have a cheap weekday lunch menu. Branches of Wienerwald and Nordsee are also reliable and inexpensive stand-bys.

Self-Catering

Supermarkets are scattered around the city. Hofer is acknowledged as the cheapest; Billa, Konsum, Spar, Löwa and Mondo sometimes have discounted ranges; and

Julius Meinl is more expensive. Typical opening hours are Monday to Friday from 7.30 or 8 am to 6.30 pm, and Saturday till noon or 1 pm. Like other shops, many open to 4 or 5 pm on the first Saturday of the month.

Outside normal shopping hours you can stock up with groceries at the main train stations, though prices are higher. Westbahnhof has a large shop (with alcohol) in the main hall open daily from 6 am to 10.50 pm; in Franz Josefs Bahnhof there's a shop open Monday to Saturday from 6 am to 10 pm, and Sunday from 8 am to noon. Shops in Südbahnhof are only tiny kiosks, but they're open daily until late. Wien Nord station has a *Billa* supermarket with late opening (to 8 pm) on Friday, and several small provision shops open daily from 5.30 am to 9 pm. Wien Mitte has a large *Interspar* supermarket (standard hours) and a reasonably sized store open daily from 5.30 am to 9.50 pm.

See the Things to Buy section later in this chapter for information on markets.

Central District
Self-Service & Budget Restaurants As you might expect, eating in the central district tends to be more expensive. If you only want a snack, try one of the many Würstel stands, or *Nordsee* has a branch on Kärntner Strasse. Near the McDonald's on Singerstrasse is a snack (*Imbiss*) shop offering half a grilled chicken for just AS32 (normal shop hours; late opening on Friday).

The most central university cafeteria is the *Music Academy Mensa*, in the Music Academy Hotel, 1 Johannesgasse 8. Weekday lunches are served between 11 am and 2 pm (1.30 pm during summer holidays), though you can also have coffee and snacks weekdays from 7.30 am to 3 pm. Main meals cost AS40 to AS55 and the salad buffet is AS19/42 for a small/large bowl. Nearby at No 3 is *Zur Fischerin Capua*, with fishing trophies on the walls and good weekday menus (lunch and evening) for around AS70, including soup. There are tables on the 1st

floor above the small bar area which is open daily.

Trzesniewski, 1 Dorotheergasse 1, is open Monday to Friday from 9 am to 7.30 pm and Saturday from 9 am to 1 pm. For a basic deli bar, where you stand in line to choose your food from the counter, this place isn't particularly cheap. Tiny (two bites and they're gone) open sandwiches with a variety of toppings are about AS8 each. But it's a famous Viennese institution and you may want to sample a few, if only to follow in Franz Kafka's mouthfuls (he was a regular here). Beer comes in equally tiny Pfiff measures.

Pizza Bizi, Rotenturmstrasse, is a convenient self-service place with hot food daily from 11 am to 1 pm. Pasta with a choice of sauces is AS65, pizzas are AS60 to AS75 and there are salads and vegetables.

Rosenberger Markt Restaurant is at 1 Maysedergasse 2. The downstairs buffet offers a fine array of meats, drinks and desserts to enable you to compile a meal for around AS100. If you really want to save schillings, concentrate on the salad or vegetable buffet: people unashamedly pile a Stephansdom-shaped food tower on small plates (AS29) for a filling feast. It is open daily from 11 am to 11 pm, and has free lockers for your bags.

Restaurant Marché Movenpick is in the Ringstrassen Galerien shopping complex, Kärntner Ring 5-7. It's almost the same as Rosenberger except the small salad/vegetable plates are only AS25. Another good feature is the pizza for AS57, where you can help yourself to a variety of toppings (available from 4 pm). There are also special deals after 9 pm. It's open Monday to Saturday from 9 am to 11 pm, and Sunday and holidays from 11 am to 10 pm.

Brezel Gwölb, 1 Ledererhof 9, offers Austrian food from AS80 to AS175 in a cobbled courtyard or a dark, cellar-like interior. It's open daily from 11.30 am to 1 am. Nearby, the air-con *China Restaurant Peking*, 1 Färbergasse 3, is open Monday to Saturday from 11.30 am to 2.30 pm and 6 to 11.30 pm. Weekday lunch specials are AS59, and other dishes start from AS78. Try the excellent Hunan spicy duck (AS95). Beer is only AS27 a Krügerl. Also good is *China Restaurant Turandot*, 1 Vorlaufstrasse 2, open daily. Weekday lunch specials are AS63, or there's an all-you-can-eat lunch buffet for AS75 (AS95 on weekends).

Mid-Range Restaurants *La Creperie* (☎ 512 56 87) has different rooms with varied and creative décor, ranging from arty odds and ends and ancient books, to a pseudo circus tent complete with clowns' faces. Meat and fish dishes are AS90 to AS235, beer is AS40 a Krügerl and wine is AS24 for an eighth of a litre. If you stick to its speciality, crêpes, eating need not be too expensive, and they're available with sweet or savoury fillings. The Florentine (AS110) is a good combination of spinach, ham, cheese and egg with a dollop of sour cream. It's at 1 Grünangergasse 10, with outside seating down the Nikolaigasse side street (open daily from 11.30 am to midnight).

Zu den 3 Hacken (☎ 512 58 95), 1 Singerstrasse 28, is a fairly rustic place with outside tables and a small room devoted to Schubert (despite the anachronistic WW II radio). Most dishes are AS105 to AS220, though Viennese dishes are cheaper (from AS86). It's open Monday to Saturday from 9 am to midnight.

Wrenkh (☎ 533 15 26), 1 Bauernmarkt 10, is a fairly up-market specialist vegetarian restaurant. Meticulously prepared dishes are AS75 to AS180 and it's open Monday to Friday from 11.30 am to 3 pm and 6 pm to midnight. It has a bar next door that's open Saturday, and there's another branch (☎ 892 33 56) at 15 Hollergasse 9.

Definitely not for squeamish vegetarians is *Weisser Rauchfangkehrer* (☎ 512 34 71), 1 Weihburggasse 4, thanks to the many hunting trophies on the wall. Meat is around AS105 to AS205 (plus a AS20 cover charge). It's an atmospheric place, mostly partitioned into small booths, and has live piano music most nights.

Griechenbeisl (☎ 533 19 77), 1 Fleischmarkt 11, is a famous tavern once frequented by the likes of Beethoven, Schubert and Brahms. Choose from the many vaulted rooms pierced by hanging antlers, or sit in the vine-fringed front garden. Viennese main dishes are AS155 to AS260 and it's open daily from 11 am to 1 am.

DO & CO (☎ 535 39 69 18), in Haas Haus at 1 Stephansplatz 12, has good food to match the good view. It specialises in fish and Thai dishes around the AS200 mark and is open Monday to Saturday from noon to 3 pm and 6 pm to midnight. There's an adjoining café, open in the afternoon.

Expensive Restaurants *Zum Kuckuck* (☎ 512 84 70), 1 Himmelpfortgasse 15, is a tiny one-room place with a vaulted ceiling. Viennese dishes are above AS200 or you can opt for multi-course gourmet menus. The kitchen is open Monday to Friday from noon to 2 pm and 6 to 11 pm.

For Japanese food, try *Kikkoman Hoshigaoka* (☎ 512 27 20), 1 Führichgasse 10. On the ground floor is a sushi bar, or go upstairs to have the food cooked in front of you on a large hot plate built into the table. The lunch menu is AS120 but otherwise expect to pay above AS200 per person, plus drinks and starters. Gourmet menus start at AS320. It is open daily except Sunday from noon to 2.30 pm and 6 to 11 pm.

Korso (☎ 515 16 546), 1 Mahlerstrasse 2, features wood-panelled elegance and opulent chandeliers. Viennese and international specialities are AS250 to AS400 and there's a vast wine cellar. Its proximity to the opera prompts it to offer a light three-course meal (AS630) for those who are replete with culture but depleted of cuisine. Opening hours are noon to 3 pm and 7 pm to 1 am, though it's closed at lunchtime on Saturdays and on Sundays in July and August.

Drei Husaren (☎ 512 10 920), 1 Weihburggasse 4, is in the same price range and is similarly formal and elegant, with soothing live piano music to aid digestion. It's closed from mid-July to mid-August; otherwise it's open daily from noon to 3 pm and 6 pm to midnight.

The North-West

Self-Service & Budget Restaurants The north-west includes numerous inexpensive places to eat near the university. The *University Mensa*, 1 Universitätsstrasse 7, has dishes from a mere AS30. Take the continuous lift to the top from the foyer. The adjoining café has the same meals and longer hours (weekdays from 8 am to 7 pm).

Close by, the *Catholic University Students' Community Mensa*, 1 Ebendorferstrasse 8, is open Monday to Friday from 11.30 am to 2 pm (closed in August). Main courses are just AS29 or AS36, and the salad buffet is AS15/28 per small/large bowl. Another good *Mensa* is open the same hours at the Afro-Asiatisches Institut, 9 Türkenstrasse 3. Three-course lunches are AS45; the café on the 1st floor is open longer hours and carries *Newsweek*.

Tunnel (☎ 42 34 65), 8 Florianigasse 39, is another student haunt. The food is satisfying and easy on the pocket, eg breakfast AS29, lunch specials AS45, spaghetti from AS38, big pizzas from AS60 and salads from AS20. Bottled beer costs from AS24 for half a litre. Tunnel is open daily from 9 am to 2 am. It also has a cellar bar with live music (see Entertainment).

Naschmarkt, on the corner of Ebendorferstrasse and Felderstrasse, has two parts. The self-service section has menus with soup for AS50 and AS55 and is open weekdays from 11 am to 2 pm. The cosier Stüberl, with outside tables, is open weekdays from 6.30 am to 2.30 pm and has similarly priced food, plus breakfast from AS28.

Vegetarisches Restaurant Légume (☎ 425 06 54), Währinger Strasse 57, has a three-course daily menu for AS98, and dishes like cheese schnitzel for AS79 (open lunchtimes only, Sunday to Friday). It's run by the adjoining health food shop, which is open Monday to Friday from 9 am to 6 pm, and Saturday from 9 am to noon.

Restaurant Jachiita, 8 Josefstädter Strasse 9, offers a rare chance to sample Japanese food without committing financial hara kiri. It hedges its bets a bit by offering Japanese (from AS80), Chinese (from AS75) and Italian (from AS60) food. The best deal is the weekday midday buffet (AS85) where you can eat your fill of any, or all, of the above. Opening hours are daily from 11 am to midnight, except in July and August when it's closed at weekends.

Mid-Range Restaurants For Thai food, try *Thai Haus*, on the corner of Veronikagasse and Hernalser Hauptstrasse. Main courses are AS80 to AS195, plus AS15 to AS35 for garnishes like rice and noodles (closed Tuesday).

Fromme Helene (☎ 406 91 44), 8 Josefstädter Strasse 53, is a small place with a cluttered salon look and good Viennese food. Midday dining is not too expensive (menus for AS70 and AS85 with soup) though evening dishes are above AS140. It's open weekdays from 8 am to midnight (except July), Saturday from 6 pm to midnight and Sunday from noon to midnight.

Wiener Rathauskeller (☎ 42 12 19) is in the Rathaus and the entrance is from the north-east corner. Enjoy the atmosphere in the arcaded Rittersaal where the walls are filled with murals and floral designs; live harp music (after 7 pm; extra charge of AS15) adds to the ambience. Down the corridor, the *Grinzinger Keller* is similar if barer, and soothes patrons with a quartet of musicians after 8 pm (extra charge of AS130 on the bill). The same Viennese and international dishes (AS88 to AS265) are offered in both halls (open 11.30 am to 3 pm and 6 to 11.30 pm, but closed Sunday and holidays).

Expensive Restaurants *Chez Robert* (☎ 43 35 44), 18 Gertrudeplatz 4, is near the Kutschkergasse stop of tram Nos 40 and 41. It's a small, quality French restaurant with many fish specialities. Main courses are AS150 to AS390 and there are several multicourse menus. It's open daily except Sunday from 5.30 to 11.30 pm (closed mid-July to mid-August).

Feuervogel (☎ 34 10 392), 9 Alserbachstrasse 21, is a Russian restaurant that has been run by the same Ukrainian family for

Top: Athena Fountain and Parlament building, Vienna
Left: Reflection of St Stephen's spire in Haas Haus, Vienna
Right: Anker Clock, Vienna

MARK HONAN

MARK HONAN

MARK HONAN

AUSTRIAN NATIONAL TOURIST OFFICE

AUSTRIAN NATIONAL TOURIST OFFICE

A	B
C	D
E	F

A: Fleischmarkt café, Vienna
B: Concert ticket sellers, Vienna
C: Schönbrunn Palace, Vienna
D: Street musicians, Vienna
E: Art-Nouveau decoration by Otto Wagner, Vienna
F: Lipizzaner stallions at the Spanish Riding School, Vienna

over 70 years. The colourful décor matches the conversational gambits (in English) of the surviving generations. The food is hearty rather than refined, but tasty nonetheless. Main courses are above AS150 and there's sometimes live music at the weekend. It's open from 7 pm to 2 am and is closed mid-July to mid-August.

The South-West
Self-Service & Budget Restaurants
Würstel stands are all over the place, but if you're in the area, wander down to the Ring end of Mariahilfer Strasse to choose between two cheap, adjacent stands engaged in cut-throat competition. The sign on one proclaims 'mein Kunde ist König' (my customer is king); the other counters with 'mein Kunde ist Kaiser' (my customer is emperor).

The *Technical University Mensa* is at 4 Resselgasse 7-9; once in the building, find the yellow area and go upstairs to the 1st floor. Good weekday lunches (11 am to 2.30 pm) are only AS28 to AS55, with several choices. Another *Mensa* is at the Academy of Fine Arts, 1 Schillerplatz 3, and is open weekdays from 9 am to 5 pm (to 3 pm on Friday). Menus are from AS39 and it's closed in July and August.

Schnitzelwirt Schmidt (☎ 93 37 71), 7 Neubaugasse 52, is the best place for schnitzels and prides itself on its enormous portions (from AS57). This informal, often hectic place is something of an institution among travellers; you really have to visit to see the size of these things. Unless you have a huge appetite, share one (they're used to supplying two plates!) and just get extra garnishes (around AS20 each). Many variations on the basic schnitzel are offered, though the high turnover means quality can be variable. Opening hours are Monday to Friday from 10 am to 10 pm and Saturday from 10 am to 2.30 pm and 5 to 10 pm.

Another good place for schnitzels is *Schnitzelhaus*, 6 Otto Bauer Gasse 24, open daily from 10 am to 10 pm. It's more of a takeaway place – rather like an Austrian version of McDonald's but without the clown. Large schnitzel burgers start at AS29.

There are other branches round town, though not in the centre.

Madal Bal, 15 Mariahilfer Strasse 160, is a healthy (no smoking or alcohol) vegetarian restaurant with background meditative music. Home-cooked meals start at AS75 and there's a salad buffet for AS35/65 (open Tuesday to Saturday from 11 am to 10 pm).

Gaunkerl, 7 Kaiserstrasse 50, serves meals from about AS55. The décor in the front room creates the illusion that you're sitting outside, complete with glowing stars and witches on broomsticks flying overhead. The illusion becomes more convincing after a couple of beers (closed Saturday lunch and Sunday). Around the corner is *Burg-Keller*, 7 Burggasse 115. It's a quiet, relaxing place with tasty Austrian cooking for AS65 to AS150. Lunch specials are excellent value – three courses for AS60 or AS80 (not Sunday; open daily from 10 am to 11 pm). There are English menus.

Amerlingbeisl, 7 Stiftgasse 8, attracts mainly young people, both as an eating (meals AS45 to AS105) and a drinking (beer AS34 a Krügerl) venue. It's open daily from 9 am to 2 pm. In summer people flock into the rear courtyard.

K & K Bierkanzlei, Windmühlgasse 20, is small, cheap and typically Viennese with its filling and straightforward daily menus costing AS55 (several choices, with soup). Opening hours are 11 am to 5.30 pm. The owner has a fondness for images of Franz Joseph and Elisabeth – their faces even appear on the salt and pepper pots. *Restaurant Pulkantaler Weinhaus*, 15 Felberstrasse 2, near Westbahnhof, is a simple place with good food (AS40 to AS110, English menus). There's a stand-up bar with several different beers (AS29 to AS32 a Krügerl), and it's open daily from 9 am to 10 pm.

Mid-Range Restaurants
Restaurant Smutny (☎ 587 13 56), 1 Elisabethstrasse 8, serves Viennese food in a Viennese environment, though the interior wall tiles are a novel touch. Dishes are filling and reasonably priced from AS80 and it's open daily from 10 am to midnight.

Ungarn-Grill (☎ 523 62 09), 7 Burggasse 97, is a Hungarian restaurant with a patio area and live Gypsy music every night. Fish, chicken, grills and other dishes are AS85 to AS180, and there's a AS11 cover charge. Opening hours are Monday to Saturday from 6 pm to 1 am. Nearby is *Glacisbeisl* in the middle of the Messepalast. It feels miles from the city centre. Ascend the path to garden tables surrounded by a trellis and vines. Salads and Viennese food are in the AS90 to AS225 range (open daily from 9 am to midnight).

Expensive Restaurants The *Beim Novak* (☎ 523 32 44), 7 Richtergasse 12, has Austrian food (AS95 to AS265) served by attentive staff, with good explanations of each dish on the English menu. Speciality of the house is Überbackene Fledermaus (bat au gratin) for AS150. The 'bat wings' are actually cuts of beef. It's closed on weekends and holidays.

Steinerne Eule (☎ 93 33 50), Halbgasse 30, has Viennese food served in lighter, more refined styles. The name means 'stone owl'; the owner has a collection of 700, some of which are on display in a cabinet, but you won't find any on the menu. Clint Eastwood had a 'great dinner' here, as he wrote in the guest book. There are several rooms and a pleasant rear courtyard. Meals cost anything from AS100, to AS580 for a gourmet menu. It's closed Sunday and Monday.

The South

The branch of *Naschmarkt* at 1 Schwarzenbergplatz 16 is buffet-style and has an outside terrace. Lunch specials are available up to 2 pm on weekdays (it's open daily until 10.30 pm).

On Wiedner Gürtel opposite Südbahnhof are several inexpensive places to eat. They include a branch of *Wienerwald* (open 8 am to 1 am daily), and a place simply called *China Restaurant*, with lunch menus (open Monday to Saturday) from AS50 including soup or a spring roll. A few doors down at No 4 is *Kristall*, open daily from 7 am to 4 am. Meals start at AS60 (English menu); the

food is surprisingly good for the price and there's plenty of it.

The *Vier Jahreszeiten Restaurant* (☎ 711 22 140) in the Hotel Inter-Continental is highly rated for gourmet food (it's closed most of July and at weekends). The sumptuous lunch buffet costs AS490 and à la carte dishes are AS195 to AS325.

The East

The *Academy of Applied Art Cafeteria*, 1 Oskar Kokoschka Platz 2, is open weekdays from 9 am to 6 pm (to 3 pm on Friday), and you can get cheap snacks and light meals. Wien Mitte station has several places for cheap and quick eating, like the *Interspar* supermarket which has a self-service restaurant upstairs (meals AS50 to AS80), open normal shop hours.

Schweizerhaus in the Prater, 2 Strasse des Ersten Mai 116, is famous for its roasted pork hocks (Hintere Schweinsstelze). A meal consists of a massive chunk of meat on the bone (AS85 for 500 grams, usually 700 to 800 grams minimum – eat alone and end up the size of two people) served with mustard and horseradish sauce. Chomping your way through vast slabs of pig smacks of medieval banqueting, but it's very tasty when washed down with draught Budweiser (the Czech stuff). It gets incredibly busy, and there are many outside tables. It's open March to October, daily from 10 am to 11 pm. Offering a similar meat orgy is *Café-Restaurant Luftberg*, nearby on Waldsteingartenstrasse.

Vegetarians will have better luck in the Prater at *Sta Cruz*, Hauptallee No 8, a large place with many outside tables in a shady garden. Latin American food costs AS76 to AS152, including many vegetarian choices (open daily 11 am to 1 am).

Steirereck (☎ 713 31 68), 8 Rasumofskygasse 2, is gourmet territory. In fact, it's considered one of the best restaurants in Austria. Different parts of the restaurant have a varied ambience, but it's pretty formal throughout. Even the toilets are stylish! Tempting main courses all top AS300 (choose from lobster, rabbit, pigeon, venison etc) yet you still have to book days in advance for the evening. The multi-course menu is AS850, or AS1350 including wine. It's open Monday to Friday.

Coffee Houses

The coffee house is an integral part of Viennese life. The story goes that the tradition started in the 17th century after retreating Turkish invaders left behind their supplies of coffee beans.

Today Vienna has hundreds (some say thousands) of coffee houses. They are a great place for observing the locals in repose and recovering after a hard day's sightseeing. Small coffees cost at least AS20 and the custom is to take your time. Most places have lots of newspapers including English and other foreign titles; as these would cost around AS30 to buy, a coffee is an excellent investment. Traditional places will serve a glass of water with your coffee.

Coffee houses basically fall into two types, though the distinction is rather blurred nowadays. A *Kaffeehaus*, traditionally preferred by men, offers games such as chess and billiards and serves wine, beer, spirits and light meals. The *Café Konditorei* attracts more women and typically has a salon look with rococo mouldings and painted glass. A wide variety of cakes and pastries is usually on offer.

Café Museum, 1 Friedrichstrasse 6, is open daily from 7 am to 11 pm and has chess, billiards, newspapers and outside tables. The building was created by Adolf Loos in 1899 but has been extensively renovated.

Café Bräunerhof, 1 Stallburggasse 2, offers free classical music on weekends from

---

Vienna Coffee

Legend has it that coffee beans were left in Austria by the fleeing Turks in 1683, and it was this happy accident that resulted in today's plethora of coffee establishments. Vienna's first coffee house opened in 1685, but it could have been emulating successful establishments already opened in Europe (Venice 1647; Oxford 1650; London 1652; Paris 1660 and Hamburg 1677), rather than having anything to do with the Turks.

Austrian coffee consumption was modest in the ensuing centuries, and only really took hold after WW II. Austrians now drink more coffee than any other beverage, gulping down 221 litres per person per year (next in line for national consumption is beer at 120 litres, followed by milk at 104, soft drinks at 84, mineral water at 76, black tea at 39 and wine at 33). Only in Finland, Sweden and Denmark is more coffee consumed per person.

Different types of coffee are:
Mocca (sometimes spelled *Mokka*) or *Schwarzer* – black coffee
Brauner – black but served with a tiny jug of milk
Kapuziner – with a little milk and perhaps a sprinkling of grated chocolate
Melange – served with milk and maybe whipped cream
Einspänner – served in a glass, with whipped cream
Masagran (or Mazagran) – cold coffee with ice and Maraschino liqueur
Wiener Eiskaffee – cold coffee with vanilla ice cream and whipped cream

Waiters usually speak English and can tell you about specialities. In particular, various combinations of alcohol may be added eg *Mozart*, with Mozart liqueur; *Fiaker*, with rum; *Mocca gespritzt*, with cognac; and *Maria Theresa*, with orange liqueur. If you find the basic coffee too strong, ask for a *Verlängerter* ('lengthened'), a *Brauner* weakened with hot water. Traditional places serve coffee on a silver tray and with a glass of water. Some types of coffee are offered in small (*kleine*) or large (*grosse*) portions. According to an old Viennese tradition, if the waiter fails to give you the bill after three requests you can leave without paying (three instantaneous requests doesn't count!). ■

3 to 6 pm, and English newspapers. It's open weekdays to 7.30 pm (to 8.30 pm in winter) and weekends to 6 pm.

Café Central, 1 Herrengasse 14, has a fine ceiling and pillars, and piano music from 4 to 6 pm. Trotsky came here to play chess. Say hello to the plaster patron near the door with the walrus moustache – a model of the poet Peter Altenberg. Opening hours are Monday to Saturday from 8 am to 10 pm.

Café Hawelka, 1 Dorotheergasse 6, is another famous coffee house. At first glance it's hard to see what the attraction is: scruffy pictures and posters, brown-stained walls, smoky air, cramped tables. At second glance you see why – it's an ideal location for people-watching. The whole gamut of Viennese society comes here, from students to celebrities; it's also a traditional haunt for artists and writers. After 10 pm it gets busy. You're constantly being shunted along to accommodate new arrivals at the table, the organising elderly Frau seizing on any momentarily vacant chair (curtail those toilet visits!) to reassign it elsewhere. Café Hawelka is open from 8 am to 2 am (from 4 pm on Sunday and holidays), and it's closed on Tuesday.

Alt Wien, 1 Bäckerstrasse 9, is a rather dark coffee house by day, attracting writers and intellectuals, and those who simply wish to be considered as such. It becomes a good drinking hall at night. Beer is AS30 for a Krügerl. Also well known for its goulash (AS75 large, AS50 small), it is open daily from 10 am to 2 am. After a hard night drinking or dancing, greet the dawn at *Café Drechsler*, 1 Linke Wienzeile 22, where you'll rub shoulders with traders at the Naschmarkt. Opening hours are 3.30 am to 8 pm (to Saturday 6 pm and closed Sunday). There are billiard tables, and meals are AS60 to AS75.

The *Hotel Sacher Café*, 1 Philharmoniker-strasse 4, behind the Staatsoper, is a picture of opulence with chandeliers, battalions of waiters and rich, red walls and carpets. It's famous for its chocolate apricot cake, Sachertorte (AS48 a slice; coffee from AS32). Its main rival in terms of torte is the

rather elegant, mirrored environment of *Demel*, 1 Kohlmarkt 14, the archetypal Konditorei establishment (open daily from 10 am to 8 pm).

Other traditional, well-known coffee houses include *Café Sperl*, 6 Gumpendorfer Strasse 11, with the *Times* newspaper and billiard tables, and two places on the Ring, both with outside tables and English newspapers: *Café Restaurant Landtmann*, 1 Dr Karl Lueger Ring 4, and *Schwarzenberg*, 1 Kärntner Ring 17, which has live piano music Tuesday to Friday from 8 to 10 pm and weekends from 4 to 10 pm.

Heurigen

Heurigen (wine taverns) can be identified by a green wreath or branch (the *Busch'n*) hanging over the door. Many have outside tables in large gardens or courtyards. Inside, these wine taverns are fairly rustic but have an ambience all their own. Heurigen almost invariably have food which you select from hot and cold buffet counters; prices are generally reasonable. It's traditionally acceptable to bring your own food, but this isn't commonly done nowadays.

Heurigen usually have a relaxed atmosphere which gets more and more lively as the mugs of wine – and customers – get drunk. Many feature traditional live music, perhaps ranging from a solo accordion player to a fully-fledged oompah band; these can be a bit touristy but great fun nonetheless. The Viennese tend to prefer a music-free environment. Opening times are approximately 4 pm (or before lunch on weekends) to 11 pm or midnight, though in the less touristy regions some may close for several weeks at a time before reopening. Similarly, some are only open in the summer, or only from Thursday to Sunday.

The common measure for Heuriger wine is a *Viertel* (one-quarter of a litre) in a glass mug, costing around AS25 to AS30, though you can also drink by the *Achterl* (one-eighth of a litre). A Viertel Gespritzer costs AS16 to AS20.

Heurigen are concentrated in the wine-growing suburbs to the north, north-west,

Drink & Be Merry

The *Heuriger* (wine tavern) tradition in Vienna dates to the Middle Ages, but it was Joseph II in 1784 who officially granted producers the right to sell wine from their premises. It proved to be one of his more enduring reforms. The term Heuriger refers not only to the tavern, but also to the year's new vintage, which officially comes of age on St Martin's Day (11 November). It continues to be Heuriger wine up to its first anniversary, at which time it is promoted (relegated?) to the status of *Alte* (old) wine. St Martin's Day is a day of much drinking and consumption of goose.

A *Buschenschank* is a type of Heuriger that can open only at certain times – a mere three weeks a year in some cases. It can only sell its own wine, either new or old, and must close when supplies have dried up. The term 'Buschenschank' is protected. Not so 'Heuriger': taverns can call themselves this if they buy wine from outside; in fact some don't even produce their own wine.

The Danube Valley is the most fertile land in Austria. Vines and fruits are grown along the river, with vineyards extending as far as the suburbs of Vienna. Austrian wine production is 80% white and 20% red. The most common variety (36%) is the dry white *Grüner Veltliner*; it also tends to be the cheapest. Other common varieties are *Riesling* and *Pinot Blanc*. *Sekt* is a sparkling wine. Some of the young wines can be a little sharp, so it is common to mix them with 50% tonic water, called a *Gespritzer*. The correct salute when drinking a Heuriger is *Prost* (cheers). But the Viennese often can't wait for 11 November to drink the new vintage, and are prepared to consume it early, as unfermented must (*Most*), partially fermented (*Sturm*), or fully fermented but still cloudy (*Staubiger*). The correct salute when drinking these versions is *Gesundheit* (health), perhaps in recognition of the risk taken by the palate. ∎

and south of the city. Once you pick a region to explore, the best approach is to simply go where the spirit moves you (or to whichever place happens to be open at the time); taverns are very close together and it's easy to visit several on the same evening.

North-West This is the best known region. The area most favoured by tourists is Grinzing (count the tour buses lined up outside at closing time), and this is probably the best area if you want live music and a lively atmosphere. However, bear in mind that this area is mostly eschewed as a tourist ghetto by Viennese. There are several good Heurigen in a row along Cobenzlgasse and Sandgasse. *Reinprecht* at Cobenzlgasse 22 is a very large place with a lively, sing-along environment. Tram D runs from the Ring and terminates at Grinzing.

From Grinzing, you can hop on the 38A bus to Heiligenstadt, towards the city centre, where in 1817 Beethoven lived in the *Beethovenhaus*, 19 Pfarrplatz 3. This has a big hall with live music and many annexes.

From Heiligenstadt it's just a couple of stops on tram D to Nussdorf, where a couple of Heurigen await right by the tram terminus. But don't just settle for these without exploring first; there are several others along Kahlenberger Strasse.

Farther west are the areas of Sievering (terminus of bus No 39A) and Neustift am Walde (bus 35A). Both these buses link up with the No 38 tram route. Ottakring is a small but authentic Heurigen area a short walk west of the tram J terminus.

North The Heurigen here are less visited by tourists and are therefore more typically Viennese, catering to a regular clientele. They are also cheaper: a Viertel costs around AS22. Live music is not the norm. Stammersdorf (terminus of tram No 31) is Vienna's largest wine-growing district, producing about 30% of its wine. From the tram stop, get on to Stammersdorfer Strasse, the next street north and running east-west. Many Heurigen are on this street in the westward direction; two good ones are *Weinhof*

Wieninger at No 78 and *Weingut Klavger* at No 14.

Strebersdorf is at the terminus of tram No 32, or about 30 minutes walk west of Stammersdorf. The Heurigen are north of the tram terminus. *Weingut Schilling*, Langenzersdorferstrasse 54, has a good reputation for wine. It's closed on odd-numbered months (January, March etc), at which time the next-door *Strauch* at No 50A is open. Another place is *Noschiel-Eckert* (☎ 292 25 96), Strebersdorfer Strasse 158.

South As in the north, tourists are less prevalent in these Heurigen. Mauer is in the south-west, on the edge of the Wienerwald. Take S1 or S2 to Atzgersdorf-Mauer then walk about one km to the taverns. Alternatively, take the U4 to Hietzing and then tram No 60 to Mauer Hauptplatz. Oberlaa is farther east. To get there, take the U1 to Reumannplatz, bus 66A or 67A to Wienerfeld, and then transfer to bus 17A. This runs along Oberlaaer Strasse where there are several Heurigen.

City Heurigen *Esterházykeller*, 1 Haarhof 1, off Naglergasse, is a busy wine cellar with cheap wine from AS22 a Viertel. Meals and snacks are available and it's open daily from 11 am (4 pm weekends) to 10 pm. In the same courtyard is *Bierhof*; it's not a Heuriger – beer is the beverage of choice.

St Urbani-Keller (☎ 533 91 02), 1 Am Hof 12, is a more expensive Heuriger, though it does have live accordion music (open daily from 6 pm to 1 am).

ENTERTAINMENT

The tourist office produces a monthly listing of concerts and other events; see also its *Vienna Scene* magazine. Publications worth referring to are the weekly magazines *City* (AS5) and *Falter* (AS23), and the Thursday edition of the *Neue Kronen Zeitung* newspaper (AS8). Blue Danube Radio has 'What's on in Vienna', broadcast in English daily at 1 pm.

Bars, Clubs & Discos

Vienna has plenty of places for a night out, and unlike some other European capital cities, you don't have to spend a lot of money in nightclubs to drink until late. Venues are by no means limited to the Innere Stadt – dozens of small bars and cafés in the 6th, 7th, 8th and 9th districts stay busy until well after midnight.

The best-known area for a night out is around Ruprechtsplatz, Seitenstettengasse, Rabensteig and Salzgries in the central zone near the Danube canal. This area has been dubbed the 'Bermuda Triangle' ('Bermuda-Dreieck') as drinkers can disappear into the numerous pubs and clubs and apparently be lost to the world. *Krah Krah*, 1 Rabensteig 8, has 50 different brands of beer (from about AS34 for a half-litre bottle) and is open daily until 2 am. Opposite is *Roter Engel*, 1 Rabensteig 5, which has live music nightly (cover charge around AS20 to AS70) and is open until 2 or 4 am.

A good jazz club is *Porgy & Bess* (☎ 512 84 38), 1 Spiegelgasse 2. It's open weekdays from 7 pm to 2 am and weekends from 8 pm to 4 am. Entry costs AS120 or more, except on Wednesday ('Session' night, AS30). Another place is *Jazzland* (☎ 533 25 75), 1 Franz-Josefs-Kai 29; entry costs from AS50 and it's closed on Monday. *P1*, 1 Rotgasse 3, is a disco that attracts a rather younger set (open to 4 or 5 am; closed Sunday).

The Volksgarten has three venues appealing to all tastes. The *Volksgarten Nightclub* has different music on successive nights (closed Tuesday) starting at about 10 pm: 'Club Student' on Thursday costs only AS60 and includes a free buffet; Friday is reggae night (AS70). There's a garden bar (drinks from AS55) and the dance-floor roof can be opened to reveal the night sky.

Somewhat bizarrely, right next door is the *Waltzer Dancing* section where serene and somewhat staid couples glide across the dance floor to 'evergreen' classics. It's open daily in summer from 4 pm with a concert followed by dancing (AS140 including a drink). In winter, dancing is every evening except Sunday and costs AS70 including a drink voucher. Participants in these diverse places can gaze in disbelief at each other's antics through the window.

The third Volksgarten venue is the *Pavillon Café*, open daily from 11 am to 2 am. It has garden tables, a DJ and food. Beer costs AS37 for half a litre. Entry is free except when there are bands or a barbecue (AS40 to AS80).

Tunnel (see Places to Eat) has a cellar bar with live music nightly from 9 pm; entry costs from AS30, to AS100 on weekends (discounts for students). On Monday there's generally a free 'Jazzsession'.

Café Käuzchen, 7 Garde Gasse 8, has interesting décor, including part of an old VW Kombi bursting out of one wall. It's open daily and is good for late-night conversation (and food) to 2 or 4 am. Breakfasts are served after 8 am.

Rincon Andino (☎ 586 56 71), 6 Münzwardeingasse 2, is a Latin American bar with live rock, soul or funk three times a week (entry is about AS80). It has lively murals, a limited menu and is open daily from 11 am to 2 or 4 am. *La Colombie* (☎ 408 30 45), 8 Laudongasse 57, is another Latin American place with good food (from AS58) and diverse events, open daily from 6.30 or 7 pm to 2 am.

BACH (☎ 450 19 70), 16 Bachgasse 21, has different events depending upon the night, with live music (usually 'alternative' bands; AS70 to AS120) and discos (anything from rave to '60s). Drink prices are reasonable and it's open from 8 pm to 2 or 4 am.

WUK (☎ 401 210), 9 Währinger Strasse 59, is an interesting venue offering a variety of events, including alternative bands, classical music, dance, theatre, children's events, political discussions and practical-skills workshops. It is government-subsidised but pursues an independent course. Prices are not high; some events are even free. There's also a Beisl in the cobbled courtyard, open daily to 2 am.

Arena (☎ 79 88 595), 3 Baumgasse 80, is another good venue, centred in a former slaughterhouse. In June and July, headline bands play on the outdoor stage (AS300); in August this space becomes an outdoor cinema instead. All year, smaller bands play in the indoor hall (AS120 to AS150), and there's sometimes theatre, dance and discussions. Keep an ear open for the once-a-month all-night parties (AS60 to AS80), eg 'Iceberg' ('70s music) and 'Badlands' (techno, heavy metal).

One of the best discos in Vienna is *U4* (☎ 85 83 18), 12 Schönbrunner Strasse 222, open nightly from 11 pm to 4 or 5 am. Drink prices aren't too bad, and there are two dancing rooms, a slide show and occasional live bands. Each night has a different style of music and attracts a different clientele. The Sunday 'Flower Power' (cover charge AS50) is a popular night featuring '60s and '70s music – too-young-to-be-hippies do amazing hair dances, flailing their flowing locks about in huge arcs. Saturday is house music (AS130); Thursday is gay night.

Gay Venues Some places popular with gays and lesbians are: *Café Berg*, 9 Berggasse 8, open daily from 10 am to 1 am; *Café Savoy*, 6 Linke Wienzeile 36, open Tuesday to Friday from 5 pm to 2 am and Saturday from 9 am to 6 pm and 9 pm to 2 am; *Why Not?*, 1 Tiefer Graben 22, a bar/disco open Friday and Saturday from 11 pm to 5 am, plus Wednesday for 'Mann intim' ('man intimate') and Sunday for Karaoke; and the *Eagle Bar*, 6 Blümelgasse 1, a men's bar with a leathery clientele.

Classical Music

Apart from bars and clubs, classical music still dominates the Viennese landscape. The programme of music events is unceasing, and as a visitor in the centre you'll continually be accosted by Mozart lookalikes trying to sell you tickets for concerts or ballets. Even some of the buskers playing along Kärntner Strasse and Graben are classical musicians.

Check with the tourist office for free events around town. There are sometimes free concerts at the Rathaus. In July and August at Rathausplatz, films of operas, operettas and concerts are shown on a large screen (free), and hundreds of Viennese turn up in their best evening attire.

Standing-room tickets (from AS20) for the Staatsoper and Volksoper go on sale one hour before the performance, as they do at the Burgtheater and Akademietheater (German-language productions; standing tickets AS15). Queue up at the venue concerned: for major productions you may have to allow two or three hours; for less important works, you can often get tickets with minimal queuing. Same-day student tickets (different queue) for these places cost AS50 for any seats left unsold, and they are available to students under age 27 who can show university ID (*not* an ISIC card). They are available 30 minutes (opera) or one hour (theatre) before productions start.

The state ticket office, charging no commission, is the Bundestheaterkassen (☎ 514 44 2959), 1 Goethegasse 1. It sells tickets for these places only and closes from July to the last week in August. Tickets are available here only seven days or less prior to the performance, and the AS50 student price is only for the cheaper seats. Credit cards are accepted. For postal bookings at least three weeks in advance, apply to the Bundestheaterverband (☎ 514 44 2653) at the same address. You pay only after your reservations are confirmed.

Operas in the *Staatsoper* (☎ 514 44 29 55) are lavish affairs, and shouldn't be missed. Advance tickets for performances are expensive at AS150 to AS800. Standing-room tickets for AS30 are in a good position at the back of the stalls, whereas those for AS20 put you in the balcony or the gallery. The Viennese take their opera very seriously and dress up accordingly. Wander around the foyer and the refreshment rooms in the interval to fully appreciate the gold and crystal interior. There are no opera performances in July and August, but the venue may be used for other events.

The other main venue for opera is the *Volksoper* (☎ 524 44 29 60), 9 Währinger Strasse 78, close to the Gürtel and the U6 line. It includes operettas and musicals in its repertoire. Standing-room tickets cost AS15 and AS20.

The Vienna Philharmonic Orchestra performs in the Grosser Saal (large hall) in the *Musikverein* (☎ 505 81 90), 1 Bösendorferstrasse 12, which is said to have the best acoustics of any concert hall in Austria. The interior is suitably lavish and can be visited by occasional guided tour. Standing-room tickets in the main hall cost AS50 but there are no student tickets. In the smaller Brahms Saal the cheapest tickets (AS60) have no view. The ticket office is open from Monday to Friday from 9 am to 6 pm, and Saturday from 9 am to noon (closed July and August).

Another major venue for classical and other music is the *Konzerthaus* (☎ 712 12 11), 3 Lothringerstrasse 20; it has three separate halls. Student tickets (for those under 27 with an ISIC card) cost half-price. The Konzerthaus ticket office is open Monday to Friday from 9 am to 7.30 pm and Saturday from 9 am to 1 pm. The Konzerthaus is closed for July and August except when it hosts Summer of Music events.

The Vienna Boys' Choir

Another famous institution, the Vienna Boys' Choir (Wiener Sängerknaben), is actually four separate choirs; duties are rotated between singing in Vienna, touring the world, resting, and perhaps even occasionally going to school. The choir was instigated in 1498 by Maximilian I and at one time numbered Haydn and Schubert in its ranks. The choir sings every Sunday (except during July and August) at 9.15 am in the *Burgkapelle* (Royal Chapel) in the Hofburg. Tickets for seats are AS60 to AS250 and must be booked weeks in advance, but standing room is free. Queue by 8.30 am to find a place inside the open doors; you can get a flavour of what's going on from the TV in the foyer. Just as interesting is the scrum afterwards when everybody struggles to photograph, and be photographed with, the serenely patient choir members.

The choir also sings a mixed programme of music in the *Konzerthaus* at 3.30 pm on

Fridays in May, June, September and October. Tickets cost AS350 to AS400, and are available through Reisebüro Mondial (☎ 588 04 141), 4 Faulmanngasse 4, not from the Konzerthaus booking office.

Theatre

There are performances in English at the *English Theatre* (☎ 402 12 60), 8 Josefsgasse 12, and the *International Theatre* (☎ 319 62 72), 9 Porzellangasse 8 (entrance Müllnergasse). Tickets at the International Theatre cost AS220 to AS250, or AS130 for students (under 26) and senior citizens, and it closes for around five weeks at the beginning of August. It has a linked venue, *Fundus*, at 9 Müllnergasse 6A.

Mime performances (avant-garde) are at the *Serapionstheater im Odeon* (☎ 214 55 62), 2 Taborstrasse 10.

If you can follow German, the prime place is the *Burgtheater* (National Theatre: ☎ 514 44 42 18) on Dr Karl Lueger Ring, though there are plenty of other theatres, like the nearby *Volkstheater* (☎ 523 35 010). The *Theater an der Wien* (☎ 588 30 265), 6 Linke Wienzeile 6, usually puts on musicals (student and standing-room tickets are available).

Spanish Riding School

Famous Viennese performers with a difference are the Lipizzaner stallions who strut their stuff in the Spanish Riding School (Spanische Reitschule). The breed was imported from Spain by Maximilian II in 1562, and in 1580 a stud was established at Lipizza, now in Slovenia. They perform an equine ballet to a programme of classical music while the audience cranes to see from pillared balconies, and chandeliers shimmer above. The mature stallions are all snow-white (though they are born dark) and the riders wear traditional garb, from their leather boots to their bicorn hats. It's a long-established Viennese institution, truly redolent of the Habsburg era.

Reservations to see the horses perform are booked up months in advance. To make a booking, write to the Spanische Reitschule,

Michaelerplatz 1, A-1010 Wien. (Buy direct – travel agents charge a 22% commission.) Otherwise, ask in the office about cancellations; cancelled tickets are sold two hours before performances. You need to be pretty keen on horses to be happy about paying AS220 to AS800 for seats or AS170 for standing room, although a few of the tricks, such as seeing a stallion bounding along on only its hind legs like a demented kangaroo, do tend to stick in the mind.

Tickets to watch them train can be bought the same day (AS80) at gate No 2, Josefsplatz in the Hofburg. Training is from 10 am to noon, Tuesday to Saturday, mid-February to the end of October, except in July and August when they go on their summer holidays (seriously!) to Lainzer Tiergarten, west of the city. Queues are very heavy early in the day, but if you try at around 11 am most people have gone and you can get in fairly quickly – indicative of the fact that training is relatively dull except for isolated high points. In July and August you can watch a film of their antics in the Palffy Palace on Josefsplatz (AS50), open daily from 10 am to 6 pm. Next door is the Stallburg (stables).

Cinema

Entry prices start at AS60; Monday is known as *Kinomontag*, when all cinema seats are this price. A number of cinemas show films in the original language. The *Austrian Film Museum* (☎ 533 70 56/4), 1 Augustinerstrasse 1, charges AS90 for day membership and entry to two films. It is closed from July to September. *Burg Kino* (☎ 587 84 06), 1 Opernring 19, has regular screenings of *The Third Man*. *De France* (☎ 317 52 36) is at 1 Schottenring 5, *Filmcasino* (☎ 587 90 62) at 5 Margaretenstrasse 78, and *Filmhaus* (☎ 54 6660) at 5 Stöbergasse 11-15.

HTU Cinestudio (☎ 588 01), 6 Getreidemarkt 9, is actually a lecture theatre in the Technical University and prices are lower than at conventional cinemas. *IMAX Filmtheater* (☎ 894 01 01) is at 14 Mariahilfer Strasse 212 and *Top Kino* (☎ 587 55 57) at 6 Rahlgasse 1.

Casino

Vienna's casino is opposite the tourist office in Kärntner Strasse. Ascend the stairs to play blackjack, roulette and other games (dress code applies; jacket and tie are available at the counter) from 3 pm to 3 am. Downstairs, slot machines are open from 11 am to midnight (no dress code).

Spectator Sport

As in any large city, there are plenty of sports. International and domestic soccer games are played at the *Praterstadion*, Meyereistrasse 7, in the Prater. The Stadthalle (☎ 98 100), Vogelweidplatz, hosts anything from tennis tournaments to water polo. Horse racing is at Freudenau, 2 Rennbahnstrasse 65; call ☎ 728 95 31 for information. Also in the Prater, there are trotting races at Krieau.

Vienna's Spring Marathon is run (jogged, walked, abandoned – depending upon the fitness of the participants) in late March or April. The route takes in Schönbrunn, the Ringstrasse and the Prater.

THINGS TO BUY

Vienna is not a place for cheap shopping but does offer numerous elegant shops and quality products. Local specialities include porcelain, ceramics, handmade dolls, wrought-iron work and leather goods. *Shopping in Vienna* is a free guide, distributed in plush hotels.

Normal shopping hours are from 8 am to 6.30 pm on weekdays and 8 am to 1 pm on Saturday. On the first Saturday of the month, stores usually open to 5 pm. Major credit cards are usually accepted. For special reductions, look for signs saying 'Aktion'. Bargaining is not the norm in shops, though you can certainly haggle when buying second-hand goods, advertised in *Bazar* or *Findegrube*; both magazines are available from pavement newsstands.

Shopping Centres

The main shopping streets in the Innere Stadt are the pedestrian-only thoroughfares of Kärntner Strasse, Graben and Kohlmarkt. Mainly up-market and specialist shops are found here. The Ringstrassen Galerien is a shopping complex off Kärntner Strasse, near the Ring. Generally speaking, outside the Ring is where you'll find shops catering for those with shallower pockets. Mariahilfer Strasse is regarded as the best shopping street, particularly the stretch between the Ring and Westbahnhof, and has large department stores like Gerngross which are mostly missing from the central zone. Other prime shopping streets are Landstrasser Hauptstrasse, Favoritenstrasse and Alser Strasse. Within the city, the best shopping centre is Lugner City, 15 Gablenzgasse, not far from the Gürtel.

The area near the church in Mexikoplatz is an interesting place to have a wander. It has many shops selling cheap electrical goods and watches, and is also known as a location for obtaining goods on the black market. Various shady types will approach you on the pavement and offer foreign currency and other deals.

For major shopping expeditions, the Viennese head south of the city to Shopping City Süd, marketed simply as SCS. It's the biggest shopping centre in Austria (some claim in Europe) and is south of the city precincts at Vösendorf, near the junction of the A21 and A2. Take the free shuttle bus departing on the hour in shopping hours from opposite the Staatsoper (near tram No 2 stop). Get a stamp in IKEA to get the return leg free. The Lokalbahn service to Baden, departing opposite Hotel Bristol in Opernring, stops at SCS (every 15 minutes; fare AS34, or AS17 if you already have a city travel card).

Markets

The biggest and best known market is the Naschmarkt, 6 Linke Wienzeile. It's a 'farmer's market', mainly consisting of meat, fruit and vegetable stalls, but there are some clothes and curios. Prices are said to get lower the farther from the Ring end you go. Opening times are Monday to Friday from 8 am to 6 pm, and Saturday from 8 am to 1 pm. The Naschmarkt is also a good place to eat cheaply in snack bars.

On Saturday from 8 am to 6 pm a flea market (*Flohmarkt*) is tacked onto the south-western end, extending for several blocks. It's very atmospheric and shouldn't be missed, with goods piled up in apparent chaos on the walkway. You can find anything you want (and everything you don't want): books, clothes, records, ancient electrical goods, old postcards, ornaments, carpets... you name it. I even saw a blow-up doll (second-hand, of course). Bargain for prices here.

Food markets are also at 16 Brunnengasse between Thaliastrasse and Gaullachergasse, and around the intersection of Landstrasser Hauptstrasse and Salmgasse.

Souvenirs & Crafts

There are various souvenir shops in the arcade connecting the old and new Hofburgs, selling artefacts such as mugs, steins, dolls, petit-point embroidery, porcelain Lipizzaner stallions and so on.

The Augarten Porcelain Factory (☎ 512 14 94), 1 Stock im Eisen Platz and 6 Mariahilfer Strasse 99, produces a variety of gifts and ornaments, including Lipizzaners. A specialist outlet for porcelain and crystal is Albin Denk, 1 Graben 13.

Österreichische Werkstätten (☎ 512 24 18), 1 Kärntner Strasse 6, has jewellery, handicrafts and ornaments. J & S Lobmeyer, at No 26, is well known for glassware, and has a small museum.

Art & Antiques

Selling works of art is big business; check the auctions at the state-owned Dorotheum, 1 Dorotheergasse 17. It was founded in 1707 by Josef I and it's interesting to watch the proceedings even if you don't intend to buy anything. Lots can be inspected in advance with the opening prices marked. If you don't have the confidence to bid you can commission an agent to do it for you. A range of objects wind up for sale, not only expensive antiques but also relatively undistinguished household nick-nacks. There are many antiques and art galleries along Dorotheergasse and the surrounding streets.

Cameras & Electrical Goods

Niedermeyer has over 40 branches in Vienna, including a huge one at 9 Alser Strasse 28-30 (☎ 43 06 020), three on Mariahilfer Strasse (Nos 51, 102 and 132), and at 1 Graben 11. Foto Nettig has over 20 branches, including at Lugner City (☎ 982 37 28), 1 Kärntner Strasse 14, 15 Mariahilfer Strasse 195, and opposite Franz Josefs Bahnhof. The larger branches of both chains also sell audio-visual and computer goods.

GETTING THERE & AWAY
Air

Vienna is the main centre for international flights – see the Getting There & Away chapter earlier in this book for details. Many airline offices are on Opernring opposite the Staatsoper, and appear in the Gelbe Seiten telephone book under *Fluggesellschaften*. Offices include:

Aer Lingus
    19 Scheibengasse 12 (☎ 369 28 85)
Air France
    1 Kärntner Strasse 49 (☎ 514 180)
American Airlines
    1 Ballgasse 5 (☎ 513 95 090)
Austrian Airlines
    1 Kärntner Ring 18 (☎ 505 57 570)
British Airways (BA)
    1 Kärntner Ring 10 (☎ 505 76 910)
Lauda Air
    1 Opernring 6 (☎ 514 770)
Lufthansa
    1 Opernring 1/R (☎ 588 360)
South African Airways (SAA)
    1 Opernring 1/R (☎ 587 15 85)
Swissair
    As for Austrian Airlines
TWA
    1 Opernring 1/R/742 (☎ 587 68 680)

Bus

National Bundesbuses arrive and depart from the Wien Mitte central bus station. Many regional destinations are serviced; routes are displayed near the Bundesbus ticket counters. For international buses, see the Getting There & Away chapter.

Train

Vienna has excellent train connections to

Europe and the rest of Austria. Check with information centres in train stations or telephone the 24-hour information line (☎ 1717) for the best way to go: not all destinations are exclusively serviced by one station and schedules are subject to change. All the following stations (except Meidling) have lockers, money-exchange, Bankomats, and places to eat and buy provisions.

Westbahnhof This is one of the main entry points to Vienna. Westbahnhof has trains to western and northern Europe and western Austria. Approximately hourly services head to Salzburg; some continue to Munich and terminate in Paris Est. Four trains a day run to Zürich (AS1066); the one departing at 9.25 pm is a sleeper service (AS1064, plus AS120 for fold-down seat, AS280 for couchette). A direct train goes to Athens at 7.05 pm (via Bucharest), and seven go to Budapest (AS326; three to four hours). Westbahnhof is also a station on U-Bahn lines U3 and U6, and many trams stop outside it.

Südbahnhof This is the other main train station. It has trains to Italy, the Czech Republic, Slovakia, Hungary (once daily to Budapest) and Poland. Direct trains depart every two hours to Graz, and four a day go to Rome via Venice and Florence. Four trains a day go to Bratislava (AS94); and five (four at weekends) go to Prague (AS410; five hours), some of which continue to Berlin. Trams D (to the Ring and Franz Josefs Bahnhof) and O (to Wien Mitte and Praterstern) stop outside. The quickest way to transfer to Westbahnhof is to take the S-Bahn to Meidling and then the U6.

Franz Josefs Bahnhof This handles regional and local trains, including trains to Tulln, Krems and the Wachau region. It also has two trains a day to Prague (AS390; 5½ hours). From outside, tram D goes to the Ring and tram No 5 goes to Westbahnhof (via Kaiserstrasse) in one direction and Praterstern (Wien Nord) in the other.

Other Stations Wien Mitte is used for local trains, and is adjacent to the Landstrasse stop on the U3. Wien Nord has local and regional trains, including the airport service which also stops at Wien Mitte. It's at the Praterstern stop on the U1. Praterstern is a hub for many tram routes. Meidling is the station for the weekday service to Eisenstadt; it is linked to the Philadelphiabrücke stop on the U6.

Car & Motorbike
Driving into Vienna is straightforward: the A1 from Linz and Salzburg and the A2 from Graz join the Gürtel ring road; the A4 from the airport leads directly to the Ring, and the A22 runs to the centre along the north bank of the Danube.

Rental Offices See the Getting Around chapter earlier in this book for a comparison of rental charges.

Hertz
    1 Kärntner Ring 17 (☎ 512 86 77). The central reservations office number in Vienna is ☎ 713 15 96.
Europcar
    1 Kärntner Ring 14 (☎ 505 29 47)
Eurodollar (ARAC Autovermietung)
    1 Schubertring 9 (☎ 714 67 17)
Avis
    1 Opernring 1 (☎ 587 62 41)
Budget
    1 Börsegasse 12 (☎ 535 09 91)

All these companies have an airport office.

Motorbike rental is at 2 Rad-Börse (☎ 24 85 95), 2 Praterstern 47. It has various Hondas available, ranging from a CB250 Nighthawk (AS590; AS2.50 per km) to a Goldwing 1500 cc (AS2990; AS6 per km). These rates are for 24 hours and include 100 km free. The weekend rates (5 pm Friday to 10 am Monday) include 200 km and are AS1390 and AS6990 respectively.

Hitching
Before you start hitching, take public transport to the main traffic routes in the suburbs. Heading west from Vienna, the lay-by across

the footbridge from the U4 Unter St Veit stop has been recommended.

Vienna has two agencies that link hitchers and drivers. Mitfahrzentrale Wien (☎ 715 00 66), 3 Invalidenstrasse 15, is open Monday to Friday from 9 am to 6 pm and Saturday to 1 pm. Examples of fares are Salzburg AS230, Innsbruck AS280, Klagenfurt AS190, Vorarlberg AS380, Brussels AS650, Cologne AS470, Frankfurt AS470 and Munich AS310. Telephone to check availability before going to the office. Lifts across Austria are limited, but there are usually many cars going into Germany. If you're offering a lift, visit the office in person. Drivers get paid the balance of the fees after the office takes its cut. Mitfahrzentrale Josefstadt (☎ 408 22 10), 8 Daungasse 1A, has similar rates.

Boat
Steamers head west and fast hydrofoils east. See the Getting There & Away and the Lower Austria chapters for details.

GETTING AROUND
To/From the Airport
Wien Schwechat Airport (☎ 711 10) is 19 km east of the city centre. The cheapest way to get to the airport is by S-Bahn on line S7. The fare is AS34, or AS17 if you have a city pass. Trains leave from Wien Nord usually at 29 and 53 minutes past the hour, calling at Wien Mitte three minutes later. The trip takes about 30 minutes and the first/last train departs at 5.09 am/9.45 pm. In the opposite direction, trains usually depart at three and 39 minutes past the hour, with the first/last service at 5.11 am/10.16 pm.

Buses run from the City Air Terminal at the Hotel Hilton to the airport every 20 or 30 minutes from 5 am (6 am in the opposite direction) to midnight, and take 20 minutes. From 1 April to 31 October buses also run hourly during the night. Airport buses run from Westbahnhof between 5.40 am and 11.40 pm every one or two hours, stopping at Südbahnhof after 15 minutes. The fare for all these buses is AS70. For more information, phone ☎ 58 00 33 369.

If taking a taxi is the only option, expect to pay around AS350; this will be the metered fare plus a AS120 supplement for the driver's return trip to the city. Cityrama (☎ 534 13 13) offers airport transfers for up to four passengers for the fixed price of AS360.

Public Transport
Vienna has a comprehensive and unified public transport network that is one of the most efficient in Europe. Flat-fare tickets are valid for trams, buses, the U-Bahn (the underground metro system) and the S-Bahn (trains to the suburbs; Inter-Rail, Eurail, and Austrian rail passes are also valid on these). Services are frequent, and you rarely have to wait more than five or 10 minutes for something to turn up. Public transport kicks off around 5 or 6 am. Buses and trams usually finish by midnight, though some S-Bahn and U-Bahn services may continue to 1 am.

Buses tend to cover a wider area than trams and always have a number followed by an 'A' or 'B'. These usually link to a tram number, eg bus 38A connects with tram 38, and bus 72A continues from the terminus of tram 72.

Night buses run on Friday and Saturday nights from 12.30 to 4 am, with half-hourly or hourly departures. All eight buses depart from Schwedenplatz; the AS25 fare is not covered by daily passes.

Transport routes are shown on the free tourist office map. For a more detailed listing, buy a map (AS15) from a Vienna Line ticket office, located in many U-Bahn stations. In addition, transport information offices are at Karlsplatz, Stephansplatz and Westbahnhof (open Monday to Friday from 6.30 am to 6.30 pm and weekends and holidays from 8.30 am to 4 pm), and at Landstrasse, Volkstheater, Philadelphiabrücke and Praterstern (open Monday to Friday from 7 am to 6.30 pm). For public transport information in German, call ☎ 7909 105.

Tickets & Passes Single tickets bought on the bus or tram cost AS20. U-Bahn stations

SIMON BRACKEN

The fiacre, a horse-drawn open carriage, is a popular tourist attraction around central Vienna

have VOR ticket machines selling single tickets for AS17 each or AS85 for a block of five.

Daily city passes (*Stunden-Netzkarte*) are the better deal for extensive sightseeing. Costs are AS50 (valid 24 hours from first use) and AS130 (valid 72 hours). An eight-day, multiple-user pass, called an *Acht-TageStreifenkarte* , costs AS265 and is valid for eight freely-chosen days for one person, one day for eight people etc. All these can be bought from ticket offices, Tabak shops and VOR machines.

Single tickets bought in VOR machines are valid for immediate use; all other tickets, no matter where bought, must be validated at the start of the journey in the blue boxes (inside buses and trams, beside U-Bahn escalators). Children aged six to 15 travel for half-price; younger children travel free. Senior citizens are eligible for special tickets. VOR machines give change for AS100 notes only – use the correct money otherwise.

Ticket offices and Tabak shops sell transferable passes: weekly (Monday to Sunday) for AS142, monthly (calender month) for AS500 and yearly for AS4700. They also sell four-single ticket blocks for AS68.

Taxi

Taxis are metered for city journeys. The flag fall starts at AS24 (AS25 on Sundays, holidays and from 11 pm to 6 am). The rate is then AS11 per km (AS13 on Sunday and public holidays) in AS2 increments, plus AS2 per 29 seconds of being stuck in traffic. The rate for trips outside the city borders is usually double but try negotiating. Taxis are found by train stations, top hotels, or can simply be flagged down in the street. There is an AS12 surcharge for phoning a radio taxi; numbers to call are ☎ 31 300, ☎ 40 100, ☎ 60 160, ☎ 81 400 and ☎ 91 011.

Car & Motorbike

Taking public transport is an easier option than driving in the city centre. Irrespective of the complications created by one-way streets, you'll find it inconvenient or expensive to park in the centre. Underground parking garages include those by the Staatsoper on Kärntner Strasse, in front of the Rathaus and at Stephansplatz. The Staatsoper garage (open 24 hours) charges AS40 per hour, AS450 for the first 24 hours and AS300 for subsequent 24-hour periods. Garages outside the Innere Stadt are cheaper.

All the Innere Stadt is now a blue parking zone (except where parking is prohibited altogether), allowing a maximum 1½ hours between 9 am and 7 pm from Monday to Friday. Vouchers (Parkschein) for parking on these streets cost AS6 per 30 minutes. Blue zones are gradually creeping into the districts bordering the Ring, though there you can still find white zones with no time restrictions on parking.

Petrol stations can be found in the city (eg on 7 Burggasse, 1 Börsegasse, and 1 Schmerlingplatz) and some are self-service. Very late at night, you may find the only stations open are near the autobahn exits. The ÖAMTC (☎ 0222-71 19 90) is at Schubertring 1-3.

Bicycle
There are 480 km of bicycle tracks in and around Vienna, including along the banks of the Danube. Pick up the Nützliche Tips für Radfahrer booklet from the tourist office, showing circular bike tours. This also lists bike-rental places (Radverleih). Westbahnhof, Südbahnhof, Wien Nord and Floridsdorf train stations all rent bikes. Returns up to midnight are possible at Westbahnhof. Bikes can be carried on the S-Bahn and U-Bahn (except U6) between certain hours. The tourist office also has a See Vienna By Bike leaflet.

Walking
The sights in the Innere Stadt can be easily seen on foot; indeed, the main arteries of

Kärntner Strasse, Graben and Kohlmarkt are pedestrian-only. To visit anything else you'd do best to buy a transport pass.

Fiacres
More of a tourist novelty than a mode of transport, fiacres (Fiakers) are traditional-style open carriages drawn by pairs of horses, and can be found lined up at St Stephen's, Albertinaplatz, and Heldenplatz at the Hofburg. Commanding prices of AS400 for a 20-minute trot, these horses must be among Vienna's richest inhabitants. Drivers generally speak English and point out places of interest en route.

Tours
Vienna Sightseeing Tours (☎ 712 46 830; fax 712 46 8377), 3 Stelzhamergasse 4/11, offers coach tours of the city and surrounds, with free hotel pick-up. Some tours take in performances (eg by the Vienna Boys' Choir and the Lipizzaner stallions). Vienna Cityrama (☎ 534 13 12; fax 534 13 22) offers a similar programme and prices. Both companies allow a child's fare only up to age 12.

Reisebuchladen (☎ 317 33 84), 9 Kolingasse 6, conducts an alternative to the normal sightseeing tour, concentrating on 'Red Vienna' and Art-Nouveau sights. It costs AS280 per person and the guide is not afraid to reveal uncomplimentary details about Vienna. Tours in English are possible, depending upon demand.

DDSG (☎ 727 50 451) offers 'Danube Sightseeing Tours' along the Danube canal, departing from Schwedenbrücke in the Ring (one a day in April and October, four a day in summer). The cost is AS200 or AS150, with discounts for families. DDSG also conducts dinner/dance cruises.

From May to October on weekends, 'old-time tram' tours depart from Karlsplatz (AS200); for information call ☎ 587 31 86. For a short guided walk see Central Vienna Walking Tour earlier in this chapter.

Burgenland

Austria and Hungary contested ownership of this region for centuries. Hungary appeared to have won out when Austria's Ferdinand III relinquished it in 1647, yet Hungary itself became wholly or partially subservient to the Habsburgs in the ensuing years. Austria finally lost control of Hungary after WW I, but the German-speaking western region of Hungary went to Austria under the Treaty of St Germain in 1919.

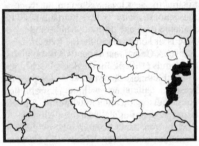

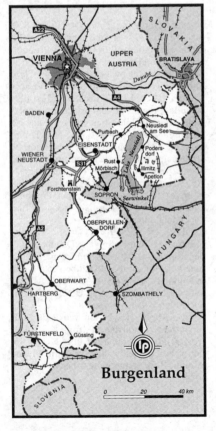

A further twist was to follow. The people of Sopron, the natural capital of the region, voted in 1921 to stay in Hungary. Some Austrians maintain that the Hungarian government manipulated the vote by importing extra Hungarian citizens on the day. The new province was named Burgenland, not for its numerous castles, but for the 'burg' suffix of the old western Hungarian district names. Eisenstadt became the capital. Across the border, Sopron has meanwhile become little more than a shopping centre for Austrians seeking lower Hungarian prices.

Burgenland is a province of tree-lined hills, vineyards and orchards. Wine production is particularly important for this agricultural province. Tasting the local wines, either over a meal or on an organised tour, is popular with visitors. The most interesting region for tourists is Lake Neusiedl and the resorts nearby.

Orientation & Information

Burgenland occupies 3965 sq km and is one-third forested. Geschriebenstein, at a mere 884 metres, is the highest point; Illmitz at 117 metres is Austria's lowest town. The province is home to 270,000 people, mostly living in the north. One-fifth of the area is owned by the Esterházys, one of the richest families in Austria.

144

Of all the regions in Austria, the province receives the fewest foreign visitors – just 803,000 overnight stays a year, little more than one-third of the figure for Lower Austria, the next least-visited province. As a consequence there is less tourist literature available than one normally finds, and what there is, is sometimes only in German.

The provincial tourist board is Burgenland Tourismus (☎ 02682-633 84 16; fax 633 84 20), Schloss Esterházy, A-7000 Eisenstadt. Personal callers are welcome (see under Eisenstadt for opening times). Pick up the *Strassenkarte*, a detailed map of the province; bicycle routes, camp sites and other attractions are marked. The board's *Burgenland Weindegustationen* leaflet gives information on wine-tasting.

Eisenstadt

• *pop 11,000* • *181 m* • ☎ *(02682)*

Eisenstadt received its town charter in 1373, and achieved greater status in 1622 when it became the residence of the Esterházys, a powerful Hungarian family. In 1648 Eisenstadt was granted the status of *Freistadt* (free city or free state). It has been the provincial capital since 1925.

Eisenstadt really milks its connection with the seminal 18th-century musician and composer Josef Haydn. 'Fascinating, not only for Josef Haydn', the town's tourist literature trumpets. Unfortunately, beyond the traces of Mozart's mentor, the sources of this fascination are somewhat obscure.

Orientation & Information

Eisenstadt lies 50 km south of Vienna. The train station is 10 minutes walk from the pedestrian-only Hauptstrasse, a street with cafés, shops and restaurants. The tourist office (☎ 67 3 90) is at Schubertplatz 1, around the side of the Hotel Burgenland. Good free maps are available, and a brochure listing hotels, private rooms and museum openings and prices. The office is open daily from 9 am to noon and 2 to 5 pm (no lunch

break in summer; closed weekends in winter).

At the other end of Hauptstrasse is the Esterházy Palace, the site of the provincial tourist office (☎ 63 384 16). The office is open daily from 9 am to 5 pm, except at weekends from 30 October to 31 April.

A post office and Bundesbus ticket office are by the cathedral at Domplatz. The main post office (Postamt 7000) is on Pfarrgasse and is open weekdays from 7 am to 7 pm, Saturday from 7 am to 4 pm, and Sunday and holidays from 8 to 10 am.

Things to See

Josef Haydn revealed that Eisenstadt was 'where I wish to live and to die'. He achieved the former, being a resident of 31 years, but it was in Vienna that he finally tinkled his last tune. He also rather carelessly omitted any directive about his preferred residency after death. His skull was stolen from a temporary grave shortly after he died in 1809, after which it ended up on display in a Viennese museum. The headless cadaver was subsequently returned to Eisenstadt (in 1932), but it wasn't until 1954 that the skull joined it.

Haydn's white marble tomb can now be

Josef Haydn was a resident of Eisenstadt for 31 years

●●● ⌒⌒ ●●● ⌒⌒ ●●● ⌒⌒ ●●● ⌒⌒ ●●●

Who's in the Money

The richest Austrian is the industrialist Alexander Kahane, with assets worth AS24 billion. Next comes the Piëch-Porsche family, with AS20 billion. The Esterházys are third on the list, with the bulk of their AS15 billion fortune in the hands of Melinda Esterházy who, despite owning some 800 sq kms of Burgenland, has opted to live in Switzerland. She is in her 70s and has no direct heirs.

Young women looking to marry into money could do worse than seek out Franz VI Mayr-Melnhof-Saurau (telephone number not available). This Austrian 18-year-old has some AS10 billion in the bank. Similarly wealthy is Karl Wlaschek, owner of the Billa supermarket chain. ■

●●● ⌒⌒ ●●● ⌒⌒ ●●● ⌒⌒ ●●● ⌒⌒ ●●●

seen in the **Bergkirche**. The church itself is remarkable for the Kalvarienberg, a unique Calvary display round the other side of the church. Life-sized figures depict the Stations of the Cross in a series of suitably austere, dungeon-like rooms. It's open between 1 April and 31 October daily from 9 am to noon and 2 to 5 pm; entry is AS20 (students AS10) and includes the mausoleum.

The **Esterházy Palace** dates from the 14th century. It was restored initially in Baroque, and later in classical style. The provincial government occupies two-thirds of the interior, and the rest can be visited by guided tour. Egotists will enjoy the multi-reflections in the mirror corridor. The highlight is the frescoed Haydn Hall; its former marble floor was replaced by an aesthetically inferior but acoustically superior wooden floor (it's rated the second-best concert hall in Austria, after Vienna's Musikverein). The hall is where Haydn conducted the orchestra on a near nightly basis; he worked for the Esterházys in this capacity from 1761 to 1790. The palace is open the same hours as the provincial tourist office. Entry costs AS20 (AS10 for students) for a 40-minute guided tour (sometimes in English, or ask for the English notes).

Haydn's former residence, **Haydn Haus**, Josef Haydn Gasse 21, is now a small museum containing Haydn memorabilia. It's open daily from Easter Sunday to 30 October; entry is AS20, students AS10 and families AS40. A reduced, combined ticket can be purchased to include admission to the **Landesmuseum**, Museumgasse 5, which otherwise costs AS30 to enter (students AS15, families AS60). The collection includes Roman mosaics, ancient artefacts, 20th-century history (with some good period posters), wine-making equipment, and a Franz Liszt room (complete with a warty death mask of the Hungarian composer). It's open Tuesday to Sunday from 9 am to noon and 1 to 5 pm. The **Jewish Museum**, Unterbergstrasse 6, is primarily concerned with the Jewish religion. It's open daily, except Monday, from early May to late October. Entry is AS30 (students AS20).

Festivals

Behind the Esterházy Palace is the large, relaxing Schlosspark, the setting for the Fest der 1000 Weine in late August.

A Haydn festival, the Haydntage, is staged (mostly in the Haydn Hall and the Bergkirche) from early to mid-September. It's the high point in Eisenstadt's cultural calendar. Contact the Haydnfestspiele Büro (☎ 61 86 60; fax 61 8 05), Esterházy Palace. Free frolics occur in the EisenSTADTfest in early June.

Places to Stay

Eisenstadt has only a few hotels, though the tourist office can help find accommodation. There are even fewer private rooms: *Toth Ewald* (☎ 64 2 22), Vicedom 5, off Domplatz, has rooms with shower/WC for about AS220 per person, with cooking facilities and a TV area. But it's full with students, except in July and August.

Gasthof Kutsenits (☎ 63 5 11), Mattersburger Strasse 30, south of the city centre, is OK if you have your own transport: singles/doubles are AS250/400, or AS300/500 with shower/WC.

Das Sportliche Haus (☎ 62 326 12),

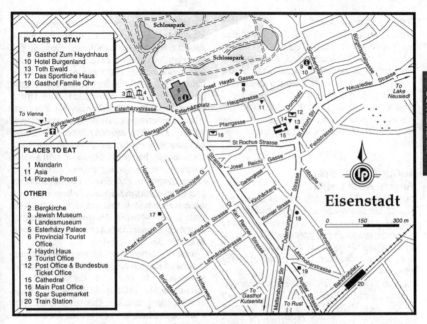

PLACES TO STAY
8 Gasthof Zum Haydnhaus
10 Hotel Burgenland
13 Toth Ewald
17 Das Sportliche Haus
19 Gasthof Familie Ohr

PLACES TO EAT
1 Mandarin
11 Asia
14 Pizzeria Pronti

OTHER
2 Bergkirche
3 Jewish Museum
4 Landesmuseum
5 Esterházy Palace
6 Provincial Tourist Office
7 Haydn Haus
9 Tourist Office
12 Post Office & Bundesbus Ticket Office
15 Cathedral
16 Main Post Office
18 Spar Supermarket
20 Train Station

Eisenstadt

BURGENLAND

Hotterweg 67, is near the city's football grounds. Rooms with shower/WC are AS295/540, rising to AS315/590 in winter (the football season). *Gasthof Zum Haydnhaus* (☎ 64 36 36), Josef Haydn Gasse 24, is conveniently situated. All rooms have private shower/WC and cost AS400/576.

The only three-star hotel is *Gasthof Familie Ohr* (☎ 62 4 81), Ruster Strasse 51, near the train station. Rooms have a shower/WC, cable TV and telephone and singles/doubles cost from AS510/780.

Hotel Burgenland (☎ 696), Schubertplatz, is the only four-star place. Rooms have all requisite facilities and cost AS1035/1490. The indoor swimming pool and sauna are free for guests.

Places to Eat
On Domplatz is a *Billa* supermarket, open Monday to Friday from 7.30 am to 6.30 pm (till 8 pm on Friday) and Saturday from 7 am to 1 pm, and there's also a Spar supermarket on Bahnstrasse.

For lunch, think Chinese: *Asia*, Hauptstrasse 32, and *Mandarin*, Wiener Strasse 2, both have excellent three-course menus from AS49 and AS55 respectively. Evening meals start from around AS75 and they're open daily.

Hidden away down Vicedom is *Pizzeria Pronti*, where decent-sized pizzas start at AS51 (closed Monday, unless it's a holiday).

The following are also worth trying for food: see Places to Stay for locations. *Gasthof Zum Haydnhaus* is open daily and has regional and Austrian dishes for AS55 to AS145, served in a vaulted dining area. *Gasthof Familie Ohr* is another good place for Pannonian (west-Hungarian) cooking (closed Monday). The *Café-Restaurant Bienenkorb* in the Hotel Burgenland is open daily and has Austrian and international dishes for AS115 to AS225, plus a cheaper lunch menu.

Getting There & Away

Trains depart from Vienna's Südbahnhof every two hours from 6.20 am (AS68; 90 minutes); you'll have to change in Neusiedl. On weekdays, a quicker option is to take the direct hourly train in the morning from Wien Meidling (AS68; 65 minutes). Buses take 70 minutes and depart from Wien Mitte (AS85). Wiener Neustadt is on the Vienna-Graz train route: buses from there to Eisenstadt take 30 minutes.

AROUND EISENSTADT
Forchtenstein Castle

This castle, 20 km south-west of Eisenstadt and 15 km south-east of Wiener Neustadt, is the best known of Burgenland's many castles. It is a large and imposing pile, topped by a circular tower and an onion dome. It was built in the 14th century and enlarged by the Esterházys in 1635, in whose hands it remains. The extensive arms and armour collection can be visited by guided tour (April to October, daily; March and November, weekends only). Franz Grillparzer's plays are performed annually in a summer festival. Call ☎ 02626-63 125 for information.

Getting There & Away Forchtenstein is not on a train line, though Bundesbuses go there from both Eisenstadt and Wiener Neustadt.

Lake Neusiedl

Bird-watchers flock to Lake Neusiedl (Neusiedler See), the only steppe lake in central Europe. It's ringed by a wetland area of reed beds, providing an ideal breeding ground for nearly 300 bird species. The mecca for ornithologists is the Seewinkel area (see the entry later in this chapter).

Lake Neusiedl is only one to two metres deep and there is no natural outlet, giving the water a slightly saline quality. The shallowness means the water warms quickly in summer. Water sports are a big draw: boats and windsurfers are for hire at resorts around the lake, and there are many bathing beaches. Beaches are invariably cordoned off and a modest fee (up to AS20) is charged for admission. Note that even if you have your own windsurfer, you have to pay a daily charge (about AS50). Swimming is also possible in some of the Seewinkel lakes. Horse riding and fishing are other popular pursuits.

For ambitious cycling tours, a cycle track winds all the way around the reed beds; you can complete the full circuit of the lake (it'll take more than one day to do this) but remember to take your passport as the southern section is in Hungary. The boat services that cross the lake will take bikes. There's a special Fahrradbus that loops round the lake once a day between Mörbisch and Illmitz, going via Neusiedl am See and all the resorts in between.

In early September the national triathlon is held at Lake Neusiedl. Watch 500 people voluntarily put themselves through hell – 42 km of running, 180 km of cycling and 3.8 km of swimming inside a nine-hour span. You could even join in: contact the Podersdorf tourist office (see the Podersdorf section in this chapter).

Lake Neusiedl is a place to be visited in summer; tourist trade is much reduced in the winter, when many hotels and restaurants close down. If you stay overnight, the VIP card, provided by the tourist office at the resort you are staying at (upon receipt of your accommodation slip), will give useful discounts, including free entry to various beaches.

NEUSIEDL AM SEE
• *pop 4000* • *133 m* • ☎ *(02167)*

Neusiedl is the region's main town, and easily accessible from Vienna. But there's no real reason to base yourself here; the smaller places round the lake are preferable – they are closer to the lake and have a more pleasant and more scenic atmosphere.

Neusiedl has a tourist office (☎ 22 29) in the town hall on Hauptplatz. The lake (where there's bathing and boating) is a 10-minute walk though the reed beds from the edge of town, or 20 minutes from Hauptplatz. Neusiedl also has a couple of museums, and a tiny ruin (the Tabor) with a view of the lake.

The tourist office will help you find somewhere to stay. The town has the region's only HI *youth hostel* (☎ 22 52), at Herbergsgasse 1. It is open from March to November, but isn't conveniently situated. By foot, it's 15 minutes from both the train station and the tourist office, and 30 minutes from the lake. Beds are AS153 (AS133 for those aged under 19); sheets are AS15. Reception is open from 8 am to 2 pm and 5 to 10 pm.

Getting There & Away
Bundesbuses leave from outside the train station, including to Seewinkel. Regular trains from Vienna's Südbahnhof take 50 minutes and cost AS68. A train ticket scores a free ride on the bus to the centre of town, which is otherwise a 20-minute walk away. Occasional buses continue to the beach after stopping at Hauptplatz.

By road, the A4 from Vienna to Bratislava passes just north of the town.

RUST
- *pop 1700* • *121 m* • ☎ *(02685)*

Rust, 14 km east of Eisenstadt, is famous for storks and wine, though its name derives from *Rüster*, the German word for elm tree.

The town's prosperity has been based on wine for centuries. In 1524 the emperor granted local vintners the right to display the letter 'R' on their wine barrels; corks today still bear this insignia.

Orientation & Information
Bundesbuses unload at the post office, 100 metres from Conradplatz, which leads to the town hall and Rathausplatz.

The tourist office (☎ 502) is in the town hall and has lists of hotels and private rooms, and can give details of wine-tasting venues. It's open Monday to Friday from 8 am to noon and 2 to 6 pm, Saturday from 9 am to 4 pm and Sunday from 10 am to noon; from October to April, the office closes from Friday noon till Monday 8 am. There's a 24-hour accommodation notice board outside.

Things to See & Do
Rust's affluent past has left a legacy of attractive burghers' houses on and around the main squares. The **Fischerkirche**, at the northern end of Rathausplatz, is the oldest church in Rust (12th to 16th century).

Storks descend on Rust from the end of March, rear their young, then fly to new pastures in late August. Many homes in the

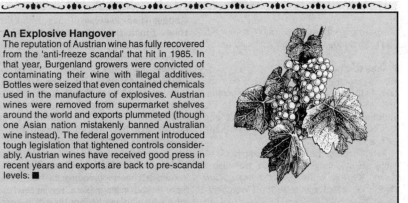

An Explosive Hangover
The reputation of Austrian wine has fully recovered from the 'anti-freeze scandal' that hit in 1985. In that year, Burgenland growers were convicted of contaminating their wine with illegal additives. Bottles were seized that even contained chemicals used in the manufacture of explosives. Austrian wines were removed from supermarket shelves around the world and exports plummeted (though one Asian nation mistakenly banned Australian wine instead). The federal government introduced tough legislation that tightened controls considerably. Austrian wines have received good press in recent years and exports are back to pre-scandal levels. ■

centre (particularly on Rathausplatz and Conradplatz) have a metal platform on the roof to entice storks to build a nest there. Recent preservation measures have seen an upturn in the formerly diminishing numbers of winged visitors: in 1994, six mothers reared 18 young. A good vantage point is attained from the tower of the Catholic church which is at the southern end of Rathausplatz. Entry is AS10 (students AS5)

The **lake** is 1.5 km down a reed-fringed road. Boat hire costs are: motor boats from AS70 (half an hour) to AS600 (one day), pedal boats from AS40 to AS420, and sailing boats from AS66 to AS540. There's also a

Many homes in Rust have a metal platform on the roof to entice storks to nest there

swimming pool (AS20 per day), mini-golf, and schools for windsurfing and sailing.

Places to Stay

Rust's *camping ground* (☎ 595) is near the lake. In the summer it costs AS45 per person, and AS35 each for a car and tent; in the shoulder seasons (April, September and October) prices are lower. There's a shop and a cheap restaurant.

Private rooms provide the cheapest beds: there are a couple of Zimmer frei places down Kraugartenweg. *Gästehaus Ruth* (☎ 277) is at Dr Ratz Gasse 1, off Weinberggasse. It has two singles and four doubles, all with shower, for AS250/440.

Pension Halwax (☎ 520), Oggauer Strasse 21, offers seven doubles for AS500 with own shower/WC. Rooms are clean and fresh, but the elderly Frau managing the pension doesn't speak English.

Stadt Rust (☎ 268), Rathausplatz 7, has doubles, some with private shower, for AS540. Its restaurant has fish specialities.

Places to Eat

Compile a picnic at the *Konsum* supermarket on Oggauer Strasse for consumption by the lake. It is open Monday to Friday from 7 am to noon and 2 to 7 pm (6 pm in winter), and Saturday from 1 am to noon.

For sit-down meals, look no farther than the many Buschenschenken around town. Many have outside tables in attractive courtyards. The tourist office can provide a list. A place with good food and wine is *Schandl* at Hauptstrasse 20, open Wednesday to Monday from 10 am to midnight. Meals cost AS70 to AS135 and wine is AS22 for a Viertel. *Kicker*, around the corner at Haydngasse 1, is open daily and sometimes has live music.

China-Restaurant Alles Gute, Zum Alten Stadttor 1, is open daily and has weekday lunch specials from AS55. The *Rathauskeller*, Rathausplatz 1, has vegetarian specialities. It's open daily, except Wednesday.

Getting There & Away

Buses run approximately hourly to/from Eisenstadt (AS34; half an hour trip). Services cease in the early evening. Rust receives many bicycle tourists, and several places in the centre rent bikes. Schiffahrt Gmeiner (☎ 493) sends boats across the lake to the shore by Illmitz (AS50).

MÖRBISCH

• *pop 2400*   •   ☎ *(02685)*

Six km down the lake from Rust, **Mörbisch** is just a couple of km short of the Hungarian border. It's worth spending an hour or so here, enjoying the relaxed atmosphere and the quaint whitewashed houses with hanging corn and flower-strewn balconies.

There's a tourist office (☎ 84 30) on the main street, Hauptstrasse 22. Staff can fill you in on the Seefestspiele, a summer operetta festival (mid-July to late August), and on the lakeside facilities. Plenty of pensions and private rooms await if you decide to stay the night. As in Rust, several Buschenschenken (on Hauptstrasse and elsewhere) will happily fill you full of food and wine.

Getting There & Away
By bus, the fare to Rust is AS17, though to/from Eisenstadt costs the same as Rust to Eisenstadt one-way: AS34. South of Mörbisch, cyclists may cross into Hungary but there's no road through for cars. To cross the border, car drivers need to return almost to Eisenstadt and then take highway 16 to Sopron.

Dreschler (☎ 88 20) sends five boats a day across the lake to Illmitz, between May and September, and also conducts a circular tour daily at 1 pm.

SEEWINKEL
Naturalists are particularly attracted to this area on the eastern shore of the lake. It's a national park of grassland and wetland interspersed with myriad small lakes. Tourist offices have information in English on the park and the species of bird that visit particular lakes.

The protected areas cannot be directly accessed by visitors, so to really get into the **bird-watching** you need a pair of binoculars. There are viewing stands along the way. Even if you're not an ornithologist, this is an excellent area to explore by foot or especially bicycle. The vineyards, reed beds, shimmering waters and constant bird calls make this an enchanting region for an excursion.

There are no hills in the Seewinkel, so a cheaper, gearless bicycle from the rental places is all you need. Another option is to go by *Pferdewagen*, a carriage pulled by ponies: tours cost AS300 or AS500 (between up to 19 people) for one or two hours.

The town of **Illmitz** is surrounded by the national park area and makes a good base. Its tourist office (☎ 02175-23 83), at Obere Hauptplatz 2-4, can provide information on both the town and Seewinkel. There are lots of pensions and private rooms available. Like Rust, Illmitz has some rooftop platforms to encourage storks to nest. The beach at Illmitz is three km from the town. From there, Gangl (☎ 02175-21 58) has all types of boats for hire. It also sends hourly ferries in the summer across the lake to Mörbisch (AS60 one-way or AS100 return; bikes carried free).

Another possible base is nearby **Apetlon** (☎ 02175-22 20 for the tourist office); Podersdorf (see the following entry) is also convenient.

PODERSDORF
● *pop 2100* ● *121 m* ● ☎ *(02177)*
Podersdorf, on the eastern shore, is not only the most popular holiday destination on the lake, but also receives more visitors than anywhere else in Burgenland. The town owes this status to its position directly on the lake shore, made possible by the absence of reed beds in the immediate area. Podersdorf therefore offers the most convenient bathing opportunities on Lake Neusiedl, with a long grassy beach (AS20, free with VIP card, available from the Podersdorf tourist office) suitable for swimming, boating and windsurfing.

The town is also within easy reach of the protected lakes in the Seewinkel area: the nearest, the Stinkersee lakes, are five km to the south. Cyclists of all ages stream along the lakeside bike trail from the town. Various places in Podersdorf rent bikes. Tauber Melitta (☎ 22 04) on Strandplatz allows you to return machines up to 9 pm (a gearless bike costs AS95 per day, or AS85 with VIP card).

The tourist office (☎ 22 27) is at Hauptstrasse 2, and can help find accommodation. It's open daily in summer and on weekdays only in winter. There's also a computer screen in the entrance (accessible daily until late evening) that shows room vacancies.

Places to Stay & Eat

It's worth booking ahead in the high season, especially for the limited number of single rooms. The *camping ground* (☎ 22 79) is by the lake and open from 1 April to 30 October; it charges AS78 per adult, AS50 for a tent and AS60 for a car.

Seestrasse, the street leading from the beach to Hauptstrasse, has many small places to stay. *Ettl* (☎ 23 66) at No 46 has the advantage of offering guests free bicycles. Rooms with shower and WC are AS200 per person. *Steiner* (☎ 23 58), close to the beach at No 89, has rooms with or without private shower for AS160 to AS180 per person. It's actually a Heuriger, with cold food, wine for AS18 a Viertel and a nightly zither player. You might find this place a bit noisy if you like to go to bed early (it quietens down at 11.30 pm).

Haus Pannonia (☎ 22 45), Seezeile 20, is a three-star place with 64 beds (but only two single rooms) for AS300 to AS360 per person, and a sauna and restaurant.

There are various places to eat near the beach, most with outside tables. *Gasthof Kummer*, Strandplatz, has good food and low prices and is open daily. *Gasthaus Zum Heiligen Urban*, on the corner of Seestrasse and Neusiedler Strasse, has a small garden: a cheap but tasty dish is the Dorschfilet (AS65), fish in batter with a generous portion of potatoes and salad.

Getting There & Away

Bundesbuses from Neusiedl am See to Podersdorf leave approximately hourly on weekdays but are infrequent on weekends; they cost AS34 and continue to Illmitz and Apetlon. Ferries cross the lake between Podersdorf and Purbach.

Styria

Occupying 16,387 sq km, Styria (Steiermark) is the second-largest province and has a population of almost 1.2 million. It encompasses mountain ranges, forested hills and green pastures. The main river, the Mur, flows through the capital city, Graz.

Graz is a major tourist attraction, but other places worth visiting in Styria include the pilgrimage site of Mariazell and the open-air museum at Stübing. The Lipizzaner stud farm at Piber and St Barbara Church at nearby Bärnbach combine to make an excellent day trip. Styria accounts for about 5% of Austria's wine production, and exploring the wine routes south of Graz is a popular excursion for those with their own transport. Styria extends as far as the Salzkammergut to the north-west, and this holiday region is dealt with in a separate chapter.

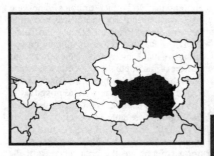

History

When Duke Ottokar IV died without an heir in 1192, Styria passed to the Babenberg duke, Leopold V, as an inheritance. Control subsequently fell to King Ottokar of

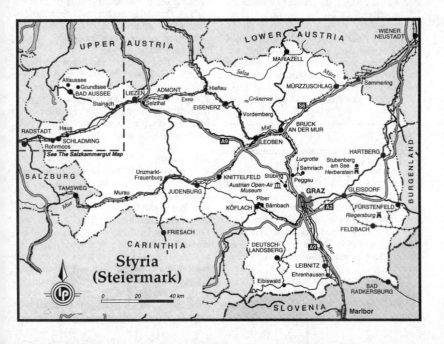

Bohemia and then (from 1276) to the Habsburgs. In the following century the population grew, but the next two centuries saw local conflicts, invasions by the Turks and Hungarians, and other troubles. The year 1480 was particularly dire; it was known as the year of the 'Plagues of God' – the Turks, the Black Death and locusts all paid unwelcome visits. Exactly 200 years later one quarter of the population of Graz was wiped out in a further epidemic of the Black Death.

The Turkish threat was removed after 1683 and the economy and infrastructure of the region were able to develop. Then, in 1779, 1805 and 1809, it was the turn of the French to invade. In WW II, the first Allied troops to liberate the area were from the Soviet Union, followed by the British, who occupied Graz until 1955.

Orientation & Information
Styria is in south-east Austria and is bordered by Slovenia. Although Graz is the capital, Bruck an der Mur is the main railhead for the region. Styria is subdivided into various tourist regions, though information on the whole province is available to personal callers at the Graz city tourist office (see below). For information sent by post, contact the provincial tourist board: Steiermark Werbung (☎ 0316-40 30 33 0; fax 40 30 33 10), St Peter Hauptstrasse 243, A-8042 Graz.

Graz

• *pop 243,000* • *365 m* • ☎ *(0316)*
The green of the parks, the red of the rooftops and the blue of the river combine to make Graz an attractive city in which to linger. It has several interesting sights and is a good base for a variety of excursions. The large student population (some 40,000 in three universities) helps to make Graz lively after dark.

Graz was considered a city as early as 1189, and in 1379 it became the seat of the Leopold line of the Habsburgs. Friedrich III, King of Germany and Holy Roman Emperor,

resided here and left his famous motto, AEIOU (*Austria est imperare orbi universo*: Austria rules the world) inscribed in various places around town. In 1564, Graz became the administrative capital of Inner Austria, an area covering present-day Styria and Carinthia, and the former possessions of Carniola, Gorizia and Istria. Once strongly fortified against Turkish attack, Graz was one of the first European cities to dismantle its city walls (1784).

Today, the second-largest city in Austria hosts prestigious fairs and festivals and has an important opera house and theatre. Graz offers a lot, but skiing is not part of the package. Strange, therefore, that the city should have sought to host the 2002 Winter Olympics. Its bid was unsuccessful.

Orientation
Graz is dominated by the Schlossberg which rises over the medieval town centre. The Mur River cuts a north-south path west of the hill, dividing the old centre from the main train station. The east train station (Ostbahnhof) is south of the old town centre and close to the exhibition centre (Messegelände) where trade fairs are held.

Tram Nos 3 and 6 run from the main station to Hauptplatz in the centre. A number of streets radiate from this square, including Sporgasse, an important shopping street, and Herrengasse, the main pedestrian thoroughfare. Jakominiplatz is a major transport hub for local buses and trams.

Information
Tourist Offices There is an information office (☎ 91 68 37) in the main train station on platform 1. It's open daily from 9 am to 6 pm (5 pm Saturday, 3 pm Sunday and holidays). The main tourist office (☎ 83 52 41 11), Herrengasse 16, is open Monday to Friday from 9 am to 7 pm, Saturday to 6 pm, and Sunday and holidays from 10 am to 3 pm. Information is held on both the city and the province. Most of it is free, although there is a charge of AS10 for the *Old Town Walk* leaflet, which has a clear map of the centre and sightseeing descriptions on the

reverse. The free monthly events guide contains lots of useful information. The provincial tourist board (see the earlier Styria Orientation & Information section) sends information on Graz by post.

Money The main train station has a money exchange office and a Bankomat. Bankomats and banks are also to be found on Herrengasse.

American Express The American Express office (☎ 0316-81 70 10) is at Hamerlingasse 6. It offers both financial and travel services and will hold mail for clients.

Post & Telecommunications The main post office is at Neutorgasse 46 (Hauptpostamt Graz, A-8010), and is open 24 hours a day for international telephones and for money exchange. Another post office (Postamt A-8020) is by the main train station at Bahnhofgürtel 48, again with many services available 24 hours.

Foreign Consulates Foreign consulates in Graz include the following:

Italy
    Herrengasse 18 (☎ 81 59 61)
Slovenia
    Friedrichgasse 6 (☎ 82 30 45)
South Africa
    Villefortgasse 13 (☎ 32 25 48)
UK
    Schmiedgasse 10 (☎ 82 61 05)

Travel Agents ÖKISTA (☎ 32 24 82) has an office at Brandhofgasse 16. The passport travel agency (☎ 91 27 16), Mariahilfer Strasse 20, is good for charter flights to the UK and stocks travel books in English.

Bookshops English-language books can be found at Englische Buchhandlung (☎ 82 62 66), Tummelplatz 7. Buch und Presse in the main train station carries many books, magazines and newspapers in English.

Medical Services The main hospital is the Landeskrankenhaus (☎ 38 50) at Auen-

bruggerplatz. Unfallkrankenhaus (☎ 50 50), Göstingersrasse 24, provides emergency treatment.

Laundry Schnellwäscherei Jakomini (☎ 81 10 20), Jakominstrasse 25, will wash and dry a four-kg load for AS120. It's open Monday to Friday from 7.30 am to 6 pm.

Hauptplatz Area

Amid the clamour and bustle of Hauptplatz lies the Renaissance-style **Rathaus** (1550). The female figures around the central fountain in the square represent the four main rivers of the region: Mur, Enns, Drau and Sann. At **Saurau Palace** on Sporgasse a figure of a Turk glares down from under the roof, while on Hofgasse the 15th-century **castle** now contains government offices. At the far end of the courtyard, on the left under the arch inscribed with AEIOU, is an ingenious double staircase (1499) – the steps diverge and converge as they spiral. Beyond the passage is a grassy area with busts of famous people associated with Graz.

The town's **cathedral** is a late-Gothic building dating from the 15th century, though it only became a cathedral in 1786. The interior combines Gothic and Baroque

Holy Roman Emperor Freidrich III left his famous motto 'AEIOU - Austria Rules the World' inscribed around Graz

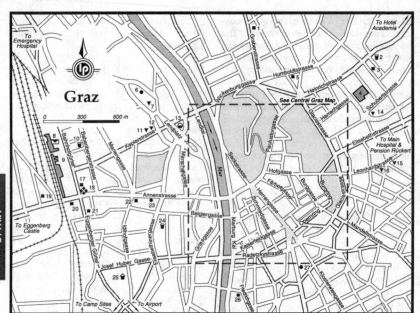

PLACES TO STAY

1	Schmid Greiner
3	Rosen-Hotel Steiermark
5	Pension Iris
17	Hotel Europa
19	Pension Lukas
20	Hotel Daniel
21	Hotel Strasser
22	Hotel Drei Raben
25	Youth Hostel

PLACES TO EAT

7	Food Market
11	La Pizza
12	Gao Ya
14	Mensa
15	Gasthaus Goldene Kugel
16	Girardikeller

OTHER

2	Bier Baron
4	University
6	Europcar
8	Post Office
9	Main Train Station
10	Babenbergerhof
13	GKB & Watzke Bus Stops
18	Forum Kaufhaus Shopping Centre
23	Billa Supermarket
24	Bang
26	Kiz-Kino
27	Laundrette

elements, with reticulated vaulting on the ceiling and many side altars. The exterior has a faded fresco showing the 1480 plagues.

The mannerist-Baroque **mausoleum** of Ferdinand II next door is a more impressive sight. It was created by an Italian architect, Pietro de Pomis, who spent nearly 20 years on the project from 1614. After his death,

Pietro Valnegro completed the structure. Inside, the exuberant stucco and frescoes were the work of Johann Bernhard Fischer von Erlach. Ferdinand, his wife, and his son are entombed in the crypt below, modestly set into the wall. Pride of place goes to the red marble sarcophagus of his parents, Charles II and Maria. However, only Maria lies within; Charles rests in Seckau Abbey, near Knittelfeld, and a former centre of the diocese of Styria. In a clever arrangement, the dome of the crypt has a hole in the centre, allowing you to look up into the larger dome above. The mausoleum is open Monday to Saturday from 11 am to noon and (May to September only) from 2 to 3 pm. Admission costs AS10 (AS5 children to 15 years).

Every day at 11 am, 3 and 6 pm figures emerge from an upper window in Glockenspielplatz to twirl to **Glockenspiel** music.

Armoury

At Herrengasse 16 is the armoury (Landeszeughaus), a sight not to be missed. It houses an incredible array of gleaming armour and weapons, enough to equip about 30,000 soldiers. Most of it dates from the 17th century, when the original armoury was built (in 1642). The purpose of the armoury was to provide a quick distribution point for equipping the local population when invasion was imminent. Some of the armour is beautifully engraved; other exhibits are crude and intimidating. The sheer weight of the metalware (such as the two-handed swords) suggests that battles were conducted in bizarre, staggering slow motion. The view from the 4th floor to the Italian Renaissance courtyard of the Styrian Parliament building (Landhaus) next door and the Schlossberg is perfect.

The armoury is open between 1 April and 31 October, Monday to Friday from 9 am to 5 pm, and on Saturday and Sunday to 1 pm. It forms part of the Landesmuseum Joanneum, Austria's oldest museum (founded 1811), whose collection is scattered in many institutions around town. Admission to each museum, including the armoury, is AS25 (AS10 for senior citizens, free for students).

Churches

Almost opposite the armoury is the **city parish church** (Stadtpfarrkirche). It's worth peeking in at the stained glass: one small panel (left of the high altar, fourth from the bottom on the right) shows Hitler and Mussolini looking on as Christ is scourged.

Mariahilf Church on Mariahilferplatz has a Baroque façade, created by Josef Hueber from 1742 to 1744. Part of the church was built by de Pomis, who is buried within.

Parks

Paths wind up the **Schlossberg** from all sides. The hike takes less than 30 minutes and rewards walkers with excellent views. Along the way there are gardens and seating terraces. At the top is an open-air theatre, a small military museum and a bell tower which dates from 1588 and formed part of the now demolished castle. Nearby is the emblem of Graz, the **clock tower** (Uhrturm). Unusually, the larger hand on the clock face shows the hours; the minute hand was added much later. The townsfolk paid the French a ransom of 2987 florins and 11 farthings not to destroy the clock tower during the 1809 invasion.

Just east of the Schlossberg is the **Stadtpark**. With its large fountain and flower beds, it's a relaxing place to sit or stroll.

Schlossberg Cave Railway

This is a good activity for those with kids. It's the longest grotto railway in Europe, and winds its way for two km around scenes from fairy tales. The entrance is on Schlossbergplatz, and it's open daily from 10 am to 5 pm (6 pm in summer). Admission prices are on a sliding scale: AS30 for one (adults or children), AS55 for two, AS75 for three, etc.

Eggenberg Castle

Schloss Eggenberg is at Eggenbergen Allee 90, four km west of the centre (take tram No 1 to Schloss Strasse, backtrack a few metres and take the first street on the right). The Eggenberg dynasty had made this site its home since the 15th century; the Baroque palace was constructed by de Pomis around the original building. He was commissioned by Johann Ulrich (1568-1634), who was celebrating the power and prestige of being appointed governor of Inner Austria in 1625.

STYRIA

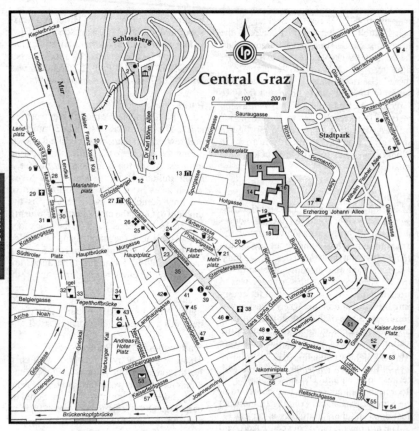

STYRIA

Astronomical themes and symbols dominate: the palace has 365 windows and 24 **state rooms** (Prunkräume). The Planet Hall is a riot of white stucco surrounding Baroque frescoes, painted by Hans Adam Weissenkircher. The frescoes portray the seven planets (all that were then discovered), the four elements and the 12 signs of the zodiac. Other rooms show mythological, classical and contemporary scenes. There's also a church, a Chinese room and games rooms. One room shows a portrait of Empress Maria Theresa, painted as a slender figure though by then she already weighed 100 kg. The

state rooms are open between 31 March and 31 October and can be visited by hourly guided tour daily from 10 am to 1 pm and 2 to 5 pm. The tour is normally in German, though if you ask at the outset the guide may give a summary in English.

The palace also houses three collections of the Landesmuseum Joanneum. The **hunting museum** (Jagdmuseum) is notable mainly for the collection of animal deformities in Room 16, such as a duck with four legs and deer with various horrible growths. The **coin collection** (Münzensammlung) has coins covering the past 2500 years and

PLACES TO STAY		OTHER		27	Alterns Palace,
7	Schlossberg Hotel				Styriarte Kartenbüro
25	Hotel Erzherzog	1	Open-Air Theatre		& Steirischer
	Johann	2	Schlossbergbahn		Herbst
31	Hotel Mariahilf	3	Military Museum		Informationsbüro
33	Grand Hotel Wiesler		& Bell Tower	28	Passport Travel Agency
47	Grazerhof	4	Café Harrach	29	Mariahilf Church
		5	ÖKISTA	35	Rathaus
PLACES TO EAT		8	Café art Scherbe	36	Kommod
		9	Brot & Spiele	37	Englische
6	Laufke	10	2 Night		Buchhandlung
21	Gamlitzer Weinstube	11	Clock Tower	38	City Parish Church
23	Fast-Food Stands	12	Schlossberg Cave	39	Armoury
30	Mohrenwirt		Railway	40	Main Tourist Office
32	Mangolds Vollwert	13	Saurau Palace	41	Landhaus Courtyard
	Restaurant	14	Schauspielhaus	42	Casino
34	Yun Hai	15	Castle	43	Hertz
45	Landhaus Keller	16	Double Staircase	44	Bus Station
52	Food Market	17	Promenade Café	46	Steirisches Heimatwerk
53	Kaiser Josef Bistro	18	Mausoleum	48	American Express
	Restaurant	19	Cathedral	49	Operncafé
54	Alt Wien	20	Glockenspiel	50	Tageskasse
55	Restaurant Athen	22	MI Bar	51	Opernhaus
56	Fast-Food Stands	24	Kölz	58	Main Post Office
57	Restaurant Gösser	26	Kastner & Öhler		
	Bräu		Department Store		

STYRIA

other antiquities, as well as the Austrian banknotes that immediately preceded the current issue. The **ancient history** (Vor- und Frühgeschichte) collection has as its prize exhibit the votive *Chariot of Strettweg* (7th century BC), a piece in bronze which is dramatically lit in a dark room.

The museums shouldn't detain visitors more than about 30 minutes each, and all are open from 1 February to 30 November, daily from 9 am to noon and 1 to 5 pm (except the history section which closes for lunch one hour later). Combined admission to the state rooms and the museums costs AS25 (students free, senior citizens AS10).

The palace is set in extensive parklands where animals such as peacock and deer roam free and Roman stone reliefs can be seen. A café is available. The grounds are open daily all year from 8 am to at least 5 pm (7 pm in summer). Admission costs AS2.

Activities

Opposite Eggenberg Castle is a sports centre with a running track, football ground and basketball court. There's a snack/buffet bar with a Kegelbahn (mini 10-pin bowling; AS10 per 12 minutes). The next stop towards town on tram No 1 will bring you to Bad Eggenberg, Janzgasse 21, open daily from 8 am to 9.30 pm. The swimming pool costs AS65 (AS35 for children, AS40 for students) and the sauna costs AS125 (AS70 for children) for a day pass. A massage costs from AS170.

In late October the Graz marathon takes place.

Organised Tours

The main tourist office organises guided walks of the city (AS65), daily in summer and on Saturday in winter.

Festivals

The Styriarte is a classical music festival held from late June to mid-July: contact the Styriarte Kartenbüro (☎ 81 29 41 22), Sackstrasse 17, A-8010. Steirischer Herbst is an avant-garde festival held during October. Events encompass music, theatre, films, exhibitions and art installations, and are staged at a dozen different locations around town. For information and tickets (AS50 to AS1200) contact Steirischer Herbst Informationsbüro (☎ 82 30 07), also at Sackstrasse 17.

The autumn trade fair, Grazer Herbstmesse International, takes place in the exhibition centre (☎ 80 88 0), Messeplatz 1, about the first 10 days in October.

Places to Stay

Bottom End Except for camp sites and the hostel, Graz has scant cheap places to stay, so try to book ahead. Even most private rooms (get the list from the tourist office) are pricey or a long way from the centre.

Waldcamping Riederhof (☎ 28 43 80), Riederhof Mantscha 1, costs AS204 for two people or AS162 for one. There's no direct public transport. *Camping Central* (☎ 28 18 31), Martinhofstrasse 3, costs AS200 for a two-person site (one-person sites are not available). Take bus No 32 from Jakominiplatz. Both camping grounds are about six km south-west of the city centre and are open from 1 April to 31 October.

The HI *youth hostel* (☎ 91 48 76), Idlhofgasse 74, has extensive lawns, but it's often full with school groups from April to June. Eight-bed dorms are AS130 per person, renovated four-bed dorms with private shower/WC are AS160, and double rooms are AS210. Sheets for the first night cost AS20. It's closed for Christmas and for up to two months afterwards. Reception is shut from 9 am to 5 pm, but the doors stay open. Laundry costs AS45 to wash and dry. There's no real curfew: after 10 pm, somebody unlocks the door on the half-hour up to 2 am, or you can get your own key (AS200 deposit). There are several good places to eat nearby – the staff will tell you where.

Five minutes from the main train station is *Hotel Strasser* (☎ 91 39 77), Eggenberger Gürtel 11. It has functional but pleasant singles/doubles for AS380/640 with private shower, or AS290/500 with hall showers. There is a reasonably-priced restaurant on the premises. Around the back of the station,

Pension Lukas (☎ 58 25 90) at Waagner Biro Strasse 8 offers a similar standard for AS250/440 or AS305/510 with shower. Breakfast isn't included – eat in the inexpensive bar/restaurant (people may warn you this is a pick-up joint, but later owners have put a stop to all that). The pension is open daily; the restaurant is closed weekends.

Schmid Greiner (☎ 68 14 82), Grabenstrasse 64, north of Schlossberg, is a cosy and old-fashioned B&B pension, but the traffic outside can be noisy. Singles/doubles are AS370/550 (cheaper in the low season), using the hall shower. Another B&B pension on a quieter street is *Rückert* (☎ 32 30 31), Rückertgasse 4. Rooms are AS380/720, or AS420/750 with shower. Take tram No 1 to Tegetthoffplatz and then walk down Hartenaugasse.

Middle *Hotel Academia* (☎ 32 35 58), Untere Schönbrunngasse 7-11, is a student residence that becomes a hotel from 1 July to 30 September. There are 170 rooms for AS440/700 with shower and modern fittings. *Rosen-Hotel Steiermark* (☎ 32 40 41), Liebiggasse 4, has the same set-up and it's closer to the university. Singles/doubles start at AS440/680.

In the old centre of town is *Grazerhof* (☎ 82 98 24) on Stubenberggasse 10. Smallish, innocuous rooms are AS460/700, or AS600/980 with private shower. The hotel borders two pedestrian streets, but the receptionist can tell you where to park.

Hotel Drei Raben (☎ 91 26 86), Annenstrasse 43, is a comfortable, convenient, mid-price hotel. Rooms with bath or shower and WC start at about AS700/1000. There are a few rooms using hall facilities for AS395/690, plus some triple rooms (AS890).

Hotel Mariahilf (☎ 91 31 630), Mariahilfer Strasse 9, has singles/doubles with private shower from AS700/1200. The rooms are large, but the standard of furnishing is variable; in some rooms it looks like the fixtures have been thrown together on a mix-and-mismatch basis – a few of those carpets

MARK HONAN

MARK HONAN

MARK HONAN

MARK HONAN

Top Left: Decorative building façade, Mariazell, Styria
Top Right: Tower detail of St Barbara Church, Bärnbach, Styria
Bottom Left: World War II memorial, by Franz Weiss, St Barbara Church, Bärnbach, Styria
Bottom Right: Art-Nouveau mosaic, Hotel Wiesler, Graz, Styria

Left:	Decorative sun dial, Velden, Carinthia
Top Right:	Winding streets, Spitz, Lower Austria
Middle:	Detail of Dürnstein's parish church spire, Lower Austria
Bottom:	Resting in the Rathausplatz, Rust, Burgenland

should have been chucked out with the Third Reich. Other rooms are quite grand.

Mid-price comfort is generally a better deal in pensions, though they tend to be farther from the town centre. An exception is *Pension Iris* (☎ 32 20 81), Bergmanngasse 10, with comfortable rooms with shower and WC for AS550/740 (closed July). Double-glazing cuts traffic noise.

Top End *Schlossberg Hotel* (☎ 80 70 0; fax 80 70 160), Kaiser Franz Josef Kai 30, is a charming four-star hotel, small enough for guests to receive personal service. Singles/doubles start at AS1500/2100; they vary in size and style but all have character. There's a sauna and fitness room (free for guests), a summer swimming pool and a rooftop terrace.

Hotel Erzherzog Johann (☎ 81 16 16; fax 81 15 15), is ideally situated at Sackstrasse 3-5, in a 400-year-old building. Large, well-furnished rooms cost from AS1280/1900, with slightly lower prices in the low season (November to March except over New Year). It's built around a pleasant, plant-strewn atrium (housing the 'winter garden' restaurant) and there's free use of the sauna. Parking is nearby.

Hotel Daniel (☎ 91 10 80; fax 91 10 85), by the main train station at Europaplatz 1, costs from AS1050/1580 and is geared more towards businesspeople than tourists (no sauna etc but has fax and computer services). If you want a sauna, stay at *Hotel Europa* (☎ 90 76; fax 90 76 606), across the road at Bahnhofgürtel 89. Plush rooms are AS1150/1600.

The only five-star hotel in town is the *Grand Hotel Wiesler* (☎ 90 66 0; fax 90 66 76), Grieskai 4. Rooms have excellent facilities though they can vary greatly in size. Costs are AS1800/2600 and guests have free use of the sauna; the solarium costs AS50.

Places to Eat
Self-Catering The main food markets are at Kaiser Josef Platz and Lendlplatz, open Monday to Saturday from 7 am to 12.30 am. There are also fast-food stands at Hauptplatz

and Jakominiplatz. Supermarkets include the large *Billa* at Annenstrasse 23 and a *Konsum* below ground in the Forum Kaufhaus department store opposite the main train station. *Laufke*, Elisabethstrasse 6, is a restaurant and delicatessen open each weekday to 11 pm.

Self-Service & Budget Restaurants There are lots of excellent-value restaurants dotted around town. The cheapest is the university *Mensa*, which is downstairs at Schubertstrasse 2-4. Main meals (including a vegetarian choice) cost AS34 to AS54, with discounts for students. Food is served Monday to Friday from 11 am to 2 pm. The café on the ground floor is open Monday to Friday from 8 am to 4 pm, and has breakfasts for AS33. There are several other cheap places near the university which are popular with students: wander down Halbärthgasse and Harrachgasse.

The Forum Kaufhaus has an *Oregano* self-service restaurant on the 1st floor. Meals start at about AS50. The Kastner & Öhler department store on Sackstrasse has a buffet-style restaurant called *Feinspitz* on the 2nd floor. Tempting arrays of food cost under AS100 per meal, and there are cheap snacks and beverages.

As ever, weekday lunches in Chinese restaurants are a great deal: you might try *Yun Hai* at Andreas Hofer Platz and *Gao Ya* at Keplerstrasse 34. *La Pizza* (☎ 91 03 22), Keplerstrasse 38, has pizzas from AS60 and a free delivery service for orders over AS120 (open daily).

Mohrenwirt, Mariahilfer Strasse 16, is a small Gasthof with snacks and meals from AS20 to AS85. Ask the server about daily specials as they're not written down. Opening times are Saturday to Wednesday from 10 am to midnight.

A good place to try Austrian cooking (and about 100 different types of beer!) is *Gästehaus Goldene Kugel*, at Leonhardstrasse 32. It's open Sunday to Friday from 9 am to 1 am. Lunch costs AS60 and AS70; evening dishes are from AS70 to AS110. Close by is *Girardikeller*, Leonhardstrasse

28, a cellar bar (free live music every second Sunday) with Austrian and Italian meals from AS50 to AS80. From Monday to Thursday it has a daily special for just AS45 or AS50. It's open daily from 2 pm (6 pm in winter) till late.

Cafeteria-style vegetable heaven can be found at *Mangolds Vollwert Restaurant*, Griesgasse 11. Salad is AS13 per 100 grams, daily dishes are AS60 to AS90, and there are various healthy desserts.

Alt Wien on Dietrichsteinplatz is a simple place with friendly staff. Meals start at about AS60 and there's a salad buffet for AS25/50 for a small/large plate. It's closed on weekends and holidays.

Mid-Price & Expensive Restaurants

Gamlitzer Weinstube (☎ 82 87 60), Mehlplatz 4, has Styrian dishes from AS80 to AS135. Try the Steinerpfandl (AS80) served in a pan: a tasty and filling combination of home-made pasta (Spätzle), cheese, minced meat and mushroom sauce. It's closed on weekends and holidays.

Restaurant Gösser Bräu, Neutorgasse 48, is a large place with many rooms, and outside tables on a terrace around the back. Food is AS65 to AS200, and there's a wide selection of Gösser beer from AS29. Opening hours are Sunday to Friday from 9 am to midnight.

Restaurant Athen (☎ 81 61 11), Dietrichsteinplatz 1, is a Greek restaurant. Prices start at about AS80 and there is live music on Friday. It's open Monday to Saturday from 11 am to midnight; Sunday and holidays from 5 pm to midnight.

For atmosphere and quality, head to the 16th-century *Landhaus Keller* (☎ 83 02 76), Schmiedgasse 9. Floral displays, coats of arms, medieval-style murals, and soft background music contribute to the historic ambience. Most dishes, including interesting Styrian specialities, exceed AS175. In the summer outside tables overlook the Landhaus courtyard. It's open Monday to Saturday from 11.30 am to midnight.

Kaiser Josef Bistro Restaurant (☎ 82 25 12), Schlögelgasse 1, is a simple-looking place that many say is the best restaurant in

Graz. The menu changes frequently and the food is French-style including a touch of nouvelle cuisine. Main dishes are above AS200; the kitchen is open from noon to 2 pm and 6 to 10.30 pm (closed Saturday evening, Sunday and for two weeks in August).

The *Grand Hotel Wiesler* (see Places to Stay) has a gourmet restaurant, as do some of the other top hotels. *Pichlmaier* (☎ 47 15 97), Petersberger Strasse 9, is a quality restaurant in the south-eastern suburb of St Peter. It serves Austrian and international dishes for about AS200 and is open daily.

Cafés & Bars Graz has several traditional coffee houses, including *Operncafé*, Opernring 22, which is open daily from 7.30 am (Sunday 9 am) to midnight. Another café is *Promenade* in the Stadtpark. The area round the university has various places where you can mix with students, such as *Café Harrach* at Harrachgasse 26. Just north of the university is *Bier Baron*, Heinrichstrasse 56, a large, busy bar with rows of gleaming silver beer pumps. Food is reasonably priced and it's open daily from 11 am (Sunday from 11.30 am) to 1 am.

Mehlplatz and Prokopigasse, in the centre of town, are full of relatively inexpensive, lively bars, which offer snacks or full meals until late. Like its Viennese parallel, this area has been dubbed the 'Bermuda Triangle'. The *MI Bar* (3rd floor) on Färberplatz gives a view of the city rooftops.

Kommod, Burggasse 15, is a bright and busy bar, often packed with students, which serves pizza and pasta from AS66; it's open daily from 5 pm to 2 am. *Café art Scherbe*, Stockergasse 2, off Lendplatz, is a more relaxed bar, with displays of objets d'art and paintings (for sale). It has a games room downstairs and is open weekdays from 10 am to 3 am. Saturday hours are noon to 3 am, and Sunday 5 pm to midnight.

Brot & Spiele at Mariahilfer Strasse 17 offers beer, food, pool tables, a cocktail happy hour (5 to 7 pm), and free live music on Thursday; it's open daily from 10 am (Sunday and holidays from 1 pm) to 2 am.

Entertainment

Graz is an important cultural centre and hosts musical events throughout the year. A ticket office (Tageskasse; ☎ 80 00), Kaiser Josef Platz 10, sells tickets without commission for the *Schauspielhaus* (theatre; ☎ 80 05) and *Opernhaus* (opera; ☎ 80 08), and dispenses information. Opening hours are Monday to Friday from 8 am to 8 pm. Students aged under 27 pay half-price at these venues. An hour before performances, students can buy leftover tickets for AS60 at the door, and anybody can buy standing-room tickets for AS25 to AS35. Normal prices are from AS40 to AS500 for the theatre (closed in July and August) and AS35 to AS480 for the opera (closed in August). Look for free 'Sommertheater' events in various venues around town.

The *Grand Hotel Wiesler* (☎ 90 66 0), Grieskai 4, is famous for its jazz brunch on Sunday from 11 am to 2 pm (October to June). It attracts well-known performers; AS330 admission includes the buffet. *Babenbergerhof*, Babenbergerstrasse 39, is a smallish bar with live jazz (free) on Monday and Tuesday. Anna, the vivacious English-speaking hostess, treats her customers as friends. It's open daily (unless she had a late night!).

2 Night, on Kaiser Franz Josef Kai, is one of the few discos in town (open weekends). *Bang*, Dreihackengasse 4, is a bar, disco and café, with a mostly (but not exclusively) gay clientele. It's open from 8 pm (Friday and Saturday from 9 pm); Thursday is for men only.

Kiz-Kino (☎ 83 56 62), Friedrichgasse 24, regularly shows films in their original language. Graz casino (☎ 28 33 66) is at Landhausgasse 10.

Things to Buy

Styria is known for painted pottery and printed linen. Other popular souvenirs include metal and china plates, steins, cow bells, dolls and statuettes. Quality handicrafts are available at Steirisches Heimatwerk at Herrengasse 10. Another souvenir shop in the town centre is Kölz,

Hauptplatz 11. Opposite is Foto Nettig, Hauptplatz 7, the photography and electrical goods chain. Close by, the Kastner & Öhler department store stocks many products.

A flea market is held at Karmeliterplatz, every third Saturday in the month from 6 am to 1 pm. Another flea market is every Saturday at Plüddemanngasse 47A.

Getting There & Away

Air The airport is 10 km south of the town centre, just beyond the A2. For flight information call ☎ 29 30 58 or 29 16 69. Several flights a day go to/from Vienna, Munich, Frankfurt and Zürich. Innsbruck and Salzburg are serviced most days.

Bus Bundesbuses depart from outside the main train station and from the bus station at Andreas Hofer Platz, where there's a bus information office. Alternatively, call ☎ 0660-80 20 (charged at the local rate) for information.

Train Call ☎ 17 17 for train information. Direct IC trains to Vienna's Südbahnhof depart every two hours (AS296; two hours 40 minutes). Trains depart every two hours to Salzburg (AS396), either direct or changing at Bischofshofen. All trains running north or west go via Bruck an der Mur, and it's sometimes necessary to change. Even if you want to go south-west to Klagenfurt you still have to first go north to Bruck; the total trip takes about 3½ hours. Trains to eastern Styria via Graz's Ostbahnhof originate at the Hauptbahnhof.

A daily direct train departs for Zagreb (AS208; 3½ hours) at 6.58 pm. The direct service to Budapest leaves at 6.18 am, though two later trains have an onward connection at Szentgottard.

Car & Motorbike The A2 from Vienna to Klagenfurt passes a few km south of the city. Leading north from the A2, the A9 passes under the city and emerges to take a north-west course to the Salzkammergut, with the

S35 branching off to Bruck an der Mur. To the south, the A9 heads to Maribor.

Car Rental Offices include: Avis (☎ 81 29 20), Schlögelgasse 10; Europcar (☎ 91 40 80), Wiener Strasse 15; and Hertz (☎ 82 50 07), Andreas Hofer Platz 1. See the Getting Around chapter for rates. Steinbauer Jeitler (☎ 91 50 83), Fabriksgasse 29, south of the town centre, has lower prices. For the cheapest group, prices are AS372 per day, AS2028 per week and AS900 for a weekend; free km included are 300, 2100 and 900 km respectively.

Getting Around
To/From the Airport Daily buses run to/from the Hotel Daniel by the main train station (AS18; 20 minutes). Departures to the airport are at 5.30 am, 3.30 pm, 4.30 pm and 5.30 pm; departures from the airport are at 1, 4, 5, 6 and 11 pm. The 5.30 am and 11 pm buses stop en route at the Grand Hotel Wiesler.

Public Transport City transport is part of a regional transport network which extends to the Styrian wine routes in the south and nearly to Bruck an der Mur in the north. Graz itself is covered by one central zone, zone 101. Single tickets for one zone (AS20) are valid for one hour, and you can switch between buses, trams and the Schlossbergbahn (castle hill railway), which runs from Sackstrasse up the Schlossberg. Ten-zone tickets, valid for up to 10 trips, are AS140. A 24-hour pass costs AS40, a weekly pass AS82 and a monthly pass AS290.

Hourly and 24-hour tickets can be purchased from the driver; other types of tickets can be purchased from Tabak shops, ticket machines or public transport windows (such as the one outside the main train station). Multi-zone tickets also are available to cover regional trains.

Other Transport Parking in areas marked as blue zones is for a maximum of three hours between 7 am and 7 pm on weekdays and from 9 am to 1 pm on Saturday; buy tickets (*Parkschein*) at Tabak shops (AS8 per 30 minutes).

To call a taxi, dial ☎ 2801, 983, 878, 889 or 1716. Taxis cost AS25 at taxi ranks or AS35 if you have to phone for one, plus AS12 per km (AS13 per km between 8 pm and 6 am).

The main train station has bicycles for hire.

Around Graz

Pick up the *Excursions Around Graz* brochure in English from the Graz tourist office. It gives plenty of ideas for trips near Graz; most are within a 40-km radius of the city.

STYRIAN WINE ROUTES
Several tours of wine routes can be taken in the Graz region. The Graz tourist office has information on the routes – ask for the Styrian Wine Routes map which gives brief descriptions of the routes and of the characteristics of Styrian wines. To explore these routes you really need your own transport. The train will take you to only one or two points along a certain route, eg it will take you to Gleisdorf, the starting point of the East Styria Roman Wine Road (Oststeirische Römerweinstrasse), but then takes a very circuitous diversion before it rejoins the main route at Hartberg. To try to follow a route by bus would be slow and tedious, involving many changes.

One possibility is to hire a bicycle in Graz and take the train to one of the stations on a wine route. Deutschlandsberg is the main town on the Schilcher Wine Road (Schilcher Weinstrasse), and can be reached by hourly train from Graz (five zones from Graz, AS78; takes one hour). The train terminates at Wies-Eibiswald, which is also the end of this wine route. Ehrenhausen is the start of the South Styria Wine Road (Südsteirischen Weinstrasse). Hourly trains also run here from Graz (five zones, AS78; takes 45 minutes). A station along the way is Leibnitz, the start of the Sausaler Wine Road (Sausaler Weinstrasse).

Deutschlandsberg
• *pop 7600* • ☎ *(03462)*
This town is the centre of the production of Schilcher, a light, dry rosé. A good view of Deutschlandsberg can be had from **Landsberg Castle**, about 25 minutes walk from the town centre. The castle also contains a museum of early history. On Corpus Christi, church altars in town are specially decorated.

The tourist office (☎ 20 11 266) is at Hauptplatz 35 in the town hall. Opening hours are Monday to Friday from 8 am to noon, though brochures are available in the town hall foyer in the afternoon.

Places to Stay & Eat Deutschlandsberg offers a choice of guesthouses or private rooms. Most are out of the town centre. Convenient but more expensive is *Gasthof Kollar-Göbl* (☎ 26 420), Hauptplatz 10, providing singles/doubles with shower/WC for AS410/670. Also on Hauptplatz is *Sorger Imbiss*, a butcher's shop with a self-service area for cheap, hot food, and *China-Restaurant Peking*, open daily, with cheap weekday lunch menus.

Various Buschenschenken beckon on the outskirts of town; these are shown on the map in the holiday brochure from the tourist office.

Ehrenhausen
• ☎ *(03453)*
Ehrenhausen is smaller and more picturesque than Deutschlandsberg, and a better place to visit if you just want a fleeting glimpse of the wine region.

Orientation & Information To walk from the train station to the tourist office (☎ 43 43), Hauptplatz 28, turn left and cross the stream, and then turn right (five minutes). It's only open Friday from 1 to 4 pm, but hotel and other information can be obtained from the Rathaus (☎ 25 07), Hauptplatz 2, during office hours. There's a bank and Bankomat

on Hauptplatz. The post office is by the station.

Things to See & Do Besides embarking from here on the South Styria Wine Road there are a couple of things to do in town. The Eggenberg family was associated with Ehrenhausen, and purchased Ehrenhausen Castle in 1543. A more interesting building, however, is the **mausoleum** of Ruprecht von Eggenberg (1546-1611), hero in battles against the Turks. It rests on a plateau above Hauptplatz, and a path leads up just to the right of the Rathaus (takes under 10 minutes). The building is white and yellow, with two large warriors gazing down from the terrace. The stucco inside is starkly white, with many embellishments clinging to the central dome and vines swirling around supporting pillars. There's a good view from the terrace down to Hauptplatz.

Before climbing up, get the key from the manse *(Pharhof)* next to the **parish church** on Hauptplatz. Take the opportunity to explore the church itself: the altars inside are vivid Baroque, with lots of gold and painted statues. Don't depart Ehrenhausen without admiring the view from the western end of Hauptstrasse: the pastel colours of the houses in the foreground, topped by the church steeple and the mausoleum crowning the hill, form a fine picture.

Places to Stay & Eat There are several private rooms available, including *Rupp Anna* (☎ 33 57), Bahnhofstrasse 9 (on the route from the train station described under Orientation & Information), with doubles for AS260 with hall shower: only two are available. Adjoining the tourist office is *Zum Goldenen Löwen* (☎ 32 19 5), Hauptplatz 28, with doubles for AS350 or AS430 with private shower.

There is a *youth hostel* (☎ 23 44), at nearby Spielfeld No 149, the next stop on the train south of Ehrenhausen. It is open from 6 January to 23 December. The next stop north, Leibnitz, has a summer *camp site* (☎ 03454-24 63).

To find somewhere to eat you need look

no farther than Hauptplatz. It offers several choices; one suitable place is *Gasthof Fleischeri*, right by the church. It has tables inside and out, and serves local food. The menu including soup is about AS60 (closed on Monday in winter). Hauptplatz also has a *Nah & Frisch* supermarket, open Monday to Friday from 7.30 am to noon and 3 to 6 pm, and Saturday from 7.30 am to noon.

AUSTRIAN OPEN-AIR MUSEUM

Seven provinces in Austria have open-air museums showing regional architecture. The Austrian Open-Air Museum (Österreichischen Freilichtmuseum) in Styria is the best to visit as you get to sample the whole country in one go. The main complex is about two km from end to end, and is arranged in order as if the visitor is walking through Austria from east to west. First comes Burgenland, then Styria, Carinthia, the Danube Valley, Salzburg, Tirol, and finally Vorarlberg. Building No 20 is a west Styrian grocery, with old-fashioned goods on display and a few modern items for sale. No 38 is a Styrian schoolhouse with a classroom and an exhibition. Other highlights include the sgraffito decorations and unified structure of the farmhouse from Upper Austria (No 58), the crisscross construction of the barn (No 56), and the Salzburg Rauchhaus (No 77), so-called because of the absence of a chimney (smoke was supposed to seep through chinks in the ceiling and dry grain in the loft).

Two to three hours is sufficient for a visit. Bring provisions for a picnic, or there's a restaurant just outside the entrance. No smoking is permitted in the complex as most buildings are timber.

The museum is open from 1 April to 31 October, daily except Monday between 9 am and 5 pm. Entry costs AS50 (AS20 for children and students). If you only want to see the exhibition hall near the entrance, admission costs AS20 (AS10). The exhibition hall gives the background to this and other open-air museums in Austria and Europe (text in German). At the entrance, buy the detailed booklet (in English) for AS25, giving a rundown on the 80-odd buildings in the complex.

A notice board by the ticket office tells when country-craft demonstrations take place. As these don't occur on a regular basis, it might be worth telephoning (☎ 03124-53 700) before planning your visit. The buildings get to look a bit similar after awhile, unless there's something happening to liven things up. At the end of September there's a special fair, Erlebnistag, with crafts, music and dancing.

Getting There & Away

There are hourly trains from Graz to Stübing (two zones, AS34; takes 15 minutes). From the train station, walk left for 20 minutes, eventually passing over the rail tracks, then under them just before the entrance. Buses go right to the museum from Graz on weekdays only, at 9 am and 12.30 pm, returning at 1.23 pm and 4.30 pm. They're operated by Watzke (☎ 0316-40 20 42), and depart from Lendplatz.

LURGROTTE

These caves at Peggau are Austria's largest. They can be combined easily with the open-air museum on a day trip from Graz (do the caves first). The temperature in the caves is about 9°C.

There are two entrances to the caves, and tours lasting about one hour are available from either end between 9 am and 4 pm (AS50; students AS45). The eastern entrance is at Semriach. Tours (☎ 03125-22 18) are conducted daily all year. Buses depart Graz from Andreas Hofer Platz. If you want also to visit the open-air museum, it's easier to use the western entrance at Peggau. Tours (☎ 03127-25 80) are between April and October, daily except Monday. Peggau is on the same train route as Stübing, except it's one zone farther from Graz (AS48). The caves are 15 minutes walk from the station.

PIBER

● ☎ *(03144)*

Piber's claim to fame is the stud farm of the

Lipizzaner stallions, three km from the small town of Köflach.

Orientation & Information

Piber is about 40 km west of Graz. Train travellers arrive first in Köflach, which has a small tourist office (☎ 25 19 70), Bahnhofstrasse 23, opposite the train station. Opening hours are Monday and Friday from 8 am to 4 pm, and Tuesday and Thursday from 8 am to 1 pm. To reach the stud farm from the tourist office, walk up Bahnhofstrasse, turn right along Hauptplatz (300 metres), and then left for a three km walk along Piberstrasse (signposted). Buses along this road are infrequent.

Piber Stud Farm

The Bundesgestüt Piber (☎ 33 23) has been in operation since 1920 and now comes under the wing of the Ministry of Agriculture. The stud farm was moved here when the original location, Lipizza, became part of Slovenia after WW I. About 40 foals are born in the farm every year, and of these only about five (stallions only) are of the right height and aptitude to be sent to the Spanish Riding School in Vienna for training, which lasts at least five years. Even before training, each stallion is worth about AS200,000. Favoured veteran stallions return to the farm to service the mares – six different breeding lines are currently in operation. Foals are born dark and take between five and 12 years to achieve their distinctive white colouring.

The farm can be visited from Easter to the end of October. The guided tour takes about 50 minutes and costs AS80 (AS30 for students and children). Tours depart between 9 and 10.15 am and 2 and 3.15 pm but only if there are at least 20 people (which they invariably are). Visitors see a film (with English commentary on the English tour) and museum exhibits, and tour the stables to meet some of the equine residents.

Places to Stay & Eat

The *Informationsblatt* brochure from the Graz or Köflach tourist office gives details of pensions and private rooms. *Gasthof Bardel* (☎ 34 22), Fesselweg 1, provides food and accommodation right by the stud farm.

Köflach has a large *KGM* supermarket at Quergasse, off Bahnhofplatz. Opening hours are Monday to Friday from 8 am to 6.30 pm and Saturday from 7.30 am to 1 pm. *China-Restaurant Beile* on Bahnhofstrasse offers lunch menus from AS45 (closed Monday and holidays). Köflach also has a gourmet restaurant, *Zum Kleinhapl* (☎ 34 94), Judenburger Strasse 6, closed Sunday noon and Monday.

Getting There & Away

Köflach is the final stop on the private railway running from Graz (takes 50 minutes; Austrian rail passes are valid, European ones aren't). The ticket for use only on this line is AS78, but it's cheaper to buy the four-zone Graz Verbandlinie ticket. GKB buses (☎ 0316-59 87 0) also make the trip from Graz, departing from Griesplatz, or sometimes Lendplatz.

BÄRNBACH

• ☎ (03142)

This small town is worth visiting primarily for the unique St Barbara Church, and can easily be combined with a trip to Piber. From the stud farm, regain Piberstrasse and then walk (buses are as elusive as Kurt Waldheim's WW II recollections) about two km east (away from Köflach). You can't miss the church on the main road. Continue in the same direction for Hauptplatz and, across the stream, the glass-making centre. A left turn at Hauptplatz will take you into Hauptstrasse and the road to the Alt Kainach Castle (two km), which contains historical exhibits.

Things to See & Do

Although built after WW II, **St Barbara Church** needed renovating in the late 1980s. About 80% of the town population voted to commission the maverick Viennese artist Friedensreich Hundertwasser to undertake the work. It was a bold move. Hundertwasser was known for his unusual concepts, particularly in discarding the straight line in previous building projects. The gamble paid off; the church is a visual treat inside and out, yet is still clearly a place of worship rather than a pseudo art gallery. The renovation was begun in 1987. Leave a donation and pick up the explanation card in English, which reveals the symbolic meaning behind the design features.

The church is surrounded by 12 gates, each representing a different faith: Hinduism, Islam etc, all connected by an uneven pathway. By the west façade is a powerful mosaic war memorial by Franz Weiss. The distinctive church steeple is topped by a gold onion dome. Features you wouldn't see in any other church include the bowed roof with green splodges along its flanks, the irregular windows, and the grass growing on the side porch roofs.

The interior also has striking and thoughtful touches: Hundertwasser's 'spiral of life' window reflects the afternoon sun onto the font; the modern art **Stations of the Cross** by Rudolf Pointer; the glass altar and podium filled with 12 layers of different types of earth representing the 12 tribes of Israel; and the harmonious ceramics surrounding the image of Christ on the Cross in the chancel.

Bärnbach has been known for glass-making for 200 years. The details of the process and the products are explained in the **Stölzle Glas Centre** (☎ 62 9 50), Hochtregisterstrasse 1. Opening times are Monday to Friday from 9 am to 5 pm, and weekends and holidays from 9 am to 1 pm. Entry costs AS55 (AS115 for a family card) and there are guided tours (in German) on weekdays at 10 am, 11 am, noon and 2 pm, and Saturday at 10 and 11 am.

Places to Stay & Eat

By the church is an information board listing accommodation and other facilities. Lodging is mostly in small guesthouses, such as *Gästehaus Lackner Hatzl* (☎ 62 5 84), Hauptstrasse 62, which charges about AS210 per person without breakfast.

Hauptstrasse has several places to eat: *Gästehaus Wolfgang Kuss* at No 8 has pizzas and local food from AS65; close by is *China-Restaurant Jang Tse Kiang*, with weekday lunch menus from just AS40. On the corner with Hauptplatz is a *Konsum* supermarket, open Monday to Friday from 7.30 am to 6 pm and Saturday from 7.30 am to noon.

Getting There & Away

Bärnbach is on the Graz-Köflach train line, one stop (five minutes) before Köflach. The train station is two km out of the town centre. To get there from St Barbara Church, go to Hauptplatz and turn right down Dr Niederdorfer Strasse; continue until the rail tracks pass under the road, then take the next left.

Northern & Western Styria

MARIAZELL

• *pop 2000* • *868 m* • ☎ *(03882)*

Mariazell is the most important pilgrimage site in Austria. It was founded in 1157 and a number of miracles have since been attributed to the Virgin of Mariazell, including Lewis I of Hungary's unlikely victory over the Turks in 1357. The town will be most crowded with pilgrims on 15 August (Assumption) and 8 September (Mary's 'name day').

Orientation & Information

Mariazell is in the extreme north of Styria, close to Lower Austria, and within the lower reaches of the eastern Alps. The train station (which rents bikes) is in St Sebastian, 15 minutes walk from Hauptplatz, the centre of Mariazell. The walk to the centre, along Wiener Strasse, takes you past a Billa supermarket and the St Sebastian tourist office (☎ 21 48; open Monday to Friday from 7 am to noon.

The Mariazell tourist office (☎ 23 66), Hauptplatz 13, reserves rooms without charging. Ask about reductions given with the guest card. The office is open Monday to Saturday from 9 am to 12.30 pm and 1.30 to

5.30 pm and Sunday from 9 am to noon. From 1 October to 30 April hours are Monday to Friday from 9 am to 12.30 pm and 1.30 to 5 pm, and Saturday to noon. The post office (Postamt 8630), Dr Leber Strasse, is just west of Hauptplatz.

Monday is the quietest day of the week, as this is when many hotels and restaurants take their rest day.

Basilica

This church on Hauptplatz is Mariazell's *raison d'être* and most visible feature. The original Romanesque church was converted to Gothic in the 14th century, then expanded and refitted as Baroque in the 17th century. The result from the outside is a claustrophobic, unbalanced look, with the original Gothic steeple bursting like a wayward skeletal limb from between two Baroque onion domes. The interior works better, with Gothic ribs on the ceiling combining well with Baroque frescoes and lavish stuccowork. Both Johann Bernhard Fischer von Erlach and his son Josef Emmanuel had a hand in the Baroque face-lift; the crucifixion group (1715) on the high altar is by Lorenzo Mattielli.

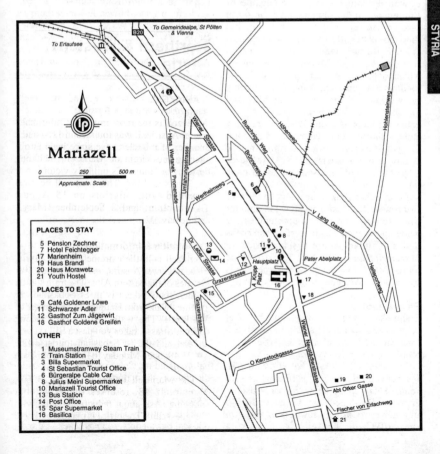

Mariazell

0   250   500 m
Approximate Scale

PLACES TO STAY
5 Pension Zechner
7 Hotel Feichtegger
17 Marienheim
19 Haus Brandl
20 Haus Morawetz
21 Youth Hostel

PLACES TO EAT
9 Café Goldener Löwe
11 Schwarzer Adler
12 Gasthof Zum Jägerwirt
18 Gasthof Goldene Greifen

OTHER
1 Museumstramway Steam Train
2 Train Station
3 Billa Supermarket
4 St Sebastian Tourist Office
6 Bürgeralpe Cable Car
8 Julius Meinl Supermarket
10 Mariazell Tourist Office
13 Bus Station
14 Post Office
15 Spar Supermarket
16 Basilica

To Gemeindealpe, St Pölten & Vienna

To Erlaufsee

STYRIA

In the centre of the church is the **Chapel of Miracles** (Gnadenkapelle), a gold and silver edifice that houses the Romanesque statue of the Madonna. Within the church is the **treasury** (Schatzkammer). It contains votive offerings spanning six centuries, mainly naive paintings (AS20, students and children AS10). The bell tower (Glockenturm) can be climbed (AS15, children AS10), though like the treasury it is closed on Monday.

Activities

Skiers have the chance to throw themselves downhill from either Gemeindealpe or Bürgeralpe. In the summer, hikers also can throw themselves down either hill, but they'd be better off following the many trails instead. **Gemeindealpe** (1626 metres) is five km north of Mariazell overlooking Mitterbach, and a chair lift ascends the mountain summer and winter, though only on weekends and holidays in May and October. The **Bürgeralpe** (1267 metres) cable car departs from Wiener Strasse, a stone's throw from Hauptplatz. The adult fare is AS60 up, AS40 down, or AS85 return. A day pass for skiers is AS235 (children AS165). A couple of restaurants await at the top.

From either peak there's a good view of **Erlaufsee**. This lake lies a few km north of Mariazell and provides opportunities for water sports such as windsurfing and scuba diving. Contact addresses are listed in *Mariazellerland von A-Z*, free from the tourist office. One way to get to the lake is by the steam Museumsbahn (AS50 return).

Places to Stay

There is a *camping ground* by the lake, costing AS35 per adult, and from AS20 each for a car and a tent. Contact the St Sebastian tourist office for reservations.

Mariazell's HI *youth hostel* (☎ 26 69), Fischer von Erlachweg 2, is 10 minutes walk south of Hauptplatz, along Wiener Neustädterstrasse. Dorm beds are AS120, or AS140 in a newer room with fewer beds and own shower/WC; the first night costs an extra

AS20. It is closed from 1 October to just before Christmas and for a week in April. There's no check-in from 1 to 5 pm and curfew is at 10 pm (get a key). Lunch and dinner are AS55 each.

Near the hostel are several options for rooms in private houses: *Haus Brandl* (☎ 28 66), Abt Otker Gasse 3 (April to September only), and *Haus Morawetz* (☎ 21 94), Abt Otker Gasse 7, are both pleasant and good value (from AS170 per person).

Marienheim (☎ 25 45), Pater Abelplatz 3, is run by nuns. Prices in this calm setting start from AS210 per person (AS310 for full board) in a room using hall shower; add AS40 for private shower. In winter there's a heating charge of AS30. *Pension Zechner* (☎ 25 81), Wiener Strasse 30, has clean, fresh rooms with shower/WC for AS240/480, plus AS30 per person in winter. Rooms facing south-west (away from the street) have a fine view.

Plenty of elegant three and four-star hotels stand on or around Hauptplatz, and there's little to choose between them. Top-of-the-range *Hotel Feichtegger* (☎ 24 16), Wiener Strasse 6, has loads of facilities, including a swimming pool; it charges about AS720 per person.

Places to Eat

There's a *Spar* supermarket on Grazerstrasse and a *Julius Meinl* near the tourist office.

Café Goldener Löwe on Hauptplatz mostly serves drinks and cakes, though it does have light meals for AS55 to AS75. Men should visit the WC upstairs to meet the Piss-Wand, a metal figure which will join in while you urinate. *Gasthof Goldene Greifen*, Wiener Neustädterstrasse 1, has a comfortable ambience and serves Austrian food for AS60 to AS120 (closed Tuesday).

Most of the hotels around Hauptplatz have a restaurant, and it's easy to compare menus before deciding. *Schwarzer Adler*, opposite the church, offers pricey fare, except for the set menu for AS75 or the vegetarian plate for AS95. *Gasthof Zum Jägerwirt*, Hauptplatz 2, looks deceptively small and cosy from the outside, but the left side has several adjoining rooms. Good, traditional dishes are mostly above AS100, except for daily specials (AS80 to AS140).

Getting There & Away

A narrow-gauge train (AS118) departs from St Pölten, 85 km to the north, every two hours or so. It's a slow 2½-hour trip, though the scenery is good for the last hour. Unless you have a car, the only way to avoid returning to St Pölten is to take the bus. There are several routes heading south, departing from the bus station (☎ 25 51) by the post office. At least four Bundesbuses a day depart for Bruck an der Mur (AS94; takes 100 minutes) with two continuing to Graz (AS144; three hours in total).

BRUCK AN DER MUR

• *pop 15,000* • ☎ *(03862)*
Bruck is at the confluence of the Mur and Mürz rivers (the Mürz is not an insignificant waterway, but they probably decided 'Bruck an der Mur und Mürz' was too much of a mouthful) and is at the junction of routes to all four points of the compass. If you're passing through, the town deserves a quick perusal.

Orientation & Information

The train station and post office (Postamt 8600) are at the eastern end of Bahnhofstrasse, and both will exchange money. There's also a Bankomat here. Walk down Bahnhofstrasse and bear left at the roundabout for the town centre, Koloman Wallisch Platz. In the centre of the square you'll find the tourist office (☎ 51 8 11). It's only a desk in a travel agency and has few brochures, but there's a computerised information board outside (with a free telephone), showing hotels, restaurants and other information. On the other side of the Mur River is the information office for the Alpenregion Hochschwab (☎ 54 7 22). It's in the Handelskammer building on An der Postwiese.

Things to See & Do

Several paths wind up to the ruins of

Landskron Castle (takes under 10 minutes). Not much remains except a clock tower and a few cannons, and you don't quite gain enough height for an enhanced view, but at least it provides a pleasant setting for a picnic. One of the paths down again leads to Bauernmarkt, where there's a food and flower market beside the 15th-century Gothic **parish church**.

The remaining sights are on Koloman Wallisch Platz. The **Rathaus** has an arcaded courtyard and a small museum. Close by is the **Kornmesserhaus**. It has an attractive open arcade with fussy ornamentation that betrays both Gothic and Renaissance influences. This late-15th century building was erected at the behest of a rich merchant, Pankraz Kornmess, for whom it is named. There are other old historic houses lining the square, though No 10 is more recent and has an Art-Nouveau façade.

On the square itself is a fine Renaissance-style **wrought-iron well** created by Hans Prasser in 1626. Also here is the **Mariensäule**, a column erected in 1710 after the town survived fire, plague and flooding.

North-west of Bruck are some Alpine lakes such as the tiny, but scenic, **Grünersee**, about 25 km from the town near the source of the Laming River.

Places to Stay & Eat

The HI *youth hostel* (☎ 53 4 65) is No 37 on Dr Theodor Körner Strasse, which runs westwards from Koloman Wallisch Platz. The church-like exterior of this place hides large dorms (AS110 for one or two nights, AS90 if three or more) and good hot showers. Reception is closed from noon to 4 pm and curfew is at 10 pm. Telephone ahead in winter to make sure it's open.

Beside the train station (take the stairs down to the left) is *Gasthof Koppelhuber* (☎ 51 6 38), Pischerstrasse 11, offering simple, bare, but large rooms using hall shower for AS300/480. Add AS50 per person if you want breakfast. *Gasthof Pension Malissa* (☎ 03862-51 1 58), Koloman Wallisch Platz 9, is a better deal,

STYRIA

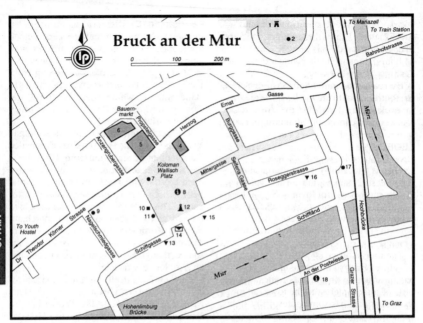

Bruck an der Mur

0   100   200 m

To Mariazell
To Train Station
Bahnhofstrasse

Bauern-markt

Gasse

Ernst

Herzog

Burggasse

Koloman Wallisch Platz

Mittergasse

Seifens Gasse

Roseggerstrasse

Schiffland

Schiffgasse

Mur

An der Postwiese

Hohenlimburg Brücke

To Youth Hostel

Dr Theodor Körner Strasse

Nagelschmiedgasse

Prochtegasse

Arzengruberstrasse

Hochbrücke

Mürz

Grazer Strasse

To Graz

PLACES TO STAY

3   Hotel Schwarzer Adler
10   Gasthof Pension Malissa

PLACES TO EAT

13   Gasthof Zur Post Riegler

15   Lackners
16   Pizza Mann

OTHER

1   Landskron Castle
2   Clock Tower
4   Kornmesserhaus
5   Rathaus
6   Parish Church

7   Wrought-Iron Well
8   Tourist Office
9   Hofer Supermarket
11   Art-Nouveau Façade
12   Mariensäule
14   Post Office
17   Billa Supermarket
18   Alpenregion Hochschwab Information Office

but there are just three doubles for AS500 with own shower/WC. The restaurant downstairs is basic and inexpensive. *Hotel Schwarzer Adler* (☎ 51 3 31), Mittlergasse 23, is cheap for a four-star place (AS580/890), if unremarkable.

The southern end of Koloman Wallisch Platz has several places to eat. *Gasthof Zur Post Riegler* at No 11 has a wide menu (AS80-180), including Styrian and vegetarian dishes, and interesting daily specials (closed Sunday). *Lackners* at No 16 has a

pizza section and a 'normal' restaurant, with reasonable prices. Roseggerstrasse leads east from here; at No 32 is *Pizza Mann*, open daily from 11 am to midnight. There's a *Hofer* supermarket on Dr Theodor Körner Strasse.

Getting There & Away

Bruck is the main rail hub for the region; all fast trains entering Graz (one hour, AS94) from the north go via Bruck. Other major destinations are: Vienna's Südbahnhof (two

STYRIA

hours, AS228), Klagenfurt (2½ hours, AS252) and Linz (three hours, AS276). Bruck train station has bicycle rental (open 24 hours), luggage lockers and a shop/snack bar.

By road, the main autobahns intersect to the south-east of the town. If you're planning to cycle along the Mur, the Alpenregion tourist office can supply some useful maps.

LEOBEN
• *pop 35,000*   • *540 m*   • ☎ *(03842)*

Leoben is a location for metallurgical industries, yet still manages to gain accolades such as 'the most beautiful town in Styria' for its floral displays and parklands. Leoben achieved fame with the peace treaty signed here in 1797 by Napoleon and Emperor Franz II.

The tourist office (☎ 440 18), Hauptplatz 12 (closed Friday afternoons and weekends), has information on the major sites. There's little of major interest in the town, although the Hauptplatz has some noteworthy sights, such as the 17th-century **Hacklhaus** with its Baroque façade. Leoben's connection with the iron industry is seen in the curious town motif (eg on the Rathaus façade), showing an ostrich eating horseshoes. Nearby, the dreary exterior of **St Xavier's Church** hides a harmonious interior of white walls and black-and-gold Baroque altars.

In the suburbs is the **Gösser Brewery** (☎ 226 21). Telephone in advance to join a free tour of the brewing process, including samples of the end product. It also has a free museum, covering the abbey and the brewing process (open weekdays).

Leoben centre has no budget beds, although you can eat cheaply in and around Hauptplatz.

Getting There & Away
Leoben is 16 km west of Bruck and is on the main rail route from there to Klagenfurt or Linz. The town centre is 10 minutes walk from Leoben train station: cross the Mur and bear right. The brewery is 1½ km south of Leoben-Göss station (only two-hourly regional trains stop).

EISENERZ
• *pop 10,000*   • *700 m*   • ☎ *(03848)*

Eisenerz is the main destination on the Styrian Iron Road (Steirische Eisenstrasse), extending north from Leoben. It's the largest ore mining centre in central Europe, extracting 8200 tonnes per day.

Orientation & Information
The town is clustered at the foot of the remarkable Erzberg (Iron Mountain). The bus station is closest to the town centre, but even the train station is little more than five minutes walk to the north. The tourist office (☎ 37 00) is at Schulstrasse 1, within the Stadtmuseum (☎ 36 15), which provides tourist information when the office is closed.

Things to See & Do
The town is attractively situated, allowing for some fine hikes along the valley. Despite some grim terraced housing near the mine, Eisenerz has a charming old town centre, particularly around Bergmannsplatz, where some buildings sport sgraffito designs. There's also a fortified Gothic church; its walls were built in 1532 to protect against the Turks. The Stadtmuseum covers folklore and mining (AS36; students AS11), and is open May to October, daily from 9 am to 5 pm.

But the main reason to come to Eisenerz is the **Erzberg**. This peak has been completely denuded by opencast stope mining, to such an extent that it resembles a step pyramid. Yet the outcome is quite beautiful, with its orange and purple shades contrasting with the lush greenery and grey crags of surrounding mountains.

The iron works can be visited in two ways. A 90-minute 'Schaubergwerk' tour burrows into the mountain to the underground mines (abandoned in 1986). Tours are usually in German (English notes) and cost AS120 (students AS60). The 'Hauly's Abenteuerfahrt' is a one-hour tour of the surface works aboard a huge truck, with fine views along the way (AS140; students AS70). A combined ticket costs AS230 (students AS110). Tours are conducted from May to October between 10 am and 3 pm; call ☎ 45 31 470 for information. The departure point is a 10-minute walk from the centre, following the course of the river.

Places to Stay & Eat

The tourist office will help you find somewhere to stay. There are few private rooms, and the only one near the centre is *Karl Moser* (☎ 24 34), Flutergasse 11, with doubles for AS260 or AS320.

Near Bergmannsplatz is *Zur Post* (☎ 22 32), Lindmoserstrasse 10, with large singles/doubles with shower/WC and TV for AS300/500. The restaurant serves good Styrian food for under AS80. Close by, *Bräustüberl* (☎ 23 35), Flutergasse 5, has rooms with shower/WC for AS250/440, and a restaurant (closed Monday).

For the cheapest eating, there's a *Konsum* supermarket, Vordernberger Strasse 6, with an *Oregano* self-service restaurant.

Getting There & Away

Two-hourly trains connect Eisenerz to Selzthal, a rail junction to the west (AS74, takes one hour; change at Hieflau). Bundesbuses go to Mariazell once a day. From Leoben, Bundesbuses go north about every two hours (AS64), via Vordernberg Markt, which is as far as you can get by train (excluding the special Vordernberg-Eisenerz 'nostalgic' train in the summer).

ADMONT

This small town at the entrance to the Gesäuse Valley is known for its Benedictine abbey. The most important part for visitors is the **abbey library** (Stiftsbibliothek), survivor of a fire in 1865 that severely damaged the rest of the abbey. It displays 150,000 volumes, and ceiling frescoes by Bartolomeo Altomonte. The best feature is the statues (in wood, but painted to look like bronze) by Josef Stammel (1695-1765), especially the *Four Last Things* series. To understand the symbolism inherent in these works, buy the leaflet in English for AS5 (the tourist office will provide a photocopy free!). Admission costs AS40 and includes entry to a couple of museums, covering natural

history, and religious art and treasures. It's open daily from 1 April to 31 October, in winter by appointment only (☎ 03613-23 12 444).

The tourist office (☎ 02613-21 64) is near the abbey church at Hauptplatz 4 (closed weekends and Monday afternoon). A HI *youth hostel* (☎ 03613-24 32) is south of the centre, sited in splendour in Schloss Röthelstein (closed from 1 November to 31 December). It's clearly visible above the trees: in the summer, walk up the trail cleared for the ski lift – the road route is much longer (no buses run). Dorms are AS175 and double rooms with shower/WC are AS295 per person. Phone ahead as it's often full with school groups (check-in from 7 am to 10 pm). There are several pensions near the abbey.

Getting There & Away

Admont is 15 km from Selzthal, on the route to Hieflau (trains run every two hours). The abbey is 10 minutes walk from the station.

MURAU

• *pop 2600* • *830 m* • ☎ *(03532)*

The Liechtenstein family was once dominant in the Murau region and built **Murau Castle** in 1250. This was taken over by the Schwarzenberg family and converted to a Renaissance building in the 17th century. There are short tours of the interior in the summer.

St Matthew's Church (Stadtpfarrkirche St Matthäus) dates from the 13th century, and it is yet another Gothic church that was remodelled in Baroque style. Both elements work well together, as in the combination of the Gothic crucifixion group (1500) and the Baroque high altar (1655). The frescoes are from the 14th to 16th centuries. Enjoy the view of the church, castle and scenic centre from across the river, near the train station.

Murau Brauerei (☎ 326 60), Raffaltplatz 19-23, may let you join a tour of the brewery if you telephone in advance. Its brewery museum opened in 1995 (AS40; closed Friday afternoon and weekends).

Skiing and hiking are enjoyed on the

nearby 2000-metre peaks, Kreischberg and Frauenalpe.

Places to Stay & Eat
If you decide to linger overnight, the tourist office (☎ 27 20) by the train station will sort out a pension or private room. The HI *youth hostel* (☎ 23 95), St Leohard Platz 4, has four-bed dorms with shower/WC for AS140 (AS115 if under 19). It closes from 31 October to 26 December, and for a few weeks after Easter. *Gasthof Bärenwirt* (☎ 20 79), Schwarzenbergstrasse 4, is central. It has rooms for AS190 per person, or AS270 with private shower/WC, and inexpensive regional food. The brewery has a restaurant and beer cellar.

Getting There & Away
Murau is on highway 96 between Tamsweg and Judenburg. Heading west to Tamsweg, you can switch to highway 97 if you want to keep by the Mur River. Murau is also on a narrow-gauge private line connecting Unzmarkt and Tamsweg (Austrian rail passes valid, Inter-Rail 50% off, Eurail not valid; departures every two hours). More of a tourist excursion than a mode of transport is the steam train that chugs to/from Tamsweg up to three times a week in the summer (AS180 return fare).

SCHLADMING
Flanked by mountain ranges to the north and south, Schladming combines with neighbouring resorts, **Rohrmoos** and **Haus**, to create a large ski area. The skiing range is 750 to 1894 metres. In summer, passes are available to ski the Dachstein Glacier (AS365 for one day). Another pass (the Top Tauern Skischeck) links this ski area with neighbouring regions – see Radstadt in the Salzburg chapter.

The town tourist office (☎ 03687-22 26 8) is at Hauptplatz 18. Schladming has a HI *youth hostel* (☎ 03687-24 53 1), Coburgstrasse 253, open all year.

Getting There & Away
Schladming is more easily reached from Salzburg province than from other places mentioned in this chapter. It is on the road and rail route that skirts the southern Salzkammergut.

Eastern Styria

This part of the province has no headline attractions, but it does have several castles surveying the undulating landscape.

STUBENBERG AM SEE
This town is a centre for water sports. There's a good lookout point from the hill above the lake, and a camp site (☎ 03176-83 90) by the water. The area between the lake and the nearby **Schielleiten Castle** is the site for a hot-air balloon festival in the second half of September. Dozens of colourful balloons rising in front of the yellow façade of the castle create a dramatic scene.

A few km south, **Herberstein Castle** (☎ 03176-28 10) adjoins a deep gorge. It has an Italianate arcaded courtyard and furnished rooms that can be toured from March to October, daily between 10 am and 5 pm. Walking down from the car park, you also pass an animal park that has 120 different species.

Places to Stay & Eat
Stubenberg is about midway between Gleisdorf and Hartberg, and either of these towns can provide a suitable base for exploring the region. The nearest HI *youth hostel* (☎ 03382-542 28) is at Klostergasse 4, Fürstenfeld, open all year. Stubenberg itself has a range of inexpensive places to stay, including private houses. Eating options in the resort include pizzeria *Erla* (☎ 03176-88 89), Buchberg 70, by the lake, which also has rooms. For more information on staying in Stubenberg, contact the tourist office (☎ 03382-88 82), on the 1st floor of the Gemeindeamt building.

Getting There & Away
From late May to late September a daily bus

runs directly to Stubenberg from Vienna's Wien Mitte bus station (takes 2½ hours). Occasional Bundesbuses to Stubenberg ply to/from Hartberg and Gleisdorf; contact ☎ 0660-80 20 for details (call charged at local rate). No train goes close to Stubenberg; the only rail track takes slow local trains that run from Graz to Hartberg, travelling a circuitous route via Gleisdorf and Fürstenfeld. By road, highway 54 connects Gleisdorf and Hartberg, from which a signposted turn-off to the north leads to Stubenberg.

RIEGERSBURG

A 13th-century castle offering fine views of the Grazbach Valley is the main attraction of this town 10 km south-west of Fürstenfeld. **Riegersburg Castle** was a crucial bastion against invading Hungarians and Turks. It now houses a couple of museums, featuring witchcraft. A war memorial is a reminder of fierce fighting in 1945, when Germans occupying the castle were attacked by Russian troops. The castle can be visited by guided tour from April to October, daily from 10 am to 5 pm.

For more information, contact the town tourist office (☎ 03153-670). The town has a HI *youth hostel* (☎ 03153-217), 3 Im Cillitor, by the old castle walls, open from 1 May to 31 October.

Getting There & Away

Several direct buses a day run from Graz (AS110; takes 90 minutes). The nearest train station is Feldbach, a 15-minute bus journey away.

Carinthia

Carinthia (Kärnten) is known primarily for its many lakes: there are 1270 within the province, of which around 200 have bathing facilities. The most famous is Lake Wörth (Wörther See), which is warmed by thermal springs. Many lakes are ideal for angling; tourist offices can give information on permits (these can be expensive) and regulations about legal seasons and the minimum size of a catch. The attraction of water sports means summer is the main season in Carinthia (it proclaims itself Austria's sunniest province), though it also offers winter sports.

Carinthia shares an area of outstanding natural beauty, the Hohe Tauern National Park, with neighbouring Tirol and Salzburg (see the following Hohe Tauern National Park Region chapter).

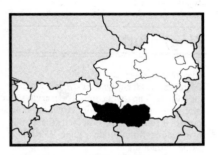

Orientation & Information

Carinthia is the fifth-largest province, with an area of 9533 sq km and a population of 548,000, 3% of whom speak Slovene. The terrain ranges from gentle hills to precipitous Alpine peaks. The main river is the Drau.

The administrative capital is Klagenfurt, but the provincial tourist board is in nearby Velden. Its address is: Kärntner Tourismus GmbH (☎ 04274-52 100; fax 52 100 50), Casinoplatz 1 A-9220 Velden. See the Velden section for directions to the office. Some of the main tourist offices in the region distribute a useful 130-page booklet, called

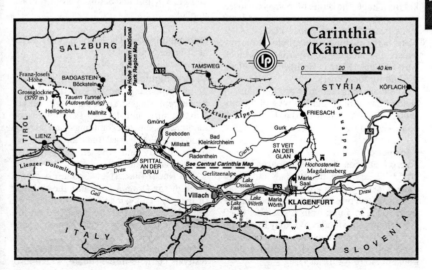

Carinthia is Captivating, which highlights major and minor sightseeing attractions with equal enthusiasm. Sport and leisure activities are also covered.

Klagenfurt

• *pop 87,000*   • *446 m*   • ☎ *(0463)*

Klagenfurt is an enjoyable city with a pleasant climate. The town centre is deserving of exploration, yet the main concession to tourism is Europa Park, especially the world-in-miniature Minimundus. Lake Wörth is a further attraction.

After twice being destroyed by fire, Klagenfurt became the capital of Carinthia in 1518, courtesy of Maximilian I. The symmetrical town plan was conceived by Domenico de Lalio, but he was only one of several architects who contributed to the Italianate flavour of the centre. The old city walls were razed in 1809 following occupation of the town by French forces.

Orientation

Klagenfurt lies 30 km from Slovenia and 60 km from Italy. The centre of town is enclosed by a square of ring roads, with Neuer Platz at its heart. North of Neuer Platz is Alter Platz, in the old town where there are narrow streets and arcaded courtyards. One block west of Neuer Platz is Heiligen Geist Platz, the hub for local buses.

The main train station is one km south of Neuer Platz. About four km west of the city centre is Lake Wörth, which has Europa Park on its eastern shore.

Information

Tourist Offices The main tourist office (☎ 53 72 23) is in the Rathaus on Neuer Platz. Opening hours are Monday to Friday from 8 am to 8 pm, and Saturday and Sunday from 10 am to 5 pm; from 15 October to 30 April, hours are Monday to Friday from 8 am to 6 pm. The staff finds rooms (no commission) and rents out bikes (AS30 for three hours or AS70 for the day).

A smaller tourist office by the entrance to Minimundus in Europa Park is open May to early October daily from 9 am to 8 pm. Another office is at Völkermarkter Strasse 225, open from mid-June to mid-September daily from 10 am to 8 pm.

Post & Telecommunications The main post office (Postamt 9010) is on the corner of Pernhartgasse and Dr Hermann Gasse, one block to the west of Neuer Platz. Opening times are Monday to Friday from 7.30 am to 8 pm and Saturday from 7.30 am to 1 pm. There's another post office (Postamt 9020) at the train station, open 24 hours a day.

Foreign Consulates Consulates include those for Hungary (☎ 50 41 41), Radetzkystrasse 50/1, and Slovenia (☎ 54 15 0), Bahnhofstrasse 22.

Travel Agency A helpful and central travel agency is Kärntner Reisebüro (☎ 56 4 00), Neuer Platz 2. Student fares are available and ISIC cards are issued (AS60). It's open Monday to Friday from 8.30 am to 12.30 pm and 2 to 5.30 pm, and Saturday from 9.30 am to noon.

Medical Services The hospital (☎ 53 80) is at St Veiter Strasse 47.

Central Sights

To take a walking tour, pick up the relevant brochure in English from the tourist office. It has a map and detailed descriptions of monuments, historic buildings and hidden courtyards. Free guided tours depart from the office in July and August, daily (except Sunday) at 10 am.

The **Neuer Platz** (New Square) is dominated by the *Dragon Fountain*, the emblem of the city. This winged beast (undergoing renovations until 1997) is modelled on the *Lindwurm* (dragon) of legend, which is said to have resided in a swamp here long ago, devouring cattle and virgins. Markets and festivals are held in the square, which also

PLACES TO STAY

7 Hotel Liebetegger
8 Jugendgästehaus Kolping
9 Hotel Moser-Verdino
19 Hotel Palais Porcia
21 Lehrerhausverein
24 Hotel Garni Blumenstöckl
28 Romantikhotel Musil

PLACES TO EAT

1 À La Carte Restaurant
3 Restaurant Akropolis

4 Zauberhutt'n
5 Gasthaus Zum Heiligen Josef
22 Gasthaus Pirker
23 Zur Chinesischen Mauer
29 Stefanitsch

OTHER

2 Stadttheater
6 Rathaus
10 Kärntner Reisebüro
11 Landhaus
12 City Bus Station
13 STW Transport Office
14 Hertz

15 Spar Supermarket
16 Main Tourist Office
17 Dragon Fountain
18 Landesgalerie
20 Spar Supermarket
25 Market Stalls
26 Main Post Office
27 Avis
30 Diocesan Museum
31 KGM Supermarket & Oregano Restaurant
32 Landesmuseum
33 Konzerthaus
34 Bus Station
35 Main Train Station

Klagenfurt

0   200   400 m

CARINTHIA

has a statue of Empress Maria Theresa dating from 1873.

Alter Platz (Old Square) is the oldest part of the city and contains a number of historic buildings. On the corner with Wiener Gasse is the 17th-century Rathaus, with an arcaded courtyard.

The 16th-century **Landhaus** stands just to the west of Alter Platz. This building is favoured with a two-storeyed courtyard and two steeples. The interior walls of its Hall of Arms (Wappensaal) are covered in paintings of 655 coats of arms belonging to the estates of Carinthia. More impressive than the walls is the ceiling, which has a gallery painted on it to give the illusion it is vaulted. It actually is perfectly flat. The scene, painted by Carinthian artist, Josef Ferdinand Fromiller (1693-1760), depicts the Carinthian estate owners paying homage to Charles VI. Stand in the centre of the room for the best effect. The Landhaus is open between 1 April and 31 September, Monday to Friday, from 9 am to noon and 12.30 to 5 pm. Entry to the Hall of Arms costs a nominal AS10 (students AS5).

Museums The **Landesmuseum** on Museumgasse reveals Carinthia's history and culture since Roman times (including a fine mosaic floor). One oddity is the *Lindwurmschädel*, a fossilised rhinoceros head which was the not-so-comely artist's model for the head of the *Dragon Fountain*. Entry costs AS30 (students AS15) and it's open Sunday from 10 am to 1 pm and other days (except non-rainy Mondays when it's closed) from 9 am to 4 pm.

The **Diocesan Museum**, in Lidmansky-gasse near the 16th-century cathedral, deals with religious art. The museum is open Monday to Saturday between May and mid-October (entry AS20). The **Landesgalerie**, Burggasse, concentrates on temporary exhibitions of recent art (AS20, children AS5). It's open Monday to Friday from 9 am to 6 pm, and 10 am to noon on weekends and holidays.

The **Mining Museum** (Bergbaumuseum), covers, would you believe it, mining (AS40,

students and senior citizens AS20, families AS80). It opens 1 April to 31 October daily from 9 am to 6 pm. Exhibits are within tunnels in the hill, and lead from the **Botanical Gardens** (free entry) at the far end of Radetzkystrasse. Adjoining the gardens is the **Kreuzbergl Church**, with mosaic Stations of the Cross on the path leading up, and hiking trails up the hill behind.

Europa Park Vicinity

Europa Park and Lake Wörth are areas for summer activities, on offer from around May to September. Balmy weather could extend the season. Buses S and K from Heiligen Geist Platz go to Minimundus, though only bus S continues the short distance to Strandbad.

Minimundus This is the most touristy offering in the park, yet quite fun, especially for kids. Detailed models of more than 150 famous international buildings on a 1:25 scale are displayed. The models are numbered, not labelled (you can pick up a catalogue for AS30). Some buildings, though, are instantly recognisable: the miniature of St Peter's Basilica in Rome is one of the most impressive. The Eiffel Tower, Statue of Liberty and Taj Mahal are also there, along with some (less famous) Austrian buildings. A café and restaurant (normal-sized) are on site. Minimundus is open daily from 9 am to 5 pm (late April and early October), 9 am to 6 pm (May, June and September) and 8 am to 7 pm (July and August; to 9 pm on Wednesday and Saturday during these months). Entry costs AS80 (children AS22).

Reptile Zoo This Reptilienzoo offers a chance to shudder at a variety of spiders, snakes and similar creatures. Brief but informative signs in English divulge facts like: spiders hear, taste and smell through their legs, and the blue poison arrow frog from Suriname, despite being under four cm long, can produce enough poison to kill 10 humans or 20,000 mice. Outside are squat crocodiles, giant turtles and model dinosaurs. It's open

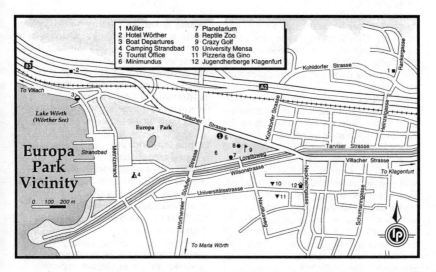

Key:
1 Müller
2 Hotel Wörther
3 Boat Departures
4 Camping Strandbad
5 Tourist Office
6 Minimundus
7 Planetarium
8 Reptile Zoo
9 Crazy Golf
10 University Mensa
11 Pizzeria da Gino
12 Jugendherberge Klagenfurt

Europa Park Vicinity

all year, daily from 8 am to 5 pm (6 pm in summer) and entry costs AS65 (students AS50, children AS30).

Strandbad This private beach on the lake has cabins (AS30), wooden piers, shady grassy areas, a nude sunbathing terrace (for men on Tuesday, Thursday and Saturday; women on other days) and a restaurant. It's open daily in the summer from 8 am to around 8 pm. A day card costs AS35 (AS15 for children) and a family card AS50 or AS80. After 3 pm entry costs AS20 (AS15 for children).

Adjoining the complex is a place for hiring rowing boats (AS24), pedal boats (AS42) and motorboats (AS66) – these prices are per 30 minutes.

Other Attractions The park is a fine place for a stroll, with winding pathways, fountains, statues and vibrant flowerbeds. There are tennis courts adjoining the park. Next to the reptile zoo is a **planetarium**, charging AS65 (children AS35) for a 45-minute show in German. Opposite there is crazy golf (AS30 per person per round), table tennis

(AS25 per hour), pool/billiards (AS10 per game) and bicycle rental (AS15 per hour, AS30 for three hours, or AS70 for one day).

The departure point for cruises on the lake is only a few hundred metres clockwise north of Strandbad. See the Lake Wörth section in this chapter for information on timetables and lakeside resorts.

Castles

Klagenfurt is ringed by castles and stately homes. The tourist office has a free map detailing routes, which is ideal if you have your own transport. These are close enough to be visited on a cycling tour. Some of the castles are covered in the tourist office's *Radwandern* cycling map, listing sights and distances. Tours (the longest being 34 km) are arranged according to specific themes.

Places to Stay

Bottom End Staying in Klagenfurt entitles visitors to a guest card, valid for various discounts and available from hotels.

Camping Strandbad (☎ 21 1 69) is in a good location by the lake in Europa Park. There is a shop with a buffet on site and

CARINTHIA

campers can use the swimming complex free of charge. The camp site is open from 1 May to 30 September and costs AS50 per adult (AS25 for children to age 14), plus AS100 for a large site (including electricity, parking and hot water) or AS20 for a small site (under 20 sq metres). In the high season, from 20 June to 20 August, the price per person rises to AS80 for adults and AS40 for children. An AS12 resort tax must be added.

The HI *Jugendherberge Klagenfurt* (☎ 23 00 20), Neckheimgasse 6, near Europa Park, has modern facilities and four-bed dorms with private shower/WC for AS170. Double rooms are AS220 per person and dinner is AS80. Reception shuts from 9 am to 5 pm, though you can leave your bags during the day. Door keys are available, and the hostel closes from mid-December to 31 January. To get there from the centre, take bus S, but check with the driver before embarking as some take a different route.

The HI *Jugendgästehaus Kolping* (☎ 56 9 65), Enzenbergstrasse 26, is a 10-minute walk east of Neuer Platz, but it's only open from 10 July to 10 September. Rooms with shower cost AS180 for a single or AS140 per person for doubles/triples; add AS20 for the first night.

There are about a dozen homes that offer private rooms, for AS160 to AS300 per person. These are mostly in the suburbs. An exception is *Lehrerhausverein*, Bäckergasse 17, with eight beds and private shower for AS212 per person. Apply to Rauter Anita (☎ 51 38 40) at Adlergasse 11, the next street east.

Hotel Liebetegger (☎ 56 9 35), Völkermarkter Strasse 8, is the only central budget hotel. Rooms start from AS220/350 for singles/doubles with just a sink, and rooms with private shower/WC cost AS400/750. Breakfast is AS50.

The other budget places are a bit out of the way. *Müller* (☎ 21 2 54), Rankengasse 21, is not too badly placed between the centre and Europa Park. Rooms are fairly plain, starting from AS260 per person, and some have private shower. The restaurant is good value and a haunt for chess players.

Middle & Top End If you have your own transport, consider staying at *Waldwirt* (☎ 42 6 42; fax 46 6 80), Josefiwaldweg 2, on the Kreuzbergl hill north-west of the city. Singles/doubles start at AS380/760 – low prices for a three-star place with swimming pool.

To stay in style overlooking Lake Wörth, go to *Hotel Wörther See* (☎ 21 1 58; fax 21 15 88), Villacher Strasse 338. Its rooms are well-presented, some with balcony, and all with cable TV, toilet and bath or shower. There's also a stretch of private beach. Singles/doubles are AS395/690, or AS540/790 in the high season.

Hotel Garni Blumenstöckl (☎ 57 7 93; fax 57 79 35), 10 Oktober Strasse 11, is in a 400-year-old building where the rooms are built around a 1st-floor courtyard. This small family-run place has rooms with bath, toilet and cable TV for around AS500/900.

On the opposite side of the junction is *Romantikhotel Musil* (☎ 51 16 60; fax 51 16 60 4), 10 Oktober Strasse 14. The historic building also has an interesting structure, with rooms grouped around an attractive oval atrium. Rooms have antique furniture and are kitted out in a variety of styles, ranging from rustic to Maria Theresa Baroque. All rooms are doubles and have modern amenities. Prices start at AS1400, with a 10% reduction for single occupancy. *Hotel Moser-Verdino* (☎ 57 8 78; fax 51 67 65), Domgasse 2, is under the same management, and has more facilities for businesspeople, despite the Art-Nouveau exterior. Singles/doubles start from AS990/1200.

Hotel Palais Porcia (☎ 51 15 90; fax 51 15 90 30), is ideally situated at Neuer Platz 13. The hotel has a sumptuous lounge on the 3rd floor, with portraits, period furniture and ornate mirrors. Most rooms match this opulence and cost from AS950/1350 to AS2400/4800.

Places to Eat

Eating cheaply in the town centre isn't too hard. Several snack stands dot the area, or you can stock up at a *Spar* supermarket either in Adlergasse or Dr Hermann Gasse. On Bahnhofstrasse there's a *KGM* supermarket with a self-service *Oregano* restaurant, where daily menus with soup are from AS55.

A fruit and vegetable market occupies Benediktinerplatz from Monday to Saturday, which is bolstered by a flower market on Thursday and Saturday morning. There are several tiny restaurants in the market arcade, where stand-up or sit-down meals are only about AS50.

Stefanitsch on Lidmanskygasse is a combination deli and stand-up snack bar, with weekday lunch specials for under AS60 (open shop hours with early closing on Wednesday). On the same street, at No 19, is *Zur Chinesischen Mauer*, a Chinese restaurant with a weekday lunch menu for about AS62 (open daily).

West of town and convenient for the youth hostel and Europa Park is the university *Mensa*, Universitätsstrasse 90, which is open to all. Cheap meals are available all year, Monday to Friday from 11 am to 2.30 pm. Virtually opposite at No 33 is *Pizzeria da Gino*, with pavement tables and tasty food for AS65 to AS120 (open daily from 11 am to midnight).

Restaurant Akropolis, Heuplatz, offers Greek food from AS70, cheap weekday lunches and occasional live music (closed Sunday). Close by, off Waaggasse, is *Zauberhutt'n*, with good Italian food from AS60 in a rustic environment (open daily). *Gasthaus Zum Heiligen Josef* is on the opposite corner; local cuisine starts at AS80 (closed Sunday and Monday in winter).

Gasthaus Pirker, on the corner of Adlergasse and Lidmanskygasse, is another place for Austrian food (from AS70 to AS130). It has a comfortable interior and a bar area. Opening hours are Monday to Friday from 8 am to midnight.

For more expensive dining, try hotel restaurants, such as that in the Hotel Musil (see Places to Stay). This hotel has its own bakery: incredibly elaborate cakes are sold in the shop and café. Fancy guzzling a Lindwurm-shaped confectionery? You can here. The restaurant in the Hotel Wörther See

(see Places to Stay) is very highly rated for regional cuisine (closed Monday lunchtime and Sunday, except in July and August).

One of the top restaurants in town is the aptly named *À La Carte* (☎ 51 66 51), Khevenhüller Strasse 3, a small, formal, expensive, but popular (reserve ahead) place. Austrian and international main courses are AS150 or more; cover charge is AS50 (closed Sunday and Monday).

Entertainment
I overheard a disgruntled young traveller describe Klagenfurt as 'the city of the dead'. She has a point. Klagenfurt has no nightlife worthy of the name – drop a pin in the centre of town on a Saturday night and you might be arrested for noise pollution. The only exception to this is around Pfarrplatz, where there are a couple of decent bars.

The *Stadttheater*, Theaterplatz 4, puts on plays, operettas and operas. Its ticket office (☎ 54 0 64) is open Tuesday to Saturday from 9 am to noon and 4 to 6 pm. Standing-room tickets are sometimes available. Other musical events are held at the *Konzerthaus*, Miesstaler Strasse 8. Pick up the yearly or monthly booklet of events from the tourist office.

Getting There & Away
Air The airport (☎ 41 5 00) has five flights a day to Vienna (with Tyrolean Airways) and two a day each to Zürich (Crossair) and Frankfurt (Tyrolean). The only other flights are chartered flights.

Bus Bundesbuses depart from outside the main train station; call ☎ 54 3 40 for route details. See the Lake Wörth Getting Around section for information on buses to resorts at the lake.

Train Trains to Graz depart every one to two hours (AS316; takes three hours); these go via Bruck an der Mur (AS252), 170 km to the north-east. Trains to western Austria, Italy, Slovenia and Germany go via Villach (AS64; takes 30 to 40 minutes, with two to four trains per hour). Heading to Ljubljana, you can lop off the trip to Villach by taking the local line from Klagenfurt to Rosenbach (AS64, 30 minutes), and continuing from there. However, these non-express trains are less frequent, so it depends upon a good connection to save any time. Call ☎ 1717 for train information.

Car & Motorbike The A2/E66 between Villach and Graz goes directly into Klagenfurt, though a section to skirt the city is under construction.

Car rental offices include: Avis (☎ 55 9 38), Villacher Strasse 1A; Europcar (☎ 51 45 38), Völkermarkter Ring 9; and Hertz (☎ 56 1 47), Villacher Strasse 4.

Getting Around

To get to the airport, take bus A from Heiligen Geist Platz in the town centre and transfer to bus F at Annabichl, which is about 2½ km north of Neuer Platz.

City buses cost AS15 for one journey (including changes) or AS36 for a day pass (available on the bus). A five-journey strip ticket costs AS60 and is available only in advance (eg from the STW transport office on Heiligen Geist Platz). Bus services are sparse in the evening so a bus timetable, free from the tourist office, is useful if you're staying out of the centre. Bus A runs from the main train station to the town centre.

The station rents bikes at the standard rate and the counter is open 24 hours. For a taxi, call ☎ 31 1 11, ☎ 35 5 55 or ☎ 21 4 44.

Lake Wörth

Lake Wörth (Wörther See) is one of the warmer lakes in the region owing to thermal springs. The average water temperature between June and September is 21°C. Summers are very hot in any case, so it's an ideal location for frolicking amid the lapping waves, or for the serious pursuit of water sports. The lake stretches from west to east;

the thin contours provide unfolding vistas on a boat trip.

The north shore has the best transport access and is the busiest side. On this side, the first main resort after Klagenfurt is **Krumpendorf**. This place has plenty of parkland and areas for tennis, golf and water sports. The tourist office, the Kurverwaltung (☎ 04229-23 13), is in the Rathaus on Schlossallee.

The next resort is **Pörtschach**, which has a distinctive tree-lined peninsula creating a curving bay on either side. Along the lake shore is a pleasant promenade lined with flowers. The resort has a golf course and the usual water sports. Contact the tourist office (☎ 04272-23 54), Hauptplatz 182, for details.

On the southern shore lies **Maria Wörth**, a small resort dominated by two churches. The largest combines Gothic, Baroque and Romanesque elements; the smaller is known as the Winter Church (12th century), and features Romanesque frescoes of the apostles. On the hill south-east of Maria Wörth is **Pyramidenkogel**, a rather ugly tower that nevertheless provides fine views of Lake Wörth and the surrounding mountain ranges. At 905 metres high, it stands 435 metres higher than the lake. It's open between April and October and entry is AS45 (children AS15).

Getting Around

Bus & Train Bundesbuses travel both sides of the lake. Bus 5179 runs between Villach and Klagenfurt about seven times a day, taking 45 minutes to cover the 23 km of the Velden-Klagenfurt leg, travelling along the north shore.

Bus 5310 goes on the south side of the lake between Klagenfurt and Velden. There are about 10 departures daily in summer, though there are fewer on Sunday and some buses don't run at all from late September to the end of May. Buses stop at all the main resorts round the lake. Bus 5316 also runs between Klagenfurt and Velden on the south side of the lake, but by a different route; take this one for Pyramidenkogel, transferring to bus

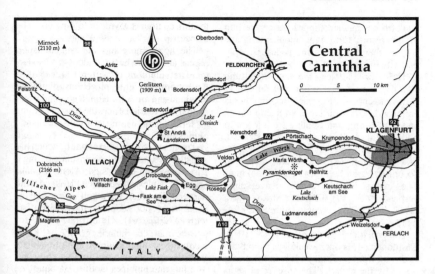

Central Carinthia

5314 at Keutscharch am See. The trip costs AS52 from either Klagenfurt or Velden.

The train line from Klagenfurt to Villach passes along the north shore of the lake. Regional trains stop at Krumpendorf, Pörtschach and Velden; express trains may stop at only one of those stations. The main roads are also on the north side: the A2/E66 and highway 83, which runs closer to the shore. On the south side, the road is classified as a main road, but it's much smaller.

Bicycle A circuit of the lake is about 50 km, well within reach of most casual cyclists, especially with an overnight stop somewhere. Bikes can be hired at the Klagenfurt, Krumpendorf, Pörtschach and Velden train stations and returned to any other. The Klagenfurt tourist office *Fahrradverleih* leaflet lists other places on the lake that rent bikes from around April to October (AS30 for three hours, AS70 for 24 hours); bikes can be returned to any of these outlets.

Boat STW (☎ 21 1 55), St Veiter Strasse 31, runs steamers on the lake from the end of April to mid-October. Boats call at both sides, stopping at Klagenfurt, Krumpendorf, Sekirn, Reifnitz, Maria Wörth, Pörtschach, Dellach, Weisses Rössl, Auen and Velden, and return by the same route. Departures are at least every two hours. The longest trip (Klagenfurt-Velden) takes one hour and 45 minutes, costs AS115 one-way and AS170 return. A stopoff is allowed en route. Alternatively, the special 'round-trip' ticket *(Rundfahrtkarte)*, also for AS170 (AS150 if purchased before boarding) allows unlimited stops en route. The same ticket for a family costs AS380 (AS330 in advance). A four-week pass costs AS400 for adults (photo required). Child fares are about half-price. STW also has evening cruises with music and dancing.

VELDEN

• ☎ *(04274)*

This resort town exudes an aura of affluence and is one of the most popular holiday destinations on the lake.

Orientation & Information

Velden is ranged round the western shoreline. The train station is about 10 minutes walk from Karawankenplatz, the central hub of the resort: turn right upon exiting the station, then left down the pedestrian way partially blocked by flower boxes.

The tourist office, the Kurverwaltung (☎ 21 03), Seecorso 2, is at the far end of Karawankenplatz. Summer opening hours are Monday to Saturday from 8 am to noon and 2 to 6 pm, and Sunday from 9 am to noon. In July and August hours are extended, in winter (mid-October to late April) they're much shorter. The office can help find accommodation but doesn't take bookings. The same applies with the Fremdenverkehrsverband (☎ 39 19), Villacher Strasse 14, a privately-funded accommodation and information office.

The provincial tourist office (☎ 52 10 0), Casinoplatz 1, is open weekdays from 8 am to 5 pm (4 pm on Friday). It is in the cream house by the church. The absence of signs makes it seem they're hiding from tourists, though they are helpful when you finally locate them.

Things to See & Do
Velden hasn't much in the way of sights, but you could linger in front of the Baroque doorway of the 16th-century former palace, now a hotel, on Seecorso. The **casino** is at Europaplatz on Am Corso and is open daily from 3 pm.

Apart from strolling around enjoying the relaxed atmosphere, the main attractions are water activities. Several **beaches** requiring an entrance fee (AS45 to AS70 per day), and rowing boats (AS40 per hour) and motorboats (AS160 per hour) are for hire. There is sailing, windsurfing, water-skiing and scuba diving.

Land activities include tennis and golf. All contact addresses and prices are given in lists available from the tourist office.

The hills north of Velden provide good views of the Karawanken mountain range to the south.

South of Velden is the Rosegg **animal park** (Wildpark; ☎ 26 74), which is open daily.

Places to Stay & Eat
In Velden you can choose between hotels, pensions, private rooms or holiday apartments. For a town of just 7500 people there's an extremely wide choice. It's best to elicit the help of one of the tourist offices. Prices are higher in summer, and these prices (per person) are quoted below.

Some of the central but still reasonably cheap pensions include: *Haus Tschebull* (☎ 26 75), Karawankenplatz 4 (from AS330); *Villa Brigitta* (☎ 20 88), Koschatpromenade 5 (AS400); *Seehaus Ogris* (☎ 20 79), Seecorso 34 (from AS450 with own shower); and *Gästehaus Rauchenwald* (☎ 26 12), Seecorso 36 (from AS490 with own shower).

Supermarkets include *ADEG* on Karawankenplatz and *Konsum* at Europaplatz. Walk along Seecorso to find various places to buy inexpensive fast food, such as *Wurstsalon* (open summer only). *Pavillon*, Seecorso 8, offers Italian food from AS78 (open noon to 1 am). *China-Restaurant Xiangianghof*, Am Corso 2A, has weekday lunch menus with starter from AS75; it's comparatively expensive for Chinese food, but still one of the cheaper options in town (open daily).

Quality regional cuisine (main courses from AS180) is served at *Hubertushof* (☎ 26 76), Europaplatz 1 (open daily with hot food till 8.30 pm). This place is also a hotel, with rooms starting at AS890 per person. Many facilities are on site, including an indoor swimming pool, sauna and fitness room.

Getting There & Away
Trains go to Villach (AS34; takes 10 to 15 minutes) every 30 minutes, and to Klagenfurt (AS48; 15 to 20 minutes) at least hourly.

Eastern Carinthia

The best sights in eastern Carinthia are north of Klagenfurt, on or close to highway 83 and the rail route between Klagenfurt and Bruck an der Mur. On either side are mountain ranges: the Seetaler Alpen and Saualpen to the east and the Gurktaler Alpen to the west.

FRIESACH
• *pop 7000*   • *636 m*   • ☎ *(04268)*

Friesach has a peaceful, unhurried air that belies the bristling fortifications on every hill top. It is Carinthia's oldest town, important for its key location on the Vienna-Venice trade route, and part of the diocese of Salzburg since 860 AD. Ensuing centuries saw invasions by the Bohemians, Hungarians, Turks and French, until the town came under the wing of the Habsburgs in 1803.

Orientation & Information
Friesach lies in the Metnitz Valley. The town centre, the picturesque Hauptplatz, is 10 minutes walk from the train station along Bahnhofstrasse: turn left upon exiting the station and follow the road as it branches right.

The tourist office (☎ 43 00), Hauptplatz 1, is open in summer, Monday to Friday from 9 am to noon and 2 to 6 pm, and Saturday from 9 am to noon. The rest of the year hours are Monday to Friday from 10 am to noon and 3 to 5 pm, and Saturday 10 am to noon.

Things to See & Do
Friesach is unique in Austria in retaining a filled moat with its ancient city walls. Flower borders seduce strollers who meander along the bank. North of the moat is a **Dominican monastery**; its 13th-century Gothic church is open to the public, and is noted for the wooden crucifix and sandstone statue of the Virgin.

Linger in Hauptplatz, an enchanting square with a Renaissance fountain. Just to the north is the **parish church**, with a fine 12th-century font and a distinctive tiled roof. To see the interior of the slender, 14th-century **Church of the Holy Blood** (Heiligblutkirche), you need to ask for the key from the manse *(Pharhof)* at the parish church.

Ranged along the hills rising above Hauptplatz stand four ancient fortifications, all providing excellent views of the town and valley. The northernmost is Geyersberg Castle; the farthest south is the Virgilienberg Ruins. The middle two are the most easily visited from the town. A path winds up by the Church of the Holy Blood to the **Rotturm Ruins**, a 13th-century tower of which little remains. A better view is from **St Peter's Church**, accessible by paths ascending from in front of the parish church. To see the Gothic interior of St Peter's Church, ask for the key in the house next door.

Behind St Peter's Church is **St Peter's Castle**, which houses the town museum, open May to October daily between 10 am and 5 pm (entry AS40, students and senior citizens AS20, children AS10). The castle is also the site for open-air theatre (anything from Shakespeare to Brecht) in summer. Obtain details and tickets (AS120 to AS200) from the tourist office.

Friesach gets all medieval in two festivals: the Altstadtfest in the first weekend of June, and the Ritterfest in mid-July. The townsfolk don ancient costumes, and duels and other events are staged.

Places to Stay
Zum Goldenen Anker (☎ 23 13), Bahnhofstrasse 3, is by Hauptplatz and has good-sized singles/doubles for AS195/350, or AS290/440 with private shower. This small Gasthof also serves limited meals (AS60 to AS110).

A country farmhouse

CARINTHIA

Weisser Wolf (☎ 22 63), Hauptplatz 8, has comfortable rooms for AS325 per person with shower and TV, and maybe WC. Food in the restaurant starts at AS90, or there's a three-course lunch menu for around AS120.

The only four-star hotel is *Metnitztalerhof* (☎ 25 10 0; fax 25 10 54), Hauptplatz 11. Singles/doubles with shower/WC and TV start at AS480/790; some have a big balcony with good views. It also has a restaurant, with outside tables overlooking the square.

Places to Eat

The *Konsum* supermarket, near the train station on Bahnhofstrasse, is open Monday to Friday from 8 am to 6 pm and Saturday from 8 am to 12.30 pm.

Explore the places round Hauptplatz, such as the hotels mentioned above. *Pizzeria Restaurant*, Langegasse 2, a left turn from the western end of Hauptplatz, has Austrian lunch specials (from AS60) or pizzas from AS80 (closed Tuesday).

Getting There & Away

Friesach is on the train line between Vienna's Südbahnhof and Villach, with express trains every hour. Bruck an der Mur (AS192) is en route. Slower trains also go to Klagenfurt every hour (AS94; takes about 55 minutes). The train station rents bicycles.

GURK

This small town, some 18 km west of the Friesach-St Veit road, is visited for its **cathedral**. It was built from 1140 to 1200 and is one of the finest examples of Romanesque architecture in Austria. The relatively plain exterior is dominated by two huge onion domes capping square-sided twin towers. The interior has Gothic reticulated vaulting on the ceiling, and most of the church fittings are Baroque or rococo. The early Baroque high altar is particularly impressive: it's laden with 72 statues and 82 angels' heads.

The frescoes in the Episcopal Chapel, dating from around 1200, are made all the more affecting by their primitive colours. The chapel can be viewed by guided tour only, daily at 1 pm from April to October. The church is open daily, all year.

Those with children might be interested in visiting the nearby **Zwergenpark**, or Dwarfs Park, populated by garden gnomes. It has a mini-railway and is open May to October (AS55; children AS25 or AS35). For information call ☎ 04266-85 20.

Getting There & Away

Gurk cannot be reached by rail, and Bundesbus No 5371 goes there from St Veit an der Glan about three times a day. Private transport makes a visit much easier: the town is on highway 93.

ST VEIT AN DER GLAN

• *pop 12,000* • *476 m* • ☎ *(04212)*

St Veit was historically important as the seat of the dukes of Carinthia from 1170 to 1518. Then the dukes skipped down the road to Klagenfurt and the town diminished in status.

Orientation & Information

St Veit is near the junction of main road routes to Villach (highway 94) and Klagenfurt (highway 83). To get to the pedestrian-only town centre from the main train station (which usually has maps to give out), walk left down Bahnhofstrasse for 600 metres and then go one block right.

The tourist office (☎ 55 55 13) is in the Rathaus at Hauptplatz 1, in the heart of the pedestrian area. It is open weekdays, plus Saturday in summer. Another tourist office (☎ 23 74) is in the circular hut with a conical roof, two short blocks north-west of the south-western end of Hauptplatz. It has better information on regional attractions, but is only open in summer.

Things to See & Do

The town centre can occupy visitors for a couple of hours. Places of interest are on the long **Hauptplatz**, with a fountain at either end and a central column, erected in 1715 to plague victims. The north-eastern fountain, the Schüsselbrunnen, is surmounted by a bronze statue, created in 1566. This figure is the town mascot: its hand is raised as if in greeting, yet at the same time a jet of water spits forth from its mouth. The south-western fountain bears a statue of local medieval poet, Walther von der Vogelweide.

The most impressive façade on Hauptplatz belongs to the Rathaus. Its Baroque stuccowork was created in 1754, and features a double-headed eagle on the pediment. St Veit (the saint, not the town) stands between the eagle's wings. Walk through the Gothic vaulted passage to admire the arcaded courtyard, complete with sgraffito designs.

Close to the town hall is the **Transport Museum** (Verkehrsmuseum), Hauptplatz 29. It does a reasonable job of making the development of transport in the region seem interesting, and displays old travel documents, motorbikes, model trains and mannequins wearing uniforms (no English text). The WW II display includes photos of bomb-damaged Villach and Klagenfurt train stations; appropriately, the guard dummy in this section sports a ludicrous Hitler moustache! It's open daily from 1 May to 15 October and entry costs AS35 (students AS20, children AS15). Close to Hauptplatz there's also a city museum (on Burggasse, in the former ducal castle) and a Romanesque parish church.

Frauenstein Castle, five km north-west of St Veit, is a 16th-century building with turrets, towers and a courtyard.

Places to Stay
In St Veit, there are inexpensive choices to stay, including private rooms. The *camp site* (☎ 21 90) is east of the centre, off Völkermarkter Strasse.

Gasthof Steirerhof (☎ 24 42), Klagenfurter Strasse 38, five minutes walk south of the centre, has adequate rooms with hall showers for AS220 per person. *Gasthof Sonnhof* (☎ 24 47), Völkermarkter Strasse 37, towards the camp site, has good rooms with shower, toilet and balcony from AS210 per person, and a good-value restaurant (closed Monday). To walk from the station in 10 minutes, exit the east side and bear right when the path joins the road.

Even the most expensive place in town, the four-star *Weisses Lamm* (☎ 23 62), Unterer Platz 4, costs only from about AS430 per person.

Places to Eat
By the main train station is a *Billa* supermarket. Nearby, at Bahnhofstrasse 32 (opposite the *Spar* supermarket), is *Pizzamax*, a cheap, takeaway pizza place. The *Interspar* supermarket on Völkermarkter Strasse has a large self-service restaurant where hot meals are from AS45 to AS80. Its salad bar costs AS10 per 100 grams. Adjoining the pedestrian zone, the *KGM* supermarket also has a cheap, self-service restaurant.

There are lots of more comfortable places to eat in the compact pedestrian area, many with outside tables. Just west of Hauptplatz is *Gasthof Traube*, with a garden and inexpensive regional food (closed Monday evening). Nearby is *Pukelsheim* (☎ 24 73), Erlgasse 11, a place for expensive, up-market Austrian and regional meals (closed Sunday and Monday).

Getting There & Away
St Veit is 33 km south of Friesach and 20 km north of Klagenfurt. Express trains on the Vienna-Villach route stop at St Veit. Fares are AS64 to Friesach and AS34 to Klagenfurt.

HOCHOSTERWITZ CASTLE
This fortress drapes itself around the slopes of a hill and is a stunning sight, especially when viewed from the north-west. The visual impact is due mainly to the 14 gate towers and their connecting walls that circle the hill to the summit. These were built from 1570 to 1586 by Georg Khevenhüller, the then owner, to protect against Turkish invasion. It all certainly looks impregnable, and the booklet (in English; AS30) outlines the different challenges presented to attackers by each gate (it's almost like a medieval forerunner to the multiple levels in computer adventure games!).

The castle itself was first mentioned in documents in 860. The small museum features family portraits and arms and armour (one suit would fit a two-metre giant). There's an inexpensive restaurant within the grounds. Entry costs AS40 (children AS20) and it's open from Palm Sunday to October, daily from 8 am to 6 pm.

Getting There & Away

Regional trains on the St Veit-Friesach route stop at Launsdorf Hochosterwitz station, a 30-minute walk from the car park and the first gate, where a lift, costing AS40, ascends directly to the castle. Infrequent buses from either Klagenfurt or St Veit will get you one km closer (to the Brückl crossroads). If you don't have time to visit, you can at least absorb the sight from the train: sit on the left if travelling south.

MAGDALENSBERG

Four km south of Hochosterwitz Castle, this 1058-metre peak provides an excellent 360° panorama from its summit. The road up approaches from the south. There's also a Roman archaeological open-air museum here (open 15 May to 15 October) and a Gothic chapel. Buses from Klagenfurt arrive once a day on schooldays (at 2.30 pm), and depart five minutes later. This means taking the bus is not viable, unless you're prepared to walk down the hill to one of the nearby villages to pick up another bus or a train.

MARIA SAAL

• *pop 3200* • ☎ *(04223)*
On a fortified hill stands the pilgrimage church of Maria Saal. Its twin spires are visible from afar.

Orientation & Information

The small town is 10 km north of Klagenfurt. The road from the train station splits in two and encloses the church hill. Behind the church is Hauptplatz, with a bank and several restaurants. The tourist office (☎ 22 14 12), Am Platz 7, is in the centre of Hauptplatz.

Things to See & Do

The **church** was built in the early 15th century from volcanic stone. Originally Gothic, it later received Romanesque and Baroque modifications. The exterior south wall is embedded with relief panels and ancient gravestones: look for the Keutschach family tombstone in red marble, and the Roman mail wagon. There are unusual outbuildings within the walled enclosure. Inside, the body of the church is nicely proportioned when looking down the nave. Overhead, the ceiling is fan-vaulted, and there are frescoes of people growing out of bulbous flowers (that's not as hallucinogenic as it sounds – it represents the genealogy of Christ). The image of the Virgin on the high altar dates from 1425; either side of the main altar are two Gothic winged altars. An explanatory pamphlet, in English, is available in the church.

About 500 metres north of the church is the **Carinthian Open-Air Museum** (Kärntner Freilichtmuseum; ☎ 28 12 or 31 66). It contains over 30 typical or historical Carinthian rural dwellings and has demonstrations of country crafts. It is open daily from 10 am to 6 pm, between about 1 May and 30 September (weather permitting). Entry costs AS50 for adults, AS120 for families and AS20 for students.

Getting There & Away

There are no official left-luggage facilities in the small train station, but the ticket clerk will guard your bags if you ask nicely. Maria Saal is on the same Vienna-Villach rail route as Friesach and St Veit, but only the slower regional trains stop here. Fares are AS34 to St Veit and AS17 to Klagenfurt. Buses run to both places from below the church.

Western Carinthia

Excluding the Hohe Tauern National Park (see the following chapter), the main points of interest in western Carinthia are close to the primary road route north, the A10/E55.

This road ultimately leads to Salzburg. It has a toll section from Rennweg to north of the Tauern Tunnel (AS190); to avoid the toll, take highway 99.

The rail route takes a more easterly course after Spittal an der Drau, before also turning north. It is shadowed by highway 106 (later 105), the road to Badgastein. However, driving this way necessitates using the railway car-shuttle service (*Autoschleuse Tauernbahn*), through the tunnel from Mallnitz-Obervellach (in Carinthia) to Böckstein (in Salzburg). The fare is AS190 one-way or AS290 return (valid two months). The price for motorbikes is AS100/160. For information on services through this tunnel, telephone ☎ 04784-600 390 in Mallnitz-Obervellach or ☎ 06434-26 63 39 in Böckstein. Departures are usually every 30 to 60 minutes (summer/winter), except at night.

VILLACH
- *pop 53,000* • *500 m* • ☎ *(04242)*

Villach is an important transport hub for routes into Italy and Slovenia. The influence of both these nations can be discerned in its ambience and inhabitants. The town has a handful of sights, and can also serve as a base for exploring Lake Ossiach and other attractions. See the later Around Villach section for details.

Orientation & Information
The old town centre is south of the Drau River. North of the river is the main train station, the bus station and a post office, all close together on Bahnhofplatz. From the well-equipped train station, walk south down Bahnhofstrasse and bear left off Nikolaigasse for the tourist office (☎ 24 4 44 0), Europaplatz 2; it's a five-minute walk. The office is open Monday to Friday from 8 am to 12.30 pm and 1.30 to 6 pm, and Saturday from 9 am to noon (also in the afternoon in July and August).

The post office is on Postgasse (Postamt 9501). It's open Monday to Friday from 7 am to 6 pm.

Things to See & Do
The yellow and blue city bus that completes a circuit of the centre every 20 minutes is free. The smaller tourist office map has English text guiding visitors through a walk of the old town. Alas, there's nothing spectacular to see. The pedestrian-only hub of the town is the long, slender Hauptplatz, at the south end of which stands **St Jacob's Parish Church**. This Gothic building has a tower (open in the summer; entry AS20), a rococo altar, carved gravestones and an unusual pulpit.

Perhaps the best sight is the **Relief of Carinthia**, housed in Schiller Park, Peraustrasse, south of the old town. This huge relief map covers 182 sq metres and shows the province on a scale of 1:10,000 (1:5000 vertically, to exaggerate the mountains). It can help you plan your trip (or track your progress) through the region, and there are some interesting photos on the walls. The building is open from 2 May to 31 October daily, except Sunday and holidays, from 10 am to 4.30 pm. Entry costs AS20 (students AS20, children free), or AS25 in combination with the **Museum der Stadt Villach** (city museum), Widmanngasse 38. Open the same hours as the relief map, the museum covers local history, archaeology, and medieval art.

The **Villacher Fahrzeugmuseum**, Draupromenade 12, displays motorcycles and cars, mostly from the 1950s and '60s. Many are crammed together, without any apparent regard for their condition or curiosity value. The bicycles with tiny motors are quite fun. Entry costs AS50 (students AS25), and it's open daily in summer, and daily except Sundays and holidays from mid-September to mid-July.

Festivals
On the first Saturday in August the pedestrian centre is taken over by a folklore festival, the Kirchtag, which is held from noon to midnight. Entry is AS60.

Places to Stay
The HI *youth hostel* (☎ 56 3 68), Dinzlweg

CARINTHIA

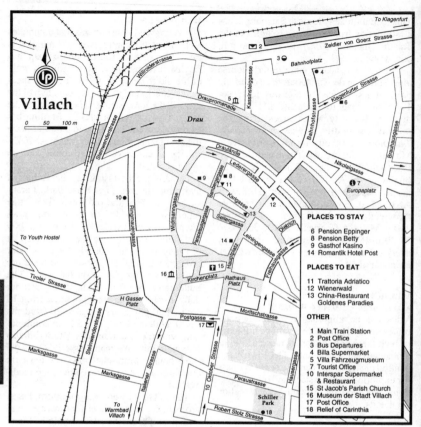

Villach

0   50   100 m

Drau

PLACES TO STAY

6 Pension Eppinger
8 Pension Betty
9 Gasthof Kasino
14 Romantik Hotel Post

PLACES TO EAT

11 Trattoria Adriatico
12 Wienerwald
13 China-Restaurant
   Goldenes Paradies

OTHER

1 Main Train Station
2 Post Office
3 Bus Departures
4 Billa Supermarket
5 Villa Fahrzeugmuseum
7 Tourist Office
10 Interspar Supermarket
   & Restaurant
15 St Jacob's Parish Church
16 Museum der Stadt Villach
17 Post Office
18 Relief of Carinthia

34, is about one km west of the pedestrian centre. Walk south from Hauptplatz, turn right at the post office on the corner of Postgasse, continue over the bridge and then bear right on St Martiner Strasse. Dinzlweg is the first on the left. The hostel has four-bed dorms with private shower/WC for AS140 per person, and dinner is AS70. Don't abuse their hospitality in the serve-yourself breakfast. Doors are open in the day (though reception is closed from 9 am to 6 pm), and getting a key means you can avoid the 10 pm curfew. There's bike rental on site (AS15 per hour or AS80 per day).

Pension Eppinger (☎ 24 3 89), Klagenfurter Strasse 6, the first left on Bahnhofstrasse when heading from the main train station, charges AS210 per person or AS250 with private shower. There's no breakfast either way. Rooms are adequate; it's off the street, through the green gate.

Pension Betty (☎ 27 2 28), Bambergergasse 3, looks plain from the outside, but the rooms are OK, if compact, and the owner's quite jolly. Singles/doubles for AS300/500 have shower/WC, and it's open all year.

Nearby is *Gasthof Kasino* (☎ 24 4 49), Kaiser Josef Platz 4, two blocks west of

MARK HONAN

MARK HONAN

MARK HONAN

Top: Outdoor café scene, Graz, Styria
Left: Arcaded courtyard, with sgraffito designs, in the Rathaus, St Viet an der Glan, Carinthia
Right: Vulture, at the Alpine Zoo, Innsbruck, Tirol

GEERT COLE

MARK HONAN

AUSTRIAN NATIONAL TOURIST OFFICE

Top: Carinthian mountain chalets
Left: Tiled roofs and spires of Graz, Styria
Right: Südtiroler Platz, Graz, Styria

Hauptplatz. Rooms are fairly large in this oldish building, and cost AS280 per person or AS350 with shower/WC (and sometimes TV). It has a garage (free for guests) and an inexpensive restaurant.

Romantik Hotel Post (☎ 26 1 01 0), Hauptplatz 26, is in a historic building with a garden and sauna (free for guests). Rooms with bath or shower, WC and satellite TV, vary in style and price, starting at AS670/1100.

Places to Eat

There's a *Billa* supermarket opposite the train station, and various snack places nearby. South of the river, slightly west of the pedestrian area on Ringmauergasse, is *Interspar*, a shopping and supermarket centre. It has a self-service restaurant, open Monday to Friday from 8.30 am to 6.30 pm (to 7.30 pm Friday) and Saturday from 8 am to 1 pm (to 5 pm on Langersamstag). Meals are cheap anyway, but there are sometimes special deals from mid-afternoon. The salad buffet is AS10 per 100 grams.

At the north end of Hauptplatz there's a *Wienerwald* with a takeaway section. On Hauptplatz itself there's *China-Restaurant Goldenes Paradies* above the Julius Meinl supermarket. It's open daily. Weekday noon menus are AS57 and AS62. An alternative is to seek out the cafés in the pedestrian centre that give a flavour of the countries farther south (particularly Italy); many have outside tables. *Trattoria Adriatico* (☎ 26 3 74), Bambergergasse, is a quality Italian place, with lunch menus from AS90 and other dishes above AS120 (closed weekends).

The *Romantik Restaurant* of the Hotel Post (see Places to Stay) has an ambience that tries to live up to its name. It's open daily and serves acclaimed regional specialities, mostly above AS160; it offers a three-course lunch menu for AS140, and a dieter's menu for AS115.

Getting There & Away

Villach is on three Austrian IC express routes, serving Salzburg (AS264, takes 2½ hours), Lienz (AS168, 70 minutes) and Klagenfurt (AS64, 30 minutes). It is also the junction at which two international EC routes diverge and head south. Direct services go to many destinations, such as Venice (AS190, 3½ hours), Ljubljana (AS116, 1¾ hours) and Zagreb (AS214, four hours). Reduced fares are available for people under 26 on these EC routes.

Villach is equally well served by roads. The autobahns cross in a confusion of slip-roads four km to the east of the centre. Various bus routes radiate from Villach; call ☎ 44 4 10 for Bundesbus information.

AROUND VILLACH

Three km south of the town centre is **Warmbad Villach**, a complex of thermal pools, heated at 33°C, and rejuvenating radioactive mineral waters, reputed to hinder the ageing process rather than causing unpleasant mutations. Nearly 40 million litres of water gush daily from six springs.

Kinetotherapy, mud baths, massages, saunas and other treatments are on offer in plush hotels, and at Kurzentrum Heilbad Thermalbad Warmbad (☎ 37 0 00), which is open all year. If you just want to enjoy the waters, it costs AS120 per day in its thermal pool (with water slide, whirlpools etc). Erlebnistherme Warmbad (☎ 37 8 89) is open all year, and entry costs AS110 (AS85 after 4 pm) to its adventure pool (with water slide etc). Zillerbad Warmbad (☎ 30 01 373), is open May to October, and its open-air pool costs AS60 (AS45 for half a day). City bus No 1 goes to Warmbad (AS17).

East of Villach many lakes, big and small, provide plenty of swimming and boating opportunities. The largest are Lake Ossiach (Ossiacher See) and Lake Faak (Faaker See). **Lake Faak** is close to the Karawanken range. **Lake Ossiach**, a long, narrow lake only four km from Villach, has a ferry service. Boats operate between mid-May and 1 October; the full circuit takes over two hours, with departures every 60 to 90 minutes in the high season. Boats also navigate the Drau River between Villach Kongresshaus and Wernberg Bad, up to four times a day between 30 April and 8 October. Both these services are operated by Ossiacher See- und Drauschiffahrt (☎ 04242-58 0 71); full tours cost AS105 and AS120 respectively, or a combined ticket is AS175.

A little north of Lake Ossiach, just off the road to Radenthein, is **Elli Riehl's Puppet World** (Puppenwelt; ☎ 04248-23 95), Winklern 14, Einöde. These cute little dolls (about 600) mainly appeal to small children; it's open from 15 April to 30 September (AS40; children AS15).

Between Villach and Lake Ossiach is **Landskron Castle** (☎ 04242 42 8 88). It is famous for its 40-minute bird-of-prey show, in which captive predators are released to soar and swoop above the crowds. Shows are conducted between May and September, daily at 11 am and 3 pm (and 6 pm in July and August) and entry costs AS50 for adults or AS20 for children. There's a great view of the castle from St Andrä, with the Karawanken peaks as a backdrop.

The backdrop to Lake Ossiach is Gerlitzen (1909 metres), one of the main areas for winter **skiing**. A day pass costs AS300. Another ski area is Dobratsch (2166 metres), in the Villacher Alpen (day pass costs AS265) west of Villach. In summer this area is ideal for hiking and mountain cycling, and at 1500 metres there's an **Alpine garden** (AS10), open mid-June to 31 August daily from 9 am to 6 pm. To get to the garden, follow the Villacher Alpenstrasse from the town. This is a toll road (AS160 for cars, AS70 for motorbikes, and bicycles free), though from about November to March no charges apply. It's closed to caravans.

Places to Stay & Eat

There are several *camp sites* by both Lake Ossiach and Lake Faak, as well as hotels, pensions, private rooms and holiday apartments. Contact the respective tourist offices for details: in St Andrä (☎ 04242-42 0 00; May to October only) for Lake Ossiach information, and in Drobollach (☎ 04254-21 85) for Lake Faak; there are offices at other lake resorts. There's also a tourist office (☎ 04242-37 2 44) in the centre of Warmbad Villach; most of the hotels there are three or

four-star. The accommodation guide obtainable from the Villach tourist office covers most of the surrounding area.

Standard Austrian inns abound. Gourmets may want to track down rather more expensive options for regional cuisine: *Das Kleine Restaurant* (☎ 04242-30 0 10) in the Warmbaderhof Hotel, Warmbad Villach, and *Karnerhof* (☎ 04254-21 88), Karnerhofweg 10, in the village of Egg on Lake Faak (closed Monday). Medieval banquets are conducted in the restaurant of Landskron Castle every Tuesday from May to September. Telephone in advance: ☎ 04242-41 5 63.

Getting There & Around

From Villach, hourly trains stop along the north shore of Lake Ossiach; trains to Lake Faak are less frequent, and to Warmbad Villach (AS17) they're half-hourly. Bundesbuses go to both lakes, but distances are so short that it's easy and more pleasant to explore the region by bicycle. Bikes can be rented at Villach, Faak am See, Bodensdorf and Steindorf train stations, and from many other places.

GMÜND
• *pop 2600* • *749 m* • ☎ *(04732)*

Gmünd's ancient city walls, still partially intact, are a reminder of its former strategic importance – it was owned by a succession of powerful rulers, not least the Archbishop of Salzburg. Gmünd was founded in the 11th century.

The walled centre is attractive, with small streets leading off Hauptplatz and running beneath a succession of arches. The most impressive old building is the 13th-century **Alte Burg** on the hill. Although it is partially in ruins, cultural events are held inside.

Also a mere stone's throw from Hauptplatz is the privately-owned **Porsche Museum**. A Porsche factory was sited in Gmünd from 1944 to 1950, and the first car to bear that famous name (a 356) was made here. One of these hand-made models is on display (only 52 were built) with around 15 other models, and a couple of the wooden frames used in construction. There's also a film (in German) on Dr Porsche's life and work. The museum is open all year, daily from 9 am to 6 pm (10 am to 4 pm from mid-October to mid-May). It's rather pricey for a small museum (AS65).

Gmünd has inexpensive private rooms as well as pensions, hotels and holiday apartments. A couple of places are on Hauptplatz, and these have affordable restaurants. There's also a restaurant in the Alte Burg (meals from AS85; open daily). The tourist office (☎ 22 22), in the Rathaus on Hauptplatz, can outline options. The staff can also tell you about Trebesing, a village with several hotels, four km down the road: 'Europe's first Babydorf' is an interesting place to stay if you have young kids.

Getting There & Away
Gmünd is not on a rail route, though buses do go there from Spittal an der Drau (AS38; takes 30 minutes), including bus No 5132 that continues north to Mauterdorf.

SPITTAL AN DER DRAU
• *pop 15,000* • *556 m* • ☎ *(04762)*
Spittal is an important economic and administrative centre in upper Carinthia. Its name comes from the original hospital and refuge, dating to the 12th century, that succoured travellers on this site.

Orientation & Information
The tourist office (☎ 34 20) is at Burgplatz 1, in the main tourist attraction, Porcia Palace. Opening hours are Monday to Friday from 9 am to 6 pm (to 8 pm in July and August) and Saturday from 9 am to 1 pm. From the train station, walk down Bahnhofstrasse and cut across Stadtpark, a 10-minute walk.

The post office near the train station is open daily from 9 am to 7 pm.

Things to See & Do
The **Porcia Palace** (Schloss Porcia) is an excellent Renaissance edifice, built between 1533 to 1597. The Italianate arcaded courtyard is particularly eye-catching. The upper floors contain a regional museum, the

Museum für Volkskultur (AS45, students AS20), which gives an effective evocation of life in the locality, covering art, artefacts, rustic crafts and culture. Note the primitive wooden skis and the crudely carved school desks. Many signs are in English. From mid-May to mid-October it's open daily from 9 am to 6 pm; otherwise hours are Monday to Thursday from 10 am to 3 pm and Friday from 10 am to 1 pm. Cultural events are also held in the palace.

Spittal's neighbourhood mountain is the **Goldeck** (2142 metres). In summer, inspiring views are easily achieved via cable car (AS145 one-way, AS195 return) or by the Goldeckstrasse toll road (AS160 cars, AS80 motorbikes; reductions with guest card). The road takes you 260 metres short of the summit; you can climb to there. In winter, the peak is the domain of skiers: a day pass costs AS330 (AS300 students and seniors, AS230 children). The cable car closes from mid-April to mid-June, and mid-September to mid-December.

Festival
One weekend in late June every odd year (1997, 1999, etc) the historical legend of Katharina von Salamanca (who is said to haunt Porcia Palace in retribution for the violent death of her son) is re-enacted in the Salamanca Festival, held in the town centre. Entry is free.

Places to Stay
The tourist office will not charge to track down accommodation. *Draufluss Camping* (☎ 24 66) is on the southern bank of the Drau River.

The HI *youth hostel* (☎ 32 52) is at Zur Seilbahn 2, near the start of the Goldeck cable car. From the train station, turn right and cross under the rail tracks. The hostel has basic cooking facilities and a good-value restaurant, but is closed from mid-November to mid-December, and for a couple of weeks in late April; check-in is from 5 pm. Dorm beds are AS130, and there are two singles (AS170) and two doubles (AS310); it is an

Spittal an der Drau

0   250   500m

PLACES TO STAY
2 Hotel Salzburg
7 Pension Hübner
9 Gasthof Weiss
11 Gasthof Brückenwirt
17 Youth Hostel

PLACES TO EAT
4 Rathaus Café
8 Hotel-Restaurant Alte Post
10 Wirtshaus Zum Spittl
15 Café Tanja

OTHER
1 Post Office
3 Forum Department Store & Restaurant
5 Porcia Palace & Museum Für Volksculture
6 Tourist Office
12 Indoor Swimming Pool
13 Post Office
14 Bus Departures
16 Train Station
18 Goldeck Cable Car

extra AS10 for nonmembers, but they don't get a guest stamp. Another HI *youth hostel* (☎ 27 01) at the Goldeck mid-station (1650 metres) is accessible only by cable car.

Gasthof Brückenwirt (☎ 27 72), An der Wirtschaftsbrücke 2, is a few minutes east of the town centre, by the Lieser River. It's a chalet-style inn with balconies and a garden. Singles/doubles are AS210/420, or AS260/520 with private shower/WC. Just over the Lieser is *Gasthof Weiss* (☎ 27 72), Edlingerstrasse 1A, charging AS250/400. A few rooms have private shower/WC; phone ahead as it's often full.

Between the train station and Porcia Palace is *Pension Hübner* (☎ 21 12), Schillerstrasse 20, run by the shop of the same name. Most rooms have private shower, some have WC, and prices are AS250 to AS330 per person, depending on the room and season (plus AS25 for single night stays). This pleasing place is open from 1 May to 30 September and has a kitchen, and free bicycles for guests.

Opposite Stadtpark, *Hotel Salzburg* (☎ 31 65), Tiroler Strasse 22, has good rooms with shower/WC and TV for AS420 to AS490 per person.

Places to Eat

Options for cheap food include snack stands and Chinese restaurants, and *Café Tanja* opposite the train station. On Neuer Platz there's a Forum department store, with a *KGM* supermarket and an *Oregano* self-service restaurant with a salad buffet, and meals for AS60 to AS80. It's open normal shop hours. *Rathaus Café*, Ebnergasse 5, has a 1st-floor outside terrace, and some meals below AS125. It's open Monday to Saturday from 7 am to midnight.

A preferable choice is *Wirtshaus Zum Spittl*, Edlinger Strasse 1. It has a welcoming interior, and serves Austrian food daily from AS72 to AS158 and pizzas in the evening (not Monday) from AS62.

Hotel-Restaurant Alte Post (☎ 22 1 70), Hauptplatz 13, has rooms, but the restaurant is the better deal, with tasty Austrian dishes from AS125. It's open daily, except Sunday, from January to April.

Getting There & Away

Spittal-Millstättersee railway station oversees an important rail junction: two-hourly IC services run north to Badgastein (AS94; 52 km) and west to Lienz (AS110; 67 km, takes one hour). Villach (AS64; takes 30 minutes) is 37 km to the south-east. The route north to Mallnitz-Obervellach yields some excellent views as the train track clings high to the side of the valley (sit on the left).

Bundesbuses and regional AVB buses leave from outside the train station, including around 12 a day to Gmünd. Call ☎ 39 16 for information.

MILLSTATT

• *pop 3100* • *604 m* • ☎ *(04766)*

Millstatt lies 10 km east of Spittal an der Drau on the northern shore of Lake Millstatt (Millstätter See). The lake is attractively situated, bordered by tree-lined hills on its southern side and a sprinkling of small resorts on its northern side.

Orientation & Information

Millstatt is approximately in the middle of the 12-km-long northern shore. The tourist office (☎ 20 22 0) is in the centre of the resort in the Rathaus, Marktplatz 8. Pick up its comprehensive *Informationen-Veranstaltungen* booklet. It covers the whole lake and gives festivals and events information, lists sports addresses and prices, transport timetables and much else. If the office is shut, get information and check room vacancies from the touch-screen computer outside.

Things to See & Do

The resort is dominated by a **Benedictine abbey**, founded in 1070. The abbey's Romanesque church has a distinctive inner doorway, complete with grotesque faces peering from the columns. The heavy Gothic ceiling vaulting vies for attention with the gold statues and Baroque altars. The fresco of the Last Judgement (1513-16), to the right of the high altar, is by Urban Görtschacher. In the arcaded courtyard stands an old linden tree; an even older tree (about 1000 years old) is outside. The abbey museum (Stiftsmuseum) deals with the history of the town and the geology of the region; it's open May to September, daily from 9 am to noon and 3.30 to 6.30 pm (entry AS20, children AS5 10).

The lake teems with possibilities for **water sports**, such as swimming, water-skiing, windsurfing, sailing, scuba diving (to a depth of 141 metres) and fishing. All types of boats are for hire. Simply walking along the Seepromenade, lined with statues and flowers, is pleasant. **Boat cruises** (☎ 20 75) on the lake are also enjoyable. From late May to mid-October you can circuit the lake; the rest of the year boats only go between Millstatt and Seeboden (AS40). The full lake circuit costs AS110 (child fares are around half-price) and takes two hours.

East of Millstatt is **Bad Kleinkirchheim**, a spa resort and winter skiing centre (AS330 for a day pass). Its tourist office (☎ 04240-82 12) can provide details.

Places to Stay & Eat

Staying in the resort earns visitors a guest card, valid for useful discounts. The summer season is from Easter to mid-October, with the highest prices (those quoted here) from June to September. Many quiet, mid-priced B&Bs are along Alexanderhofstrasse and Tangernerweg, to the west of the resort centre. Millstatt has some winter tourism, but most hotels, pensions and private rooms close at this time. The winter hibernators don't open until May, including the places mentioned below – rely on the touch-screen outside the tourist office to tell you what's available.

Cheap and central is *Gasthof Zum Brunnen* (☎ 20 80), Marktplatz 30, with basic rooms starting at AS190 per person, and rising to AS240 per person for the few rooms with shower/WC. The single supplement is AS30. Nearby, *Haus Aigner-Haberl* (☎ 21 11), Mirnockstrasse 39, has only doubles with hall shower for AS360. There's a café downstairs.

Haus Josef Pleikner (☎ 20 36), Seemühlgasse 57, has rooms for AS295 to AS350 per person, most with private shower/WC. It has parking facilities and private lake access. Next door is *Pizzeria Peppino* (closed Sunday), with pizzas from AS61, plus schnitzels and spaghetti.

Seemühlgasse is between Kaiser Franz Josef Strasse and the boat station. Several restaurants overlook the water, but they're more expensive.

For self-catering, there's a *Konsum* supermarket, not far from the lakeside at the corner of Kaiser Franz Josef Strasse and Überfuhrgasse. It is open Monday to Friday from 8 am to noon and 3 to 6 pm, and Saturday from 8 am to noon.

Hotel-Restaurant See-Villa (☎ 21 02), Seestrasse 68, has a good restaurant where main dishes, including fish specialities, are above AS140 (open daily). Menu prices are reduced by 20% if you stay here: rooms start at AS420 per person, and have bath or shower, toilet, telephone and balcony.

Getting There & Away

Regular Bundesbuses or regional AVB buses depart from outside Spittal train station, and take under 20 minutes to reach Millstatt (AS30). Some buses continue to Bad Kleinkirchheim (takes 40 minutes). The road from Spittal stays close to the lake shore. Buses to Villach go via Radenthein.

Hohe Tauern National Park Region

Austria's highest peak and tallest waterfall, the longest glacier in the eastern Alps, snow-capped crags, lush valleys, soaring bearded vultures, skipping ibexes, burrowing marmots – all this and more awaits the visitor to the Hohe Tauern National Park (Nationalpark Hohe Tauern), accessible by roads twisting through some of the finest views in the country.

Orientation

In 1971 Carinthia, Salzburg and Tirol agreed to the creation of a national park. Regions were added in stages until now it is Europe's largest national park, comprising 1786 sq km. Salzburg has contributed 804 sq km, Tirol 610 sq km, and Carinthia 372 sq km. The most famous route in Austria, the Grossglockner Road, starts in Salzburg and ends in Carinthia. Its apotheosis is at the site of the mighty Grossglockner (3797 metres), which straddles the border between East Tirol and Carinthia. On the western side of the park stands the region's second-highest peak, the Grossvenediger (3674 metres), the high point of the border between East Tirol and Salzburg.

The boundaries of the park are extremely irregular, but can loosely be considered split into three sections: west of the Felber Tauern Road (containing Grossvenediger), the vicinity of Grossglockner, and the eastern portion between Mallnitz and Badgastein. Zell am See and Badgastein border the park and are covered in this chapter. Lienz (see the Tirol chapter) is another good jumping-off point for the park.

Information

The Hohe Tauern National Park is open all year and there's no admission charge. However, most of the roads to and through the park have toll sections, and some will be impassable or closed in winter (see Getting There & Away later in this chapter). This is a protected nature area but not a wilderness

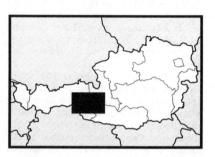

area: 60,000 people live within its borders in 29 communities.

All tourist offices in places bordering the park have information on Hohe Tauren, including the offices in Lienz, Zell am See and Krimml. They should be able to provide free maps of the park. The *Experience in Nature* map (in English) shows information offices and overnight accommodation spots. It also highlights many tour suggestions, with descriptions on the reverse side.

The main centre for dispensing information on the park is the Office of the National Park Council: Evidenzstelle des National-park-Rates (☎ 04875-51 61 17; fax 51 61 20), Rauterplatz 1, Matrei, A-9971 Ostirrol. Matrei also has an information office and a museum; the town is on the southern side of the Felber Tauern Road. The national park office (☎ 06565-65 58 0) in the north-west is at Neukirchen, in Salzburg. Another national park office is at Mallnitz (☎ 04784-25 5 15). See the Heiligenblut entry in this chapter for more addresses.

Things to See & Do

Hiking and enjoying the unspoiled environment are the main activities in the park. Freytag & Berndt produces nine 1:50,000 hiking maps covering the national park and surrounding areas. As this is a conservation area, there are several things *not* to do, like straying from the marked trails, littering, lighting fires or disturbing the flora and fauna.

The park has more than 300 mountains above 3000 metres, and 246 glaciers. There are also numerous rivers, lakes, waterfalls and ravines. For information on the Grossglockner Road, see the entry in this chapter.

Another popular excursion is to **Grossvenediger**, a peak permanently coated with ice and snow and flanked by glaciers. The closest you can get by road is the Matreier Tauernhaus Hotel (1512 metres), at the southern entrance to the Felber Tauern Tunnel. You can park here and gain fine views of the mountain within an hour's walk. A more athletic option is to park at the Hopffeldboden parking area, south of Neukirchen, and walk south along the Obersulzbach Valley. It is a 10-hour walk to Grossvenediger, with a mountain refuge about halfway. Another possibility is to

approach from the south. There's a car park at Hinterbichl, at the end of the road running west from Matrei. It's a similar distance to Grossvenediger, again with a mountain refuge along the way.

Skiing areas are just beyond the borders of the park, such as at Zell am See and Badgastein.

Places to Stay & Eat

Camping is not permitted within the park, though there is a *camp site* at Matrei (☎ 04875-51 11), and two more on the road leading west from there (one is open all year).

For short excursions to the park, it's easy to base yourself somewhere like Zell am See or Lienz. Within the park, some small-scale guesthouses provide food and accommodation, but they are widely scattered. If you plan to undertake major hiking expeditions you should schedule your overnight stops in advance. The Edelweisshütte (☎ 06545-

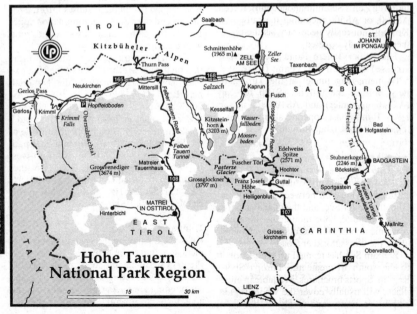

Hohe Tauern National Park Region

425) on Edelweiss Spitz has information on regional Alpine huts, as do most of the tourist offices.

On the food front, regional specialities include Erdapfelnidei (potato noodles), Fleischkrapfen (meat-filled dumplings) and Kasnocken (cheese dumplings).

Getting There & Away

The authorities are determined to limit the flow of traffic through the park. It is possible that private vehicles will one day be banned altogether. This is certainly envisaged for the Grossglockner Road, where visitors would have to rely on buses or shuttle taxis. See the following Grossglockner Road section for information on travelling this route in the meantime. Getting about by Bundesbus is made more attractive by the Nationalpark Ticket, available from early June to early October, and valid for 10 days free travel on bus routes in and around the park, particularly routes to/from Lienz and Zell am See. It also gives reductions on various cable-car fares (eg Zell's Schmittenhöhebahn). It costs AS400, or AS500 including the railway to Krimml (not really necessary, as the bus to there is already covered).

The Felber Tauern Road (Felbertauernstrasse) is open all year. There is a 5304-metre-long tunnel at the Tirol-Salzburg border: the toll is AS190 for cars (AS110 in winter) and AS100 for motorbikes. Bundesbuses operate along this road (eg the Lienz-Kitzbühel route).

ZELL AM SEE

• *pop 8000* • *758 m* • ☎ *(06542)*

Zell am See is ideally situated. It enjoys a picturesque location between its namesake lake, the Zeller See, and the concave slopes of the Schmittenhöhe mountains. It's also a convenient base for excursions, including along the Grossglockner Road.

Zell am See has teamed up with **Kaprun** to the south to create the Europa Sports Region. Sports brochures, available in either place, will usually cover the whole region. Kaprun is pretty and lively. It has good

access to ski slopes, but isn't so convenient for water pursuits.

Orientation

Zell am See lies on the west bank of the Zeller See. Almost adjacent to the main resort is Schüttdorf, barely clinging to the south side of the lake; it is generally cheaper for accommodation.

Information

The tourist office, or Kurverwaltung (☎ 26 00 0), is at Bruckner Bundesstrasse 1, five minutes walk from the train station. It is open Monday to Friday from 8 am to noon and 2 to 6 pm, and Saturday from 8 am to noon. In the high season, hours lengthen, and include Saturday afternoon and Sunday morning. In the foyer is an accommodation board with a free telephone (accessible daily from 8 am to midnight).

On Postplatz is the post office (Postamt 5700), open Monday to Friday from 7.30 am to 6.30 pm and Saturday from 7.30 to 11 am (10 am in winter).

If you want to stay in Kaprun, contact its tourist office (☎ 06547-86 43 0) for accommodation advice. You should get the guest card wherever you stay.

Skiing

This region has a long skiing history. In 1927 the first cable car in Salzburg province (the fifth in Austria) was opened on Schmittenhöhe, and the first glacial ski run was opened on Kitzsteinhorn in 1965. The Europa Sports Region comprises 55 cable cars and lifts, giving access to over 130 km of runs for all ability ranges. General ski passes cost AS760 for a two-day minimum (reductions for senior citizens, children and in the low season). Ski buses are free for ski pass holders. Ski rental prices are AS80 to AS170 per day.

On **Schmittenhöhe** (1965 metres), the cable car goes almost to the top. Other cable cars from Zell am See ascend to the ridge on either side of the main peak. These operate approximately from mid-December to mid-April. There are several black (difficult) runs that twist between the tree-lined flanks of the mountain. For weather conditions, call ☎ 36 94, or check the live TV pictures shown in valley cable stations.

Kaprun is the closest resort to the **Kitzsteinhorn**, offering year-round glacier skiing. Start early in the day during the high season to avoid long queuing times. Ascent options include the Gletscherbahn underground railway, or the cable car that soars over the glacier and up to 3039 metres (less than 200 metres from the summit). In winter, a day pass for Kitzsteinhorn costs AS400 (AS390 low season) for skiers or AS250 (AS205) for non-skiers. In winter, first-timers can try a cheap taste of skiing on the Maiskogel lift, costing from AS125 (after 2 pm). The short Lechnerberglift costs just AS18 for one ride. For weather conditions on the Kaprun slopes, call ☎ 06547-84 44.

Other Activities

The tourist office can provide maps and information on cycling and hiking. From Schmittenhöhe you can gaze at 30 peaks over 3000 metres. The **Pinzgauer Spaziergang hike** from here takes less than seven hours and exploits to the full the magnificent view. There is very little change in altitude along the way. You descend via the Schattbergbahn cable car to Saalbach (which is another excellent skiing area), and take the Bundesbus back from there to Zell am See (the last departure is at 6.35 pm, or 7.28 pm on Saturday). From June to mid-October there are guided hikes from Schmittenhöhe to other places. These are free with the lift ticket (AS170 up, AS120 down, or AS215 return; reductions with guest card).

Golf and tennis are among the other sports offered in the region. In the centre of town on Steinergasse is a swimming pool complex (☎ 33 88), with an adventure swimming pool, saunas, steam room and massage, as well as 10-pin bowling and an ice stadium. It is open daily from 10 am to 10 pm.

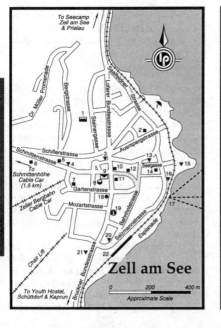

PLACES TO STAY

2	Hotel Salzburgerhof
5	Wilhelmina
6	Haus Haffner
7	Hubertus
10	Zum Hirschen
11	Gasthof Steinerwirt
12	Sporthotel Lebzelter
14	Buchner

PLACES TO EAT

3	Prima SB
4	Ampere
13	Wienerwald
15	Grand Hotel
16	Seestüberl
20	China-Restaurant Wang Hai
21	Restaurant Kupferkessel

OTHER

1	Swimming Pool Complex
8	Bundesbus Station
9	Post Office
17	Boat Departures
18	Spar Supermarket
19	Tourist Office
22	Train Station

HOHE TAUERN NATIONAL PARK

In winter the lake is frozen over. In summer (late May to early October), boats depart from Zell am See Esplanade and complete a 40-minute circuit of the lake (AS70, children AS38). Boats also shuttle passengers across the lake, occasionally stopping at the camp site (AS20 one-way, AS35 return). Rowing boats, pedal boats and motorboats can be hired from April to October. Anglers need to apply for a fishing permit. Of the other resorts around the lake, Thumersbach has a water-skiing school and Prielau has a sailing and windsurfing school.

Another option for water lovers is rafting on the Salzach River. Rafting Centre Taxenbach (☎ 06543-352), 20 km east of Kaprun, charges AS480 for a two-hour trip. Bundesbus No 3441 goes there, and trains go to Taxenbach-Rauris from Zell am See.

Alpine Reservoirs

South of Kaprun is a series of reservoirs within a picturesque setting of Alpine peaks. There are hiking paths and restaurants in the vicinity. The southernmost of the accessible reservoirs, the **Mooserboden** (2036 metres), stores 84.9 million cubic metres of water; two-thirds of this quantity is meltwater from the Pasterze Glacier in the Hohe Tauern National Park, which arrives via a 12-km-long tunnel from another reservoir farther south. Mooserboden has two dams at its northern end and an electricity plant. Water spills down to the Wasserfallboden reservoir (1672 metres), and is then pumped up again to create yet more electricity. The smooth arches of the dams provide a striking contrast to the rugged irregularity of the mountain peaks. Near Kaprun is the Klamm reservoir and the main stage power plant.

The Mooserboden reservoir is a viable day trip from Zell am See; the total return cost by public transport (late May to late September) is AS180. Buses go beyond the Klamm reservoir and as far as the Lärchwand funicular (if you're driving you can only go as far as Kesselfall; park there and continue by bus). The Lärchwand funicular ascends 431 metres and connects with another bus to Mooserboden.

Festivals

Zell am See celebrates a full calender of seasonal events, including two lake festivals. The first, in mid-July, has sports events, and the second, in early August, has music and costume parades.

Places to Stay

Bottom End *Seecamp Zell am See* (☎ 21 15), Thumersbacher Strasse 34, Prielau, is near the shoreline (head clockwise from the town) and open year-round. It charges AS85 per person and at least AS50 per site. *Camping Südufer* (☎ 56 2 28), Seeuferstrasse 196, south of the lake, is cheaper.

The HI youth hostel, *Haus der Jugend* (☎ 57 18 5), Seespitzstrasse 13, Schüttdorf, is a 15-minute walk anti-clockwise around the lake. Exit the train station on the lake side ('Zum See') and take the footpath along the shore (it's moderately lit, but safe). Turn left at the end. Beds in four-bed dorms with own shower/WC and lockable lockers cost AS160 for one night or AS135 per night for longer stays. Those over 26 pay an overnight tax of AS9.50 in summer or AS8.50 in winter. The food is good – order dinners (AS65) by 5 pm. Getting a key circumvents the curfew and day closure; check-in is from 4 pm. It closes from late October to late December.

Nearby Kaprun also has a HI *youth hostel* (☎ 06547-85 07), at Nikolaus Gassner Strasse 448 (closed in September).

Private rooms are another cheap option in Zell am See. *Haus Haffner* (☎ 23 96), Schmittenstrasse 29, is close to the centre (just west of the Zeller Bergbahn cable car) and has 12 rooms available. Singles/doubles are AS215/390 using hall shower or AS260/480 with own shower/WC. Nearby, *Wilhelmina* (☎ 26 07), Schmittenstrasse 14, is a B&B with rooms from AS290/540, some with own shower.

Buchner (☎ 26 36), Seegasse 12, is right in the centre of town on a pedestrian street, though there's parking around the back. Rooms are average-sized, with wood furnishings, and some have a balcony. Prices with hall shower are AS300 per person

(AS320 in winter) or AS350 with own shower/WC. *Hubertus* (☎ 24 27), Gartenstrasse 4, is a chalet-style place near the Zeller Bergbahn cable car, and charges similar prices.

Middle & Top End The price difference between the low and high seasons (the latter is quoted here) is more marked in this category. Some prices drop in summer.

Near the youth hostel, *Seepension Arabella* (☎ 57 24 5), Seespitzstrasse 30, offers breakfast buffet, and rooms with shower/WC, telephone and TV from AS450/700.

The central *Gasthof Steinerwirt* (☎ 25 02), Schlossplatz 1, has rooms with shower and TV from AS420 per person. It's by the pedestrian zone but has parking. Nearby, *Sporthotel Lebzelter* (☎ 24 11), Dreifaltigkeitsgasse 7, has better rooms and good hotel facilities, including a sauna and cellar bar. Prices start at AS760/1420.

Krone (☎ 57 42 1), Kitzsteinhornstrasse 16, is away from the lake in Schüttdorf, but has excellent facilities for the price, including sauna, steam bath, fitness room and a small swimming pool. Rooms with own shower/WC in this chalet-style place are AS710/1320.

Zum Hirschen (☎ 24 47; fax 24 47 99), Dreifaltigkeitsgasse 1, has sauna, steam bath, solarium etc, and is in an ideal central location. Prices start at AS1050/1900 for singles/doubles.

Hotel Salzburgerhof (☎ 28 28 0; fax 28 28 66), Auerspergstrasse 11, is equally central. It's a big chalet with a rustic-style interior, even down to the traditional garb worn by staff. All modern comforts are provided, such as well-equipped rooms, indoor swimming pool, sauna and fitness room (all free for guests), and ample parking. Prices start at AS1200/2200.

Places to Eat

There are several supermarkets, including a *Spar* just along from the tourist office (late opening to 7.30 pm on Friday). Farther north, at Loferer Bundesstrasse 3, is a very cheap self-service place, *Prima SB*. It has a good choice of Austrian menus for around AS50 to AS100 including soup or dessert. Evening opening times depend upon demand (usually to 10 pm in the high season, 7 pm in the low season; closed Sunday).

In front of the train station is a *snack bar* selling pastries, soup and pizza slices (AS18 to AS28). Next door is *China-Restaurant Wang Hai* with dishes from AS80 (open daily until 11.30 pm); the weekday lunch menu (AS55 to AS75) comes with soup or spring roll and rice. A branch of *Wienerwald* (☎ 06565-65 58 0) is on Seegasse.

Seestüberl is a tiny place on Salzmannstrasse, by the train tracks. The whole building shakes as trains rumble past. It has a rough-and-ready atmosphere but is good value. Daily menus start at AS70 and there are fish specialities (open daily from noon to 10 pm).

Restaurant Kupferkessel, a little south of the tourist office at Bruckner Bundesstrasse 18, is a former petrol station and retains the old forecourt. It has varied seating areas around a central bar and a youthful ambience (but not exclusively so). The menu is varied, covering pizza and pasta (AS70 to AS120), fish (AS120 to AS140), steaks (AS98 to AS225) and Austrian food (AS85 to AS120), and there's a salad bar. Opening hours are 11 am (5 pm Sunday) to 2 am.

Ampere (☎ 23 63), Schmittenstrasse 12, has a bar on the ground floor and a classy restaurant upstairs. It has regular festivals where different types of cuisine are served; main courses are usually more than AS175. Lunches are not served. It is closed on Sunday and for two weeks each in early May and in late November.

Similarly priced is the Zirbenstube ('pine room') of *Zum Hirschen* (see Places to Stay), which serves quality Austrian fare in a wood-panelled interior. It closes in the low season. The quality restaurant in the *Hotel Salzburgerhof* (see Places to Stay) has main courses at around the AS240 mark. The restaurant in the *Grand Hotel* (☎ 23 88), Esplanade 4, is another culinary temple.

Entertainment
Zell am See has a reasonable choice of bars and discos. Popular with the après-ski crowd are *Ampere* (see Places to Eat), and *Bier-Keller*, Kirchgasse 1, a bar with 33 tempting brews (open 8 pm to 3 am).

Getting There & Away
Zell am See is on the hourly IC rail route connecting Salzburg province and Tirol. Destinations include Salzburg (AS168; takes 1½ hours), Kitzbühel (AS94; 45 minutes) and Innsbruck (AS228; two hours). It is also at the head of the narrow-gauge rail line to Krimml Falls (see the following entry). The train station rents bikes.

Bundesbuses leave from outside the train station and/or from the bus station, behind the post office. They run to various destinations, including Kaprun (AS24 each way), Krimml Falls (approximately hourly) and Salzburg (about four a day). Some buses are covered under the Nationalpark Ticket.

Zell am See is on highway 311 heading north to Lofer, where it joins the 312 connecting St Johann in Tirol with Salzburg (passing through Germany). Zell am See is also just a few km north of an east-west highway, linking St Johann im Pongau to Tirol (via the Gerlos Pass).

KRIMML FALLS
About 55 km west of Zell am See, these triple-level falls are an inspiring sight and attract hordes of visitors in summer. In winter, the slopes above the village of Krimml become a ski area, and the falls just one more static lump of ice.

Orientation & Information
The Krimml Falls (Krimmler Wasserfälle) are on the north-western edge of the national park, within the protected area.

Krimml village, at an elevation of 1076 metres, is about 500 metres north of the path to the falls, on a side turning from highway 165, which goes towards the falls; there are parking spaces (about AS40 per day) near the path up, which branches to the right just before the toll booths for the Gerlos Pass road (see the section later in this chapter).

In the village centre by the white church is the tourist office (☎ 06564-239). Opening hours are Monday to Friday from 8 am to noon and 2.30 to 5.30 pm, and Saturday from 8 to 10 am. In the low season hours are much reduced. Next door is the post office. There's another information office on the way up to the falls.

Viewing the Falls
The Krimml Falls path (Wasserfallweg) is four km long. The combined height of the falls is 380 metres, over three main sections connected by a fast-flowing, twisting river and rapids. This lessens the immediate impact, but also means you can ascend for 1½ hours or more and enjoy ever-unfolding views. The highest free fall of water is 65 metres in the lower falls. The middle section is mostly dissipated into a series of mini-falls, the highest being 30 metres. The upper level has a free fall of 60 metres. The trail is steep in parts but many elderly people manage the incline.

Five minutes after setting out on the path you reach the ticket and information offices. Entry costs AS10 (AS5 for children) between May and October; the rest of the year there's no charge as the offices are not staffed. Within two minutes you reach the first viewpoint of the lower falls, where a curtain of spray beats down onto a plinth of rock. Every few minutes further small paths deviate from the main trail and offer alternative viewpoints of the falls; each gives a worthwhile perspective. The excellent view back towards Krimml can often be seen through the treetops.

After about an hour the Gasthof Schönagel (1300 metres) is reached, where you can take refreshments and buy souvenirs. This point is just above the middle level of the falls. After five to 10 minutes the terrain opens out and you can see the final, upper level of the falls. A steep, further 20 minutes will bring you to the top of that level (known as the Bergerblick viewpoint), for a

HOHE TAUERN NATIONAL PARK

truly memorable view over the lip of the falls and back down to the valley.

If you deviate to all or most of the viewpoints on the way up, it'll take about two hours to reach Bergerblick – more if you stop for food. A fast, straight descent can take as little as 40 minutes. If you're unable or unwilling to walk up to the falls, a national park taxi can take you to the upper levels; call ☎ 06564-228 or 356 from Krimml. Private cars are not allowed on this route.

Places to Stay & Eat
Unless you want to continue hiking past the third level and along the Krimmler Ache, Krimml is easily visited as a day trip from Zell am See. There are places to stay either in the village or on the way up to the falls; the Krimml village tourist office can advise on options.

Near the church in Krimml is an *ADEG* supermarket, useful for compiling a picnic. There are snack stands and restaurants (neither cheap nor extortionate) on the walk to the falls.

Getting There & Away
Krimml can be reached from either the west or the east. The only rail route is the narrow-gauge Pinzgauer Lokalbahn from Zell am See. It calls at many places (including Schüttdorf, near the Zell am See youth hostel) on its pleasant trip through small villages and cow pastures (AS94, takes 90 minutes). Departures are approximately hourly with the last train back to Zell am See at 5.37 pm. The only drawback is that the train leaves you three km short of the falls – walk or take the bus (AS21) from there. The regular Bundesbus from Zell am See (AS94 each way; last return bus at 6.10 pm) takes you right into Krimml, only a few hundred metres short of the path to the falls. The Krimml Falls path starts near the beginning of the Tauernradweg (cycle path), which goes to Salzburg (175 km) and Passau (325 km).

GERLOS PASS
This pass (1507 metres) is north-west of Krimml and is a scenic route to the Ziller Valley (Zillertal). Initially starting from Krimml, there are fine views of the whole extent of the Krimml Falls; later, peaks and Alpine lakes are on display. There is a toll charge to use this route (for cars: AS90 one-way or AS150 day-return; motorbikes: AS50 one-way or AS80 day-return).

Bundesbuses make the same trip to the Ziller Valley (AS169 return; last bus to Zell am Ziller at 4.10 pm). By car, you can avoid using the toll road by taking the old route, signposted 'Alte Gerlosstrasse'. From Krimml, get on this 11-km stretch of road at Wald im Pingau, a few km east (on the road to Zell am See) and join the new Gerlos road just west of the toll section.

GROSSGLOCKNER ROAD
The Grossglockner Hochalpenstrasse (High Alpine Road) was built between 1930 and 1935, yet since the Middle Ages this has been an important trading route between Italy and Germany. The present road takes visitors on a magical 50-km journey between 800 to 2500 metres high, crossing a range of geographical and climatic conditions. Pick up the informative Grossglockner Hochalpenstrasse *Seeing Nature* leaflet, available from tourist offices or the Grossglockner Bundes-

The chamois, a small antelope found in the mountains

bus itself. There are a dozen restaurants along the route, some with rooms available.

Even before reaching the national park, the trip south from Zell am See is picturesque. Cows graze in green fields and white peaks appear over the steep sides of the valley. At Fusch is an Alpine game reserve (AS50; AS30 for children) with more than 200 animals (open daily, May to November). The admission price includes a bird-of-prey show, at 11 am and 3 pm from June to September, and at 3 pm in May.

Once through the toll gate, the road rises steeply. At 2260 metres there's an Alpine nature reserve (free). A little farther on and up is Fuschertörl (2428 metres), where there's Dr Franz Rehrl Haus (a restaurant), and excellent views on both sides of the ridge. From here a two-km side road (no coaches allowed) goes up to **Edelweiss Spitz** (2571 metres), where there's an even better panorama.

Continuing south, the road descends, then rises again. At Knappenstube (2450 metres) there are traces of medieval gold mining. The peak of activity was in 1557 when 900 kg of gold was found here; much of it swelled the already bulky coffers of the archbishopric of Salzburg. Hochtor (2503 metres) is the highest point on the road, then there is a steady descent to Guttal (1950 metres). Here the road splits: to the left is Heiligenblut and the route to Lienz, to the right is the Glacier Road (Gletscherstrasse). This nine-km-long road ascends to Franz Josefs Höhe (2369 metres), the viewing area for Grossglockner.

Taking the Glacier Road, the initial views down to the Heiligenblut Valley are fantastic, yet you soon concentrate on the approaching massif of Grossglockner itself (sit on the left for the best views). At **Franz Josefs Höhe** there are places to park, eat, sleep and buy souvenirs. The Grossglockner looms from across a vast tongue of ice, the Pasterze Glacier. The cracks and ridges in this 10-km-long mass of ice create a marvellous pattern of light and dark. Steps lead down to the edge of the glacier, or an easier option is to take the Gletscherbahn (AS55 one-way, AS90 return; departures every 10 minutes). There

are several walks that can be taken from Franz Josefs Höhe. The most popular is the Gamsgrubenweg, winding above the glacier and leading to a waterfall; allow up to 1½ hours return.

Getting There & Away

The Grossglockner Road (highway 107) is open to traffic from May to November, daily between 5 am and 10 pm. It is a toll road from Fusch to just north of Heiligenblut. The one-day charge is AS350 for cars and AS230 for motorbikes, with a AS20 reduction in the low season in either case. An eight-day pass (consecutive days) costs AS450 and AS300; two freely-chosen days costs AS480 and AS320. You can walk or cycle along the road free of charge. The hills are steep (up to 12% gradient), but hardy mountain cyclists manage the trip. For recorded information on road conditions, call ☎ 04824-26 06.

Franz Josefs Höhe is accessible from north and south by Bundesbus. Toll charges are included in the ticket price. The fare from Zell am See is AS130 one-way or AS219 return. One bus departs at 9.50 am between the beginning of June and early October. It arrives at 12.25 pm, giving you two hours and 20 minutes at the site before the bus returns to Zell am See. On the trip, the bus stops for 45 minutes at the Alpine nature show. If desired, you can skip this and walk 15 to 20 minutes up the hill to Dr Franz Rehrl Haus. The bus stops here, so you can pick it up again (same ticket) once you've admired the view. Warn your driver before you do this.

From Lienz, the bus to Franz Josefs Höhe costs AS124 one-way and AS179 return. Between mid-June and 1 October, a bus departs Lienz at 7.45 am, arriving at Franz Josefs Höhe at 10 am, and departing for the return journey at 2.35 pm.

Between early July and early September additional buses run in both directions, so you can plan a longer stay in the park without needing an overnight stop. You needn't necessarily return whence you came. In the main season, you can get from Zell am See to Lienz (or vice versa) for AS175 in the same day, and still have sufficient time at Franz Josefs Höhe.

HEILIGENBLUT
• *pop 1300* • *1300 m* • ☎ *(04824)*

Heiligenblut is both a summer and winter resort, close to the borders of the national park.

Orientation & Information
This beautifully situated village is 39 km north of Lienz. The tourist office (☎ 20 01 21) is on the main street, close to the 'Hotel Post' bus stop. It's open from Monday to Friday from 9 am to 6 pm, except in the low season (closed noon to 4 pm) and the high season (open Saturday). Close by, in the Gästehaus Schober, is a national park information office (☎ 27 00), with information and museum exhibits. From mid-June to 1 September the Bergführerinformationsbüro operates from the same office, giving advice on climbing and hiking.

Things to See & Do
Heiligenblut's **church** was built between 1430 and 1483; its slender pale steeple is visible from far away on the Glacier Road. The church's ceiling and altar are both late-Gothic in style, and there are many statues of saints. The high altar is winged, with intricate figures carved in relief. The tabernacle is purported to contain a tiny phial of Christ's blood, hence the name of the village (Heiligenblut means 'holy blood').

Most of the **skiing** above the resort is done from the Schareck (2604 metres) and Gjaidtroghöhe (2969 metres) peaks. A one-day lift pass costs AS335, or AS250 after noon. Lift coupons are also available. Mountaineering is another local pursuit.

Places to Stay & Eat
Camping (☎ 20 48) is from mid-May to mid-October. There's a HI *youth hostel* (☎ 22 59) at Hof 36, near the church and below the ADEG supermarket. It is closed from 1 October to 26 December and costs AS140 for a dorm bed (reception is closed from 9 am to 5 pm).

See the tourist office about hotels, pensions, private rooms, apartments and farmhouses. At the budget end, prices start at about AS190 per person in winter, or AS170 in summer.

Restaurants are not too expensive. *Café Dorfstüberl* is near the tourist office, and has pizza and Austrian food from about AS85 (open daily).

Getting There & Away
In addition to the Bundesbuses to Franz Josefs Höhe, four or five buses a day run year-round to/from Lienz (AS68 one-way, AS122 return; takes 70 minutes).

BADGASTEIN
• *pop 6000* • *1100 m* • ☎ *(06434)*

Badgastein is the chief resort in the scenic north-south Gastein Valley (Gasteiner Tal). Badgastein's fame rests on its radon-rich hot springs, which have attracted cure-seekers since the Middle Ages.

Orientation & Information
Badgastein clings to the valley slopes; this means there are lots of hills and plenty of scenic vantage points. Tumbling through the centre in a series of waterfalls is the valley river, the Gasteiner Ache.

The train station is on the west side of town. The town centre, Kongressplatz, is down the hill to the east: make your way down near the Hotel Salzburger Hof. You can save some leg-work by finding the car park at the top of Haus Austria and taking the lift down.

To reach the tourist office (☎ 25 31 0) on Mozartplatz go left from the train station exit and walk down the hill. It is open Monday to Friday from 8 am to 6 pm (9 am to noon and 2 to 5 pm in off-season). It's also open Saturday and Sunday, depending on demand. Staff will find accommodation without charging (guest card available).

The post office (Postamt 5640) is next to the train station, and is open Monday to Friday from 8 am to 8 pm and Saturday from 8 to 10 am.

Things to See

Badgastein became popular in the 19th century and many of the building façades reflect the grandeur of that era. From near the Wasserfallbrücke (waterfall bridge), a path ascends. At the upper bridge, take Kötschachtaler Strasse and follow it eastwards round to the Hotel Schillerhof: here you have one of the best views of the town and the valley. Work your way down via paths and roads to the small church with the dark tiled roof. This is **St Nicholas' Church**, built in the 14th and 15th centuries round a central pillar. It is Gothic in style and charmingly simple inside, with an uneven flagstone floor and faded, childlike murals.

The **Gasteiner Museum** is on the 2nd floor of Haus Austria in the town centre and is open daily from 10.30 am to noon and 3.30 to 6 pm (AS20, or AS15 with guest card). It displays minerals, paintings, crafts, and photos of historic events and famous visitors (including a shot of the infamous Goebbels taken in 1938). There are also models and costumes of the **Perchten Festival** where participants wear tall, incredibly elaborate hats. This occurs every four years on 6 January (the next is in 1998). You can see more festival paraphernalia on the 3rd floor of Haus Austria (free access).

Badgastein

0   150   300 m

To Bockstein & Sportgastein

PLACES TO STAY

1	Pension Laura
4	Christian
5	Hotel Mozart
7	Hotel Schillerhof
16	Hotel Salzburger Hof
22	Bergfriede
25	Haus Erika
27	Youth Hostel

PLACES TO EAT

8	Brasserie
10	Café Weissmayr
11	Le Café de Gastein
13	China-Restaurant Zum Mandarin
15	Hotel Elisabethpark Restaurant
17	Bayer Imbiss
26	Imbiss Stube

OTHER

2	St Nicholas' Church
3	Tourist Office
6	Stubnerkogelbahn
9	Casino
12	Kur und Kongresshaus
14	Gasteiner Museum & Haus Austria
18	Post Office
19	Train Station
20	Spar Supermarket
21	Felsenbad
23	KGM Supermarket
24	Graukogelbahn

HOHE TAUERN NATIONAL PA

Health Treatments

The tourist office will provide copious information in English on the beneficial effects of Badgastein treatments. The radon-enriched water is the product of 3000 years of geological forces. Back then it was merely rain water. Now, apparently, it has the ability to revitalise and repair human cells, alleviate rheumatism, improve male potency, reduce female menopausal problems, and much else. No doubt patients emerge from treatments not only feeling fully refreshed, but also able to explain Einstein's theory of relativity while simultaneously leaping tall buildings with a single bound. The radon is absorbed through the skin and retained by the body for nearly three hours.

The waters of the hot springs are piped to all major hotels and pensions, which offer their own health treatments. **Felsenbad** (☎ 22 23), opposite the train station, has an indoor swimming pool (dug into sheer rock) and several steaming outdoor pools. Admission includes the saunas and lockers and costs AS130 (children AS65). Curative massages in its Thermalkurhaus (☎ 27 110) cost AS190 or AS240. It is open daily from 9 or 9.30 am to 8 pm or later (up to 11 pm).

The Gastein water can also be drunk to beneficial effect: imbibe at the Kur- und Kongresshaus in the centre of town.

Activities

In the winter, **skiing** is strongly highlighted. The whole Gastein Valley is covered by the Gastein Super Ski Pass, giving access to 50 lifts (800 to 2800 metres) and 250 km of ski runs. Most runs are intermediate level. The pass is valid for a minimum of three days and costs AS780 to AS1040, depending upon the season (bus and train transfers included). Badgastein's main peaks are the Stubnerkogel (2246 metres) and the Graukogel (2492 metres). A ski pass for only Badgastein and Bad Hofgastein (see the Around Badgastein section in this chapter) costs AS290 to AS390 for one day or AS230 to AS300 after 11.45 am. Cross-country skiing is also popular.

In summer, both peaks are excellent for **hiking**. The two sections of the Stubnerkogelbahn (near Hotel Schillerhof) cost AS155 up, AS55 down, or AS180 return. The full trip on the Graukogelbahn (near the train station) is the same price.

Places to Stay

Bottom End Phone ahead in the off-season as many places close at that time. There are two camp sites a couple of km north of Badgastein in Kötschachdorf (accessible by Bundesbus). Both are open year-round: *Camping Azur* (☎ 27 90) and the much smaller *Camping Gasteinerblick* (☎ 21 78).

The HI *youth hostel* (☎ 20 80), Ederplatz 2, is 10 minutes walk from the train station: turn right, take the first path right under the train tracks, cross the river, take the left of the two forking paths then continue in the same direction till you see the sign to your right. It's open all day (10 pm curfew) and year-round; beds are AS140 in summer and AS180 in winter. It even has a sauna (AS45).

There are many private rooms which you can find by walking around (eg behind the KGM supermarket) – the tourist office leaflet lists some. *Haus Erika* (☎ 22 16), Stubnerkogelstrasse 40, near the cable car, has 12 rooms, all with private shower/WC, from AS200 to AS300 per person. The friendly owner (minimal English spoken) has many interesting pictures on the walls.

Pension Laura (☎ 52 10), Bismarckstrasse 20, is a small place by St Nicholas' Church, open year-round. It has cheerful rooms with own shower, and there's a sauna and radon baths on the premises. Prices are AS270/490 for singles/doubles and AS690 for triples.

Bergfriede (☎ 20 11), Waggerlstrasse 23, is a pension with its own restaurant. It has only double rooms, for AS400 with hall shower or AS560 with private shower (either a room cubicle or en suite bathroom). The furnishings are almost museum pieces: rustic and old-fashioned, with painted designs. The writer Karl Heinrich Waggerl was born in this house in 1897.

Middle & Top End *Christian* (☎ 32 11 0), on Kaiser Franz Josef Strasse near the tourist office, is a lively place charging AS400 per person for rooms with own shower/WC. It's worth visiting in the evening for the MTV bar/café, which has pool and table football.

Hotel Mozart (☎ 26 86 0) is nearby at Kaiser Franz Josef Strasse 25 (around the corner from Mozartplatz). It has pleasant singles/doubles for AS550/960 with high ceilings, shower/WC and cable TV, and a radon bath on site (AS120).

Hotel Schillerhof (☎ 25 81), Kötschachtaler Strasse 5, has fine views, very low prices and an outdoor swimming pool. It also offers thermal bathing and various heath and fitness treatments (AS50 to AS320). Fresh, clean rooms vary in size and facilities; only some have a balcony, all have at least a shower. Prices per person start from AS550 in the low season and AS690 in the high season.

Hotel Salzburger Hof (20 37 0), at Grillparzerstrasse 1, is not quite as good value as Schillerhof but it's much more convenient for the train station. Rooms are standard for four-star class, though the singles are a little too compact for comfort. Prices start from AS1150/1900 to AS1550/2700 depending on the season. There is live music in the bar three times a week in summer and nightly, except Saturday, in winter. The hotel has a health centre with a thermal pool, sauna, massage and mud bath, but all these cost extra.

Places to Eat

Supermarkets include the *Spar* opposite the train station, and *KGM*, farther along the same road towards the youth hostel.

Finding cheap prepared food will be a struggle, though there are a few places around. *Imbiss Stube*, Schareckstrasse 15, near the youth hostel, has basic Austrian food for under AS85 (open Monday to Saturday from 9.30 am to 1.30 pm and 3 to 7 pm). *Bayer Imbiss*, on Grillparzerstrasse between the train station and Hotel Salzburger Hof, is a self-service place open Monday to Friday from 8.30 am to 6.30 pm, and Saturday from

8.30 am to 5 pm. It serves snacks and simple meals for AS49 to AS85 and has a deli counter and salad bar.

Pension Laura (see Places to Stay) has good, unpretentious food and an eclectic clutter on the walls. Pizzas and Austrian dishes are AS65 to AS118.

China-Restaurant Zum Mandarin, by the Wasserfallbrücke, has half a dozen weekday lunch menus with soup or spring roll for AS80; other meals are above AS95. It is open daily from noon to 2.30 pm and 6 to 11 pm.

Le Café de Gastein, Kongressplatz, has a comfortable ambience and sofa seating. It serves drinks, refreshments, and some meals for AS78 to AS149 (open daily from 9 am to 10 pm). At *Café Weissmayr*, nearby on Kaiser Franz Josef Strasse, dishes are from AS85 to AS185 and there's a three-course menu for AS125. Food is available daily from 11 am to 9 pm.

Hotel Mozart (see Places to Stay) has a restaurant with a range of meals and prices. Some daily specials are under AS100 and the three-course menu is AS140.

The *Bahnhof Restaurant* is a quality, comfortable and popular place, despite its relatively humble location in the train station. Dishes are mostly above AS100 and the three-course menu (available lunch and dinner) is affordable and filling (AS128). The kitchen is open daily from 11 am to 2 pm and 5 to 9 pm.

The restaurant in the five-star *Hotel Elisabethpark* (☎ 25 52 0), Kaiser Franz Josef Strasse 5, has an excellent reputation with prices to match. Another gourmet choice is *Brasserie* (☎ 51 0 15), Kaiser Franz Josef Strasse 16 (closed lunchtime and on Sunday). The food (AS150 to AS270) combines Austrian and French styles. The restaurant is usually closed over summer, though it has a café terrace (good views) that stays open.

Getting There & Away

Express trains trundle through Badgastein every two hours, connecting the resort to points both north and south, eg Salzburg (AS156; 1¾ hours), Innsbruck (AS296;

three hours), and Spittal-Millstättersee (AS94; 50 minutes). There are good views on the right of the train from Badgastein to Bad Hofgastein. Travelling south, also sit on the right, as the view is good after the tunnel. The train station rents bikes.

To take your car south, you need to use the railway car shuttle service through the tunnel that starts at Böckstein (AS180 one-way). See Western Carinthia in the Carinthia chapter for more details.

AROUND BADGASTEIN

Three km south of Badgastein, at the head of the Gastein Valley, is **Böckstein** (1131 metres), a village with a museum and a Baroque church. It also has a medieval gold mine which has been converted into a health treatment centre, the Gasteiner Heilstollen (☎ 37 53). Patients are delivered by a small tunnel train 2½ km into the mountain, where they take their cure (AS610 per trip). A full cure takes at least 10 trips over three weeks (reserve well in advance), and it's open mid-January to late October.

Leading west from Böckstein is a toll road (AS45, but included in skiing pass) to **Sportgastein** (1588 metres), a recently created centre for skiing and other sports. Seven km north of Badgastein is **Bad Hofgastein** (858 metres), another spa centre, with good winter sports facilities. Badgastein, Bad Hofgastein and Böckstein are all linked by both bus and rail; Bundesbus No 3230 continues to Sportgastein only twice a day.

There are two access roads to the national park (with parking spaces at the terminus): the road to Sportgastein is one; the other turns east just south of Badgastein and follows the Kötschachtal.

Tirol

The province of Tirol (sometimes spelled Tyrol) is the engine that drives Austrian tourism: in 1992 it catered for nearly 43 million overnight stays by foreigners, over twice as many as its nearest rival, Salzburg province. The reason they all come is, of course, the Alps. This is classic Austrian scenery, with quaint wooden chalets sprinkled amid the foothills of precipitous peaks.

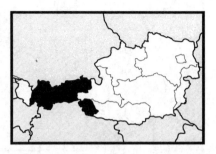

Numerous highly developed resorts offer myriad sporting opportunities, particularly skiing. In summer, hiking takes over, but winter remains the busiest season. The more sedentary visitor can simply enjoy the magnificent views and fresh Alpine air.

The Tiroleans are a proud lot, as evident in the traditional saying: 'Bisch a Tiroler, bisch a Mensch' – 'If you're Tirolean, you're a (real) person'. The implication is that if you're not Tirolean you don't really count, but this isn't a put-down of foreigners, it's more a dig at their fellow Austrians (particularly the Viennese). They could easily adapt the saying to: if you're in Tirol, you're somewhere.

History

Despite the difficult Alpine terrain, Tirol has experienced influxes of tribes and travellers since the Iron Age. In 1991, the 5500-year-old body of a man was discovered preserved in ice in the Ötztal Alps. The Brenner Pass (1374 metres) made it possible for the region to develop as a north-south trade route.

Emperor Maximilian's fondness for Innsbruck increased the region's status. Under his rule (1490-1519) Innsbruck became an administrative capital and centre for arts and culture. The duchy of Tirol was ruled from Vienna after the death of Archduke Sigmund Franz in 1665.

Bavaria, which for many centuries had contested control of parts of northern Tirol, attempted in 1703 to capture the whole province. The Bavarians, in alliance with the French (during the War of the Spanish Succession), reached as far as the Brenner Pass before being beaten back.

Another French-Bavarian alliance during the Napoleonic Wars saw Tirol incorporated into Bavaria. In 1809 Andreas Hofer led a successful fight for independence, only to have Vienna return Tirol to Bavaria under a treaty later that year. Hofer continued the struggle, and was shot by firing squad on Napoleon's orders on 20 February 1810.

A further blow was dealt by the Treaty of St Germain (1919), under which prosperous South Tirol was ceded to Italy and East Tirol was isolated from the rest of the province.

Orientation & Information

Various river valleys thread their way through the Alpine ranges that crowd the skyline. The most important is the Inn Valley, which provides the main east-west passage through the province.

Tirol is an ideal playground for skiers, hikers, mountaineers and anglers, and the tourist offices release plenty of glossy material to promote these pursuits. The *Mountains* brochure has enticing photographic imagery and details on hiking itineraries, mountain huts and mountaineering schools. The provincial tourist board, Tirol Werbung (☎ 0512-53 20; fax 53 20 174), is at Maria Theresien Strasse 55, A-6010 Innsbruck. This is the office for postal

213

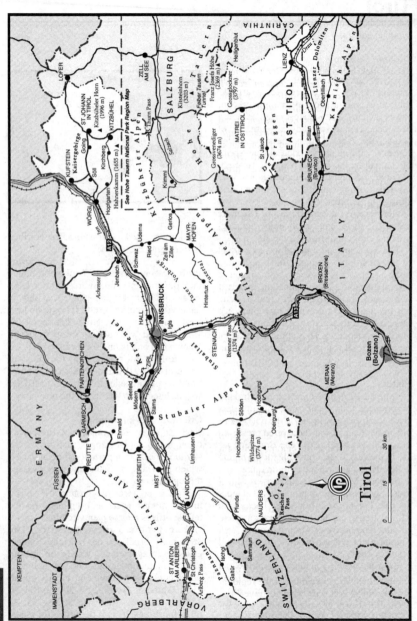

and telephone enquiries; there is no office for personal callers.

Tirolean Cuisine
Specialities include *Tiroler Gerstlsuppe*, a barley soup; *Gebackene Schinkenfleckerl*, soufflé with square noodles and ham; *Schlutzkrapfen*, ravioli filled with spinach and cheese; *Tiroler Rindersaftbraten*, sliced braised beef with parmesan; *Tiroler Saftgulasch*, a goulash with diced bacon that is often served with polenta; and *Tiroler Kirchtagskrapfen*, fritters filled with dried pears, prunes and poppy seed.

Getting Around
In 1995 Tirolean public transport underwent extensive reorganisation. The transport authority is now the Verkehrsverbund Tirol (VVT). Its head office (☎ 0512-36 59 20) is at Bodem Gasse 9, Innsbruck. Many fares came down as a result of the new system, but it's now quite complicated, with different types of ticket available for each journey. Double-check to make sure you're buying the most economical ticket for your purposes. A brochure (in German only) explains the options. Prices cover journeys on city buses, trams, Bundesbuses and ÖBB trains.

Streckenkarten tickets are 'ordinary' tickets, priced according to distance. The minimum price is A17 for a single or AS28 for a day return; the maximum for any trip in Tirol (including to/from East Tirol) is AS132 or AS212. Additionally, Tirol is divided into 12 overlapping transport regions, each with its own passes *(Netzkarten)* for unlimited travel. However, Innsbruck is treated as a special case, even though it apparently comes within three regions. A pass for any region (excluding travel within Innsbruck city) is AS130 per day or AS230 for a week, or it's AS260 (AS500) for all 12 regions. To add travel in Innsbruck city to one of the three regional cards that cover the Innsbruck vicinity there's a small extra charge. Travel in other towns is covered under the regional passes, but if you *only* want to travel in a particular town get a city pass instead, costing AS28 for a day or AS60 for a week.

Monthly and yearly tickets are also available, and there are reductions for children, senior citizens and families.

Innsbruck

• *pop 120,000* • *575 m* • ☎ *(0512)*
Innsbruck dates from 1180, when the small market settlement on the north bank of the Inn expanded to the south bank. The expansion was made possible by a bridge that had been built a few years previously and gave the settlement its name, 'Ynsprugg'.

In 1420 Innsbruck became the ducal seat of the Tirolean line of the Habsburgs. Emperor Maximilian I built many of the monuments that survive today. Archduke Ferdinand II and Empress Maria Theresa also played a part in shaping the city. More recently, the capital of Tirol has become an important winter sports centre, and it staged the Winter Olympics in 1964 and 1976.

The diverse attractions of the city, coupled with beautiful scenery and top-class skiing, make Innsbruck a destination that offers something for everybody.

Orientation
Innsbruck is in the valley of the Inn River, scenically squeezed between the northern chain of the Alps (the Karwendel) and the Tuxer mountains (Tuxer Vorberge) to the south. Extensive mountain transport facilities surround the city and provide ample hiking and skiing opportunities, particularly to the south and west. The centre of town is very compact, with the main train station (Hauptbahnhof) just a 10-minute walk from the pedestrian-only, old town centre (Altstadt). The main street in the Altstadt is Herzog Friedrich Strasse, which connects to Maria Theresien Strasse. It's a major thoroughfare but closed to private transport.

Innsbruck's exhibition centre is on Ingenieur Etzel Strasse, one km north of the Hauptbahnhof.

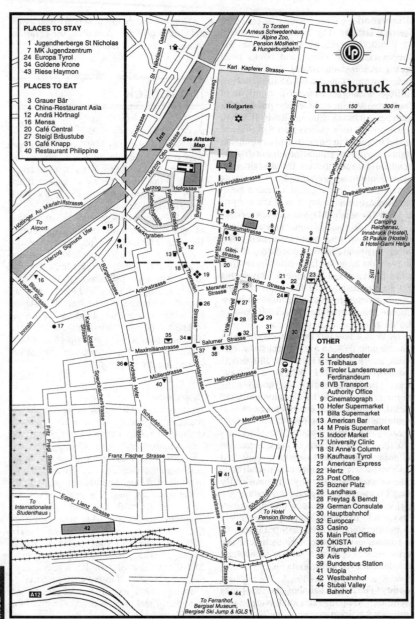

PLACES TO STAY
1 Jugendherberge St Nicholas
7 MK Jugendzentrum
24 Europa Tyrol
34 Goldene Krone
43 Riese Haymon

PLACES TO EAT
3 Grauer Bär
4 China-Restaurant Asia
12 Andrä Hörtnagl
16 Mensa
20 Café Central
27 Steigl Bräustube
31 Café Knapp
40 Restaurant Philippine

OTHER
2 Landestheater
5 Treibhaus
6 Tiroler Landesmuseum Ferdinandeum
8 IVB Transport Authority Office
9 Cinematograph
10 Hofer Supermarket
11 Billa Supermarket
13 American Bar
14 M Preis Supermarket
15 Indoor Market
17 University Clinic
18 St Anne's Column
19 Kaufhaus Tyrol
21 American Express
22 Hertz
23 Post Office
25 Bozner Platz
26 Landhaus
28 Freytag & Berndt
29 German Consulate
30 Hauptbahnhof
32 Europcar
33 Casino
35 Main Post Office
36 ÖKISTA
37 Triumphal Arch
38 Avis
39 Bundesbus Station
41 Utopia
42 Westbahnhof
44 Stubai Valley Bahnhof

Innsbruck

0   150   300 m

To Torsten Ameus Schwedenhaus, Alpine Zoo, Pension Mösheim & Hungerburgbahn

Hofgarten

See Altstadt Map

To Camping Reichenau, Innsbruck (Hostel), St Paulus (Hostel) & Hotel-Garni Helga

To Airport

To Internationales Studenthaus

To Hotel Pension Binder

To Ferrarihof, Bergisel Museum, Bergisel Ski Jump & IGLS

TIROL

Information

Tourist Offices The main tourist office (☎ 53 56), Burggraben 3, sells ski passes and public transport tickets, and books hotel rooms (AS30 commission). It also sells a three-day museum card for AS150 (students AS90), entitling the bearer to free entry to 11 museums within a three-day period (this includes Ambras Castle and the Hofkirche).

The tourist office offers plenty of free and useful literature in English. The city map has sight descriptions around the edge and useful practical information on the reverse. The *High Mountains, Terrific Town* brochure contains even greater detail. Opening hours are Monday to Saturday from 8 am to 7 pm, and Sunday and holidays from 9 am to 6 pm.

'Club Innsbruck' is a guest card, obtainable free from your accommodation place, which provides various discounts. It also allows you to go on free, guided mountain hikes from June to September. This should not be confused with the visitor's card, which gives transport and admission benefits, but must be purchased (AS360 from the tourist office).

There is a hotel reservation centre in the Hauptbahnhof (☎ 58 37 66), open daily from 9 am to 9 pm (8 am to 10 pm in the high season) which can help with other information. At the Hauptbahnhof, the youth waiting room *(Jugendwarteraum)* can also give useful tips on sights, entertainment and HI accommodation. It is closed from mid-July to mid-September; hours are otherwise Monday to Friday from 11 am to 7 pm and Saturday from 10 am to 1 pm.

Other offices for information and hotel reservations are at the city approach of the main highways: those on the autobahn to the east and west, and the one on the Brenner Pass road, are open March to November, daily from noon to 7 pm (to 9 pm from July to September). The one on Kranebitter Allee to the west is open mid-June to 30 September, daily for the same hours.

Money The Hauptbahnhof has exchange facilities (compare rates and commission between the ticket counters and the office) and a Bankomat. The tourist office also exchanges money.

Post & Telecommunications The main post office is at Maximilianstrasse 2 (Hauptpostamt A-6010), and is open daily 24 hours. Another post office is at Brunecker Strasse 1-3, just to the right upon exiting the Hauptbahnhof. It is open Monday to Saturday from 7 am to 9 pm, and Sunday from 9 am to noon.

Foreign Consulates These include:

British Consulate
    Matthias Schmid Strasse 12/I (☎ 58 83 20)
German Consulate
    Adamgasse 5 (☎ 59 6 65)
Italian Consulate
    Conradstrasse 9 (☎ 58 13 33)
Swiss Consulate
    Höhenstrasse 107 (☎ 29 22 21)

Bookshops Freytag & Berndt (☎ 57 24 30), Wilhelm Greil Strasse 15, sells many maps, plus some travel books and novels in English. It is open Monday to Friday from 8.30 am to 12.30 pm and 2 to 6 pm, and Saturday from 9 am to noon.

Travel Agencies American Express (☎ 58 24 91), Brixnerstrasse 3, with full travel agency and financial services, is open Monday to Friday from 9 am to 5.30 pm and Saturday to noon. ÖKISTA (☎ 58 89 97), Andreas Hofer Strasse 16, is open Monday to Friday from 9.30 am to 5.30 pm

Medical Service The University Clinic (☎ 50 40) is at Anichstrasse 35.

Laundry Waltraud Hell (☎ 34 13 67), Amraserstrasse 15, east of the train line, costs from AS95 to wash and dry. Opening hours are Monday to Friday from 8 am to 6 pm and Saturday from 8 am to 1 pm.

Walking Tour

Start by absorbing the Baroque façades along Herzog Friedrich Strasse. Most of these buildings were built in the 15th and 16th centuries. They make a fine picture, with the impressive Nordkette mountains soaring behind to the north. The fussy rococo ornamentation of the Helblinghaus, the last building on the left as you walk north, was created in the 18th century.

For an overview of the city, climb the 14th-century **city tower** (Stadtturm), also in Herzog Friedrich Strasse. It's open from 1 March to 31 October, daily from 10 am to 5 pm (to 6 pm in July and August). Entry costs AS20 (students AS10). Combined tickets are available which include the small Olympic Museum across the square (AS32).

The **Olympic Museum** (AS22; students AS11) shows videos of the winter games hosted by the city, but its **Golden Roof** (Goldenes Dachl) is of more interest; it comprises 2657 gilded copper tiles which shimmer atop a Gothic oriel window (built in 1500). Emperor Maximilian used to observe street performers from the 2nd-floor balcony, which has a series of scenes depicted in relief (including, in the centre, the emperor himself with his two wives). The balustrade on the 1st floor shows eight coats of arms.

Behind the Golden Roof is **St James' Cathedral** (Dom zu St Jakob). Its interior is over-the-top Baroque. Much of the sumptuous art and stuccowork were completed by the Asam brothers from Munich, though the picture above the high altar of the Madonna is by the German painter, Lukas Cranach the Elder.

Returning south along Herzog Friedrich Strasse, continue along the equally imposing Maria Theresien Strasse. The tall, slender **St Anne's Column** (Annasäule) was erected in 1706 to mark the repulsing of a Bavarian attack in 1703. The Virgin Mary stands at the top; St Anne is depicted at the base. Next, to the left, is a fine Baroque façade belonging to the **Landhaus**, built in 1728 and now the seat of the provincial government. Another 200 metres brings you to the 1765 **Triumphal Arch** (Triumphpforte), which commemorates the marriage of the then emperor-to-be, Leopold II.

Hofburg

The Hofburg (Imperial Palace) dates from 1397, but was rebuilt and extended several times since. A major influence was Maria Theresa, who imposed her favourite Baroque and rococo styles. For a self-guided tour (AS50; students AS30), departing on the hour, buy the booklet in English for AS25. From June to September there's the option of taking instead the multilingual guided tour for AS70 (lasts one hour). The grand rooms are decorated with numerous paintings of Maria Theresa and family; the faces of her 16 children all look identical – maybe the artist was intent on avoiding royal wrath from sibling rivalry in the beauty stakes. The impressive **Giant's Hall** (Riesensaal) is a 31-metre-long state room with ceiling frescoes and much marble, gold and porcelain embellishment. The palace, next to St James' Cathedral, is open daily from 9 am to 5 pm, except from mid-October to mid-May when it closes on Sunday and holidays.

Hofkirche

The Hofkirche (Imperial Church) is opposite the Hofburg, on Burggraben. It contains the massive but empty sarcophagus of Maximilian I, decorated with scenes of his life. Most of these reliefs were created by Flemish sculptor Alexander Colin (1527-1612), who also did the kneeling bronze figure of the emperor (1584). The tomb is considered the finest surviving example of German Renaissance sculpture, though the overall display is only a partial realisation of the initial plans. The Renaissance metal grille was designed by Georg Schmiedhammer, from Prague, in 1573. Maximilian is actually buried in Wiener Neustadt.

The twin rows of 28 sombre, giant bronze figures which flank the sarcophagus are memorable, if strangely unsettling. Habsburgs and other dignitaries are depicted. The dullness of the bronze has been polished to a sheen in certain places by the sheer number of hands that have touched it; a certain private part of Emperor Rudolf is very shiny indeed! King Arthur (König Artur), the legendary English king, was designed by

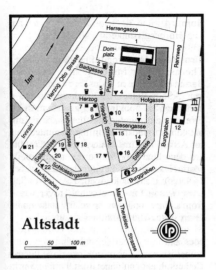

Altstadt

0   50   100 m

Albrecht Dürer, as were the images of Theoderic of the Ostrogoths and Count Albrecht IV.

The tomb of Tirolean hero Andreas Hofer (1767-1810) is also in the church. The stairs by the entrance lead to the **Silver Chapel** (Silberne Kappelle), wherein stands an image of the Virgin with embossed silver. Inside are also the tombs of Archduke Ferdinand II and his commoner wife.

The Hofkirche is open daily to 5 pm (5.30 pm in July and August) and entry costs AS20 (students AS14). Combined tickets (AS50; students AS39) are available which include the adjoining **Folk Art Museum** (Volkskunst Museum). This collection includes utensils and musical instruments, though most space is devoted to a series of rooms from Tirolean dwellings. It is open Monday to Saturday from 9 am to 5 pm, and Sunday from 9 am to noon. Admission to the museum alone costs AS40 (students AS25).

Ambras Castle

South-east of the town centre, this fine Renaissance castle can easily occupy visitors for several hours. Archduke Ferdinand II acquired the castle the year he became ruler

of Tirol (1564), and greatly extended the original building, shifting the emphasis from fortress to palace. He was responsible for creating the impressive Renaissance **Spanish Hall**, a long room with a wooden inlaid ceiling, and frescoes of Tirolean nobles gazing from the walls. The grisaille (painted in grey relief) courtyard of the upper castle is also noteworthy.

Ferdinand was the instigator of the Ambras Collection which has three main elements. The **Armour Collection** (Rüstkammer) has mostly 15th-century armour, plus Ferdinand's wedding armour (which inexplicably lacks a lapel for the carnation). The **Art & Wonders Collection** (Kunst- und Wunderkammer) is more interesting. Some beautiful objects are on display here, alongside many oddities. The *Nuremberg Plate* (1528) seems innocuous at first glance, but closer inspection reveals several perpetrators doing something unmentionable to a victim's posterior. The **Portrait Gallery**

(Portraitgalerie) has room upon room of portraits of Habsburgs and other nobles. No 158 (Room 10) shows a whiskered Charles VIII masquerading as a peasant, wearing a hat masquerading as an armchair. Maria Anna of Spain (No 126, Room 22) wins the prize for the most ludicrous hairstyle. When Habsburg visages begin to pall, unwind by strolling in the extensive gardens.

Opening hours from 1 April to 31 October are Wednesday to Monday from 10 am to 5 pm; admission costs AS60 for adults (students and children AS30). From 27 December to 31 March you can only visit the interior by guided tour in German (AS20 plus admission fee), departing at 2 pm on weekdays. To get there, take tram No 6 or bus K. The terminus of tram No 3 also gets you reasonably close. Another option is to take the special shuttle bus from the Landhaus on Maria Theresien Strasse (AS30 return), departing on the hour in summer and at 1.45 pm only in winter.

Bergisel

On the southern outskirts of Innsbruck, Bergisel was the site of the famous battle in 1809 where Hofer defeated the Bavarians. The **Bergisel Museum** contains memorials to Tirolean freedom fighters from this and other battles (open March to October; AS25, or AS15 for students).

Alpine Zoo

The zoo is north of the Inn River on Weiherburggasse. It features a comprehensive collection of Alpine animals, including amorous bears and combative ibexes. It is open daily from 9 am to 6 pm (5 pm from late September to late March). Admission costs AS60 for adults (students and children AS30). Walk up the hill to get there or take the Hungerburgbahn (the funicular to Hungerburg), which is free if you buy your zoo ticket at the bottom.

By the Hungerburgbahn lower station is a circular building; within is the **Rundgemälde**, a 1000-sq-metre panorama painting of the Battle of Bergisel. It's open

from 1 April to 30 October, daily from 9 am to 5 pm; admission costs AS26.

Tiroler Landesmuseum Ferdinandeum

This museum, at Museumstrasse 15, houses a good collection of art and artefacts, including Gothic statues and altarpieces, and a collection of Dutch and Flemish masters. The original reliefs from the Golden Roof are to be found here. In the basement is a relief map of Tirol, on a scale of 1:20,000. Opening hours are May to September daily from 10 am to 5 pm (Thursday also from 7 to 9 pm); October to April, Tuesday to Saturday from 10 am to noon and 2 to 5 pm, and Sunday and holidays from 9 am to noon. Entry costs AS50 (students AS30).

Markets

There is a large indoor market selling flowers, meat and vegetables by the river in Markthalle, Herzog Sigmund Ufer. It is open Monday to Saturday from 7 am to 1 pm. Every Saturday morning a flea market appears outside.

Skiing

Innsbruck has five main ski areas, and most have been used in Olympic competitions. All are connected by ski buses which are free of charge to anyone with the 'Club Innsbruck' card. The closest to the city is the Hungerburg area, to the north. The others are to the south or the west: Igls, Mutters, Tulfes and Axamer Lizum. Skiing is varied, with most runs geared to intermediates. At Bergisel there's a ski jump which, rather disconcertingly, overlooks a graveyard.

A one-day ski pass costs from AS250 to AS350, depending on the area; the cheapest is for the Glungezer lifts on Monday to Friday. There are also two general passes valid for several days and extending to areas such as the Arlberg and Kitzbühel. The general passes are sold by the tourist office; buy other passes at the ski lifts. One-day rental of skis, boots and poles starts at AS270 for downhill and AS175 for cross-country.

You can ski year-round at the Stubai Glacier, which is a popular excursion from

Innsbruck's five main ski areas have all been used in Olympic competitions

Innsbruck. Seefeld is also easily within reach from the city. See the Around Innsbruck section later in this chapter.

Hiking

Above the Hungerburgbahn soars the two-section Nordkette cable car, reaching the Hafelekar belvedere at 2334 metres. This whole area is ideal for hiking and taking in fine views. A three-day hiking pass can be purchased for AS400, which is also valid for the Patscherkofl cable car in Igls. Special evening services to Seegrube (1905 metres, the mid-station on Nordkette) are operated so that the lights of Innsbruck can be enjoyed from above; ☎ 29 33 44 for information.

Language Courses

The university conducts German language courses in July and August. Three weeks (60 hours) costs AS5000 and six weeks (120 hours) is AS9800. Contact Innsbrucker Hochschulkurse Deutsch (☎ & fax 58 72 33), Universität Innsbruck, Innrain 52, A-6020 Innsbruck. German courses are also offered at ISICO (☎ 57 21 60; fax 57 72 63), Colingasse 3, A-6020 Innsbruck, between April and November, except in July and August.

Organised Tours

Sightseeing bus tours of the city depart daily at noon from outside the Hauptbahnhof. They last two hours and cost AS160 (children AS75, or free if under six). In the summer tours also depart at 10 am and 2 pm, and a shorter version is available (AS130). Tourist offices and specified travel agents make tour bookings.

Festivals

The best-known annual event is the series of early music concerts conducted over two weeks in the latter half of August. Baroque operas dominate and prices are around AS150 to AS500. The venues include Ambras Castle, Landestheater and the Hofburg. The tourist office sells tickets from mid-March. Before this time, apply to Ambraser Schlosskonzerte, Schöpfstrasse 20, A-6020 Innsbruck.

From 26 November to 22 December, a Christmas market is sited in the Altstadt.

Places to Stay

The tourist office has lists of private rooms in Innsbruck and Igls in the range of AS150 to AS250 per person. Igls is south of town; get there by tram No 6 or bus J.

Camping *Camping Innsbruck Kranebitten* (☎ 28 41 80), Kranebitter Allee 214, is west of the town centre and open from April to October. Prices are AS61 per person, AS35 for a tent and AS35 for a car. There is a restaurant on site.

Hostels A convenient hostel for the centre is *Jugendherberge St Nicholas* (☎ 28 65 15), Innstrasse 95. Reception is also here for the *Glockenhaus* hostel, up the hill at Weiherburggasse 3, which has more secluded singles/doubles for AS300/380 with private shower. The hostel is HI-affiliated but it seems more like an independent backpacker place. Unfortunately, it's not very clean, the shower (AS10 for a token) situation is dire, and the 'pay-up-or-get-out' wake-up call is not particularly friendly. Dorm beds are AS115 for the first night and AS100 for additional nights, including sheets but not breakfast. Reception is closed from 10 am to 5 pm. Get a key for late nights out. The attached restaurant is open to all and is a good place for socialising. The food is so-so, comprising spaghetti bolognese (AS65), Wiener schnitzel (AS85), and rather stingy egg and bacon breakfasts (AS55). The hostel has a bar, rents bikes and offers excursion packages. You can walk here from the Hauptbahnhof, or take the half-hourly bus K from outside the station.

Two HI hostels down Reichenauerstrasse are accessible by bus No O from Museumstrasse. *Innsbruck* (☎ 34 61 79), at No 147, is in a modern, block-like building. It costs AS135 the first night and AS105 thereafter (AS6 less if you're aged under 18). Curfew is at 11 pm, and the place is closed from 10 am to 5 pm. It has a kitchen, and a laundry which costs AS45 (however, these small machines take nearly *three hours* to wash and dry). *St Paulus* hostel (☎ 34 42 91), at No 72, has large dorms for AS95 and sheets for AS20. Breakfast costs AS25, and kitchen facilities are available. Curfew is at 10 pm (but you can get a key) and the doors are locked from 10 am to 5 pm. The hostel is only open from mid-June to mid-August.

Two other hostels to try in summer are: *MK Jugendzentrum* (☎ 57 13 11), centrally situated at Sillgasse 8A, which has beds for AS140 and sheets for AS10 (open from July to mid-September); and the HI *Torsten Arneus Schwedenhaus* (☎ 58 58 14), at Rennweg 17B, where beds cost AS100, breakfast is AS45 and sheets are AS20 (open July and August).

Student Rooms As in Vienna, student accommodation is reborn as tourist hotels in the summer, from July to August or September.

Internationales Studenthaus (☎ 501 or 59 47 70), Rechengasse 7, is the most conveniently situated. It's right by the university and has 616 beds. Singles/doubles with private shower and WC cost AS370/660, or it's AS300/500 using the hall showers.

Hotels & Pensions *Riese Haymon* (☎ 58 98 37), Haymongasse 4, is south of the Hauptbahnhof. It has long, spacious rooms with a sofa, stuccowork on the ceiling and lots of character. The rooms vary in quality, so ask to see a selection. The best rooms are mostly in the older part of the building. Singles/doubles sharing the hall shower cost AS330/550, and doubles with private shower start at AS640. Reception is open between 7 am and 11 pm in the adjoining restaurant. On Saturday, when the restaurant is closed, phone ahead or look for the cleaner on the 1st floor.

Ferrarihof (☎ 58 09 68), Brennerstrasse 8, is south of town, just off the main road. Rooms are AS240/480 with either private or hall shower. Reception is in the bar downstairs from 7 am to midnight. There is plenty of car parking space.

Up the hill towards the zoo is *Pension Paula* (☎ 29 22 62), Weiherburggasse 15. Per-person prices are AS260, or from AS310 with private shower, and parking is no problem.

On the other side of the zoo in a residential area is *Pension Möslheim* (☎ 26 71 34), at Oberkoflerweg 8, Mühlau, with singles/doubles for just AS200/400, using hall showers. Reception is next door at No 4, but telephone ahead as it's usually full with long-term students (English not spoken).

Middle & Top End *Hotel-Pension Binder* (☎ 33 43 60), Dr Glatz Strasse 20, is behind the Hauptbahnhof, close to the route of tram No 3. This amenable place has doubles from AS760, with shower/WC, TV and telephone. Doubles using hall shower start at AS560. Singles are AS480, or AS340 using hall shower.

Hotel-Garni Helga (☎ 26 11 37), Brandlweg 3, is north-east of town across Grenobler Brücke and just off highway 171, the road to Salzburg. Bus O runs close by. Rooms with shower and WC start at AS470 per person, and the hotel has a sauna and indoor swimming pool.

Goldene Krone (☎ 58 61 60), Maria Theresien Strasse 46, is near the Triumphal

Arch, conveniently sited for both the old town and the Hauptbahnhof. Smallish but well equipped singles/doubles start at AS840/1280 in this three-star place. In the three-star category, the pick in the Altstadt is *Weisses Kreuz* (☎ 59 479), Herzog Friedrich Strasse 31, which has rooms for AS420/780, or AS700/1080 with private shower/WC. The 'superior' doubles for AS1160 are worth the extra cost. This 500-year-old inn played host to Mozart when he was 13, and all the rooms are spacious, well presented and comfortable. Prices drop slightly in winter. If it's full, try the *Hotel Happ* (☎ 58 29 80) across the street at No 14. It's slightly more expensive and almost as atmospheric. Pre-book on Sunday when the reception is closed.

The four-star *Goldener Adler* (☎ 58 63 34; fax 58 44 09), Herzog Friedrich Strasse 6, has welcomed many famous people through its portals in the last 600 years – see the plaque by the entrance. All the public access areas have loads of character, rather more than the modern, comfortable, but somewhat sanitised rooms. Prices start at AS1080/1600.

Hotel Innsbruck (☎ 59 8 68; fax 57 22 80), Innrain 3, is near the river in the old town. Good hotel facilities include a sauna (AS80), swimming pool (free) and garage parking (AS150). Rooms start at AS1100/1400.

The only five-star place in town is *Europa Tyrol* (☎ 59 31; fax 58 78 00), opposite the Hauptbahnhof at Südtiroler Platz 2. The rooms (from AS1350/1950) and lobby are as grand as you would expect, and it has a top-class restaurant.

Places to Eat

For further suggestions on where you can eat, see the Innsbruck Entertainment section.

Self-Catering There's a large *M Preis* supermarket on Innrain near the Altstadt, open Monday to Friday from 8 am to 6.30 pm and Saturday from 8 am to noon. A *Billa* and a *Hofer* are close together on Museumstrasse.

Self-Service & Budget Restaurants Like Vienna, Innsbruck has various snack stands

providing cheap filling fodder such as sausages, chips and burgers. Some of these only come out at night to reel in the going-home-half-drunk trade.

Andrä Hörtnagl, Maria Theresien Strasse 5, is the self-service restaurant of the supermarket around the corner on Burggasse. Snacks are from AS26, main dishes from AS55 and there's a salad buffet (AS13 per 100 grams). It's open weekdays to 6.30 pm and Saturday to 1 pm.

Another inexpensive option is the deli shops which offer hot and cold food. *Neuböck*, on Herzog Friedrich Strasse, is one such place (open daily). *Café Knapp*, Salurner Strasse 4, near the Hauptbahnhof, has cheap weekday lunch menus. The station itself has one of the *Rosenkavalier* restaurant chain, where meals start about AS65.

The university *Mensa*, Herzog Sigmund Ufer 15, on the 1st floor, serves good weekday lunches (with a vegetarian option) between 11 am and 2 pm (1.30 pm on Friday). Sometimes it's open Saturday too. There a choice of self-service or the slightly more expensive section where you are waited on. Either way you can eat well for under AS70. The Mensa is closed at Easter and over Christmas/New Year.

The *China-Restaurant Asia* is at Angerzellgasse 10. It offers excellent three-course weekday lunch specials – you get a lot of food for just AS59. It is open daily from 11.30 am to 4.30 pm and 6 pm to midnight. Another Chinese restaurant is *Lotos*, Seilergasse 5, in the Altstadt. It also has three-course lunch specials but with a wider choice (AS58 to AS85; not Sunday). It's open daily.

Notwithstanding the Chinese challenge, *Don Camillo* offers the best budget eating in the Altstadt. It is on the corner of Marktgraben and Seilergasse, and is a standard Austrian bar/restaurant. Decent-sized portions include pizza from AS65, pasta from AS58, and tasty Austrian food from AS78. Opening hours are Monday to Saturday from 11 am to 1 am, and Sunday from 5 to 11 pm.

Restaurant Philippine (☎ 58 91 57), Müllerstrasse 9, is a specialist vegetarian restaurant, decked out in light colours. It has a wide selection of main dishes in the range of AS75 to AS180, and an extensive salad buffet for AS52/94 for a small/big plate. It is open Monday to Saturday from 10 am to midnight (the kitchen closes at 10.30 pm). English menus are available.

There are a couple of places to try on the east side of the train line. *Sirene*, Reichenauerstrasse 95, has Austrian and pasta meals. It's not too expensive if you stick to the daily specials (from AS75). Opening hours are Monday to Saturday from 8 am to midnight. Not far away is *Café Intermezzo*, Nicolussistrasse 12, a small place frequented by locals, with tasty meals for around AS80.

Mid-Price & Expensive Restaurants *Café Central*, Gilmstrasse 5, is a Viennese-style coffee house. It has English newspapers, daily menus (with soup) from around AS90, and piano music on Sunday from 8 to 10 pm. It opens daily from 8 am to 11 pm.

Most places in the Altstadt are a little on the pricey side, and generally serve a combination of Tirolean, Austrian and international food. *Gasthaus Goldenes Dachl*, Hofgasse 1, provides a civilised environment for tasting Tirolean specialities such as Bauerngröstl, a pork, bacon, potato and egg concoction served with Krautsalat (AS118). It is open daily from 8 am to midnight.

Steigl Bräustube, Wilhelm Greil Strasse 25, has almost a beer hall atmosphere, though it's a bit too restrained to really qualify. Steigl beer is AS32 for half a litre and food is around AS80 to AS170 (closed Sunday).

Grauer Bär, Universitätsstrasse 5, offers creative cuisine in an arcaded room. Prices are AS85 to AS220 and there's a three-course menu for about AS125 (open daily).

Weisses Rössl (☎ 58 30 57), Kiebachgasse 8, in the Altstadt, is good for regional food for around AS90 to AS180 (daily menus and 'senior' meals are cheaper). It's closed on Sunday and holidays. Opposite is *Hirschenstuben* (☎ 58 29 79) at No 5. It has vaulted rooms and a menu that encompasses both local and Italian dishes (AS85 to AS225). It is closed Monday lunchtime, Sunday, and mid-June to late July. Both these places get busy in the high season, so reserve ahead.

For up-market eating, *Restaurant Altstadtstüberl* (☎ 58 23 47), Riesengasse 13, is one of the best places to try Tirolean food. Main dishes vary with the availability of seasonal ingredients, and cost in the region of AS120 to AS240. It's closed on Sundays and holidays.

Goldener Adler (see Places to Stay) has three restaurants, all with main courses at around AS135 to AS265. The two on the 1st floor are the more elegant, but the cellar-style Goethe Stube (open evening only) on the ground floor has the added attraction of a plucking zither player from 7 pm. The restaurants are open daily.

Entertainment

Ask at the tourist office about 'Tirolean evenings' (AS200 for brass bands, folk dancing, yodelling and one drink). Innsbruck has its own symphony orchestra; it and other ensembles perform regularly in various venues. Ambras Castle hosts a series of classical music concerts in summer. Between late May and late September there is medieval brass music performed from the Golden Roof balcony, every Sunday at 11.30 am.

The *Landestheater* (☎ 52 07 44), Rennweg 2, has year-round performances ranging from opera and ballet to drama and comedy. Get information and tickets (commission charged) from the tourist office.

Cinematograph (☎ 57 85 00), Museumstrasse 31, shows independent films in their original language. Tickets are around AS60. Cinemas around town are cheaper on Monday, when all seats are AS50.

Utopia (☎ 58 85 87), Tschamlerstrasse 3, has something going on most nights in the downstairs cellar bar, whether live music or other events. It's open Thursday to Saturday; entry costs AS60 to AS200 (AS20 reduction for students). There's also a café, open Monday to Saturday from 5 pm to midnight. Some fixtures from its former incarnation as

Left: Austria's national flag with the country's highest peak, Grossglockner, in the background, at Dr Franz Rehrl Haus, Hohe Tauern National Park
Right: Ibex statue at Dr Franz Rehrl Haus, Hohe Tauern National Park
Bottom: The road leading to Dr Franz Rehrl Haus, Hohe Tauern National Park

MARK HONAN

MARK HONAN

MARK HONAN

MARK HONAN

Top Left: Gauderfest, Zell am Ziller, Tirol
Top Right: Musician at the Gauderfest, Zell am Ziller, Tirol
Bottom Left: Ceremonial parade, Innsbruck, Tirol
Bottom Right: Annual festival, Mayrhofen, Tirol

a factory are still in place, creating an unusual environment.

Treibhaus (☎ 58 68 74), Angerzellgasse 8, has live music most nights (in a circus-style tent in summer). Entry costs AS150 to AS200, though free jazz enlivens Sunday lunchtimes. There's also a play area for kids, and pizzas are great value (from AS50/70 for small/large). Opening times are 11 am to 1 am, except Sunday when it's 10.30 am to 6 pm or later.

A place popular with students is *Elferhaus* (☎ 58 28 75), Herzog Friedrich Strasse 11. It's a long, narrow bar and restaurant with occasional live music (free entry). Food costs from AS70 to AS98 and there is a wide selection of beer from Austria and elsewhere (from AS36 for half a litre). This place gets very busy and stuffy; it's open daily from 10 am to 1 am.

A more affluent clientele frequents the *Club Filou*, Stiftgasse 12, in the Altstadt. This bright, chic bar and restaurant is open daily from 6 pm to 4 am. The darker, downstairs bar is open from 6 pm; here the music's louder and there's dancing later. In either section the drinks are expensive (AS38 a glass of wine, AS48 a small beer).

The *American Bar*, Maria Theresien Strasse 10, is below the Orangerie Café. Drinks are pricey, but there's a DJ on Friday and Saturday nights and a dancing area. It is open from 10 pm to 4 am and features a broad range of modern music.

Dom Café-Bar, Pfarrgasse 3, is a busy, dimly-lit drinking establishment in the Altstadt, with good pizzas and other dishes from AS85. It is open daily 5 pm to 1 am.

Innsbruck has a *casino* at Landhausplatz, open daily from 3 pm.

Things to Buy
Tirolean crafts include embroidered fabrics, wrought iron and glassware. There are many souvenir shops in the cobbled streets of the Altstadt offering loden hats, wood carvings, grotesque masks and other products. The Innsbruck Heimatwerk shop is in Meraner Strasse. Swarovski Haus in Herzog Friedrich Strasse sells crystal ware. Kaufhaus Tyrol,

Maria Theresien Strasse 33, is a large department store.

Getting There & Away
Air The small airport (☎ 22 5 25), Fürstenweg 180, is four km to the west of the town centre. Tyrolean Airlines (☎ 22 22 77) is the main carrier and flies daily to Vienna, Amsterdam, Frankfurt, Paris and Zürich. Air UK has direct scheduled flights to/from London Stansted on Wednesday and Thursday (UK£169).

Bus Bundesbuses leave from by the Hauptbahnhof. The bus ticket office is near the youth waiting room in the smaller of the station's two halls.

Train The Hauptbahnhof is the most convenient Innsbruck station, though some local trains also stop at the Westbahnhof (which is actually in the south) and at Hötting (to the west).

Fast trains depart every two hours for Bregenz and Salzburg. From Innsbruck to the Arlberg, most of the best views are on the right-hand side of the train. Regular express trains head north to Munich (via Kufstein) and south to Verona. Departures are hourly to Kitzbühel (AS132).

Three trains a day go to Lienz, passing through Italy. Two are 'corridor' trains (AS132; no passport necessary, no disembarking in Italy). The 12.43 pm train is an international train, which means you'll need to show your passport. The fare for this train is AS202, as it's not fully covered under the new VVT ticket (see the introduction to this chapter) and if you're travelling on an Austrian rail pass you must pay for the Italian section (AS74).

For train information, call ☎ 1717, daily from 7 am to 9 pm.

Car & Motorbike The A12 and the parallel highway 171 are the main roads heading west and east. Highway 177, to the west of Innsbruck, heads north to Germany and Munich. The A13 is a toll road (AS130) running south through the Brenner Pass to

Italy. En route you cross the Europabrücke (Europe Bridge); this is 777 metres long and passes over the Sill River at a height of 190 metres, making it Europe's highest bridge. Toll-free highway 182 follows the same route, passing under the bridge.

Car Rental Offices include: Avis (☎ 57 17 54), Salurner Strasse 15; Budget (☎ 58 84 68), Michael Gaismayr Strasse 7; Eurodollar (☎ 34 31 61), Amraserstrasse 84; Europcar (☎ 58 20 60), Salurner Strasse 8; and Hertz (☎ 58 09 01), Südtiroler Platz 1.

Getting Around
To/From the Airport The airport is four km to the west of the town centre. To get there, take bus F, which leaves every 20 minutes from Maria Theresien Strasse (AS18). Taxis charge around AS100 for the same trip.

City Transport Tickets on buses and trams cost AS20 (from the driver; valid upon issue), or AS50 for a block of four (in advance). Tickets bought in advance must be stamped in the machines at the outset of the journey. Advance-purchase passes are AS28 for one day and AS100 for one week (Monday to Sunday). They're not valid for the Hungerburgbahn. The fine for riding without a ticket is AS470 (the AS3000 fine mentioned on signs is if you're taken to court). Advance tickets can be purchased from Tabak shops and the IVB transport authority office (☎ 53 07 103) at Museumstrasse 23. The IVB office can also issue VVT tickets (see the introduction to this chapter).

You can park without restriction on unmarked streets, but most streets near the town centre have a blue line. This means you can park for a maximum of 1½ hours; the charge is AS5 for 30 minutes, AS10 for an hour and AS20 for 90 minutes – get tickets from the pavement dispensers. Parking is free on these streets from 6 pm to 8 am, and at weekends and holidays.

Taxis cost AS52 (AS57 at night), plus about AS18 per km. Numbers for radio taxis are ☎ 53 11 and ☎ 45 5 00.

Bike Rental The office in the Hauptbahnhof is open daily from 6.30 am to 11 pm between April and October, depending on the weather.

Around Innsbruck

If you're staying in Innsbruck, consider buying travel tickets to the following places, as they include Innsbruck city travel (eg a one-day return to Hall is AS44 on this basis).

IGLS
Igls is just a few km south of Innsbruck, at the terminus of tram No 6 (Innsbruck city tickets are valid). This charming and picturesque resort achieved world notice as a site for the 1976 Winter Olympics, for which a toboggan and bobsleigh run was built. Igls is covered under the Innsbruck ski pass. It has a tourist office (☎ 0512-37 71 01) which can help with accommodation.

HALL IN TIROL
● *pop 13,000* ● *574 m* ● ☎ *(05223)*

Nine km east of Innsbruck lies Hall. It enjoyed past importance from its salt mines, and now seeks a new role as a tourist destination. The tourist office (☎ 62 69) will do its best to convince you that this is not a futile endeavour; it's open weekdays and Saturday morning. Hall has an attractive old town centre, and it's certainly viable to pay a visit on the way to or from Innsbruck.

If you do stop off, explore the area round Oberer Stadtplatz, the centre of the town. The 15th-century **Rathaus** is distinctive and has a courtyard with crenated edges, and mosaic crests. Ascend the stairs and turn left to view an impressive wood-panelled room. Across the square, the **parish church** (13th century) has an off-centre chancel, and is predominantly Gothic in style. Less than 200 metres to the east is the **Ladies Abbey** (Damenstift), founded in 1557 and graced by a Baroque tower.

A little south of the centre is **Hasseg Castle**, with the tower that has become an emblem of the town. It had a 300-year career as a mint for silver coins (*Thalers*, the ancestor of dollars). The castle is now a municipal museum that elucidates the town's history (AS35 for a tour, Innsbruck museum card valid). It's open April to October, daily except Sundays and holidays.

Getting There & Away
Highway 171 goes almost through the town centre, unlike the A12/E45 which is over the Inn River to the south. The train station is about one km south-west of the centre; it is on the main Innsbruck-Wörgl train line, but only regional trains stop there. Innsbruck can also be reached by bus; buses skirt the town centre and also stop near the train station.

SCHWAZ
• *pop 11,000* • *535 m* • ☎ *(05242)*
Schwaz, 18 km east of Hall, is another former mining town, except that silver and copper was the bounty sought (much of it finding its way to the Hall mint). During its heyday (15th and 16th centuries), it was the second most populous town in Tirol after Innsbruck. Houses built during these prosperous years survive in and around the central Stadtplatz.

For information on the town, contact the tourist office (☎ 32 40).

Things to See & Do
The large **parish church** (15th century) bears 15,000 copper tiles on its roof. Although the church has a Gothic structure, it has been fitted out as Baroque inside. A similar combination can be seen in the **Franciscan Church**, which has 15th-century wall paintings in the cloisters, depicting Christ's Passion.

About one km east of the town is a former **silver mine** (Schau Silberbergwerk). This can be perused by visitors, on a 45-minute tour conducted after a mini-train ride into the mountain (AS130; children AS65). It's open daily from 1 January to 15 November.

Glacier-Watching
With fears of global warming, glaciers are increasingly under scrutiny. Of the world's supply of fresh water, 80% is stored in ice and snow, and 97% of this is in Antarctica and Greenland. Glaciers are also important in the rest of the world. Without glacier meltwater, many areas at the foot of high mountain ranges would be desert or steppes. In Austria, most glaciers are in Tirol and Vorarlberg. The Pasterze Glacier in the Hohe Tauern National Park is the largest in the eastern Alps.

There's much more to glaciers than lumps of ice. They begin as snow, which over the course of years is compressed to firn (sometimes called névé). About 10 metres of fresh snow makes one metre of firn, which eventually evolves into ice. Surprisingly, ice takes longer to form in 'cold' glaciers (ie those below 0°C) than in 'temperate' glaciers. Glaciers are filled with air bubbles, created during the transformation of snow to ice, and the gas content of these bubbles may be modified by water flows in a temperate glacier.

The ice at the bottom of glaciers (in the ablation zone) may be centuries old, making it possible to measure past environmental pollution. The eruption of Krakatoa volcano in Indonesia in 1883 can be measured in glacial ice, and there are traces of the 1977 Sahara dust storms in Alpine glaciers. The peak of nuclear testing and fallout, 1963, is a benchmark year in dating glacial ice.

Glaciers are always moving; whether retreating (shrinking) or advancing (growing), the ice always moves down the valley. You might think the movement so slow as to be insignificant. Not so. The pylon feet of glacier ski lifts are set in the ice and may have to be repositioned several times a year, as is the case on the Kitzsteinhorn Glacier in Salzburg province. Over summer, huge crevasses open in the ice and must be filled before skiing starts in winter. But they can still be hazardous – never leave the marked trails when skiing on glaciers. Ice avalanches from glaciers are another significant hazard. ∎

Getting There & Away

Schwaz is on the same transport routes as Hall. Similarly, only regional trains stop; to/from Innsbruck takes 25 minutes and costs AS92 for a 'spar' return (AS100 including Innsbruck city transport).

STUBAI GLACIER

Year-round skiing is possible on this glacier – a popular excursion from Innsbruck – and the pistes are varied enough for most skiers. The summer skiing area is 2900 to 3300 metres high. Hikers are attracted to the network of footpaths lower down in the valley. The Stubai Valley (Stubaital) runs south-west, and branches off from the Brenner Pass route a little south of the Europabrücke. The glacier itself is about 40 km from Innsbruck.

The journey takes 1½ hours by bus No 1 from outside Innsbruck Hauptbahnhof (tickets from the driver). There are approximately hourly departures and the last bus is back at 5.30 pm. Stubai Glacier ski passes are AS420 for one day or AS285 for half a day. Many places in Innsbruck offer complete packages to the glacier, which work out only a little more expensive than going it alone. The tourist office has the cheapest deal: AS660 includes transport, lift passes and equipment rental.

SEEFELD

• *pop 2800* • *1180 m* • ☎ *(05212)*

This prosperous, attractively situated resort hosted the Olympic Nordic skiing competition in 1964 and 1976. Seefeld is popular all year, but especially in winter.

Orientation & Information

Seefeld lies between Innsbruck and the German border on the Seefeld Saddle (Seefelder Sattel), a high glacier-formed channel through the Northern Limestone Alps.

From the train station (which rents bikes for AS150/200 with/without a train ticket), walk west along Bahnhofstrasse for three minutes to reach the main square, Dorfplatz. On the north side is the tourist office (☎ 23 13), Klosterstrasse 43, open Monday to Friday from 8.30 am to 12.15 pm and 3 to 6.15 pm, and Saturday from 8.30 am to 12.15 pm. The high-season hours are Monday to Saturday from 8.30 am to 6.30 pm, and Sunday from 10 am to 12.30 pm and (November to February) 4 to 6 pm.

The post office (Postamt 6100) is also on Klosterstrasse.

Things to See & Do

The **Parish Church of St Oswald** dates from the 15th century. Above the Gothic doorway is a tympanum, depicting the 14th-century martyrdom of St Oswald and the miracle of the host (an event which caused the church to become a pilgrimage site). Other features include the winged Gothic altar, the wooden font and the fine ceiling vaulting in the chancel. Ascend the inside stairs to view the Chapel of the Holy Blood (Blutskapelle), with paintings by Michael Huber and some 18th-century stuccowork.

Seefeld greets plenty of affluent, fur-clad tourists, who take leisurely strolls round the streets and footpaths, or opt for a horse-drawn carriage. The walk south to the Wildsee (lake) is pleasant, or climb the small hill behind St Oswald's for good views of the resort, the lake and surrounding peaks. For longer hikes, enquire at the tourist office about its summer excursions (AS150).

Downhill **skiing** is mainly geared towards intermediates and beginners. The local ski pass costs AS315 (AS210 for children) for one day. The two main areas are Gschwandtkopf (1500 metres) and Rosshütte (1800 metres), the latter being reached by a funicular and thereafter connecting to higher lifts and slopes on the Karwendel range. The resort's speciality is cross-country skiing: 200 km of trails *(Loipe)* across the valley. They go all the way to **Mösern**, five km distant, where there are excellent views of the Inn River and peaks beyond.

Olympia is a complex of saunas and indoor and outdoor heated pools (with a water slide) open daily. The pools are open from 9.30 am to 10 pm and entry costs AS85 (children AS40) with the guest card reduction, or AS150 (AS110) to include the saunas (these are open from 1 pm). Massages are also available.

Seefeld has a **casino** near the train station, for those tourists who feel weighed down by their bulging pockets (it's open from 3 pm daily).

Places to Stay

The tourist office will search for accommodation free of charge, and will answer telephone enquiries on this matter daily except Sunday from 8.30 am to 8 pm. Check with the office on what's left open in the off

season (not much!). A guest card is available for overnighters.

The cheapest option is a room in one of the many private houses, though in these, as in hotels and pensions, prices will be higher in the winter. In fact, more up-market places have four price levels through the year; the highest (quoted here) may be nearly double off-season prices, and stays of under three days might incur a surcharge. Many top-end hotels offer discounts on green fees for the golf course.

Landhaus Seeblick (☎ 23 89), Innsbrucker Strasse 165, overlooks the Wildsee. Most

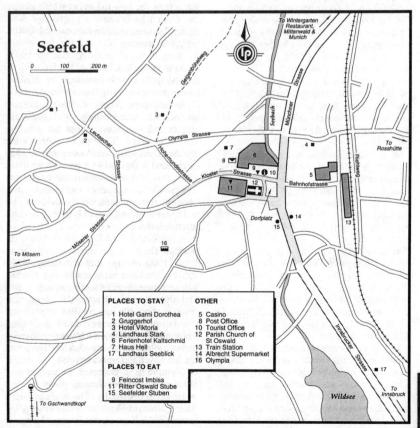

PLACES TO STAY
1 Hotel Garni Dorothea
2 Gruggerhof
3 Hotel Viktoria
4 Landhaus Stark
6 Ferienhotel Kaltschmid
7 Haus Hell
17 Landhaus Seeblick

PLACES TO EAT
9 Feincost Imbiss
11 Ritter Oswald Stube
15 Seefelder Stuben

OTHER
5 Casino
8 Post Office
10 Tourist Office
12 Parish Church of St Oswald
13 Train Station
14 Albrecht Supermarket
16 Olympia

TIROL

rooms have a view to this side and have wood balconies. Recent renovations equipped all rooms with shower/WC (AS330 per person).

Three minutes walk north of the tourist office is *Landhaus Stark* (☎ 21 04), Andreas Hofer Strasse 144, with an annex above the bank. Rooms per person cost AS230, or AS400 with private shower/WC. Nearby at Olympiastrasse 290 is *Haus Hell* (☎ 26 60). It's only a small place, but there's an indoor swimming pool; rooms have shower/WC and TV and cost from AS480 per person.

A little to the west of here is *Gruggerhof* (☎ 32 54), Leutascher Strasse 64, where rooms have balcony and sink and cost from AS200 to AS250 per person (hall showers). On the hill above is *Hotel Garni Dorothea* (☎ 25 27), No 391. This three-star place has a swimming pool, sauna and other facilities. Prices are AS570 to AS720 per person for rooms with shower/WC and TV.

The four-star *Ferienhotel Kaltschmid* (☎ 21 91), No 101, behind the tourist office, also has good facilities (swimming pool, sauna, fitness room etc). Rooms vary greatly in size and price (AS890 to AS1850 per person).

A hint that Seefeld is a haven for big spenders is the fact that it boasts seven five-star hotels, as compared to just one in Innsbruck. *Hotel Viktoria* (☎ 44 41; fax 44 43), Geigenbühelweg 589, is small and cosy with just 14 suites, each reflecting a different epoch. Prices start at AS2400 per person.

Places to Eat

Feincost Imbiss on Dorfplatz is a store that sells cheap, hot food to eat in or take away. Wiener schnitzel and salad is AS73, and a half-chicken and chips is AS69. Opening hours are Monday to Friday from 8.30 am to 12.30 pm and 3 to 6 pm, and Saturday from 8.30 am to 12.30 pm.

Dorfplatz has plenty of other places to eat, mostly in the mid-price category. Leading south from Dorfplatz is Innsbrucker Strasse, where there's an *Albrecht* supermarket. Opposite is *Seefelder Stuben*, with Austrian and Italian food for about AS80 to AS200, served between 11 am and 11 pm (closed in

off-season). A little farther along on the same side of the road are a couple of pizzerias.

The *Bahnhof Restaurant* in the train station is a bit rough-and-ready, attracting male drinkers and card players, but also serves big platefuls of tasty food from AS79. Try the Tiroler Gröstel (AS89), a heaped fry-up of meat, potatoes, and onion, served with a bowl of salad. It's open daily to 9 pm.

The five-star Hotel Tümmlerhof (☎ 25 71), Münchner Strasse 215, has *Wintergarten*, a gourmet restaurant. The food is nouvelle cuisine with regional flourishes, and the kitchen is open Thursday to Tuesday from noon to 1.30 pm and 7 to 8.30 pm. The *Ritter Oswald Stube* in the Hotel Kloserbräu (☎ 26 21), Klosterstrasse 30, is also gourmet quality, and conveniently central (closed in the off season).

Getting There & Away

Seefeld is 25 km north-west of Innsbruck, just off highway 117, the route into Germany. The road stays on the floor of the Inn Valley till it rises sharply (1:7 gradient) near Zirl. The train track starts climbing the north side of the valley much sooner after departing Innsbruck, providing spectacular views across the whole valley (sit on the left). Trains depart hourly and take 40 minutes (AS48 one-way, AS84 return). To Germany from Seefeld, train fares are AS44 to Mittenwald and AS78 to Garmisch-Partenkirchen.

EHRWALD

Ehrwald's crowning glory is the **Zugspitze** (2962 metres), which marks the border between Austria and Germany, and looms mightily over the village. A modern, fast cable car (AS385 return) flies to the top, where there's a restaurant and a magnificent panorama. All the main Tirolean mountain ranges can be seen, as well as the Bavarian Alps and Mt Säntis in Switzerland. North of the Zugspritze is Garmisch-Partenkirchen, Germany's most popular ski resort, which also offers access to the mountain summit.

Ehrwald is linked to other resorts in Austria (including Seefeld) and Germany (including Garmisch-Partenkirchen) under the Happy Ski Pass, available for a minimum of three days (AS910; AS650 for children).

For information on accommodation and other activities, contact the tourist office (☎ 05673-23 95) in the town centre. Staff will book rooms for no fee, or there's an accommodation board with a free telephone.

Getting There & Away

By train, you have to pass through Germany. Some maps still show a non-express 'corridor route' from Innsbruck to Ehrwald; however, this service has been withdrawn. You can still get to Ehrwald by train, but Austrian rail pass holders will have to pay for the German leg of the journey (AS72). In the other direction, trains come from Reutte (AS48), but Reutte itself can be reached by rail only from Germany.

Drivers can follow either rail route, or approach from the south via the Fern Pass (1216 metres); it's open all year and has a maximum gradient of 1:8. Bundesbuses go to/from Reutte (AS48) and Imst (AS60, via Nassereith).

Western Tirol

The Inn River slices east-west through mountain ranges until Landeck, at which point it twists south and goes into (or more accurately, flows out of) Switzerland. The Arlberg ski region traverses the provincial border between Tirol and Vorarlberg, and is covered in the Vorarlberg chapter later in this book.

STAMS

Stams is a small town visited primarily for its **Cistercian abbey**, founded in 1273 by Elizabeth of Bavaria, mother of Conradin, the last of the Hohenstaufens. The exterior is dominated by two sturdy Baroque towers, added in the 17th century. The most impressive feature of the interior is the high altar (1613): the intertwining branches of this version of the 'tree of life' support 84 saintly figures surrounding an image of the Virgin. Near the entrance is the *Rose Grille*, an exquisite iron screen made in 1716.

The town's tourist office (☎ 05263-65 11) can give more information.

Getting There & Away

Stams is in the upper Inn Valley, on the rail route between Innsbruck and Landeck, but only regional trains stop there. From Innsbruck, train fares are: AS60 one-way, AS106 return, or AS112 return including Innsbruck city transport. Both the A12/E60 and highway 171 pass near the abbey.

THE ÖTZTAL

The Ötztal is the most densely populated of the three river valleys that run north from the Ötztal Alps until they drain into the Inn River. The **Ötztal Alps** (Ötztaler Alpen) guard the border to Italy, and are home to numerous glaciers that shimmer between soaring peaks. The highest summit in the region is Wildspitze (3774 metres). Mountaineers, hikers and skiers can find plenty to occupy themselves. Contact the various tourist offices about accommodation; prices are 30% to 50% lower in summer.

The Ötztal is dotted with villages, in picturesque locations along the banks of the Ötztaler Ache. At Umhausen it is possible to walk to the **Stüben Falls** in about 40 minutes: take the path by the tourist office (☎ 05255-52 09).

One of the most popular resorts for skiers is **Sölden** (1377 metres), which has a mountain annex, Hochsölden (2090 metres). Some of the pistes are long and demanding; the Tiefenbach Glacier is included on the local lift pass. The Gaislachkogel cable car rises to 3058 metres and provides sweeping views of the whole Ötztal Alps. A mountaineering school, Hochalpine Bergsteigerschule Sölden (☎ 05254-25 46), is at Windau 511, A-6450 Sölden. There's a mountain guides office in the resort: Tiroler Berg- und Skiführerverband, Postfach 28 (☎ 05254-23 40). The tourist office (☎ 05254-22 12 0) can also help.

Three km beyond Sölden is **Zwieselstein**,

Frozen Fritz

In September 1991 German hikers in the Ötztal Alps came across the body of a man preserved within the Similaun Glacier. Policemen and forensic scientists were summoned to the scene. They carelessly hacked the body out of the ice, not yet aware of the importance of the find. The body had been found some 90 metres within Italy, but was appropriated by the Austrians and taken to Innsbruck University to be studied.

Although a Swiss woman identified the body as that of her father, who had disappeared on the glacier in the 1970s, experts initially decided it was about 500 years old: the ice man, nicknamed 'Otzi' or 'Frozen Fritz', was thought to have been a soldier serving under Archduke Ferdinand. Carbon dating, however, revealed he was nearly 5500 years old, placing him in the late Stone Age.

Fritz became big news. More so because the state of preservation was remarkable: even the pores of the skin were visible. In addition, Fritz had been found with 70 artefacts, including a copper axe, bow and arrows, charcoal and clothing. Over the next couple of years, he was thoroughly examined and analysed. Physiologically he was found to be no different to modern humans. His face was reconstructed, right down to his dark hair and blue eyes. X-Rays showed he had suffered from arthritis and frostbite, and his ribs had been broken. He had died between late August and late September.

Despite these discoveries, the experts could not agree on what had brought Fritz up 3000 metres into the Alps. Perhaps he had sheltered in a cave from a wintry squall, but frozen to death. Or had been a Shaman, communing with spirits in the cave. A hunter, taking flight? A shepherd, returning with his herd to Italy from the summer pastures in Austria? And what had he been doing with a copper axe, when he predated the Bronze Age? Conflicting theories raged back and forth.

Not everybody was worried about these details. Several Austrian and Italian women contacted the university and requested they be impregnated with Fritz's frozen sperm. The scientists were unable to oblige. Although he was well-preserved in many respects, Fritz no longer had a penis. 'We don't know if it's shrunk or has been eaten by an animal', one scientist explained. Poor Fritz would not become the oldest father in the world. ■

where the Ventertal River branches to the south-west. Paths lead up to Wildspitze from the end of this valley.

Farther south is **Obergurgl** (1930 metres), another well-known skiing resort, and the highest parish in Austria. Pistes are mostly for beginners and intermediates and continue right to the edge of the village. Hohe Mut (2659 metres) is a justly famous lookout, accessible by chair lift. Obergurgl is actually at the head of the valley, but the road doubles back on itself and rises to **Hochgurgl** (2150 metres). Here the pistes are a little steeper and the views equally spectacular. One tourist office (☎ 05256-258) and one ski pass (AS420 for one day) cover both resorts.

Just beyond Hochgurgl, where the road makes a sharp right-hand turn, is another viewing point, the **Windegg Belvedere** (2080 metres). The road continues into Italy where it joins the course of the Timmelsbach River.

Getting There & Away

No trains enter the valley. Stop off at Ötztal on the Innsbruck-Landeck IC route and pick up a Bundesbus from there. In the summer and winter high seasons, buses depart approximately hourly (only two-hourly in the low season) and go as far as Obergurgl (AS88; takes 90 minutes). From approximately mid-July to mid-September two morning buses continue as far as Timmelsjoch, on the Italian border.

If you have your own transport, you should be able to get at least as far as Hochgurgl all year, but the road beyond into Italy is generally blocked by snow in winter.

REUTTE

• *pop 5300* • *854 m* • ☎ *(05672)*

Reutte is the administrative capital of the Ausserfern district. You might pass through the town if you're going to Füssen (home of King Ludwig's castles) or Ehrwald, but there's no compelling reason to linger. The tourist office (☎ 23 36), Untermarkt 34, will try to convince you otherwise, especially with reference to nearby skiing and hiking.

The town has a HI *youth hostel* (☎ 30 39), Prof Dengel Strasse 20, open mid-June to late August.

Getting There & Away

Train routes to/from Reutte go via Germany. Bundesbuses provide direct connections to the rest of Tirol; ☎ 25 58 for information.

Bundesbuses also go to Füssen in Germany (AS30 or AS54 for a day return; takes 40 minutes).

Highway 314, the main north-south road, passes a couple of km to the east of the town.

IMST

• *pop 7500* • *830 m* • ☎ *(05412)*

Imst is beautifully situated and has a couple of interesting buildings in the old centre. It's mainly known for its **Shrovetide festival**, the Schemenlaufen, which takes place every four years (1996, 2000 etc). The centrepiece of this occasion is a colourful procession of 'ghosts', which the less credulous spectator will realise are actually locals wearing elaborate costumes and masks.

Fantasy Castles

Some of Germany's prime attractions are a short trip by car or bus from Reutte, including the fantastic castles of Ludwig II (1845-86), last king of Bavaria and cousin to the Empress Elisabeth. Ludwig was found drowned in suspicious circumstances in Lake Starnberg. Perhaps it was as well that he died without heirs, for he was at least a couple of Brot slices short of a Bavarian breakfast. The so-called 'mad monarch' had three obsessions in life: Richard Wagner, swans and building castles. The first two are clearly seen in the decorations of the third.

Ludwig's most famous creation is Neuschwanstein, a mishmash of architectural styles that inspired Walt Disney's Fantasyland castle. It is beautifully situated on a pine-clad hill, with a backdrop of shimmering peaks and a deep blue lake. Images of swans are everywhere, including in light fittings, door handles and basin taps. A large painted image on the walls of Ludwig's study indicates that his musings were generally less than erudite: it shows Ludwig being intimately attended to by near-naked nymphs. The setting for the scene is a grotto, which is exactly what Ludwig had built in the next room.

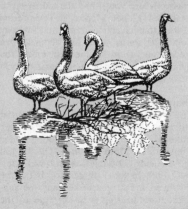

A little way down the hill is Hohenschwangau Castle. This was not built by Ludwig but is where he lived as a child. Structurally it is not as eccentric as its neighbour, but it is still well worth a visit. The castles are situated a few km from Füssen and are accessible by guided tour in English (entry is DM9 for each castle). Füssen is about 15 km north of Reutte.

Farther east is Ludwig's Linderhof Castle. This is visited mainly for its grounds, particularly the ludicrous Wagner-inspired golden conch boat. Entry to the castle costs DM7. To get there from Reutte, take the minor road that skirts the north shore of the Plansee. ■

The tourist office (☎ 24 19) is at Johannesplatz 4.

Getting There & Away

Imst is linked to other parts of Austria by Bundesbus (☎ 22 66 for information), which is how you can get from the nearest train station, Imst-Pitztal (AS17); departures are approximately every 40 minutes and it takes eight minutes to complete the three-km trip. The town is slightly to the north of the main east-west roads (the A12 and highway 171).

LANDECK

• *pop 7500* • *816 m* • ☎ *(05442)*

Landeck is an important transport junction, guarding the routes to Vorarlberg, Switzerland and Italy. The town has been standing sentinel for centuries, as proved by its hillside fortifications.

Orientation & Information

Landeck is split into several spread-out communities. The town centre proper is east of the right-angle bend of the Inn River, where that river converges with the Sanna. The train station is 1½ km to the east: upon exiting, walk left, and stay on the same side of the river (even though the main built-up area seems to be on the other side).

The main street in the centre is Malserstrasse, where you'll find the tourist office (☎ 62 3 44), open Monday to Friday from 8.30 am to noon and 2 to 6 pm, and Saturday from 8.30 am to noon. Ask about its free guided tours from May to September. You can change money here, as well as in the post office (Postamt 6500) opposite.

Things to See & Do

The **parish church**, behind the tourist office, was built in 1493, and displays Gothic features such as network vaulting and a winged altar (16th century). On the hill above stands **Landeck Castle**. It was originally built in the 13th century, but a fire destroyed it 500 years later, and the subsequent rebuilding was not true to the original form. It now contains a museum of local history (open May to October). There's

a fine view of the valley from the castle tower.

Like everywhere in Tirol, Landeck attracts the odd skier or two. Free ski buses go to nearby Zams, where the Venet cable car rises to Krahberg (2208 metres). The **ski** area is not huge, but it has runs for all abilities; a ski pass costs AS470 for a minimum two days. In the summer (Landeck's main season), the same area is ideal for **hiking**; the cable car costs AS130 one-way or AS150 return.

Landeck also offers river rafting and kayaking: contact Sport Camp Tirol (see the entry in Places to Stay).

Places to Stay

The town offers a guest card for stays of three days or more.

Sport Camp Tirol (☎ 46 6 36), Mühlkanal 1, off Flirstrasse, on the north bank of the Sanna River, is open year-round. Prices are AS50 per person, AS31 for a car, and AS35 or more for a tent. It also has a couple of bungalows at AS158 per person.

The best option for a cheap bed is to search for a room in a private house. The most likely hunting area is west of the Inn and south of the train line. Here you'll find *Landhaus Zangerl* (☎ 62 6 76), Herzog Friedrich Strasse 14, with four rooms with balcony, including two with private shower/WC. Prices start from just AS140 in summer and AS150 in winter.

On Fischerstrasse, 200 metres north of the tourist office, is *Gasthof Greif* (☎ 62 2 68). It has a restaurant, garden and plenty of parking spaces. Singles/doubles start at AS350/560, and have toilet and bath or shower.

Tourotel Post (☎ 69 11), Malserstrasse, is attached to and run by the Wienerwald restaurant (see Places to Eat). It provides renovated, comfortable rooms with shower/WC, TV and telephone from AS710/1020, and there's a fitness room and sauna on the premises.

Places to Eat

There are various places to eat along

Malserstrasse near the post office. This street also has two supermarkets, a *Hofer* and a *Spar*.

Prima, Malserstrasse 36, is a self-service place with a varied menu. Daily specials including soup cost AS62, AS72 and AS85, and there's a salad buffet and pastries. It is open Monday to Friday from 8 am to 6 pm and Saturday from 8 am to 1 pm (5 pm on Langersamstag).

Wienerwald is close to the tourist office. It has the usual chicken-oriented meals (for around AS100; open daily 7 am to midnight).

For more expensive, quality cuisine, try the restaurant in the four-star *Hotel Schrofenstein* (☎ 62 3 95), on Malserstrasse 31 (closed November to mid-December).

Getting There & Away
Landeck stands on the east-west IC express train route, 50 minutes from Innsbruck (AS128) and one hour and 50 minutes from Bregenz (AS192). Bundesbuses head in all directions, departing from outside the train station, and/or from the bus station in the town (where the train track crosses the Inn); ☎ 64 4 22 for information. Several bus routes go south down the Inn Valley: bus No 4216 goes to the Swiss customs-free zone of Samnaun (AS88; takes 1½ hours); bus No 4220 goes to Scoul-Tarasp in Switzerland (1¾ hours); and bus No 4224 goes to Nauders, where you can transfer to an Italian bus to Merano in Italy (total trip at least 3¾ hours).

The A12/E60 into Vorarlberg passes by Landeck, burrowing into a tunnel as it approaches the town. Highway 315, the Inn Valley road, passes through the centre of town and stays on the east side of the river.

THE INN VALLEY
The Inn Valley (Inntal) extends for 230 km within Tirol. Its initial stretch, south of Landeck, is the only section not shadowed by railway tracks. There's little of major interest on this part, though **Pfunds** is picturesque. Many homes here are similar in design to those found in the Engadine, a region in Graubünden, Switzerland, farther up the Inn Valley.

South of Pfunds, you have the choice of continuing along the Inn and into Switzerland, or turning left to Nauders, and thereafter into South Tirol (Italy) by way of the Reschen Pass (1508 metres; open year-round). Either road offers a corniche section with fine views.

Places to Stay
Pfunds has a HI *youth hostel* (☎ 05474-52 44), Haus Dangl, No 347; it's open all year, but note the limited check-in time (5 to 7 pm only). The small tourist office (☎ 05474-52 29), near the bus stop, can give you directions.

Getting There & Away
Regular buses go from Landeck, through the valley and into Switzerland and Italy. See the Landeck entry in this chapter.

THE PAZNAUN VALLEY
The Paznaun Valley (Paznauntal) runs the same course as the Inn Valley, except farther to the west. It's divided from its more famous neighbour by the Samnaun mountain chain. The main settlement in the valley is **Ischgl** (population 1100; altitude 1400 metres). This attractive resort is considered one of Austria's best ski areas, despite (or because of) its relative isolation. It shares its skiing pass (AS440 for one day; reductions for seniors and children) with Samnaun, a duty-free area in Switzerland. Its tourist office (☎ 05444-52 66) can tell you more.

Getting There & Away
Only a secondary road (188) runs along the valley, which crosses into Vorarlberg at Bielerhöhe (good views). This pass at 2036 metres is closed in winter, and to caravans at all times; there's a toll of AS40 per occupant for car drivers and AS70 for motorbikes. The road rejoins the main highway near Bludenz. Regular Bundesbuses travel along the valley as far as Galtür (10 km beyond Ischgl); they originate in Landeck.

North-Eastern Tirol

This part of the province is dominated by two east-west mountain chains, the Kitzbühel Alps (Kitzbüheler Alpen) and the Zillertal Alps (Zillertaler Alpen). A road and rail route between Innsbruck and Salzburg diverts into Germany near Kufstein; an alternative route that dips south between the Kitzbühel Alps is slower but more scenic.

THE ZILLER VALLEY

The Ziller Valley (Zillertal) is well developed for summer and winter sports. It is one of the most densely populated valleys in the region and attracts plenty of tourists.

The Ziller Valley runs south between the Tux Alps and the Kitzbühel Alps. Guarding the entrance to the valley is Jenbach (population 6000), which stands on the north bank of the Inn River. The broad valley has the narrow Ziller River meandering along its length. Small resorts provide all amenities, but attractive cow pastures, chalets and church spires are offset by unsightly lumber yards and electricity pylons. The farthest resort, at the head of the valley, is Mayrhofen.

All the resorts have a tourist office. The magazine *Zillertaler Gästezeitung* (partially in English) covers the valley in great detail, listing sights, events, and much practical information.

There are five camp sites within the valley. Uderns, about one-third of the way into the valley, has a HI *youth hostel* (☎ 05288-20 10), Finsingerhof, Finsing 73, open all year. Accommodation prices at most places are usually slightly higher in the winter. Wherever you stay, enquire about a guest card.

Activities The main **skiing** resort is Mayrhofen (see entry later in this chapter); but there is downhill and cross-country skiing elsewhere. The Super Ski Pass covers all 154 lifts in the valley; it is valid for a minimum of four days and costs AS1130 (children

AS670) or AS1410 (AS840) to include the glacier cable car. Ski buses connect resorts.

Hiking is strongly emphasised in summer. Between early June and early October it is possible to buy a six-day 'Z' hiking ticket, valid for 12 cable cars (one return per day) within the valley; it costs AS370 (children AS185) or AS650 (AS325) to include the valley train and buses. The Z *Wanderticket* booklet has ideas for hikes. A famous network of trails is the Zillertaler Höhestrasse in the Tux Alps. Trails lead from the resorts of Ried, Kaltenbach, Aschau, Zell and Ramsau. Mountain huts at around 1800 metres provide overnight accommodation.

Other sporting possibilities include rafting on the Ziller River, tennis, paragliding and cycling. The Ziller and its tributaries are also good for fishing, but permits are only valid for certain stretches.

Festival From late September to early October the cow herds are brought down from the high pastures, an event known as the Huamfahrerfest. The cows wear elaborate headdresses for the occasion, and the clanging of cow bells accompanies the efforts of amateur musicians. In Zell they come down on Rosenkranz (rosary) Saturday, a variable date. In Mayrhofen it's always the second Saturday in October, when the sprawling *Krämermarkt* takes over the village centre. Its wares include food, curios, crafts and cow bells.

Getting There & Away The Ziller Valley is serviced by a private train line, the Zillertalbahn. For information, call ☎ 05244-53 53 0, in Jenbach, the departure point of trains and buses. A steam train *(Dampfzug)* runs twice a day: to the last stop, Mayrhofen, it takes 80 minutes and costs AS114 one-way or AS166 return. If you just want to get from A to B, take the normal train *(Triebwagen)*. From Jenbach to Mayrhofen takes 55 minutes and costs AS52 one-way or AS94 return. Departures from Jenbach are 50 minutes past the hour between 6.50 am and 6.50 pm. Austrian rail passes are valid (except on the steam train) but Eurail and Inter-Rail are not.

Buses also run down the valley every hour or so; the last departure from Jenbach is 8.50 pm and the last from Mayrhofen is 6.50 pm.

Zell am Ziller
• *pop 1900*   • *580 m*   • ☎ *(05282)*

A former gold mining centre and now the main market town in the valley, Zell am Ziller (also known as Zell im Zillertal) retains its sense of fun, especially during the Gauderfest.

Orientation & Information The tourist office (☎ 22 81) is at Dorfplatz 3A, near the train tracks: from the Zell am Ziller train station, turn right along Bahnhofstrasse and go right at the end, a five-minute walk. The office is open Monday to Friday from 9 am to noon and 2 to 6 pm; in the summer it also opens on Saturday.

At the other end of Dorfplatz is the post office, with bus stops at the rear.

Things to See & Do Off Dorfplatz is the **parish church**, built in 1782 to an unusual circular design, with side altars all the way around. Interior wall scenes in gentle pastel colours were painted by Franz-Anton Zeiller (1716-93). Outside, most of the graves feature similar but distinctive black metal crosses with tracery surrounds.

Pizza-Air is not some fancy new delivery service for Italian food; it offers piloted **paragliding** trips of three to 25 minutes duration (AS700 to AS1500). It is based in Pizza-Café Reiter (☎ 22 89 0), Zellbergeben 4, on the west side of the Ziller River.

One round of the Paragliding World Cup is held in Zell in late May. The tourist office will provide copious information on all activities, such as free guided hikes in summer.

Festival Wafting around hot air currents (with or without the aid of a paraglider) is not recommended after a bellyful of Gauderbier, an incredibly strong beer (reputedly over 10% alcohol) brewed specially for the Gauderfest. This festival takes place on the first weekend in May (admission around AS70 per day), and participants show off long-established rural skills such as playing music, dancing and drinking heavily. On Sunday is the lavish main procession (participants wear historic costumes) and wrestling (separate bouts for humans and rams).

Places to Stay & Eat *Camping Hofer* (☎ 22 48) is at Gerlosstrasse, east of the train tracks. It is open all year and costs AS55 per person, and AS60 for a site.

Rooms in chalet-style homes are found everywhere in and around Zell. *Gästehaus Wolf* (☎ 44 36), Rosengarten 12, is five minutes walk from the tourist office, east of the train tracks (take Rosengartenweg from opposite the Spar supermarket). Singles/ doubles with hall shower are AS160/280 in summer and AS180/320 in winter, and there are balconies and a relaxing garden. An apartment (AS700 between four) is on the top floor.

Früstückspension Kerschdorfer (☎ 25 11) Unterdorf 18, is by the river, three minutes from Dorfplatz. It has pleasant rooms for AS280/510 with private shower/WC, sometimes a balcony too. There's also a TV room and a 1st-floor terrace, overlooking tennis courts and trees.

If you have more money to spend, look to the hotels on or near Dorfplatz, such as *Hotel Bräu* (☎ 23 13), with well equipped rooms for AS720/1320, off-street parking and a sauna (free for guests). Its restaurant has wood panelling, old stoves and a mid-price menu with Austrian and international dishes.

On Bahnhofstrasse is a *Konsum* supermarket, open Monday to Friday from 7.30 am to noon and 3 to 6.30 pm, and Saturday from 7.30 am to noon. Large pizzas at *Café Reiter* (see Things to See & Do) are mostly AS95 to AS115, and it's a good après-ski place.

Perhaps the best place for a cheap feed is *SB Restaurant*, Unterdorf 11, a self-service place on Dorfplatz, open daily from 11 am to 9 pm. It has snacks, soups and salads, plus

TIROL

daily specials for around AS80 to AS105. It's an annex to the *Zeller Stube*, a Gasthaus serving large portions (AS80 to AS210).

Getting There & Away The Triebwagen train costs AS20 (takes 13 minutes) to Mayrhofen and AS48 (takes 44 minutes) to Jenbach. There are special reduced fares on the Gauderfest weekend. Zell am Ziller is the start of the Gerlos Pass route to the Krimml Falls; most Bundesbuses start from Mayrhofen.

Mayrhofen
• *pop 3000* • *630 m* • ☎ *(05285)*
A picturesque chalet village, Mayrhofen guards the approach to four Alpine valleys.

Orientation & Information Leading from the train station is Am Marktplatz. On the far side of the Marktplatz is Durster Strasse, on which stands Europahaus, a convention centre. Inside is the tourist office (☎ 23 05), open Monday to Friday from 8 am to 6 pm, Saturday from 8 am to noon and 3 to 6 pm, and Sunday from 10 am to noon. The low season hours depend on demand. Pick up the comprehensive *Mayrhofen from A-Z*; it's free and in English. Outside Europahaus is an electronic 24-hour accommodation board.

Things to See & Do Mayrhofen offers legion **skiing** and **hiking** opportunities. It also has the Zillertal mountaineering school (☎ 28 29) at Hauptstrasse 458. Enquire at the tourist office about guided hikes (free with guest card). Return cable car fares on Ahorn and Penken are AS140 in summer; the peaks and valleys all around provide fine vistas.

Mayrhofen's local ski pass, valid for lifts on Ahorn, Penken and Horberg (28 ski lifts in total), costs AS340 for one day. The resort also provides easy access to year-round skiing on the Huntertux Glacier, on which an altitude of 3250 metres can be reached. In winter, a day pass costs AS420 and free ski buses go there (a 20-km, 45-minute trip). In summer, a day pass costs AS320 but there are

fewer lifts and Bundesbus is the only transport (hourly, AS84 return).

There's a swimming pool complex (☎ 25 59) at Waldbadstrasse, with indoor and outdoor pools, an aquaslide, whirlpools and saunas. The white-water rafting school (☎ 81 82) is at Gstan 18.

Keep an eye out for events staged in the Europahaus, such as Tirolean evenings. There are free tours of the hydroelectricty plant on Friday morning.

Places to Stay *Campingplatz Kröll* (☎ 25 80), in the north of the village at Laubichl, is open all year and costs AS55 per person, plus AS25 each for a car and tent. Its Gästehaus has singles/doubles for AS180/320, or AS260/520 with private shower/WC.

Most other accommodation is in chalet-style properties, whether pensions, private rooms, holiday apartments or farmhouses. The best budget deal in the village centre is the family-run *Gästehaus Fischnaller* (☎ 23 47), Hauptstrasse 410. There are no signs on this white house, just look for the number. Rooms are plain but quite sizeable; singles/doubles using hall showers are AS190/340 (closed in off-season).

Landhaus Alpenrose (☎ 22 19), Wiesl 463, is in a quieter location but still reasonably central. All but one room has a balcony, and there are parking places. Rooms cost AS200/440; singles have a shower cubicle in the room, whereas the doubles mostly have a proper bathroom. A single for AS130 has no access to a shower.

Also quiet but still convenient is *Pension Mozart* (☎ 24 85), Durst 266, with rooms with shower/WC for AS300/520. *Hotel-Garni Central* (☎ 23 17), Hauptstrasse 449, has modern, comfortable rooms with shower/WC in a chalet-style house for AS390/740 in the high season. Apartments can work out cheaper, depending on how many people stay there (maximum of four), and they have a bathroom, kitchen, telephone, TV and balcony.

Places to Eat Supermarkets include

Konsum and *Spar*, both on Brandberg Strasse.

The tiny *Pizza & Strudel* on Hauptplatz is a takeaway place with a few tables outside. Choices include spaghetti bolognese for AS63 and Wiener schnitzel for AS78, and it's open Monday to Friday from 9.30 am to 10 pm and Saturday from 9.30 am to 6 pm.

China-Restaurant Singapore, Scheulingstrasse 371, is open daily from 11.30 am to 2.30 pm and 5.30 pm to midnight. It offers a range of lunch menus with starters from AS65 (one list is daily, the other is weekdays only). The English menus are a help.

Just off Am Marktplatz on Schwendaustrasse is *Zur Kaiserbründl*, open daily from 9 am to 1 am. Pizzas and Austrian food are AS80 to AS190 and there's a garden patio, and a cheap takeaway pizza counter. *Café Edelweiss*, Brandbergstrasse 352, serves a similar range and standard of food for AS75 to AS225.

Gourmets in search of Tirolean and international dishes might try the rather presumptuously-named *Die Gute Stube* in the plush Hotel Elisabeth (☎ 29 29), Einfahrt Mitte 432. It's open daily and main dishes are AS180 to AS260.

Getting There & Away Bundesbuses to Krimml Falls via Zell am Ziller and the Gerlos Pass depart three to five times a day between late May and late September. The fare is AS88 (AS176 return) and the journey takes 90 minutes. See Krimml Falls in the preceding Hohe Tauern National Park Region chapter for more on this route.

LAKE ACHEN

Lake Achen (Achensee) is the largest lake in Tirol, about nine km long and one km wide. But size isn't everything – its beautiful situation amid forested mountain peaks is what draws tourists in the summer. A private cogwheel steam train makes the trip from Jenbach (AS140 one-way, AS220 return); the Bundes-Netzkarte and the Austrian Puzzle pass are valid, but other rail passes are not. There are three to five departures a day between 1 May and late October. Boat tours of the lake cost AS120 and take 90 minutes, and the departure from Seespitz is co-ordinated with the arrival of the train from Jenbach. There are several resorts around the lake offering water and winter sports.

KITZBÜHEL
* *pop 12,400* * *762 m* * ☎ *(05356)*

Kitzbühel was founded way back in the 9th century BC. It developed as a copper and mining centre, and is now a fashionable and prosperous winter resort. It's a place where you're assailed by plenty of glitz and glamour – not least in the tourist brochures. These have reached new heights in recent years: the 1994-95 *Winter Live* brochure was a heady kaleidoscope of tempting images, complete with a scratch-and-sniff page issuing a fresh scent of Alpine pines.

Orientation & Information

The main train station is one km north of the hub of the resort, Vorderstadt. The tourist office (☎ 21 55/22 72), Hinterstadt 18, is in the pedestrian-only part of the town centre. It is open Monday to Friday from 8.30 am to noon and 2.30 to 6 pm, and Saturday from 8.30 am to noon. In the summer and winter high seasons, hours are weekdays from 8 am to 7 pm and weekends from 10 am to noon and 4 to 8 pm. The staff dispense lots of information in English; the pocket-sized *Kitzbühel Portrait*, produced summer and winter, will tell you everything about activities and events. To find accommodation, pick up the hotel guide and/or make use of the electronic accommodation board outside, with free telephone. The guest card for overnighters offers various discounts in summer, but no such benefits apply in winter.

Opposite the tourist office is a travel agency, Eurotours (☎ 71 30 4), Rathausplatz 5, which is open daily in the high season and changes money. Ask here if the Tirolean show has restarted (tickets formerly cost AS140 including a drink).

The post office (Postamt 6370) is on Josef Pirchl Strasse.

TIROL

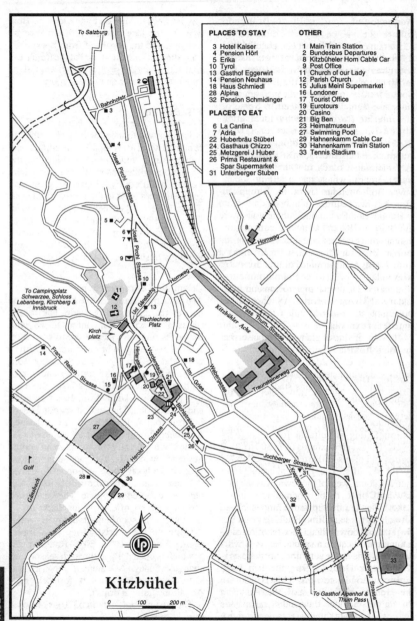

PLACES TO STAY

3 Hotel Kaiser
4 Pension Hörl
5 Erika
10 Tyrol
13 Gasthof Eggerwirt
14 Pension Neuhaus
18 Haus Schmiedl
28 Alpina
32 Pension Schmidinger

PLACES TO EAT

6 La Cantina
7 Adria
22 Huberbräu Stüberl
24 Gasthaus Chizzo
25 Metzgerei J Huber
26 Prima Restaurant &
     Spar Supermarket
31 Unterberger Stuben

OTHER

1 Main Train Station
2 Bundesbus Departures
8 Kitzbüheler Horn Cable Car
9 Post Office
11 Church of our Lady
12 Parish Church
15 Julius Meinl Supermarket
16 Londoner
17 Tourist Office
19 Eurotours
20 Casino
21 Big Ben
23 Heimatmuseum
27 Swimming Pool
29 Hahnenkamm Cable Car
30 Hahnenkamm Train Station
33 Tennis Stadium

To Salzburg

Bahnhofstr

Josef Pirchl Strasse

To Campingplatz
Schwarzsee, Schloss
Lebenberg, Kirchberg &
Innsbruck

Josef Pirchl Strasse

Josef Pirchl Strasse

Hornweg

Hornweg

Kitzbüheler Ache

Pass Thurn Strasse

Franz Reisch Strasse

Kirch platz

Fischlechner Platz

Untere Gänsbachg

Vorderstadt

Hinterstadt

Im Gries

Weberstrasse

Traunsteinerweg

Josef Herold Strasse

Bichlstrasse

Golf

Gänsbach

Hahnenkammstrasse

Jochberger Strasse

Klausengasse

Ehrenbachgasse

Jochberger Strasse

To Gasthof Alpenhof &
Thurn Pass

Kitzbühel

0   100   200 m

Things to See

Picturesque gabled houses dominate the pedestrian centre – get that camera clicking! Kitzbühel has a couple of interesting **churches** just north of Vorderstadt. The parish church was built in the 15th century; Gothic features remain (eg the nave) despite the subsequent Baroque face-lift. Some of the interior frescoes are by local artist Simon-Benedikt Faistenberger (1695-1759), who added to the work of his grandfather. Faistenberger also had a hand in the adjoining Church of Our Lady (Liebfrauenkirche), which has a sturdy square tower. Both churches are off the Kirchplatz, near the town centre.

If you've more money than you need (unlikely in Kitzbühel), you can always lighten your pockets in the **casino** near the tourist office in Hinterstadt (open nightly from 7 pm). A rather more cultural diversion is provided by a visit to the **Heimatmuseum**, Hinterstadt 34, displaying sections on local history and winter sports (AS30; AS5 for students). It's open Monday to Saturday from 9 am to noon.

The tackier side of glamour can be seen in the **Miss Austria** beauty pageant, held over two days in early March. Late July sees tennis stars compete in the **Austrian Open**, which is held at the tennis stadium just off Jochberger Strasse.

Activities

Skiing Skiing is suitable for all activity levels. The ski area extends from 800 to 2000 metres and offers 160 km of pistes accessed by 64 ski lifts. The Hahnenkamm (1655 metres), south-west of the town, was the first downhill piste to be opened in Austria (1928). On the ridge up and behind is a huge network of runs and lifts. The Hahnenkamm professional downhill ski race takes place in January, and is quite a spectacle.

Across the valley to the north-east is Kitzbüheler Horn (1996 metres), with mostly intermediate runs. This is also the favoured mountain for snowboarders. The ski region includes the peaks around the nearby resort of Kirchberg (see the entry

later in this chapter), and extends as far as Thurn Pass in the south, the gateway to Salzburg province and the Felber Tauern Tunnel.

A one-day general ski pass costs AS370 in the high season (approximately Christmas, New Year and February to mid-March) and AS360 at other times. Use of ski buses is included. The two-day pass (AS710) includes free entry to the swimming pool. A day's equipment rental is around AS180 for downhill or AS105 for cross-country skiing.

Hiking Dozens of summer walking trails surround the town and provide a good opportunity to take in the scenery; a free map from the tourist office shows routes. Get a head start to the heights with the three-day cable car pass for AS320 (AS420 including Bundesbus trips). Individual ascent tickets are AS150 (AS130 with guest card) on either Hahnenkamm or Kitzbüheler Horn, and the descent is free with the ascent ticket. Children pay half-price. Of the two peaks, vista vultures generally consider the view to be superior from Kitzbüheler Horn: the jagged Kaisergebirge range dominates to the north, and beyond the Kitzbüheler Alps the Grossglockner and Grossvenediger are visible in the south.

There is an **Alpine flower garden** with free admission on the slopes of the Kitzbüheler Horn, open in the summer. You can drive up as far as the Alpenhaus: the toll of AS30 per car and AS20 per person allows a reduction in the restaurant there. The 120 different types of flower bloom at different times: most are in the spring (June), and summer (mid-July to mid-August), though some tardy species wait till autumn (September). Hahnenkamm has a free museum, open summer and winter.

Places to Stay

Bottom End A single-night surcharge (AS20 to AS40) usually applies on top of published rates, but try to negotiate in the low season. Prices are higher at Christmas and in February, July and August – peaking in the winter high season, which are the prices quoted here.

Campingplatz Schwarzsee (☎ 28 06), Reither Strasse 24, is on the shores of the lake of the same name. It is open year-round and costs a hefty AS70 to AS80 per person, plus AS88 basic fee. The site is about three km north-west of the centre; local trains stop at Schwarzsee.

Many private homes have rooms available. They offer up to 10 beds apiece; AS200 per person is usual though farther-flung farmhouses will be cheaper. *Haus Schmiedl* (☎ 27 48), Im Gries 15, is basic, but only one block east of Vorderstadt; singles/doubles are AS200/360 with hall shower. A real bargain is *Hotel Kaiser* (☎ 47 08), Bahnhofstrasse 2, by the main train station, a backpacker-oriented place with rooms as cheap as AS140/200, or AS195/200 with private shower. A similar place is *Gasthof Alpenhof* (☎ 45 07), Aurach 176, but it's four km south-east of town.

Pension Hörl (☎ 31 44), Josef Pirchl Strasse 60, has simple but pleasant rooms from AS260/480, or AS300/560 with shower.

Pension Schmidinger (☎ 31 34), at Ehrenbachgasse 13, has rooms for AS240 per person, or AS300 with shower. The owner, Barbara, said she would give a discount to students with this book. *Pension Neuhaus* (☎ 22 00), Franz Reisch Strasse 23, is also near the centre of the resort. It has singles/doubles from AS450/800 at half-board (AS250/450 for B&B in summer). This place not only welcomes motorcyclists, it gives them a discount. Both pensions are usually open in the off season.

Middle & Top End The atmospheric *Gasthof Eggerwirt* (☎ 24 55), Untere Gänsbachgasse 12, has a painted façade and is conveniently down the steps from the churches. Singles/doubles with private shower/WC are AS700/1280, and parking is available. It is closed in November and for a couple of weeks after Easter. Close by is *Tyrol* (☎ 24 68 0), Josef Pirchl Strasse 14, where similar-quality rooms cost from AS750/1440 on a half-board basis.

Alpina (☎ 27 31), Hahnenkammstrasse 4A, is near the Hahnenkamm cable car station. Rooms in this chalet-style place have shower/WC, TV and balcony and start from AS1045/1990, with substantial reductions in the low season.

Erika (☎ 48 85), Josef Pirchl Strasse 21, has excellent facilities, such as an indoor swimming pool, sauna, steam bath, solarium and massage. Rooms in this period building have shower/WC and cable TV, and half-board starts at AS1350/2400.

Places to Eat

There is a *Julius Meinl* supermarket behind the tourist office on Franz Reisch Strasse. The *Spar* supermarket, Bichlstrasse, is slightly cheaper.

Metzgerei J Huber, Bichlstrasse, is a shop with sit-down tables and some inexpensive snacks and hot food. Along the road is *Prima*, a branch of the self-service chain, open daily in season from 9 am to 10 pm. In the low season it closes at 7 pm, at 2 pm on Saturday and all day Sunday. It offers the best cheap food in town, with menus starting at AS35, a salad bar and a comfortable, clean environment. *Huberbräu Stüberl*, Vorderstadt 18, serves good Austrian cooking and a menu (AS85 to AS115) with soup and dessert. After the kitchens close around 9.30 pm it remains popular with drinkers till about midnight. Beer is AS30 for half a litre and it's open daily.

There are a couple of places near the post office that are less crowded than those in the centre, and are open in the off season. *Adria* has Italian food from AS62, and is open daily. Next door is *La Cantina*, with Mexican food from AS70 to AS100, along with appropriate beverages such as tequila and sangria (open Tuesday to Sunday after 5 pm).

Gasthaus Chizzo, Josef Herold Strasse 2, is a good place to try Austrian food from AS90 to AS245 (open daily). It's served in a large room with lots of wood decor, and there's a bar area.

Gasthof Eggerwirt (see Places to Stay) offers quality local cuisine from AS100 to

AS240 in frescoed rooms. The three-course daily menu is around AS150.

For excellent if pricey food, head northwest out of town to *Schloss Lebenberg* (☎ 43 01 0) on Lebenbergstrasse. It's closed from mid-October to early December, and serves Austrian, international and vegetarian meals.

Book ahead in season for *Unterberger Stuben* (☎ 21 01), a rustic-style but elegant restaurant at Wehrgasse 2 (closed Wednesday lunch, Tuesday, and in the low season). It has a wide menu, with dishes from AS95 to a gourmet extravaganza for AS830. Try the Kohlroulade auf Trüffelkartoffel (cabbage stuffed with veal, with truffles and mashed potato) for AS175.

Entertainment
Kitzbühel has many discos and pubs – several are on Hinterstadt. You can meet other English-speakers at *Big Ben* on Vorderstadt, or at the *Londoner* on Franz Reisch Strasse, a bar usually crammed with young drinkers.

Getting There & Away
There are approximately hourly train departures from Innsbruck to Kitzbühel (AS156; takes 1¼ hours) and Salzburg (AS228; 2½ hours). Regional trains between Wörgl and Zell am See stop at Hahnenkamm train station, which is closer to the town centre than the main Kitzbühel station.

Getting to Lienz is awkward by train: two changes are required and it takes more than four hours. The bus is direct and takes only two hours. It leaves from outside the main train station daily at 5 pm (AS139; buy the ticket from the driver), with extra buses at weekends. By bus to Kufstein costs AS80 (AS128 return) and takes one hour, though there are only one or two departures a day.

Heading south to Lienz, you pass through some marvellous scenery. Highway 108 (the Felber Tauern Tunnel) and highway 107 (the Grossglockner Road, closed in winter) both have toll sections; for details, see the preceding Hohe Tauern National Park Region chapter.

KIRCHBERG
• ☎ *(05357)*
This resort provides access to the same ski slopes as Kitzbühel and is a slightly cheaper base than its famous neighbour. As one skier described it, people wear Swatches not Rolexes. For this reason, many travellers looking for work in the ski season base themselves here. Some start out at *Pension Astrid* (☎ 29 49), behind the train station on Rafflweg. It provides beds for just AS120 per person for job seekers who arrive in autumn. The rest of the year it costs from AS150 to AS280 per person for large rooms with own shower, WC and balcony. The blue-green house at Kitzbüheler Strasse 47, nicknamed the *Green House* (☎ 39 05), offers cheap long-term accommodation, and has a couple of new apartments for shorter stays (from about AS200 per person, with shower/WC and kitchen).

The tourist office (☎ 23 09) is at Hauptstrasse 8, and there's an accommodation board outside with a free telephone.

There are several cheap snack places in the centre, and *Max & Moritz*, Lendstrasse, is a self-service restaurant with a sun terrace. Along the same road is *La Bamba*, a bar with Mexican food and a pool table (open from 5 pm). Although smaller than Kitzbühel, Kirchberg can be lively at night. English-speakers crowd into the *Londoner* pub on Schlossergasse.

Getting There & Away
Ski buses make the six-km trip from Kitzbühel every 10 or 15 minutes during the day. Bundesbuses run in the summer. By train (hourly) it takes 10 minutes (AS17), with departures up to 10.05 pm.

ST JOHANN IN TIROL
• *pop 6500* • *660 m* • ☎ *(05352)*
Ten km north of Kitzbühel, St Johann is a typical Tirolean chalet resort. **Skiing** is suitable for all abilities, but especially intermediates; a general ski pass costs AS330 (children AS175). The Baroque **parish church** (1723-32) has paintings and

stuccowork by Simon-Benedikt Faistenberger.

Places to Stay & Eat

To find somewhere to stay, go to the tourist
office (☎ 22 18), Poststrasse 3, which has an
accommodation board outside with a free
telephone.

The Huberbräu brewery has been soothing parched throats in St Johann since 1727.
The best place to imbibe is the *Huberbräu
Bräustuberl*, Brauweg 2, above the brewery
itself. The square tower is clearly visible,
five minutes walk to the left of the train
station. Light or dark beer is AS28 for half a
litre, and there's typical, inexpensive pub
food available. It's open daily from 10.30 am
to 10 pm. There's a good view over the town
from tables inside or out.

Getting There & Away

St Johann is on the IC rail route from Zell am
See to Innsbruck, and is the stop before
Kitzbühel when travelling west. It is also at
an important road junction, where the north-
south highway 161 intersects with the
east-west highway 312. Bundesbuses
between St Johann and Kitzbühel are frequent.

WÖRGL

• *pop 8500* • *511 m* • ☎ *(05332)*
This town has nothing of tourist interest but
it is an important transport junction. At
Wörgl, the two-hourly 'corridor' train (via
Germany) to Salzburg splits off from the
hourly express route that stays in Austria.
Road routes also split, with the A12 taking
the more northerly route through Germany.
Highway 311 stays with the other train line,
but drivers have a third option to Salzburg,
highway 312 via St Johann and Lofer, which
also passes through a section of Germany.
Any car with EU and particularly Austrian
number plates shouldn't experience any
delay crossing the border.

Contact the tourist office (☎ 76 00 7),
Bahnhofstrasse 4, if you anticipate having to
spend the night in Wörgl.

KUFSTEIN

• *pop 14,000* • *503 m* • ☎ *(05372)*
Tourists are drawn to Kufstein, near the
German border, by its lakes and medieval
castle.

Orientation & Information

Kufstein is the northernmost Austrian town
in the Inn Valley. The train station is on the
west bank of the Inn River, a short stroll from
the core of the town, Stadtplatz, on the east
bank.

The tourist office (☎ 62207), Münchner
Strasse 2, is across the street from the train
station. It's open Monday to Friday from
8.30 am to 12.30 pm and 2 to 5 pm, and
Saturday from 9 am to noon; hours are
extended during the peak summer period.
The office makes room reservations without
charging commission. If you decide to stay
overnight, ask for the guest card, which has
different benefits in summer and winter.
Many shops accept payment in Deutschmarks.

The post office (Postamt 6332) is on
Oberer Stadtplatz and is open Monday to
Friday from 7 am to 8 pm and Saturday from
7 to 11 am.

Things to See & Do

Control of the town has been hotly contested
through the ages between Tirol and Bavaria.
The first recorded reference to Kufstein's
fortress was in 1205, when it was owned by
Bavaria. Kufstein swapped hands twice
before Maximilian I took the town for Tirol
in 1504. The bulky Emperor's Tower
(Kaiserturm) was added to the castle's
defences in 1522. In 1703 the town was razed
by fire during a siege by the Bavarians. The
siege failed, but the Bavarians belatedly won
the prize in 1809 during the Napoleonic
Wars, only to have it returned to Austria five
years later by the Congress of Vienna.

The fortress dominates the town from its
hill overlooking Stadtplatz. There is a lift to
the fortress (AS25 return, closed in winter),
but the 15-minute walk up is not demanding.
Roam the castle ramparts and grounds (open
all year) for fine views of the valley below.

The **Heimatmuseum** in the castle has a bit of everything but can only be visited by guided tour, which lasts around 1¼ hours. Entry to the Emperor's Tower is included, as is access to the Heroes Organ (Heldenorgel), a massive instrument with 4307 pipes and 46 organ-stops. Keep an ear out for recitals at noon and (between 1 June and 15 September) 6 pm – the music can easily be heard from Stadtplatz. The tour costs AS25 (students AS20), and there are five a day (except Monday) from April to late October. In July and August tours are daily and more frequent.

The **lakes** around Kufstein are an ideal destination for cyclists; you can rent bikes in the train station. Bundesbuses visit some of the lakes – get a timetable from the tourist office. The smaller, closer lakes are in the wooded area west of the Inn River, where there's a network of walking trails. Hechtsee, three km to the north-west, and Stimmersee, 2½ km to the south-west, are both attractively situated, and both have swimming areas with entrance fees. Hechtsee is flanked by two other lakes, Egelsee and Längsee. The larger lakes such as the Walchsee, Hintersteinersee and the Thiersee are farther afield, to the east.

Places to Stay

There is a *camp site* (☎ 636 89), Salurner Strasse 36, by the river. It charges AS44 per person, and AS30 each for a tent and a car.

For budget beds, elicit the help of the tourist office in choosing a private room in a town house or farmhouse. Most prices are between AS160 and AS220 per person.

Gasthof Zellerhof (☎ 624 15), Schluiferstrasse 20, has singles/doubles using hall shower from AS230/420. It is behind the train station (take the footbridge over the tracks) and has parking places and a restaurant on site (closed Tuesday).

Hotel Gisela (☎ 645 20), Bahnhofplatz 4, is an oldish building opposite the train station, and has rooms from AS280/540, or AS320/600 with private shower.

A few blocks south-east of the castle are a couple of places on Mitterndorfer Strasse.

Pension Striede (☎ 623 16) at No 20 costs AS285 per person, and is attached to an orthopaedic centre. Hospital-like rooms have a private shower/WC, and a balcony or access to the large garden. *Fremdenheim Maier* (☎ 622 60) at No 13 costs AS300 per person, also with private shower/WC. It has a bar and restaurant (closed Saturday afternoon and Sunday).

To stay in the centre of town, go to *Hotel Gasthof Goldener Löwe* (☎ 621 81), Oberer Stadtplatz. This attractive place has a restaurant and nearby garage parking, and rooms (from AS460/760) are equipped with shower/WC, TV and telephone.

Places to Eat

Less than 200 metres north of Oberer Stadtplatz, along Reischsstrasse, is the Inntal Center, with shops and a large supermarket. On the 1st floor *(not* the ground floor café with the same name) is a *Prima* self-service restaurant with a terrace. It has the usual wide choice offered by this chain, plus daily menus with soup or dessert for AS68 and AS85 (open normal shopping hours).

If you don't want to eat at Prima or in your hotel restaurant, the area to explore is Unterer Stadtplatz. It's a pleasant pedestrian area, with several restaurants with outside tables, and the prices aren't too bad. There's even a *Spar* supermarket at No 27 for those picnics: it's open Monday to Friday from 8 am to 6.30 pm and Saturday from 7.30 am to 1 pm.

Café Restaurant Auracher, Unterer Stadtplatz 11, has Austrian dishes from about AS65, including daily specials and a reduced-price 'seniors' meal. It has a pizza restaurant attached (pizzas from AS65). Across the street is *Café Hell*, open daily to 6 pm. It provides a range of cakes and ice creams, but also serves some meals between 11 am and 2 pm, eg spaghetti bolognese for AS78 and schnitzels from AS92. The best thing about this place is the outside terrace overlooking the river.

Getting There & Away

Kufstein is on the main Innsbruck-Salzburg

'corridor' train route; trains to Salzburg (AS264; takes 1¼ hours) run only every two hours, but those to Innsbruck (AS128; 50 minutes) are hourly, as some trains funnel down from Germany (Munich is on a direct line, a little over an hour away).

To Kitzbühel (AS78, change at Wörgl) usually takes under an hour. The easiest road route is also via Wörgl.

One or more Bundesbuses a day go to Lienz; they take 3¼ hours and call at Kitzbühel 75 minutes after departure. Buses leave from outside the train station.

KAISERGEBIRGE

Running east of Kufstein is the Kaisergebirge range, a rugged landscape extending as far as St Johann in Tirol, and more than 2300 metres high. It exercises hikers, mountaineers and skiers alike. The Kaisergebirge is actually two ranges, split by the eastward Kaiserbach Valley. The northern range is the Zahmer Kaiser (Tame Emperor) and the southern is the Wilder Kaiser (Wild Emperor). No medals for guessing which has the smoother slopes. The cable chair up Wilder Kaiser from Kufstein costs AS85 (AS115 return).

There is a mountaineering school in Going, a resort on highway 312: Bergsportschule Kaisergebirge (☎ 05358-27 50), Sonnseite 187, A-6353 Going.

SÖLL

• *720 m*

Just 10 km south of Kufstein, Söll is a well-known ski resort. It had a reputation for attracting boozy, boisterous visitors who were at least as interested in après-ski as *actuel-ski*. Recently, however, the resort has attempted to move more upmarket and regain its traditional Tirolean charm, with some success.

The highest skiing area overlooking the resort is Hohe Salve at 1829 metres. A one-day ski pass for Söll lifts costs AS320. Söll has combined with neighbouring resorts Itter, Hopfgarten, Kelchsau, Westendorf and Brixen to form the huge Skiwelt area (88 lifts, 250 km of pistes), for which a one-day pass costs AS330, including use of ski buses.

The tourist office (☎ 05353-52 16) will tell you more.

Getting There & Away

Söll is on highway 312 between Wörgl and St Johann in Tirol. It is not on a train line, but Bundesbuses run from Wörgl every couple of hours (fewer on Sunday). Free ski buses run from Kufstein.

East Tirol

East Tirol (Osttirol) covers 2020 sq km and has a population of 42,000. It is a region circled by mighty Alpine ranges, including the Lienzer Dolomites (Lienzer Dolomiten) and the Carnic Alps (Karnische Alpen) to the south. This factor, together with the loss of South Tirol to Italy after WW I, has made East Tirol somewhat isolated from the rest of Tirol. The opening of the Felber Tauern Tunnel in 1967 improved access to fellow Tiroleans, but the region retains strong social and economic links with its eastern neighbour, Carinthia. The Hohe Tauern National Park accounts for over 25% of East Tirol's territory. See the Hohe Tauern chapter for details, including information on routes north to Salzburg province.

Skiing resorts in East Tirol include St Jakob, Sillian and Obertilliach. Obertilliach is on highway 111, on the south side of the Lienzer Dolomites. Sillian is near the Italian border, on the main highway 100 heading east from Lienz. St Jakob is farther north, on a much more precipitous and spectacular route into Italy, crossing a 2052-metre-high mountain pass in the Defereggen.

LIENZ

• *pop 13,000* • *686 m* • ☎ *(04852)*

The administrative capital of East Tirol, Lienz combines winter sports and summer hiking with a relaxed, small-town ambience. The jagged Dolomites crowd the southern skyline. Lienz has been inhabited since

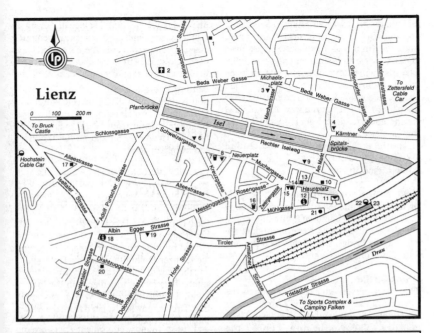

PLACES TO STAY

1 Frühstückspension
   Doris
5 Pension Gretl
10 Hotel Traube
13 Hotel Garni Eck
14 Pension Lugger
17 Haus Egger
20 Gästehaus Masnata

PLACES TO EAT

3 China-Restaurant
   Szechuan
4 Goldener Fisch
6 Gasthof Neuwirt
8 Pizzeria Azzurro
9 Restaurant Tiroler
   Stub'n
15 Adlerstüberl Restaurant
19 Imbisstube Ortner

OTHER

2 St Andrew's Church
7 Café Wha
11 Post Office
12 Tourist Office
16 Okay Café
18 Regional Tourist Office
21 Spar Supermarket
22 Bus Departures
23 Train Station

Roman times, and was granted a town charter in 1252.

Orientation & Information

The Italian influence is evident in Lienz (it's 40 km from the border): restaurants usually offer Italian menu translations ahead of English, and various shopkeepers proclaim their facility in that language.

The town centre is within a 'v' formed by the junction of the rivers Isel and Drau. The pivotal Hauptplatz is directly in front of the train station; three other squares lead from it. Hauptplatz has lots of parking – it's a Kurzparkzone with a 90-minute limit during indicated hours.

Tourist Offices The local tourist office (☎ 65 2 65) is just off Hauptplatz, at Europaplatz 1. It's open Monday to Friday from 8 am to noon and 2 to 6 pm, and Saturday from 9 am to noon. In the summer and winter high seasons (June to September and mid-December to Easter) it also opens Saturday from 5 to 7 pm and Sunday from 10 am to noon and (summer only) 5 to 7 pm. The staff will reserve accommodation (even private rooms) free of charge; if they're shut, use the accommodation board outside (free telephone). Wherever you stay, ask your host for the guest card, and get it stamped at the tourist office.

The regional tourist office, the Osttirol Werbung (☎ 65 3 33; fax 65 3 332), is at Albin Egger Strasse 17.

Post & Telecommunications The post office (Postamt 9900; money exchange available) is on Hauptplatz, virtually opposite the train station. Its opening hours are Monday to Friday from 7 am to 8 pm and Saturday from 7 to 11 am.

Bruck Castle
This well-preserved castle overlooks the town from the west. It is the former seat of the counts of Görtz and was built in the 13th century. The castle now houses the **Heimatmuseum**, which exhibits local crafts and folklore. It includes a Romanesque chapel (15th century) sporting colourful frescoes. The museum also displays 19th and 20th-century art by East Tirolean artists. A whole gallery is devoted to Albin Egger-Lienz (1868-1926), who dwelt on themes of toil, conflict and death. Expunge his morose vision with the view from the castle tower. The museum is open between Palm Sunday and 31 October, Tuesday to Sunday from 10 am to 5 pm, except between mid-June and mid-September when it is open daily from 10 am to 6 pm. Admission costs AS45 (students AS20).

St Andrew's Church
The Stadtpfarrkirche St Andrä stands over the Isel River. This impressive Gothic building is noted for its murals (some dating to the 14th century), the organ loft (1616) with winged organ, and two 16th-century tombstones, sculpted in red Salzburg marble. There's also a 'Schöne Madonna' (1430),

displaying the classic 'S' stance of this style. Albin Egger-Lienz is buried in the memorial chapel in the graveyard. There's a good view of the Dolomites from the church area – visit in the early evening when the peaks catch the sun.

Activities
Downhill **skiing** takes place on the **Zettersfeld**, with mostly medium to easy runs. The Zettersfeld cable-car station is north of the Isel (a free bus runs from the train station in summer and winter). The top section of the cable car is complemented by five ski lifts between 1660 and 2278 metres. **Hochstein** (2057 metres) is another skiing area, with its cable-car station west of the centre. One-day ski passes for all local lifts are AS290 and the ski lifts are open from 1 December to Easter, depending on snow. There are also several cross-country trails in the valley. Dolomintenlauf is a famous cross-country skiing championship that takes place on the third Sunday in January. Downhill ski rental costs from AS190 (including boots) and cross-country equipment costs around AS120.

In the summer, good **hiking** trails await in the mountains or along the valley to surrounding villages. Ask for the tourist office's *Hiking Tips* brochure. The cableways come back into service for the summer season: Hochstein, which is open late May to mid-September costs AS130 return for both sections of the chair lift; Zettersfeld (open mid-June to early October) costs AS130 return, or AS160 including the chair lift. A seven-day pass for Zettersfeld and Hochstein is AS440. Children pay half-price.

South of the Drau River is a sports complex with a stadium, swimming pool and tennis courts. Radiating from Lienz there are cycling paths for city and mountain bikes.

Festivals
On the second weekend in August Lienz hosts its annual Stadtfest, when it costs AS50 to enter the town centre to view and partake in the celebrations. Summer also sees a series of events portraying Tirolean culture, and

free concerts on Hauptplatz (at 8 pm on Wednesday, Saturday and Sunday).

Places to Stay

Bottom End *Camping Falken* (☎ 64 0 22), Eichholz 7, is south of the Drau, and closed from November to mid-December. High-season prices are from AS75 for a site and AS75 per person.

Lienz offers plenty of private rooms and a single night's stay is often possible. Prices start at around AS130, though the cheapest choices are a little way out of town. *Haus Egger* (☎ 48 7 72), Alleestrasse 33, is quiet, fairly central and excellent value at AS160 per person (up to 10 beds are available). You eat breakfast with the family and will be plied with food until you beg for mercy.

Pensions are pretty cheap, too. Near St Andrew's Church is *Frühstückspension Doris* (☎ 70 1 33), Dr Breitner Strasse 6. It's in a quiet location (except for the church bells!), with a garden and parking spaces (English not spoken). Rooms average AS225 per person, including private shower or the extra charge for the hall shower.

Pension Gretl (☎ 62 1 06), Schweizergasse 32, has big singles/doubles for AS245/450 with own shower/WC, off-street parking, and a couple of apartments. It's closed from 1 October to 31 May. Ring the bell to the ceramics shop if nobody's about (it's run by the same family).

Pension Lugger (☎ 62 1 04), Andrä Kranz Gasse 7, is plain but adequate, and right in the town centre. Doubles are AS400 with private shower, but without breakfast. There's just one single for AS250 using the hall bathroom.

Middle & Top End *Gästehaus Masnata* (☎ 65 5 36), Drahtzuggasse 4, has a couple of modern, spacious doubles (AS500 or AS520 with private WC/shower or bath), and three excellent apartments (sleeping two or three) with kitchens, for AS520 in winter or AS480 in summer. The minimum stay for the latter is at least a week.

The *Hotel Garni Eck* (☎ 64 7 85) has been run by the same family for 500 years. It has large rooms with high ceilings, shower/WC, sofa and comfortable chairs, nicely decorated corridors, big breakfasts and an excellent location on Hauptplatz, all for just AS450 per person in double rooms (no single supplement). The newer rooms are an extra AS50, but are not so 'in' with the character of the place.

Hotel Traube (☎ 64 4 44; fax 64 1 84), Hauptplatz 14, is an atmospheric, stylish hotel with a rooftop indoor swimming pool. Large rooms have all amenities and per person prices start at AS790 in winter and AS990 in the summer high season. Ask about special package deals.

Places to Eat

Supermarkets include the *ADEG* on Hauptplatz and the *Spar* by the tourist office.

The speciality at *Imbissstube Ortner*, Albin Egger Strasse 5, is grilled chicken (that's almost all it does, if the inside section is out of use). Although quite greasy, they're coated with delicious spices: the smell of the chickens sizzling on the spit outside is enough to make vegetarians join Meat Eaters Anonymous. This simple place is open daily from 10 am to 9 pm. A half-chicken *(Hendl)* is just AS32.

China-Restaurant Szechuan, north of the Isel in Marcherstrasse, is open daily and has a choice of weekday lunch menus for AS55. Pizzerias are another inexpensive option. Prices at *Pizzeria Azzurro*, Schweizergasse 3, start at AS60, and it has an adjoining bar with pool tables (open daily).

The *Adlerstüberl Restaurant*, Andrä Kranz Gasse 5, is a good place to try Tirolean specialities, from around AS80. Opening hours are daily from 8.30 am to midnight. *Restaurant Tiroler Stub'n*, Südtiroler Platz 2, also has tasty regional dishes above AS80, including the filling Tirolerstub'n Platte (AS440 for two). There are lots of outside tables overlooking the square, and it serves food daily till 11 pm.

Gasthof Neuwirt, Schweizergasse 22, has local, Austrian and grilled dishes from AS95 to over AS200, and a daily vegetarian menu. There are many different rooms; on the walls of the Fischerstube is a rogue's gallery of stuffed fish that didn't quite make it onto the dinner plate. The fish that do, are very appetising: the Forelle Neuwirt (trout) for AS145 swims under a sea of mushrooms and tomatoes. Another Gasthof with a good restaurant is *Goldener Fisch*, at Kärntner Strasse 9.

One of the best restaurants in town is in the *Hotel Traube* (see Places to Stay). Meat and fish dishes are AS175 to AS240, or there's a three-course set menu for around AS200. The hotel also has a cheaper Italian restaurant (both are open daily).

Entertainment

In the summer, there are occasional rock concerts in Hauptplatz (entrance fee payable).

The *Okay Café* in the Creativ Centre off Zwergergasse is a dark and smoky bar where beer costs around AS34 for half a litre. In the back room, there are concerts ranging from rock to avant-garde every week (AS150 to AS220). It is open Monday to Friday from 5 pm to 1 am, and Saturday and holidays from 7 pm.

Café Wha, Schweizergasse 22, is rather self-consciously trendy, but if you're young enough (at 25 you'll probably feel too old) it's worth a visit for drinks and music (open daily from 6 pm to 1 am).

Getting There & Away

Bus Buses leave from in front of the train station. The ticket and information office (☎ 67 0 67) is open Monday to Friday from 7.45 to 8.15 am and 4 to 6.30 pm. There are bus connections to the East Tirol resorts of St Jakob, Sillian and Obertilliach. To Kufstein and Kitzbühel the bus is quicker and more direct than the train. For getting to the Hohe Tauern National Park, see the preceding chapter.

Train Most train services to the rest of Austria go east via Spittal-Millstättersee, where you usually have to change trains. Trains to Salzburg take about three hours (AS296). This is also a route to Innsbruck, changing at Schwarzach-St Veit. However, a quicker and easier route to Innsbruck is to go east, via Sillian and Italy. Austrian rail passes are valid for the whole trip only on the two 'corridor' trains *(not* the one at 1.38 pm) – see under Innsbruck earlier in this chapter for more on this. Lienz train station rents bikes and changes money.

Car & Motorbike To head south by car, you must first divert west or east along highway 100, as the Dolomites are impassable sentries. See the Hohe Tauern National Park Region chapter for information on toll routes north.

Vorarlberg

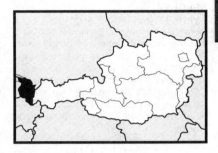

The small state of Vorarlberg extends from the plains of Lake Constance in the north to the Silvretta group of Alpine peaks in the south. It provides many outdoor activities and access to Liechtenstein, Switzerland and Germany. The provincial capital, Bregenz, annually hosts a spectacular music festival.

The local people speak an Alemmanic dialect of German, which is closer to Swiss-German than to 'ordinary' German. This is a lingering legacy of Alemmani settlers who arrived in 14 AD. In the early 15th century, Vorarlberg suffered great damage during the Appenzell War with the Swiss Confederation. Relations with its neighbour improved later: in 1918 the state became independent of Tirol and sought union with Switzerland, a move blocked by the Allied powers in the postwar reorganisation of Europe.

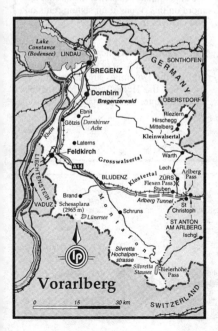

Orientation & Information

At 2600 sq km, Vorarlberg is the smallest Austrian province (except for Vienna), and is home to 331,000 people. The Arlberg skiing region is split between Vorarlberg and Tirol, and is covered in this chapter.

The provincial tourist board is Vorarlberg-Tourismus (☎ 05574-42 52 50; fax 42 52 55), Römerstrasse 7/I, A-6901 Bregenz. Prospective visitors with children should contact the office in advance for details of the many activities for kids throughout the province in July and August. Also ask for the A3-size map of Vorarlberg, with sightseeing information (in English) on the reverse side.

Getting Around

Transport in Vorarlberg is divided into five overlapping regions, covering the northwest (Rheintal), west (Oberland), south (Bludenz), south-west (Walgau) and northeast (Bregenzerwald). Kleinwalsertal in the east is not covered. To travel in each region costs AS70 (families AS100) for a day card or AS150 for one week. For all regions a travel pass costs AS120 (families AS160) per day or AS220 for a week. Children and seniors pay half-price. Passes are available for city transport in Bregenz, Dornbirn, Feldkirch, Bludenz and Götzis; day passes are AS26 (families AS35) and one-week passes are AS54.

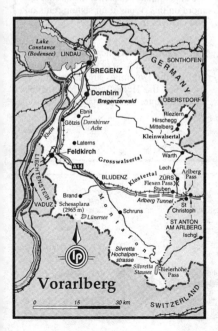

VORARLBERG

For further transport information, contact the provincial Verbundbüro (☎ 05572-33 6 60), Zollgasse 10, Dornbirn.

BREGENZ
• *pop 24,700* • *352 m* • ☎ *(05574)*

Bregenz is a compact provincial capital. It was the seat of the counts of Bregenz after the 8th century and was part of Bavaria during the Napoleonic Wars.

The town's most compelling attraction is Lake Constance (Bodensee), which provides the setting for the annual music festival that places Bregenz firmly on the cultural map of Austria.

Orientation & Information
Bregenz is on the eastern shore of Lake Constance. The town centre is about 10 minutes walk from the train station. Local buses also make the trip (AS12, or AS24 for a day card); bus No 1 continues to the Pfänder cable car.

The newer part of town is near the boat landing stage; the older part, known as the Oberstadt, is inland. The tourist office (☎ 43 39 10), Anton Schneider Strasse 4A, is open Monday to Friday from 9 am to noon and 1 to 5 pm, and Saturday to noon. During the July-August festival, hours are Monday to Saturday from 9 am to 7 pm and Sunday

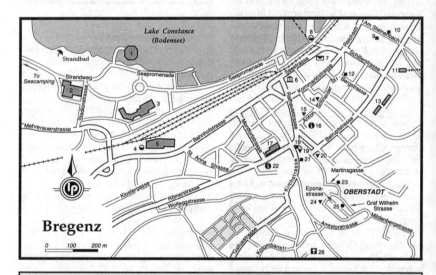

Bregenz

Lake Constance (Bodensee)

PLACES TO STAY		19	Alte Weinstube Zur Ilge	7	Post Office
		20	Gasthaus Maurachbund	8	Boat Departures &
9	Pension Paar	24	Deuring-Schlössle		Ticket Office
10	Hotel Germania			11	Pfänder Cable Car
12	Pension Traube	**OTHER**		16	Tourist Office
13	Youth Hostel			17	GWL Shopping Centre
18	Hotel Krone	1	Festival Stage	22	Provincial Tourist Office
21	Hotel Kinz	2	Indoor Pool	23	Martinsturm
		3	Casino	25	Rathaus
PLACES TO EAT		4	Bus Station	26	Old St Gallus Parish
		5	Train Station		Church
14	Restaurant Charly	6	Vorarlberg		
15	Brauhaus		Landesmuseum		

from 4 to 7 pm. It has good city maps, and listings of accommodation, consulates and activities. It also sells fishing permits for the lake. The provincial tourist office (see the chapter introduction) is open Monday to Friday from 9 am to noon and 1 to 6 pm.

The post office (Postamt 6900) is on See-strasse and is open daily until 9 pm.

Things to See & Do

The old town certainly merits a stroll; follow the walking route described in the tourist office leaflet. Quaint homes with shutters and frescoes line cobbled streets; some houses are built into the old city walls.

The centrepiece and town emblem is the bulbous, Baroque **Martinsturm** (St Martin's Tower), built in 1599. It's the largest onion-dome in central Europe. On the ground floor is the church, with 14th-century frescoes, and on the upper floors is a small military museum, with the benefit of good views. It's open over Easter and from May to September daily, except Monday, from 9 am to 6 pm.

Nearby is the half-timbered **Old Rathaus** built in 1662 by Baroque architect Michael Kuen. Farther south, off Thalbachgasse, the **Parish Church of St Gallus** has a plain exterior, but the Baroque and rococo interior is surprisingly light and delicate.

The **Vorarlberg Landesmuseum**, Korn-marktplatz 1, outlines the region's history and culture, and has a collection of works by Swiss-born artist Angelika Kauffmann (1741-1807). It is open from Tuesday to Sunday, 9 am to noon and 2 to 5 pm, and costs AS15 (students AS5). The **casino**, behind the train station, is open daily from 3 pm.

The **Pfänder** (1064 metres) offers an impressive panorama of the lake and beyond; to the east, the Allgäu Alps can be seen. A cable car to the top operates daily all year (except during maintenance) from 9 am to 6 pm (to 7 pm in summer). Fares are: up AS77, down AS55 and return AS110. Walk south through the woods from the top station to find a viewing table. At the top there is also a bird-of-prey show *(Greifvogelflugschau)* from early May to late September, daily at

Window frescoes decorate the quaint homes lining Bregenz's cobbled streets

11 am and 2.30 pm (AS40, children AS20), and an animal park (free entry).

A bathing complex is just to the west of the train station. The open-air **Strandbad** is open mid-May to September (AS31). It has lakeside access, a couple of pools and a self-service restaurant. Entry to the **indoor pool** (Seehallenbad) costs AS40 (open in winter, closed Monday).

Sailing and **diving** are on offer at Lochau, five km north of town.

Festival

The Bregenz Festival takes place from late July to late August. Operas, orchestral works and theatrical productions are performed from a vast, open-air floating stage *(See-bühne)* on the edge of the lake, behind the train station. Contact the Kartenbüro (☎ 49 20 223), Postfach 311, A-6901, about nine months before the festival, for information and tickets (costing anything from AS150 to AS1600).

Places to Stay

Seecamping (☎ 71 8 95/6), Bodangasse 7, is a lakeside site three km west of the train station. Prices are AS55 each per person, tent

The Bregenz festival is famous for its orchestral and theatrical productions

and car, and it's open from mid-May to mid-September; there are cheaper camp sites slightly inland.

The HI *youth hostel* (☎ 42 8 67), Belruptstrasse 16A, is open from 1 April to 30 September. Yes, it is those two long sheds that look like army barracks. Beds are AS116, plus AS24 or AS12 for sheets if required. It's closed from 9 am to 5 pm: reception (5 to 8 pm) is in the farthest hut, below which is a small room (door to left of the stairs) where you can leave your bags or wait during the day. Avoid the 10 pm curfew by getting a key.

Private rooms cost around AS200 per person and are invariably good value; some are scenically situated on the lower slopes of the Pfänder. These, and holiday apartments, appear on the tourist office hotel list. Stays under three days may not be possible, or will incur a surcharge. The tourist office will book rooms for AS30 commission, which is an especially useful service during the festival. Expect prices to be higher during the festival than those quoted here.

Hotel Krone (☎ 42 1 17), Leutbühl 3, is ideally central, though the building is literally cracking in two (it shouldn't fall down just yet). The prickly, elderly Frau keeps the place open all year. Doubles (from AS500 using hall shower, or AS640 with private shower/WC), are huge and well-kept. There are no singles.

Pension Traube (☎ 42 4 01), Anton Schneider Strasse 34, is in a cosier building, but is closed in winter. Singles/doubles are AS350/660 using hall showers. It has inexpensive weekday lunches in the restaurant (closed Sunday).

Pension Paar (☎ 42 3 05), Am Steinenbach 10, is a two-star place near the boat landing stage. It has rooms for AS350/640 using hall showers, and is closed from October to May. Move up one star to *Hotel Kinz* (☎ 42 0 92), Kirchstrasse 9-11. Rooms with private shower/WC are AS480/800. It has a restaurant which is open daily, except Tuesday.

Hotel Germania (☎ 42 76 60), Am Steinenbach 9, is a four-star place yet tries to attract cyclists. It has a bike workshop, sells accessories and organises bike tours (rental available). It also has garage parking, a fitness room and sauna, all free for guests. Healthy meals are offered in the quality restaurant (closed Sunday evening and Monday). Singles/doubles start at AS790/1190 and have bathroom, TV and telephone.

Places to Eat

Some of the places mentioned under Places to Stay are worth trying for food.

There's a *Familia* supermarket downstairs in the GWL shopping centre on Römerstrasse. This has a self-service café-restaurant with meals for AS54 to AS110, and a salad buffet for AS10 per 100 grams. Opening hours are Monday to Friday from 9 am to 6 pm and Saturday from 9 am to 1 pm (4 pm on Langersamstag). There's a more expensive restaurant on the 1st floor.

Restaurant Charly (☎ 45 9 59), Anton Schneider Strasse 19, serves good pizza and pasta from AS65 (closed Thursday). It gets busy, so you may need to reserve a table. Nearby in the same street is *Brauhaus*, with a couple of rooms with a beer hall atmosphere and a restaurant. There are two menus – the cheaper has meals from AS75, including national dishes. It's open daily from 9 am to 1 am.

Gasthaus Maurachbund, Maurachgasse 11, is a good place for Austrian food, with main dishes from AS88 to AS190 (closed Thursday). Perhaps an even better choice is *Alte Weinstube Zur Ilge*, up the road at Maurachgasse 6 (open daily). It has similar prices but is more atmospheric. The menu includes old standards and daily specials.

The best restaurant in Bregenz is *Deuring-Schlössle* (☎ 74 8 00), Ehregutaplatz 4. This elegant building in the old town (rooms available) is the refined setting for gourmet dishes from around AS285, including fish from the lake. You can opt to have a different specially selected glass of wine with each course of a multi-course menu. The kitchen is open from 11.30 am to 12.45 pm and 6.30 to 9.30 pm (closed Monday).

Getting There & Away
For Rheintalflug flights (see the Getting Around chapter earlier in this book) go to Bahnhofstrasse 10 (☎ 48 8 00).

Bundesbuses to destinations in Vorarlberg leave from outside the train station. Trains to Munich (AS371) go via Lindau; trains to Constance (AS154) go via the Swiss shore of the lake. There are also regular departures to St Gallen and Zürich. Trains to Innsbruck (takes under three hours) depart every one to two hours. Trains are more frequent as far as Bludenz (AS78), calling at Feldkirch en route (AS54); for return trips to both places buy a day card. The train station has a bike rental counter open daily from 6 am to 9.40 pm, and a train information office.

Boat services operate from late May to late October, with a reduced schedule from late March. For information, call ☎ 42 8 68. From Bregenz to Constance by boat (AS138 or DM20; via Lindau) takes about 3½ hours and there are up to six departures per day. Eurail, Inter-Rail and Austrian rail passes give you 50% off fares. Special boat excursions are also operated out of Bregenz in the

---

Lake Constance Excursions

Lake Constance (Bodensee) is a major summer holiday region for Austria, Germany and Switzerland. As well as many water sports, there are interesting sights round the lake which can easily be visited by boat tour from Bregenz. There are plenty of youth hostels and cosy guesthouses if you want to stay overnight.

Considered in anticlockwise order (the direction the boats travel), the closest place to Bregenz is **Lindau** in Germany. This island village has a Bavarian lion monument and an old Rathaus with murals. **Friedrichshafen** is where Graf Zeppelin built his overgrown cigar-shaped balloons, an achievement commemorated in the town's Zeppelin museum. Picturesque **Meersburg** has many half-timbered houses built in the classical German style, and two castles overlooking the vineyard-patterned hills. **Überlingen** has the Cathedral of St Nicholas, with a four-storey high altar (17th century) and a dozen side altars. **Constance** (Konstanz), the largest town on the lake, is linked to Meersburg by car ferry, and has a Gothic cathedral and a lively student population. The flower island of **Mainau** is close by.

Switzerland has fewer points of interest around the lake. The Swiss annex of Constance, **Kreuzlingen**, has nothing of great sightseeing importance. **Arbon** has a historical museum in a 16th-century castle, and some half-timbered houses. **Rorschach** has a craft museum in its historic Kornhaus. A short train ride from Rorschach is **St Gallen**, with an excellent late-Baroque cathedral and adjoining rococo library, plus many buildings with oriel windows in the old town centre.

The international **Bodensee Festival** takes place from early May to early June. Most events (concerts, cabaret, theatre etc) are on the German side of the lake. The Bregenz tourist office has a comprehensive timetable of Bodensee boats, trains and buses. ■

summer by ÖBB (same concessions apply). Schedules are available from the boat station, train station or tourist office.

A Lake Constance pass (AS336 for 15 days) entitles the holder to purchase half-price tickets on boats, trains and buses. Holders can buy transferable day passes (AS231 per set of three) valid for free travel on boats. Enquire also about the Bodensee family card, allowing free travel for children.

There is a Mitfahrzentrale (☎ 61 1 00), which links hitchhikers and car drivers, at Bildsteiner Strasse 7 in Wolfurt, four km to the south. The office is open weekdays from 10 am to 6 pm and Saturday from 10 am to noon. It usually has cars going to Vienna (hitchers pay AS395, drivers get AS297) and Germany.

BREGENZERWALD

This is the area round Bregenz. It is less wooded than the name implies ('Wald' means 'forest'), being a combination of tree-lined hills, small villages and open pastures. Skiing (both downhill and cross-country) and hiking are popular. The most dramatic natural feature is the **Rappenloch Gorge** (Rappenlochschlucht), through which the raging Dorbirner Ache flows.

The best source of information on exploring the gorge is the tourist office (☎ 05572-22 1 88) in the Rathaus in nearby **Dornbirn**. Dornbirn itself is the largest town in Vorarlberg (population 40,000) but has no major tourist sights.

Getting There & Away

IC trains stop at Dornbirn on their way to/from Bregenz, eight minutes away. Otherwise, private transport, Bundesbus, bike or foot is the way to explore the region. The bus from Dornbirn to Ebnit will take you close to the Rappenloch Gorge.

FELDKIRCH
• *pop 27,000* • *450 m* • ☎ *(05522)*
Feldkirch has a long history: its town charter was granted in 1218, yet 'Feldkirichun' appeared in records as early as 842. It's also the gateway to Liechtenstein, a parcel-sized

principality to the west famous for its postage stamps and wines.

Orientation & Information

The town centre is eight minutes walk south of the train station (turn left upon exiting). The tourist office (☎ 73 4 67), Herrengasse 12, is in the centre; Herrengasse leads off from the cathedral and Domplatz. Opening hours are Monday to Friday from 8 am to noon and 2 to 6 pm, and Saturday from 9 am to noon. It reserves rooms free of charge.

The post office (Postamt 6800) is opposite the train station.

Things to See & Do

The town retains an aura of its medieval past, with old patrician houses lining the squares in the centre, and a couple of towers surviving from the ancient fortifications. Both Neustadt and Marktplatz have arcaded walkways. The **cathedral**, known as St Nicholas' Church, has late-Gothic features and fine stained glass. The painting to the right of the altar is by local boy Wolf Huber (1480-1539), a leading member of the Danube school.

The 12th-century **Schattenburg** dominates the town, and can be reached by stairs or road. This castle was the seat of the counts of Montfort until 1390. Extensive views can be enjoyed from the keep, and the museum (AS25, students AS10; closed Monday and from November to February) has religious art and historical artefacts. The castle is also the setting for folklore evenings.

There's an **animal park** *(Wildpark)*, in which 200 species roam, about one km to the north-west of the town centre. Entry is free.

Ski slopes are at **Laterns**, with lifts up to 1785 metres. It's just 15 minutes away by car. Alternatively, take the ski bus (calling at the town, the train station and the hostel) which is free if you buy that day's ski pass (AS290; family cards available) from the driver.

Festivals

Since 1993 Feldkirch has hosted the Schubertiade summer music festival, formerly held at Hohenems. This annual event

Top: The Schattenburg, Feldkirch, Vorarlberg
Bottom: The Seeschloss Ort at Gmunden on Traunsee, in the Salzkammergut

MARK HONAN

Parish Church of St Oswald, Seefeld, Tirol

is a justly famous celebration of Schubert's work. Bookings are accepted from June of the preceding year, and it's often necessary to book this far ahead. Contact Schubertiade Feldkirch GmbH (☎ 38 0 01; fax 38 0 05), Schubertplatz 1, Postfach 625, A-6803 Feldkirch.

Other festivals include a **wine festival** on the second weekend in July and a **juggler's festival** on the first weekend in August. In winter there's a Christmas market.

Places to Stay

Waldcamping (☎ 74 3 80) offers a quiet location for summer and winter camping in Gisirigen; take bus No 2 from the train station to the last stop.

The HI *youth hostel* (☎ 73 1 81), Reichsstrasse 111, is 1.5 km north of the train station (bus No 2 trundles past) in a historic building that formerly served as an infirmary. It has been completely modernised inside and has good facilities. Beds are AS130 and there may be a AS20 heating surcharge. Curfew is at 10 pm; reception is closed and the doors are locked from 9.30 am to 5 pm. The hostel shuts from 1 November to early January and at Easter.

Private rooms are an economical alternative, but you'll find hotels and pensions surprisingly expensive – Switzerland may be nearby but that's no excuse to charge Swiss prices. The best deals are away from the town centre: *Gasthof Engel* (☎ 72 0 56), Liechtensteiner Strasse 106, is just under two km south-west of the centre in Tisis. It provides singles/doubles for AS320/500 using hall shower, and has a restaurant (closed Monday).

In the centre, *Gasthof Lingg* (☎ 72 0 62), overlooking Marktplatz from Kreuzgasse, has just one single (AS405) and two doubles (AS750), with private shower/WC. It's closed Monday.

Hotel Central Löwen (☎ 72 0 70; fax 72 0 705), Neustadt 17, has good-sized modern rooms with TV and en suite bathroom. Prices are AS660/1020 for singles/doubles and include the sauna and steam bath. *Hotel Bären* (☎ 25 50; fax 72 5 77), Bahnhof-

strasse 1, is of similar quality and charges upwards of AS540/880(closed Sunday).

Places to Eat

In the town centre, at Neustadt 19, is a *Familia* supermarket. A larger supermarket and general store (selling anything from microwaves to car tyres) is *Interspar*, St Leonhards Platz, open weekdays from 9 am to 6.30 pm (to 7.30 pm on Friday) and Saturday from 8 am to 1 pm. It has a cheap café with meals from AS60.

For the best prices, go to *Löwen City*, Neustadt 17, which has self-service meals from AS50. It's open Monday to Friday from 9 am to 6 pm, and Saturday from 9 am to 2 pm. The salad buffet costs AS12 per 100 grams.

Two mid-price places to try for Austrian food and ambience are *Johanniterhof*, Marktgasse 1, and *Gasthof Lingg* (see Places to Stay).

Another place for good food but without excessive prices is the restaurant inside the Schattenburg (closed Monday).

Getting There & Away

Two buses (one at weekends) per hour depart for Liechtenstein from in front of the train station. To reach Liechtenstein's capital, Vaduz (AS30; 40 minutes away), change buses in Schaans. Liechtenstein has a customs union with Switzerland so you will pass through Swiss customs before entering Liechtenstein. Trains to Buchs on the Swiss border pass through Schaans, but only a few stop there. Buchs has connections to major destinations in Switzerland, including Zürich and Chur. Bundesbuses to destinations in Vorarlberg also depart from outside the train station.

Feldkirch is on the main road and rail route between Bregenz and Tirol.

BLUDENZ

• *pop 14,000* • *588 m* • ☎ *(05552)*

Bludenz is a pleasant, unassuming town, standing at the meeting point of the Klostertal, Montafon, Brandnertal, Grosswalsertal and Walgau valleys.

VORARLBERG

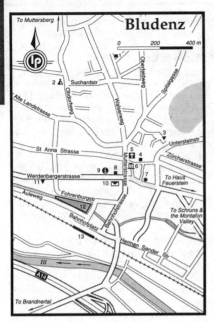

1. Landhaus Muther
2. Camping Seeberger
3. Schlosshotel
4. Haus Manahl
5. Parish Church of St Lawrence
6. City Museum
7. SB Restaurant & Familia Supermarket
8. Altdeutsche Stuben
9. Tourist Office
10. Post Office
11. Restaurant Fohrenburg
12. Suchard Chocolate Factory
13. Train Station

It was granted its town charter in 1274 and was the seat of the Habsburg governors from 1418 to 1806. A former silver-mining centre, the arrival of the railways in the late 19th century allowed the town to become an important commercial base. At the same time there was an influx of settlers from the Val Sugana, in northern Italy, resulting in today's Italianate ambience. Textiles, chocolate and beer are Bludenz's main industries.

Orientation & Information

The town centre is on the northern bank of the Ill River. The tourist office (☎ 62 1 70), Werdenbergerstrasse 42, is five minutes walk from the train station: walk up Bahnhofstrasse and turn left after the post office (Postamt 6700), also on Werdenbergerstrasse. The tourist office is open Monday to Friday from 8 am to noon and 2 to 5 pm. Post office hours are Monday to Friday from 7 am to 8 pm (cash counters till 5 pm) and Saturday from 8 am to noon. Both will change

money. East of the tourist office is a small pedestrian-only area.

Things to See & Do

One of Bludenz's most enjoyable features can't even be seen. Almost anywhere you wander in the centre, the rich, enticing scent of chocolate will tug at your nostrils. The **Suchard chocolate factory** is right opposite the train station; it doesn't conduct tours but there is a shop where you can buy the produce at below normal prices (open to the public Monday 1.30 to 4.30 pm and Tuesday to Thursday 9.15 to 11.30 am). Chocolate also plays an important part in the children's **Milka chocolate festival** in mid-July; 1000 kg of the stuff is up for grabs in prizes.

For other attractions, join one of the free city tours organised by the tourist office; they depart from the tourist office at 11 am on Tuesday between June and September. The most distinctive architectural feature in town is the **Parish Church of St Lawrence** (St Laurentiuskirche). It was built in 1514 and has an unusual octagonal onion-dome spire. Several covered staircases lead to the church; one has a war memorial within. There's also a **city museum** at Kirchgasse 9, open June to September (closed Sunday).

Bludenz is a good base for exploring the surrounding valleys. There are 15 **skiing** areas within a 40-km radius. Free ski buses to/from Bludenz are often included in ski passes (eg with the AS335 one-day pass for Sonnenkopf). A private train takes skiers in 20 minutes to Schruns (AS24, Austrian rail passes valid), a resort to the south-east. Hiking and cycling are other popular activities. A cable car (☎ 66 8 38) goes up to Muttersberg at 1384 metres (AS80 return).

Places to Stay

Ask for the guest card if you stay overnight in town. *Camping Seeberger* (☎ 62 5 12), Oberdorfweg 9, is open all year. It costs AS200 for a two-person site, and is about 600 metres north-west of the centre.

The tourist office won't charge a commission to reserve a bed. Private rooms are the best value for budget travellers, even though a AS30 per day surcharge usually applies for stays under three days. *Haus Manahl* (☎ 67 6 55), Herrengasse 11, is in the heart of town. The house is actually a few steps up from Herrengasse, with the No 11 on the garden fence. It has four doubles (hall showers) for AS416; single occupancy costs AS268.

Rooms in the suburbs give more for your money but are less convenient. *Haus Feuerstein* (☎ 32 0 32), Schillerstrasse 22, costs AS230/380 for singles/doubles, or AS250/420 with private shower. The house is about one km east of the pedestrian centre. *Landhaus Muther* (☎ 65 7 04), Alemannstrasse 4, is a similar distance north-west and costs from AS370/640 for rooms with own shower/WC.

Next to the tourist office, *Altdeutsche Stuben* (☎ 62 0 05; fax 62 0 056), Werdenbergerstrasse 40, has good, three-star rooms for AS540/800, with private shower/WC, TV and telephone.

Places to Eat

In the pedestrian-only town centre is the Kronenhaus department store at Werdenbergerstrasse 34. Inside is a *Familia* supermarket, open Monday to Friday from 8.30 am to 6 pm and Saturday from 8 am to 1 pm (4 pm on Langersamstag). Upstairs is the *SB* self-service restaurant, with meals for AS60 to AS115, including two daily menus and a salad buffet. It serves alcohol and is open for hot food from Monday to Friday, 11 am to 4.30 pm.

Altdeutsch Stuben (see Places to Stay) has a restaurant serving Austrian food in comfortable, rustic surroundings (AS95 to AS220 per main course). The lunch menu with soup is around AS90. There's also a takeaway counter for cheap snacks.

Restaurant Fohrenburg, Werdenbergerstrasse 53, is a large place with several sections, including garden seating. It has Austrian food for AS80 to AS210, but the main attraction is the many varieties of local Fohrenburger beer (from AS32 per half a litre). That's hardly surprising as the brewery is across the road. Opening hours are Monday to Saturday from 9 am to midnight and Sunday from 9 am to 11 pm.

Schlosshotel (☎ 630 16), Schlossplatz 5, is the only four-star hotel and has one of the best restaurants in town.

Getting There & Away

Bludenz is on the east-west IC rail route, two hours from Innsbruck (AS204) and 45 minutes from Bregenz (AS78).

The east-west A14 passes just south of the river and the town centre. The Silvretta Road, leading to Silvretta Stausee (reservoir) and the Bielerhöhe Pass (2036 metres) into Tirol, heads south-east from Bludenz along the Montafon Valley. There's a toll for cars of AS40 per adult to cross the pass (AS70 for motorbikes).

Bundesbuses run down all five valleys, intersecting at Bludenz. Call ☎ 627 46 14 for information.

BRANDNERTAL

The Brand Valley runs south-west of Bludenz. Thirteen km from Bludenz is the resort of **Brand** (elevation 1037 metres). It offers accommodation and winter sports (AS335 for a day skiing pass; reductions for youth and senior citizens). There have been good reports about the ski school. Contact the tourist office on ☎ 05559-55 50 for more information.

The climbing road from Brand provides good views and ultimately leads to below the **Lünersee** (sounds like a mad name for a lake). To reach the lake, at 1907 metres, you have to make a 400-metre ascent by cable car (mid-May to mid-October only). The Lünersee has been dammed to produce hydroelectric power. Overlooking the lake is the Schesaplana peak (2965 metres), straddling the Swiss border. It can be climbed from the lake in about three hours.

Getting There & Away
Bundesbuses go hourly as far as Brand Innertal, a 40-minute journey. The further 20 minute-trip (six km) to the Lünerseebahn cable car station is run only in the summer, as the road (1:8 gradient) is often blocked by snow in winter.

KLEINWALSERTAL
This oddity of a place is more German than Germany. It's in the east of Vorarlberg, encircled by German territory to the north, west and east. Furthermore, access from the south is precluded by the towering Allgäu Alps, meaning the only way in or out is through Germany. Inevitably, the cultural and economic links of the place are with Germany rather than Austria. The Deutschmark is a more shopkeeper-friendly currency than the schilling, and yes, they even speak German.

As you can only get in or out through Germany, the area is treated as de facto German territory when it comes to customs and border controls: you'll see it marked on maps as *Zollanschlussgebiet* (customs connection area) or *Zollausschlussgebiet* (customs exclusion area), depending upon the orientation of the cartographer. This special status has existed since 1891.

The region was settled by migrants from the Swiss canton of Valais (Wallis) in about 1300. The isolation of the area meant traditional culture, crafts and costume held sway until well into the 20th century. Nowadays, however, the population mainly ministers to the needs of affluent skiers.

Orientation & Information
The Kleinwalsertal occupies about 100 sq km, and has three main resorts: Riezlern (1100 metres), Hirschegg (1124 metres) and Mittelberg (1218 metres). Together they

provide plenty of variety for downhill skiers (30 lifts linked by one ski pass) and cross-country skiers (over 40 km of trails). Although the valley is scenically rewarding, it's probably not worth the effort of getting here unless you're a ski enthusiast. Nevertheless, each resort has a tourist office which will try to convince you otherwise; the largest is in Hirschegg (☎ 05517-51 14 0).

Hotels and restaurants are expensive; the only cheaper accommodation is in the mountains above the resorts.

Getting There & Away
The only road to/from Kleinwalsertal is highway 201 that goes north to Oberstdorf and Sonthofen. A right turn at Sonthofen (highway 199) leads to Reutte, in Tirol. A few km farther north on the 201 is Immenstadt, where highway 308 will allow you to re-enter Vorarlberg.

The easiest access by public transport is the Bundesbus from Reutte. The nearest rail line terminates at Oberstdorf.

Arlberg Region

The Arlberg region, shared by Vorarlberg and neighbouring Tirol, comprises several linked resorts and is considered to have some of the best skiing in Austria. St Anton is the largest and least elitist of these fashionable chalet resorts. But even there, budget travellers can kiss their savings goodbye.

The winter season is long, with snow reliable till about mid-April. Summer is less busy (and less expensive), though still popular with hikers. Even so, some of the restaurants, bars and discos that swing during the ski season are closed. Most others will close between seasons, and open for summer from late June to October. Many pensions and some hotels do likewise.

Skiing
A single ski pass covers the whole region. It is valid for 88 ski lifts, giving access to 260 km of prepared pistes and 180 km of high

Alpine deep snow runs. Passes cost AS455 for one day, AS1230 for three and AS2190 for seven. Skiers staying in Lech, Zürs, Stuben, St Anton and St Christoph get a reduction of 5% to 10% on passes of six days or more, and low-season passes are also about 10% cheaper. The low seasons run from late November to pre-Christmas, early to late January, and early to late April. Other versions of tickets are available, such as a cheaper beginner's ticket or a points-system ticket. Children get reductions on all tickets, but senior citizens only on some types.

Downhill equipment rental in the resorts starts at AS170 for skis and poles, and AS80 for boots.

Getting There & Away

St Anton is on the main rail route between Bregenz (AS84) and Innsbruck (AS124), less than 1½ hours from either place. St Anton is close to the eastern entrance of the Arlberg Tunnel, the toll road connecting Vorarlberg and Tirol. The tunnel toll is AS150 for cars and minibuses. You can avoid the toll by taking the B197, but no vehicles with trailers are allowed on this winding road.

Getting Around

Bundesbuses go between St Anton and Lech, stopping at St Christoph and Zürs en route. There are about nine a day in winter, reducing to three a day in summer; the full trip costs AS36, or AS68 return. Taking a minibus taxi is another option, and can be shared between up to eight people: from St Anton to Lech costs AS550.

ST ANTON AM ARLBERG
• *pop 2200* • *1304 m* • ☎ *(05446)*
This is the largest resort, enjoying an easygoing atmosphere and vigorous nightlife. Actually across the border in Tirol, St Anton has been characterised by its large proportion of Australasian 'ski bums' who work through the ski season, though their presence is likely to be diminished by Austria's EU status,

which will make it easier for those from EU countries to obtain work.

St Anton's main problem is its popularity: try to avoid the weekend crowds.

Orientation & Information

St Anton is strung out along the north bank of the Rosanna River. Both the centre (a pedestrian-only zone) and most of the ski lifts are near the train station. Farther east and on the north side of the rail tracks is the area called Nasserrein. Farther east still is St Jakob, with its own train station (only two local trains a day stop there) but no ski lifts.

The tourist office (☎ 226 90) is in the Arlberg Haus, 300 metres from the train station and back from the road. It's open daily in the high season and Monday to Friday between seasons, with hours adjusting to demand. Outside is an accommodation board, hotel lists and free telephone, so you can sort out somewhere to stay at any time.

The post office (Postamt 6580) is near the Rosanna River, off the northern end of the pedestrian zone.

Activities

St Anton went down in skiing history as the place where Hannes Schneider pioneered the Arlberg method in the early 20th century. The resort offers some of the best **skiing** in Austria for experts, with many black (difficult) runs, both on and off-piste. In fact, St Anton is one of the best resorts in Austria for off-piste skiing on powder snow. Cable cars go all the way up to Valluga (2811 metres), from where experts can go off-piste all the way to Lech (with a ski guide only). There are nursery slopes on Gampen (1846 metres) and Kapall (2333 metres), but generally the skiing is not suited to beginners.

Snowboarders favour the Rendl area, on the south side of the Rosanna River. Lifts on this side go as high as Gampberg (2407 metres). St Anton also allows the opportunity to **toboggan** down a two-km track, starting from the Rodelhütte restaurant and ending near the Alte St Anton restaurant. Rent the toboggans at the top (AS40 plus

VORARLBERG

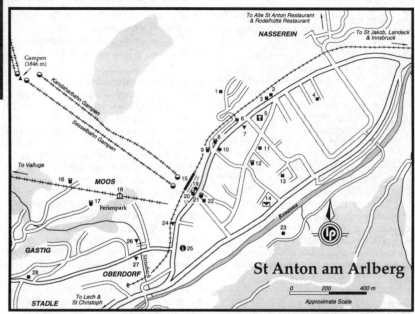

To Alte St Anton Restaurant
& Rodelhütte Restaurant

NASSEREIN

To St Jakob, Landeck
& Innsbruck

Gampen
(1846 m)

Kandaharbahn Gampen

Sesselbahn Gampen

To Valluga

MOOS

Ferienpark

GASTIG

Rosanna

OBERDORF

Streiflach

To Lech &
St Christoph

STADLE

St Anton am Arlberg

0   200   400 m

Approximate Scale

PLACES TO STAY

1 Haus am Fang
2 Enzian
3 Tiroler Frieden
4 Josefine
6 Pirker
11 Moostal
13 Stockibach
22 Sporthotel
28 Karl Schranz Hotel

PLACES TO EAT

7 Fuhrmann Stube
24 Pomodoro
26 Fahrner Stub'n
27 Floriani's

OTHER

5 St Anton Church
8 Chic Bar
9 Amadeus
10 Spar Supermarket

12 Underground
14 Post Office
15 Train Station
16 Krazy Kanguruh
17 Mooser Wirt
18 Museum
19 Nah & Frisch
   Supermarket
20 Piccadilly
21 Drop In
23 Musikpavilion
25 Tourist Office

AS100 deposit) and hand them back at the bottom.

Six km to the west of St Anton is **St Christoph** (1800 metres), a much smaller place with only a half-dozen or so hotels, all expensive. It has lifts going to Galzig (2185 metres), which is also accessible directly from St Anton.

In the summer, **hiking** takes over from skiing. A Wanderpass valid for all lifts costs

AS350 for one week or AS700 for the whole summer season. A version of the one-week pass costs AS490 and includes admission to the swimming pool and other attractions.

Other activities include indoor swimming, sauna, massage, ice skating, tennis and squash. St Anton has a **museum** in the Ferienpark, devoted to the history of skiing and local culture (AS20, reduced admission with guest card).

Places to Stay

There are nearly 200 B&B places in and around St Anton (and a similar number of holiday apartments). Prices are significantly higher in winter, which is the per-person price range quoted here. Many places have six different prices levels through the year – two in summer and four in winter. Summer prices are up to 50% lower than those in winter. Short stays usually incur a surcharge.

There's not a great deal to chose between the simpler B&Bs in terms of value for money, but watch for those that charge extra to use a hall shower (places listed below don't). To make a choice based on location you'll need the tourist office brochure showing prices and map positions – this is especially necessary as there are no street names! Booking ahead will save a lot of frustration in peak times. Otherwise, check the accommodation board for vacancies.

Bottom End Generally, the farther from the town centre, the cheaper it gets. St Jakob's main street has *Schuler* (☎ 31 08), at No 33 and *Sailer* (☎ 28 14), at No 120. Both cost around AS230 with hall shower; Sailer has some rooms with private shower. The Nasserein area is also slightly cheaper.

Not far from the pedestrian area, beyond St Anton Church in the main street, is *Enzian* (☎ 24 03), with rooms with private shower for AS260 to AS350. Next door is *Tiroler Frieden* (☎ 23 45). It's full with groups for most of the winter, but gives summer prices (AS150 per person, plus AS20 to use the hall shower) to those looking for work in November. *Josefine* is a little farther north, just off the main street. It's a friendly place, with just a few singles/doubles with hall shower from AS250 to AS290; winter only.

Stockibach (☎ 20 72) has rooms with private shower from AS290 to AS380; it's down the turn-off by the church. The place is open even in the off season, but is full in February and March with Swedish groups.

Middle & Top End The following are mid-price pensions, with clean modern rooms with shower/WC and cable TV, and a sauna

on site. *Pirker* (☎ 23 10), No 241, is north of the pedestrian zone on the main street and costs from AS400 to AS550; there's a restaurant next door. *Moostal* (☎ 28 31), No 487, is nearby and costs from AS400 to AS490; all rooms have a telephone but there's a AS70 charge to use the sauna. *Haus am Fang* (☎ 35 43), north of the main street, has a genial hostess and rooms from AS400 to AS600. All these places have apartments available, but Pirker has no single rooms.

Sporthotel (☎ 31 11), No 52, is a Best Western four-star hotel in the pedestrian zone, with an indoor swimming pool, sauna, and lots of other facilities included in the price (AS1200 to AS1880). *Karl Schranz Hotel* (☎ 2 97 70), up on the hill across the train tracks, is better value (also four-star) than Sporthotel, though it lacks the swimming pool and is a 15-minute walk from the town centre. This Tirolean-style place is owned by the famous skier and costs AS900 to AS1250 for half board (credit cards not accepted). Reception closes at 8 pm. The public restaurant is the Jägerstube, serving good, local fare to 9 pm.

Places to Eat

Some of the bars mentioned under entertainment also serve food. Restaurants and bars are described in *St Anton Revue*, a detailed free magazine in English available from the tourist office.

Self-caterers have a choice of supermarkets, including two branches of *Nah & Frisch* in the pedestrian zone; one is open Sunday afternoon. So is the nearby *Spar* supermarket. This has the added bonus of a deli counter with hot lunches from Monday to Saturday to take away (AS50 to AS75), though the store is shut from noon to 2 pm. The only other way to save money on food is to frequent the few takeaway stands in town, such as the one in front of the tourist office.

Restaurants have few or no dishes below AS100. English speakers favour *Pomodoro*, in the pedestrian zone, where pizzas start at AS80 (open from 6 pm to midnight; closed in summer). *Floriani's*, across the train tracks, also has pizzas at similar prices (open from 6 pm; closed Monday).

The *Pasta Restaurant* in the train station is another fairly inexpensive choice, and has a quieter ambience than the pizza places; it sometimes has reduced prices in the early evening. *Fuhrmann Stube*, north of the pedestrian zone, is a family-friendly place with good-value Austrian food (open daily).

Fahrner Stub'n (☎ 23 53), opposite Floriani's, is open from 3 or 5 pm (closed in summer). This small, comfortable place serves good Tirolean food for around AS120 to AS240. The cheapest thing on the main menu, but still an excellent choice, is Mariniertes Hirschfilet (AS105) – thinly sliced stag and vegetables in a rich sauce, served in a wok, and with rice.

Most of the top hotels in the resort have quality restaurants, which are also open for the summer season. *Brunnenhof* (☎ 22 93), in St Jakob, has the reputation of being one of the best restaurants in Arlberg; dishes are around AS180 to AS290 (closed May to November).

Entertainment

Lively après-ski bars on the lower slopes include *Krazy Kanguruh* (cheapish food, too) and *Mooser Wirt* (with live music). In the centre of the village is *Piccadilly*, with live music. *Underground* is another good venue (cover around AS40; free in the low season). It has two parts, each with live music: a bar downstairs and a ground floor bistro with decent food (open from 4 pm). Night clubs include *Drop In* (AS80 entry; free in the low season), and they're open from around 9 pm to 3 am. The *Chic Bar* in the Hotel Schwarzer Adler has karaoke (that's not necessarily a recommendation).

All the above places are closed throughout summer. An exception is *Amadeus*, a comparatively cheap bar (beer is AS38 for half a litre) with pool tables, darts and taped rock music (open 4 pm to 2 am).

Getting There & Away

For train information, call ☎ 22 42. Bundesbuses depart from opposite the tourist office.

Local buses go to outlying parts of the resort (eg St Jakob), and these are free with the guest card.

WESTERN ARLBERG

The following resorts are all within Vorarlberg. The northernmost is **Lech** (1450 metres). This up-market resort is a favourite with royalty (notably the UK's Princess Diana), film stars, and anybody who likes to pretend to be such from behind dark glasses. Ski runs are predominantly medium and easy, with some advanced off-piste possibilities. A cable car goes up Rüflikopf (2362 metres), but most of the lifts and runs are on the opposite side of the valley, on the Zuger Hochlicht (2377 metres). The Lech ski school (☎ 05583-23 55) can arrange helicopter skiing (AS3000 for three people). Lech's tourist office (☎ 05583-21610) is in the centre of the resort, on the main road. It's open daily in the high season.

Six km to the south lies **Zürs** (1716 metres), a smaller resort, but with its own tourist office (☎ 05583-22 45) on the main street. A cable car ascends to Trittkopf (2423 metres); across the valley the Zürsersee goes to 2206 metres, where there's a lake and a further lift to whisk you to 2450 metres.

One km south of Zürs is the Flexen Pass (1773 metres), after which the road splits: the west fork leads to **Stuben** (1407 metres), and the right fork leads to Tirol and St Christoph.

Places to Stay

The cheapest options are in private rooms or holiday apartments, but it's wise to book in advance. If you just arrive on spec, seek the help of the local tourist office; the Lech and Zürs offices each have an accommodation board and free telephone that are always accessible.

Despite its up-market profile, Lech has a HI *youth hostel* (☎ 05583-24 19) two km to the north-east of the main resort, in the village of Stubenbach. It is closed in May, June, October and November. It costs AS260 (AS130 in summer) and check-in is from 4 pm.

Pension Lorenz Guido has rooms from

AS310 (AS160 in summer) per person: it's north of the Lech River, just west of the centre. A bargain place in the centre, near the church, is *Sandbur* (☎ 05583-22 30), charging from AS480 per person in winter and only AS180 in summer. It has four doubles and one single, all with private shower/WC and cable TV.

Places to Eat
Eating cheaply in Lech is all but impossible, unless you stock up at one of the two *supermarkets* in the centre (both are closed from 12.30 to 3 pm on weekdays). *Hager Metzgerei* is closed the same lunch hours, and serves hot and cold meats, including grilled chicken; it's east of the post office. Farther along this road is *Charly Pizza*, where most pizzas cost AS100 or more (open daily).

In the centre of Lech, by the Rüflikopf lift, is *Haus Ambrosius*, with a few choices under AS100, including a salad buffet. But if you have the money, there are lots of quaint places where you can eat very well.

In Zürs, the *Sporthotel Zürser See* sometimes has live lunchtime music to entertain its al fresco diners.

Getting There & Away
The Flexen Pass is open all year, but has been known to be blocked in winter. Lech can also be approached from the north, via the turning at Warth (1494 metres). Infrequent Bundesbuses travel this route in summer, terminating at Reutte.

Salzburg Province

Salzburg province (Salzburger Land) has something for everyone. The city of Salzburg draws visitors from near and far; it is a tourist magnet second only to Vienna. To the east of the city is a sublime landscape of mountains and lakes, the Salzkammergut (covered in the following Salzkammergut chapter). To the south are found mightier mountain ranges, towering above ski villages, cascading waterfalls and spa resorts. Salzburg province also has the lion's share of the Hohe Tauern National Park. This park, together with attractions in the south such as Krimml Falls, is covered in the Hohe Tauern National Park Region chapter earlier in this book.

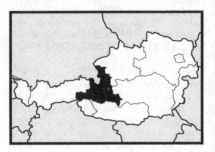

History

Salzburg, the provincial capital, was the chief town in the region as far back as Roman times. In about 696 St Rupert established a bishopric in Salzburg, which was subsequently elevated to an archbishopric with authority over the dioceses of Bavaria.

The archbishops increasingly became involved in temporal matters and in the 13th century were granted the title of Princes of the Holycity Roman Empire. The powers of the archbishop-princes extended to an area up to twice the size of present-day Salzburg province and included parts of Bavaria and Italy.

Economic strength was built on mining: there were some gold mines (now within Tirol and Carinthia) but salt, the so-called 'white gold', had been more important since Celtic times. This is acknowledged in various place names (eg 'Hall' in Celtic or 'Salz' in German). See the following Salzkammergut chapter for more on salt mining in Austria.

Wolf Dietrich von Raitenau (1578-1612) was one of Salzburg's most influential archbishops, and instigated the Baroque reconstruction of the city. However, an unsuccessful dispute with powerful Bavaria over the salt trade led to his imprisonment, during which he died.

Paris Lodron (1619-53) managed to keep the principality out of the Thirty Years' War. Salzburg was also neutral during the War of the Austrian Succession a century later, but about this time its power and prosperity began to diminish. During the Napoleonic Wars, Salzburg was controlled by France and Bavaria, before becoming part of Austria in 1816.

Orientation & Information

Salzburg province is roughly triangular, totals 7154 sq km and is home to 482,000 people. It shares borders with Germany and Italy.

The main river is the Salzach, which originates in the south-west of the province, flows east, turns north at St Johann im Pongau, and marks the border with Germany north of Salzburg city.

The provincial tourist board is Salzburger Land Tourismus GmbH (☎ 0662-62 05 06 0; fax 62 30 70), Alpenstrasse 96, A5033 Salzburg, Postfach 8. This office primarily deals with marketing and postal or telephone enquiries; personal callers should go to the office in the same building as the Salzburg tourist office (see the following Salzburg city entry).

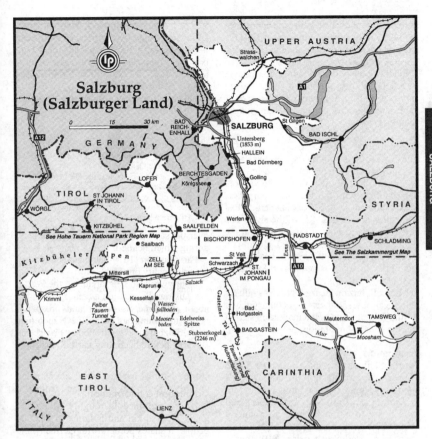

Salzburg (Salzburger Land)

Salzburg

- *pop 144,000* • *425 m* • ☎ *(0662)*

Salzburg is in a breathtaking setting and contains magnificent architectural treasures. The Baroque spires of the old town, with the Hohensalzburg Fortress rising behind, are an unforgettable sight. The city's descent to poverty in the 18th century was a blessing in disguise: it ensured that the historic buildings which now attract high-spending tourists were repaired rather than replaced. Another fortuitous factor in Salzburg's

tourist pre-eminence was the birth in 1756 of one Wolfgang Amadeus Mozart. The city that gave the composer scant encouragement during his lifetime now can't get enough of him (or the influx of high-spending music lovers).

The influence of Mozart is everywhere. There is Mozartplatz with its Mozart statue, the Mozarteum (music academy), Mozart's Birthplace and Mozart's Residence. His music dominates alike grand festivals and the more humble outpourings of street musicians. Chocolate confections and liqueurs are even named after him. Devotees of a rather different musical genre are also drawn to the city in surprising numbers: in 1964 the city and nearby hills were alive to filming of *The Sound of Music*.

Salzburg also offers plenty for budget travellers. It costs nothing to walk around and take it all in. Entering churches, courtyards and gardens places no demands on shallow pockets.

Orientation

The city centre is split by the Salzach River. The old part of town, mostly pedestrian-only, is on the left bank (known as linkes Salzachufer), with the Hohensalzburg Fortress dominant on the Mönchsberg. Most attractions are on this side of the river. The new town, the centre of business, is on the right bank (rechtes Salzachufer), along with most of the hotels. You may also hear people talk of the old town as being on the south or west bank.

Mirabellplatz on the right bank is a hub for both local buses and city and country tours. A little farther north is the main train station and the Bundesbus station.

Information

Tourist Offices The main office (☎ 84 75 68) is at Mozartplatz 5, in the old town. It's open daily from Easter to October from 9 am to 7 pm (8 pm from May to October), and from 9 am to 6 pm Monday to Saturday between November and Easter. Note that its town map, *Stadtplan*, costs AS10; this is almost identical to the free *Hotelplan*, though the former has a street index and practical information on the reverse side. The free *Salzburg Sights* leaflet details opening hours and admission fees of important sights. The tourist office will book rooms in hotels and pensions, but not in private houses; commission is AS30. In the same office is a ticket service (☎ 84 03 15) for events around town (commission charged).

The provincial tourist office (☎ 84 32 64) is in the same building, to the right after you go through the door. It is open Monday to Saturday from 9 am to 6 pm.

Salzburg Information (☎ 88 9 87; fax 88 9 87 32), Auerspergstrasse 7, deals with marketing and congress enquiries, and will send out literature; it doesn't usually deal with personal callers. Opening hours are Monday to Thursday 7.30 am to 5 pm, and Friday from 7.30 am to 3 pm

Other information offices are at arrival points to the city:

Main train station, platform 2A (☎ 87 17 12); open daily from 9 am to 8 pm (8.30 am to 9 pm from 1 May to 31 October)

Flughafen, at the airport near the BP petrol station, Innsbrucker Bundesstrasse 95 (☎ 85 24 51), west of the city; open Easter to 31 May, Monday to Saturday from 9 am to 6 pm, and June to October, daily from 9 am to 7 pm

Salzburg Mitte, Münchner Bundesstrasse 1, in the north-west (☎ 43 22 28); open Easter to 31 October, daily from 9 am to 8 pm (7 pm before May), and Monday to Saturday from 11 am to 5 pm the rest of the year

Salzburg Süd, at Park & Ride Parkplatz, Alpensiedlung Süd, Alpenstrasse, in the south (☎ 62 09 66); open the same hours as Mitte

Salzburg Nord, Autobahnstation Kasern, on the A1 from the north-east (☎ 66 32 20); open from Easter to 31 October, Monday to Saturday from 9 am to 7 pm (daily 9 am to 8 pm in July and August)

Money Normal banking hours are Monday to Friday from 8 am to noon, and from 2 to 4.30 pm, though some branches and exchange offices are open longer, particularly in the summer. Currency exchange at the main train station is available daily from 7 am to 10 pm in summer, and 7.30 am to 9 pm in winter. At the airport, money can be exchanged daily at the exchange booth from 8 am to noon and 12.30 to 4 pm, and at the information office from 4 to 8 pm. Bankomats are all over the place. Some places will accept payment in Deutschmarks, but make sure the conversion rate is competitive.

Post & Telecommunications The post office at the main train station (Bahnhofspostamt A-5020) is open daily 24 hours (including for money exchange), but poste restante is only open from 6.20 am (7 am on

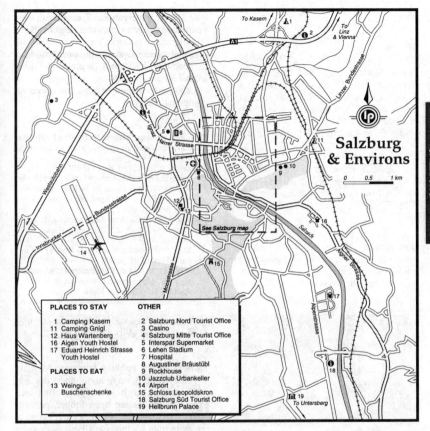

PLACES TO STAY

1 Camping Kasern
11 Camping Gnigl
12 Haus Wartenberg
16 Aigen Youth Hostel
17 Eduard Heinrich Strasse
    Youth Hostel

PLACES TO EAT

13 Weingut
    Buschenschenke

OTHER

2 Salzburg Nord Tourist Office
3 Casino
4 Salzburg Mitte Tourist Office
5 Interspar Supermarket
6 Lehen Stadium
7 Hospital
8 Augustiner Bräustübl
9 Rockhouse
10 Jazzclub Urbankeller
14 Airport
15 Schloss Leopoldskron
18 Salzburg Süd Tourist Office
19 Hellbrunn Palace

Sunday) to 10 pm. In the town centre, the main post office (Hauptpostamt A-5010), Residenzplatz 9, is open Monday to Friday from 7 am to 7 pm, and Saturday from 8 to 10 am.

Foreign Consulates Offices are usually open Monday to Friday from 9 am to noon; exceptions are noted below. Countries represented include:

Czech Republic
  Bergerbräuhofstrasse 27 (☎ 87 96 24)

Germany
  Bürgerspitalplatz 1-II (☎ 84 15 910)
Italy
  Alpenstrasse 102-II (☎ 62 52 33); Monday to Friday from 10 am to noon
South Africa
  Out of town at Buchenweg 14, Elsbethen-Glasenbach, A-5061 (☎ 62 20 35); Monday to Friday from 8 am to 1 pm and 2 to 5 pm
Switzerland
  Alpenstrasse 85 (☎ 62 25 30); Monday to Thursday from 8 am to noon and 2 to 4 pm, and Friday from 8 am to noon
UK
  Alter Markt 4 (☎ 84 81 33)

USA
    Herbert von Karajan Platz 1 (☎ 84 87 76);
    Monday, Wednesday and Friday from 9 am to
    noon

Travel Agents American Express (☎ 84 25 01) is next to the tourist office at Mozartplatz 5. Amex travellers' cheques are exchanged free of charge; the minimum commission for other cheques is AS40. It's open Monday to Friday from 9 am to 5.30 pm, and Saturday to noon.

ÖKISTA (☎ 88 32 52), Wolf Dietrich Strasse 31, is open Monday to Friday from 9.30 am to 5.30 pm. Young Austria (☎ 62 57 580), Alpenstrasse 108A, is open Monday to Friday from 9 am to 6 pm, and Saturday to noon.

Bookshops Motzko (☎ 88 33 11), Elisabethstrasse 1, stocks English-language books. Across the road, on Rainerstrasse, is its travel branch, Motzko Reise. At the main train station is a Buch und Presse shop, with international newspapers and magazines.

Medical Services & Emergency The hospital, St Johanns-Spital (☎ 44 82 0), is at Müllner Hauptstrasse 48, just north of the Mönchsberg. The police headquarters (☎ 63 83 0) is at Alpenstrasse 90.

Gay & Lesbian The Homosexuelle Initiative, HOSI (☎ 43 59 27), has a branch at Müllner Hauptstrasse 11. It runs a bar at this address on Tuesday, Wednesday, Friday and Saturday evenings.

Laundry At Wasch Salon, Südtirolerplatz, opposite the train station, it costs AS118 to wash and dry a six-kg load. It's open weekdays from 7 am to 7 pm and Saturday from 7 am to 1 pm. The laundrette a few doors away is for dry cleaning.

SIMON BRACKEN

Pondering the next move in a giant chess game on Kapitelplatz

SIMON BRACKEN

The reverential pose of this statue aptly marks the site of the 9th-century St Peter's Abbey

Walking Tour

Take time to wander around the many plazas, courtyards, fountains and churches in the Baroque old town. Start by absorbing the bustle of Domplatz and the adjoining Kapitelplatz and Residenzplatz. The hubbub from the market competes with the clip-clop of horses' hooves and the rhythms of classical and folk street artists. Portrait painters add to the scene. Residenzplatz also has a Glockenspiel that chimes at 7 am, 11 am and 6 pm; tours are conducted of the interior.

The vast **cathedral** on Domplatz has three bronze doors symbolising – from left to right as you face them – faith, hope and charity. Built from 1614 to 1657, this was the first building north of the Alps to exhibit the Italian Baroque style. Inside, admire the dark-edged stucco, the dome and the Romanesque font where Mozart was baptised. The church has a museum, the Dommuseum, containing ecclesiastical treasures and oddities (open daily from early May to mid-October; AS40, students AS10).

From here, turn left at the first courtyard off Franziskanergasse for **St Peter's Abbey**, dating from 847 AD. This church is remarkable for its Baroque ostentation. It's like a dozen churches have been plundered to fit this one out: the walls are crammed with emotive paintings, swirling stucco and 15 side altars. There's also a fine organ with a clock and statues. The graveyard contains catacombs, and 20-minute tours are conducted every hour in the high season, much less frequently in the low season (AS12; students AS8).

Back in Franziskanergasse is the **Franciscan Church**, revealing Gothic, Romanesque and Baroque elements spanning the 13th to 18th centuries. The best feature is the Baroque high altar (presumed to be by Johann Bernhard Fischer von Erlach) complementing the carved Madonna by Michael Pacher.

The western end of Franziskanergasse opens into Max Reinhardt Platz, where you'll see the back of Fischer von Erlach's

SALZBURG

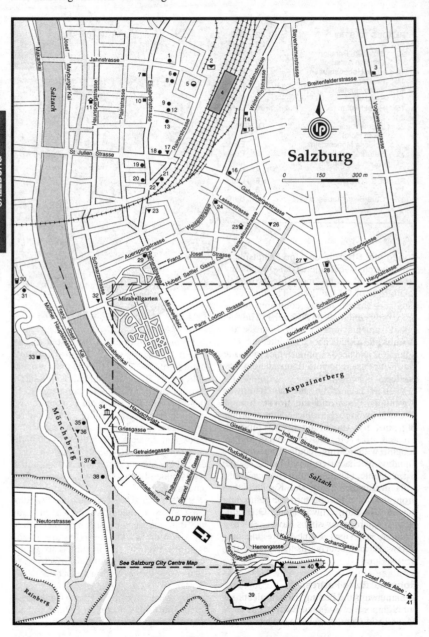

SALZBURG

Collegiate Church on Universitätsplatz. This church is considered an outstanding example of Baroque, more for its overall structure than for the décor. The interior is bare and almost austere compared to the fussy ornamentation of St Peter's. The few embellishments don't overly impress: the cherubs and clouds above the altar are a bit ridiculous and need cleaning – the clouds are grey with dust. The gold figures below lack subtlety.

Walk left after exiting the church to reach Sigmunds Platz and the **horse trough** (Pferdeschwemme), a rather elaborate drinking spot for the archbishops' mounts. Created in 1700, this is a horse-lovers' delight, with rearing, equine pin-ups surrounding Michael Bernhard Mandl's 'horse tamer' statue. (There are also 'horsey' fountains in Residenzplatz and Kapitelplatz.) From the horse trough, turn the corner and join the bustling crowds along **Getreidegasse**, where many shops have distinctive wrought-iron signs. Some interesting passageways and courtyards lead from this street.

Hohensalzburg Fortress
In many ways the Festung Hohensalzburg is the high point of a visit to Salzburg. It takes about 15 minutes to walk up the hill, or you

can use the Festungbahn funicular (AS22 up, AS32 return) from Festungsgasse 4. The castle was extended by the archbishops over many centuries. By far the greatest influence on its present structure was Leonhard von Keutschach, Archbishop of Salzburg from 1495 to 1519. His symbol was the turnip, and this peculiar motif appears 58 times around the castle, usually as a wall relief. Admission is AS30 (AS15 for students under 27, but it's worth paying extra for the multilingual guided tour (AS30; students AS20) which allows entrance to parts of the castle not otherwise accessible.

The 40-minute tour covers grisly torture chambers, the lookout tower, and impressive state rooms (featuring a fine tiled stove, Gothic carvings and Leonhard's state-of-the-art en suite toilet). At the end, you're left to roam around the two small museums covering history, arms, WW II photos and more tools of the torture trade. Allow 30 to 40 minutes for both museums.

If you don't join the tour you can still enjoy the sweeping views, explore the courtyards, see a slide show (regular showings in English) and visit the terrace café. The outlook over the city is simply stupendous. The view to the south is of Alpine peaks, including the Untersberg (1853 metres); in the foreground, the isolated house in the middle of the big field once belonged to the archbishop's groundkeeper, though tour guides will tell you it was the home of the shunned official executioner.

The castle is open daily: between November and March from 9 am to 5 pm; in April, May, June and October from 9 am to 6pm; and between July and September from 8 am to 7 pm. However, the museums shut earlier, and if you take a late tour they may be closed by the time you finish; it's possible to see the museums before doing the tour.

Below the castle, on its eastern side, is **Nonnberg Convent**, founded by St Rupert around 700 (the oldest convent in German-speaking lands). Its church is late-Gothic.

Museums & Galleries

The outstanding **Museum of Natural History** (Haus der Natur) is at Museumplatz 5. You could spend many hours wandering round its diverse and well-presented exhibits. In addition to the usual flora, fauna and mineral displays, it has good hands-on

Forever Young

Born in 1756, Wolfgang Amadeus Mozart was only 35 when he died in 1791, yet composed some 626 pieces: 24 operas, 49 symphonies, over 40 concertos, 26 string quartets, seven string quintets and numerous sonatas for piano and violin. Praise for his music came from many quarters – Haydn believed him to be the 'greatest composer' and Schubert effused that the 'magic of Mozart's music lights the darkness of our lives'.

Mozart was born in Salzburg and started his career at a young age. His musician father, Leopold, taught him how to play the harpsichord at age three. Two years later, Leopold gave his son a small violin, but without musical instruction. A few days afterwards, young Mozart asked a quartet if he could join in. The musicians laughingly agreed, but were amazed when the prodigy played his part perfectly. One went as far as to call it witchcraft. Mozart senior was quick to exploit his son's astounding talent. Along with Wolfgang's sister, Nannerl (four years older and also exceptionally gifted), they toured Europe, giving recitals and receiving plaudits wherever they went.

At age six, Wolfgang performed for Empress Maria Theresa at Schönbrunn. By age eight he had toured London, Paris, Rome, Geneva, Frankfurt and the Hague. Four sonatas were published before he turned nine, and he could write down complex pieces after just one hearing. In 1770, though only 14 years old, Mozart was appointed director of the archbishop of Salzburg's orchestra but departed for Paris in 1777 after an argument with his employer. In 1781 he settled in Vienna. Here Mozart had his most productive years, with his music encompassing light-hearted and joyous themes, dramatic emotions and melancholic gloom.

Although always productive, Mozart was a compulsive gambler and lost large sums of money at billiards, ninepins and cards. He was also something of a ladies' man – at age 24 he proclaimed, 'If I had married everyone I jested with, I would have well over 200 wives'. On 4 August 1782 he married Constanze Weber in St Stephen's Cathedral (although he apparently had a deep affection for her opera-singer sister, Aloysia).

Mozart was dispatched to the earth on a rainy December day after a meagrely attended and frugal funeral. His body was wrapped in a sack and doused with lime (an imperial decree to prevent epidemics) before being buried in a ditch in the Cemetery of St Mark in Vienna.

The film *Amadeus* (1985) by Milos Forman & Peter Shaffer, portrayed Mozart as infuriating, enthusiastic, volatile, emotionally immature and effortlessly gifted, an interpretation perhaps not far removed from the truth (though Mozart once announced that nobody had worked harder than himself at studying musical composition). ■

exhibits on physics and astronomy, plus bizarre oddities such as a stomach-churning display of deformed human embryos. There are also many tropical fish and an excellent reptile house with lizards, snakes and alligators. It even has an inexpensive terrace café with a lunch menu. The museum is open daily from 9 am to 5 pm, and admission costs AS45 (students AS30).

Overlooking Residenzplatz, the **Residenz** was built from 1596 to 1619. This less than modest home allows you to see the Baroque luxury which the archbishops endured while they sweated over sermons about humility and charity. Rottmayr created some of the frescoes, which are well complemented by rich stuccowork and furnishings. It can be visited by guided tour only, daily in July and August and Monday to Friday the rest of the year (AS45; students and seniors AS35). Entry to the **Residenz Gallery** costs the same, or get a combined ticket for AS70. European art from the 16th to 19th centuries is on display and includes good Dutch and Flemish works. It's open daily from 10 am to 5 pm (closed Wednesday from October to March).

The **Rupertinium**, Wiener Philharmoniker Gasse 9, has 20th-century art in its not particularly stunning permanent collection, but most space is devoted to temporary exhibitions. The building dates from the 17th century. Entry costs AS40 (students AS20) It's open daily in summer and Tuesday to Sunday the rest of the year, always with late opening (to 9 pm) on Wednesday.

The **Carolino Augusteum Museum**, Museumplatz 1, has an interesting collection, covering local history with recourse to paintings by local artists, Roman mosaics, Gothic statues and utensils. There are some good room interiors, but no signs in English. Entry costs AS40 (students AS20), and it is usually closed on Monday, with late opening (to 8 pm) on Tuesday.

There are two Mozart museums; they're popular but expensive for what they are. **Mozart's Birthplace** (Geburtshaus), Getreidegasse 9, is where he lived for the first 17 years of his life (AS62; students and

seniors AS47). It contains musical instruments, sheet music and other memorabilia of the great man, including the mini-violin which he used as a toddler. **Mozart's Residence** (Wohnhaus), Makartplatz 8, where he lived for seven years from 1773, tells much the same story. The house is to be restored to its original structure during 1996 (it had been damaged in WW II) and the Mozart 'sound and film' show moved in. It's expected combined tickets with Mozart's Birthplace will be available when the restoration is complete.

Mirabell Palace

Schloss Mirabell, in Mirabellgarten, was built by the worldly prince-archbishop Wolf Dietrich for his mistress, Salome Alt, in 1606. Salome bore the archbishop at least 10 children (sources disagree on the exact number – poor Wolf was presumably too distracted by spiritual matters to keep count himself). Johann Lukas von Hildebrandt gave the building a more Baroque appearance in 1727. Its attractive gardens featured in *The Sound of Music*, and this is a great place to relax. A most harmonious (and oft photographed) view is obtained from the northern end. A dwarfs garden is also at this end. Concerts and other extravaganzas are held in the palace. Take a look inside at the marble staircase, which is adorned with Baroque sculptures by George Raphael Donner.

From the palace, cross Makartplatz and peek into the **Holy Trinity Church** (Dreifaltigkeitskirche). It was created by Johann Bernhard Fischer von Erlach at the end of the 17th century; the dome fresco by Rottmayr depicts a congested celestial scene.

Mausoleum of Wolf Dietrich

This restored mausoleum, in the graveyard of the 16th-century St Sebastian Church on Linzer Gasse, has some interesting epitaphs. In a wonderful piece of arrogance, the archbishop commands the faithful to 'piously commemorate the founder of this chapel' (ie himself) and 'his close relations', or expect 'God Almighty to be an avenging judge'.

SALZBURG

SALZBURG

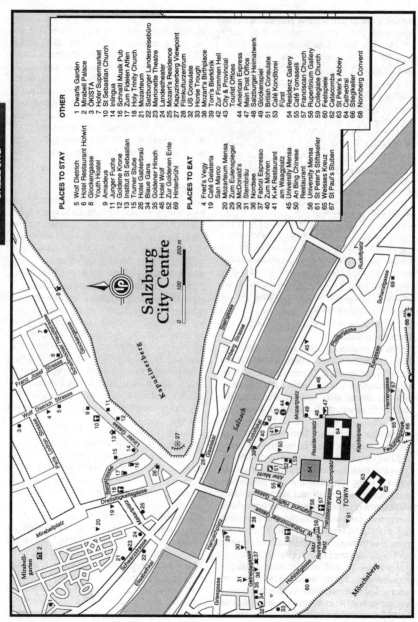

Salzburg City Centre

0   100   200 m

PLACES TO STAY

5   Wolf Dietrich
6   Hotel Restaurant Hofwirt
8   Glockengasse
    Youth Hostel
9   Amadeus
11 Junger Fuchs
12 Goldene Krone
13 Institut St Sebastian
15 Trumer Stube
26 Hotel Gablerbräu
34 Blaue Gans
35 Goldener Hirsch
46 Hotel Wolf
52 Zur Goldenen Ente
69 Hinterbrühl

PLACES TO EAT

4   Fred's Vegy
19 Café Gelateria
    San Marco
20 Mozarteum Mensa
29 Zum Eulenspiegel
30 McDonald's
31 Sternbräu
36 Nordsee
37 Fabrizi Espresso
40 Zum Mohren
41 K+K Restaurant
    am Waagplatz
45 University Mensa
50 University Mensa
56 An Bing Chinese
    Restaurant
61 St Peter's Stiftskeller
65 Weisses Kreuz
67 St Paul's Stuben

OTHER

1   Dwarfs Garden
2   Mirabell Palace
3   ÖKISTA
7   Hofer Supermarket
10 St Sebastian Church
14 Inlingua
16 Schnaitl Musik Pub
17 Zum Fidelen Affen
18 Holy Trinity Church
21 Mozarteum
22 Salzburger Landesreisebüro
23 Marionette Theatre
24 Landestheater
25 Mozart's Residence
27 Kapuzinerberg Viewpoint
28 Filmkulturzentrum
32 US Consulate
33 Horse Trough
38 Mozart's Birthplace
39 Tom's Bierklinik
42 Zur Frommen Hell
43 City & Provincial
    Tourist Offices
44 American Express
47 Main Post Office
48 Salzburger Heimatwerk
49 Glockenspiel
51 British Consulate
53 Café Konditorei
    Fürst
54 Residenz Gallery
55 Café Tomaselli
57 Franciscan Church
58 Rupertinum Gallery
59 Collegiate Church
60 Festspiele
62 Catacombs
63 St Peter's Abbey
64 Cathedral
66 Stieglkeller
68 Nonnberg Convent

Mozart's father and widow are buried in the graveyard.

Walks
The old town is squeezed between the Kapuzinerberg and Mönchsberg hills, both of which have a good network of footpaths. There is a viewpoint at the western end of the Kapuzinerberg, with ramparts which were built during the Thirty Years' War: climb up in 10 minutes from the stairs near the south end of Linzer Gasse. On Mönchsberg, consider walking from the Hohensalzburg Fortress down to the Augustinian brewery.

Language Courses
Inlingua (87 11 01), Linzer Gasse 17, offers courses in the German language. A two-week beginners course costs AS4930 for 40 lessons of 45 minutes each, with new starts every month. Other places to try are IFK Deutschkurse (☎ 87 65 95 0), Franz Josef Strasse 19; and the summer school (88 24 70), Dreifaltigkeitsgasse 9.

Organised Tours
One-hour walking tours of the old city leave from the main tourist office (AS80) daily except Sunday at 12.15 pm. Coach tours of the city and environs usually have free hotel pick-up. Some also leave from Mirabellplatz, including the renowned Sound of Music Tour.

The Oscar-winning film was a flop in Austria, but this tour is by far the most popular with English-speaking visitors. Tours last three to four hours and cost around AS300. They take in major city sights featured in the movie and include a visit to the Salzkammergut. If you go with a group with the right mix of tongue-in-cheek enthusiasm, as I did, it can be brilliant fun. I have fond memories of loutish youths (and older) skipping in the summer house, chanting 'I am 16 going on 17', and manic Julie Andrews impersonators flouncing in the fields. On the other hand, people who have gone with a serious group have reported it quite dull. A lot depends on the approach of the guide;

make sure they don't deviate from the itinerary unless you want them to.

Other organised tours explore Bavaria, salt mines, the city and the Salzkammergut. Tours are conducted by various agencies, the most prominent of which are Salzburg Panorama Tours (☎ 87 40 29) and Salzburg Sightseeing Tours (☎ 88 16 16); both are on Mirabellplatz. The Sound of Music Tour arranged through the Jugendgästehaus (see Places to Stay) is about the cheapest.

Festivals
The Salzburg International Festival takes place from late July to the end of August, and includes music ranging from Mozart (of course!) to contemporary. This is the high point in Salzburg's cultural calendar, and a time when the city takes on a new vitality. Just beware of the crowds. Several events take place each day in different locations, and prices vary from AS50 to AS4200. As many as 175 orchestral, operatic and theatrical events are staged. Most sell out months in advance. Write for information as early as September to: Kartenbüro der Salzburger Festspiele, Postfach 140, A-5010 Salzburg. People under 26 years are eligible for reduced-price deals. Try checking closer to the event for cancellations. Some venues sell standing-room tickets either one day or 45 minutes before performances (AS50 to AS200). Enquire at the ticket office, Hofstallgasse 1. Opening hours during the festival are daily from 10 am to noon and 3 to 5 pm.

Other important music festivals are at Easter (Osterfestspiele for one week) and the Whit Sunday weekend (Pfingstkonzerte). There's Mozart Week in late January, and music concerts in Hellbrunn, performed in historic costumes, from early May to mid-September.

Places to Stay – bottom end
Accommodation is at a premium during the Salzburg Festival, so be prepared to book ahead (and to pay even higher prices than the summer prices quoted here). In more expensive places, prices in winter usually come

down. The tourist office's *Hotelplan* lists hotels, pensions, hostels and camping grounds.

Camping *Camping Kasern* (☎ 50 5 76), Carl Zuckmayer Strasse 4, just north of the A1 Nord exit, costs AS55 per adult and AS30 each for a car and tent. *Camping Gnigl* (☎ 64 14 44), Parscher Strasse 4, east of Kapuzinerberg, is only open mid-May to mid-September, but costs less.

Hostels – Right Bank If you're travelling to party, head for the *International Youth Hotel* (☎ 87 96 49), Paracelsusstrasse 9. Although neighbour complaints have forced this place to calm down a little, it still has a sociable atmosphere, with loud music and cheap beer (AS25 for half a litre), and no school groups. The staff are almost exclusively young native English-speakers. It's often full: phone reservations are accepted the day before but not earlier. Beds per person are AS120 (eight-bed dorm), AS140 (four-bed dorm, own key) and AS160 (double room, own key). There is a 1 am curfew and it's open all day, with check-in any time. Showers cost AS10, lockers AS10 and sheets (if required) are AS20. Breakfast costs AS30 to AS55, and dinner AS60 to AS75. The hotel also organises outings and shows *The Sound of Music* daily.

The HI *youth hostel* (☎ 87 62 41) at Glockengasse 8 has large dorms and a tendency to be overrun by noisy school groups, but it's the cheapest hostel in town. Beds in large dorms are AS125 (AS115 after the first night); dinner is AS68. Curfew is at midnight, and reception is shut from 9 am to 3.30 pm (the dining room stays open). The hostel is open from 1 April to 30 September. It's conveniently situated and has student discounts for the Sound of Music Tour.

The HI *youth hostel* (☎ 87 50 30) at Haunspergstrasse 27, near the train station, is only open in July and August. Beds costs AS135 in four-bed dorms, and reception is from 7 am to 2 pm and 5 pm to midnight. *Institut St Sebastian* (☎ 87 13 86), Linzer

Gasse 41, is attached to the church, literally and administratively. Prices per person for rooms with private shower/WC are AS210 (dorms) up to AS340 (singles). Some longterm students stay in this recently renovated place. Get a key for unlimited access. Reception is closed from noon to 5 pm on weekdays and 10 am to 5 pm on weekends.

If everywhere is full in town, try the HI *youth hostel* (☎ 62 32 48) at Aigner Strasse 34, in the southern suburb of Aigen. There's nothing wrong with it except its outlying location (take bus No 49 from the centre), and the 11 pm curfew. It's open all year, and dorm beds cost AS135. You can check in from 5 pm.

Hostels – Left Bank The *Naturfreundehaus* (☎ 84 17 29), Mönchsberg 19, also signposted as the Gästehaus Bürgerwehr, is clearly visible high on the hill between the fortress and the casino. Take the footpath up from near Max Reinhardt Platz, or the Mönchsberg lift (AS15 up, AS25 return) from A Neumayr Platz. It offers four-bed dorms for AS110 (showers AS10) and has marvellous views. It's open all day, but with a 1 am curfew. The café provides breakfast from AS30 and hot meals from AS68 to AS110. It's open from about mid-May to 1 October, but it depends on the weather (phone ahead).

The HI *Jugendgästehaus* (☎ 84 26 700) at Josef Preis Allee 18 is large, modern, busy and comfortable. Eight-bed dorms are AS145, four-bed rooms are AS195 per person and two-bed rooms are AS245 per person, all with a AS10 surcharge for a single night's stay. Telephone reservations aren't accepted, so turn up at 11 am to be sure of a bed – reception is only open in small shifts during the rest of the day. It has good showers, free lockers and bike rental for AS85 per day. Curfew is at midnight. Its daily Sound of Music tours are the cheapest in town, at AS230, and leave at 8.45 am and 1.30 pm. The film is also shown daily (AS5).

South of town is a year-round HI *youth hostel* (☎ 62 59 76) at Eduard Heinrich Strasse 2; beds are AS135 (six-bed dorms).

Bus No 51 will get you within 400 metres (stop: Polizeidirektion). Reception hours are 7 to 9 am and 5 to 11 pm.

Private Rooms These aren't quite the bargain they are elsewhere in Austria: they cost a minimum AS250 per person anywhere near the city centre. Ask for the tourist office's list of private rooms and apartments.

If you're prepared to travel, Kasern, north of the city, offers better value. There are several places with private rooms on the Kasern Berg. They can be reached by bus No 15 or train, followed by a walk up the hill. Representatives from some places may even pick you up from the local train station (Salzburg-Maria Plain). *Mathilde Lindner* (☎ 45 66 81), Berg 64, has doubles for AS180 and dorms for AS160 per person, plus an all-you-can-eat breakfast.

Hotels & Pensions *Sandwirt* (☎ 87 43 51), Lastenstrasse 6A, is behind the main train station and back from the street (behind the post office building). Singles/doubles are AS280/440 and triples AS570 with hall shower; doubles/triples with private shower are AS500/630 and quads AS800. Don't be put off by the musty smell in the corridor – the rooms are clean and reasonably large and there's courtyard parking.

Nearby is *Hotel Merian* (☎ 870 06 11), Merianstrasse 40, a student residence that welcomes tourists from July to September. Singles/doubles with hall shower are AS240/370.

Elizabeth Pension (☎ 87 16 64) is on Vogelweiderstrasse 52. The rooms are average and the street is fairly noisy but the building is just around the corner from the Breitenfelderstrasse stop of bus No 15, which heads for the town centre every 15 minutes. Rooms are from AS300/420 with hall shower, or AS350/520 with shower cubicle in the room. The owners are gradually renovating the house.

Junger Fuchs (☎ 87 54 96), Linzer Gasse 54, has singles/doubles for AS260/400 and triples for AS500 (AS15 charge for the hall shower in summer only) without breakfast.

The rooms are simple but a fair size and it's in a convenient location. Room rates are the same all year.

Places to Stay – middle

Right Bank Near the train station is *Pension Adlerhof* (☎ 87 52 36), Elisabethstrasse 25. Some rooms are modern with pine fittings, other have old-style painted furniture, and there's a Baroque breakfast room. Singles/doubles are AS500/700 with private shower/WC or AS400/600 using hall facilities. Parking is limited.

Goldene Krone (☎ 87 23 00 1), Linzer Gasse 48, has rooms with private shower for AS570/970; some rooms have church-like groined ceilings, which add a bit of character.

Amadeus (☎ 87 14 01) is across the road at No 43-45. It has similar facilities but with cable TV. Prices are about AS700/1150 for rooms with private shower. This place must have the bluest breakfast room in the country.

Closer to the river is *Trumer Stube* (☎ 84 7 76), Bergstrasse 6. This family-run place offers clean and pleasant rooms with shower/WC and cable TV for around AS700/1000.

Hotel Restaurant Hofwirt (☎ 87 21 72), Schallmooser Hauptstrasse 1, has three-star rooms (AS760/1290) and free private parking.

Left Bank *Haus Wartenberg* (☎ 84 42 84), Riedenburger Strasse 2, is a small, friendly, family-run place. Telephone for prices: it used to have budget rooms with old painted wardrobes, but the son is planning renovations that will leave only large, mid-price doubles with shower/WC (expected to be around AS850). It's walking distance from the old town, and there are many buses along Neutorstrasse.

The following places are in the old town: the convenience means you pay significantly more. Parking can be limited, though many places have an arrangement for reduced prices at parking garages.

Hinterbrühl (☎ 84 67 98), Schanzlgasse

SALZBURG

12, is fairly basic, but is still one of the cheapest places in the old town. Singles/doubles are AS370/470 using hall shower, and breakfast is AS50. Reception is in the restaurant downstairs, open daily from 8 am to midnight.

Blaue Gans (☎ 84 13 17) is at Getreidegasse 43, and good value. Prices start at AS450/750, or AS500/950 for rooms with private shower.

Hotel Wolf (☎ 84 34 53 0), Kaigasse 9, charges from AS680/980. Appealing rooms are kitted out in modern or rustic style, and have shower/WC and cable TV.

All rooms in *Zur Goldenen Ente* (☎ 84 56 22), Goldgasse 10, have private bath/shower and TV but prices (from AS720/980) depend upon size and situation. This 700-year-old house retains some original features. Reception is open daily.

Places to Stay – top end
All places mentioned here provide rooms with private bath or shower, WC, TV and telephone.

Lasserhof (☎ 87 33 88; fax 87 33 88 6), Lasserstrasse 47, is a small place with singles/doubles from AS930/1540, some with balcony. There's street or garage parking (AS50), and guests have free use of bicycles. The excellent rustic-style apartment is a real home from home (from about AS900 per person; accommodates between three or four people).

Wolf Dietrich (☎ 87 12 75; fax 88 23 20), Wolf Dietrich Strasse 7, has good facilities, including an indoor pool, sauna, solarium, bar and restaurant, though the TVs aren't satellite. With rooms from AS790/1360, it's one of the cheapest four-star hotels. Garage parking costs AS95.

Nearby, *Hotel Gablerbräu* (☎ 88 9 65; fax 88 9 65 55), Linzer Gasse 9, has reasonable-sized rooms (AS1070/1740), though some are without TV, and a lobby area on each floor.

Hotel Hohenstauffen (☎ 87 21 93; fax 87 21 93 51), Elisabethstrasse 19, is convenient for the station. Stylish rooms are all different

– some even have a four-poster bed. Rooms are AS990/1490 and parking is no problem.

Goldener Hirsch (☎ 84 85 11; fax 84 33 49), Getreidegasse 37, is a classy five-star hotel. There are 73 rooms in three houses; they vary in size and colour scheme but are all in rustic style. Rooms cost from AS2200/3300. The valet parking service is AS250 per day.

Schloss Mönchstein (☎ 84 85 55 0; fax 84 85 59), Mönchsberg Park 26, is as palatial as the name suggests. Its pastoral, isolated setting favours those with their own transport, and it has a tiny chapel that's popular for weddings. Prices start at AS2200/2900 per person, or AS2400 in the low season.

Places to Eat
Salzburg need not be expensive for food. Quick, hot snacks or meals can be had at various deli shops and outdoor food stands. *Ridder*, in Rainerstrasse, provides half a chicken for AS32. The Shell garage nearby, on St Julien Strasse, has a shop open 24 hours, with snacks, provisions and alcohol.

The main train station has *Eurosnack* (a burger and schnitzel place) and a *Rosenkavalier* restaurant. A *McDonald's* is at Getreidegasse 26, with a *Nordsee*, the fast fish chain, nearby at Getreidegasse 27. Between sightseeing, nip into *Eduscho*, Getreidegasse 34 (and elsewhere); a small, strong cup of coffee costs only AS7, but you'll have to stand.

You can also eat at some of the places mentioned in the Entertainment section.

Self-Catering On Universitätsplatz and Kapitelplatz there are market stalls and food stands. Also in the old town, there's a small *Konsum* supermarket at Getreidegasse 25. On the right bank, there are several supermarkets on Schallmooser Hauptstrasse, including a *Hofer*. A *Billa* is close to the train station. A fruit and vegetable market occupies some of Mirabellplatz on Thursday mornings.

Self-Service Restaurants The best budget deals are in the university Mensas. Menus for students (show ISIC card) start as low as AS30; others pay around AS45 to AS65. Lunches are served from 11.30 am to 2 pm, but don't leave it too late as the better choices run out. They're closed at weekends.

The *Mozarteum Mensa* can be reached via the Preussner Hof stairway in the Aicher Passage or from Mirabellgarten. On the left bank there are three university *Mensas*. The most convenient is in the courtyard at Sigmund Haffner Gasse 11; the café is open weekdays from 8 am to 6 pm (3 pm Friday). The Mensa at Rudolfskai 42 has the same menus and opening times.

North-west of the old town, by the Lehen Stadium, is a large *Interspar* supermarket, with cheap hot meals and a weekday menu including soup for AS54. Opening hours are Monday to Friday from 8 am to 6.30 pm (7.30 pm on Thursday), and Saturday from 8 am to 12.30 pm (5 pm on Langersamstag).

Budget Restaurants – Right Bank *Café Gelateria San Marco*, Dreifaltigkeitsgasse 13, is a small place, good for cheap Italian food (from AS50). It's open Monday to Saturday from 9 am to 10 pm.

Restaurant Wegscheidstuben (☎ 87 46 18), Lasserstrasse 1, has a three-course menu for AS110, available lunchtime and evening. It offers traditional Austrian cooking (AS85 to AS155), which is popular with locals, and it's open Tuesday to Saturday from 8 am to midnight and at Sunday lunchtime.

One of the few vegetarian places in town is *Vollwertkost Spezialitäten*, Schwarzstrasse 33, also called Fred's Vegy. It's a shop and snack bar with a salad buffet from AS33, and a lunch menu for AS73, including soup. It is open Monday to Friday from 10.30 am to 6 pm. There's another *Fred's Vegy* at Wolf Dietrich Strasse 17.

Reform Haus Gfrerer, Lasserstrasse 18, is a shop selling health food and natural products. It serves lunch specials for just AS37 and a salad buffet for AS30/50 a small/large plate. There are sit-down tables (open normal shop hours).

Budget Restaurants – Left Bank Salzburg

has its share of Chinese restaurants. Some, like *An Bing*, Goldgasse, have inexpensive weekday lunch menus.

Blaue Gans (see Places to Stay) has a restaurant serving Austrian and Mexican specialities from AS75, and three-course meals from AS85. There's live music on Thursday (closed Wednesday in the low season). Its Mexican tavern (open from 8 pm; closed Tuesday and Wednesday) is more atmospheric, and has live music – often jazz – on Friday and Saturday.

Weisses Kreuz (☎ 84 56 41), Bierjodlgasse 6, has Austrian food above AS100, but a better choice is its Balkan specialities. Djuvec (rice, succulent pork and paprika) for just AS70 is excellent, or try the Balkan Plate (a selection of five dishes) for AS120. It's a small place, so reservations are advised in summer (closed Tuesday in winter).

It's almost as if they're trying to keep *St Paul's Stuben*, Herrengasse 16, a secret. It's the yellow house, completely anonymous but for the 1st-floor terrace tables. Pasta and tasty pizzas (from AS72 to AS94) are served upstairs until late. Sitting together on long tables makes it easy to meet the students who drink there. It's open daily from 6 pm to 1 am.

Fabrizi Espresso, Getreidegasse 21, is a café in a small, pretty courtyard. This calm retreat serves a few hot meals (about AS90) as well as cakes and snacks. It is open daily until 7 pm (6 pm on Sunday).

Weingut Buschenschenke, Neutorstrasse 34, is a wine tavern of the type normally found in wine-growing regions. Compile a meal from the hot and cold buffets (open daily from 4 pm to midnight).

Mid-Price Restaurants – Right Bank *Café-Bistro Tabasco*, Rainerstrasse 25, has a tempting array of international and Austrian dishes (AS90 to AS240). The salad buffet is AS62 per bowl. This comfortable family-oriented place is open daily to midnight.

K+K StieglBräu Restaurant, Rainerstrasse 14, has several large rooms, a good choice of beer and a garden. The food is

Austrian (AS92 to AS230) and there's a salad bar.

Restaurant Hofwirt (see Places to Stay) serves à-la-carte meals for around AS100 to AS220. If you go there at lunchtime you can enjoy the set two-course meal for AS75 (three courses for AS175 on weekends).

Mid-Price Restaurants – Left Bank *Sternbräu*, in a courtyard between Getreidegasse 36 and Griesgasse 23, is a bit touristy, but it has a nice garden and many rooms. It serves good Austrian food and fish specials from AS80 to AS210. Opening hours are daily from 8 am to midnight. The adjoining courtyard has a self-service place for salads and *La Stella* restaurant for Italian food.

St Peter's Stiftskeller, in a courtyard by St Peter's Abbey, is also rather touristy, but the outside tables are a fine place to relax on a sunny day, to the accompaniment of live accordion music. There are also many inside rooms; main dishes cost from AS95 to AS255 (open daily).

The atmospheric, rustic restaurant at *Zur Goldenen Ente* (see Places to Stay) offers exotic dishes such as fillet of wild boar (AS205). Meals start at AS100 and it is closed at weekends.

Zum Mohren (☎ 84 23 87), Judengasse 9, is a cellar restaurant with some eye-catching decorative features. Most main dishes are above AS170, though if you stick to vegetarian food or the set menu you can eat from about AS90 (closed Sunday).

West of Mönchsberg is *Restaurant Wartenberg* (☎ 84 84 00), in Haus Wartenberg (see Places to Stay). It has an informal atmosphere and simple décor. The frills are reserved for the food, which has a good reputation. There are some cheaper choices, but most main dishes are well above AS130; lamb is a speciality of the house (closed Sunday and holidays).

Expensive Restaurants *K+K Restaurant am Waagplatz* (☎ 84 21 56), Waagplatz 2, has something for most people: outside tables, medieval parties in the cellar, and cheapish food in the casual ground floor Stüberl. Upstairs, the restaurant is more formal and restrained. Quality Austrian fare is around AS165 to AS260 (open daily), and there's a varied selection of wines and spirits.

Zum Eulenspiegel (☎ 84 31 80), Hagenauerplatz 2, by Mozart's Birthplace, is on several floors. It has pleasant surroundings and good food from AS150 to AS260 (though the cartoon menus betray downmarket leanings).

Café Winkler (☎ 84 77 38), Mönchsberg 32, has the advantage of providing good views with very appetising food. It's one large room split into two sections (refer to the overhead signs). In the restaurant area, main courses are AS195 or more, plus AS35 cover charge. The café section has food from AS100 and no cover charge. It's closed Sunday evening and Monday, and has live piano music Thursday to Saturday evenings.

The restaurant in the *Goldener Hirsch* (see Places to Stay) has good gourmet food for about AS250. The hotel also has *s'Herzl*, a less formal rustic restaurant, with food from AS105. It shares some of the same dishes as its gourmet sibling, except they are much cheaper here!

At the top of the range is the *Paris Lodron* restaurant in Schloss Mönchstein (see Places to Stay). Enjoy lavishly prepared food in an opulent setting, all shining silverware and soft classical music. Most dishes top AS300 and are presented with pride and panache.

Entertainment

Music & Theatre The *Marionette Theatre* (☎ 87 24 06 0), Schwarzstrasse 24, has been delighting visitors for 80 years. These ingenious puppets sing and dance to recordings of famous operas and ballets from May to September, as well as at Christmas, Easter, and during Mozart Week in January. Tickets are pricey at AS250 to AS400. Less frivolous musical events are staged at the next-door *Mozarteum* (☎ 87 31 54).

The *Landestheater* (☎ 87 15 12 0), Schwarzstrasse 22, sometimes has musicals and ballets as well as plays. The *Festspiele* (festival halls; ☎ 84 25 41), Hofstallgasse 1, is the main venue for operas and operettas, and is built into the sheer sides of the Mönchsberg.

Szene (☎ 84 34 48), Anton Neumayr Platz 2, puts on avant-garde productions in summer, encompassing dance, theatre and music. *Jazzclub Urbankeller* (☎ 87 08 94, or ☎ 62 22 54 for recorded information), Schallmooser Hauptstrasse 50, has live jazz every Friday from 8 pm to midnight (AS80 to AS200)

The *Kongresshaus* (☎ 88 9 87 0), Auerspergstrasse 7, has occasional cultural and artistic presentations and business conferences. The *Rockhouse* (☎ 88 49 14), Schallmooser Hauptstrasse 46, is Salzburg's main venue for rock and pop bands.

Bars & Clubs *Augustiner Bräustübl*, Augustinergasse 4-6, proves that monks can make beer as well as anybody. The quaffing clerics have been running this huge beer hall for years. It's atmospheric and Germanic, even though mostly filled with tourists. Beer is dispensed from the self-service counter, either in litre (AS48) or half-litre (AS24) mugs. Meat, bread and salad ingredients (pricey) are available in the shops in the foyer. Eat inside or in the large, shady beer garden. It's open daily from 3 pm (2.30 pm on holidays and weekends) to 11 pm.

Stieglkeller (☎ 84 26 81), Festungsgasse 10, is another beer hall. It's even more touristy, as indicated by the live Sound of Music show (AS350) in the summer, but there is a good garden overlooking the town. Food costs between AS88 and AS160. Opening hours are daily from 10 am to 10 pm.

Salzburger Weissbierbrauerei, on the corner of Rupertgasse and Virgilgasse, is a small brewery creating its own very palatable dark and cloudy brew. Everyone drinks this by the half-litre (AS34) in the shady courtyard of the *Bräustüberl*, and there are pretzels and cuts of meat. It's open daily from 11 am (10 am on weekends) to 11 pm. Also on the premises is the *Bräugasthof Rupertihof*, open Monday to Friday from 5 pm to midnight and Saturday from 6 pm to 1 am.

Zum Fidelen Affen, Priesterhausgasse 8, is popular and like a small beer hall. There's limited food for around AS90 (open from 5 pm to midnight).

The *Schnaitl Musik Pub* at Bergstrasse 5

Salzburg's Marionette Theatre has been delighting visitors for 80 years

has a young and lively local clientele and live rock or independent music every second Thursday or Friday from October to June. The cover charge is AS60 to AS80 on music nights. There's also a disco every second Saturday (AS30). The pub is open daily in summer from 7.30 pm to 2 am, and in winter from 6.30 pm to 1 am.

The liveliest area for bars, clubs and discos is the area near the Radisson Hotel on Rudolfskai. *Tom's Bierklinik*, in a passage at Rudolfskai 22, allows the indecisive to dither over a choice of 131 types of beer (open daily from 8 pm to 3 am). In the next passage along, *Zur Frommen Hell* has more of a student feel, and serves good food in winter (open Monday to Saturday from 8 pm to 2 am). Between the two passages is the self-consciously trendy *Vis-à-Vis* bar (open daily, 7 pm to 3 or 4 am). The vicinity of the Mönchsberg lift (elevator) is also a good place to explore for late-night bars.

Other Entertainment To experience the best of Salzburg's coffee-house culture, go to Alter Markt. *Café Tomaselli* is the city's most famous café; *Café Konditorei Fürst* is opposite and also worth a visit. Both have English-language newspapers, lots of cakes and outside tables.

Filmkulturzentrum (☎ 87 31 00), Giselakai 11, has non-mainstream films in the original language (AS85). Salzburg's *casino* is open from 3 pm in Schloss Klessheim in the north-west.

Casino Salzburg is one of Austria's leading soccer teams, and plays at the Lehen Stadium, Schumacherstrasse. The team attracts a lot of juvenile support and crowd trouble is almost unknown; tickets cost from AS200. Bus Nos 1, 2 and 27 go there from the main train station.

Things to Buy

Not many people leave without sampling some Mozart confectionery. Chocolate-coated combinations of nougat and marzipan cost AS4 to AS6 and are available individually or in souvenir packs. These are sold throughout Austria, but it's only in Salzburg that you find whole window displays devoted to Mozart merchandise, with the chocolate joining force with liqueurs, mugs and much else.

Getreidegasse is the main street for shopping and souvenirs. Elsewhere in the old town, souvenir shops are La Point, Alter Markt 1, and round the corner at Kopfberger, Judengasse 14. Salzburger Heimatwerk (☎ 84 41 19), Residenzplatz 9, has glassware, metalware, china, sells Austrian fabrics and has a tailoring service.

Getting There & Away

Air The airport (☎ 85 80 0) has regular scheduled flights to Amsterdam, Berlin, Brussels, Frankfurt, London, Paris, Zürich and elsewhere, including main Austrian cities. Austrian Airlines (☎ 87 55 44 0) has an office at Schrannengasse 5, which it shares with Swissair, and British Airways (☎ 84 21 08) has one at Griesgasse 29. Lauda Air (☎ 84 54 30) is at Getreidegasse 38.

Bus Bundesbuses depart from outside the main train station, on Südtirolerplatz. Timetables are displayed, or call ☎ 167 for information. There's also a Bundesbus information office at the train station, with the entrance by Eurosnack. There are at least four bus departures a day to Kitzbühel (AS118; 2¼ hours), changing at Lofer. Buses to Lienz run only from July to September (AS217, change at Franz Josefs Höhe; services in summer only). Numerous buses leave for the Salzkammergut between 6.30 am and 8 pm – destinations include Bad Ischl (AS94), Mondsee (AS52), St Gilgen (AS60) and St Wolfgang (AS88).

Train Salzburg is well served by IC and EC services. For train information, call ☎ 17 17, daily from 7 am to 8 pm. Tickets (no commission) and train information are also available at Salzburger Landesreisebüro (☎ 88 28 21 16), Schwarzstrasse 11.

Fast trains leave hourly for Vienna's Westbahnhof (AS396; takes three hours 20 minutes), travelling via Linz (AS192; one hour and 20 minutes). The express service to

Klagenfurt (AS 316; three hours) goes via Villach.

The quickest way to Innsbruck is by the 'corridor' train through Germany via Kufstein (no passport required and no disembarkation possible in Germany); trains depart every two hours and the fare is AS336 (takes two hours). There are trains every 30 to 60 minutes to Munich (AS274, but ask about special weekend deals; takes about two hours), some of which continue to Karlsruhe via Stuttgart. German customs is passed in the station before boarding.

Car & Motorbike Three autobahns converge on Salzburg and form a loop round the city: the A1 from Linz and Vienna and the east, the A8/E52 from Munich and the west, and the A10/E55 from Villach and the south. The quickest way to Tirol is to take the road to Bad Reichenhall in Germany and continue to Lofer (highway 312) and St Johann in Tirol.

Car Rental Offices include: Avis (☎ 87 72 78), Ferdinand Porsche Strasse 7; Budget (☎ 87 34 52), Rainerstrasse 17; Eurodollar (☎ 46 81 338), Kaiserschützenstrasse 7; Europcar (☎ 87 42 74), Gabelbergerstrasse 3; and Hertz (☎ 87 66 74), Ferdinand Porsche Strasse 7. Kadal (☎ 62 00 06), Alpenstrasse 2, is a local operator.

Hitching Getting a lift to Munich is notoriously difficult. Consider taking the bus or train across the border before you waste too much time on the autobahn slip road.

Getting Around
To/From the Airport Salzburg airport is just four km west of the city centre at Innsbrucker Bundesstrasse 95. Bus No 77 stops near the airport tourist office and terminates at the main train station. This bus runs from around 7 am to 10 pm and doesn't go via the old town – a taxi to the airport from there would cost about AS120.

Public Transport Single bus tickets cost AS21 from the bus driver, but it's cheaper to

buy a book of tickets from Tabak shops: a book of five costs AS70. The 24-hour pass valid for all city buses (including those to/from Hellbrunn) is excellent value at AS30. Prices are 50% less for children aged six to 15 years; those under six years travel free.

The transport information office (☎ 62 05 51 553) is at Griesgasse 21. Bus routes are shown on city and hotel maps: bus Nos 1, 2, 6 and 51 start from the main train station and skirt the pedestrian-only old town.

A 'bus taxi' (AS27) operates nightly from 11.30 pm to 1.30 am. Hanuschplatz is the departure point for set routes on the left bank, and Theatergasse for routes to the right bank.

Taxi Taxis cost AS30 (AS40 from 10 pm to 5 am) to start, plus AS10 per km inside the city or AS20 per km outside the city. To book a radio taxi, call ☎ 87 44 00 or ☎ 17 15.

Car & Motorbike Driving in the city centre is hardly worth the effort. Parking places are limited and much of the old town is only accessible by foot. The largest car park near the centre is the Altstadt Garage under the Mönchsberg. Attended car parks cost around AS25 per hour. Rates are lower on streets with automatic ticket machines (blue zones): a three-hour maximum applies (AS42, or AS7 for 30 minutes).

Bicycle Bike rental (standard rates) in the main train station is open 24 hours. The bikes for rent in Residenzplatz in summer are much more expensive (AS60 for one hour, AS190 for a day).

Fiacre Rates for a fiacre for up to four passengers are AS350 for 25 minutes and AS680 for 50 minutes. They are lined up on Residenzplatz.

Around Salzburg

Hellbrunn, Gaisberg and Untersberg are best visited as an excursion from Salzburg.

Hallein and Werfen can also be visited as a day trip or explored in a more leisurely fashion en route to sights farther south. Between Hallein and Werfen, another excursion is to the Golling Falls (Gollinger Wasserfall).

HELLBRUNN

Four km south of Salzburg's old town is the popular **Hellbrunn Palace**, built in the 17th century by bishop Marcus Sitticus, a nephew of Wolf Dietrich. The grounds contain many ingenious trick fountains and water-powered figures. They were installed by the bishop and are activated by the tour guides, who all seem to share the bishop's infantile sense of humour. Expect to get wet!

This section of the grounds is open daily from April to October, with the last tour at 4.30 pm (later in summer). Tickets cost AS48, (students AS24), and include entry to the main palace (Baroque in style) and the small Folklore Museum (open from 9 am to 5 pm), which is inside the Month (Monat) Palace, on the hill. Depending on who you believe, the name for this tiny palace comes from either the time it took to build, or the duration of its occupation per year. To visit the main palace only costs AS20 (students AS10).

There is no charge to stroll round the attractive gardens, which are open from February to November (until 9 pm in summer). **Hellbrunn Zoo** is in the grounds. It is naturalistic and open-plan: the more docile animals are barely confined. Enclosures are in a line below a cliff. The zoo is open daily from 8.30 am to 6 pm (4 pm from October to March). Admission costs AS60 (students AS35).

Getting There & Away

Bus No 55 stops directly outside the palace every half-hour (AS21). Pick it up from Salzburg's main train station or Rudolfskai in the old town. The last bus back to the city is at 9.10 pm.

GAISBERG

The Gaisberg (1288 metres) is east of Salzburg. A lookout point provides an excellent panorama of the town and the Salzkammergut. Unless you have your own transport, the only way up is to take the Albus Bus from the north end of the Aicher Passage, Mirabellplatz. It departs at 10.30 am (AS30 each way, takes 30 minutes) and returns at 2.30 pm. From November to March the bus only goes as far as Zistelalpe, six minutes drive short of the Gaisberg stop. A school bus also departs Salzburg at around noon, Monday to Saturday; the driver *might* let you on.

UNTERSBERG

This is the peak to the south of the town, and reaches to a height of 1853 metres. The panorama of Tirolean and Salzburg Alpine ranges is more spectacular than from Gaisberg. The summit is accessible by a cable car (AS100 up, AS90 down, or AS170 return), which runs year-round except for about three weeks from mid-April and six weeks from late November. Get to the valley station by city bus No 55 to St Leonhardt (AS37).

HALLEIN

• *pop 15,400* • *461 m* • ☎ *(06245)*

Hallein is primarily visited for the salt mine at Bad Dürrnberg, on the hill above the town. The town was once settled by Celts, who provided its name ('hall' meaning 'salt' in old Celtic).

Orientation & Information

The train station is east of the Salzach River: walk ahead, bear left and then turn right to cross the river for the town centre (five minutes). The tourist office (☎ 85 3 94), Unterer Markt 1, is in the pedestrian zone, and is open Monday to Friday from 8 am to 4.30 pm. Information via computer screen is accessible out of hours. There's also a summer tourist kiosk on Mautorpromenade, Pernerinsel (turn right on the Stadtsbrücke bridge), open daily from 4 to 9 pm.

The post office (Postamt 5400) is opposite the train station.

Things to See & Do

The sale of salt from the **Bad Dürrnberg mine** filled Salzburg's coffers with money during its ecclesiastical principality days. It is believed inhabitants here were mining salt as many as 4500 years ago, but production has now been replaced by guided tours (AS160; students AS140); see the Salzkammergut chapter for more details. At this mine there's the bonus of a short boat trip on the salt lake. The mine is open daily from mid-April to late October, and the last tour leaves around 5 pm, depending upon demand. Overalls are supplied. Call ☎ 852 85 15 for information. See the following Getting There & Away section for transport to/from the mine.

Hallein has some elegant 17th and 18th-century houses in Salzach style, and a **Celtic Museum** (Keltenmuseum) at Pflegerplatz 5. In addition to Celtic artefacts, the museum covers the history of salt extraction and local folklore (expected to reopen May 1996 after renovations).

Festival

The Halleiner Stadtfestwoche is 10 days of celebration in late June: a AS50 ticket gains admission to all events, which include live music, street theatre, clowns and processions.

Places to Stay

Hallein has a HI *youth hostel* (☎ 80 3 97), Schloss Wispach, Wiespachstrasse 7, open 1 April to 30 September. It's 15 minutes walk from both the station (signposted) and the town centre, but at least staying there allows you to pay just AS10 to swim in the Freibad next door (AS50 normally). This former stately home has beds in large dorms for AS140 (AS150 for a single night). There's a shower/WC on every floor and good breakfasts. Reception is closed from noon to 5 pm (6 pm Sunday).

In the town centre, *Gästehaus Sandwirt* (☎ 80 7 13), Lindorferplatz 8, has singles/doubles using hall showers for AS220/400, and inexpensive food (closed Sunday). *Gasthof Bockwirt* (☎ 80 6 23),

Thunstrasse 12, is within the pedestrian zone with parking nearby. Big, old-fashioned rooms with shower/WC are AS400/750. Frau Eder, one of the owners, is a lively character.

Places to Eat

In front of the station on Bahnhofstrasse is a *Hofer* supermarket; a *Billa* supermarket is near the tourist office summer kiosk. At the beginning of the pedestrian zone on the main street is *China-Restaurant Asia*, open daily. A few metres farther along the main street is *Prima*, a self-service place with lots of menus from just AS35. It's open weekdays from 9 am to 6.30 pm, and Saturday from 8 am to 1.30 pm (6 pm on Langersamstag).

Just beyond the pedestrian zone, to the left, is *Gästehaus Unterholzerbräu*, Oberhofgasse 4, serving Austrian food, fish and grills for AS75 to AS190 (closed Tuesday).

Getting There & Away

Hallein is a half-hour bus or train ride from Salzburg (the station rents bikes). If you don't have a car, the easiest way to reach Bad Dürrnberg is to take the cable car, which is a signposted 10-minute walk from the train station. The AS230 (students AS200) return fare includes entry to the mines (AS105 excluding the mine). A cheaper option is the 15-minute bus ride (AS24) from outside the station; departures are synchronised with train arrivals. You could also hike to the mine, but it's a steep 40-minute climb: from the tourist office, walk up to the church with the bare concrete tower, turn left along Ferchl Strasse, and follow the sign pointing to the right after the yellow Volksschule building.

BERCHTESGADEN

Although this town is in Germany, it is easy to visit from Salzburg. It achieved fame (or perhaps notoriety) for the **Eagle's Nest**, a retreat built by Adolf Hitler on the Kehlstein summit. The **Salzbergwerk** (☎ 08652-6 00 20) north of town proves the Germans are also able to turn salt into money – proceeds from Berchtesgaden have long contributed to Bavaria's power and wealth. Popular tours follow a similar schedule to those in Hallein and the Salzkammergut, but, depending on exchange rates, a tour should be cheaper here: DM16 (around AS110) for adults; children half-price.

Five km south of Berchtesgaden is the **Königssee**, an attractive lake providing boat tours and a scenic setting for hikes. This area is a national park and a few devotees maintain it offers some of the best hiking in Germany.

If you plan to stay overnight in or around Berchtesgaden, contact the town tourist office (☎ 08652-50 11), opposite the train station in Königsseer Strasse, for advice.

Getting There & Away

Berchtesgaden is 30 km south of Salzburg on highway 160. Direct buses run from the city, or it's less than an hour by rail (take a Munich train and change at Freilassing). Salzburg tour operators offer a half-day tour of Berchtesgaden, the Eagle's Nest and the Königssee.

WERFEN
• *pop 3000* • *525 m* • ☎ *(06468)*

Picturesque Werfen provides access to a topline attraction, the Eisriesenwelt ice caves.

Orientation & Information

The town stands on the north side of the Salzach River, five minutes walk from the train station: cross the river and head towards the castle. The tourist office (☎ 388) is on Hauptstrasse, in the centre of the town. It is open Monday to Friday from 9 am to 5 pm, except in July and August when it's open to 7 pm, and weekends from 5 to 7 pm. It can book accommodation and charges no commission.

Eisriesenwelt Caves

The Eisriesenwelt Höhle in the mountains are the largest accessible ice caves in the world. They contain 30,000 sq metres of ice and about 42 km of passages have been explored. During a 75-minute tour some immense caverns are visited, containing some beautiful and elaborate ice shapes. Unfortunately, the powerful illumination provided by a series of magnesium flares is all too brief. The caves were first entered in 1879 but it was Alexander von Mörk who pioneered the most extensive exploration, and his ashes lie in an urn in the 'cathedral' cave.

Take warm clothes because it can get cold inside, and you need to be fairly fit (older people may find the stairs a bit difficult because of the altitude). The caves are open from 1 May to early October. The tour (in German) visits about one-fiftieth of the caves and costs AS80. See the following Getting There & Away section for transport to/from the caves. See also the Dachstein ice caves in the Salzkammergut chapter.

Hohenwerfen Fortress

The Hohenwerfen Fortress stands on the hill above the village. Originally built in 1077 for an archbishop of Salzburg, the present building dates from the 16th century. The entry fee includes an exhibition (displays change periodically), and a guided tour of the interior (in English only if there's sufficient demand), which covers the chapel, dungeons, arsenal and belfry. The best part is a dramatic falconry show in the grounds. The walk up from the village takes 20 minutes. It can be visited daily from Easter to 31 October, and entry costs AS100 (students AS90).

Both the fortress and the caves can be fitted into a day-trip from Salzburg if you start early; visit the caves first, and be at the fortress by 3 pm for the falconry show.

Places to Stay & Eat

Private rooms are from about AS150 per person. There are three places on Hirschenhöhstrasse, the street behind Gasthof Lebzelter.

Guesthouses are reasonably priced, too. *Eisriesenwelt* (☎ 228), Hauptstrasse 44, has rooms from AS180 to AS220, depending on whether they have a sink, shower, or shower/WC; single occupancy incurs a surcharge of AS30. *Goldener Hirsch* (☎ 342),

MARK HONAN

MARK HONAN

MARK HONAN

MARK HONAN

Top Left: Statue by the cathedral doorway, Salzburg
Top Right: Fiacres for hire, Residenzplatz, Salzburg
Bottom Left: Window display of Mozart confectionery, Salzburg
Bottom Right: Sights at the Hellbrunn Zoo, Salzburg

MARK HONAN

MARK HONAN

MARK HONAN

MARK HONAN

MARK HONAN

A	B
C	D
E	

A: Hohensalzburg Fortress and old town, Salzburg
B: Roof of the cathedral, Salzburg
C: Mirabellgarten, Salzburg
D: Hellbrunn Palace, Hellbrunn, Salzburg
E: Salzburg city by night

Hauptstrasse 28, has slightly better singles/doubles for AS270/500 with shower; the place has a garden.

There are several places to eat along the main street that aren't too expensive, such as *Bella Grotta Pizzeria*, Hauptstrasse 39. It has pizzas from AS58, outside tables and is open daily.

If you have the money, go to *Zur Stiege* (☎ 256), Hauptstrasse 10. Its restaurant has a very good reputation, and there are rooms with shower/WC and TV from AS330 per person.

Gasthof Lebzelter Obauer (☎ 212), Hauptstrasse 46, also has rooms (from AS550 per person), which have all the comforts expected of a four-star place. But it's really known for its restaurant, acclaimed as one of the finest in the whole country. Reserve in advance, especially as rest days vary.

Getting There & Away

Werfen can be reached from Salzburg by highway 10. By train from Salzburg takes 50 minutes. Getting to the caves is a bit of an effort, though the trip yields fantastic views. A minibus service (AS65 return) from the station operates along the steep, six-km road to the car park, which is as far as cars can go. A 15-minute walk brings you to the cable car (AS100 return); from the top station it is a 15-minute steep walk to the caves. Allow at least four hours return from the station, or three hours from the car park (peak-season queues may add an hour). The whole route can be hiked, but it's a hard four-hour ascent, rising 1100 metres above the village.

Southern Salzburg Province

The principal attractions in the south are covered in the Hohe Tauern National Park Region chapter. The following places are worth a look if you're passing through the south-east of the province.

TAMSWEG
- *pop 5000* • *1024 m* • ☎ *(06474)*

Tamsweg is the main town in the Lungau region. If you're passing through you may want to stop off to look at **St Leonard's Church**, a 15th-century Gothic structure sited on a hill outside the town. It has some impressive stained glass windows, particularly the so-called gold window (Goldfenster), on the right of the chancel. After the discovery of a statuette of St Leonard, an event depicted by the gold window, the church became a well-known pilgrimage site.

In the centre of town, the attractive **Marktplatz** is lined by rustic-style inns. Also here is the 16th-century Rathaus, a rather grander, turreted edifice.

Tamsweg is known for its **Samson Procession** on the weekend after Corpus Christi. The biblical character and other famous figures are depicted in giant size and paraded through the streets. If you want to visit at this time, seek the advice of the tourist office (☎ 416), in the Rathaus, about accommodation.

Getting There & Away

Tamsweg is at the terminus of a private rail line that branches off from the Vienna-Klagenfurt main line at Unzmarkt. See Murau in the Styria chapter for transport details.

The town is a 10-km detour from highway 99 connecting Radstadt and Spittal an der Drau.

MAUTERNDORF
- *pop 1600* • *1122 m*

Both a summer and winter resort, Mauterndorf has the added attraction of a **castle**. This was built by the archbishops of Salzburg in the 13th century on the site of a Roman fort. In 1339 the castle chapel (with Gothic frescoes) was added, and in 1452 a winged altar was installed. The castle has a regional museum, and is the site for various cultural events. It is believed that in the Middle Ages the main road passed directly through the castle courtyard. This facilitated the collecting of tolls from road users, but presumably also entailed a defence risk. The locals were lucky not to encounter a Trojan horse trundling along the road.

Moosham, six km south of Mauterndorf, has a castle formerly owned by the archbishops of Salzburg.

Getting There & Away
Mauterndorf is on highway 99. Bundesbuses go along this route, but Mauterndorf is not on a train line.

RADSTADT
• *pop 4000* • *856 m* • ☎ *(06452)*
Radstadt retains much of its medieval fortifications, but most visitors flock to participate in winter skiing.

Orientation & Information
The town centre is uphill from the train station: a town plan in the station foyer shows the best paths. The tourist office is in the centre at Stadtplatz 17, open Monday to Friday, 8 am to noon and 2 to 6 pm, and Saturday from 9 am to noon. In the winter additional hours are Saturday 4 to 6 pm and Sunday from 9 to 11 am. The tourist office will book rooms for no commission, including cheap private rooms (no minimum stay). Next door is an accommodation board with a free telephone, accessible daily from 7 am to midnight.

Things to See & Do
The walled centre of town, with three round turrets, is an impressive sight. One tower, the **Kapuzinerturm**, houses a museum dealing with local history and culture (open June to September). There is another museum in **Schloss Lerchen**(closed April and May). The **parish church**, recently renovated, combines Gothic and Romanesque elements and has an interesting graveyard.

Radstadt and six neighbouring skiing areas combine to form the huge **Sportwelt Amandé** skiing area; 120 lifts give access to 320 km of pistes, mostly suitable for inter-

mediates and beginners. A high-season lift pass costs AS350 for one day. If this doesn't give you enough choice, you can opt instead for the Top Tauern Skischeck, a pass valid for 320 lifts (880 km of runs) in Salzburg province and Styria; it costs AS1870 for six days or AS1990 for seven days.

As always, the same mountains attract hikers in summer. Overlooking Radstadt to the north is the **Rossbrand** (1770 metres). If you ascend wearing rose-tinted spectacles, you might believe the tourist office's claim that this is the most famous viewpoint in the eastern Alps.

Places to Stay
Radstadt has a few hotels, guesthouses and pensions, but by far the most beds are provided by numerous private homes, farmhouses and holiday apartments. The tourist office will help you track down the best deals.

There are cheaper places, but if you just want something central and decent, try *Gasthof Torwirt* (☎ 55 41), Hoheneggstrasse 12, costing AS320/600 for singles/doubles, or *Hotel Post* (☎ 43 06), Stadtplatz 8, costing from AS500/840. Both offer rooms with shower/WC and cable TV, though Hotel Post has more on-site facilities, including a restaurant.

Places to Eat
Close to the tourist office, on Hoheneggstrasse, are two *Spar* supermarkets.

China-Restaurant Mauer, Schernbergstrasse 15, offers weekday lunch menus for under AS70, including soup or spring roll (open daily). *Gasthof Löcker*, next door at No 13, provides Austrian food for AS68 to AS125 (closed Tuesday). This place also has rooms with shower and toilet for AS260/520.

3P, near the parish church on Karl Berg Gasse, is a pub with pool tables that also serves some food.

Getting There & Away
Radstadt receives two-hourly IC trains running between Innsbruck and Graz (takes

about three hours to either place). Kitzbühel, Zell am See and Bruck an der Mur are also along this route.

From Radstadt, highway 99 runs into Styria. This climbs to the Radstädter Tauern Pass at 1739 metres and is not recommended for caravans. Just to the west is a busier north-south route, the A10/E55, which avoids the high parts by going through a six-km tunnel.

The Salzkammergut

This 'earthly paradise,' as described by Franz Joseph I, is a popular holiday region to the east of Salzburg. The lure of the many lakes means summer is the main season, but winter has its attractions too. It's an area where you can simply relax and take in the scenery, or get involved in the numerous sports and activities on offer. In summer, hiking and water sports are favoured; in winter, some hiking paths stay open but downhill and cross-country skiing are more popular.

A winter ski pass is available from ski lift stations for the Salzkammergut-Tennengau region, which includes 140 cable cars and ski lifts in 21 ski resorts. It costs AS1420 (children AS900) for five days, AS1630 (AS1030) for six days, AS1750 (AS1100) for seven days and AS2450 (AS1550) for 10 days. It is also valid for a number of free ski buses. Look for low-season offers: in 1994-95 purchasers of a six or seven-day pass during most of January and after mid-March received a free extra day.

If you plan to fish, be sure to check with the local tourist office about permits, permitted seasons and other regulations – these vary from lake to lake and can be quite specific. At Wolfgangsee, for example, fishing is allowed from the bank or a boat, but not between 10 pm and 6 am, and live bait is allowed but not multiple fishing equipment.

Orientation

In this region of mountains and lakes, most taller mountains are in the south and most larger lakes in the north. The Salzkammergut is split between three provinces. Upper Austria takes the lion's share, including the largest lake, Attersee, its two neighbours, Mondsee and Traunsee, and the ever popular Hallstätter See in the south. Bad Ischl, also in Upper Austria, is the geographical and administrative centre of the Salzkammergut. East of Hallstätter See is a small region

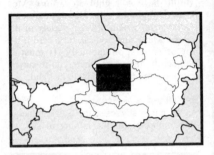

within Styria, comprising Bad Aussee and its lakes. Salzburg province has most of Wolfgangsee, and some less important lakes to the west and north-west.

Information

The Salzkammergut has its own tourist board, Salzkammergut Tourismusverband (☎ 06132-26 9 09), Kaltenbachstrasse 36, A-4820 Bad Ischl. The office is hard to find and doesn't have an outside sign – they're geared to field written or telephone enquiries rather than service personal callers.

In addition to the local tourist offices – there is one in almost every resort – the provincial tourist offices can help, though they usually only hold resort brochures for their own region within the Salzkammergut. See the Salzburg, Upper Austria and Styria chapters for addresses and opening times of these offices. The provincial tourist office in Salzburg city has a lot of information on the area, including bus and train schedules and a list of camping grounds. The Upper Austria provincial tourist office in Linz also has a good supply of brochures. In Styria, information is held in the main Graz tourist office (for personal callers) and the provincial office (for information by post), also in Graz.

The Salzkammergut is dotted with hostels and affordable hotels, but the best deal is probably a room in a private home or farmhouse – despite the prevalence of single-night surcharges. Tourist offices can supply lists of private rooms, as well as details of Alpine huts at higher elevations. Most resorts have a holiday/guest card (*Gästekarte*) which offers a variety of discounts. Make sure you ask for a card if it is not offered spontaneously. It must be stamped by the place where you're staying (even at camping grounds) to be valid.

Salt Mines

As its name suggests, the Salzkammergut was important for the mining of salt, the 'white gold' that gave the region its prosperity. Mines at Hallstatt, Bad Ischl and Altaussee are still in production. Salt mining is a lengthy process: it takes 10 to 15 years for the brine in each new section to reach a height and saturation level at which it is economical to pump it out: brine from these mines goes to Ebensee where the salt is extracted. Only 10% ends up as table salt; the rest is used for industrial purposes.

All three mines offer tours, each slightly different but adhering to a similar formula: visitors don mining overalls, take a mini-train ride to the mine and slide down wooden

tunnels. Beyond this, the content of tours is pretty thin and they're rather expensive. If you can only afford one guided tour in the mountains, I'd recommend the ice caves at Obertraun instead.

Getting Around

The main rail routes pass either side of the Salzkammergut, but the area can be crossed by regional trains on a north-south route. You can get on this route from Attnang Puchheim on the Salzburg-Linz line. The track from here connects Gmunden, Traunkirchen, Ebensee, Bad Ischl, Hallstatt and Obertraun. After Obertraun, the railway continues east via Bad Aussee before connecting with the main Bischofshofen-Graz line at Stainach-Irdning. It takes 2¼ hours to complete the 108 km from Attnang Puchheim to Stainach-Irdning (and the trains are often late). A few small stations along this route are unstaffed (marked 'Hu' on timetables); at these you'll have to pay on the train. Attersee is also accessible by rail.

Regular bus services connect all towns and villages in the area. Timetables are displayed at stops, and tickets can be bought from the driver. Enquire about special tickets: in previous summers, a good deal has been the Salzkammergut ticket, providing four days of specified train and bus travel within a 10-day period. See the Salzburg Getting There & Away section for more bus information.

Passenger boats ply the waters of the Attersee, Traunsee, Mondsee, Hallstätter See and Wolfgangsee.

To reach the Salzkammergut from Salzburg by car or motorbike, take the A1 or highway 158. Travelling north-south, the main road is highway 145 (known as the Salzkammergut Bundesstrasse), which closely follows the rail line for most of its length.

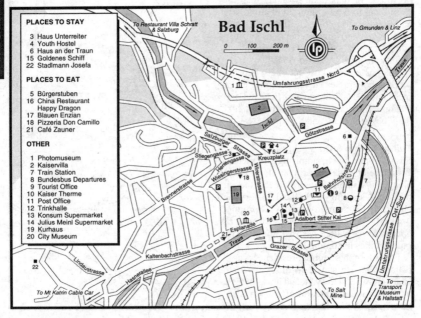

Bad Ischl

PLACES TO STAY

3 Haus Unterreiter
4 Youth Hostel
6 Haus an der Traun
15 Goldenes Schiff
22 Stadlmann Josefa

PLACES TO EAT

5 Bürgerstuben
16 China Restaurant
   Happy Dragon
17 Blauen Enzian
18 Pizzeria Don Camillo
21 Café Zauner

OTHER

1 Photomuseum
2 Kaiservilla
7 Train Station
8 Bundesbus Departures
9 Tourist Office
10 Kaiser Therme
11 Post Office
12 Trinkhalle
13 Konsum Supermarket
14 Julius Meinl Supermarket
19 Kurhaus
20 City Museum

Bad Ischl

• *pop 13,000* • *468 m* • ☎ *(06132)*

This spa town's reputation snowballed after Princess Sophie took a treatment to cure her infertility in 1828. Within two years she had given birth to Franz Joseph I; two other sons followed. Rather in the manner of a salmon returning to its place of birth, Franz Joseph made an annual pilgrimage to Bad Ischl, making it his summer home and hauling much of the European aristocracy in his wake. However, deviating from salmon behaviour, Franz Joseph returned to his spiritual home to make not love but war – usually on deer, but ultimately on the whole world.

Orientation & Information

Bad Ischl town centre is compactly contained within a bend of the Traun River.

The tourist office, or *Kurdirektion* (☎ 235 200), is close to the train station at Bahnhofstrasse 6. It is open Monday to Friday from 8 am to 6 pm, Saturday 9 am to 4 pm and Sunday from 9 to 11.30 am. The guest card (*Kurkarte*) gives reductions on many admission prices, though this is offset by the nightly *Kurtaxe* (AS12 to AS19).

The post office (Postamt 4820) is nearby on Bahnhofstrasse. There are money changing facilities at the post office and train station. The train station also rents bikes daily between 5 am and 8.10 pm.

Things to See & Do

Stroll around town, admiring the plentiful Biedermeier-style buildings; if you walk along the Esplanade you'll reach the **city museum**, dealing with local history and culture (AS30; closed Monday). For longer walks, refer to the tourist office's *Die Spaziergänge* leaflet. Also ask about the free guided hikes in summer.

Franz Joseph's summer residence was the **Kaiservilla**. He stayed in this villa for 60 years, from 1854 to 1914, and it was here that he signed the declaration of war on Serbia that started WW I. The emperor had the habit

Emperor Franz Joseph I made an annual pilgrimage to Bad Ischl, where he had a summer villa

of getting up for his daily bath as early as 3.30 am – not a typical regimen for someone on holiday. The villa was his hunting lodge (though rather grand for that purpose) and contains an obscene number of hunting trophies; most of his victims are now no more than antlers on the wall, but the 2000th (!) chamois he shot is presented in its stuffed entirety.

The villa can be visited only by guided tour, which is given in German, but there are written English translations. The tour takes 40 minutes, costs AS88, and includes entry to the Kaiserpark grounds (which costs AS35 on its own). The Kaiservilla is open 1 May to 30 October, daily from 9 am to noon and 1 to 7 pm; from Easter to 30 April it's open weekends only.

The small **Photomuseum**, nearby in the

park in the Marmorschlössel building, has some interesting old photographs and cameras (entry AS15; students AS10). It's open from 1 April to 31 October, daily from 9.30 am to 5 pm.

Bad Ischl's local peak is **Mt Katrin** (1542 metres), which provides views and hiking trails. In summer, the cable car costs AS159 return. In winter, the mountain offers downhill skiing (AS214 for a day pass). The town also has some cross-country skiing trails.

There's a **salt mine** (*Salzbergwerk*) to the south of town in Perneck: walk there in 40 minutes or take the infrequent bus; tours cost AS120, and they're conducted daily from 1 April to 30 September. For information, call ☎ 23 9 48 31. Also in the south, in Sulzbach, is a **transport museum** (Museum Fahrzeug), open daily from 1 April to 31 October (AS60).

The tourist office has information on health treatments, such as those in the Kaiser Therme (☎ 23 3 24 11), 1 Bahnhofstrasse. To get a taste of the salubrious waters (AS13 a cup), visit the **Trinkhalle** (drinking hall) on Auböckplatz (open in the summer), or the Kaiser Therme.

Festivals

Free 'spa concerts' are usually performed twice a day (except Tuesday) during summer; the tourist office has a list of venues and times. An operetta festival takes place in July and August; for advance details and reservations call ☎ 23 8 39, or write to: Büro der Operettengemeinde Bad Ischl, Wiesingerstrasse 7, A-4820. After 1 July, phone ☎ 23 7 66.

Places to Stay

The tourist office will phone round for rooms without a charge.

The HI *youth hostel* (☎ 26 5 77) is at Am Rechensteg 5, in the town centre behind Kreuzplatz. Beds (one to five per room) are AS130 and dinner is AS60. Reception is only open from 8 to 9 am and 5 to 7 pm, and there's a 10 pm curfew.

Haus Unterreiter (☎ 46 072), Stiegengasse 1, is a private house run by an elderly

Frau who doesn't speak English. She has four singles and two doubles for around AS140 per person – an excellent deal. Baths cost AS20 and there are TVs in most rooms. Go through the arch and climb the stairs at the back of the small Nah & Frisch supermarket. Many other homes offer private rooms, but none so central.

B&B pensions offer reasonable value. *Stadlmann Josefa* (☎ 23 1 04), west of town at Masteliergasse 21, has basic rooms from AS170 per person, though some have private shower. *Haus an der Traun* (☎ 23 4 72) is just to the right of the station, at Bahnhofstrasse 11. It has attractive rooms at AS320 per person with radio, TV and balcony, or AS370 including private shower/WC; prices drop in the low season and rise for short stays.

Goldenes Schiff (☎ 24 2 41; fax 24 2 41 58), Adalbert Stifter Kai 3, overlooks the river and offers four-star comfort from just AS480/840 in the low season and AS560/1060 in the high season (river views cost extra). The hotel has a solarium and parking places, and they're proud of their horsehair mattresses.

Places to Eat

A *Julius Meinl* supermarket is on Pfarrgasse, but the *Konsum* on Auöckplatz is cheaper.

The *China Restaurant Happy Dragon*, on Adalbert Stifter Kai by the Schröpferplatz bridge, overlooks the river and has outside tables. It has lunch menus for AS64 (not Sunday or holidays) and other dishes for about AS85 (open daily); the food is above average. *Pizzeria Don Camillo*, Wiesingerstrasse 5, has good-value pizza and spaghetti from AS55 and salads from AS35 to AS73. It's also open daily, and has outside tables overlooking the Kurpark (and a couple of double rooms available).

For Austrian food, try *Bürgerstuben* at Kreuzplatz 7, off the street in a courtyard. It has white walls, lots of plants, and meals in the range of AS90 to AS170 (closed Sunday in the low season). The salad buffet costs AS40 or AS60.

Blauen Enzian, Wirerstrasse 2, is also

back from the main street. This informal place offers a varied menu (AS80 to AS170 per dish) covering pasta, regional and national food and salads (closed Sunday in the low season). It has an adjoining bar that's open from 8 pm to 4 am (closed Sunday and Monday).

Sample imperial elegance on the Esplanade at *Café Zauner*, open 1 May to 30 September. Gourmets may want to head two km out of town (north-west) to *Restaurant Villa Schratt*, (☎ 27 6 47), Steinbruch 43 (closed Tuesday and Wednesday).

Getting There & Away

Bundesbuses leave from outside the train station. There are hourly buses to Salzburg (AS94) between 5.05 am and 8.10 pm, via St Gilgen. To St Wolfgang (AS42), you have to change at Strobl at weekends (the bus will be waiting, and the same ticket is valid). Buses run to Hallstatt every one to two hours (AS48; 50 minutes). Three buses a day go to both Mondsee and Obertraun.

Trains depart hourly. It costs AS34 to Hallstatt but, unlike the bus, you must add the cost of the boat (see the Hallstatt Getting There & Away section). The fare to Salzburg by train is AS180, via Attnang Puchheim.

Most major roads in the Salzkammergut go to or near Bad Ischl; highway 158 from Salzburg and the north-south highway 145 intersect just north of the town centre.

Southern Salzkammergut

The Dachstein mountain range provides a 3000-metre backdrop to the lakes in the south. Transport routes go round rather than over these jagged peaks.

HALLSTÄTTER SEE

This lake, at an elevation of 508 metres, is the big draw in the south. Hallstatt is the most famous resort and receives hordes of day-trippers. Just five km round the lake lies Obertraun, the closest resort to the Dachstein ice caves. Either place would make a suitable base to explore the locality.

From the beginning of May to the beginning of September, three boats a day embark on a circular excursion round the lake (AS80), a 75-minute trip (disembarkation possible).

Hallstatt
• ☎ *(06134)*

Hallstatt has a history stretching back 4500 years. The Hallstatt Period (800-400 BC) refers to the early Iron Age in Europe, and was named after the settlers who worked the salt mine (near the mine entrance, 2000 flat graves were discovered dating from 1000 to 500 BC). In 50 AD, the Romans were also attracted by the rich salt deposits, but nowadays the village is prized mainly for its picturesque location.

Orientation & Information Seestrasse is the main street; some other streets are mere pedestrian paths. Turn left from the ferry to reach the tourist office (☎ 8208), Seestrasse 169. It is open Monday to Friday from 9 am to 5 pm and weekends from 10 am to 2 pm; from September to June it is closed at weekends and for one hour at noon. The office sells an invaluable information brochure for AS10, which includes accommodation; the regional office should provide this for free. It also sells a hiking guide in English. Guest-card benefits for staying in the village include reduced admission to the Dachstein ice caves.

The post office (Postamt 4830) is around the corner from the tourist office.

Things to See & Do Hallstatt is set in idyllic, picture-postcard scenery, wedged between the mountains and the lake. The tour buses that roll in only stay a few hours and then the village returns to a calmer state. Join everyone else strolling down the quaint streets, snapping up souvenirs and photographs in equal measure.

The Catholic **parish church** was built in the 15th century and has Gothic frescoes and two winged altars: the better one shows saints Barbara and Katharina, with Mary in the middle (1510). Don't miss the macabre **Bone House** (Beinhaus; entry AS10) by the church; it contains rows of neatly stacked skulls, upon which have been painted flowery designs and the names of their former owners. These human remains have been exhumed from the too-small graveyard since 1600.

The village has two small **museums**, one devoted to local history (the Prähistorisches Museum) and the other to local crafts and fauna (the Heimatmuseum). They're worth a look, although signs are only in German. Combined entry costs AS40 (reductions for students and guest-card holders).

Above the village on the Salzberg (salt mountain) are the **saltworks**. Tours (usually in German, plus a short English film) dwell on the fate of a 3000-year-old miner, found preserved in the salt in 1735. It's open from early April to late October, daily from 9.30 am. The last tour is at 4.30 pm from the end of May to late September; at other times it's at 3 pm. Entry costs AS130 (AS115 with guest card). The funicular costs AS95 return (AS80 with guest card). It takes you to **Rudolf's Tower** (where there's an excellent view from the public terrace), 15 minutes walk from the mine. Alternatively, either of two scenic hiking trails will get you to the tower in 45 minutes.

Gasthof Hallberg is the base for Hallstatt's **scuba diving** school, and the **ski** school is at the Gasthof Zauner Seewirt; see Places to Stay & Eat.

Hallstatt has an unusual **Corpus Christi procession**: the shoreline is so crowded that some participants take to the water in boats.

Places to Stay & Eat Some private rooms in the village are only available in summer; others require a minimum three-night stay. The tourist office will willingly ring round for you, or there's an accommodation board with free phone in Lahn (the southern part of the village), which has the cheapest private rooms.

Campingplatz Höll (☎ 83 29), Lahn-

strasse 6, Lahn, costs AS50 per person, AS35 per tent and AS28 per car. It's open from 1 May to 30 September.

The HI *youth hostel* (☎ 82 12), Salzberg-strasse 50, is open from around 1 May to 30 September, depending on the weather. Beds cost AS100 and (if required) breakfast and sheets another AS25 each. Nonmembers don't pay extra; some dorms have many beds and are cramped. Day check-in is sometimes possible, and getting a key avoids the 10 pm curfew.

TVN Naturfreunde Herberge (☎ 83 18), Kirchenweg 36, is just below the road tunnel, by the waterfall. It has dorm beds for AS110, plus AS35 each for sheets and breakfast (if required). As in the hostel, some rooms are OK, others are cramped. It's run by the *Zur Mühle Gasthaus*, which is in the same building. Zur Mühle has the best prices in the village: pizza and pasta from AS65 and Austrian food from AS70. It's closed on Wednesday, so you can't check into TVN on that day (or from 2 to 4 pm any day).

Frühstückspension Seethaler (☎ 84 21), Dr Morton Weg 22, has central rooms for AS185 (AS205 if single night) with a lake view, but barely adequate hall showers.

Go to *Bräu Gasthof* (☎ 82 21), Seestrasse 120, for Austrian food in an old-fashioned atmosphere (or sit outside by the lake). Lunchtime specials start from AS105, and other dishes from AS85. It's open daily, but only from 1 May to 31 October. Double rooms with private WC and shower reflect the same style, and are available all year for AS800.

There are a couple of *Konsum* supermarkets in the village, and *Kongress Stuberl* by the tourist office is another good place to eat (meals from AS85).

Gasthof Hallberg (☎ 82 86), Seestrasse 113, has pizzas and Austrian food for AS85 to AS160. It also has a few rooms for AS400 per person with private WC and shower. *Gasthof Zauner-Seewirt* (☎ 82 46), Markt-platz 51, is run by the same family. It has good rooms with shower/WC, TV and telephone, some with a balcony and a view of the lake; singles/doubles are AS620/1040

(AS840/1480 for half-board). The restaurant is known for its good food (especially fish) and wines. Dishes are above AS100, and it's closed from 1 November to Christmas.

Getting There & Away There are around six buses a day to Obertraun and Bad Ischl, but none after 6 pm. To get to the youth hostel upon arriving, get off at the 'Lahn' bus stop, by the stream at the southern end of the road tunnel; for the centre and the tourist office, get off at the 'Parkterrasse' stop.

The train station is across the lake (at least nine trains a day to/from Bad Ischl; total trip 45 minutes). The private boat service from there to the village (AS20) doesn't leave till the train has arrived from both directions. Car access into the village is restricted: from early May to late October, electronic gates are activated. Staying overnight gives free parking, and a pass to open the gates.

Obertraun
• ☎ *(06131)*

This spread-out village appears to be totally enclosed within a crater of mountains; it's a trick of perspective, but a pleasing one.

┅┅┅┅┅┅┅┅┅┅┅┅┅┅┅┅┅

Dachstein or Werfen?
Unless you're a caving buff, you'll probably want to see either the caves at Dachstein or those at Werfen, but not both. The costs involved are about the same, so how to choose between them?

Werfen, in Salzburg, is undeniably the more impressive in terms of sheer scale. Dachstein is said to have more beautiful ice formations, but this is probably only because they are better lit and the tour allows more time to study them. Dachstein is also less physically strenuous, and has the advantage of tours in English. In either case, the view across the valley from the cave mouth is excellent.

Political purists may get excited about another difference: the Dachstein caves are managed by the local authority, whereas Werfen is a private enterprise. ∎

┅┅┅┅┅┅┅┅┅┅┅┅┅┅┅┅┅

Orientation & Information Obertraun is on the north bank of the Traun River, at the start of the narrow and steep-sided valley leading east to Bad Aussee. The tourist office (☎ 351) is in the Gemeindeamt, open Monday to Friday from 8 am to noon and 2 to 4 pm, and in season, Saturday from 9 am to noon. The Dachstein ice caves are south of the river, a pleasant 20-minute walk through the woods (take path No 7; signposted).

The resort guest card gives useful discounts.

Dachstein Caves The best of these caves are the **Giant Ice Caves** (Riesen-Eishöhle). Ask at the ticket office about tours in English. The caves are millions of years old and extend for nearly 80 km in places. The ice itself is no more than 500 years old but is increasing in thickness every year – the 'ice mountain' is eight metres high, twice as high as when the caves were first explored in 1910. There are some unusual and beautiful formations, such as the 'ice chapel'.

The **Mammoth Caves** (Mammuthöhle) are basically more of the same except without the ice formations, and the tour is in German only. But they are worth seeing, if only for the atmospheric slide show projected within a far cavern, accompanied by swelling music mingling with the sound of ceaselessly dripping water.

Both sets of caves are 10 minutes walk from the first stage of the Dachstein cable car (station Dachsteinhöhlen) at 1350 metres, near which is found the ticket office for the caves. The cable car operates every 20 minutes; a return ticket costs AS155. Entry costs AS79 for each cave, or AS110 for a combined ticket, and they're open from 1 May to mid-October. Each tour takes nearly an hour; be at the ticket office by 3 pm in summer and 2 pm in autumn as the *latest* time to do both tours.

The **Koppenbrüllerhöhle** is part of the same Dachstein cave system, and is down the valley towards Bad Aussee. This water-filled cave can be visited by guided tour (AS70) from 1 May to 30 September.

Other Attractions The Dachstein cable car has three stages, the highest being **Krippenstein** at 2109 metres; various viewpoints and walking trails await, which provide excellent views of the Dachstein range to the south and Hallstätter See to the north. In winter this is also a ski region (AS285 for a one-day pass). The restaurant here is not too expensive.

Obertraun also has a grassy beach area (free entry) with changing huts, a small waterslide, a children's play area and boat rental.

Places to Stay & Eat Look for the many private rooms and holiday apartments in the village. *Campingplatz Hinterer* (☎ 265) is by the lake, south of the river.

The HI *youth hostel* (☎ 360), Winkl 26, is 15 minutes walk from the train station: cross the river and take the first street on the left. It costs AS85 (AS70 if aged under 19) plus AS10 for short stays and AS50 for sheets (if required). Those aged under 19 save AS5 on the price of breakfast (AS45), lunch (AS70) and dinner (AS60). Reception is open from 9 am to 1 pm, when you can leave your bags, but you can only check in between 5.30 and 7.30 pm. Get a key to avoid the 10 pm curfew.

Other than this, places to stay and eat are limited to a few guesthouses. *Gasthof Höllwirt* (☎ 394), Hauptstrasse 29, costs AS330 per person with private shower. It has a good restaurant, with daily specials for AS65 to AS115 and other meals for AS75 to AS195 (closed Wednesday).

Obertrauner Hof (☎ 456), Hauptstrasse 90, has a range of prices depending upon the length of stay and season. Expect to pay around AS300 per person using hall shower or AS370 with private shower. The restaurant is also good, and has similar prices to Höllwirt; look for the good-value 'theme' meals (closed Tuesday).

Near the beach and boat station is a skittles alley (*Kegelbahn*) with pizzas for AS60 to AS90 (until 11 pm). By the tourist office there's a *Konsum* supermarket, open Monday to Friday from 7.30 am to noon and 3 to 6 pm, and Saturday from 7 am to noon.

Getting There & Away Buses between Hallstatt and Obertraun are patchy, with only six or fewer running per day. But it's possible to hitch, or the walk takes 50 minutes. Five boats per day take 25 minutes to go between Obertraun and Hallstatt (AS35).

Obertraun-Dachsteinhöhlen is the train station for the village, and it rents bicycles. Obertraun-Koppenbrüllerhöhle is the station for the water cave, and trains only stop here when the caves are open in summer.

BAD AUSSEE
• *pop 5000* • *650 m* • ☎ *(06152)*
Bad Aussee provides access to two lakes, as well as being a health resort. Everywhere in town there's the sound of rushing water, emanating from the swiftly-flowing Traun.

Orientation & Information
Bad Aussee is the chief Styrian town in the Salzkammergut. The train station is two km south of the town, which has Kurhausplatz at its centre. The tourist office (☎ 523 23) is near the centre, at the corner of the adjoining Kurpark – the park is the geographical point (*Geografischer Mittelpunkt*) on which the whole country would pivot. It is open Monday to Friday from 8 am to noon and 2 to 5 pm, except in July and August when hours are weekdays from 8 am to 7 pm, and weekends from 8 am to noon. Across the street is the post office (Postamt 8990), with a bus information counter.

Things to See & Do
Four km north of the town is **Altausseer See**, a small lake with the village of Altaussee on its west side. From the village there is access to the Altaussee salt mines, where art treasures were secreted during WW II. Tours (AS120) are conducted daily: at 10 am and 4 pm from 1 April to 31 October, and at 2 pm the rest of the year; call ☎ 03662-713 32 51 for information. A scenic road, the Panoramastrasse, climbs most of the way up Loser (1838 metres), the main

peak overlooking the lake. The toll for the return trip is AS43 for cars plus AS60 per person, and AS50 for motorbikes (accessible in winter with snow chains).

Five km east of Bad Aussee is the **Grundl-see**, a longer, thinner lake, with a good viewpoint at its western end, and walking trails and water sports (including a sailing school). Extending from the eastern tip of the lake are two smaller lakes, the Toplitzsee and Kammersee; boats tour all three from May to September (AS120 for the full tour). Call ☎ 03622-86 13 for information.

Bad Aussee itself has a couple of Gothic

churches, and a **Heimatmuseum**, covering local history and salt production, housed in the 17th-century Kammerhof on Chlumeckyplatz. Sauna, swimming pool and health treatments are at the Kurzentrum (☎ 532 030).

Festival
Ascension Day, usually around late May/early June, sees the start of the four-day Narzissenfest.

Places to Stay & Eat
At the east end of Grundlsee, in Gössl, are

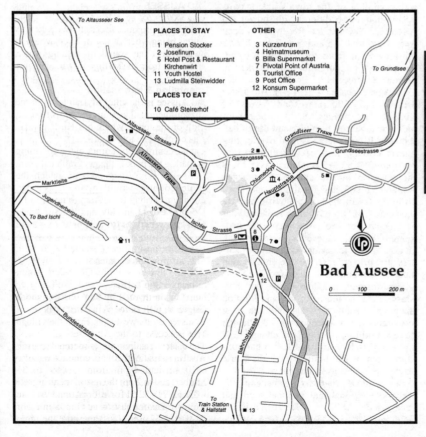

PLACES TO STAY
1 Pension Stocker
2 Josefinum
5 Hotel Post & Restaurant
    Kirchenwirt
11 Youth Hostel
13 Ludmilla Steinwidder

PLACES TO EAT
10 Café Steirerhof

OTHER
3 Kurzentrum
4 Heimatmuseum
6 Billa Supermarket
7 Pivotal Point of Austria
8 Tourist Office
9 Post Office
12 Konsum Supermarket

Bad Aussee

0   100   200 m

THE SALZKAMMERGUT

two camp sites: call ☎ 03622-81 81 or ☎ 03622-86 89. A HI *youth hostel* (☎ 03622-86 29) is nearby in Wienern, open May to October. Many homes around Altausseer See and Grundlsee offer cheap private rooms; these and pensions are listed in the Bad Aussee brochure.

The tourist office makes no charge for helping find accommodation. *Ludmilla Steinwidder* (☎ 55 1 24), Bahnhofstrasse 293, 600 metres towards the station from town, has private rooms for about AS180 per person.

The HI *youth hostel* (☎ 03622-52 2 38), Jugendherbergsstrasse 148, is a modern white building on the town's hill. It costs AS145 in a four-bed dorm with shower and AS160 also with toilet. Reception is open from 8 am to 1 pm and 5 to 7 pm. It's 15 minutes walk from the centre by road, though there's a shorter footpath (marked on the tourist office map).

Pension Stocker (☎ 52 4 84), Altausseer Strasse 245, 500 metres north-west of Kurhausplatz, charges AS200 per person for rooms with sturdy furniture and use of hall showers. It has a large garden overlooking tennis courts, and off-street parking. *Josefinum* (☎ 52 1 24), Gartengasse 13, is the bargain in the centre. It charges AS226/452 and has 13 singles and three doubles (twin beds), all with private shower/WC. It's run by nuns so be on your best behaviour (no smoking inside bedrooms). Telephone ahead for evening arrival. Other places in the centre with private facilities are pricey: refer to the information touch-screen outside the tourist office.

Supermarkets include *Konsum*, Bahnhofstrasse, near the tourist office, and *Billa* on Hauptplatz. Hauptplatz also has the most restaurants (often attached to hotels), though there's nothing particularly cheap. *Café Steirerhof*, Ischler Strasse 81, is a bar open from 7 pm. It has limited food; the house pizza (AS90) has lots of toppings. *Restaurant Kirchenwirt*, Kirchengasse 62, has good regional and national food and good prices (AS78 to AS175). It's in the Hotel Post (☎ 53 5 55; fax 53 6 66), which

has rooms for AS660/1160, with shower/WC and cable TV.

Getting There & Away
Bad Aussee is on the rail route from Bad Ischl to Stainach-Irdning, with trains running hourly. Regular buses go from the train station to both lakes (AS21), calling at Bad Aussee en route (AS17).

GOSAUSEE
This small lake is flanked by some impressively precipitous peaks, like the Gosaukamm (2459 metres). The view is good from the lake, and there's also a cable car that goes up to Zwieselalm from mid-May to mid-October (AS125, AS85 in the low season). Before reaching the lake, you pass through the village of **Gosau**, where there's a tourist office (☎ 06136-82 95). Gosau also has a HI *youth hostel* (☎ 06136-35 20), house No 168, open year-round.

Getting There & Away
Gosau is at the junction to the only road to the lake, and can be reached by highway 166 from Hallstätter See. Bundesbuses go to the lake from Bad Ischl, via Steeg on Hallstätter See, every one to two hours.

Northern Salzkammergut

The main lakes of interest are Traunsee – with the three resorts of Gmunden, Traunkirchen and Ebensee – and Wolfgangsee, home to the resorts of St Wolfgang and St Gilgen as well as the Schafberg peak.

TRAUNSEE
The eastern flank of this lake (the deepest in Austria at 192 metres) is dominated by rocky crags, particularly Traunstein at 1691 metres high. The resorts are strung along the western shore and are connected by rail. Boats operated by Traunsee Schiffahrt (☎ 07612-52 15) tour the shoreline, from

Gmunden to Ebensee, regularly between mid-May and late September, and infrequently a month either side. The full one-way trip costs AS65 (children AS45) or AS150 (AS90) for a day pass. The famous paddle-steamer *Gisela* (once boarded by Franz Joseph) takes to the waves in July and August on holidays, Thursdays and weekends (a surcharge applies).

Gmunden
• *pop 12,700* • *440 m* • *☎ (07612)*

Gmunden is known for its castles and ceramics. It was established in 909 and received a town charter in 1278. Gmunden was a former administration centre both for the Habsburgs and the salt trade.

Orientation & Information The town centre is on the west bank of the Traun River, and has the Rathausplatz at its heart. Close by is the tourist office (☎ 43 05), Am Graben 2, open Monday to Friday from 8 am to 6 pm, and Saturday (and Sunday in July and August) from 10 am to 6 pm. Hours from mid-September to mid-May are Monday to Friday from 8 am to noon and 2 to 6 pm. The

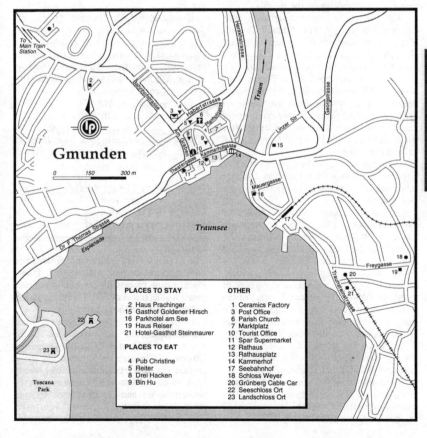

Gmunden

0   150   300 m

Traun

Traunsee

Toscana Park

PLACES TO STAY
2 Haus Prachinger
15 Gasthof Goldener Hirsch
16 Parkhotel am See
19 Haus Reiser
21 Hotel-Gasthof Steinmaurer

PLACES TO EAT
4 Pub Christine
5 Reiter
8 Drei Hacken
9 Bin Hu

OTHER
1 Ceramics Factory
3 Post Office
6 Parish Church
7 Marktplatz
10 Tourist Office
11 Spar Supermarket
12 Rathaus
13 Rathausplatz
14 Kammerhof
17 Seebahnhof
18 Schloss Weyer
20 Grünberg Cable Car
22 Seeschloss Ort
23 Landschloss Ort

office will find rooms without charging. The post office (Postamt 4810) is 200 metres up the hill on Bahnhofstrasse.

Things to See & Do Start explorations in the **Rathausplatz**, which has the Rathaus, complete with a ceramic Glockenspiel that chimes tunes at 10 am, noon, 2, 4 and 7 pm. More ceramics can be seen in the nearby **Kammerhof**, open Tuesday to Saturday from 10 am to noon and 2 to 5 pm, and Sunday and holidays from 10 am to noon (AS15, children free). As well as antique Gmunden ceramics, it covers local history and has an art gallery on the top floor.

Walks along the Esplanade are enjoyable. Head south for 1½ km to reach Toscana Park, a protected nature area on a peninsula. A castle is here (Landschloss Ort; now a forestry school), which is connected by a causeway to another castle, **Seeschloss Ort**. This 17th-century castle, jutting into the lake, is clearly visible from the Esplanade and forms a fine picture. Close up, the need for renovation is evident, though it does have an attractive arcaded courtyard and a small chapel (free entry).

In the town centre is the **parish church**, a Gothic building remodelled as Baroque and noted for an altar (1678) by Thomas Schwanthaler.

Off Bahnhofstrasse, midway between the Hauptbahnhof and the centre, is a **ceramics factory** (☎ 54 41), Keramikstrasse 24, which has free guided tours in July and August on Tuesday and Thursday at 9.30 am. More porcelain, and other valuable artefacts, can be seen in the elegant environment of **Schloss Weyer**, Freygasse 27, east of the Traun. Entry costs AS45 and it's open Tuesday to Saturday from 10 am to noon and 2 to 6 pm, and Saturday from 10 am to 1 pm.

The town has schools for sailing, water-skiing and windsurfing, and a beach (AS40 per day) just south of Toscana Park.

Gmunden provides access to the **Grünberg** lookout, at 984 metres high. A cable car ascends from the east side of the lake (AS110 return), or it's easy to walk up.

Places to Stay Private rooms are the best deal for budget travellers. *Haus Prachinger*, (☎ 55 7 43), Kaltenbrunerstrasse 36, is along the tram route from the station, and has eight beds for AS145; it costs AS25 to use the hall shower. *Haus Reiser* (☎ 72 4 25), Freygasse 20, is near Schloss Weyer, and has five doubles and one triple room; prices are AS190 per person, or AS240 with private shower.

Gasthof Goldener Hirsch (☎ 43 86), Linzer Strasse 4, is conveniently central, near the eastern bank of the Traun. Rooms with shower/WC and telephone start at AS310 per person, and the restaurant has a garden.

Hotel-Gasthof Steinmaurer (☎ 42 39), Traunsteinstrasse 23, is near the sailing school and the base of the Grünberg cable car. Rooms have shower/WC, telephone and balcony, and cost from AS400 to AS600 per person. The hotel has a private beach and the restaurant has outside seating.

Parkhotel am See (☎ 42 30; fax 42 30 66), Schiffslände 17, is by the eastern bank of the Traun. It's a four-star place with rooms from AS640 to AS940 per person; hotel facilities include a garage, restaurant and private beach.

Places to Eat There's a large *Spar* supermarket at Franz Josef Platz; it's open Monday to Thursday from 8 am to 6 pm, Friday from 7 am to 7.30 pm, and Saturday from 7.30 am to 1 pm (5 pm on Langersamstag).

For snacks, there are a couple of stands on the Esplanade, or there's *Reiter* on Rinnholz Platz, a meat store with cheap hot and cold meals and a couple of tables; eat lunch early or late as it closes from 1 to 3 pm.

Pub Christine, Tagwerker Strasse 1, is a small, simple place with Austrian food on the lunch menu for just AS58 (closed Sunday). Otherwise, the cheapest lunch deals are at several Chinese restaurants in the centre, such as *Bin Hu* on Kirchengasse, with 19 two-course weekday lunches from AS55 to AS75 (open daily).

Drei Hacken, Am Graben 10, has a nice

shady garden and palatable food. The menu is standard Austrian fare (including daily specials with soup) from AS70 to AS160, and wines by the Pfiff. It's open daily.

Getting There & Away Three rail lines converge on Gmunden. Two loop down from Lambach on the Linz-Salzburg route, and terminate at Gmunden Seebahnhof, the closest station to the town centre. But Lambach is bypassed by express trains, and one of these lines is for goods trains only, and the other is a private line requiring a change at Vorchdorf-Eggenberg. This means that Gmunden Hauptbahnhof, on the Salzkammergut Attnang-Puchheim to Stainach-Irdning line, is the easiest to get to.

Getting Around The Hauptbahnhof (which rents bikes) is two km north-west of the town centre: a tram goes from outside it to Franz Josef Platz, every 15 minutes from 5.30 am to 8.45 pm. Single tickets cost AS14, but get a day card (*Tagesnetzkarte*) for AS20, which is also valid for the two local bus lines. A family day card costs AS30.

Traunkirchen
• *pop 1500* • ☎ *(07617)*
Traunkirchen is an attractive hamlet on a spit of land about halfway along the western shore of the Traunsee.

Orientation & Information The small but helpful tourist office in the town centre, the Tourismusbüro (☎ 234), is part of the Gemeindeamt building. Staff can provide accommodation listings, sights information in English, and a useful hiking map (free) with English text. The office is open from June to September, Monday to Friday from 8 am to noon and 2 to 5 pm, and Saturday from 8 am to noon, and the rest of the year on weekday mornings only.

Things to See & Do The main point of interest in the village is the **Fisherman's Pulpit** (Fischerkanzel) in the parish church. It was carved from wood in 1753 and depicts the miracle of the fishes, with the apostles

standing in a tub-shaped boat and hauling in fish-laden nets. The composition, colours (mostly silver and gold) and detail (even down to wriggling, bug-eyed fish) create a vivid impression. The church has some good Baroque altars, and portraits of the apostles (Judas is notable for his absence). The church was built by the Jesuits before their suppression in 1773.

The spire on the hill belongs to the **Johannesberg Chapel** which was built in the 14th century or earlier. On the south side of the hill (the opposite side to the parish church) is a war memorial.

Festival **processions** take place on 5 January and Corpus Christi.

Places to Stay & Eat Ask the tourist office to help find accommodation (no commission). There is a *camping ground* (☎ 22 81) by the lake at Viechtau, north of the resort; it's open from May to September.

Haus Reithner (☎ 24 45) is midway between the train station and the tourist office, and has a garden and balconies. Per-person prices are AS175 with hall shower or AS205 with private shower. *Seepension Hüthmayr* (☎ 23 53) is also central and right by the lake. Prices are AS215, or AS240 with shower.

On the main street, 100 metres from the tourist office, is *Goldener Hirsch* (☎ 22 60), an inn offering rooms with shower and WC for AS310 per person. The restaurant has good Austrian food, including fish specialities, for around AS70 to AS120 (closed Thursday).

Even closer to the tourist office is a *Konsum* supermarket, open Monday to Friday from 7.30 am to noon and 3 to 6 pm, and Saturday from 7.30 am to noon.

Getting There & Away Traunkirchen is on the north-south train line, 12 km from Gmunden (AS34) and five km from Ebensee (AS17). To reach the centre from the unstaffed train station, Traunkirchen Ort (it's closer than the Traunkirchen station), take the path that passes under the tracks (a five-minute walk).

Ebensee

- *pop 9000* • ☎ *(06133)*

This town is on the southern shore of the Traunsee.

Orientation & Information Ebensee is mostly on the east bank of the Traun, though the town centre is on the west bank. This is where you'll find the tourist office (☎ 80 16), at Hauptstrasse 34 by the Landungsplatz train station. Opening hours are Monday to Friday from 8 am to noon and 2 to 5 pm, extending to 7 pm in July and August, including Saturday.

Things to See & Do There is little to see in the town. Instead, take the cable car that climbs up to **Feuerkogel** (1585 metres), with walking trails across a flattish plateau. Within an hour's walk is Alberfeldkogel (1708 metres) with an excellent view over the two Langbath lakes. The cable car leaves hourly and costs AS135 up, AS95 down, or AS185 return. Feuerkogel also provides access to winter **skiing** (medium to easy slopes).

The tourist office will give you details of the many **water sports** on offer, such as fishing, scuba diving, windsurfing and sailing.

Places to Stay & Eat Ask for the local guest card if you stay in the resort. Around a dozen homes offer private rooms for about AS150 per person; these are listed in the tourist office's accommodation brochure.

The HI *youth hostel* (☎ 66 98), Rindbach-strasse 15, is 15 minutes walk anticlockwise round the lake. Newly renovated dorms with own shower/WC cost AS110 to AS135 per person.

Gasthof Himmel (☎ 54 63), Berggasse 27, and *Gasthof Kofler* (☎ 53 42), Berggasse 1, each charge AS220 per person and both have a restaurant. So does *Gasthof Rosenstüberl* (☎ 52 76), Berggasse 21; rooms cost from AS290 per person and have a private shower, WC and TV. Berggasse is near the tourist office: head south-west on Hauptstrasse,

then take the first street on the right, the first left, and the first right again.

Midway between the two train stations, on Bahnhofstrasse, are two supermarkets, a *Billa* and *Konsum*, and *China-Restaurant Jasmin*, which has cheap weekday midday menus (open daily).

Getting There & Away The train station for the centre and the landing stage is Ebensee-Landungsplatz. The larger Ebensee station is less than 15 minutes walk to the south. The town is 17 km north of Bad Ischl (AS34) and the same distance south of Gmunden.

ATTERSEE

The largest lake in the Salzkammergut is flanked by hills, with mountains in the south. Resorts cling to the shoreline, offering the usual water leisure activities. The main resort is **Attersee**, which has a museum and a couple of churches. Its tourist office (☎ 07666-77 19) is at Nussdorferstrasse 15.

From early July to early September, there are two boat circuits of the lake: a 75-minute tour (AS65) from Attersee town explores the north, and a 2½-hour tour (AS110) commences from **Weyregg** and heads south.

Weyregg has a HI *youth hostel* (☎ 07664-27 80), Weyregg 3, open from 1 April to 30 October.

Getting There & Away

Two lakeside towns are connected to the rail network, each by a line branching from the main Linz-Salzburg route (though only regional trains stop): for Kammer-Schörfling change at Vöcklabruck and for Attersee town change at Vöcklamarkt.

WOLFGANGSEE

This lake is easily accessible from Salzburg, and receives hordes of summer and weekend visitors escaping the city. In addition to the two main resorts, St Wolfgang and St Gilgen, it has **Strobl** on the eastern shore (population 2750), a pleasant but unremarkable place. It's at the start of a scenic toll road (AS30) to Postalm (1400 metres). Wherever you stay, ask about the local guest card.

An hourly ferry service operates from Strobl to St Gilgen between May and early October, stopping at various points en route. Services are more frequent during the high season from mid-June to mid-September; some boats may also operate in April and October. The St Wolfgang to St Gilgen leg takes 40 minutes (AS48) and boats sail from about 8 am to 6 pm (7.30 pm in the high season). Schedules are about an hour later in the opposite direction. These boats, like the cogwheel railway up Schafberg, are run by the federal railway, and rail card validity is the same for both: holders of Eurail or Bundes-Netzkarte passes ride free, and an Inter-Rail pass secures a 50% reduction.

St Wolfgang
• *pop 2500* • *549 m* • ☎ *(06138)*
St Wolfgang was founded in 976 by the Bishop of Regensburg, Germany (who was later canonised) and has achieved renown as a place of pilgrimage.

Orientation & Information The main streets are Pilgerstrasse and Michael Pacher Strasse, which join by the pilgrimage church. The tourist office (☎ 22 390), Pilgerstrasse 28, is between the church and the post office (where Bundesbuses stop). It's open Monday to Friday from 8 am to noon and 2 to 5 pm and, in July and August, Monday to Saturday from 8 am to 6 pm.

Things to See & Do The major sight is the **pilgrimage church**, built in the 14th and 15th centuries. This incredible church is virtually a gallery of religious art, with altars (Gothic to Baroque), a showy pulpit, fine organ and many statues and paintings. The best piece is the winged high altar made by Michael Pacher between 1471 and 1481, which has astonishing detail on the carved figures and Gothic designs. The church wardens were once so protective that the wings were kept closed except for important festivals. Now they are always open, except for eight weeks before Easter.

The double altar by Thomas Schwanthaler is also excellent. This Baroque creation was commissioned in 1675, reputedly to replace Pacher's effort which was by then considered 'old fashioned' and slated for destruction. According to this apocryphal story, it was Schwanthaler himself who persuaded the then abbot to retain Pacher's high altar as well. The church is open daily from 7.30 am to 6 pm.

Beside the church is a bronze **fountain** from 1515. A lengthy inscription includes rather condescending advice to poor pilgrims: if they can't afford wine, they should 'make merry' with the fountain's waters.

A tourist office booklet (free) details the many **water sports** on offer. A few minutes walk anticlockwise round the lake is the start of the Schafberg railway.

Places to Stay *Camping Appesbach* (☎ 22 06), Au 99, is on the lakeside, one km from St Wolfgang in the direction of Strobl. It's open from Easter to 30 September and costs AS60 per person (plus tax), from AS50 for a tent and AS30 for a car.

St Wolfgang has some good *private rooms*

THE SALZKAMMERGUT

Pacher's Religious Art
Michael Pacher was the dominant figure in Austrian religious art in the 15th century. He was born in Bruneck (South Tirol, now in Italy) in 1435 and died in Salzburg in 1498. His work was rooted in traditional Bruneck art, but he also absorbed Dutch and, in particular, northern Italian influences. Pacher was a master of perspective and colouring and gave an impression of fluidity and movement to his statue groups. This is seen in his altar in the pilgrimage church at St Wolfgang. In creating this altar, as in several others, Pacher was aided by his brother Friedrich.

Pacher's style was much imitated, eg in the impressive altar in Kefermarkt. His paintings and carvings are found in many museums, such as the Landesmuseum Ferdinandeum in Innsbruck (where Friedrich Pacher's work is also featured) and the Orangery of the Lower Belvedere in Vienna. ■

(from AS140 per person), either in village homes or in farmhouses on the surrounding hills. Lists are available from the tourist office, which will phone places on your behalf.

Gästehaus Raudaschl (☎ 25 61), Pilgerstrasse 4, opposite the tourist office, has singles/doubles from AS270/480 with private shower/WC, plus some doubles using hall shower for AS380.

Gasthof Rudolfshöhe (☎ 23 48), Aschau Strasse 36, is five minutes walk from the centre, to the north-east, up the small hill near the tunnel. It has a sunny restaurant terrace and ample parking. Rooms have shower/WC and TV and cost from AS190 to AS250 per person (with or without private shower). This place is sometimes invaded by British tour groups.

St Wolfgang's most famous hotel is the *Weissen Rössl* (☎ 23 06), Im Stöckl 74, which, as the White Horse Inn, was the setting for Ralph Benatzky's operetta of the same name. Rustic-style rooms have modern amenities, and start from AS950/1400. Service is good, and the restaurant is also highly regarded.

Places to Eat Buy picnic materials at the *Konsum* supermarket 100 metres from the Schafberg cogwheel railway ticket office, towards the village centre. There are smaller supermarkets in the centre.

The main street has plenty of options, ranging from cheap snack joints to quaint touristy restaurants. The centre is compact enough to explore before making a choice. *Pizzeria Mirabella*, Pilgerstrasse 152, has 1st-floor tables overlooking the street; pizzas cost from AS73 and are served from 11.30 am to 3 pm and 6.30 to 9.30 pm. *Schnitzelwirt*, Marktplatz, specialises in schnitzel variations (open 11 am to 11 pm).

Gasthof Rudolfshöhe (see Places to Stay) has an excellent menu offering Hungarian, Austrian, Indian and vegetarian food from AS65. In the summer, it has a barbecue on Monday (with folk music) and goulash on Friday evenings.

Getting There & Away The only road to St Wolfgang approaches from the east. The Bundesbus service from St Wolfgang to St Gilgen (AS42) and Salzburg (AS88) goes via Strobl, where you must change buses. Wolfgangsee ferries stop at the village centre (the Markt) and at the Schafberg railway.

Schafberg

Wolfgangsee is dominated by this 1783-metre mountain on the northern shore. The summit has a hotel, restaurant and phenomenal views over mountains and lakes (especially Mondsee, Attersee and, of course, Wolfgangsee). If you don't fancy the three to four-hour hike from St Wolfgang, ascend by the cogwheel railway which runs from May to early October. Departures are approximately every 1½ hours during the day, but the trip is so popular that you probably won't be able to get on the next departure: queue early, get your ticket for a specified train, and then go for a wander along the lake or in St Wolfgang.

The train trip takes 40 minutes to reach the top station, which is only a few metres short of the hotel and viewing point. The fare is AS140 up, AS120 down, or AS250 return. Combined tickets with the boat are available.

St Gilgen
• *pop 3000* • ☎ *(06227)*

St Gilgen is only 29 km from Salzburg, and this ease of access has greatly helped its popularity. Apart from the scenic setting, there is little to see in the town. Near the Rathaus is the house where Mozart's mother was born, and it now contains a few memorials to the musician.

The local tourist office (☎ 348), Mozartplatz 1, is in the Rathaus, open daily in July and August, weekdays and Saturday morning the rest of summer, and only Monday to Friday the rest of the year.

Like all lakeside resorts, St Gilgen offers water sports, such as windsurfing, waterskiing and sailing. The Strandbad, just to the north of the landing stage, is a beach with an admission fee. A little farther, beyond the yacht club, is a small beach with a grassy area (free).

The mountain rising over the resort is **Zwölferhorn** (1520 metres); a cable car will whisk you to the top (AS120, or AS180 return) where there are good views and hikes. Skiers ascend in winter; for information on the ski school, contact Pepi Resch (☎ 275), Liam 136, St Gilgen.

Places to Stay & Eat St Gilgen has a good HI *youth hostel* (☎ 365) at Mondseestrasse 7. It's almost like a hotel in its facilities and attitude, though it does receive the usual school groups. Prices are from AS100 to AS250 per person (plus resort tax), in anything from singles to 10-bed dorms, with or without WC and lake view (but always with shower). Reception hours are 8 to 9 am and 5 to 7 pm, but the doors are open during the day. Ask for a key to avoid the 11 pm curfew.

The tourist office will help find somewhere to stay, or there's an accommodation board, available 24-hours daily, opposite the bus station. The cheaper places (private rooms etc) are mostly away from the centre, though *Kendlerhof* (☎ 72 54), Streicherplatz 6, is just off the pivotal Mozartplatz, and has good breakfasts and solicitous hosts. Singles/doubles are AS300/540, or AS360/640 with shower (reductions in the low season, supplements for short stays). It's open from 1 May to 31 October.

Gasthof Rosam (☎ 591), Frontfestgasse 2, two minutes from the St Gilgen boat station, charges AS320/520 for rooms with shower and WC. There are large portions of good Austrian food for AS70 to AS130 in the small restaurant area (kitchen to 9 pm). It's open from Easter to 31 October.

Pizzeria Bianco, Ischler Strasse 18, by the lake, has pizza (from AS60) and pasta (from AS55), plus a salad buffet (closed on Monday in winter). *China-Restaurant Hong Kong*, Schwarzenbrunner Strasse, just off Mozartplatz, has weekday lunch menus from AS55. *Gasthof Zur Post* (☎ 75 09), Mozartplatz 8, is recommended for slightly pricier regional food (about AS85 to AS190) in a rustic-style restaurant. Rooms cost AS450 per person (with shower/WC and cable TV).

Getting There & Away St Gilgen is 50 minutes from Salzburg by Bundesbus (AS60), with hourly departures until 7.05 pm. The bus station is near the base station of the cable car. Highway 154 provides a scenic route north to Mondsee.

MONDSEE
• *pop 2000* • *493 m* • ☎ *(06232)*

The Mondsee is noted for its warm water; this factor, coupled with its closeness to Salzburg (30 km away), makes it a popular lake for swimming and other water sports. The village of Mondsee is on the northern tip of the crescent-shaped lake. The tourist office (☎ 22 70) is at Dr Franz Müller Strasse 3, between the church and the lake. It's open daily in summer, and weekdays only the rest of the year.

Segelschule Mondsee (☎ 21 75), Robert Baum Promenade 3, is the largest sailing school in Austria. It offers sailing and windsurfing courses, and boat/board rental (from A100/80 per hour).

The main cultural interest in the village is the 15th-century **parish church**. The Baroque façade was added in 1740. This large church achieved brief fame when featured in the wedding scenes of *The Sound of Music* movie, but it's worth visiting in any case for its many altars and statues.

Next door, within rooms of the former abbey, is a **museum** devoted to local history and crafts, including archaeological finds from the so-called 'Mondsee Culture' in the late Stone Age to early Bronze Age (AS25; students AS12). It's open daily from 1 May to mid-October, and weekends and holidays to the end of October.

Places to Stay & Eat
For lists of hotels and restaurants, go to the tourist office. Mondsee has a HI *youth hostel* (☎ 24 18), Krankenhausstrasse 9, open year-round. *Gasthof Grüner Baum* (☎ 23 14), Herzog Odilo Strasse 39, has large doubles with own shower/WC for AS600. There's no

check-in when the restaurant is closed from 2 to 5 pm and on Tuesday.

Imbiss Café, M Guggenbichler Strasse 5, with a stand-up buffet section, is between the bus station and the church. It has sausage snacks and Austrian meals for AS25 to AS130 (closed Sunday). On Marktplatz are several pricier places with good atmosphere and food. Try *Gasthof Blaue Traube* (☎ 22 37), which also has rooms (AS410 per person).

Getting There & Away
Plenty of Bundesbuses run to/from Mondsee, including an hourly service from Salzburg (AS52) that takes 40 to 55 minutes.

Upper Austria

Upper Austria (Oberösterreich) occupies almost 12,000 sq km and is home to more than 1.3 million people. The province's most important holiday area is the lakes and mountains of the south (see the Salzkammergut chapter). Elsewhere, Upper Austria offers abbeys, quaint and attractive towns in the north and east, and a not-so-attractive reminder of Nazi occupation, the Mauthausen concentration camp. Adolf Hitler was born in the province, in Braunau. His favourite city was Linz, for which he had great (unrealised) plans, including making it the architectural jewel of the Danube. Here he wanted to retire to, had he not been forced to retire sooner than planned in a Berlin bunker.

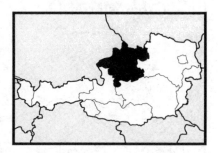

Orientation & Information

Upper Austria is a mostly flat province, with the mighty Danube River slicing through the region from west to east. The river is an important trade artery, but this section is less scenic than the stretch farther east in Lower Austria.

The provincial capital and industrial heartland is Linz, which is also the location of the provincial tourist board, the Landesverband für Tourismus in Oberösterreich (☎ 0732-60 02 21 0; fax 60 02 20), Schillerstrasse 50, A-4010 Linz.

Linz

• *pop 203,000* • *266 m* • *☎ (0732)*

Linz is an industrial town and a busy Danube port; important industries are iron, steel and chemicals. The southern suburbs show a depressing skyline of belching smokestacks, but past these you'll find a surprisingly charming and picturesque old town centre.

In Roman times Linz was a fortified camp called Lentia, and soon achieved importance for its position on trade routes. Linz was

granted the status of regional capital in 1490 by Friedrich III, who was then a resident of the town.

Orientation

Linz lies on both sides of the Danube, with the old town and sights on the south bank. Hauptplatz, a spacious square, is the hub. It is mostly car free, and abuts Landstrasse, a shopping street with a pedestrian-only section. The train station is about one km to the south and has good facilities (and probably the most expensive lavatories in the country – AS6.50 a go!).

Information

Tourist Offices The tourist office (☎ 2393 1777), Hauptplatz 5, is open Monday to Friday from 7 am to 7 pm, and weekends from 8 to 11.30 am and 12.30 to 7 pm. From 1 November to 30 April it opens an hour later and closes an hour earlier. Staff will search out accommodation without charging a fee.

Another information office, in the Sparda Bank in the train station, opens Monday to Friday from 8 am to 7 pm, Saturday from 8 am to noon and 3 to 5 pm, and Sunday from 8 am to noon.

Personal callers are welcomed at the provincial tourist office (see the chapter introduction), which is open Monday to

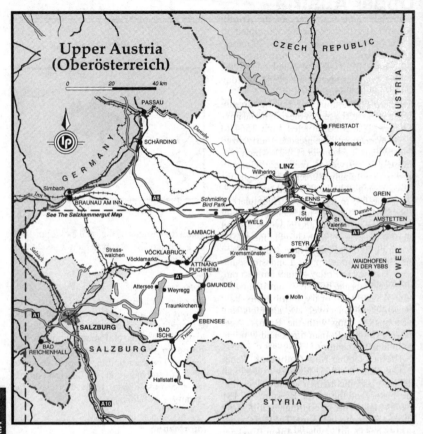

Upper Austria (Oberösterreich)

CZECH REPUBLIC

AUSTRIA

GERMANY

PASSAU

SCHÄRDING

Danube

FREISTADT

Kefermarkt

LINZ

Wilhering

Simbach

Inn

BRAUNAU AM INN

See The Salzkammergut Map

A8

Schmiding
Bird Park

Mauthausen

ENNS

GREIN

Danube

AMSTETTEN

A25

St
Florian

St
Valentin

A1

WELS

LAMBACH

Kremsmünster

STEYR

Sierning

LOWER

WAIDHOFEN
AN DER YBBS

Strass-
walchen

VÖCKLABRUCK

Vöcklamarkt

ATTNANG-
PUCHHEIM

A1

Attersee

Weyregg

GMUNDEN

Traunkirchen

Molln

A1

Salzach

SALZBURG

Traun

EBENSEE

BAD
ISCHL

BAD
REICHENHALL

SALZBURG

Hallstatt

A10

STYRIA

Thursday from 8 am to noon and 1 to 4.30 pm, and Friday from 8 am to noon.

Post & Telecommunications The main post office (Postamt 4020), opposite the train station and to the left, is open 24 hours a day. Another post office (Postamt 4010) is in Domgasse.

Travel Agencies American Express (☎ 66 90 13) is at Bürgerstrasse 14, and opens Monday to Friday from 9 am to 5.30 pm and Saturday from 9 am to noon. It has full financial and travel agency services, and charges no commission on any travellers' cheques (even non-Amex).

ÖKISTA (☎ 77 58 93) is at Herrenstrasse 7: it's open Monday to Friday from 9.30 am to 5.30 pm.

South Bank

Follow the walking tour of the town centre outlined in the tourist office's pamphlet (in English).

The large **Hauptplatz** is surrounded by Baroque buildings, including the old Rathaus, which retains some earlier Renaissance elements. A focus is the **Trinity column** (Dreifaltigkeitssäule) sculpted in Salzburg marble in 1723. This 20-metre-high Baroque pillar commemorates deliverance from war, fire and plague. A flea market occupies Hauptplatz every Saturday from 7 am to 2 pm.

Just off Hauptplatz is the **Landhaus**, Klosterstrasse, the seat of the provincial government. It was constructed from 1564 to 1571. Wander into the arcaded courtyard to see the *Planet Fountain* (1582), which predated the arrival of the great German astronomer Johann Kepler, who taught for 14 years in a college once sited here.

Up the hill to the west of Hauptplatz is **Linz Castle**. The castle has been periodically rebuilt since 799 AD and provides a good view of the many church spires in the centre. Friedrich III once resided here. It also houses the **Schlossmuseum**, or Landesmuseum, open Tuesday to Friday from 9 am to 5 pm, and weekends and holidays from 10 am to 4 pm (AS25; temporary exhibitions cost extra). Displays cover art, artefacts and weapons, starting with the Bronze Age, passing through Roman times, and winding up in the 19th century.

The neo-Gothic **New Cathedral** (Neuer Dom), built in 1855, features exceptional stained glass, including a window depicting the history of the town. Its spire, at 131 metres high, is the second-highest in Austria after St Stephen's in Vienna. The **Old Cathedral** (Alter Dom) is where Anton Bruckner had a 12-year stint as church organist. The church is 17th-century Baroque, with the usual stucco and marble décor.

Other churches described in the tourist office's walking tour include the **Minorite Church** that features paintings on the side altars by Johann Schmidt of Krems, and the **parish church**, with a tomb containing the heart of Friedrich III.

Linz has its share of greenery. **Danube Park** trails alongside the river and boasts unusual metal sculptures, and the **botanical garden** (Botanischer Garten) flaunts a plethora of cacti and orchids (AS10 entry; kids free).

North Bank

Clearly visible on the north bank is the **Pöstlingberg** (537 metres), providing fine views. At the summit is a twin-spired Baroque church dating from the 18th century. The walk up is gentle, or you can take the Pöstlingbergbahn that runs every 20 minutes till 8 pm. It costs AS40 return (or AS48 including a ride on tram No 3 to the lower station – get these tickets from the tourist office). At the top is a grotto railway (AS40; children AS20), that meanders past scenes from fairy stories. It runs from the Saturday before Palm Sunday to 2 November.

The **Neue Galerie** at Blütenstrasse 15 exhibits German and Austrian art from the 19th and 20th centuries, with the likes of Klimt and Schiele well represented. Entry costs from AS30, depending on the exhibition. It's open daily from 10 am to 6 pm (10 pm on Thursday), except from June to September when it's closed from 1 pm Saturday and all day Sunday.

Festivals

The famous Brucknerfest is held during September, for which tickets are AS220 to AS900, or AS40 to AS50 for standing room. It is held primarily at the city's premier music venue, Bruckner Haus (☎ 77 52 30), Untere Donaulände 7, Postfach 57, A-4010. The Brucknerfest kicks off with Klangwolken Weekend in Danube Park, where concerts are transmitted live (and free) to Hauptplatz, and lasers sear the night sky.

Other festivals are Ars Electronica (technology festival with avant-garde music) in late June, and a Linz city festival late May.

Places to Stay

Camping Linz *camp site* (☎ 30 53 14) is out of town to the south-east, at Wiener Strasse 937, Pichlinger See. It's open all year and has a restaurant.

Hostels There are three HI hostels in Linz. The *Jugendgästehaus* (☎ 66 44 34), Stanglhofweg 3, is about one km west of the train station, near Linz Stadium. Its two-bed

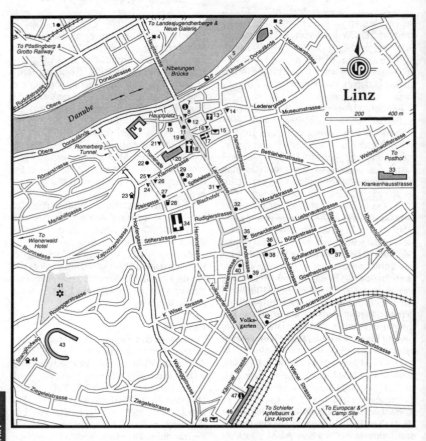

rooms are AS195 per person, and four-bed rooms are AS145.

The *youth hostel* (☎ 78 27 20), Kapuziner-strasse 14, is nearer the centre. It has beds, without breakfast, for AS90 to AS130, depending on whether you're aged over 19 and/or need sheets. This small hostel (36 beds) has a kitchen and laundry, and no curfew. It's like being invited into the owner's home: you can use the TV and stereo, but phone ahead if you're planning to arrive after 6 pm, as he likes to go out every now and then.

The *Landesjugendherberge* (☎ 23 70 78) at Blütenstrasse 23, on the north bank, has beds from AS115, without breakfast.

You should be able to check in at these hostels during the day, except at Kapuziner-strasse on weekends, when you'll have to wait until 5 pm.

Budget Hotels & Pensions There aren't many budget places in town. The cheapest hotel (singles/doubles for AS220/410 using hall shower; no breakfast) is *Schiefer Apfel-baum* (☎ 65 31 73), at Hanuschstrasse 26. It's inconveniently south of the train station,

PLACES TO STAY		26	El Mexicano	22	Landestheater
		31	Klosterhof	27	Spar Supermarket
2	Trend Hotel Linz	35	Stadtwirt	28	Café Ex-Blatt
4	Landgraf Suites			29	ÖKISTA
10	Goldener Anker	**OTHER**		32	Billa Supermarket
19	Wolfinger			33	Krankenhaus
23	Youth Hostel	1	Pöstlingbergbahn	34	New Cathedral
30	Schwarzen Bären	3	Bruckner Haus	36	Hertz
44	Jugendgästehaus	5	Danube Park	37	Provincial Tourist Office
		6	DDSG Station	38	American Express
PLACES TO EAT		7	Tourist Office	39	Avis
		9	Linz Castle	40	Casino
8	Mangolds	11	Trinity Column	41	Botanical Garden
14	Goldenes Kreuz	12	Rathaus	42	Mondo Supermarket
16	Wachauer Weinstube	13	Parish Church	43	Linz Stadium
21	Kremsmüsterer Stuben	15	Post Office	45	Post Office
24	Linzer Stuben	17	Old Cathedral	46	Main Train Station
25	Nihonya	18	Minorite Church	47	Tourist Office
		20	Landhaus		

though bus No 14 or 15 from there will get you close.

Wienerwald (☎ 77 78 81), Freinbergstrasse 18, is next to the western terminus of bus No 26, 1.5 km from the town centre. It has a restaurant (serving the usual chicken dishes) and ample parking. The rooms are reasonably-sized and good value for the price: AS270/470 using hall shower or AS330/550 with private shower. Credit cards are accepted.

Middle & Top End Hotels *Goldener Anker* (☎ 77 10 88) at Hofgasse 5, off Hauptplatz, has singles/doubles for AS315/590, or AS445/780 with private shower. It's not bad value considering its central location, though the surrounding bars can be a little noisy. Breakfast, if required, costs AS80 per person.

Schwarzen Bären (☎ 77 24 77), Herrenstrasse 9-11, provides comfortable if unremarkable accommodation in a convenient location. Prices start at AS480/720, or AS680/880 with private shower. Garage parking costs AS50 per night.

Wolfinger (☎ 77 32 91; fax 77 32 91 55), Hauptplatz 19, is a stylish place in the pedestrian zone. The historic ambience is accentuated by archways, stuccowork and period furniture. Rooms with shower/WC and TV start at AS820/1200.

Landgraf Suites (☎ 23 64 41 0; fax 23 08 41), Hauptstrasse 12, on the north bank, is a newly renovated four-star hotel with a neo-Gothic façade. All rooms are suites and include a kitchenette; prices start at AS950/1500.

Trend Hotel Linz (☎ 76 26 0; fax 76 26 2), Untere Donaulände 9, by the Bruckner Haus, has an office-block appearance. Facilities include an indoor swimming pool. Rooms cost AS1190/1490 and have good views.

Places to Eat
Linz is the home of a tempting cake, the Linzer Torte. Supermarkets include the *Spar* at Steingasse, the *Mondo* at Blumauerplatz, and *Billa* on Landstrasse. There are plenty of cheap Würstel stands lining the Volksgarten on Landstrasse.

The train station has several places to eat, such as the *Bierstube*, with light meals from AS60. Outside and to the right is a stall selling drinks, alcohol, fruit and groceries (open daily from 8 am to 10 pm).

Mangolds, Hauptplatz 3, is a vegetarian restaurant open from 10 am to 8 pm (4 pm on Saturday; closed Sunday). Self-service meals start from just AS40 and the salad buffet is AS14 per 100 grams.

UPPER AUSTRIA

Goldenes Kreuz, Pfarrplatz 11, is behind the parish church. It provides Austrian food at good prices (from AS60), plus fish, spaghetti and grilled dishes. It's closed Saturday and Sunday.

Wachauer Weinstube, Pfarrgasse 20, is a wine tavern with a fairly limited choice of food (from AS65). Watch the locals playing cards in the evening. It's open 10 am to midnight (closed Sunday and holidays).

On the corner of Waltherstrasse and Klammstrasse is a cluster of good restaurants, including a Chinese place. *El Mexicano*, also known as *Don Camillo*, Klammstrasse 3, serves Mexican and Italian food (large pizzas, generous toppings) from around AS80. It's open daily, but not for lunch on weekends, Friday and holidays. *Nihonya*, Klammstrasse 12, has pricey Japanese dishes (AS130 to AS200). But when *isn't* Japanese food pricey? When you go there for lunch! The weekday menu starts at AS78.

Linzer Stuben (☎ 77 90 28), Klammstrasse 7, has mid-price (AS165 to AS215) Austrian cuisine in a comfortable environment. This place is a real bargain at weekday lunchtime, when there's a daily special for just AS59. Opening hours are Monday to Saturday from 11 am to 2.30 pm and 5 pm to midnight.

Klosterhof, on the corner of Bischofstrasse and Landstrasse, is a large and popular eatery in a 17th-century building, where each dining room has a different ambience. It's open daily from 8 am to midnight, and has lunch from AS75 and evening dishes between AS90 and AS180.

Stadtwirt (☎ 78 51 22), on the corner of Bismarckstrasse and Landstrasse, has good-quality Austrian fare from AS90 and all the frills (ruffled napkins, candlesticks etc) and a shady garden. It's closed on Saturday evening and Sunday.

The expensive choice for gourmets is *Kremsmünsterer Stuben* (☎ 78 21 11), at Altstadt 10. Typical Austrian dishes (more than AS185) have been adapted to suit more refined tastes. This place is closed Sunday and Monday.

Entertainment

Café Ex-Blatt, on the corner of Steingasse and Waltherstrasse, caters to students, as do many bars in the centre. It has pizza for AS76 and a beer for AS36, and is open daily to at least 1 am.

The *Posthof* (☎ 77 05 48), Posthofstrasse 43, is a centre for contemporary music, dance and theatre, particularly avant-garde events. Programmes at the *Landestheater* (☎ 76 11 100), Promenade 39, are generally more traditional.

There is a *casino* in the Hotel Schillerpark, Rainerstrasse 2-4; it's open daily from 3 pm. *Linz Stadium* (☎ 57 3 11), Roseggerstrasse 41, stages sports events and major pop concerts.

Getting There & Away

Air Linz airport handles mostly national and charter flights. Austrian Airlines and Swissair (☎ 77 00 55 57) share an office at Schubertstrasse 1. For general flight information call the airport on ☎ 07721-72 7 00 224.

Bus Bundesbuses depart from near the train station, either from the stands to the right or from beyond the small park. Allow sufficient time to locate your departure point. For bus information, call ☎ 16 71.

Train Linz is on the main rail route between Vienna and Salzburg, with express trains hourly in both directions. Slower trains also service this and other routes. From June to September express trains depart for Prague twice a day, though only one is direct (AS302 each way, or AS428 for a special four-day return); the rest of the year three changes are required. For train information call ☎ 17 17 between 7.30 am and 8 pm daily.

Car & Motorbike The city has equally good road connections. The east-west A1/E60 passes a little to the south of the city; the A7 branches north from there and skirts the old city centre.

Boat The DDSG station (☎ 77 10 90) is at Untere Donaulände 10, on the south bank just east of Nibelungen Brücke (bridge). Services to Vienna (AS832; 11 hours) and Passau (AS248; 6½ hours) operate from mid-May (late April for Linz-Passau) to late September. There is one departure daily in each direction, with regular stops en route.

Getting Around

Linz airport is 12 km south-west of the town. An airport bus departs from outside the train station at 5.45 am (not Sunday; AS50) and there's no return service. If you don't fancy a AS230-odd taxi fare from central Linz, get an hourly train to Hörsching (AS17; direction: Salzburg) and then get a taxi or walk 30 minutes.

Public transport includes trams (such as the No 3 between the train station and Hauptplatz) and buses. Single tickets cost AS18, available from pavement dispensers, as are day passes (AS35: correct change required) – drivers *don't* sell tickets. Tabak shops sell a six-ride, multi-user ticket for AS72, and the day pass. The tourist office sells two-day (AS80) and three-day (AS100) passes that include the Pöstlingbergbahn.

Linz has offices for all the major car hire firms including: Avis (☎ 66 28 81), Schillerstrasse 1; Europcar (☎ 60 00 91), Wiener Strasse 91; and Hertz (☎ 78 48 41), Bürgerstrasse 19.

Bike rental in the train station is open 24 hours a day.

Around Linz

The following places can be visited on day trips from Linz, but to fully experience the character of these towns, you should plan to stay overnight. If you enjoy rococo interiors, consider also visiting the **Cistercian abbey** at Wilhering, nine km west of Linz, on the south bank of the Danube. The abbey church is breathtaking for its extremely elaborate but delicate ornamentation.

MAUTHAUSEN
• *pop 4500*

Nowadays Mauthausen is a pleasant small town on the north bank of the Danube, but its status as a quarrying centre prompted the Nazis to site a concentration camp (*Konzentrationslager*) here. Prisoners toiled in the granite quarry and all too often perished on the so-called Stairway of Death (Todesstiege) leading from the quarry to the camp. Some 200,000 prisoners died or were executed in the camp from 1938 to 1945. The museum tells the story of this and other camps (eg at Ebensee and Melk) using German text, charts, artefacts and many harrowing photos. Visitors can see the inmates' living quarters (each designed for 200, but housing up to 500) and gas chambers. In the camp and on the approach to the quarry are numerous poignant memorials to the deceased.

The camp is open from February to mid-December, 8 am to 4 pm (last entry at 3 pm), and charges an entry fee: AS15, or AS5 for students. I suggest visitors register a protest at the gate about this attempt to profit from war crimes. In other countries, camps such as Auschwitz and Dachau have free entry.

On the way through Mauthausen, pause for awhile in the centre. A pink house on the main road has a scene in relief showing a sadistic dentist at work. Round the corner, facing the Danube, is a building with a colourful façade and some distinctive features, such as the giant spider's web on the metal gate.

Mauthausen has places to stay and eat; get details from the tourist office (☎ 07238-2023) in the Freizeitzentrum (leisure centre) on the main road.

Getting There & Away

Mauthausen train station is east of the town centre and can be reached from Linz in about half an hour (AS64 one-way, or AS104 for a day return), depending upon connections in St Valentin. The station rents bikes, which eases the five km journey to the camp (signposted KZ Mauthausen). If you want to walk, you can do it in 40 minutes: walk through the town and then take the signposted Fussweg to the right after the Freizeitzentrum (bikes can go this way too).

The bus from Linz (AS52) takes 55 minutes and gets you about three km closer to the camp than the train. Another option is to take the boat from Linz (AS85 one-way, AS164 return; 75 minutes there, 90 minutes back).

ST FLORIAN
• pop 4500 • ☎ (07224)

This town has one of the best abbeys in Upper Austria, if not the whole country, and is easily accessible from Linz. St Florian was a Roman who converted to Christianity and was drowned in the Enns River (in 304) for his pains. In many Austrian churches, he is represented wearing Roman military uniform and dousing flames with a bucket of water.

Orientation & Information
St Florian is a market town 15 km south-east of Linz. The centre of town is Marktplatz, where there's a small tourist office (☎ 56 90) at No 3, open Monday to Friday from 9 am to 1 pm. The post office (Postamt 4490) is also here.

Augustinian Abbey
The Baroque spires of this abbey are visible from anywhere in town. The abbey dates from at least 819 and has been occupied by the Augustinians since 1071. The Baroque appearance was created from 1688 to 1751 by Carlo Carlone and Jakob Prandtauer. The main entrance, framed by statues, is particularly impressive, especially when bathed in the afternoon sun.

The interior is accessible by guided tour (one hour), which takes in lavish rooms, resplendent with rich stucco and emotive frescoes. They include 16 emperor's rooms – once occupied by visiting popes and royalty, a library containing 125,000 volumes, and Prince Eugene's Room, with an amusing bed featuring carved Turks. The Marble Hall is dedicated to Eugene, who defeated the Turks in many battles.

The high point of the interior is **Altdorfer Gallery**, with 14 paintings by Albrecht Altdorfer (1480-1538) of the Danube school. There are eight scenes of Christ and four of St Sebastian – all vivid and dramatic, and with an innovative use of light and dark. Altdorfer cleverly tapped into contemporary issues to depict his biblical scenes (eg one of Christ's tormentors is clearly a Turk).

The **abbey church** is almost overpowering in its extensive use of stucco and frescoes. The altar is made from 700 tonnes of Salzburg marble, and the huge organ (1774) was once the largest in Europe. Bruckner was a choir boy in St Florian and church organist from 1850 to 1855. He is buried in the crypt below his beloved organ. Also in the crypt are the remains of 6000 people, their bones and skulls stacked in neat rows.

Abbey tours cost AS55 (AS45 for students), and are conducted from Easter to 1 November, daily at 10 and 11 am and 2, 3 and 4 pm. They are usually in German (notes in English), though phone ahead (☎ 89 02 0) to see if you can join an English tour. The church can be visited without joining a tour.

Attached to the abbey is the **Fire Brigade Museum** (Historisches Feuerwehrzeughaus), open 1 May to 31 October, daily except Monday from 9 am to noon and 2 to 4 pm. It displays historic fire engines, hoses, buckets and other firefighting paraphernalia (AS25, students AS15).

Schloss Hohenbrunn
Less than two km west of town is Schloss Hohenbrunn, built from 1722 to 1732 in Baroque style; the architect was Jakob Prandtauer. More of a stately home in appearance than a castle, it houses a fairly interesting museum of hunting (Jagdmuseum). Blood sports are celebrated in art, ornaments, implements, weapons and even the castle stuccowork. In 1995 the collection was extended to include fishing. It is open from 1 April to 30 October, from 10 am to noon and 1 to 5 pm, and costs AS30 (students AS20). It's closed on Mondays that aren't public holidays.

Places to Stay & Eat

St Florian has about six small-scale places to stay, and these are displayed on a board outside the tourist office. *Zum Goldenen Pflug* (☎ 42 26), Speiserberg 3, near the abbey gates, has singles/doubles with shower from AS300/530 and triples from AS750.

Gasthof Erzherzog Franz Ferdinand (☎ 42 45 0), Marktplatz 13, costs from AS390/800/1170, and the rooms have shower, TV, radio and usually a toilet.

There's a small *Spar* supermarket at Marktplatz, and a much larger one in the west part of town by the Lagerhaus bus stop. *Gasthaus Goldener Löwe*, Speiserberg 9, by the abbey gates, serves Austrian food for AS55 to AS110. It has a courtyard and garden and is closed on Wednesday.

Down the hill at Linzer Strasse 11 is *China-Restaurant Chi Wan*. It shuns the usual garish décor of its ilk, but the food is typically Chinese; the lunch menu (AS52 to AS65) comes with soup and rice (open daily). Nearby, on the corner with Speiserberg, is *Gasthof Zur Traube*, with Austrian food and a menu with soup for AS68 (closed Friday lunch and Thursday).

Getting There & Away

St Florian is not accessible by train. Bundesbuses depart from outside the Linz main post office, and take 25 minutes to reach St Florian (AS34). Several buses do the trip (frequent departures), but allow a few minutes to locate the right bus, as they won't have St Florian marked on the front. Buses to Sierning and Molln call at Hohenbrunn after St Florian (AS38 from Linz).

STEYR

• *pop 39,000* • *310 m* • ☎ *(07252)*

Like Linz, Steyr has an attractive town centre, despite its heavy industries, and was the first town in Europe to have electric street lighting (1884). The iron industry has been the backbone of its prosperity since the Middle Ages. Steyr made armaments in WW I and WW II, and was bombed for its trouble in 1944. During the Allied occupation it was

Composer, Franz Schubert (1797-1828) once lived in Steyr

a frontier town between the US and Soviet zones.

Orientation & Information

The picturesque town centre is contained within the converging branches of the Enns and Steyr rivers. The train station is eight minutes walk from the pivotal Stadtplatz, where the tourist office (☎ 53 2 29) can be found in the Rathaus, at Stadtplatz 27. Opening hours are Monday to Friday from 8.30 am to 6 pm, Saturday from 8.30 am to noon (2 pm in December and May to September), and Sunday from 10 am to 3 pm.

To the left of the main train station is the main post office (Hauptpostamt 4400), open Monday to Friday from 7 am to 8 pm and Saturday from 8 am to 11 pm. It'll change money during these hours, but not travellers' cheques. There is another post office at Grünmarkt 1, adjoining Stadtplatz, and several Bankomat machines.

Things to See & Do

Steyr's main points of interest are clustered on or around Stadtplatz. A 17th-century fountain is at the centre of the long, narrow square. One of the most noteworthy buildings is the 18th-century **Rathaus**, which has a church-like belfry and a rococo façade. Opposite, at No 32, is the **Brummerlhaus**, a symbol of the town with its Gothic appearance and steep gable. It dates from the 13th century and has recently been restored.

Other buildings round the square have distinctive arcades and courtyards – some are incorporated within modern businesses: wander into the bank at No 9 and the clothes shop at No 14. You can admire the fine façade of **No 12** and see where Franz Schubert lived at No 16.

Two highly visible buildings at the north end of the Stadtplatz area are Schloss Lamberg, which was restored as Baroque in 1727 after a fire damaged the town centre, and Michaelerkirche (1635; just across the Steyr River where it meets the Enns) which has a large gable fresco.

At the south end of Stadtplatz is **St Mary's Church**, a mix of Gothic and Baroque, with an extremely ornate high altar and pulpit. Alcoves for the side altars are rich in stucco; the one to the left of the entrance has a statue of St Florian.

A little way up the hill is the **parish**

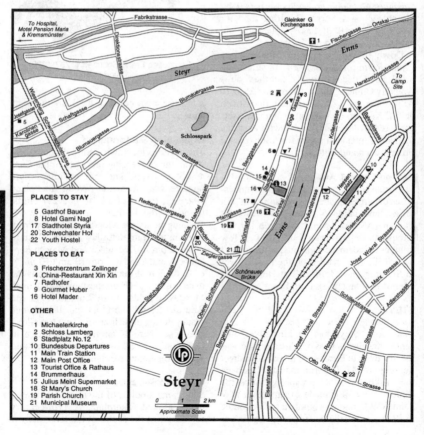

PLACES TO STAY

5 Gasthof Bauer
8 Hotel Garni Nagl
17 Stadthotel Styria
20 Schwechater Hof
22 Youth Hostel

PLACES TO EAT

3 Frischerzentrum Zellinger
4 China-Restaurant Xin Xin
7 Radhofer
9 Gourmet Huber
16 Hotel Mader

OTHER

1 Michaelerkirche
2 Schloss Lamberg
6 Stadtplatz No.12
10 Bundesbus Departures
11 Main Train Station
12 Main Post Office
13 Tourist Office & Rathaus
14 Brummerlhaus
15 Julius Meinl Supermarket
18 St Mary's Church
19 Parish Church
21 Municipal Museum

Steyr

0   1   2 km

Approximate Scale

UPPER AUSTRIA

MARK HONAN

MARK HONAN

MARK HONAN

MARK HONAN

Top Left: The view from Krippenstein, the Salzkammergut
Top Right: Cogwheel railway, Schafberg, the Salzkammergut
Bottom Left: Moonrise from St Gilgen, the Salzkammergut
Bottom Right: Bones and skulls in a crypt, St Florian Abbey, Upper Austria

MARK HONAN

MARK HONAN

MARK HONAN

MARK HONAN

Top Left: Colourful buildings, Dürnstein, Lower Austria
Middle: Weissenkirchen and surrounding vineyards, Lower Austria
Bottom: Terracotta arches of Schallaburg Castle, Lower Austria
Right: Parish church spire, Dürnstein, Lower Austria

church, a Gothic creation from the 15th century. It shares some features with St Stephen's in Vienna, just as it shared the same architect, Hans Puchsbaum, but it's a much cruder work. Down the steps is the **municipal museum**, in the 17th-century Innerberger Stadel, Grünmarkt 26. It has displays of history, culture and folklore, including mechanical puppets. Entry is free and it's open 10 am to 3 pm, except Monday and (November to March) Tuesday.

Places to Stay

There is a *camping ground* (☎ 68 0 08) at Kermatmüllerstrasse 1A, Münichholz, to the north of town on the east bank of the Enns (take bus No 1 from the centre). It is open from May to September and costs AS70 plus AS40 per person.

The HI *youth hostel* (☎ 45 5 80), Hafner Strasse 14, is behind the station: pass under the tracks via Damberggasse, take the second street on the right after the overpass bridge and then bear right on Viktor Adlerstrasse. It's closed over Christmas and New Year and costs just AS76 (AS69 if aged under 19); reception is open from 3 pm on weekdays and 5 pm on weekends.

Other than these options, budget travellers will have a problem in Steyr. The few cheap choices (including private rooms) are inconveniently away from the centre. *Motel Pension Maria* (☎ 61 0 62), Reindlgutstrasse 25, to the west, is a short walk beyond the Krankenhaus (where bus No 2 stops). Singles/doubles cost AS255/550 and triples AS650, all with own shower/WC (closed Friday).

Hotel Garni Nagl (☎ 52 9 76), Kollergasse 1, off Bahnhofstrasse, charges AS300/500/690, with private shower. *Gasthof Bauer* (☎ 54 4 41), Josefgasse 7, is on an island in the Steyr River, accessible from the town centre. This small place has rooms with shower/WC for AS300/560 (closed Tuesday).

Schwechater Hof (☎ 53 0 67), Werndl Strasse 1, behind the parish church, has singles/doubles for AS550/830, with shower/WC, cable TV and telephone.

Stadthotel Styria (☎ 51 5 51), Stadtplatz 40, is the next category up, with rooms for AS720/1040, and offers a sauna and solarium.

Places to Eat

Stadtplatz has a *Julius Meinl* supermarket, open Monday to Friday from 8 am to 6 pm and Saturday from 7.30 am to 12.30 pm (and 2 to 5 pm on Langersamstag). Stadtplatz also has an open-air market on Thursday morning.

Gourmet Huber, Bahnhofstrasse 3, will not, despite its name, attract too many gourmets. It's a small, simple place, offering snacks and meals for less than AS60 (open Monday to Friday from 9.30 am to 6 pm).

China-Restaurant Xin Xin, Enge Gasse 20, has weekday lunch menus with soup from AS55 (closed Monday at lunchtime). Nearby at No 13, *Frischerzentrum Zellinger* is a shop serving inexpensive hot food.

Hotel Mader (☎ 53 3 58), Stadtplatz 36, has a restaurant offering reliable and enjoyable regional cuisine for more than AS100, either inside or in the garden (closed Sunday). Along the square, *Radhofer*, Stadtplatz 9, also serves good food (closed Sunday and Monday).

Getting There & Away

By train, Steyr is 40 minutes from Linz (AS78); it's direct every second hour, or change at St Valentin. Trains continue south into Styria. Steyr train station has a restaurant, bike rental, left-luggage and a travel information office.

Bundesbuses leave from outside the station to the right, where there's a bus information booth open Monday to Friday from 7.40 am to 3 pm. Just two buses a day go to St Florian. Steyr is on highway 115, the road branching from the A1/E60 and running south to Leoben.

WELS

• *pop 54,000* • *317 m* • ☎ *(07242)*
Wels is an agricultural hub with an appealing and historic centre. Most of the countryside comes to town at the agricultural fair and

Volksfest carnival, which together take over Wels in early September in even years (1996 etc).

The tourist office (☎ 43 4 95) is at Stadtplatz 55.

Things to See & Do

The focal point of the town is the long **Stadtplatz**, lined with historic buildings and eye-catching façades. Branching off are several attractive courtyards (eg at Stadtplatz 34). Written or audio (AS20) tours of the centre are available from the tourist office. At the western end of Stadtplatz, in the former leather workers' district, is a tower, the **Ledererturm** (1618), and at the eastern end is the parish church, with a fine Romanesque porch and Gothic stained glass. Opposite the church, Stadtplatz 24 bears paintwork from 1570 and was once occupied by Salome Alt, the mistress of Salzburg's prince-archbishop Wolf Dietrich.

Behind No 14 is the stately **Kaiserliche Burg** where Maximilian breathed his last in 1519. It now houses a museum: among the exhibits are two room interiors (rustic and Biedermeier), and some ingenious small puppets activated from underneath. North of the tourist office, at Pollheimer Strasse 17, is the **Stadtmuseum**, containing Roman finds, including the *Venus of Wels*, a small, beautiful bronze statue. Both museums are free and closed on Monday, and in the afternoon on weekends and holidays.

Places to Stay & Eat

The tourist office can help you find somewhere to stay. The HI *youth hostel* (☎ 67 2 84), Dragonerstrasse 22, is five minutes walk from Stadtplatz and opens all year (check-in from 5 pm).

The town has many cheap places to eat, including two self-service restaurants: *SB Am Eck* at Bahnhofstrasse 13, and *Reiter* at Stadtplatz 63 (both open normal shop hours). Stadtplatz has other restaurants for a range of tastes and budgets, and there's a *Spar* supermarket just beyond the Ledererturm. A surprising number of Chinese restaurants are in the town centre. *Pfeffermühle* (☎ 45 5 97),

Gärtnerstrasse 7, by the train station on the north side, is another. It has a garden, weekday lunch menus from AS59, off-street parking, and singles/doubles with private shower for AS320/580.

Getting There & Away

The train station (which rents bikes) is less than 15 minutes walk north of Stadtplatz. The bus station is in front of the train station. The town is on the express rail route between Linz and Salzburg, just 16 minutes (AS48) south-west of Linz.

LAMBACH

The small town of Lambach is 10 km southwest of Wels. Its **Benedictine abbey** was founded in 1056, though much of the present edifice dates from the 17th century, when the church was rebuilt in Baroque style. The abbey has a theatre (the only one of its kind in Austria), but more striking are the Romanesque frescoes from the 11th century. They are extremely well preserved and betray styles of south-eastern Europe, unusual in Austria. They can only been seen by guided tour; ☎ 07245-83 55 for information. The tourist office (☎ 07245-83 55) can also provide details.

Getting There & Away

Lambach is on the Linz-Salzburg rail route, but unlike Wels, IC and EC trains don't stop here. Pick up a local train from Wels (AS13; takes 11 minutes).

SCHMIDING BIRD PARK

This is Austria's largest bird park (*Vogelpark*), with 350 different species. It also has an interesting ethnological museum. Combined admission costs AS80 and it's open from 1 April to 31 October, daily from 9 am to 5 pm.

The park is about seven km north-west of Wels, accessible by bus No 2438 from there (infrequent on weekends). Alternatively, Haiding train station on the Passau route is about 30 minutes walk from the park.

KREMSMÜNSTER

Another **Benedictine abbey** is at Kremsmünster, overlooking the Krems Valley. Although it was established in 777, it too owes much to Baroque remodelling in the early 18th century. Stuccowork and frescoes are much in evidence in the church, library and **Emperor's Hall** (Kaisersaal). The most acclaimed piece in the treasury is the *Tassilo Chalice*, made of gilded copper and donated to the monks by the Duke of Bavaria in about 780. These sights can be visited by a regular one-hour guided tour (AS45, students AS20; only two daily in winter). In the **observatory tower** (Sternwarte) are wide-ranging museum collections. This can be visited by a separate guided tour taking 90 minutes, from 1 May to 31 October only (AS50, students AS20). Also of interest are the five fish ponds from the late 17th century, sporting statues and arcades (AS10 entry).

About 1.5 km east of Kremsmünster is a **motorcar museum** in Schloss Kremsegg (limited opening hours). The Kremsmünster tourist office (☎ 07583-72 12), Rathausplatz 1, will tell you more.

Getting There & Away

Kremsmünster is on the IC rail route from Linz to Graz, going via Selzthal (direct trains every two hours). Kremsmünster Markt station is reached after 25 minutes from Linz (AS34).

FREISTADT

- *pop 6700* • *560 m* • ☎ *(07942)*

This medieval fortified town is one of the main sights in the Mühlviertel region. Freistadt was important for its position on the salt route to Bohemia.

Orientation & Information

The compact town centre is within the old city walls. Right in the centre is Hauptplatz, with a small tourist office (☎ 29 74) at No 12. It is open Monday to Friday from 9 am to noon and 2 to 5 pm, and (May to September) Saturday from 9 am to noon. The office

will make reservations without charging, including bookings for private rooms.

Immediately to the west of the city wall is the main north-south route, highway 125, called Linzer Strasse in the south, Promenade where it abuts the old centre, and Prager Strasse in the north. A post office (Postamt 4240) is at Promenade 11.

Things to See & Do

The city walls with several gates and turrets are mostly intact and surrounded by a grassy fringe. **Hauptplatz** has some interesting buildings with ornate façades. On the south side of the square is the 14th-century parish church, which is Gothic with a Baroque tower. Waaggasse, just west of Hauptplatz, has striking buildings, including some with sgraffito designs.

Just beyond the north-east corner of Hauptplatz is a **castle** (1390), with a square tower topped by a tapering red-tiled roof. Inside is the **Heimathaus**, a regional museum (AS10) open for tours from Tuesday to Friday (and Saturday from May to October). It contains the usual historical and cultural displays, and a collection of 600 works of engraved and painted glass (*verre églomisé*).

The town has had a **brewery** since 1777, and now makes Freistädter Bier. Free group tours of the premises at Promenade 7 are available, including a taste of the produce. Phone ahead (☎ 57 77) to join a tour; office hours are Monday to Thursday from 7 am to noon and 1 to 4.30 pm, and Friday from 7 am to noon.

Places to Stay

There is a *camping ground* (☎ 24 26) just outside the old centre, to the east of the Feldaist River.

The HI *youth hostel* (☎ 43 65), Schlosshof 3, is in front of the castle, open June to September. Reception is open from 5 to 8 pm, and the doors are locked during the day. Private rooms (about AS150 per person) are on the tourist office's hotel list.

Frühstückspension Hubertus (☎ 23 54), Höllplatz 3, in the south-west corner of the old centre, has singles/doubles with own shower/WC for AS230/400; it has a café and parking places. *Pension Pirklbauer* (☎ 24 40), Höllgasse 2-4, has similar rooms for AS220/380, and a garden.

Hotel Zum Goldenen Adler (☎ 21 12; fax 21 12 44), Salzgasse 1, in the historic centre, has the best facilities in town, including an outdoor pool and terrace, sauna and solarium. Rooms have shower/WC, telephone and cable TV and cost AS495/790.

Places to Eat

Two large supermarkets, *Hofer* and *Spar*, are opposite each other on Linzer Strasse. In the old town, on Eisengasse, there's a *Julius Meinl*. Next door is *Haider Imbiss*, serving snacks and small meals for AS18 to AS59. It often has weekly culinary themes and is open Monday to Friday from 7.30 am to 6 pm and Saturday from 7 am to 12.30 pm.

On Salzgasse is *China-Restaurant Rosstall*, with a weekday lunch menu from AS49 (closed Wednesday). There's another Chinese restaurant and a pizzeria just north of the Bühmertor (gate) on Schmiedgasse.

For tasty regional specialities, try the restaurant (closed Tuesday) in the *Hotel Zum Goldenen Adler* (see Places to Stay).

Getting There & Away

Freistadt is on a direct rail route from Linz (AS94 one-way or AS162 return); departures are two-hourly and take 70 minutes. This line wriggles its way north to Prague. Czech rail fares are lower than those in Austria, so you can save money by buying (in Czech currency) onward tickets once you've crossed the border.

Freistadt train station is three km southwest of the centre: to avoid the walk and not rely on infrequent buses, hire a bike from the station.

Highway 125, the main route from Linz, passes adjacent to the walled centre and continues towards Prague.

KEFERMARKT

There's one main reason to visit Kefermarkt: the **Church of St Wolfgang**. Although not as famous as the pilgrimage church in the village of St Wolfgang, its Gothic altar (the Flügelaltar) is of comparable beauty and similar design. The identity of the 15th-century sculptor is not known. The altarpiece of limewood is 13.5 metres high, with lattice-work fronds rising towards the ceiling. At the centre are three expressive figures, carved with great skill (left to right as you face them): St Peter, St Wolfgang and St Christopher. The wings of the altar bear religious scenes in low relief. The rest of the decorations in the church are Baroque. It closes at about 5.30 pm.

Places to Stay & Eat

If you want to stay, there are a couple of places down the hill from the church at Oberer Markt. *Hosner* (☎ 07947-62 20) has singles/doubles for AS250/400 with shower. No arrivals are accepted on Tuesday when the restaurant is shut. *Zehethofer*, close by, is cheaper for Austrian fare (AS55 to AS100).

Getting There & Away

Kefermarkt is 10 km south of Freistadt and the church is 10 to 15 minutes walk from the train station. The fare from Freistadt is AS17. If you hire a bike at Freistadt station you can return it at Kefermarkt station (or vice versa), though this will cost an extra AS40.

BRAUNAU AM INN
• *pop 17,000* • *352 m* • ☎ *(07722)*

Isolated from the rest of the province, Braunau has achieved unwanted attention as the birthplace of Hitler.

Orientation & Information

Braunau is within easy distance of the German border: from the central Stadtplatz, simply walk across the bridge over the Inn River and there you are. On the German side is the linked town of Simbach.

From the train station to Stadtplatz is 10 minutes walk: go right upon exiting, take a semi-left under the road bridge and continue along Linzer Strasse. Stadtplatz is straight on, but following the 'i' sign to the right will bring you to an unstaffed information centre, with an accommodation board and free telephone, leaflets, and free backpack-sized lockers.

The tourist office (☎ 26 44), Stadtplatz 9, in the Volksbank, is open Monday to Friday from 9 am to noon and (from May to September) 2.30 pm to 5.30 pm.

Things to See & Do

Braunau's sights should occupy you for more than a couple of hours – follow the walking tour of the centre prescribed by the tourist office (notes in English). **Stadtplatz** is a long square lined with elegant homes in pastel shades, and a 13th-century gate tower at the southern end. The spire of **St Stephen's Church** is one of the tallest in Austria – to find out how tall, you'll have to measure it yourself: the tourist office claims it is 100 metres; guidebooks variously describe it as 99, 96 or 95 metres. Close by is **St Martin's Church**, containing a war memorial.

The walking tour omits **Hitler's Geburtshaus** (birth house) at Salzburger Vorstadt 15, just south of Stadtplatz. Hitler was born here in 1889 with the unprepossessing moniker of Adolf Schicklgruber. His family remained a further two years before moving to Linz. In 1938, when Hitler stormed through Braunau at the head of his troops and tanks, he did not stop at his old house.

The town tries to play down its Hitler connection. The *Führer* is ignored in most tourist literature. No plaque marks his birthplace, although in 1989 a belated, oblique acknowledgment came with the placing of a lump of stone from Mauthausen on the pavement outside the house. Even this fails to mention Hitler: its German inscription reads 'For peace, freedom and democracy. Never again fascism.'

Festival

Braunau adopts a more light-hearted face in late September, when it hosts its own version of Munich's beer-driven Oktoberfest.

Places to Stay

There's camping at the *Freizeitzentrum*

(☎ 73 57), in the south of town, off Salzburger Strasse. It's open from 1 April to 30 September.

In the centre is a HI *youth hostel* (☎ 23 21 247), Palmplatz 8. It's part of a church (Bürgerspitalskirche), with the entrance on the south side; reception is from 6 pm. Telephone ahead in winter to make sure it's open. Breakfast is optional and costs extra.

Ideally situated at Stadtplatz 23 is *Hotel Gann* (☎ 32 06), with a ground-floor bar. Singles/doubles cost AS330/550 with private shower/WC, or AS230/400 using a hall shower. Equally convenient is the nearby *Gasthaus Puchmayr* (☎ 32 73), Johann Fischer Gasse 6. It's a smaller place, charging AS290/490 with private shower/WC.

By the train station is *Gasthof Gfrörer* (☎ 33 20), Bahnhofstrasse 50, with rooms for AS310/510 with shower/WC and telephone.

Places to Eat

There's a *Billa* supermarket at Am Berg, off Salzburger Vorstadt, and a *Julius Meinl* on Stadtplatz.

Stadtplatz has a range of places to eat, including *Harry's Pub* at No 24 with cheap fast food. Another place is *Reiter* at No 15, a small fast-food joint attached to a deli shop, open Monday to Friday from 9 am to 6 pm (1 pm on Wednesday) and Saturday from 9 am to noon. It has a lunch menu with meals for AS36 to AS72. *Bogner's* at No 47 has outside tables and Mexican specialities. There's also a cheap pizzeria (closed Wednesday) round the corner from Harry's Pub, and *China-Restaurant Kotaradja*, Johann Fischer Gasse 6, with weekday lunches from AS52.

A place offering good regional dishes (AS70 to AS170) is *Gasthaus zum Schiff*, Stadtplatz 3 (closed Monday and Tuesday from October to April).

Getting There & Away

Braunau is the terminus of the regional train service from Steindorf bei Strasswalchen

(AS64; takes 45 minutes). Steindorf is on the Linz-Salzburg IC rail route. To take a train from Braunau to Simbach in Germany costs AS17; trains go from there to Munich. Cars to Munich can take highway 12 (the E552).

Braunau receives plenty of touring cyclists (and the train station rents bikes): the town is on the Inntal Radweg, following the Inn River through Germany and down to Innsbruck, and in the other direction reaching the German border town of Passau (where further cycling routes follow the Danube). Another bike track follows the Salzach River to Salzburg.

Lower Austria

Lower Austria (Niederösterreich) is rather overshadowed by Vienna. Although the province surrounds the city, all things, it seems, revolve round the national capital. Literature from the provincial tourist office takes pride in the fact that Lower Austria is 'The Province on Vienna's Doorstep'. This stepping-stone status is underlined by such advice as to stay in the Wienerwald (Vienna Woods) while (commence fanfare...) visiting Vienna.

Efforts to forge a separate identity were not helped by Vienna's former status as Lower Austria's provincial capital, while also the federal capital and having its own provincial government. In 1986 St Pölten became the capital of Lower Austria, and the task of exploiting the province's accessibility to Vienna, without being overwhelmed by its closeness, began in earnest.

It's not a futile endeavour. Lower Austria does have plenty to offer in its own right: the Danube Valley is justly praised for its wines, castles and abbeys, the Wienerwald attracts hikers and spa seekers, and Semmering is a famous holiday region in the south.

Bratislava, the capital of Slovakia, has been included in this chapter as it is an easy and popular excursion from Lower Austria or Vienna.

Orientation & Information

Lower Austria is the country's largest province, covering 17,174 sq km, and has the largest population (1.5 million) of any region except Vienna. Geographically, it is dominated by the Danube Valley, which is also the focus of tourism. The land is relatively flat and fertile (it has the highest percentage of land under cultivation in Austria) though mountains reach 2000 metres high in the south.

St Pölten is gradually absorbing most of the administrative functions of the province, but the Lower Austria Information Centre

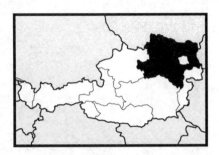

(☎ 0222-53 33 114; fax 53 110 6060), Heidenschuss 2, A-1010, is still in Vienna. Direct all written enquiries to this address. St Pölten's city tourist office holds only limited information on the province.

St Pölten

• *pop 50,000* • *267 m* • ☎ *(02742)*

Nearly 2000 years ago, St Pölten was known as Aelium Cetium, but the town all but disappeared with the departure of the Romans. The arrival of the Augustinians in the 8th century saw it regain importance, and the country's newest provincial capital has the oldest municipal charter, granted in 1159. It also has a smattering of Baroque buildings: Baroque master Jakob Prandtauer was once a resident.

Orientation & Information

The town centre is a compact, mostly pedestrian-only area to the west of the Traisan River. The tourist office (☎ 53 3 54), inside the Rathaus on Rathausplatz, is five minutes walk from the main train station. Opening hours are Monday to Friday from 8 am to 6 pm and, Easter to 31 October, also Saturday from 9.30 am to 6.30 pm and Sunday from

Lower Austria
(Niederösterreich)

0   25   50 km

1.30 to 6.30 pm. Ask for the *St Pölten In-Guide*, an excellent map with restaurants, hotels, pubs and sights marked. Next to the tourist office is a travel agency, with an accommodation map and free telephone.

The train station (which has money-exchange counters open daily and a Bankomat) has a similar accommodation facility outside.

The post office (Postamt 3100) is near the train station. Opening hours are Monday to Friday from 7 am to 8 pm, Saturday from 7 am to 4 pm, and Sunday and holidays from 8 to 10 am.

Things to See & Do

Follow the walking tour of the town centre outlined in English in the tourist office's *Sankt Pölten barock* leaflet, or hire its taped walking tour for AS20. The architecture is not exclusively Baroque – Kremser Gasse 41 has an Art-Nouveau façade by Josef Olbrich, the creator of the Secession building in Vienna.

Rathausplatz is the hub of the town and has at its centre a **Trinity column**, constructed in 1782. Several eye-catching buildings line the square, including the rococo **Franciscan Church**, completed in

1770. This has side altar paintings by Kremser Schmidt.

Close to Rathausplatz are several places of interest, including the **Institut der Englischen Fräulein** on Linzer Strasse, a convent founded in 1706, with a classic Baroque façade, and frescoes by Paul Troger in the chapel. The tiny **Museum im Hof**, Hess Strasse 4, dwells on recent history, particularly from a worker's viewpoint (free entry; open 9 am to noon on Wednesday, Friday and Saturday).

Across the road is the **Municipal Museum**, Prandtauerstrasse 2, covering history from Roman times to the mid-19th century (AS20, students AS10; open Tuesday to Sunday from 9 am to 5 pm). There's a cultural centre (with music and other events) in the same building. The house at Rathausgasse 2 has a Baroque façade, complete with a relief of Schubert (the composer was a frequent visitor).

Herrenplatz has a small morning market (daily except Sunday), which expands into the adjoining Domplatz on Thursday and Saturday. Domplatz was the heart of the ancient Roman town. The **cathedral** has a 77-metre-high tower and much Baroque ornamentation. The interior, with lashings of fake marble and gold, was by Prandtauer. Note the painted figure that seems about to fall on you if you stand before the altar, and the hole in the organ that captures the stained glass image behind. Many of the paintings are by Daniel Gran, who lived at Wiener Strasse 8 for awhile. Prandtauer lived at Klostergasse 1, north of Domplatz.

There's a sports and leisure complex to the north-east of the town, by the Ratzersdorf Lake. For nightlife venues, pick up the tourist office's *In Szene* brochure.

Places to Stay

The *camping ground* (☎ 51 5 10) is three km north-east of the centre in the Freizeitpark, and is open year-round.

Budget options are limited. There is a HI *youth hostel* (☎ 73 0 10) at Kranzbichlerstrasse 18, but this was closed in 1995 for renovations and may never re-open.

Fuchs (☎ 72 9 46), Europaplatz 7, five minutes walk south of Rathausplatz, could do with a spruce-up too. It's merely adequate: singles/doubles with a sink but no access to a shower are AS180/340, and doubles with shower cubicle are AS380. Optional breakfast is AS30. Also on Europaplatz is *Mariazellerhof* (☎ 76 9 95), providing rooms with shower/WC, cable TV and telephone from AS300 to AS460 per person. Apartments are also available, but reception is closed from 10 am to 5 pm.

Gasthof Graf (☎ 52 7 57), Bahnhofplatz 7, opposite the station, has rooms with or without private shower and WC, and charges from AS300 to AS450 per person. It has a cheapish restaurant, a garden and parking.

Stadthotel Hausereck (☎ 78 3 86) is near the pedestrian zone at Schulgasse 2. This Art-Nouveau place has comfortable rooms with shower/WC, cable TV and telephone for AS640/880. It has a lift, restaurant and arrangements for parking.

Metropol (☎ 70 700 133), Schillerplatz 1, is the only central four-star hotel, charging AS940/1480, but the standardised rooms aren't much better than Hausereck's.

Places to Eat

Cheap eating is less of a problem. Behind the train station at Daniel Gran Strasse 13 is an *Interspar* shopping centre, with a supermarket and self-service restaurant (menus from AS50). The train station itself has a *Eurosnack* fast-food outlet, open daily until 9 pm.

Just within the pedestrian area of Kremser Gasse is a branch of *Nordsee*, with eat-in or takeaway fish meals from about AS65 (open Monday to Friday from 8.30 am to 6.30 pm, and Saturday from 8.30 am to 1.30 pm).

The town also has a handful of Chinese restaurants: *Ten-An*, Fuhrmannsgasse 15 (closed Monday), and *Tai-Yang*, Schneckgasse 12 (open daily), are both central and have weekday lunch menus from AS53.

For Austrian food, there's plenty of choice: *Gasthaus Bamberger*, Kremser Gasse 22, has dishes for AS60 to AS100. The

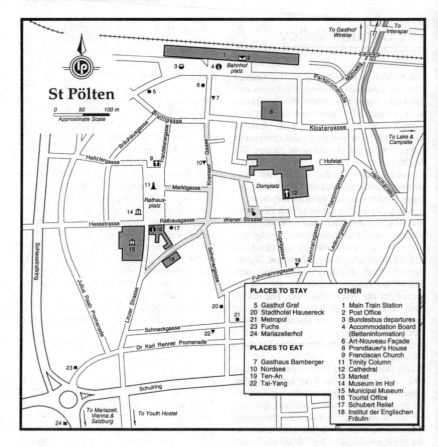

St Pölten

0   50   100 m
Approximate Scale

PLACES TO STAY
5   Gasthof Graf
20 Stadthotel Hausereck
21 Metropol
23 Fuchs
24 Mariazellerhof

PLACES TO EAT
7   Gasthaus Bamberger
10 Nordsee
19 Ten-An
22 Tai-Yang

OTHER
1   Main Train Station
2   Post Office
3   Bundesbus departures
4   Accommodation Board
    (Betteninformation)
6   Art-Nouveau Façade
8   Prandtauer's House
9   Franciscan Church
11 Trinity Column
12 Cathedral
13 Market
14 Museum im Hof
15 Municipal Museum
16 Tourist Office
17 Schubert Relief
18 Institut der Englischen
    Fräulin

kitchen closes at 8 pm on weekdays and 1 pm on weekends.

About one km north of the station at Mühlweg 64 is *Gasthof Winkler* (☎ 64 9 44), a more elegant place with good regional and seasonal dishes for AS80 to AS240 (closed Monday and Sunday evening). At Sunday lunchtime there's an extensive buffet for AS150.

Getting There & Away

St Pölten is 60 km west of Vienna, 35 minutes along the hourly express train route from Vienna's Westbahnhof (AS102) to Linz (AS150) and Salzburg (AS336). From St Pölten, trains run north to Krems and south to Mariazell.

St Pölten has equally good road connections: the A1/E60 passes a few km south of the city, and the S33 branches from there, bypasses the city to the east, and continues to Krems.

The east-west highway 1 passes through the city centre, from which highway 20 branches south to Mariazell. Bundesbuses depart from outside the train station.

The Danube Valley

The historical importance of the Danube (Donau) Valley as a corridor between east and west ensured that control of this area was hotly contested. There are hundreds of fortresses in Lower and Upper Austria, including many monasteries and abbeys with defences to match conventional castles. The Wachau section of the Danube, between Krems and Melk, is the most scenic, with villages, forested slopes, vineyards and imposing fortresses at nearly every bend.

A popular way to explore the region is by boat. DDSG operates steamers along the Danube west of Vienna from early April to late October. Commentary en route (in English) highlights points of interest. See the Getting There & Away chapter for more details. Inevitably, the boats are usually packed for the Wachau section. The stretch from Krems to Vienna is less interesting; the scenery is flatter and there are fewer fortresses, though you do pass through a couple of locks, and the entry into Vienna is quite enjoyable.

The Danube flows from west to east and you need to be prepared for longer sailing times when travelling upstream. Return fares are approximately 50% more than the one-way fares quoted here; fares combining the boat and the train or bus are also available. Eurail passes are valid for DDSG boats, and Inter-Rail gets 50% off. Discounts also apply for families and senior citizens. Bikes can be taken on board for AS35. If you have a boat ticket and rent a bike from the DDSG office the cost is also AS35 per day, and these bikes are transported free.

The route by road is also scenic. Highway 3 links Vienna and Linz and stays close to the north bank of the Danube for much of the way. Cycling is extremely popular in summer. There is a bicycle track along the south bank from Vienna to Krems, and along both sides of the river from Krems to Linz. East from Vienna, a bicycle track runs north of the river to Hainburg. Pick up the useful *Lower Danube cycle track* leaflet, in English, free from most tourist offices in the region.

The rail track that runs along the north bank of the Danube takes slow local trains (2nd class only). It makes 33 stops on the 120-km, three-hour trip between Krems and St Valentin, including at Dürnstein, Weissenkirchen, Spitz, Grein and Mauthausen. Some of the small stations are unstaffed, where you must buy a ticket on the train.

The guest card for the Wachau and Nibelungengau region gives a host of benefits for anyone staying in the region (approximately between Ybbs and Krems). If you stay in one resort you can get the benefits for *all* resorts: particularly useful is

Johann Strauss Jnr (1825-99), composer of the *'Blue Danube'* waltz; the famous river runs through Lower Austria

one day's free bike rental in Melk (apply to the Melk tourist office). There's also a 10% reduction on DDSG fares. Cards are provided with your accommodation, and are funded by the nightly resort tax of around AS10, which is usually included in the price of your room. The Wachau-Nibelungengau regional office (☎ 02732-85 6 20; fax 73 0 74 85) is at Undstrasse 6, A-3504 Krems.

Danube Valley attractions are covered below in order from west to east.

WEST OF MELK

Grein, in Upper Austria, is a small town on the north bank of the river, and has a castle (mostly 15th century) with a fine arcaded courtyard. On the premises is a museum devoted to navigation and shipping on the Danube, open 1 May to 31 October (closed Monday).

About 15 km south of Grein is **Amstetten**, the main town in the vicinity (population 22,000). It has little of tourist interest, though it is on both the A1 and the main rail route (express trains stop here) between Linz and Vienna. The Ybbs River, a tributary of the Danube, skirts the south of the town.

Continuing south another 25 km, you reach **Waidhofen an der Ybbs**, a stunningly attractive riverside town, with historic gabled houses, arcaded courtyards and several onion domes reaching skywards. It can be reached by train from Amstetten in 30 minutes, en route to Eisenerz (see the Styria chapter).

Travelling eastward along the Danube from Grein, you soon pass into Lower Austria and a rocky, wooded section of the river. After Ybbs, the next boat stop is at Marbach. Three km along a road that wriggles northwards from here is the pilgrimage church of **Maria Taferl**. This Baroque creation with two onion domes was the work of Jakob Prandtauer.

About five km north-east of Maria Taferl, taking minor roads, is **Artstetten**, notable for a castle that has been much modified in the last 700 years. It was formerly owned and occupied by Archduke Franz Ferdinand, to whom a museum is devoted (open daily from 1 April to 2 November). The assassination of the archduke and his wife sparked WW I. The tomb of the unlucky pair is in the church. Artstetten is three km north of Klein Pöchlarn, which is across the river from its larger cousin, Pöchlarn. There's no bridge, but these places are linked by ferry: Danube steamers stop at the Pöchlarn side.

MELK
• *pop 5000* • *211 m* • ☎ *(02752)*

Lying in the lee of its imposing monastery-fortress, Melk is an essential stop on the Danube trail.

Historically, the site of Melk was important for both the Romans and the Babenbergs. In 1089 the Babenberg margrave Leopold II donated the castle to the Benedictines, who converted it into a fortified abbey. Fire accounted for the original edifice, which was completely rebuilt from 1702 to 1738 by Prandtauer and his follower, Josef Munggenast. Extensive restorations were planned for completion in 1996.

Orientation & Information
The train station is 300 metres from the town centre. Walk 50 metres down Bahnhofstrasse to reach the post office (Postamt 3390), where money exchange is available to 5 pm on weekdays and 10 am on Saturday. Turn right for the youth hostel or carry straight on, taking the Bahngasse path, for the central Rathausplatz.

Turn right at Rathausplatz for the tourist office (☎ 23 07 32) on Babenbergerstrasse 1. In summer it's open weekdays from 9 am to noon and 2 to 6 pm, and weekends from 10 am to 2 pm, with hours extending to daily from 9 am to 7 pm in July and August. In April and October weekend hours are restricted to Saturday until 2 pm. It closes completely in November and December, and for the rest of the winter it's open if and when staff are there. The office will make room reservations (AS100 refundable deposit).

Benedictine Abbey
The Benedictine abbey (Stift Melk) dominates the town from its commanding hill site,

and provides an excellent view from the terrace. Visitors can roam the abbey buildings alone, but guided tours (up to two a day in English) highlight interesting details and are well worth the small extra charge.

The huge **abbey church** is enclosed by the buildings, but still dominates the complex with its twin spires and high octagonal dome. The inside is Baroque gone mad, with endless prancing angels and gold twirls, but is still extremely impressive. The theatrical high altar scene, depicting St Peter and St Paul (the patron saints of the church), is by Peter Widerin. Michael Rottmayr did most of the ceiling paintings, including those in the dome.

Other high points are the library and the mirror room: both have painted tiers on the ceiling (by Paul Troger) to give the illusion of greater height. The ceilings are slightly curved to aid the effect. Imperial rooms, where various dignitaries stayed (including Napoleon), contain museum exhibits.

The abbey is open from the Saturday before Palm Sunday to All Saints' Day from 9 am to 5 pm, except between May and September when it closes at 6 pm. Entry costs AS50, or AS25 for students aged under 27 years, and the guided tour is AS15. During winter it may only be visited by guided tour (☎ 23 12). If you also want to visit Schallaburg Castle, get a combined ticket.

Other Buildings

Other interesting buildings around town are mostly from the 16th and 17th centuries. Try the **walking tour** outlined in the tourist office pamphlet, particularly along the pedestrian-only Hauptstrasse and Sterngasse. Don't miss the excellent façade of the Altes Posthaus at Linzer Strasse 3-5.

Festival

The Melker Sommerspiele in July and August features open-air theatre.

Places to Stay & Eat

Camping Melk is on the west of the canal where it joins the Danube, and is open from around April to October. Charges are AS35 per person, AS35 per tent and AS25 for a car. The reception is in the restaurant *Melker Fährhaus* (☎ 32 91), Kolomaniau 3, open Wednesday to Sunday (daily in summer) from 8 am to midnight. When it is closed, just camp and pay later. The restaurant has good lunchtime menus including soup from AS75. Self-caterers can stock up at the *Spar* supermarket, in the town centre at Rathausplatz 9.

The HI *youth hostel* (☎ 26 81), Abt Karl Strasse 42, painted in pastel pink and green, has good showers and four-bed dorms. Beds are AS164 (AS139 for those aged under 19 years), or AS144 (AS119) for stays of three nights or more. The reception and main doors are closed from 10 am to 5 pm, but during the day you can reserve a bed and leave your bags behind the door to the left of the entrance. The hostel is closed from 1 November to 31 March and is 10 minutes walk from the station.

The tourist office accommodation leaflet lists private rooms, which are quite good value, even though most are away from the centre. *Gasthof Goldener Stern* (☎ 22 14), Sterngasse 17, offers good prices for the centre: singles/doubles are AS290/500 (less for longer stays) and rooms are quite large, with hall showers. The restaurant is closed Tuesday in summer and weekends in winter. *Gasthof Weisses Lamm* (☎ 29 69), Linzer Strasse 7, has doubles for AS550 with private shower/WC.

Gasthof Goldenen Hirschen (☎ 27 52), Rathausplatz 13, is a 16th-century house with renovated singles/doubles (private shower/WC) from AS320/560. Its *Rathauskeller* restaurant has daily menus, with soup, for about AS90, and other dishes from AS75 (open daily).

Gasthof Baumgartner (☎ 24 19), Bahnhofstrasse 12, is by the train station. Its restaurant is basic and caters to locals, but serves a good Wiener schnitzel, chips and salad for AS75, and beer is just AS26 a Krügerl. There are tables inside and out, and it's open daily from 7 am to midnight.

Hotel Goldener Ochs (☎ 23 67), Linzer

Strasse 18, is an old house, but has large rooms with modern furnishings, private shower/WC and cable TV: prices are AS620/920, less in the low season. The place has a restaurant, garden, sauna (free for guests) and solarium.

Melk's gourmet restaurant is in *Stadt Melk* (☎ 25 47), Hauptplatz 1, where main dishes cost AS245 to AS275. The proprietor maintains an extensive wine cellar. Stylish rooms in this four-star place are AS680/920.

Getting There & Away
Boats leave from the canal by Pionierstrasse, 400 metres to the rear of the monastery. The 5½-hour boat journey from Melk to Vienna costs AS530; Krems is reached after less than two hours. Bicycle rental is available in Melk at both the train and boat stations.

A direct train departs Vienna's Westbahnhof (AS118) at 8.44 am and arrives at Melk at 9.47 am; if you take this you can explore the abbey and/or Schallaburg Castle before taking an afternoon boat back to Vienna. The only direct train in the opposite direction departs Melk at 4.02 pm. All other trains involve changing at St Pölten and take more than two hours.

SCHALLABURG CASTLE
This splendid Renaissance castle-cum-palace, five km south of Melk, is an easy and rewarding excursion. The architectural centrepiece is a two-storey, arcaded Renaissance courtyard with marvellous terracotta arches. The rich red-brown carvings set against whitewashed walls cry out to be photographed. There are some 400 terracotta images, completed in 1572-73. The largest figures support the upper storey arches – note the court jester snickering in the corner. Below these are pictorial scenes and a series of mythological figures and masks. Pay AS10 for a commentary that explains the significance of some of the images. Prestigious exhibitions are held in the castle, a different one each year.

The castle is open from 1 May to 31 October, and entry to the complex and exhibition costs AS60, AS40 for seniors and

AS20 for students. A reduced combination ticket with Melk's monastery costs AS95. There's an excellent, mid-price restaurant in the castle.

Getting There & Away
Schallaburg can be reached by infrequent Bundesbus (AS30). Hiring a bike from Melk train station gives more flexibility.

MELK TO DÜRNSTEIN
In addition to the many vineyards, peaches and apricots are grown on this 30-km-long passage of the Danube. Even the steepest hills are terraced and cultivated.

Shortly after departing Melk you pass the 12th-century **Schönbühel Castle**, standing high on a rock on the south bank, which officially marks the beginning of the Wachau region. There's also a Servite monastery from the 17th century. Immediately afterwards, on the same side, are the ruins of **Aggstein Castle** (12th century), built by the Kuenringer family. These so-called 'robber barons' are said to have imprisoned their enemies on a ledge of rock (the Rosengärtlein), where the hapless captives faced starvation, unless they opted for a quicker demise by throwing themselves into the abyss below.

On the opposite bank **Willendorf** soon appears, where the 25,000-year-old sandstone statuette of Venus, now in Vienna's Museum of Natural History, was discovered; another statuette made from a mammoth tusk was found here.

A farther five km brings **Spitz** into view, a peaceful village with attractive houses. The parish church at Kirchenplatz is unusual for its chancel, which is out of line with the main body of the church. Another noteworthy feature is the 15th-century statues of the 12 apostles lining the organ loft; most wear an enigmatic expression, as if being tempted by an unseen spirit to overindulge in the communion wine. It's a Gothic church with crisscross ceiling vaulting, yet has Baroque altars. The fountain in front and the vine-covered hills rising behind make a pretty picture. The Tausendeimerberg hill is so-named for its reputed ability to yield a thousand buckets of wine per season. The tourist office (☎ 02713-23 62) in the village centre can give information about accommodation.

Six km farther along the north bank is **Weissenkirchen**. Its centrepiece is a fortified parish church on a hill. This Gothic church was built in the 15th century and has a Baroque altar. The garden terrace, if open, provides good views of the Danube. Below the church is the charming Teisenhoferhof arcaded courtyard, with a covered gallery and lashings of flowers and dried corn. The Wachau Museum is here and has work by artists of the Danube school. It's open from 1 April to 31 October (closed Monday) and entry costs AS20 (students AS10). The tourist office (02715-26 00) is in the village centre.

After Weissenkirchen the river sweeps to the right and yields a fine perspective of Dürnstein.

Getting There & Away
DDSG boats stop at Aggsbach-Dorf, Spitz and Weissenkirchen. The Wachau railway runs along the north bank, connecting all the villages on that side. Krems to Spitz costs AS34; Spitz train station rents bikes. Drivers wishing to stay close to the river can choose a road on either bank.

DÜRNSTEIN
- ☎ (02711)

One of the prime destinations in the Wachau, Dürnstein achieved 12th-century notoriety by its imprisonment of King Richard the Lion-Heart of England.

Orientation & Information
From the train station, walk ahead and then right for the village walls (five minutes). En route you pass the tourist office (☎ 200), in a little hut in the corner of the east car park. It's only open in the afte,rnoon from April to October. The landing stage is below the dominating feature of the village centre, the blue-and-white parish church.

Things to See & Do
High on the hill, commanding a marvellous view of the curve of the Danube, stand the ruins of **Kuenringer Castle**, where Richard was incarcerated from 1192 to 1193. His crime was to have insulted Leopold V; his misfortune was to be recognised despite his disguise when journeying through Austria on his way home from the Holy Lands; and his liberty was achieved only upon the payment of a huge ransom of 35,000 kg of silver (which partly funded the building of Wiener Neustadt). It was here that the singing minstrel Blondel attempted to rescue his sovereign. The hike from the village takes 15 to 20 minutes.

In the village, Hauptstrasse is a cobbled street with some picturesque 16th-century houses and wrought-iron signs. The Augustinian monastery was founded in 1410, and received its Baroque face-lift in the 18th century (overseen by Josef Munggenast, among others). The **parish church**, often called the abbey church (*Chorherrenstift*), has been meticulously restored since 1985. The exterior has plenty of saints and angels adopting pious poses on and around the pristine steeple; the interior effectively combines white stucco and dark wood balconies. Kremser Schmidt did many of the ceiling and altar paintings. Entry costs AS20 and includes access to the porch overlooking the Danube and a photo exhibition detailing the renovations. It's open daily from 9 am to 6 pm from 1 April to 31 October.

East of the centre is **Kuenringerbad**, a swimming and sports complex.

Places to Stay & Eat
Pension Altes Rathaus (☎ 252), Hauptstrasse 26, is reached through an attractive courtyard. Singles/doubles are AS370/480, (AS470/580 with shower/WC). *Pension Böhmer* (☎ 239), at Hauptstrasse 22, has slightly smaller rooms with shower/WC for AS350/550. Private rooms are cheaper, eg *Maria Wagner* (☎ 232), at Hauptstrasse 41, costs AS195 per person.

For food, try *Gasthof Sänger Blondel*

(☎ 253), Klosterplatz, with many rooms and a shady courtyard (closed Monday), or the cheaper and plainer *Goldener Strauss*, Hauptstrasse 18 (closed Tuesday). Sänger Blondel also has rooms from AS660/920 with private shower/WC.

Gartenhotel-Weinhof (☎ 206) is actually a pair of four-star hotels, side by side about one km west of the centre, sharing the same ownership and prices (from AS620/860). Guests enjoy numerous facilities, including a heated swimming pool, sauna, garden and restaurant.

Alter Klosterkeller is a Buschenschank on Anzuggasse, just outside the village walls and overlooking the vineyards. Wine is AS20 a Viertel and a selection of cold snacks and meals are served (AS25 to AS75). Opening hours are from 3 pm (2 pm on weekends) and it's closed Tuesday and Wednesday.

Getting There & Away
Steamer fares are AS84 to Krems and AS238 to Melk. The boat station is just below the monastery. By train, the fare is AS17 to either Krems or Weissenkirchen.

KREMS
• *pop 23,000* • *202 m* • ☎ *(02732)*
Krems lies on the north bank of the Danube, surrounded by terraced vineyards. It was first mentioned in documents in 995, and has been a centre of the wine trade for most of its history.

Orientation & Information
Krems comprises three linked parts: Krems to the east, the smaller settlement of Stein (formerly a separate town) to the west, and the connecting suburb of Und. Hence the Austrian joke: *Krems Und Stein sind drei Städte* (Krems and Stein are three cities).

The centre of Krems itself stretches along a pedestrian-only street, Obere and Untere Landstrasse. The tourist office (☎ 82 6 76) is between Krems and Stein at Undstrasse 6, in the Kloster Und building. It's part of the Austropa travel agency, and sells packages to nearby attractions. Opening hours are

Monday to Friday from 8 am to 6 pm, and (Easter to 31 October) weekends as well from 10 am to noon and 1 to 6 pm. Room reservations are made without charge, and there's a free phone and accommodation board outside.

The main post office (Postamt 3500) is west of the train station on Brandström-strasse 4.

Things to See & Do
There are several Renaissance and Baroque houses lining Untere and Obere Landstrasse in Krems, and Steiner Landstrasse in Stein; a peaceful stroll along these streets is rewarding. Quaint courtyards hide behind some of the old façades, and the odd remnant of the city walls remains. The distinctive **Steinertor** on Obere Landstrasse dates from the 15th century and is the town emblem. Near the **Linzertor** in Stein is the house occupied after 1756 by the artist Martin Johann Schmidt, often known as Kremser Schmidt.

Krems has several churches worth a peek inside. The **St Veit Parish Church**, on the hill at Pfarrplatz, is fitted out in Baroque style, though it had earlier Gothic and Romanesque incarnations. The ceiling frescoes are by Kremser Schmidt. The 15th-century **Piarist Church** (Piaristenkirche), behind St Veit's on Frauenbergplatz, has Gothic vaulting, huge windows and Baroque altars.

The **Dominican Church**, Dominikanerplatz, is an atmospheric site for the Krems Historical Museum. This has two main strands: religious and modern art (with plenty of paintings by Kremser Schmidt), and an exposition of wine-making (AS20); it's open April to October, daily except Monday. The **Minorite Church** in Stein is used for temporary exhibitions.

The street plan from the tourist office details other points of interest. Wine buffs can enjoy wine-tasting daily in the Kloster Und (AS130), the home of a wine college. Weingut Stadt Krems, Stadtgraben 11, allows free tastings prior to possible purchase.

PLACES TO STAY
4 Haus Hietzgern
9 Hotel Alte Poste
17 Youth Hostel
18 Camping Donau
21 Frühstückspension
   Einzinger

PLACES TO EAT
3 Zur Wiener Brücke
5 Schwarze Kuchl

OTHER
1 Weingut Stadt Krems
2 Piarist Church
6 St Veit Parish Church
7 Dominican Church
8 Spar Supermarket
10 Steinertor
11 Hofer Supermarket
12 Train Station
13 Bundesbus Departures
14 Main Post Office
15 Konsum Supermarket
16 Tourist Office & Klosterund
19 Boat Station
20 Minorite Church

Krems

Danube

STEIN

Festivals

In August every year Krems hosts its Niederösterreichische Landesmesse, a folklore festival, expanding to international scope every odd year (1997 etc). The annual Donau festival of the arts runs from mid-June to early July.

Places to Stay

Camping Donau (☎ 84 4 55) at Wiedengasse 7, near the boat station, is open from mid-April to 31 October and costs AS50 per person, from AS30 for a tent and AS40 for a car.

The HI *youth hostel* (☎ 83 4 52) is at Ringstrasse 77, and has excellent facilities for cyclists, such as a garage and repair service. Beds in four or six-bed dorms with own shower/WC are AS160. The doors are closed from 9 am to 5 pm, check-in is from 5 to 8 pm, and it's open from 1 April to 30 September.

In other places, a surcharge of AS10 to AS30 for a single night's stay is common. As ever, private rooms are a good deal, and these are listed in the tourist office's accommodation brochure. *Haus Hietzgern* (☎ 76 1 84), Untere Landstrasse 53, is ideally central and has an Art-Nouveau façade. There are two doubles and two triples for AS230 per person, with private shower/WC, available from 1 June to 31 August.

Frühstückspension Aigner (☎ 84 5 58), Weinzierl 53, is a *Weinbau* (wine producer) and there's a Heuriger next door. Doubles with private shower/WC and TV are AS260 (AS350 for single occupancy). Bundesbuses go along this road, though it's less than 20 minutes walk from the train station.

In Stein, *Frühstückspension Einzinger* (☎ 82 3 16), Steiner Landstrasse 82, offers similar-standard doubles from AS540, and singles with private shower (not WC) for AS320.

Hotel Alte Poste (☎ 82 2 76), Obere Landstrasse 32, is a 500-year-old house. It has good singles/doubles for AS290/560, or AS460/680 with private shower, grouped round an enchanting courtyard.

Gourmet-Hotel Am Förthof (☎ 83 3 45), Förthofer Donaulände 8, 500 metres west of Stein, is a small hotel with an outdoor swimming pool. Rooms (all with bath or shower, toilet and TV) cost from AS650/1200 to AS750/1400, depending on the size and season.

Places to Eat

Krems has several supermarkets: *Spar* at Obere Landstrasse 15, *Hofer* nearby on Sparkassegasse, and *Konsum* near the train station.

Where Untere and Obere Landstrasse join there are several cheap snack bars serving bread and sausage or pizza slices. *Schwarze Kuchl*, Untere Landstrasse 8, has food for around AS50 to AS90, and there is a good choice at the salad bar (AS42 or AS62). It's open weekdays from 8 am to 7 pm, and Saturday from 8 am to 1 pm.

The restaurant *Zur Wiener Brücke*, also called Gasthof Klinglhuber (☎ 82 1 43), Wiener Strasse 2, has terrace seating overlooking the canal. Tasty Austrian food costs around AS100 to AS160 (there are a few cheaper choices), and it is open daily from 7 am to midnight.

Hotel Alte Poste (see Places to Stay) has a pleasant restaurant, and tables in the even more pleasant courtyard. Dishes start from AS90 and local wine from AS30 per quarter litre. It's open daily.

As its name implies, the *Gourmet-Hotel Am Förthof* (see Places to Stay) is also a good place to eat, particularly for regional specialities. Prices are AS90 to AS300 (open daily; kitchen to 9.30 pm).

Don't omit a visit to a Heuriger; they are mostly out of the centre but provide an authentic experience in eating and drinking. They are only open for two or three-week bursts during the year: get the timetable from the tourist office.

Getting There & Away

Three or four Bundesbuses a day to Melk leave from outside the train station. The fare is AS64 and it takes 65 minutes. Buses also go between Krems and Stein. Trains to

Vienna cost AS119 and take about an hour to Franz Josefs Bahnhof.

The boat station (☎ 82 0 50) is 20 minutes walk from the train station towards Stein on Donaulände. There are up to three departures a day to Melk between 10.30 am and 2.30 pm. It costs AS238 and takes three hours.

Bikes can be rented at the train station, camping ground and some hotels. Bicycle tourists are very welcome in Krems; some hotels have bike garages and repair facilities.

AROUND KREMS

Six km south of Krems is **Göttweig Abbey**, founded in 1083 and given to the Benedictine order 11 years later. The abbey's position on a hill makes its towers and onion domes clearly visible from afar (and you can view to afar from the garden terrace or the restaurant in the abbey grounds). What remains today is mostly the Baroque work begun in 1719 following a devastating fire. The plans for rebuilding were never fully realised, resulting in an asymmetric but impressive complex. The abbey church has ceiling frescoes (1739) by Paul Troger; Kremser Schmidt also contributed to the church and to the imperial apartments, which are part of the abbey buildings. Guided tours of the abbey (AS40) are conducted from April to October.

Less than 30 km north of Krems are a few worthwhile sights. The most important is the Benedictine **Altenburg Abbey**, founded in 1144. In the ensuing centuries it was all but destroyed by plundering hordes, until extensive Baroque rebuilding began in 1650. The abbey library (with ceiling frescoes by Paul Troger) and the crypt (with frescoes by Troger's pupils) are among the most impressive examples of their kind in Austria. The abbey church was created by Josef Munggenast from 1730 to 1733. The church contains some of Troger's best frescoes (in the central dome, and above the high and side altars). The gilded organ dates from 1773. The abbey buildings can be visited on a 60-minute guided tour, conducted daily from Easter to 31 October (AS50, students AS30).

For information call ☎ 02982-34 51. The church is accessible without taking a tour.

From Krems, a few km short of Altenburg, is **Rosenburg Castle**, a multi-turreted edifice built from the 14th to the 17th centuries (daily tours from 1 April to 15 November). A similar distance west of Altenburg is **Greillenstein Castle**, built in the late 16th century, but with an entrance tower added in 1700 (tours of the interior are held from 1 April to 31 October daily).

South-west of these sights is the **Waldviertel**, a less visited forested region, ideal for off-the-beaten-track hiking.

Getting There & Away

Rosenburg is on a rail line that runs north from Krems (takes 55 minutes). For the other destinations you'll have to rely on Bundesbuses if you don't have your own transport; call ☎ 82 3 60 in Krems for information. For Göttweig Abbey, the bus leaves from outside Krems train station at 1.30 pm and returns at 4.15 pm.

TULLN

• *pop 11,300* • *180 m* • ☎ *(02272)*

Formerly a Roman camp called Comagena, and named as a town settlement in 791, Tulln trumpets itself as the 'Birthplace of Austria', and was in effect the nation's first capital.

Orientation & Information

Tulln is 29 km west of Vienna, on the south bank of the Danube River. The centre of town is the pedestrian-only Hauptplatz. The tourist office (☎ 58 36) is one block north at Minoritenplatz 2. It's open 1 May to 31 October on weekdays from 9 am to noon and 2 to 6 pm, and weekends from noon to 6 pm; for the rest of the year, hours are weekdays only from 8 am to noon. The office reserves rooms without charging commission.

Tulln train station (with bike rental) is 15 minutes walk south-east of Hauptplatz; from the station, turn right into Bahnweg, right at Brückenstrasse, and left on Wiener Strasse. Tulln Stadt is an S-Bahn station, just five minutes walk south of Hauptplatz along Bahnhofstrasse.

Things to See & Do

Next to the tourist office in the Minoritenkloster is a new complex of museums, the **Tullner Museen**. Collections cover the city's history, both ancient and modern (including geology and Roman finds); one section deals with fire-fighting. Admission to all parts costs AS30 (AS20 for seniors and students) and it's open Wednesday to Friday from 3 to 6 pm, Saturday from 2 to 6 pm, and Sunday from 10 am to 6 pm.

On the riverside is the **Egon Schiele Museum**, open Tuesday to Sunday from 9 am to noon and 2 to 6 pm (4 pm in winter). Admission costs AS30 (AS20 for seniors and students). It tells vividly the life story of the Tulln-born artist – ask for the extensive English notes. Schiele is famous for his provocative nudes and he was briefly imprisoned following the seizure of 125 erotic drawings of children. Appropriately, the premises are a former jail and contain a mock-up of his cell (though Schiele was actually jailed in Neulengbach). There are 100 of his works on display (plus copies), mostly sketches and early paintings.

Churches of interest include the newly restored **Minorite Church** (18th century) and the **Parish Church of St Stephen** (12th-century Romanesque, with alterations to Gothic and Baroque). Behind the latter is a polygonal funerary chapel dating from the 13th century, with frescoes depicting some not very evil-looking devils. The crypt below was formerly filled with exhumed bones.

The town offers a variety of sports near the Yachthafen (yacht harbour), to the west of the centre. The swimming pool complex costs AS40 per day (students AS30). The tourist office has plenty of information for cyclists.

Places to Stay & Eat

The *Donaupark Camping Ground* (☎ 52 00) is open from mid-May to early October; it's east of the centre near the river. A site (including parking) costs AS50, plus AS50 per person.

Beside the river and half a km west of the Egon Schiele Museum is *Alpenvereins*

Herberge (☎ 26 92), with dorm beds for AS148 or a mattress on the floor for AS118 (open 1 May to 31 October). Lunches in the basic restaurant are cheap and not bad.

Some families offer private rooms for about AS200 per person, identified in the tourist office list. *Gasthof Zum Grünen Baum* (☎ 25 05), Wiener Strasse 43, has five rooms with private shower, and charges AS250 per person. It's in Langenlebarn, four km towards Vienna, and has a restaurant and parking spaces.

Hotel-Restaurant Zur Rossmühle (☎ 24 11), Hauptplatz 13, has an imperial aura and a veritable jungle of plants in the lobby (complete with tweeting birds). Singles/doubles have high ceilings and shower/WC and TV, and start from AS430/860. The restaurant is good quality, with interesting presentations of national dishes for around AS130 to AS270 (open daily).

China Restaurant Asia, Brudergasse 5, off Hauptplatz, has good weekday lunch menus from AS56, with plenty of food (open daily). For good Austrian cooking, go to *Albrechts-stuben*, Albrechtsgasse 24, with three-course lunch menus from AS60, and other meals for AS70 to AS180. This place has a garden and is frequented by locals (closed Monday).

There is a *Hofer* supermarket on Hauptplatz.

Getting There & Away

Tulln is reached by train or S-Bahn (line 46) from Vienna's Franz Josefs Bahnhof (AS51). The train is quicker (25 minutes), but only stops at the main Tulln station, while the S40 stops at Tulln Stadt. Heading east, trains go to Krems (AS68) or St Pölten (AS74). The road from Vienna is highway 14, going via Klosterneuburg.

KLOSTERNEUBURG

• ☎ (02243)

Overlooking the river at Klosterneuburg is a large **Augustinian abbey**, founded in 1114. The abbey buildings are mostly Baroque and can be visited by a 45-minute guided tour every day (AS50; students AS15). The abbey church is also Baroque, despite its neo-

Gothic spires. An annex to the church is St Leopold's Chapel, which has the *Verdun Altar,* covered in 51 enamelled panels showing biblical scenes. It was made in 1181 by Nicholas of Verdun and is an unsurpassed example of medieval enamel work.

Klosterneuburg has a year-round camp site (☎ 85 8 77) by the Danube. A HI *youth hostel* (☎ 83 5 01), Hüttersteig 8, in the Maria Gugging district, is accessible by bus from the train station; it's open from 1 May to mid-September.

Getting There & Away
Klosterneuburg is on the S-Bahn route from Vienna to Tulln: Klosterneuburg-Kierling is the station closest to the abbey (AS34 from Franz Josefs Bahnhof). Alternatively, hike there from Kahlenberg (at the end of bus No 38A from Vienna).

PETRONELL
• *pop 1250* • *190 m* • ☎ *(02163)*

The village of Petronell lies close to the Danube, 38 km east of Vienna. In Roman times it was the site of Carnuntum, a regional capital believed to have had 60,000 inhabitants. Ruins extend towards Bad Deutsch-Altenburg, four km to the east.

Orientation & Information
Petronell train station is one km south of the main street, Hauptstrasse. The tiny tourist office (☎ 22 28) is on the 1st floor of the post office at Kirchengasse 57 and is open Monday and Friday from 8 am to noon and Wednesday from 8 am to 4 pm.

Bad Deutsch-Altenburg's tourist office (☎ 02165-62 4 59) is at Badgasse 17.

Things to See & Do
Relics of former glories are not particularly stunning, but together they make a reasonably diverting day. They include a grass-covered amphitheatre that formerly seated 15,000, the palace ruins (Palastruine), and an archaeological park on the site of the old civilian town. This park is being reconstructed in Roman style, and is open daily from 1 April to 31 October; ☎ 28 82 for information.

The **Heidentor** (Heathen Gate) was once the south-west entrance to the city and now stands as an isolated anachronism amid fields of corn. The small Petronell museum is open May to September, only on weekends and holidays from 10 am to 4 pm.

Bad Deutsch-Altenburg has a larger museum devoted to the Carnuntum era, at Badgasse 40-46; it is open Tuesday to Sunday from 10 am to 5 pm (7 pm Friday). Bad Deutsch-Altenburg is also a health spa, with iodine sulphur springs (28°C).

Tiny **Rohrau**, six km south of Petronell, is the birthplace of Josef Haydn. Signs will point you to the house where it happened: it's now a museum (☎ 02164-22 68) devoted to the composer (AS20; closed Monday). The 16th-century Harrach Castle in Rohrau has a private art collection (AS45; open April to October except Monday).

Places to Stay & Eat
Gasthof Zum Heidentor (☎ 22 01), Hauptstrasse 129, has singles/doubles for AS300/500 with shower, WC and TV. The restaurant offers a lunch menu for AS60 with soup (not Sunday; closed Monday), and has a beer garden and children's play area. A *Konsum* supermarket is nearby on Hauptstrasse.

Hotel Marc Aurel (☎ 22 85), Hauptstrasse 173, is a three-star place charging AS500/710 for rooms with shower/WC but no TV. The restaurant has plenty of Austrian dishes under AS100.

Bad Deutsch-Altenburg has a wider choice of places to stay. At the cheaper end, try *Pension Mittermayer* (☎ 02165-62 8 74), Badgasse 20, with rooms from AS200 per person using hall shower. *Pension Riedmüller* (☎ 02165-62 4 73 0), Badgasse 28, charges AS285 per person (private shower/WC) and has a restaurant. *Hotel-Restaurant König Stephan* (☎ 02165-64 7 11) is good for mid-price regional food (open daily).

Getting There & Away

From Vienna, an hourly train (S7) departs Wien Nord station at 29 minutes past the hour, calling at Wien Mitte station three minutes later. The fare is AS68, or AS51 if you already have a Vienna city travel pass. Bad Deutsch-Altenburg station is an extra zone from Vienna, so the fare is AS85 (AS68 with pass). Rohrau can be reached by Bundesbus.

The cycle path from Vienna goes along the north bank of the Danube, crosses to the south at Bad Deutsch-Altenburg, and continues into Slovakia.

BRATISLAVA (SLOVAKIA)

The capital of Slovakia is 65 km east of Vienna and a popular day trip. People come here to shop and eat, not because the quality and range are particularly good but because prices are so much lower than in Vienna. In mid-1995 the exchange rate was about AS1 to 2.7 Slovak koruna (crowns). In a supermarket or a restaurant a crown would buy at least as much as a schilling would in Austria. Money is easily changed in Austria or Slovakia (at the boat station or banks).

Orientation & Information

The centre and the sights are north of the Danube. From the boat station, walk left 200 metres, turn right into Mostová, continue past the National Theatre on the right, and through the next intersection until you reach Panská. The tourist office (☎ 333 715) is 100 metres to the left at No 18, and can sell you a city guide for Sk15 and help with accommodation. Most museums are closed on Monday. On SNP square is the large Dom Odievania department store.

Things to See & Do

Bratislava hasn't the charm of Prague or Budapest; the old centre was scarred by soulless Soviet-style edifices, and the sea of standardised apartment blocks to the south is a depressing sight. **Bratislava Castle** stands on the hill but it has little to excite the visitor except a historical museum and the view from the top. There are many other museums, the best being the **Municipal Museum** in the old town hall, featuring artefacts, decorated rooms and torture chambers.

The **SNP bridge** is an absurd lopsided structure with a restaurant at the top. A lift will whisk you up there, where you can enjoy a beer, the view and the unnerving quivering of the floor as the traffic rumbles below and the wind buffets the windows.

Historical resonances are best experienced in the **cathedral**, where 11 Habsburg kings were crowned, and the **Primatial Palace**, where Napoleon signed a peace treaty with Franz I in 1805.

Places to Eat

There are several options by the National Theatre, including an Italian place with outside tables, and Chinese food and burgers in the small arcade.

For typical Slovak food and a typical queue-oriented set-up, go to *Diétna Jedálen Restaurant* (closed Sunday), where you can eat and drink for about Sk40. A supermarket with alcohol is opposite. *U Dežmára* has good food and a comfortable ambience, yet is still very cheap by Austrian standards. It's down the Podjazo passage, leading west from Venturská.

Getting There & Away

DDSG runs two fast hydrofoils each way between Vienna and Bratislava (AS210, takes one hour). Departures are from mid-April to mid-October daily (except Monday to Wednesday in the low season). A one-day package including city tour and lunch costs AS580 (reservations required).

To spend more time in Bratislava, take the last bus back to Vienna at 8.30 pm from the Mlynské Nivy bus station (Sk92; 1½ hours); you can get your ticket from the driver. The bus fare from Wien Mitte station in Vienna to Bratislava is the same price – but in schillings! Buses go along highway 9, passing through Petronell and Vienna airport.

Wienerwald

The Wienerwald (Vienna Woods) is a place to get off the beaten track and enjoy nature. **Hiking** is popular, with numerous trails meandering through the trees. **Schöpfl** (893 metres) is the highest point, and has a panoramic lookout (with an Alpine hut open year-round). The signposted hike to Schöpfl lookout takes about two hours, starting from the car park off the Hainfeld-Laaben road, near the Klammhöhe Pass. Walking and cycling trails are shown on the free *Wienerwald Wander- und Radkarte*, available free from the Lower Austria Information Office and the Baden tourist office.

Attractive settlements speckle the Wienerwald, such as the wine-growing centres of Perchtoldsdorf, Mödling and Gumpoldskirchen. Enquire at the respective tourist offices about accommodation. The tourist board for the Wienerwald (☎ 02231-21 76) is at Hauptplatz 11, Purkersdorf, A3200, just west of Vienna. **Mödling** (population 19,000) achieved favour with the artistic elite escaping from Vienna: Beethoven's itchy feet took him to Hauptstrasse 79 from 1818 to 1820; and Schönberg stayed at Bernhardgasse 6 from 1918 to 1925. Mödling tourist office (☎ 02236-26 7 27) is at Elisabethstrasse 2, behind the town hall.

Mayerling has little to show now, but the bloody event that occurred there still draws people to the site. The Carmelite convent can be visited on a daily guided tour (AS15).

Six km to the north-east is **Heiligenkreuz**, where Maria's grave can be seen. The 12th-century Cistercian abbey here is the final resting place (in the chapter house) of most of the Babenberg dynasty which ruled Austria until 1246. The church and the cloister both combine Romanesque and Gothic styles. The abbey museum contains 150 clay models by Giovanni Giuliani, a Venetian sculptor who also created the Trinity column in the courtyard. Tours of the abbey buildings are conducted daily and cost AS35 (students AS20). Maria's grave can be seen

without joining the tour. Heilingenkreuz's tourist office (☎ 02256-22 86) is near the abbey.

Between Mödling and Heiligenkreuz, boat tours can be taken of Europe's largest underground lake, **Seegrotte Hinterbrühl** (☎ 02236-26 3 64). The site was used by the Nazis in WW II to build armaments. The tours (in English) last 45 minutes and cost AS46 (children AS23). Hinterbrühl is open daily, April to October from 8.30 am to noon and 1 to 5 pm, and November to March from 9 am to noon and 1 to 3.30 pm; ☎ 02236-26 3 64 for information.

Getting There & Away
To explore this region, it's best if you have your own transport. Trains skirt either side of the woods and the Bundesbus service is patchy. Bus No 902 runs every 90 minutes or so between Baden, Heiligenkreuz and Mayerling. Mödling receives S-Bahn and regional trains running between Vienna's Südbahnhof and Baden, and a bus goes from Mödling to Hinterbrühl. The main road through the area is the A21 that loops down from Vienna, passes by Heiligenkreuz, then curves north before joining the A1 just east of Altlengbach.

BADEN
- *pop 24,000* • *230 m* • ☎ *(02252)*

On the eastern edge of the Wienerwald, the spa town of Baden has a long history. The Romans were prone to wallow in its medicinal springs. Beethoven came here many times in hope of a cure for his deafness. The town flourished in the early 19th century when it was adopted by the Habsburgs as their favourite summer retreat. Baden mostly closes down in winter, including the museums.

Orientation & Information
The centre is 10 minutes walk north-west of the train station: cut across the small park to Bahngasse and then bear right on the pedestrian-only Wassergasse. The tourist office (☎ 86800 310), Hauptplatz 2, is open Monday to Saturday from 9 am to noon and

2 to 6 pm, and Sunday and holidays from 9 am to noon. From November to Easter, hours are Monday to Friday from 8 am to noon and 1 to 5 pm.

Things to See & Do

Baden exudes health and 19th-century affluence, an impression endorsed by the many Biedermeier-style houses. The impressive **Trinity column** on Hauptplatz dates from 1714.

The town attracts plenty of promenading Viennese on the weekends. All and sundry make for the **Kurpark**, a magnificent setting for a stroll. Rows of white benches are neatly positioned under manicured trees in front of the bandstand, and elaborate flower beds complement monuments to famous artists (Mozart, Beethoven, Strauss, Grillparzer etc). The *Undine Brunnen* (fountain) is a fine amalgam of human and fish images. Free spa concerts (*Kurkonzerte*) are performed in the bandstand from May to September, usually daily except Monday at 4.30 pm. In bad weather concerts move inside to the nearby Bistro Café of the casino. The casino itself has gaming tables (open from 3 pm; dress code) and slot machines (from 1 pm; no dress code). An ID is required for entry.

The **Emperor Franz Josef Museum,**

Mystery at Mayerling

It's the stuff of lurid pulp fiction: the heir to the throne found dead in a hunting lodge with his teenage mistress. Fiction became fact in Mayerling on 30 January 1889, yet for years the details were shrouded in secrecy and denial. Even now a definitive picture has not been established – a flurry of books was produced to commemorate the 100th anniversary of the tragedy, and Empress Zita claimed publicly that the heir had been murdered.

The heir involved was Archduke Rudolf, 30-year-old son of Emperor Franz Joseph, husband of Stephanie of Coburg, and something of a liberal, fond of drinking and womanising. Rudolf's marriage was little more than a public façade by the time he met the 17-year-old Baroness Marie Vetsera in the autumn of 1888. The attraction was immediate, but it wasn't until 13 January the following year that the affair was consummated, an event commemorated by an inscribed cigarette case, a gift from Marie to Rudolf.

On 28 January, Rudolf took Marie with him on a shooting trip to his hunting lodge in Mayerling. His other guests arrived a day later; Marie's presence, however, remained secret. That night the valet, Loschek, heard the couple talking until the early hours, and at about 5.30 am a fully-dressed Rudolf appeared and instructed him to get a horse and carriage ready. As he was doing his master's bidding, two gun shots resounded. He raced back to discover a lifeless Rudolf on his bed, with a revolver by his side. Marie was on her bed, also fully clothed and also dead. Just two days earlier Rudolf had discussed a suicide pact with a former mistress. Apparently he hadn't been joking.

Almost immediately the cover-up began. Count Hoyos, a guest at the lodge, told Marie's mother that Marie had killed both herself and the archduke with the aid of poison. The official line was proffered by Empress Elisabeth, who claimed Rudolf had died from heart failure. Publicly, there was no hint of suicide or a mistress. The newspapers swallowed the heart-failure story, though a few speculated about a hunting accident. Only some years later was Rudolf's suicide letter to his wife published in her memoirs. In it, he talked of going calmly to his death.

Throughout the lies and misinformation, the real victim was Marie. How much of a willing party she was to suicide will never be known. But it is clear that to the imperial family she represented, not a tragically curtailed life, but an embarrassing scandal to be discreetly disposed of. Her body was left untouched for 38 hours, after which it was loaded into a carriage in such a manner as to imply that it was a living person being assisted, rather than a corpse beyond help. Her burial was a rude, secretive affair, during which she was consigned to an unmarked grave (her body was later moved to Heiligenkreuz). Today, the hunting lodge is no more and a Carmelite nunnery stands in its place. ■

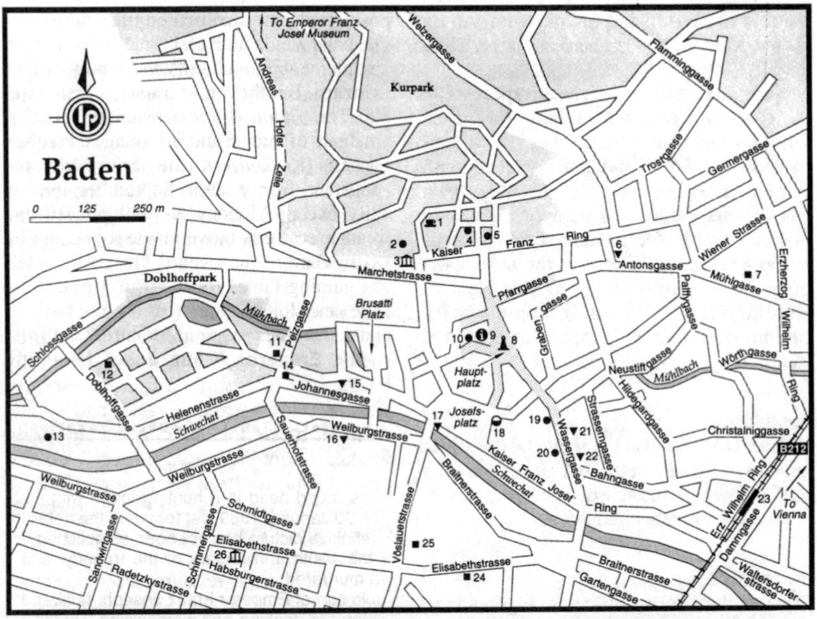

PLACES TO STAY

7 Pension Garni Margit
11 Hotel Rauch
12 Hotel Schloss
    Weikersdorf
14 Nihonya
24 Pension Maria
25 Lakies

PLACES TO EAT

6 Gasthaus Zum
   Reichsapfel

15 Ackerl's Badner Stüberl
16 Hotel Sauerhof
17 Wan Zhen
21 Venezia
22 Nakowitsch

OTHER

1 Bistro Café
2 Casino
3 Doll and Toy Museum
4 Bandstand
5 Undine Brunnen
8 Trinity Column

9 Tourist Office
10 Beethoven's House
13 Strandbad
18 Lokalbahn Station
19 Billa Supermarket
20 Familia Supermarket
23 Train Station
26 Rollett Museum

Hochstrasse 51, out of town to the north, displays local folklore (AS20, students AS15; closed Monday). The **Rollett Museum**, Weikersdorfer Platz 1, south-west of the centre, covers aspects of the town's history (eg bomb damage in WW II). The most unusual exhibit is the collection of skulls, busts and death masks amassed by the founder of phrenology, Josef Gall (1752-

1828). This apparently cranky science, which held that criminal characteristics could be inferred from the shape of the skull, links disturbingly with modern claims of the discovery of a 'criminal gene'. The museum is closed on Monday and entry costs AS20 (students AS10). Beethoven's former house at Rathausgasse 10 has Beethovenesque exhibits (AS15; limited opening hours).

There's also a doll and toy museum (AS15; closed Monday) at Erzherzog Rainer Ring 23.

Baden's reputation as a health spa rests on its 15 **hot springs**, with a daily flow of 6.5 million litres. The waters emerge at a temperature of 36°C and are enriched with sulphur, chlorine and sulphates. The town has various indoor and outdoor pool complexes suitable for medicinal or frivolous purposes. Predominantly in the latter category is the Strandbad, to the west at Helenenstrasse 19-21, complete with sulphur and normal pools, plus imported sand.

Festivals
In June a rose festival is held in the Rosarium gardens and an operetta festival begins. May to September is the season for trotting races (*Trabenen*; entry around AS30).

Places to Stay
Outside the tourist office is a good map showing the locations of hotels and restaurants. Unfortunately, the few private rooms are the only option for those on a tight budget; get a list from the tourist office. *Lakies* (☎ 41 1 11), Vöslauerstrasse 11, just south of Josefsplatz, has singles with shower for AS180, and one double. The *Nihonya* Japanese restaurant (☎ 24 3 03), Johannesgasse 1, has large if fairly bare rooms with shower for AS250 per person (one week's notice preferred).

Pension Garni Margit (☎ 89 7 18), Mühlgasse 15-17, is eight minutes walk east of Hauptplatz. It has a homey ambience and a garden but the singles/doubles for AS300/550 have no access to a shower. Pay AS380/600 or more for private facilities. *Pension Maria* (☎ 87 9 37), Elisabethstrasse 11, off Vöslauerstrasse, has rooms for AS400/680, with shower/WC, and sometimes TV. There's a small swimming pool.

Hotel Rauch (☎ 44 5 61), Pelzgasse 3, west of Hauptplatz, is next to the Doblhoffpark in a typical Baden building with high ceilings. Rooms (with WC and mini-baths)

cost up to AS480/800, depending on the size and season.

Hotel Schloss Weikersdorf (☎ 48 3 01), Schlossgasse 9-11, also adjoining the park, has a genuine castle ambience and fixtures, which is usually reflected in room furnishings. Singles/doubles with shower/WC and cable TV start at AS825/1350, though the cheaper rooms are in the building with the sauna and indoor swimming pool (both free for guests).

Places to Eat
On Wassergasse there are *Familia* and *Billa* supermarkets. On the same street by Bahngasse is *Nakowitsch*, a self-service place serving sausage snacks and simple Austrian meals for under AS85. It's open weekdays (not Wednesday) from 7 am to 6 pm and Saturday from 7 am to 1 pm. There's a similar place on Brusatti Platz (except it's closed lunchtimes), where there are also market stalls.

Several Chinese restaurants provide inexpensive fare: *Wan Zhen*, Braitnerstrasse 1, has weekday lunch menus from AS59 and outside tables overlooking the Schwechat River. *Venezia*, Wassergasse 29, is an Italian restaurant with bigger-than-the-plate pizzas for AS42 to AS100. Both are open daily.

Ackerl's Badner Stüberl, Gutenbrunnerstrasse 19, has mid-price food (closed Tuesday). The plush *Hotel Sauerhof* (☎ 41 2 51 6), Weilburgstrasse 11-13, has a quality restaurant, serving international dishes for above AS200. It's open only in the evening, except for its Sunday lunchtime buffet.

Baden is not known for its nightlife, but to combine wine and dining, ask the tourist office for the opening schedule of the various Heurigen.

Gasthaus Zum Reichsapfel, Spiegelgasse, is like a small beer hall, with several varieties of ale on tap. It also serves Austrian meals from AS70, plus cheap vegetarian dishes.

Getting There & Away
IC trains don't stop at Baden, but regional and S-Bahn services run to/from Baden about twice an hour from Vienna's Südbahn-

hof (AS51; 20 to 25 minutes). The same trains also go to Wiener Neustadt. The Lokalbahn tram goes from Vienna's Kärntner Ring (opposite Hotel Bristol) to Josefsplatz in Baden three times an hour and takes 64 minutes (AS51). On this service, Austrian rail passes are valid but European passes aren't.

North-south road routes, highway 17 and the A2, pass a few km to the east of the town.

Southern Lower Austria

This region includes the edge of the Alps, the highest and best-known peak being Schneeberg at 2075 metres high. In the south-east are several mountains approaching 2000 metres high, such as Hochkar and Ötscher (both have chair lifts).

WIENER NEUSTADT
• *pop 40,000* • *265 m* • ☎ *(02622)*
The city, then known simply as Neustadt (new city) or Nova Civitas, was built by the Babenbergs in 1194. It became a Habsburg residence in the 15th century, courtesy of Friedrich III. His son, Maximilian I, was born in the town. Wiener Neustadt was severely damaged in WW II and only 18 homes were unscathed. Historic buildings that were damaged have been restored.

Orientation & Information
The centre of town is the large Hauptplatz, where you'll find the tourist office (☎ 23 5 31) at No 3, in the Rathaus complex. It is open Monday to Friday from 8 am to noon and 1 to 5 pm, and Saturday from 8 am to noon. Most of the streets leading off Hauptplatz are pedestrian-only.

The train station is less than one km to the south-west. It has bike rental, a travel agency and a Bankomat. Next door is the main post office (Hauptpostamt 2700), open Monday to Friday from 7 am to 7 pm, Saturday from 7 am to 4 pm, and Sunday and holidays from 8 to 10 am.

Things to See & Do
The tourist office doesn't have a great deal of information in English, but at least there's its free *Cultural Promenade* booklet, describing central sights and locating them on a map.

Spacious **Hauptplatz** is lined with elegant buildings, not least the three parts of the Rathaus, featuring an arcade and colourful crests. An outdoor market fills the square daily except Sunday, though the busiest days are Wednesday and Saturday. East of Hauptplatz is **Neukloster**, a 14th-century Gothic church with striking Baroque fittings.

The Romanesque **cathedral** (built in 1279 but subsequently much rebuilt) has a rather bare and grey exterior, and two severe-looking square towers. The interior has an unbalanced look, caused by the chancel being out of line with the nave, and the asymmetric arch that connects the two. Wooden apostles peer down from pillars, and there's a Baroque high altar and pulpit.

The imposing **castle** on Burgplatz houses a military academy, founded by Empress Maria Theresa in 1752, and later commanded by young Rommel, before he became a foxy Nazi general. The castle with its four towers dates from the 13th century, though it had to be completely rebuilt after WW II. Within the complex is **St George's Church**, with a fine late-Gothic interior. Maximilian I, who was born in the castle, is buried under the altar. On the outside wall is the Wappenwand, comprising 15th-century carvings of 107 coats of arms. This wall was all that survived WW II bombs (the stained glass had already been removed to the Altaussee salt mines). The statue below the window is of Friedrich III, whose AEIOU motto also appears on the wall. The military guard will show you round (ring on the bell if the door's shut).

At the eastern end of the Stadtpark is a **water tower** (Wasserturm), built from 1909 to 1910. Its shape intentionally apes the gilded goblet (*Becher*) donated to the townsfolk by King Matthias Corvinus of Hungary, after he took the town in 1487. A copy of this chalice can be seen in the **Stadtmuseum**

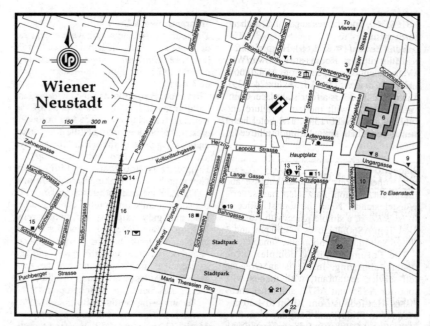

Wiener Neustadt

PLACES TO STAY

11 Hotel Zentral
15 Gasthof Friedam
18 Hotel Corvinus
21 Youth Hostel

PLACES TO EAT

1 Oregano Restaurant

3 Stargl-wirt
8 Stüberl zum Ungartor
9 China-Restaurant
    Hong Kong
12 Weisses Rössl

OTHER

2 Stadtmuseum
4 Sport Café

5 Cathedral
6 Hospital
7 Billa Supermarket
10 Neukloster
13 Tourist Office
14 Bundesbus Departures
16 Train Station
17 Main Post Office
19 Billa Supermarket
20 Castle
22 Water Towers

(AS30, open Tuesday to Friday, and Sunday morning), at the intersection of Wiener Strasse and Petersgasse; the original is in the Rathaus.

Wiener Neustadt is a convenient base for an excursion to Schneeberg (see later entry).

Places to Stay

The HI *youth hostel* (☎ 29 6 95), Promenade 1, is the white house in the Stadtpark, near the water tower. It has rooms with one to four beds (36 in total) with modern bathroom

facilities and a kitchen. The price is AS125.50, plus S30 for breakfast. Get a key for late entry. Check-in is from 5 to 8 pm on the 1st floor, but phone ahead as it's a one-woman show, and she may not always be around; the place is often full anyway.

Wiener Neustadt has just five hotels and pensions. The only budget choice, and an excellent one, is *Gasthof Friedam* (☎ 23 0 81), Schneeberggasse 16, five minutes walk behind the train station. Singles/doubles with shower cubicle and sink cost just

AS190/360, and the restaurant has a cheap lunch menu.

Hotel Zentral (☎ 23 1 69), Hauptplatz 27, is ideally situated. Rooms have shower/WC, TV and telephone and cost from AS420/660.

Hotel Corvinus (☎ 24 1 34; fax 24 1 39), Bahngasse 29-33, is a four-star place. Comfortable rooms with modern furniture and facilities are AS880/1340. The hotel has a sauna, steam bath and whirlpool (all free for guests).

Places to Eat

Billa supermarkets are on Bahngasse and Hauptplatz. Hauptplatz also has several Würstel stands. Near the tourist office is *Weisses Rössl*, a simple place with Austrian food from AS60. It closes at 8.30 pm, and is closed Saturday afternoon and Sunday.

The Forum shopping complex is on Baumkirchnerring. Inside is an *Oregano* self-service restaurant, with menus with soup for AS55 and AS72, and other cheap dishes. Hot food is from 10 am to 4.30 pm, Monday to Friday, and Saturday from 8.30 to 11.30 am (4.30 pm on Langersamstag). An adjoining café is open slightly longer.

To the east, Baumkirchnerring becomes Eyerspergring. On this street is *Sport Café*, with snooker and pool tables (open daily from 2 pm to midnight), and *Stargl-wirt*, a specialist place for schnitzels (AS85 to AS130; closed Saturday evening and Sunday).

Ungarngasse, running east from Hauptplatz, has two good places to eat. *China-Restaurant Hong Kong* at No 27 has weekday lunch menus from AS52, including a starter (open daily). *Stüberl Zum Ungarntor*, at No 21, has tasty Austrian food (AS75 to AS120) and special dishes, which are chalked on a board (closed Monday).

Getting There & Away

By train, Wiener Neustadt costs AS85 from Vienna's Südbahnhof (takes 30 minutes; three departures per hour). Approximately hourly trains go to the Hungarian shopping town of Sopron (AS51, takes 45 minutes) and Austrian rail passes are valid for the whole trip. Bundesbuses depart from the north end of the train station, including to Eisenstadt.

The city has excellent road links: options from Vienna include the A2 or highway 17.

SEMMERING
• *1000 m* • ☎ *(02664)*

This spread-out mountain resort is famed for its clean air. Semmering became a favourite with moneyed tourists at the turn of the century.

Shopping Spree

When Hungary's borders opened in 1989, the Viennese flocked to Sopron (Ödenburg) to shop. Just eight km from the Austrian border, Sopron was Eastern Europe's first free trade shopping zone and prices were a fraction of those in Vienna's plush boulevards. Sopron had been a picturesque medieval town, but quickly changed to meet the new demand. It spawned 36 supermarkets (foie gras was highly prized, as was the cheap wine, spirits and cigarettes) and 24 fashion boutiques. There were also 127 dentists – an incredible number, but dental work was being described by happy punters as half the price as in Austria and twice as good.

Sopron is near Lake Neusiedl, about an hour's drive south-east of Vienna. From Wiener Neustadt or Eisenstadt, it's only half an hour away. South of Sopron, in Hungary is another well-known shopping city, Szombathely (Steinamanger). It's less than 15 km from the border and within easy reach of Austrian towns like Gussing, Oberwart, Fürstenfeld and Hartberg.

Even in these days of more liberalised markets, Hungary is much cheaper and a popular shopping excursion for Austrians. The Hungarians, meanwhile, come to Austria for more reliable electrical goods. ■

Orientation & Information

Semmering sits on a south-facing slope above the Semmering Pass. There's no real centre to the resort: it's mostly ranged along Hochstrasse which transcribes an arc above the train station. Parking is not a problem.

Outside the train station (which has a restaurant and left luggage, but no bike rental) there's a map. If you take the paths directly up to the ridge, in 20 minutes you reach the Kurverwaltung tourist office (☎ 23 26 80), Gemeindeamt, Hochstrasse 32, open Monday to Thursday from 8 am to noon and 1 to 4 pm, and Friday from 8 am to noon. If instead you go left and follow the paths to 'Passhöhe', you reach the Tourismusregion tourist office (☎ 25 39) in about the same time. It's on the 1st floor above the bank, where Hochstrasse branches from highway 306, and is open Monday from 8.30 am to 2 pm, and Tuesday to Friday from 8.30 am to 4 pm.

Things to See & Do

Outdoor activities are the resort's main draw, including **hiking**: get the *Wanderkarte* map (text in German) from the tourist office. Overlooking Semmering to the south is the **Hirschenkogel** (1340 metres), up which a chair lift trundles (AS45 up, AS25 down or AS55 return). It attracts hikers or skiers (AS290 for a day pass), depending on the season, and there's a restaurant at the top. A day pass for all three local ski regions costs AS305.

The resort has a golf course (☎ 24 71), mini-golf, a ski school (☎ 24 71 or ☎ 85 38), tennis, and a swimming pool and sauna complex (in the five-star Hotel Panhaus).

An excursion can be made to the north along the scenic **Höllental** (Hell's Valley), a deep, narrow gorge created by the Schwarza River. Along the route from Semmering (by winding, local roads) you pass the Raxblick viewpoint. A little farther on is Hirschwang, where in 1926 Austria's first cable car was built. You can ascend to 1540 metres (AS155 return) for a 360° panorama. Hirschwang is where you join the Höllental.

Places to Stay & Eat

Most places close during the off season (after Easter until sometime in May, and in November). Semmering has few options for budget travellers, other than a couple of private rooms. Unless stated otherwise, all the places below are conveniently situated on Hochstrasse, between the two tourist offices.

Haus Mayer (☎ 22 51), No 257, has good-value rooms for AS220 to AS250 per person with shower and balcony, but only takes non-smokers.

Haus Tonn (☎ 22 64), No 108, charges AS180/340 for singles/doubles using hall shower, or AS540 for doubles with private shower.

Pension Löffler (☎ 23 04), No 174, has good, largish rooms for AS350/600, with shower, WC and TV. Cable TV is available for a AS50 surcharge. Its restaurant has good food for AS60 to AS125, and some outside tables. There's a three-course lunch menu for AS110 and a two-course deal for senior citizens for AS85.

Hotel-Restaurant Berghof (☎ 23 20), No 271, has pleasant rooms with shower/WC and TV for AS370/740; doubles also have a balcony. Austrian food costs around AS70 to AS140 and it's round the corner from the regional tourist office.

The family-run *Hotel-Restaurant Belvedere* (☎ 22 70), No 60, has excellent facilities for a three-star place: use of the swimming pool, sauna and solarium are all included in the price, and there's a large garden and patio area. Rooms have shower/WC, TV and balcony, and cost from AS390 per person in summer or AS480 in winter. The restaurant (open daily) has appetising regional dishes from AS80 to AS240, including fish and seasonal specialities.

The more expensive hotels are mostly higher up the road, near and beyond the Kurverwaltung tourist office. Opposite the regional tourist office is a *Konsum* supermarket, open Monday to Friday from 7.30 am to noon and 3 to 6 pm, and Saturday from 7 am to noon.

Paraglider's Nemesis

You're unlikely to see any paragliders leaping into the Breite Ries, as the swirling currents of wind within this jagged chute of rock are too dangerous. Even highly experienced fliers would find it difficult, if not impossible, to control their descent. A Puchberg schoolmaster related to me the following scene he'd witnessed:

A policeman observed a paraglider preparing to jump into the jaws of the Briete Ries. He warned the man of the dangers but the paraglider was unconcerned. On the contrary, he boasted that he relished the challenge. When the policeman insisted it was too dangerous the man became aggressive. 'I'll do what I like,' he asserted. 'It's not illegal. You can't stop me just because you're a policeman.'

'I'm not stopping you because I'm a policeman,' was the reply. 'I'm stopping you because I'm a knowledgeable man.' But the paraglider continued with his preparations. The policeman tried a different approach. 'Watch,' he said, and threw a roll of toilet paper into the chasm. The ribbon of paper rapidly unfurled and became a swirling dervish as the wind snatched it this way and that. It was violently ripped to shreds before it fell from view.

The paraglider watched the demonstration and then quietly packed his gear away. He had suddenly become very meek, realising the policeman had probably saved his life. ■

Getting There & Away

From Semmering, the rail route to the northeast passes through some impressive scenery of precipitous cliffs and forested hills (sit on the right). The track, incorporating many bridges and tunnels, was Europe's first Alpine railway and was completed in 1854 by Karl Ritter von Ghega. The most scenic section is the 30-minute stretch between Semmering and Payerbach (AS48). The trip to Semmering from either Vienna's Süd-bahnhof (direct service) or Graz (change at Mürzzuschlag) costs AS252, though only regional trains stop.

By road (highway 306), the Semmering Pass at 985 metres marks the border between Lower Austria and Styria. Excursions along the Höllental are easiest if you have your own transport. Bundesbuses do go to Hirschwang and Raxblick, but departures are infrequent.

SCHNEEBERG

The popular ascent up Schneeberg by cogwheel steam train is a full day excursion, providing excellent views and good hikes. The top station, Hochschneeberg, is at 1795 metres. Close by is a hotel and restaurant, and also a viewing terrace by a small chapel dedicated to the Empress Elisabeth. From the station, a path leads to Klosterwappen and Fischerhütte; these places are each about a 70-minute hike from the station, and 20 minutes from each other.

The path to both is initially the same. After 30 minutes it splits: the steeper left-hand path goes to **Klosterwappen** (2075 metres), identified by a radar and a cross on the ridge. This fork provides the best view of the Raxealpe range and the upper reaches of the Höllental, with the ribbon-like road winding its way on the far side of the valley. A path goes down into the valley, but a flattish walk along the ridge will bring you to the *Fischerhütte* self-service restaurant (food till 7 pm). Up the hill behind the restaurant is the Kaiserstein viewpoint (2061 metres), with a beehive-shaped monument to Emperor Franz I. The most impressive part of the view is the Breite Ries, a bowl-shaped area of erosion with stark grey and red cliffs.

Getting There & Away

A special leaflet (in English) giving times of the Schneeberg cogwheel train is available at many train stations. Trains operate from late April to early November, and the full ascent from Puchberg am Schneeberg to Hochschneeberg takes 85 minutes (AS150 up, AS120 down, AS250 return). Austrian rail passes are valid. Many trains depart, but only if there's the demand (which there usually is). Guaranteed ascents are at 8.40 and 11.55 am, with descents at 12.40 and 4 pm, with further guaranteed trains running in July and August. The journey time from Wiener Neustadt to Puchberg is 50 minutes. Puchberg itself has places to stay and eat.

For more information about the trains, or special all-in tickets (including overnight accommodation and/or meals), contact the Puchberg train station on ☎ 02636-22 25 0.

To walk from Puchberg up to Hochschneeberg takes three hours or more. Klosterwappen is on the long-distance hiking path, the Nordalpenweg. This path goes from Lake Constance to the Wienerwald.

Glossary

Abfahrt – departure (trains)
Achterl – eighth-litre (drinks)
Ankunft – arrival (trains)
ANTO – Austrian National Tourist Office
Apotheke – pharmacy
Ausgang – exit
Autobahn – motorway
Autoreisezug – motorail train

Bad – bath (spa resort)
Bahnhof – train station
Bahnsteig – train station platform
Bankomat – automated teller machine
Bauernhof – farmhouse
Bezirk – (town or city) district
Biedermeier period – 19th-century art movement in Germany and Austria; applies particularly to a decorative style of furniture from this period
Bierkeller – beer cellar
Brauerei – brewery
Bundesbus – state bus
Bundesländer – federal province (government)
Bundesrat – Federal Council (upper house – government)
Buschenschank – wine tavern

Dirndl – traditional skirt

Eingang, Eintritt – entry
EU – European Union

Fahrplan – timetable
Ferienwohnungen – self-catering holiday apartments
Flohmarkt – flea market
Flugpost – air mail
Föhn – hot, dry wind which sweeps down from the mountains, mainly in early spring and autumn
FPÖ – Freedom Party (political party)

Glockenturm – clock tower
Glockenspiel – carillon
Gästekarte – guest card

Gästehaus/Gasthaus – guesthouse
Gasthof – inn
Gendarmerie/Polizei – police
Gondelbahn – gondola

Heuriger – wine tavern
Hauptbahnhof – main train station
Hauptpost – main post office

Imbiss – snack bar

Jugendherberge/Jugendgästehaus – youth hostel

Kaffeehaus/Café Konditorei – coffee house
Konsulat – consulate
Kurzparkzone – short-term parking zone

Landesmuseum – provincial museum
Landtag – provincial assembly (government)
Langlauf – cross-country skiing
Langersamstag – 'long' Saturday, when shops may open up to 5 pm on the first Saturday of the month
Luftseilbahn – cable car

Maut – toll (or indicating a toll booth)
Mehrwertsteuer (MWST) – value-added tax
Mensa – university restaurant
Mitfahrzentrale – hitching organisation

Nationalrat – National Council (lower house – government)

ÖAMTC – national motoring organisation
ÖAV – Austrian Alpine Club
ÖBB – Austrian federal railway
ÖKISTA – student travel agency
ÖVP – Austrian People's Party (political party)

Parkschein – parking voucher
Pedalos – paddle boats
Pfarrkirche – parish church

Postamt – post office
Postlagernde Briefe – poste restante

Rathaus – town hall
Ruhetag – 'rest day', on which a restaurant is closed

Schlepplift – ski lift
Schlossberg – castle hill
Schrammelmusik – popular Viennese music for violins, guitar and accordion
Secession movement – early 20th-century movement in Vienna seeking to establish a more functional style in architecture; led by Otto Wagner (1841-1918)
Selbstbedienung (SB) – self-service (restaurants, laundries etc)
Sesselbahn – chair lift
SPÖ – Social Democrats (political party)
Stadtmuseum – city museum
Standseilbahn – funicular
Studentenheime – student rooms

Tabak – tobacconist
Tagestellar/Tagesmenu – the set meal or menu of the day in a restaurant
Telefon-Wertkarte – phonecard
Tierpark – zoo

Urlaub – holiday

Vienna Circle – group of philosophers centred on Vienna University in the 1920s and 1930s
Vienna Group (Wiener Gruppe) – literary/art movement formed in the 1950s, whose members incorporated surrealism and dadaism in sound compositions, textual montages and actionist happenings
Viertel – quarter-litre (drinks)

Wäscherei – laundry
Würstel Stand – sausage stand

Zimmer frei/Privat Zimmer – private rooms (accommodation)

Index

LONELY PLANET PHRASEBOOKS

Nepali phrasebook

Ethiopian Amharic phrasebook

Latin American Spanish phrasebook

Ukrainian phrasebook

Greek phrasebook

Vietnamese phrasebook

Building bridges,
Breaking barriers,
Beyond babble-on

Listen for the gems

Speak your own words

Ask your own questions

Master of your own image

- handy pocket-sized books
- easy to understand Pronunciation chapter
- clear and comprehensive Grammar chapter
- romanisation alongside script to allow ease of pronunciation
- script throughout so users can point to phrases
- extensive vocabulary sections, words and phrases for every situations
- full of cultural information and tips for the traveller

'...vital for a real DIY spirit and attitude in language learning' – Backpacker

'the phrasebooks have good cultural backgrounders and offer solid advice for challenging situations in remote locations' – San Francisco Examiner

'...they are unbeatable for their coverage of the world's more obscure languages' – The Geographical Magazine

---

Arabic (Egyptian)
Arabic (Moroccan)
Australia
  Australian English, Aboriginal and Torres Strait languages
Baltic States
  Estonian, Latvian, Lithuanian
Bengali
Burmese
Brazilian
Cantonese
Central Europe
  Czech, French, German, Hungarian, Italian and Slovak
Eastern Europe
  Bulgarian, Czech, Hungarian, Polish, Romanian and Slovak
Egyptian Arabic
Ethiopian (Amharic)
Fijian
Greek
Hindi/Urdu

Indonesian
Japanese
Korean
Lao
Latin American Spanish
Malay
Mandarin
Mediterranean Europe
  Albanian, Croatian, Greek, Italian, Macedonian, Maltese, Serbian, Slovene
Mongolian
Moroccan Arabic
Nepali
Papua New Guinea
Pilipino (Tagalog)
Quechua
Russian
Scandinavian Europe
  Danish, Finnish, Icelandic, Norwegian and Swedish

South-East Asia
  Burmese, Indonesian, Khmer, Lao, Malay, Tagalog (Pilipino), Thai and Vietnamese
Sri Lanka
Swahili
Thai
Thai Hill Tribes
Tibetan
Turkish
Ukrainian
USA
  US English, Vernacular Talk, Native American languages and Hawaiian
Vietnamese
Western Europe
  Basque, Catalan, Dutch, French, German, Irish, Italian, Portuguese, Scottish Gaelic, Spanish (Castilian) and Welsh

LONELY PLANET JOURNEYS

JOURNEYS is a unique collection of travel writing – published by the company that understands travel better than anyone else. It is a series for anyone who has ever experienced – or dreamed of – the magical moment when they encountered a strange culture or saw a place for the first time. They are tales to read while you're planning a trip, while you're on the road or while you're in an armchair, in front of a fire.

JOURNEYS books catch the spirit of a place, illuminate a culture, recount a crazy adventure, or introduce a fascinating way of life. They always entertain, and always enrich the experience of travel.

THE GATES OF DAMASCUS
Lieve Joris
Translated by Sam Garrett

This best-selling book is a beautifully drawn portrait of day-to-day life in modern Syria. Through her intimate contact with local people, Lieve Joris draws us into the fascinating world that lies behind the gates of Damascus. Hala's husband is a political prisoner, jailed for his opposition to the Assad regime; through the author's friendship with Hala we see how Syrian politics impacts on the lives of ordinary people.

Lieve Joris, who was born in Belgium, is one of Europe's leading travel writers. In addition to an award-winning book on Hungary, she has published widely acclaimed accounts of her journeys to the Middle East and Africa. *The Gates of Damascus* is her fifth book.

'Expands the boundaries of travel writing' – Times Literary Supplement

KINGDOM OF THE FILM STARS
Journey into Jordan
Annie Caulfield

Kingdom of the Film Stars is a travel book and a love story. With honesty and humour, Annie Caulfield writes of travelling in Jordan and falling in love with a Bedouin. Her book offers fascinating insights into the country – from the traditional tent life of nomadic tribes to the first woman MP's battle with fundamentalist colleagues. *Kingdom of the Film Stars* unpicks some of the tight-woven Western myths about the Arab world, presenting cultural and political issues within the intimate framework of a compelling love story.

Annie Caulfield, who was born in Ireland and currently lives in London, is an award-winning playwright and journalist. She has travelled widely in the Middle East.

'Annie Caulfield is a remarkable traveller. Her story is fresh, courageous, moving, witty and sexy!' – Dawn French

LONELY PLANET TRAVEL ATLASES

Lonely Planet has long been famous for the number and quality of its guidebook maps. Now we've gone one step further and in conjunction with Steinhart Katzir Publishers produced a handy companion series: Lonely Planet travel atlases – maps of a country produced in book form.

Unlike other maps, which look good but lead travellers astray, our travel atlases have been researched on the road by Lonely Planet's experienced team of writers. All details are carefully checked to ensure the atlas corresponds with the equivalent Lonely Planet guidebook.

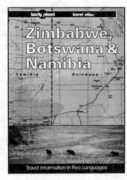

The handy atlas format means no holes, wrinkles, torn sections or constant folding and unfolding. These atlases can survive long periods on the road, unlike cumbersome fold-out maps. The comprehensive index ensures easy reference.

- full-colour throughout
- maps researched and checked by Lonely Planet authors
- place names correspond with Lonely Planet guidebooks
  – no confusing spelling differences
- legend and travelling information in English, French, German, Japanese and Spanish
- size: 230 x 160 mm

Available now:
Chile & Easter Island • Egypt • India & Bangladesh • Israel & the Palestinian Territories •Jordan, Syria & Lebanon • Kenya • Laos • Portugal • South Africa, Lesotho & Swaziland • Thailand • Vietnam • Zimbabwe, Botswana & Namibia

---

LONELY PLANET TV SERIES & VIDEOS

Lonely Planet travel guides have been brought to life on television screens around the world. Like our guides, the programmes are based on the joy of independent travel, and look honestly at some of the most exciting, picturesque and frustrating places in the world. Each show is presented by one of three travellers from Australia, England or the USA and combines an innovative mixture of video, Super-8 film, atmospheric soundscapes and original music.

Videos of each episode – containing additional footage not shown on television – are available from good book and video shops, but the availability of individual videos varies with regional screening schedules.

Video destinations include: Alaska • American Rockies • Australia – The South-East • Baja California & the Copper Canyon • Brazil • Central Asia • Chile & Easter Island • Corsica, Sicily & Sardinia – The Mediterranean Islands • East Africa (Tanzania & Zanzibar) • Ecuador & the Galapagos Islands • Greenland & Iceland • Indonesia • Israel & the Sinai Desert • Jamaica • Japan • La Ruta Maya • Morocco • New York • North India • Pacific Islands (Fiji, Solomon Islands & Vanuatu) • South India • South West China • Turkey • Vietnam • West Africa • Zimbabwe, Botswana & Namibia

The Lonely Planet TV series is produced by:
Pilot Productions
Duke of Sussex Studios
44 Uxbridge St
London W8 7TG UK

Lonely Planet videos are distributed by:
IVN Communications Inc
2246 Camino Ramon
California 94583, USA

107 Power Road, Chiswick
London W4 5PL UK

Music from the TV series is available on CD & cassette.
For video availability and ordering information contact your nearest Lonely Planet office.

PLANET TALK

Lonely Planet's FREE quarterly newsletter

We love hearing from you and think you'd like to hear from us.

*When...*is the right time to see reindeer in Finland?
*Where...*can you hear the best palm-wine music in Ghana?
*How...*do you get from Asunción to Areguá by steam train?
*What...*is the best way to see India?

For the answer to these and many other questions read PLANET TALK.

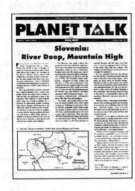

Every issue is packed with up-to-date travel news and advice including:

- a letter from Lonely Planet co-founders Tony and Maureen Wheeler
- go behind the scenes on the road with a Lonely Planet author
- feature article on an important and topical travel issue
- a selection of recent letters from travellers
- details on forthcoming Lonely Planet promotions
- complete list of Lonely Planet products

To join our mailing list contact any Lonely Planet office.

Also available: Lonely Planet T-shirts. 100% heavyweight cotton.

LONELY PLANET ONLINE

Get the latest travel information before you leave or while you're on the road

Whether you've just begun planning your next trip, or you're chasing down specific info on currency regulations or visa requirements, check out Lonely Planet Online for up-to-the minute travel information.

As well as travel profiles of your favourite destinations (including maps and photos), you'll find current reports from our researchers and other travellers, updates on health and visas, travel advisories, and discussion of the ecological and political issues you need to be aware of as you travel.

There's also an online travellers' forum where you can share your experience of life on the road, meet travel companions and ask other travellers for their recommendations and advice. We also have plenty of links to other online sites useful to independent travellers.

And of course we have a complete and up-to-date list of all Lonely Planet travel products including guides, phrasebooks, atlases, Journeys and videos and a simple online ordering facility if you can't find the book you want elsewhere.

www.lonelyplanet.com
or
AOL keyword: lp

LONELY PLANET PRODUCTS

Lonely Planet is known worldwide for publishing practical, reliable and no-nonsense travel information in our guides and on our web site. The Lonely Planet list covers just about every accessible part of the world. Currently there are eight series: *travel guides, shoestring guides, walking guides, city guides, phrasebooks, audio packs, travel atlases* and *Journeys* – a unique collection of travel writing.

EUROPE

Amsterdam • Austria • Baltic States & Kaliningrad • Baltic States phrasebook • Britain • Central Europe on a shoestring • Central Europe phrasebook • Czech & Slovak Republics • Denmark • Dublin • Eastern Europe on a shoestring • Eastern Europe phrasebook • Finland • France • Greece • Greek phrasebook • Hungary • Iceland, Greenland & the Faroe Islands • Ireland • Italy • Mediterranean Europe on a shoestring • Mediterranean Europe phrasebook • Paris • Poland • Portugal • Portugal travel atlas • Prague • Russia, Ukraine & Belarus • Russian phrasebook • Scandinavian & Baltic Europe on a shoestring • Scandinavian Europe phrasebook • Slovenia • Spain • St Petersburg • Switzerland • Trekking in Greece • Trekking in Spain • Ukrainian phrasebook • Vienna • Walking in Britain • Walking in Switzerland • Western Europe on a shoestring • Western Europe phrasebook

NORTH AMERICA

Alaska • Backpacking in Alaska • Baja California • California & Nevada • Canada • Florida • Hawaii • Honolulu • Los Angeles • Mexico • Miami • New England • New Orleans • New York, New Jersey & Pennsylvania • Pacific Northwest USA • Rocky Mountain States • San Francisco • Southwest USA • USA phrasebook • Washington, DC & the Capital Region

CENTRAL AMERICA & THE CARIBBEAN

Bermuda • Central America on a shoestring • Costa Rica • Cuba • Eastern Caribbean • Guatemala, Belize & Yucatán: La Ruta Maya • Jamaica

SOUTH AMERICA

Argentina, Uruguay & Paraguay • Bolivia • Brazil • Brazilian phrasebook • Buenos Aires • Chile & Easter Island • Chile & Easter Island travel atlas • Colombia • Ecuador & the Galápagos Islands • Latin American Spanish phrasebook • Peru • Quechua phrasebook • Rio de Janeiro • South America on a shoestring • Trekking in the Patagonian Andes • Venezuela

Travel Literature: Full Circle: A South American Journey

ANTARCTICA

Antarctica

ISLANDS OF THE INDIAN OCEAN

Madagascar & Comoros • Maldives & Islands of the East Indian Ocean • Mauritius, Réunion & Seychelles

AFRICA

Arabic (Moroccan) phrasebook • Africa on a shoestring • Cape Town • Central Africa • East Africa • Egypt • Egypt travel atlas• Ethiopian (Amharic) phrasebook • Kenya • Kenya travel atlas • Morocco • North Africa • South Africa, Lesotho & Swaziland • South Africa, Lesotho & Swaziland travel atlas • Swahili phrasebook • Trekking in East Africa • West Africa • Zimbabwe, Botswana & Namibia • Zimbabwe, Botswana & Namibia travel atlas

Travel Literature: The Rainbird: A Central African Journey • Songs to an African Sunset: A Zimbabwean Story

MAIL ORDER

Lonely Planet products are distributed worldwide. They are also available by mail order from Lonely Planet, so if you have difficulty finding a title please write to us. North American and South American residents should write to Embarcadero West, 155 Filbert St, Suite 251, Oakland CA 94607, USA; European and African residents should write to 10 Barley Mow Passage, Chiswick, London W4 4PH; and residents of other countries to PO Box 617, Hawthorn, Victoria 3122, Australia.

NORTH-EAST ASIA

Beijing • Cantonese phrasebook • China • Hong Kong, Macau & Guangzhou • Hong Kong • Japan • Japanese phrasebook • Japanese audio pack • Korea • Korean phrasebook • Mandarin phrasebook • Mongolia • Mongolian phrasebook • North-East Asia on a shoestring • Seoul • Taiwan • Tibet • Tibet phrasebook • Tokyo

Travel Literature: Lost Japan

MIDDLE EAST & CENTRAL ASIA

Arab Gulf States • Arabic (Egyptian) phrasebook • Central Asia • Iran • Israel & the Palestinian Territories • Israel & the Palestinian Territories travel atlas • Istanbul • Jerusalem • Jordan & Syria • Jordan, Syria & Lebanon travel atlas • Middle East • Turkey • Turkish phrasebook • Yemen

Travel Literature: The Gates of Damascus • Kingdom of

ALSO AVAILABLE:

Travel with Children • Traveller's Tales

INDIAN SUBCONTINENT

Bangladesh • Bengali phrasebook • Delhi • Hindi/Urdu phrasebook • India • India & Bangladesh travel atlas • Indian Himalaya • Karakoram Highway • Nepal • Nepali phrasebook • Pakistan • Rajasthan • Sri Lanka • Sri Lanka phrasebook • Trekking in the Indian Himalaya • Trekking in the Karakoram & Hindukush • Trekking in the Nepal Himalaya

Travel Literature: In Rajasthan • Shopping for Buddhas

SOUTH-EAST ASIA

Bali & Lombok • Bangkok • Burmese phrasebook • Cambodia • Ho Chi Minh City • Indonesia • Indonesian phrasebook • Indonesian audio pack • Jakarta • Java • Laos • Lao phrasebook • Laos travel atlas • Malay phrasebook • Malaysia, Singapore & Brunei • Myanmar (Burma) • Philippines • Pilipino phrasebook • Singapore • South-East Asia on a shoestring • South-East Asia phrasebook • Thailand • Thailand travel atlas • Thai phrasebook • Thai audio pack • Thai Hill Tribes phrasebook • Vietnam • Vietnamese phrasebook • Vietnam travel atlas

AUSTRALIA & THE PACIFIC

Australia • Australian phrasebook • Bushwalking in Australia • Bushwalking in Papua New Guinea • Fiji • Fijian phrasebook • Islands of Australia's Great Barrier Reef • Melbourne • Micronesia • New Caledonia • New South Wales & the ACT • New Zealand • Northern Territory • Outback Australia • Papua New Guinea • Papua New Guinea phrasebook • Queensland • Rarotonga & the Cook Islands • Samoa • Solomon Islands • South Australia • Sydney • Tahiti & French Polynesia • Tasmania • Tonga • Tramping in New Zealand • Vanuatu • Victoria • Western Australia

Travel Literature: Islands in the Clouds • Sean & David's Long Drive

THE LONELY PLANET STORY

Lonely Planet published its first book in 1973 in response to the numerous 'How did you do it?' questions Maureen and Tony Wheeler were asked after driving, bussing, hitching, sailing and railing their way from England to Australia.

Written at a kitchen table and hand collated, trimmed and stapled, *Across Asia on the Cheap* became an instant local bestseller, inspiring thoughts of another book.

Eighteen months in South-East Asia resulted in their second guide, *South-East Asia on a shoestring*, which they put together in a backstreet Chinese hotel in Singapore in 1975. The 'yellow bible', as it quickly became known to backpackers around the world, soon became *the* guide to the region. It has sold well over half a million copies and is now in its 8th edition, still retaining its familiar yellow cover.

Today there are over 180 titles, including travel guides, walking guides, language kits & phrasebooks, travel atlases and travel literature. The company is one of the largest travel publishers in the world. Although Lonely Planet initially specialised in guides to Asia, we now cover most regions of the world, including the Pacific, North America, South America, Africa, the Middle East and Europe.

The emphasis continues to be on travel for independent travellers. Tony and Maureen still travel for several months of each year and play an active part in the writing, updating and quality control of Lonely Planet's guides.

They have been joined by over 70 authors and 170 staff at our offices in Melbourne (Australia), Oakland (USA), London (UK) and Paris (France). Travellers themselves also make a valuable contribution to the guides through the feedback we receive in thousands of letters each year.

The people at Lonely Planet strongly believe that travellers can make a positive contribution to the countries they visit, both through their appreciation of the countries' culture, wildlife and natural features, and through the money they spend. In addition, the company makes a direct contribution to the countries and regions it covers. Since 1986 a percentage of the income from each book has been donated to ventures such as famine relief in Africa; aid projects in India; agricultural projects in Central America; Greenpeace's efforts to halt French nuclear testing in the Pacific; and Amnesty International.

'I hope we send the people out with the right attitude about travel. You realise when you travel that there are so many different perspectives about the world, so we hope these books will make people more interested in what they see. These are guidebooks, but you can't really guide people. All you can do is point them in the right direction.'
– Tony Wheeler

LONELY PLANET PUBLICATIONS

Australia
PO Box 617, Hawthorn 3122, Victoria
tel: (03) 9819 1877 fax: (03) 9819 6459
e-mail: talk2us@lonelyplanet.com.au

USA
Embarcadero West, 155 Filbert St, Suite 251,
Oakland, CA 94607
tel: (510) 893 8555 TOLL FREE: 800 275-8555
fax: (510) 893 8563
e-mail: info@lonelyplanet.com

UK
10 Barley Mow Passage, Chiswick,
London W4 4PH
tel: (0181) 742 3161 fax: (0181) 742 2772
e-mail: 100413.3551@compuserve.com

France:
71 bis rue du Cardinal Lemoine, 75005 Paris
tel: 1 44 32 06 20 fax: 1 46 34 72 55
e-mail: 100560.415@compuserve.com

World Wide Web: http://www.lonelyplanet.com